Beijing

"All you've got to do is decide to go and the hardest part is over.

So go!"

TONY WHEELER, COFOUNDER – LONELY PLANET

THIS EDITION WRITTEN AND RESEARCHED BY

Daniel McCrohan

David Eimer

Contents

Plan Your Trip 4

Explore Běijīng 48

Understand Běijīng 203

Survival Guide 243

Běijīng Maps 282

(left) **Food p34** A delicious highlight of any trip to Běijīng

(above) **Chinese tea p77** Traditional tea ceremony

(right) **Forbidden City p54** Dragon relief carving on a city wall

Welcome to Běijīng

Inextricably linked to its glorious, notorious past, yet hurtling towards a power-charged future, Běijīng is as complex as it is compelling.

Mouth-watering

Food is an obsession for the Chinese and the dazzling array of dishes you'll encounter in Běijīng reflects the joy locals take in eating. Dining out is the main social activity; it's in restaurants that Beijingers hang out with friends, romance each other, hold family reunions and do business, and the variety of restaurants here is mesmerising. Local menus will have you salivating over succulent Peking duck, delicious dumplings and awesome noodles, but there's also food from every corner of China (and beyond). From fiery Sìchuānese to Turkic-inspired Uighur cuisine, Běijīng's restaurants have it covered.

Antique

Few places on earth can match the extraordinary historical panorama on display in Běijīng. There are six Unesco World Heritage Sites in this city alone (just one less than the whole of Egypt). At its heart is the magnificent Forbidden City, a royal palace like no other. Běijīng is also home to sublime temples that aspire to cosmological perfection, while the city centre is criss-crossed by enchanting, ancient *hútòng* that teem with life today, as they did hundreds of years ago. And, to cap it all, the awe-inspiring Great Wall snakes its way across the hills north of town.

Eye-catching

It's not just the ancient architecture that wows tourists. Běijīng is also home to some of the world's most innovative modern buildings. The world's leading architects clamber for the chance to make their mark on this new global powerhouse, and jaw-dropping structures like the CCTV Building, Galaxy Soho, the NCPA concert hall and the Olympic Stadium are clear signs that Běijīng is not shy about proclaiming its status as China's capital. Like the temples and palaces of the ancient past, and the imposing socialist realist monuments of the 1950s, these latest additions are built on a scale that screams 'look at me!'.

Culture Hub

The nation's top artists, writers, movie-makers and musicians converge in Běijīng, making it *the* place to take the pulse of China's rapidly evolving cultural scene. With top-class museums, galleries galore, and an increasing number of music venues, there's enough to keep you busy day and night. Běijīng is also the centre for the traditional Chinese performing arts. Whether it's the mystique of Peking opera, tumbling acrobats or the graceful lines of Chinese classical dance that entrances you, the capital has it and more.

Why I Love Běijīng

By Daniel McCrohan, Author

I love the food, the abundance of restaurants, the cheap beer and the lack of table manners. I love the *hútòng*, the parks and the taichi. I love drinking tea (proper tea; not Tetley), playing table tennis, flying kites, and being able to cycle everywhere, even to the Great Wall! Most of all, though, I love Běijīng's capacity to surprise. After a decade of living here, I still find something unexpected almost every day: a phrase I hadn't heard, a mannerism I hadn't noticed, a new shop, a new bar, or even, when I'm especially lucky, a long-abandoned temple I never knew existed.

For more about our authors, see p304.

Above: Food stalls at Dōnghuámén night market (p73)

Běijīng's Top 13

The Great Wall (p170)

1 China's most famous landmark, and one of the world's superlative manmade sights, the Great Wall snakes its way across northern China for almost 9000km, but nowhere beats Běijīng as a base for mounting your assault. Scattered throughout the municipality are more than a dozen fragmented stretches, from the perfectly chiseled to the charmingly dilapidated. You can get to them by bus, by train, by taxi...even by bicycle. And the adventurous can hike along it for days. GREAT WALL AT JĪNSHĀNLǏNG

The Great Wall

Forbidden City (p54)

2 The largest palace complex in the world, the Forbidden City is the be-all and end-all of dynastic grandeur, with imposing halls, splendid gates and age-old relics. No other place in Běijīng teems with so much history, legend and imperial intrigue. You could spend hours wandering its vast squares and high-walled passageways, which lead to delightful courtyards, gardens and minimuseums, and give you plenty of time to contemplate the enormity of shuffling your way around the place that 24 emperors of China called home.

Forbidden City & Dōngchéng Central

2

4

Tiān'ānmén Square *(p62)*

3 The world's largest public square is a vast desert of paving stones at the heart of Běijīng. It's also a poignant epitaph to China's democracy movement, which was quashed by the People's Liberation Army here in June 1989. The stringent security can be off-putting, but such is its iconic status, few visitors leave Běijīng without coming here. Get up early and watch the dawn flag-raising ceremony, or wander by later on to see the surrounding buildings lit up at night. GREAT HALL OF THE PEOPLE

Forbidden City & Dōngchéng Central

Hútòng *(p222)*

4 The heart and soul of Běijīng are its *hútòng*: the intoxicating alleyways that criss-cross the centre of the city. Still home for many locals, these unique lanes not only tie the capital to its ancient past – some lanes date back almost 800 years – but offer the chance to experience Běijīng street life in all its raucous and cheerful glory. Wandering or cycling the *hútòng* during the day, and returning at night to some of the many bars and restaurants that now inhabit them, is an essential part of any visit to Běijīng.

Historic Hútòng

Temple of Heaven Park *(p108)*

5 The ultimate expression of the eternal Chinese quest for order, Temple of Heaven Park contains sheer geometric perfection: a series of stunning shrines – including the iconic Hall of Prayer for Good Harvests – where the sons of heaven, China's emperors, came to pray for divine guidance. Everything about them – colour, shape, sound – has an esoteric significance that's mind-boggling to contemplate. Surrounding them is a delightfully soothing park, where locals come to stroll, sing and dance, or to just sit under the gnarled cypress trees planted here hundreds of years ago. HALL OF PRAYER FOR GOOD HARVESTS

Temple of Heaven Park & Dōngchéng South

Lama Temple *(p84)*

6 Central Běijīng's largest, most important and most atmospheric Buddhist temple, the serene Lama Temple used to be home to legions of monks from Mongolia and Tibet and was where the reincarnation of the Panchen Lama was determined. These days it is still an active temple, although tourists now outnumber the monks. There are five beautiful central halls, the last of which houses the world's largest sandalwood Buddha.

Drum Tower & Dōngchéng North

Summer Palace *(p159)*

7 The imperial summer playground, the Summer Palace is a beguiling, superbly landscaped collection of temples, pavilions, gardens, lakes, bridges and corridors. Less formal than the Forbidden City, there is still more than enough elegance and beauty in its many structures to take your breath away. Clamber up Longevity Hill, pausing for breath at the various temples that dot it, for splendid views across Běijīng, or promenade around Kūnmíng Lake and imagine what it must have been like to have had this place all to yourself.

Summer Palace & Hǎidiàn

6

Peking Duck *(p35)*

8 You can't leave Běijīng without sampling its most iconic dish. Once reserved for emperors and mandarins, Peking duck began to feature on the menus of the lower orders at the beginning of the 20th century. Now there are a number of specialist *kǎoyā* (roast duck) restaurants and the dish – juicier and more flavoursome than the crispy duck you get back home – is as much a part of Běijīng's fabric as the streets themselves.

Eating

Drum & Bell Towers *(p86)*

9 Standing watch over one of the most charming corners of Běijīng (although developers have their eyes on it), these two magnificent ancient towers, facing each other on either side of a small public square, used to be the city's official timekeeper, with drums and bells beaten and rung to mark the times of the day. Climb the Drum Tower to listen to a body-rumbling performance played out on replica drums or climb either tower for a bird's-eye view of the surrounding *hútòng*.

Drum Tower & Dōngchéng North

Chinese Performing Arts *(p26)*

10 Whether it's the chance to experience the intricate, highly stylised Peking opera, or tumbling, spinning and high-wire-walking acrobats, to say nothing of shaven-headed Shàolín monks showing off their supreme fighting skills, Běijīng is a great place to catch a show. There are performances every night of the week, giving you no excuse to miss out. And don't be put off by the language barrier: most shows are easy to follow. Acrobatics in particular is a stunning spectacle. CHÁOYÁNG ACROBATIC THEATRE

Arts

Hòuhǎi Lakes *(p120)*

11 These three interconnected lakes are one of the great outdoor areas in Běijīng and a prime spot to watch, and join, the locals at play. Ringed by bars and restaurants, the lakes themselves provide much of the entertainment. In the summer, flotillas of pedalos take to the water. During the winter, the lakes are the best place in the capital to ice skate. Then there's fishing, kayaking and swimming (for the brave). But perhaps the most amenable option is simply meandering around them, enjoying the sight of Beijingers letting their hair down. TOURISTS ON A BOAT AT HÒUHǍI LAKE

Běihǎi Park & Xīchéng North

10

Pānjiāyuán Market *(p154)*

12 Save some time at the end of your trip to visit this treasure-filled outdoor market and head home with armfuls of unusual souvenirs. Pānjiāyuán is the best place in Běijīng to shop for arts, crafts and (mostly fake) antiques, and even if you don't want to buy anything, it's fun to wander through the clutter.

Sānlǐtún & Cháoyáng

798 Art District *(p140)*

13 Housed inside the cavernous buildings of a disused electronics factory, 798 has become the city's premier art district. It celebrates its proletarian roots via retouched red Maoist slogans decorating gallery interiors and statues of burly, lantern-jawed workers dotting the lanes, while the voluminous factory workshops are ideally suited to ambitious projects requiring lots of space. Cafes dot the streets, making this a pleasant spot for lunch before you plug yourself in to the world of China's leading artists.

AN ARTIST IN HER STUDIO IN 798 ART DISTRICT

Sānlǐtún & Cháoyáng

What's New

Courtyard Hotels

The city's ever-growing brood of impossibly charming courtyard hotels means that staying in the capital has never been more attractive. Notable new additions include friendly Jǐngshān Garden Hotel, chic Hulu Hotel and peaceful Graceland Yard, housed in the grounds of a small 500-year-old temple. (p194)

72 Hours Visa Free

Běijīng now has a 72-hour visa-free policy for visitors in transit. You must have a confirmed flight to another country in order to qualify, and you cannot leave the municipality of Běijīng.

Dadu Museum of Art

This huge art gallery – located somewhat incongruously in the tree-lined *hútòng* Guozijian Jie – was about to open at the time of research, and was poised to become the city's premier gallery for contemporary Chinese oil paintings. (p93)

Shǐjiā Hútòng Museum

Hútòng buffs will love this new little museum, which offers a refreshingly honest and informative look at the history of the courtyard-filled neighbourhood surrounding historic Shijia Hutong. (p71)

Temple Hotel

Part of a five-year-long renovation project that was recognised by Unesco, this unique heritage hotel is housed within the large grounds of an abandoned, 250-year-old Buddhist temple, and is the most unusual addition to Běijīng's long list of luxury lodgings. (p195)

Galaxy Soho

Běijīng continues to be a breeding ground for state-of-the-art architecture, but its latest high-profile addition – the deliciously curvy, space-station-lookalike Galaxy Soho – courted controversy when it touched down in an old *hútòng* neighbourhood near Zhìhuà Temple. The outcry from heritage-protection activists didn't stop it being shortlisted for an international RIBA (Royal Institute of British Architects) award, though.

New Subway Lines

The city's already hugely impressive subway system continues to expand with a number of new lines being built in the past couple of years, and plenty more under construction.

Public-Transport Price Hike

Rumours of a substantial increase in bus and subway fares were rife at the time of research. Authorities were expected to ditch the cheap-as-chips, set-price fares in favour of the Shànghǎi model, based on journey distance.

Wángfǔjǐng Facelift

For a long time, Běijīng's most famous shopping street, Wangfujing Dajie, has been a dowdy old strip of nondescript malls (Oriental Plaza being the sparkling exception), but a massive makeover for two other malls – Běijīng apm and Intime Lotte – has added some extra pizazz. (p76)

For more recommendations and reviews, see **lonelyplanet.com/beijing**

Need to Know

For more information, see Survival Guide (p243).

Currency
Yuán (¥; 元)

Language
Mandarin

Visas
Seventy-two hours visa-free for passengers in transit. Otherwise, visas required for almost all nationals. A 30-day visa is standard. One extension is usually possible.

Money
Most ATMs accept foreign cards. Most large banks change money. Credit cards are not widely used (apart from in hotels and shopping malls), so carry cash at all times.

Mobile Phones
Local SIMs can be used in non-locked phones. Local phones are cheap. Smartphones can use China's 3G and 4G networks (with roaming charges) or Běijīng's many free wi-fi spots.

Time
GMT plus eight hours

Tourist Information
Tourist information offices are aimed at domestic tourists. Foreigners are better off using hotels or, better still, hostels.

Daily Costs

Budget: less than ¥200
- Hostel dorm: ¥50–80
- A meal in a locals' restaurants: ¥20–40
- Bus or subway tickets: ¥1–2 (before price restructure)

Midrange: ¥200–750
- Standard private room: ¥200–500
- A meal in a midrange restaurant: ¥40–80
- Short taxi trip: ¥15
- Admission to main sights: ¥20–60

Top end: more than ¥750
- Luxury accommodation: ¥1000-plus
- A meal at an international restaurant: ¥100-plus
- Drinks at cocktail bars: ¥50–80
- Guided tours: ¥200–1000

Advance Planning

Three months before Check vaccinations are up to date. Sort out your visa. Start learning Mandarin.

One month before Decide which neighbourhood to base yourself in. Scout around for hotel deals. Look into possible tours and courses.

One week before Book your accommodation, tours and courses. Consider possible day trips.

Useful Websites

The Beijinger (www.thebeijinger.com) Eating and entertainment listings, blog posts and forums.

Timeout Běijīng (www.timeoutbeijing.com) Main rival to The Beijinger. Similar content, but better-looking website.

Běijīng Cream (http://beijingcream.com) Lighthearted Běijīng-based blog covering China-wide current affairs.

Sinica Podcast (http://popupchinese.com) Popular, uncensored current-affairs podcast based in Běijīng.

Air Pollution (http://aqicn.org/city/beijing) Real-time Air Quality Index (AQI) readings for Běijīng (and other cities).

Lonely Planet (www.lonelyplanet.com/china/beijing) Destination information, hotel bookings, online forum and more.

WHEN TO GO

April to May and October to November are pleasant. December to February is dry and very cold. June to September (peak season) is hot, but rain offers respite.

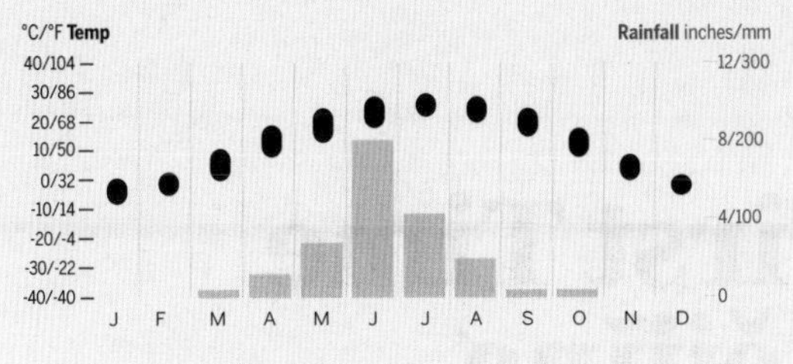

Common Scams

Teahouse Invitations Refuse invitations to teahouses from sweet-talking girls around Tiān'ānmén Sq or Wangfujing Dajie – it's an expensive scam.

Art Exhibitions Similar invitations by 'art students' see tourists pressured into buying overpriced art.

Rickshaws Riders at the North Gate of the Forbidden City are particularly unscrupulous. The ¥3 trip really is too good to be true – it'll end up costing you ¥300!

Taxis If any city-centre driver refuses to *dǎ biǎo* (use the meter), find another taxi. Note, for long journeys, eg to the Great Wall, you'll have to negotiate a fee.

How Much?

- *Bāozi* (steamed dumpling) from street stall ¥1 to ¥2
- Hour in internet cafe ¥3 to ¥5
- Large bottle of local beer from a shop ¥4
- Small bottle of local beer from a bar ¥20
- Half-litre bottle of mineral water ¥1 to ¥2
- Lamb skewer ¥1 to ¥3
- Bananas from a market stall ¥4 per *jīn* (500g)
- Bicycle rent per day ¥30
- Repairing a puncture ¥3

Sleeping

Hostels are best value, with traveller-friendly facilities and good English-language skills. Courtyard hotels are wonderfully atmospheric, and plant you right in the thick of the *hútòng* action, but they lack the facilities (pool, gym etc) of top-end hotels in similar price brackets.

You can book rooms over the phone, or directly through hotel websites.

Useful Websites

airbnb (www.airbnb.com) Private rooms for short-term (even daily) rent.

booking.com (www.booking.com) Hotels and hostels.

ctrip (www.english.ctrip.com) Discounted hotels.

Couch Surfing (www.couchsurfing.org) Stay with locals for free.

Hostel Bookers (www.hostelbookers.com) Hostel bookings, ratings and reviews.

MONEY-SAVING TIPS

Travel Card (交通一卡通; *jiāotōng yīkǎtōng*; refundable deposit ¥20) Saves 60% on all bus fares. Can be used on the subway, but without discounts (may change with proposed new price structure). Obtained from subway stations.

Museum Pass (博物馆通票, *bówùguǎn tōngpiào*; www.bowuguan.bj.cn; ¥120) Worth it if you're staying a while. Gets you up to 50% discounts on more than 60 sights (not just museums) across the city.

Beijing on a Budget Smartphone app for cost-conscious travellers.

For much more on **sleeping**, see p191.

First Time Běijīng

For more information, see Survival Guide (p253)

Checklist

- ➡ Secure your visa
- ➡ Make hotel bookings
- ➡ Have name and address of your hotel printed out in Chinese characters
- ➡ Put your name down for any classes or courses
- ➡ Check your mobile phone is unlocked, so you can use a local SIM card
- ➡ Tell your bank you'll be using your cards in China

What to Pack

- ➡ Phrasebook and/or Chinese dictionary
- ➡ Skin moisturiser (Běijīng can be incredibly dry)
- ➡ Smog mask
- ➡ Sun hat and sunscreen in summer
- ➡ Woolies in winter
- ➡ Shoes with good grip for Great Wall hikes
- ➡ Small rucksack for day trips

Top Tips for Your Trip

- ➡ Learn as much Chinese (Mandarin) as you can before you come.
- ➡ Rent a bike. Běijīng is a great city to explore by bicycle.
- ➡ Have the name and address of wherever you're going each day written down in Chinese characters before you go out. And bring your hotel business card with you, so you can find your way home.
- ➡ Try as much variety of Chinese food as you can. Běijīng has every culinary base covered, from imperial Peking Duck to fiery Sichuanese, so grab some chopsticks and tuck in. Oh, and don't listen to anyone who tells you to avoid the street food – terrible advice.

What to Wear

Jeans and shirt or T-shirt is fine for much of the year. Shorts are OK in summer. It gets very hot in mid-summer, so don't forget a sun hat (as well as sunscreen and mosquito repellent) and a lightweight raincoat for sudden downpours. Winter is a different ball game. Wear plenty of layers: thermal underwear, thick shirt, jumper, gloves, woolie hat and a down jacket, plus thick-soled shoes or boots. At any time of year, you'll need shoes with good grip for Great Wall hiking.

Be Forewarned

- ➡ Air quality can be a problem, especially if you're particularly sensitive to pollution. Consider wearing a smog mask, and check the air quality index (www.aqicn.org).
- ➡ Try to avoid visiting during national holidays (especially May Day and National Day) as the main sights can get ridiculously crowded. Conversely, Chinese New Year is relatively quiet, as most people spend time with their families.
- ➡ Be on your guard for unscrupulous taxi drivers (always insist on using the meter), rickshaw riders (always clearly agree on a fee first), and English-speaking Chinese people who approach you around major tourist sights, offering to show you to a teahouse or an art gallery (an expensive scam).

Money

ATMs are everywhere, and many accept foreign bank cards. Visa and MasterCard are most readily accepted. Don't expect to be able to use a foreign card to make purchases (the exceptions are at hotels, top-end restaurants and modern shopping malls) – always carry cash too.

For more information, see p259.

Bargaining

Bargaining is common in shops (apart from supermarkets), and expected in markets. But there are no hard and fast rules. In shops, you'll only be able to knock a small amount off the asking price, but in markets – especially souvenir markets – you can bargain your socks off. Remember to keep negotiations lighthearted, and be prepared to walk away; that's usually when you'll hear the genuine 'last price'.

Tipping

Tips are never asked for, or expected. The only time you should ever consider tipping is in top-end luxury hotels or in top-end international restaurants. Don't be pressured into tipping tour guides – giving them extra on top of their fee is entirely optional.

Language

Less people than you think speak English in Běijīng, and most people speak none at all (taxi drivers, for example). However, many people who work in the tourist industry do speak at least some English (particularly in hotels and hostels), so, as a tourist, you'll be able to get by without speaking Chinese. That said, you'll enrich your experience here hugely, and gain the respect of the locals, if you make a stab at learning some Chinese before you come.

1 Where would you go for yum cha?

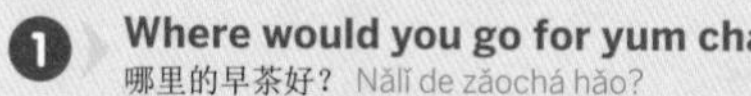

哪里的早茶好？ Nǎlǐ de zǎochá hǎo?

When in China, make sure you find the right place for what has to be the signature dining experience in Chinatowns the world over.

2 Please bring a knife and fork.

请拿一副刀叉来。 Qǐng ná yī fù dāochā lái.

Don't be afraid to ask for cutlery at a restaurant if you haven't quite mastered the art of eating with chopsticks.

3 Can I get a discount (for the room)?

这（房间）能打折吗? Zhè (fángjiān) néng dǎzhé ma?

In China, always bargain for a hotel room – discounts of 10% to 50% off the rack rate are the norm, available by simply asking at reception.

4 I'd like to hire a bicycle.

我想租一辆自行车。 Wǒ xiǎng zū yīliàng zìxíngchē.

Bikes are a great option for getting around Chinese cities and tourist sites. They can also be invaluable for exploring the countryside.

5 Can you write that in Pinyin for me?

请用拼音写。 Qǐng yòng Pīnyīn xiě.

If you find Chinese script intimidating, Pinyin (the official system for writing Mandarin in the Roman alphabet) is your next best option.

Etiquette

Generally speaking, China is pretty relaxed when it comes to etiquette.

➡ **Greetings and goodbyes** Shake hands, but never kiss someone's cheek. Say *'nǐ hǎo'* to greet someone, and *'zài jiàn'* to say goodbye.

➡ **Asking for help** To ask for directions, say *'qǐng wèn...'* ('can I ask...'). Say *'duìbuqǐ'* ('sorry') to apologise.

➡ **Eating and drinking** Help fill your neighbour's plate or bowl at the dinner table. Toast the host and others at the table. At the start of dinner, wait until toasting begins before drinking from your glass. Offer your cigarettes around if you smoke. Always offer to pay for the meal, or for drinks at a bar, but don't fight too hard over the tab if someone else wants to pay.

Getting Around

For more information, see Transport (p244)

Bicycle (自行车; zìxíngchē)

The most fun and often the quickest way to get around. Almost every road has a bike lane. Bike rental per day is ¥30 to ¥50.

Walking (走路; zǒulù)

The best way to see Běijīng's *hútòng* (narrow alleyways).

Subway (地铁; dìtiě)

Quick, modern and easy to use (all signage is in Chinese and English), but often overcrowded, so don't expect a seat. Costs ¥2 per trip, but price hike expected.

Bus (公共汽车; gōnggòng qìchē)

Dirt cheap and extensive, but difficult for non-Chinese speakers to negotiate, and often overcrowded. Costs ¥1 per trip, with travel card ¥0.4. Price hike expected.

Taxi (出租车; chūzūchē)

Cheap by Western standards, but at certain times hard to find, and traffic jams can really slow things down. Flag fall is ¥13.

Cycle/Motor Rickshaw (三轮车; sānlúnchē)

Great fun, but fares have to be negotiated (rickshaws don't have meters) so tourists are sometimes heavily overcharged.

Key Phrases

dǎ dī (打的) To take a taxi (colloquial)

dǎ biǎo (打表) To use the meter

qù ____ duōshǎo qián? How much to ____ ?

zuò chē (坐车) To take a bus

qù ____ ma? Does this go to ____ ?

mǎi piào (买票) To buy a ticket

yīkǎtōng (一卡通) Travel card

shuā kǎ (刷卡) To swipe a travel card

xià chē (下车) To get off any vehicle

dào le! (到了) We've arrived!

kuài dào le (到了) We're nearly there.

dǔ chē (堵车) Traffic jam

zū zìxíngchē (租自行车) To rent a bicycle

yǒu suǒ ma? (有锁吗?) Do you have a bike lock?

dǎ qì (打气) To pump up a tyre

Key Routes

Buses 专1 and 专2 These two handy buses do clockwise circuits of the Forbidden City, looping south to Qiánmén, via Tiān'ānmén Sq.

Subway Lines 1 and 2 For 30 years, until 2002, these were Běijīng's only two subways lines. They're still the most useful for tourists, between them taking in the Forbidden City, Tiān'ānmén Sq, the Drum Tower, the Lama Temple, the main train station and the two shopping hubs of Xīdān and Wángfǔjǐng.

How to Hail a Taxi

➡ It's almost always best to simply hail a passing taxi from the side of the road.

➡ A red '空车-for hire' sign will be illuminated in the front windscreen when a taxi is free.

➡ Your hotel may be able to help arrange a taxi for day trips, out of town.

TOP TIPS

➡ Go right to the very end subway carriages for a bit more breathing space (but still probably no seat).

➡ Every subway platform has public toilets at one end.

➡ If a taxi driver refuses to *dǎ biǎo* (use the meter), get out and find another one.

➡ Taxi drivers don't speak English, so always have the name and address in Chinese characters of the place you're going to. And don't forget your hotel's business card, so you can find your way home again!

When to Travel

➡ **Rush hour** Roughly 7.30am to 8.30am and 6pm to 7pm. This is when the subway is heaving, but it's also very tough to find a cab that's free. Avoid these times if you can, or cycle.

➡ **Rainstorms** Taxis are always hard to find when it's raining.

➡ **Evening** In areas where there are lots of bars and restaurants, it can be hard to find a taxi from around 8pm to 10pm.

Etiquette

➡ Do give up your seat for children or the elderly, even if it seems as though others aren't prepared to do so.

➡ Passengers of all ages (not just kids) rush to any spare seats the moment the subway doors open.

➡ Don't expect people to let you off your subway carriage before they get on.

➡ Bus and subway passengers expect to be allowed to move right to the door in preparation for getting off at the next stop.

Tickets & Passes

➡ At the time of research, Běijīng was expecting a large hike in public transport fares. For a long time, fares had been set at ¥2 for any single journey on the subway, and ¥1 for any city-centre bus trip (¥0.4 with a travel card). This was expected to change to a system based on distance travelled.

➡ It's worth getting a free travel card (一卡通; *yīkǎtōng;* deposit ¥20) at any subway station or large bus station. It makes subway travel more convenient (and may make it cheaper if subway fares rise as expected) and gives you 60% off all bus rides, including those out to the Great Wall. You can recharge them at many (but not all) subway stations and bus-station ticket kiosks.

➡ Children under 1.2m in height travel for free, but each must be accompanied by a fee-paying adult.

For much more on **getting around**, see p251.

ARRIVING IN BĚIJĪNG

Běijīng Capital International Airport The Airport Express (¥25, 30 minutes, 6.30am to 11pm) links up with the subway system (Lines 10 and 2). If taking a taxi (¥80 to ¥100), use the official taxi rank only.

Běijīng Train Station On subway Line 2.

Běijīng West Train Station On subway Line 9.

Běijīng South Train Station On subway Line 4.

Top Itineraries

Day One

Temple of Heaven Park & Dōngchéng South (p106)

You're jet-lagged anyway, so what the heck? Get up at the crack of dawn and head straight for **Temple of Heaven Park**. Běijīng is blessed with some fabulous city parks, but this is arguably the most captivating of all, and early morning, when it's filled with locals rather than tourists, is the best time to visit. Don't miss the park's crowning edifice, the magnificent **Hall of Prayer for Good Harvests** – Ming-dynasty architectural perfection.

Lunch Traditional noodles at Old Běijīng Zhájiàng Noodle King (p113).

Forbidden City & Dōngchéng Central (p52)

Join the crowds of domestic tourists on their pilgrimage-like tour of China's most famous public space, **Tiān'ānmén Square**, before spending the afternoon exploring the immense palace grounds of the **Forbidden City**.

Dinner Take a short walk to cute courtyard restaurant Little Yúnnán (p73).

Drum Tower & Dōngchéng North (p82)

Start your evening with cocktails in **Mao Mao Chong**, just a short walk north of Little Yúnnán, before catching some live music at **Jiāng Hú** or **Mao Livehouse**.

Day Two

The Great Wall (p170)

Make an early start. You're heading for the Great Wall at **Zhuàngdàokǒu**. It's not the most remote section of the Wall, but it still takes a while to get there by bus, via Huáiróu.

Lunch Stop for lunch at Zǎoxiāng Yard (p179), a small village guesthouse.

The Great Wall (p170)

Leave the village, and follow the stony pathway up to the Great Wall. When you hit the Wall, turn right and begin the steep, 45-minute hike to the top (where you'll get fabulous views of the Wall snaking off into the distance), before descending (15 minutes) to the main road by **Huánghuā Chéng Great Wall**. You can climb another section of the Wall here, if you like, or just catch a bus back to Huáiróu.

Dinner Authentic Běijīng grub at Bàodǔ Huáng (p144), near the bus terminus.

Sānlǐtún & Cháoyáng (p138)

If you've still got any energy left, hop in a taxi to **Dos Kolegas**, where you can catch a gig in the large beer garden.

Day Three

Drum Tower & Dōngchéng North (p82)

After an exhausting second day, ease yourself into Day Three with a calming stroll around the incense-filled courtyards of the **Lama Temple** before visiting the equally peaceful **Confucius Temple**. Grab a coffee at nearby **Cafe Confucius** before heading for lunch.

Lunch Great value set-menu at Xù Xiāng Zhāi Vegetarian Restaurant (p97).

Drum Tower & Dōngchéng North (p82)

Stroll through the *hútòng* to the magnificent **Drum Tower**. Catch one of the drumming performances here before hopping across the square to climb the equally majestic **Bell Tower**.

Dinner Stroll south for an evening meal in the intriguing Royal Icehouse (p127).

Běihǎi Park & Xīchéng North (p116)

Listen to some live jazz at nearby **East Shore Jazz Cafe**, before drinking the night away by the lakeside, at the Hòuhǎi Bar Strip.

Day Four

Summer Palace & Hǎidiàn (p157)

Head to the western outskirts for a morning trip to the **Summer Palace**, where the imperial court used to decamp to flee Běijīng's midsummer heatwaves. Food options are poor here (although it's great picnic territory), so have lunch at 798 Art District, where you'll be spending the afternoon.

Lunch At Cafe (p152): the original, and still one of the best artists hang-outs.

Sānlǐtún & Cháoyáng (p138)

Spend the rest of the afternoon at **798 Art District**: wander the galleries, stop for coffee and chat to young artists, while keeping your eye out for quirky souvenirs.

Dinner Head to Lìqún Roast Duck Restaurant (p113) for Peking duck.

Dashilar & Xīchéng South (p130)

Spend your last evening in Běijīng being wowed by the city's best performance artists. If it's Peking opera you fancy, there's nowhere better than **Húguǎng Guild Hall**. Acrobatics more your thing? Head to **Tiānqiáo Acrobatics Theatre**. Can't decide? Try the mixed-performance shows at **Lao She Teahouse**.

If You Like...

Imperial Architecture

Forbidden City Sitting at the very heart of Běijīng, this vast 9000-room palace made up of hundreds of buildings is China's best-preserved reminder of its imperial past. (p54)

Temple of Heaven Park This fabulous imperial park is home to the sublime Hall of Prayer for Good Harvests – the most perfect surviving example of Ming-dynasty architecture. (p108)

Summer Palace A harmonious marvel of landscaping on the outskirts of the city which features hilltop temples and elegant pavilions all set around a lake. (p159)

Drum & Bell Towers Dating back to the Mongol occupation of Běijīng and still standing guard over the surrounding *hútòng* (narrow alleyways). (p86)

Gate of Heavenly Peace Chairman Mao's portrait may adorn it, and he proclaimed the founding of the People's Republic of China (PRC) from atop it, but this was the largest gateway to the old imperial city. (p65)

Workers Cultural Palace Not a very promising name, but this little-visited and quiet park was once an important place of worship for China's emperors, and is home to some superb imperial-era halls. (p65)

Southeast Corner Watchtower Splendid Ming-dynasty structure that rises above the last remaining stretch of the former city walls. (p111)

Prince Gong's Residence An imperial-style home and the

Silk at a Běijīng market

finest example of a traditional courtyard house, only on a very grand scale. (p120)

Foreign Legation Quarter Imperial, but in the Western fashion rather than the Chinese; an incongruous slice of colonial-era European architecture in Běijīng. (p67)

Ming Tombs The Unesco-protected final resting place of 13 of the 16 Ming-dynasty emperors showcases some of Běijīng's largest and most-impressive imperial structures. (p184)

Parks

Fragrant Hills Park Superb in the early autumn, when Beijingers flock here to see the maple leaves turn red against the green backdrop of the hills. (p161)

Běihǎi Park Hire a boat and spend a lazy day floating on the lake, or just amble around watching the locals at play. (p118)

Temple of Heaven Park A prime spot for people-watching, as Běijīng's senior citizens dance or practise taichi in the shade of thousands of ancient cypress trees. (p108)

Jǐngshān Park Climb the man-made hill for fine views over the Forbidden City. (p65)

Rìtán Park A soothing escape from the hustle of the nearby CBD, fly a kite by the altar to the sun that's located here. (p141)

Dìtán Park Home to Běijīng's most popular temple fair during the Spring Festival. (p88)

Hòuhǎi Lakes Not strictly a park, but still one of the most happening open spaces in Běijīng; a playground by day, and nightlife hub come sundown. (p120)

Markets

Pānjiāyuán Market Hands-down the most fun market in the city, a chaotic jumble of antiques, calligraphy, carpets, curios, furniture and Mao memorabilia. (p154)

Mǎliándào Tea Market All the tea in China, or at least most of it, with tea shops galore around it for those in search of tea sets. (p137)

Silk Market Still one of the essential stops for many visitors to the capital, its collection of counterfeit clothes and bags is as popular as the genuine silk sold here. (p153)

Hóngqiáo (Pearl) Market Pearls and more pearls, of wildly different quality, as well as all manner of ephemera. (p115)

Temples

Lama Temple A former royal palace that is now home to chanting monks, this impressive, ornate complex is Běijīng's most popular Buddhist temple. (p84)

Confucius Temple Lovely, tranquil retreat from the hustle of Běijīng's chaotic streets and surrounded by atmospheric *hútòng*. (p88)

Dōngyuè Temple Perhaps the strangest temple in the capital, certainly the most morbid, this thought-provoking and very active Taoist shrine has halls dedicated to ghosts and the god who manages the 18 levels of hell. (p141)

White Cloud Temple Founded in AD 739, White Cloud Temple is the headquarters for China's Taoists and home to a fabulous temple fair during Spring Festival. (p124)

For more top Běijīng spots, see the following:

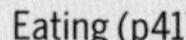

- Eating (p41)
- Drinking & Nightlife (p43)
- Entertainment (p45)
- Shopping (p47)

Fǎyuán Temple Secluded and very ancient shrine, dating back to the 7th century AD, and still busy with worshippers. (p132)

Wǔtǎ Temple A distinct oddity, with its five striking pagodas, and more reminiscent of an Indian temple than a Chinese one. (p163)

Fine Dining

Brian McKenna @ The Courtyard The setting right by the Forbidden City couldn't be better – book ahead for a window seat – and the food and wine list are top class. (p74)

Temple Restaurant A contemporary European menu and a fabulous location in the grounds of a former temple. (p74)

Lost Heaven The subtle flavours of Yúnnán province served up in the swanky surrounds of the former Foreign Legation Quarter (p113)

Duck de Chine A France-meets-China take on the capital's favourite bird in industrial-chic surroundings. (p147)

Capital M Classic Mediterranean meets North African dishes and views over Tiān'ānmén Sq at this Běijīng outpost of a celebrated Shànghǎi restaurant. (p114)

Source Swish Sìchuān, with the spices toned down for Western palates, in a delightful courtyard house in the heart of *hútòng* land. (p98)

Běijīng Dàdǒng Roast Duck Ultramodern restaurant promising the leanest roast duck in the capital. (p74)

O'Steak Relaxed, French-run steak house with superior cuts of meat and a top-class wine list. (p148)

Okra Minimalist in design, but the best sushi in the capital. (p148)

Museums & Galleries

Capital Museum Běijīng's finest, containing superbly informative galleries on the evolution of the city and its customs, and all in a bright, user-friendly environment. (p124)

798 Art District A maze of galleries devoted to the weird and wonderful world of Chinese contemporary art; be prepared to be alternatively bemused and captivated. (p140)

Poly Art Museum The place to see some of the ancient treasures, including incredible bronzes, that weren't pillaged by invading armies in the 19th century. (p69)

Běijīng Police Museum Brothels, opium dens, class traitors, gangsters and spies; the past and present Běijīng underworld revealed in all its fascinating, sometimes gruesome, glory. (p67)

Military Museum Something of a propaganda exercise perhaps, but plenty of detail on China's martial past and lots and lots of guns, swords, tanks, missiles and planes. (p166)

Běijīng Ancient Architecture Museum Little-visited but excellent museum housed in a former Ming-dynasty temple that offers a great guide to how the imperial city was built. (p132)

Red Gate Gallery The original gallery devoted to modern Chinese art, and still trailblazing with the artists it showcases. (p111)

National Museum of China Newly renovated, extensive trawl through 5000 years of Chinese history and culture. (p64)

Chinese Performing Arts

Tiānqiáo Acrobatics Theatre Perhaps the finest tumbling, spinning, high-wire-walking show in town, and less touristy than other venues. (p134)

Húguǎng Guild Hall Fantastic, historic venue for Peking opera, with the audience close to the action and superb balconies overlooking the stage. (p135)

National Centre for the Performing Arts One of the key hubs of Běijīng cultural life, as well as one of the city's most striking buildings, with China's top orchestras and classical dance troupes regular performers. (p128)

Lao She Teahouse A little bit of everything takes place here on a nightly basis: Peking opera, shadow-puppet and folk-music performances especially, but also crosstalk: traditional Běijīng stand-up comedy. (p135)

China Puppet Theatre Shadowplay and puppetry every weekend, and a great place to take kids who've had enough of sightseeing. (p102)

Live Music

Yúgōng Yíshān Chinese and foreign bands and electronic knob-twiddlers, as well as an audience-friendly vibe, make this the top venue for seeing live music in the capital. (p101)

Mao Livehouse Big enough to make you feel like you're at a real event, but small enough to still feel intimate; a sound booking policy and a cracking sound system. (p101)

East Shore Jazz Café The number-one spot in town for jazzers with a prime location by the side of the Hòuhǎi Lakes; a relaxed feel and cool tunes late into the night. (p128)

Dos Kolegas A little bit out of the way, but this is a grungy gem of a venue that puts on a lot of the local punk and alternative bands. (p152)

Jiāng Hú Intimate courtyard venue for local indie and rock bands. (p101)

Temple Bar The owners are tattooed and pierced metal and punk fiends, but all sorts of bands take to the stage at this friendly place. (p101)

Jiāng Jìn Jiǔ A cafe by day that puts on a lot of folk and ethnic minority acts, especially Uighur and Mongolian, which you won't hear anywhere else once the sun goes down. (p101)

What? Bar Years ago this tiny place was just about the only venue in town; it still has loads of character and it's a good place to see up-and-coming new bands. (p75)

Month by Month

TOP EVENTS

Spring Festival, January/February

International Literary Festival, March

Midi Festival, April

National Day, October

Běijīng Music Festival, October

January

Běijīng shivers at the beginning of the year, with temperatures dipping to −10°C or below. But there are far fewer visitors in town, so this is a great time to see the Forbidden City without the crowds. Head to the Hòuhǎi Lakes for ice skating.

Western New Year

元旦; Yuándàn

With the Spring Festival as their New Year bash, the Chinese treat the Western New Year on 1 January as an excuse just to party and have fun. But don't expect any fireworks.

February

Not a good month for air pollution, and it can be bitterly cold, but Spring Festival means winter is drawing to a close.

Spring Festival

春节; Chūn Jié

As big as Christmas in the West, the family-oriented, 15-day Spring Festival is the year's most joyous celebration. Fireworks illuminate the night sky, while firecrackers are let off seemingly nonstop. Spend time with a Chinese family if you can, or visit a temple fair (庙会; *miàohuì*): try Dōngyuè Temple (p141) or White Cloud Temple (p124). 2016: 8 February. 2017: 28 January. 2018: 16 February.

Lantern Festival

元宵节; Yuánxiāo Jié

Celebrated on the final day of Spring Festival, this tastiest of festivities sees locals devour delicious *yuánxiāo* (glutinous rice dumplings with sweet fillings), while fireworks and firecrackers explode all over town.

Valentine's Day

情人节; Qíngrén Jié

China has its own festival for lovers (Qīxī; 七夕; held on the seventh day of the seventh month of the lunar year), but it's not nearly as popular as the Western version, held here on 14 February too. Book ahead if you want to eat out. And be sure to buy your Valentine 11 roses, not 12.

March

It's almost time to put away the winter wardrobe. The domestic tourists who came for the Spring Festival have gone, but foreign ones are arriving in numbers.

International Literary Festival

国际文学节; Guójì Wénxué Jié

This excellent festival sees writers and bibliophiles convening at the Bookworm

THE CHINESE CALENDAR

China follows both the *yánglì* (Gregorian) and the *yīnlì* (lunar) calendars. Traditional Chinese festivals are calculated according to the lunar calendar and fall on different days each year according to the Gregorian calendar.

(www.chinabookworm.com) for a two-week bonanza of readings and talks. With a very strong line-up of international authors and local writers, it's one of the key cultural events of the year. Get tickets early. Capital M Literary Festival (www.m-restaurantgroup.com/capitalm), also in March, has a similarly impressive program.

Guanyin's Birthday

观世音生日, Guānshìyīn Shēngrì

Held on the 19th day of the second moon, the birthday of Guanyin, the Buddhist Goddess of Mercy, is a fine time to visit Buddhist temples. 2016: 26 March; 2017: 16 March.

April

One of the nicest months of the year to be in Běijīng, as a fresh wind keeps the sky clear and snowflake-like poplar seeds and willow catkins *(liǔxù)* flutter through the air. It's getting warmer.

Tomb Sweeping Day

清明节, Qīngmíng Jié

This official public holiday falls on 5 April (4 April in leap years). People visit and clean the graves of their departed relatives, placing flowers on tombs and burning ghost money for the departed; you'll see ghost money being burned on pavements around the city.

Midi Festival

迷笛音乐节, Mídí Yīnyuè Jié

China's longest-running music festival normally takes place in Hǎidiàn (or sometimes in Tōngzhōu on the eastern outskirts of Běijīng) on the last weekend of April. Both domestic and international bands and electronic acts play. It's a great chance to mingle with local music fans.

Spring Flower Shows

花展, Huā Zhǎn

Flower-loving locals flock to Zhōngshān Park (p66) and Jǐngshān Park (p65) in April and May, when the parks' tulip and peony flower shows are in full bloom.

May

The temperature starts to rise as the fiercely hot and humid Běijīng summer approaches. May also marks the beginning of the peak tourist season.

May Day

五一, Wǔyī

May Day on 1 May kicks off a much-needed three-day national holiday for Chinese, who swamp tourist sights the length and breadth of the nation.

June

Hot and sweaty days and balmy nights. But this month is also the peak time for rainfall in Běijīng. The main tourist sites are packed.

Dragon Boat Festival

端午节, Duānwǔ Jié

Held on the fifth day of the fifth lunar month (usually June), dragon boat races are sometimes staged on Běijīng's reservoirs and you'll see people all over town scoffing *zòngzi* (delicious parcels of sticky rice and meat or veggies wrapped in a bamboo leaf). 2015: 20 June; 2016: 9 June; 2017: 30 May.

SURGE Art Běijīng

北京艺术节, Běijīng Yìshùjié

Held at different venues from year to year, this art fair (www.surgeart.com) showcases emerging contemporary Chinese artists and acts as a platform for them to sell affordable art.

September

The crowds are thinning out a little at the main tourist sites and the heat has mercifully relented. But this month sometimes sees major gatherings of the Chinese Communist Party (CCP) in the capital, which means enhanced security around Tiān'ānmén Sq.

Mid-Autumn Festival

中秋节, Zhōngqiū Jié

Also known as the Moon Festival, the Mid-Autumn Festival is marked by eating *yuèbǐng* (moon cakes), gazing at the full moon and family reunions. 2015: 27 September; 2016: 15 September; 2017: 4 October.

October

Autumn is a fine time to visit Běijīng as it enjoys high clear skies and perhaps its best weather of the year. It can feel crowded, though, as domestic visitors descend on the capital during Golden Week.

Top: Decorations at Dìtán Park (p88) during Spring Festival
Bottom: Folk musicians at Spring Festival, Dōngyuè Temple (p141)

National Day

国庆节, Guóqìng Jié

Crowds flock to Tiān'ānmén Sq for a huge party on 1 October, followed by a massive week-long national holiday where the Chinese blow their hard-earned savings on travelling and enjoying themselves in what is known as Golden Week.

Běijīng Music Festival

北京国际音乐节, Běijīng Guójì Yīnyuè Jié

Usually staged throughout October, this classical-music festival (www.bmf.org.cn) showcases foreign orchestras and musicians and has become increasingly high-profile in recent years. It's a must for Běijīng culture vultures.

December

Běijīng can feel gloomy once winter descends and it becomes relentlessly cold. But a white Christmas is a real possibility, and you can strap on the ice skates and take to the Hòuhǎi Lakes, although sometimes they don't freeze sufficiently until January.

Christmas Day

圣诞节, Shèngdàn Jié

Not an official Chinese festival perhaps, but Christmas is a significant event on the commercial calendar, when Běijīng's big shopping zones sparkle with decorations and younger Chinese get into the Yuletide spirit.

With Kids

The Chinese have a deep and uncomplicated love of children and openly display their affection for them. Běijīng may have less child-friendly facilities than equivalent-sized cities in the West, but the locals will go out of their way to accommodate your kids.

Need to Know

- **Discounts** Kids are often half price; those under 1.2m in height are usually free.
- **Bike seats** Rent baby seats and helmets from Bike Be ijing (p251).
- **Seatbelts** Only in the front of taxis, so consider sitting up here with your child on your lap.
- **Getting Lost** Always arm your child with your hotel's business card.
- **Cots** Only available in top-end hotels.

Toddlers

Parks

Toddlers will love exploring the dinky pathways of Běijīng's parks and dancing along to bands of local singers. Parks are also perfect for family picnics. Try Temple of Heaven Park (p108), Jǐngshān Park (p65), Rìtán Park (p141) or **Cháoyáng Park** (朝阳公园; Cháoyáng Gōngyuán).

Young Kids

Lakes

Běihǎi Park (p118) has a large boating lake. The lakes at Hòuhǎi (p120) also provide pedal-boats, and in winter they freeze over and become central Běijīng's biggest playground. Rent ice-skates, ice-bikes and even ice bumper cars! The rest of the year, try Le Cool Ice Rink (p156) in the China World Shopping Mall.

Swimming

For water slides, try the outdoor pools at Cháoyáng Park, **Tuánjiéhú Park** (团结湖公园; Tuánjiéhú Gōngyuán) with its mini-beach, or Qīngnián Hú Park (p105). For something bigger, head to the huge indoor Happy Magic Water Park (p156).

Toys

The Toy Market behind Hóngqiáo (Pearl) Market (p115) is full of cheap toys that whiz, whir, beep and flash.

Arts & Crafts

At Jīngchéng Bǎixìng (p103) kids can have a go at painting, or even making, their own traditional Chinese clay figures.

Kite-Flying

Buy a handmade kite at Three Stone Kite Shop (p129) and head to one of the parks to join the legion of kite-flying enthusiasts.

Museums & Shows

Try the vast China Science & Technology Museum (p144) or the Běijīng Natural History Museum (p111), which has dinosaurs! Kids will love the China Puppet Theatre (p102) or an acrobatics show.

Teenagers

Hiking & Cycling

Older kids will love the adventure of hiking along the Great Wall; just be sure they know the dangers. Cycling tours around the *hútòng* (narrow alleyways) can also be fun. Try hooking up with Bike Běijīng (p251).

Like a Local

Eat pancakes off a cycle rickshaw, use a shuttlecock for keepie-uppies, and walk backwards, barefoot, along pebbled pathways; you're in Běijīng now, where people do things a bit differently.

MATT MUNRO / LONELY PLANET ©

Cooking *yóutiáo* (fried dough sticks)

Eating

Běijīng Cuisine

Běijīng has pretty much every type of world cuisine covered – be it Chinese or international – but there are still a few restaurants knocking out genuine old-Běijīng tucker.

Breakfast

Skip the expensive fry-up and coffee in your hotel and head to any restaurant that has bamboo baskets stacked up at its entrance between 6am and 8.30am. This indicates that they do dumplings. Order *'yītì bāozi'* (a basket of dumplings) with *'yīwǎn zhōu'* (a bowl of rice porridge), and tuck in. You'll pay less than one US dollar. Other favourite breakfast combos here include *yóutiáo* (油条; fried dough sticks) with *dòujiāng* (豆浆; soy milk); and *húndùn* (馄炖; wonton soup) with *shāobing* (烧饼; sesame-seed roasted bun).

Snacks & Street Food

Things to look out for in the evenings include *yángròu chuàn* (羊肉串; lamb skewers) – any place with a large red neon 串 sign does them. During the day, look for *jiānbing* (煎饼; savoury pancakes), sometimes cooked off the back of a cycle rickshaw.

Food Markets

Western-style supermarkets are on the rise, but thankfully there are still some atmospheric food markets in Běijīng where you can stock up on fresh fruit as you watch locals pick their favourite frogs and fish. Try Rùndélì Food Market (p127) near Hòuhǎi Lake or Xīnmín Food Market (p96), just north of the Drum Tower.

Park Life

Group Dancing

Locals often congregate in parks for a hearty singsong or a good old dance. Large-group formation dancing, accompanied by heavily amplified, patriotic songs, is the order of the day, and passers-by are always welcome to join in. Note, it isn't just parks that attract group dancing. Any large paved area of the city, especially public squares (although not Tiān'ānmén Sq), are prime locations come early evening.

Flying Kites

The all-time classic Chinese pastime is as popular as ever and Běijīng's parks are a great place to join in. Buy a kite – try Three Stone Kite Shop (p129), or Tiān Yì Goods Market (p104) – then head to any park; the northeast corner of Temple of Heaven Park (p108) is a good spot.

Games

Card games are very popular, as is *jiànzi,* an oversized shuttlecock that's used for keepie-uppies. Older people enjoy the soothing nature of *róulìqiú* (taiji softball). Whatever the game, locals are almost always happy for you to join in. So, don't just stand there taking photos; play!

Working Out

All Běijīng parks have exercise areas with low-tech apparatus, such as pull-up bars and leg curls. Hòuhǎi Exercise Park (p125) is a popular lakeside version. Some areas include a pebble path. Try walking barefoot along them; good for your circulation, apparently, especially if you do it backwards.

Taichi

You'll notice some trees in parks have a worn out ring of bare ground around the base of their trunk. This marks out the tree as a taichi spot. Every day, usually early in the morning, someone will come to this tree to perform his or her preferred taichi movements. It's fascinating to watch.

Other Activities

Cycling

Cyclist numbers are declining, but they are still huge, and cycling along with the masses is a great way to feel like you are a part of the everyday city flow. It's also the perfect way to explore Běijīng's *hútòng* (narrow alleyways).

Table Tennis

It's easy to understand how China dominates world table tennis when you see how easily available the sport is. Schools have whole floors of buildings dedicated to table tennis, and there are free-to-use tables dotted around the city, in most parks and most residential areas. If you fancy being on the wrong end of a ping-pong thrashing, head to Jǐngshān Table Tennis Park (p79). Hòuhǎi Exercise Park (p125) also has tables.

Ice Swimming

Every day of the year a group of dedicated Beijingers go swimming in the lakes at Hòuhǎi (p120). Nothing strange about that, until it gets to December, when temperatures plummet and the lake freezes over. Instead of taking a winter break, they rise early each morning, smash a hole in the ice and go for the coldest swim imaginable. Head to Hòuhǎi Exercise Park (p125) if you want to watch or, heaven forbid, take a plunge yourself.

Nightlife

KTV

Bars and clubs are a Western influence. Most locals just go for a slap-up meal if they fancy a night out. If they do go anywhere after dinner, it's usually to a karaoke joint, aka KTV. You're locked away in your own private room, so it's pretty boring on your own, but if you get the chance to join a group of Chinese friends, take it; the Chinese enthusiasm for belting out pop classics is incredible, and most KTV joints have an English song list available too.

Báijǐu

We don't recommend you drink this stuff – it is lethal – but the few old Beijingers who are serious drinkers tend only to drink *báijiǔ* (白酒), a potent liquor made from sorghum. If you do get goaded into a *báijǐu* session at a local restaurant (no one drinks *báijǐu* in bars), take care. The protocol is to down glassfuls in one hit, while declaring '*gānbēi!*' (dry glass!), so getting blind drunk doesn't take long.

For Free

Běijīng may not appear at first sight to be a city overburdened with freebies. But dig a little deeper and you'll find a plethora of places to see, things to do and worthwhile experiences to be had that don't involve cash changing hands.

Free Activities

Hòuhǎi Lakes

Join the locals promenading around the lakes (p120), watch the kite-flying or have a game of table tennis.

Hútòng

Walk your shoes off through the myriad ancient alleyways.

Parks

Jǐngshān Park (p65), Zhōngshān Park (p66), Dìtán Park (p88) and Workers Cultural Palace (p65) are fun to explore and cost just ¥2 to ¥5 to enter.

798 Art District

One of the very best freebies in town, this art district (p140) inhabits a former factory.

Free Museums & Galleries

To get in for free, bring your passport.

Capital Museum

The best museum (p124) in the city, with a host of galleries and exhibits.

Military Museum

Guns, planes, rockets and tanks (p166).

National Museum of China

Come to this excellent museum (p64) to see 5000 years of Chinese history.

China Art Museum

Absorbing art exhibitions from across China (p67).

Shǐjiā Hútòng Museum

The story of one of Běijīng's most historic *hútòng* neighbourhoods (p71).

Lu Xun Museum

The life and times of the father of modern Chinese literature (p124).

Free Sights

Tiān'ānmén Square

Stroll around, catch the flag-raising and lowering ceremonies at dawn and dusk, and watch the kite-flying in the world's largest public square (p62).

Chairman Mao Memorial Hall

It doesn't cost a thing to shuffle reverently past the Great Helmsman's mummified remains in this memorial hall (p64). Open mornings only.

Foreign Legation Quarter

Enjoy a complimentary walk past the imposing European architecture (p67).

Ming City Wall Ruins Park

The sole remaining section of the Ming-dynasty walls that once enclosed Běijīng, this slice of history comes gratis (p111).

Free Wednesdays

On Wednesdays, the first 200 visitors get free entrance to Zhìhuà Temple (p69), Xiānnóng Altar (p132), Wǔtǎ Temple (p163) and Wànshòu Temple (p161).

Stretching dough to make noodles

Eating

Běijīng is a magnificent place for culinary adventures. With upwards of 60,000 restaurants here, you can enjoy the finest local dishes, as well as eating your way through every region of China. Some of your most memorable Běijīng experiences will take place around the dining table. So do as the locals do – grab those chopsticks and dive in.

Peking duck

NEED TO KNOW

Price Ranges

The following price ranges represent the cost of a meal for one person.

$ up to ¥40
$$ ¥40 to ¥100
$$$ over ¥100

Opening Hours

Běijīng restaurants are mostly open from around 10am to 11pm, although there are a few that run 24/7. Many shut after lunch and reopen at 5pm. Generally, Chinese eat much earlier than Westerners, lunching from 11am and having dinner at about 6pm.

Menus

Be warned that some restaurants in tourist areas still fob off foreigners with an English menu (英文菜单; *yīngwén càidān*) that has higher prices than the Chinese menu (中文菜单; *zhōngwén càidān*). Generally, though, most places have picture and/or English menus now.

Service

With the exception of upmarket restaurants, service can often be erratic and/or lackadaisical. Unless you're in a restaurant that serves foreign food, don't expect the waiting staff to speak English.

Smoking

There are nonsmoking signs in most Běijīng restaurants these days, but that doesn't mean they are adhered to. Smoking is still commonplace in many eateries. Our listings note if an establishment is tobacco-free.

Tipping

Tipping is not standard practice in Běijīng. Leave a tip in a local restaurant and the waiter will likely come after you, saying you've forgotten your change. Some upmarket Western places, though, do tack on a service charge to the bill, as do high-end hotel restaurants.

Peking Duck

You'd have to be quackers to leave Běijīng without trying Peking duck (北京烤鸭; *Běijīng kǎoyā*), the capital's most iconic dish. Its origins go back as far as the 13th century and the Yuan dynasty, when it was listed in royal cookbooks. But it wasn't until imperial rule in China came to an end in 1911 that most ordinary people got the chance to try it, when the former palace cooks set up roast duck restaurants around Běijīng.

Chefs go through a lengthy process to prepare the duck. First the birds are inflated by blowing air between the skin and body. The skin is then pricked and boiling water poured all over the duck. Sometimes the skin is rubbed with malt sugar to give it an amber colour, before being hung up to air dry and then roasted in the oven. When roasted, the flesh becomes crispy on the outside and juicy on the inside. The bird is then meticulously cut into slices and served with fermented bean paste, light pancakes, sliced cucumbers and green onions.

Vegetarians & Vegans

China has a 1000-year-plus tradition of Taoist and Buddhist philosophers who abstained from eating animals. But with an equally long history of poverty and famine in China, eating meat is a sign of status and many Chinese regard vegetarianism as a strange Western concept.

However, there are an increasing number of vegetarian (吃素的人; *chīsùderén*) eateries, while many Buddhist temples also have vegetarian restaurants. Nevertheless, vegetarian food often consists of 'mock meat' dishes made from tofu, wheat gluten and vegetables. Some of the dishes are almost works of art, with the ingredients sculpted to look like spare ribs or fried chicken and 'bones' created from carrots and lotus roots.

Top: *Yáng zá* (sheep intestine) for sale at Dōnghuámén night market

Left: Traditional north-China hotpot

Etiquette

Strict rules of etiquette don't really apply to Chinese dining, with the notable exception of formal banquets. Table manners are relaxed and get more so as the meal unfolds and the drinks flow. By the end, the table can resemble a battlefield, with empty bottles, stray bones and other debris strewn across it.

Many foreigners get asked if they mind dishes that are *là* (辣; spicy). If you don't want very spicy, say '*bú yào tài là*' (not too spicy). The Chinese believe that a mix of tastes, textures and temperatures is the key to a good meal, so they start with cold dishes and follow them with a selection of hot meat, fish and vegetable dishes. Waiters will expect you to order straightaway after sitting down and will hover at your shoulder until you do. If you want more time, say '*wǒ huì jiào nǐ*' (I'll call you).

Rice often arrives at the end of the meal but if you want it before, just ask. The mainland Chinese dig their chopsticks into communal dishes, or spoons will be used to ladle out the food, but don't root around for a piece of food. Instead, identify it first and go directly to it without touching what's around it. Bones can be deposited in your side dish, or even on the table itself. If you're in doubt about what to do, just follow the example of the people around you.

Běijīng Bites

Off the main roads is a world of steaming food stalls and eateries teeming with activity. Eat this way and you will be dining as most Beijingers do. Breakfast can be easily catered for with a *yóutiáo* (油条; deep-fried dough stick), a sip of *dòuzhī* (豆汁; bean curd drink) or a bowl of *zhōu* (粥; rice porridge). Other snacks include the crunchy, pancake-like *jiānbǐng* (煎饼). The heavy meat-filled *ròubǐng* (肉饼; cooked bread filled with finely chopped pork) are lifesavers and very cheap. A handy vegetarian option is *jiǔcài bǐng* (韭菜饼; bread stuffed with cabbage, chives, leek or fennel and egg). *Dàbǐng* (大饼; a chunk of round, unleavened bread sprinkled with sesame seeds) can be found everywhere, and of course there's *mántou* (馒头; steamed bread).

Hóngshǔ (红薯; baked sweet potatoes) are cheap and filling and sold during winter. *Málà tàng* (麻辣烫) is a spicy noodle soup that's very warming in winter, and has chunks of *dòufu* (豆腐; bean curd), cabbage and other veggies – choose your own ingredients from the trays. Also look out for *ròu jiāmó* (肉夹馍), a scrumptious open-your-mouth-wide bun filled with meat, chilli and garlic shoots. But perhaps the most ubiquitous Běijīng snack is *kǎo yángròu chuàn* (烤羊肉串; lamb kebabs), which are sold throughout the city at all times of the day and night.

Desserts & Sweets

The Chinese do not generally eat dessert (甜点; *tiándiǎn*), but fruit is considered an appropriate end to a good meal. Western influence has added ice cream to the menu in some restaurants, but, in general, sweet stuff is consumed as snacks and is seldom available in restaurants.

Regional Cuisines

All of China's cuisines converge on Běijīng, from far-flung Tibet to the hardy northeast, the arid northwest and the fecund south. The most popular cooking styles are from Sìchuān, Shànghǎi, Hong Kong, Guǎngdōng (Cantonese) and Běijīng itself. If you want to explore China's full compendium of cuisines, Běijīng is *the* place to start.

BĚIJĪNG

Běijīng's native cuisine (京菜; *jīngcài*) is classified as a 'northern cuisine' and is in one of the four major styles of cooking in China. Peking duck apart, many popular dishes, such as hotpot (火锅; *huǒguō*), have their origins in Mongolia and arrived in the wake of Genghis Khan. Běijīng's bitter winters mean that warm, filling dishes are essential. Typically, they are made with wheat or millet, whose most common incarnations are delicious dumplings (饺子; *jiǎozi*) or noodles, which are preferred to rice in the capital. Vegetables are more limited, so there is a heavy reliance on freshwater fish and chicken; cabbage and turnips, as well as yams and potatoes, are some of the most ubiquitous vegetables found on menus.

Two of the region's most famous culinary exports – Mongolian barbecue and Mongolian hotpot – are adaptations from Mongol field kitchens. Animals that were hunted on horseback could be dismembered and cooked with wild vegetables and onions using soldiers' iron shields on top of hot coals as primitive barbecues. Alternatively, each soldier could use his helmet as a pot, filling it with water, meat, condiments and

Eating by Neighbourhood

vegetables to taste. Mutton is now the main ingredient in Mongolian hotpot.

Roasting was once considered rather barbaric in other parts of China and is still more common in the northern areas. The main methods of cooking in the northern style, though, are steaming, baking and 'explode-frying' (爆炒; *bàochǎo*), a rapid method of cooking in which the wok is superheated over a flame and the contents tossed in for a swift stir-frying.

SÌCHUĀN

Famed as China's fieriest food, Sìchuān cuisine (川菜) should be approached with caution and lots of chilled H_2O or beer. A concoction of searing red chillis (introduced by Spanish traders in the early Qing dynasty), star anise, peppercorns and pungent 'flower pepper' (花椒; *huājiāo*), a numbing herb peculiar to this cuisine, Sìchuān dishes are simmered to allow the chilli peppers time to seep into the food. Meats are often marinated, pickled or otherwise processed before cooking, which is generally by stir- or explode-frying.

Landlocked Sìchuān is a long way from the coast, so pork, poultry, legumes and *dòufu* (豆腐; bean curd) are commonly used, and supplemented by a variety of wild condiments and mountain products, such as mushrooms and other fungi, as well as bamboo shoots. Seasonings are heavy: the red chilli is often used in conjunction with Sìchuān peppercorns, garlic, ginger and onions. Hallmark dishes include camphor-smoked duck (樟茶鸭; *Zhāngchá yā*), Granny Ma's bean curd (麻婆豆腐; *Mápó dòufu*) and spicy chicken with peanuts (宫保鸡丁; *gōngbǎo jīdīng*).

CANTONESE

Cantonese cuisine (粤菜) is what non-Chinese consider to be 'Chinese' food, largely because most émigré restaurateurs originate from Guǎngdōng or nearby Hong Kong. Cantonese flavours are generally more subtle than other Chinese styles and there are very few spicy dishes. Sweet-and-sour and oyster sauces are common. The Cantonese are almost religious about the importance of fresh ingredients, which is why so many restaurants are lined with tanks full of finned and shelled creatures. Stir-frying is by far the favoured method of cooking, closely followed by steaming. Dim sum (点心; *diǎnxīn*), now a worldwide Sunday institution, originated in this region; to go *yum cha* (饮茶; Cantonese for 'drink tea') still provides most overseas Chinese communities with the opportunity to get together at the weekend. Dim sum can be found in restaurants around Běijīng.

Expensive dishes – some that are truly tasty, others that appeal more for their 'face' value – include abalone (鲍鱼; *bàoyú*), shark's fin (鱼翅; *yúchì*) and bird's nest (燕窝; *yànwō*). Pigeon (鸽子; *gēzi*) is a Cantonese speciality served in various ways, but most commonly roasted.

SHÀNGHǍI

Generally sweeter and oilier than China's other cooking styles, Shànghǎi cuisine (上海菜) features plenty of fish and seafood, especially cod, river eel and shrimp. Fish is usually *qīngzhēng* (清蒸; steamed) but can be stir-fried, pan-fried or grilled. Crab-roe dumplings (蟹黄饺子; *xièhuáng jiǎozi*) are another Shanghainese luxury. *Dàzháxiè* (大闸蟹; hairy crabs) are a Shànghǎi speciality between October and December. They are eaten with soy, ginger and vinegar and downed with warm Shàoxīng rice wine. They are delicious, but can be fiddly to eat. The body opens via a little tab on the underside (don't eat the gills or the stomach).

Several restaurants specialise in cold salty chicken, while drunken chicken gets its name from being marinated in Shàoxīng rice wine. *Bāo* (煲; clay pot) dishes are braised for a long time in their own casserole dish. Shànghǎi's most famous snack is *xiǎolóngbāo* (小笼包), small dumplings containing a meaty interior bathed in a scalding juice.

Vegetarian dishes include *dòufu;* cabbage in cream sauce; *mèn* (焖; braised) *dòufu;* and various types of mushrooms,

Diners enjoy a communal meal at a busy Dashilar restaurant

MǍIDĀN!

The Chinese pride themselves on unwavering generosity in public and the arrival of the bill (买单; *mǎidān*) among a group of diners is an excuse for some elaborate histrionics. People push each other aside and almost fight for the right to pay, but generally it is the host who does and if he doesn't he will lose face.

Splitting the bill is less common here than in the West, so if you invite someone out for dinner, be prepared to foot the bill. And remember that most places will expect you to settle it in hard cash; only top-end restaurants take credit cards.

including *xiānggū báicài* (香菇白菜; mushrooms surrounded by baby bok choy). Tiger-skin chillies (虎皮尖椒; Hǔpí Jiānjiāo) are a delicious dish of stir-fried green peppers seared in a wok and served in a sweet chilli sauce. Fried pine nuts and sweet corn (松子炒玉米; *sōngzǐ chǎo yùmǐ)* is another common Shanghainese dish.

UIGHUR

Uighur cuisine (新疆菜) reflects the influences of Xīnjiāng's chequered past. Yet, despite centuries of sporadic Chinese and Mongol rule, the strongest influence on ingredients and methods is still Turkic or Middle Eastern, which is evident in the reliance on mutton for protein and wheat as the staple grain. When rice is eaten, it is often in the Central Asian version of pilau *(plov)*. Nevertheless, the infusion of Chinese culinary styles and ingredients makes it probably the most enjoyable region of Central Asia in which to eat.

Uighur bread resembles Arabic *khoubz* (Indian naan) and is baked in ovens based on the *tanour* (Indian tandoor) model. It is often eaten straight from the oven and sprinkled with poppy seeds, sesame seeds or fennel. Uighur bakers also make excellent *girde nan* (bagels). Wheat is also used for a variety of noodles. *Laghman* (拌面; *bàn miàn*) are the most common: noodles cooked al dente, thick and topped with a combination of spicy mutton, peppers, tomatoes, eggplant, green beans and garlic. *Suoman* are noodle squares fried with tomatoes, peppers, garlic and meat, sometimes quite spicy. *Suoman goshsiz* is the vegetarian variety.

Kebabs, both shashlik (羊肉串; *yángròu chuàn*) and tandoori styles, are common, as they are throughout the Middle East and Central Asia. *Samsas* or *samsis* (烤包子; *kǎo bāozi*) are the Uighur version of samosas: baked envelopes of meat. Meat often makes an appearance inside *chuchura* (dumplings; 饺子汤; *jiǎozi tāng*), which can be steamed or fried.

Foreign Fancies

Běijīng's emergence as a true world city has revolutionised its dining scene. Now, a whole host of ambitious chefs have descended on the capital, meaning that if you're pining for a taste of home, you won't have to travel too far to find it.

Korean and Japanese restaurants are especially plentiful, and there are many places specialising in contemporary Mediterranean cuisine, as well as standard Western comfort food such as pizza, pasta, steaks and hamburgers. But whether you're hankering for Afghan or Turkish food, a burrito or a rogan josh, it's being served somewhere in the city. For restaurant listings, check the monthly expat magazines.

Self-Catering

Even the most selective chef will be able to find just about any ingredient desired in Běijīng. But if you're staying in an apartment, you might be stumped by the lack of an oven; Chinese cooking doesn't call for them.

If you're after Western food, the following supermarkets and stores cater for foreigners and stock such esoteric delights as imported cheese, French wine, English tea and peanut butter.

Carrefour (6b Beisanhuan Donglu; ⌚8.30am-10.30pm; S Liufang) Carrefour stocks just about everything you might need, as well as providing ATMs and taking credit cards. Its supermarkets are open every day and are always crowded.

Olé Map p298 (48 Dongzhimenwai Dajie, Basement Ginza Mall; ⌚10am-10pm; S Dongzhimen) Olé is a reliable supermarket chain, with a number of branches around town. This branch is in the Ginza Mall in Dōngzhímén.

April Gourmet Map p298 (1st fl, Lianbao Mansion, Xingfucun Zhonglu; ⌚8am-midnight; S Dongsi Shitiao) April Gourmet caters for Westerners craving a taste of home. Cheese, fresh bread, butter, wine, sauces, Western soups, coffee, milk, meats and frozen food are all available. This branch stays open till midnight.

Lonely Planet's Top Choices

Dàlǐ Courtyard (p98) Beautiful courtyard restaurant with Yúnnán specialities.

Běijīng Dàdǒng Roast Duck Restaurant (p74) The leanest duck in town in a busy and bright setting.

Nàjiā Xiǎoguǎn (p145) Old-school Běijīng place with an esoteric menu of Manchu favourites.

Duck de Chine (p147) Peking duck with a French flavour in a swish environment and super service.

Bǎihé Vegetarian Restaurant (p96) Inventive dishes at one of Běijīng's few veggie eateries.

Best by Budget

¥

Tàn Huā Lamb BBQ (p95) Roast your own leg of lamb at this *hútòng* hang-out.

Zhāng Māma (p93) Super-popular Sìchuān restaurant and excellent value.

Bocata (p145) Fine sandwiches and salads and fantastic chips at this popular lunch spot.

Bāozi Pù (p95) Long-standing dumplings and noodles place.

Yàn Lán Lóu (p144) Muslim restaurant with great hand-pulled noodles.

¥¥

Jīn Dǐng Xuān (p97) Tasty dim sum and open 24 hours.

Xiǎo Wáng's Home Restaurant (p146) Běijīng institution with a China-wide menu.

Vineyard Café (p98) Family-friendly, expat fave.

Xù Xiāng Zhāi Vegetarian Restaurant (p97) Historic setting and lunch and early-evening set-price buffets.

Jīngzūn Peking Duck (p145) Not just duck but a huge variety of dishes.

¥¥¥

Duck de Chine (p147) Standout Peking duck in an artfully designed space.

Temple Restaurant (p74) Fantastic setting, flawless food and service.

Lost Heaven (p113) Top-notch Yúnnán dishes.

Capital M (p114) Specialises in Mediterranean classics.

Brian McKenna @ The Courtyard (p74) Ultimate location next door to the Forbidden City.

Best Peking Duck

Lìqún Roast Duck Restaurant (p113) Ramshackle setting but serves a superb bird.

Biànyífāng (p115) Old-school Peking duck and sees fewer foreigners than other places.

Duck de Chine (p147) Fancy-pants Peking-meets-Paris duck.

Jīngzūn Peking Duck (p145) An unpretentious introduction to Běijīng's most famous dish.

Qiánmén Quánjùdé Roast Duck Restaurant (p114) Always crowded but the duck is top quality.

Best Dumplings

Din Tai Fung (p145) Famed Taiwanese restaurant and shrine to dumplings in all their forms.

Bǎoyuán Dumpling Restaurant (p144) Multicoloured dumplings that delight the kids.

Dūyīchù (p113) Serving up seasonal favourites since the mid-Qing dynasty.

Hángzhōu Xiǎochī (p73) Cheap eats close to the Forbidden City.

Gǒubùlǐ (p134) Eight different types to choose from and all delicious.

Best Hotpot

Yáng Fāng Lamb Hotpot (p94) Classic Běijīng-style hotpot.

Little Sheep (p96) Mongolian hotpot on bustling Ghost St.

Lǎo Chē Jì (p167) Dry hotpots are the house speciality.

Chóngqìng Kǒngliàng Huǒguō (p96) Very fiery hotpot for spice fiends.

Róng Tiān Sheep Spine (p94) Down-to-earth eatery but delicious food.

Best Regional

Crescent Moon Muslim Restaurant (p71) Arguably the finest Uighur eatery in Běijīng.

Jíxiángniǎo Xiāngcài (p146) Spicy Húnán cuisine and always busy.

Chuān Bàn (p72) Fire fiends love this authentic, tongue-numbing Sìchuān place.

In & Out (p145) The best of southwestern China's many great dishes are on offer here.

Golden Peacock (p167) Southeast Asian–influenced Dai cuisine from Yúnnán Province.

Best Noodles

Yàn Lán Lóu (p144) Dishes from China's noodle heartland.

Liu Family Noodles (p134) Cheap and cheerful, but excellent noodles.

Old Běijīng Zhájiàng Noodle King (p113) Traditional noodles and a local hotspot.

Drinking & Nightlife

It's amazing to contemplate, as you sip a martini in the latest hotspot or dance to a big-name European DJ, but until 20-odd years ago there weren't any bars or nightclubs, outside a few hotels, in Běijīng at all. Now, as more and more locals take to partying, the capital is home to an increasing number of sophisticated nightspots.

Hútòng Bar-Crawling

In the last couple of years, a whole host of bars have sprung up in the ancient heart of the city with former courtyard homes converted into some of the finest and liveliest drinking destinations in town. They range from bohemian joints to distinctly chic cocktail bars. Nanluogu Xiang lane led the way in making the *hútòng* (narrow alleyways) an integral part of the city's nightlife; now many *hútòng* across Dōngchéng North are almost as popular.

Drink Like a Local

Although wine and whisky are gaining ground among the middle classes, the two most popular alcoholic drinks in Běijīng remain *píjiǔ* (beer) and *báijiǔ,* a pungent, potent white spirit with a unique taste that few foreigners can stomach. The commonest brews are Yanjing Beer (the local favourite), Běijīng Beer and Tsingtao. None are very distinguished, and all are weaker than most foreign beers. You can pick up a large bottle of Yanjing or Tsingtao, the closest to a European-style lager, for around ¥4 on the streets; Běijīng Beer is usually served on tap.

KARAOKE

Karaoke is the number-one leisure pastime in China and there are well over 100,000 karaoke, or KTV, joints across the country. As alien as it can seem to be singing along to a TV in front of people, karaoke is one of the best ways of getting to know the locals. And you'll be surprised at how quickly crooning cheesy pop standards becomes addictive.

Běijīng Clubland

Most of the capital's nightclubs are as much places for drinking as they are for dancing so, despite the increasing numbers of international DJs who fly in, many local punters aren't too interested in what is on the turntables. Much of what you hear will be mainstream house and hip-hop. But a few local DJs do their best to promote more eclectic sounds and stage parties in various venues around town. Check the local listings magazines for details.

Drinking & Nightlife by Neighbourhood

- **Drum Tower & Dōngchéng North** *Hútòng* bars and cafes aplenty on and off Gulou Dongdajie.
- **Běihǎi Park & Xīchéng North** The shores of the Hòuhǎi Lakes are awash with bars.
- **Sānlǐtún & Cháoyáng** Clubbing central and also home to upmarket cocktail bars.
- **Summer Palace & Hǎidiàn** The Wǔdàokǒu district of Hǎidiàn is Běijīng's student heartland and buzzes come nightfall.

Lonely Planet's Top Choices

Apothecary (p149) Huge range of cocktails lovingly made from fresh ingredients.

El Nido (p99) Always jammed and the archetypal neighbourhood *hútòng* bar.

Lantern (p150) The best DJs in town and an authentic, sweaty underground vibe.

Migas Bar (p149) Wildly popular roof terrace in the summer and a hip crowd.

Great Leap Brewing (p149) Join the hordes sipping on home-brewed ales.

Best Hútòng Bars

El Nido (p99) Brilliant in the summer, when you can drink outside.

Ball House (p99) One of the most unique drinking spaces in Běijīng.

Great Leap Brewing (p99) Craft beers in a courtyard setting.

Mao Mao Chong Bar (p99) Creative cocktails, a laid-back vibe and decent pizzas.

If (p99) Offbeat design (and crowd) and a cool roof terrace.

Best Cocktail Bars

Apothecary (p149) Much-imitated but it's hard to beat the quality of the drinks here.

Ichikura (p150) In-the-know bar with the widest range of whiskies in Běijīng.

Parlor (p149) In 1920s Shànghǎi speakeasy-style, deliberately tucked away.

Revolution (p149) Mao-themed cubbyhole of a bar with knowledgeable bartenders.

Janes and Hooch (p149) Hip hang-out for cashed-up locals and expats.

Best Clubs

Spark (p150) True hotspot and rammed at the weekend.

Lantern (p150) Genuine underground club vibe and top DJs.

Destination (p151) Běijīng's only real gay club.

Mix (p151) Mainstream hip-hop for a younger crowd.

Chocolate (p150) Gloriously over-the-top Russian-style nightclub that gets going after midnight.

Best Cafes

Zá Jiā (p99) Cool cafe-cum-bar housed in a historic former Taoist temple.

Await Cafe (p128) Heavenly coffee and cakes in a superb space.

Irresistible Cafe (p100) The name says it all and good food too.

Alley Coffee (p75) Courtyard cafe that's ideal for a Forbidden City coffee break.

Bridge Café (p167) Twenty-four-hour hang-out with decent drinks and food and friendly staff.

Best Neighbourhood Bars

Tree (p150) Great range of foreign brews and excellent pizzas too.

Paddy O'Shea's (p151) The best spot to catch live sport in the capital.

Hippo (p100) Cubbyhole of a bar with many foreign beers.

First Floor (p149) Pub-like vibe in the heart of Sānlǐtún's bar zone.

NEED TO KNOW

Opening Hours

Most bars in Běijīng open in the late afternoon and close at 2am. But many stay open longer, especially on weekends, while others shut up shop around midnight. Cafes open much earlier and sometimes close early, too. Clubs can go all night, depending on their mood.

Prices

The cost of drinking in Běijīng's bars depends very much on your personal tastes. If you want to gargle with a Guinness, you'll pay more (¥40 to ¥50) than if you drink a bottle of Tsingtao (¥20 to ¥25). Mixed drinks start at around ¥35 in most bars, but in a swanky place expect to pay Western prices, ¥60 and up, for a proper cocktail. Many bars, though, have happy hours (usually 5pm to 8pm) when you can imbibe more cheaply.

Best Craft Beers

Great Leap Brewing (p149) Běijīng's original brew masters.

Slow Boat Brewery Taproom (p75) A dozen draft beers available.

NBeer Pub (p128) Big range of imported beers and there are local ones on tap.

Big Smoke (p150) Home base of Jīng A Brewing, the capital's finest brewers.

Entertainment

Běijīng is the cultural capital of China and by far the best place to be if you're interested in seeing anything from ballet and contemporary dance, to jazz or punk bands. Then there's the traditional local pastimes such as Peking opera (jīngjù) *and acrobatic shows, as well as movies, theatre and Běijīng's various sports teams.*

Live Music

While there might be an instinctive Chinese fondness for Taiwanese boy bands, Beijingers have always been at the forefront of the more soulful end of the Chinese music scene. Now, you can find all sorts of bands – indie, alternative, punk, metal, folk and jazz – lifting roofs every night of the week in venues that range from Qing dynasty courtyards to open-air cinemas. Come summer, Běijīng hosts the odd open-air festival too. Sadly, though, the capital remains a backwater for international rock and pop acts, very few of whom make it out here.

Acrobatics & Peking Opera

Two thousand years old, Chinese acrobatics (杂技; *zájì*) is one of the best shows in town and there are daily performances at a number of different theatres. Look out too for the legendary, shaven-headed Shàolín monks, who pass through the capital regularly to put on displays of their fearsome fighting skills.

Far more sedate, but equally intriguing, is Peking opera, also known as Běijīng opera. It might seem impenetrable to foreigners, its mystique reinforced by the costumes, singing style and, of course, the language, but live performances are actually relatively easy to follow. Plot lines are simple (rather like Shakespearean tragedy, including the low comic relief) and the shows are a more interactive experience than you might imagine.

Spectator Sport

The Chinese are avid football *(zúqiú)* fans, with many supporting the top teams in England, Italy and Spain. The China Super League is emerging as a force of its own in Asia, with increasing numbers of foreign players arriving to lift standards. The local heroes are the Běijīng Guo'an, who play their home games at the Workers Stadium in front of some of China's most vocal fans.

Even more popular than football is basketball. A number of Chinese players have followed in the footsteps of national icon Yao Ming to play in the NBA. The capital's team is the Běijīng Ducks; they draw a big crowd at the Wǔkēsōng Arena in Hǎidiàn.

Entertainment by Neighbourhood

- **Forbidden City & Dōngchéng Central** Prime district for culture vultures, with classical music, opera and theatre venues.
- **Drum Tower & Dōngchéng North** Home to many of the best live-music venues in town.
- **Běihǎi Park & Xīchéng North** Key cultural hub thanks to the impressive National Centre for the Performing Arts.
- **Dashilar & Xīchéng South** The Húguǎng Guild Hall is the most atmospheric Peking opera venue of them all.
- **Sānlǐtún & Cháoyáng** Acrobatics shows galore and movie multiplexes.

Lonely Planet's Top Choices

Yúgōng Yíshān (p101) Great space and super booking policy make this the number-one spot for live music.

National Centre for the Performing Arts (p128) Extraordinary building that is now Běijīng's cultural centre.

Tiānqiáo Acrobatics Theatre (p134) The most agile and graceful acrobats in town.

Húguǎng Guild Hall (p135) Beautiful and historic venue to watch Peking opera in.

Dos Kolegas (p152) Make the trip here to catch all sorts of alternative bands in a truly bohemian setting.

Best for Alternative, Punk & Metal Bands

Dos Kolegas (p152) Fantastic venue with a large outdoor area that jumps in the summer.

Temple Bar (p101) Local and foreign bands of all varieties at this raucous spot.

Mao Livehouse (p101) Local and foreign bands at one of the few midsized venues in the city.

What? Bar (p75) Pint-sized club that's good for catching up-and-coming acts.

Star Live (p102) Great space for both international bands and dance parties.

13 Club (p168) Metal fans flock to this suitably grimy place.

Best for Folk & Jazz Bands

Jiāng Jìn Jiǔ (p101) Folk and ethnic minority bands from China's far-flung reaches.

East Shore Jazz Café (p128) The most amenable place in town to catch local and foreign jazzers.

Jiāng Hú (p101) Lovely, intimate courtyard setting to hear Chinese bands.

Modernista (p100) Hipster hang-out with live jazz and swing dancing.

Best for Classical Music & Dance

Forbidden City Concert Hall (p76) Superb acoustics and a romantic ambience.

Poly Plaza International Theatre (p153) Ambitious venue stages Chinese and Western plays, ballet, opera and folk music.

National Library Concert Hall (p168) A top spot for Chinese classical dance.

Best for Peking Opera

Cháng'ān Grand Theatre (p76) *The* place for true Peking opera aficionados.

Húguǎng Guild Hall (p135) This magnificent venue is the most atmospheric in all Běijīng.

Mei Lanfang Grand Theatre (p128) Traditional performances in a modern setting.

Líyuán Theatre (p135) A good place for your first Peking opera experience.

Lao She Teahouse (p135) Peking opera, but also shadow plays and traditional folk music.

Best for Acrobatics & Plays

Universal Theatre (p152) Home to the China National Acrobatic Troupe.

Cháoyáng Theatre (p153) Touristy, but the show is consistently impressive.

Red Theatre (p115) Nonstop kung fu fighting as a boy learns how to be a warrior monk.

China Puppet Theatre (p102) Shadow plays and puppets and very family-friendly.

Pénghāo Theatre (p101) Super, intimate venue in the heart of *hútòng*-land.

NEED TO KNOW

Opening Hours

Ballet, classical music and Chinese folk or contemporary dance performances generally start at 7.30pm at the big concert hall venues. Acrobatics and opera houses often have two shows a day, starting at 5.15pm or 6.30pm and then again at 7.30pm. Live-music venues mostly open their doors around 8pm and don't close till the wee hours.

Information

Check the monthly expat magazines, which can be picked up around town, for the latest news on events and who is playing when and where.

Prices & Tickets

Some live-music venues don't levy an entrance fee, but if a popular local band or any international act is playing they will, and it's advisable to reserve tickets in advance. You'll need to book ahead if a famous foreign orchestra or ballet company is in town too.

Shopping

Whether you're a diehard shopaholic or a casual browser, you'll be spoiled for choice in Běijīng. Join the locals in their favourite pastime at any number of shiny shopping malls, markets and specialist shopping streets. Then there are the pavement vendors and itinerant hawkers. All ensure that keeping your cash in your pocket is increasingly difficult.

Arts, Crafts & Antiques

Běijīng is a great place to pick up curios such as embroidered purses, paper cuttings, wooden and bronze Buddhas, paper lanterns, Chinese musical instruments and kites. Carpets, jade and pearls of varying quality can be found in abundance too.

Remember it's not just DVDs and clothes that are pirated in China: antiques, ceramics and carpets get the facsimile treatment too, so be wary before paying for that supposed Ming-dynasty vase. Be aware, too, that technically items dating from before 1795 cannot be exported from China.

Clothing

Sīchóu (silk) is an important commodity in Běijīng and excellent prices for both silk fabrics and clothing can be found. If you have the time, there are excellent tailors who will turn your silk into made-to-measure clothing, such as traditional Chinese gowns (*qípáo*, or *cheongsam* in Cantonese). *Yángróngshān* (cashmere) from Inner Mongolia is also a good buy in Běijīng.

Contemporary Art

With Chinese contemporary art still in demand from collectors around the world, artwork can be a great investment. If you're here in June, the annual Affordable Art Fair held in the 798 Art District is a fine place to find reasonably priced work. Otherwise, visit reputable galleries like Red Gate Gallery. Realistically, you'll need to spend at least $1000 for a piece by an up-and-coming artist that is likely to increase in value.

Tea

You can pick up any of China's huge variety of teas in Běijīng, as well as the tea sets you'll need to sample them in the proper local fashion. Prices range dramatically, depending on the type of tea, or the design of the tea set. But no matter your budget, you'll be able to find a brew to sip long after you've returned home.

Shopping by Neighbourhood

- **Forbidden City & Dōngchéng Central** Wangfujing Dajie is Běijīng's premier shopping street.
- **Drum Tower & Dōngchéng North** Trendy and offbeat boutiques abound in this area.
- **Temple of Heaven Park & Dōngchéng South** Come here for Hóngqiáo Market and its oceans of pearls, as well as the refurbished Qiánmén shopping street.
- **Dashilar & Xīchéng South** Some of the city's oldest emporiums, and the antiques, arts and crafts hub of Líulìchǎng.
- **Sānlǐtún & Cháoyáng** Malls galore and home to most of Běijīng's finest markets.

Lonely Planet's Top Choices

Shard Box Store (p154) Utterly unique exquisite shard boxes in all sizes.

Ruifúxiáng (p136) All kinds of silk in every conceivable pattern.

Plastered 8 (p103) Ironic T-shirts with Běijīng-centric themes.

Three Stone Kite Shop (p129) Glorious handmade kites at this family-run place.

Yuèhǎixuān Musical Instrument Store (p136) Esoteric instruments from across China.

Best Markets

Pānjiāyuán Market (p154) By far the best place in town for arts, crafts and antiques.

Mǎliándào Tea Market (p137) A great place to wander for China's favourite drink.

Hóngqiáo (Pearl) Market (p115) Famed for its pearls, but good for clothes too.

Centergate Como (p168) Come here for computers, software and phones.

Best Clothing Stops

Sānlǐtún Yashow Clothing Market (p154) Clothes in larger sizes and accessories.

Silk Market (p153) The silk is one of the few genuine items on sale at this Běijīng institution.

Sānlǐtún Village (p153) Eye-catching mall with both midrange and high-end brands.

3.3 Shopping Centre (p154) Trendy boutiques and accessories for the style-conscious.

77th Street (p129) Where Běijīng's teens and students come to shop.

Best Shopping Streets

Wangfujing Dajie (p76) The most prestigious shopping street.

Liulichang Xijie (p136) Antiques, calligraphy and Chinese paintings.

Dashilar (p136) Home to some of the capital's oldest stores.

Nanluogu Xiang (p88) Crazy at weekends, but fine for souvenir-hunting.

Qianmen Dajie (p112) Refurbished street with midrange brands and some silk.

Yandai Xiejie (p129) Souvenirs, fake antiques and a few more-quirky outlets.

Best for Gifts

Shard Box Store (p154) Porcelain fragments from antique vases reshaped into jewellery.

Jīngchéng Bǎixìng (p103) Traditional clay figurines, and you can make your own, too.

Plastered 8 (p103) Fun and stylish Běijīng-themed T-shirts.

Three Stone Kite Shop (p129) Beautiful hand-painted kites.

Esy Dragon Gift Shop (p103) Souvenirs in all sizes and prices.

Xían Yàn Tāng (p136) Traditional shadow puppets, framed or ready for play.

Best for Art

798 Art District (p140) Galleries galore in Běijīng's art centre.

Red Gate Gallery (p111) First contemporary gallery in Běijīng.

Róngbǎozhāi (p137) Traditional scroll and ink paintings, as well as inks, brushes and paper.

UCCA Design Store (p154) Prints and paintings from some of China's best-known artists.

NEED TO KNOW

Opening Hours

Most shops in Běijīng open earlier than in the West and close later; they usually open between 8am and 8.30am and shut between 9pm and 10pm. Open-air markets generally run from dawn to around sunset, but might open later and close earlier.

Bargaining

Always remember that foreigners are likely to be quoted an inflated price in Běijīng. Prices in malls are fixed, but haggling is standard practice in markets. It's always best to bargain with a smile on your face. Remember, the point of the process is to achieve a mutually acceptable price, not to screw the vendor into the ground.

Paying

Most large department stores take Western credit cards, but many smaller ones only accept Chinese ones. Markets deal in cash only.

Best for Tea

Mǎliándào Tea Market (p137) All the tea in China and cheap tea sets nearby too.

Famous Tea of China (p104) Friendly emporium selling tea in pre-wrapped parcels.

Ten Fu's Tea Culture House (p71) A museum showcasing Chinese tea and a good place to buy it too.

Celadon Story (p76) Perfect, pale-green porcelain tea sets.

Explore Běijīng

BĚIJĪNG'S TOP SIGHTS

Neighbourhoods at a Glance

❶ Forbidden City & Dōngchéng Central p52

This historic neighbourhood is the very heart of Běijīng. Packed with essential sights, and some fabulous accommodation options, it is the area you'll likely be spending much of your time in. Imperial palaces, temples, socialist-realist architecture, parks and museums jostle for space here, but it's also where you'll find the capital's most famous shopping street, Wangfujing Dajie.

❷ Drum Tower & Dōngchéng North p82

The *hútòng* (narrow alleyways) in this part of town are the most numerous and best-preserved and offer a fantastic insight into

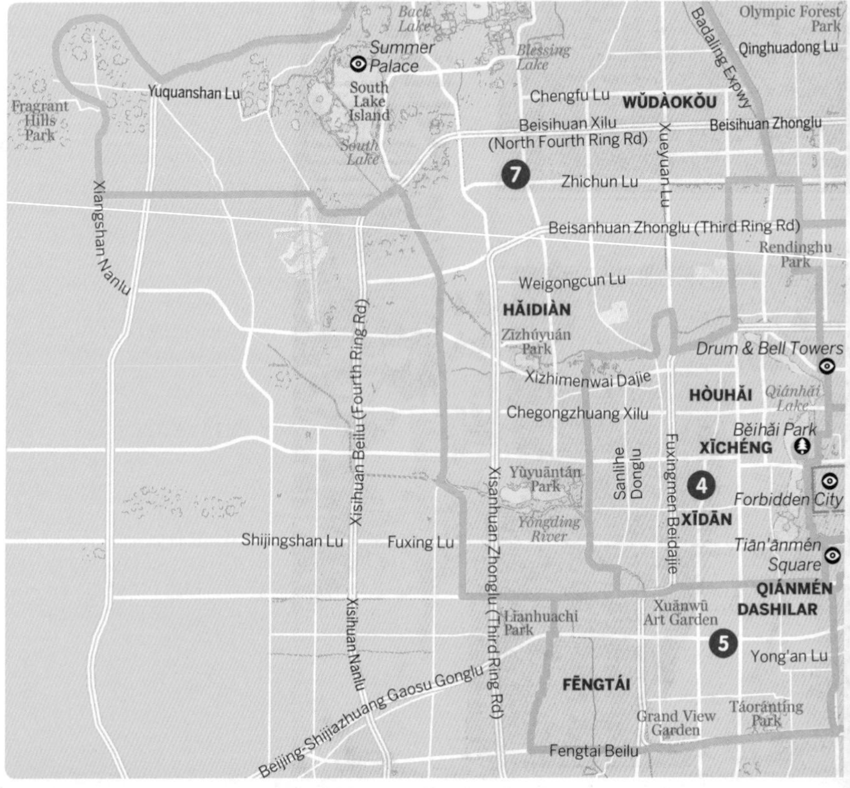

local life. Many, like Nanluogu Xiang and Fangjia Hutong, are also home to an ever-increasing number of hip bars and restaurants. With some lovely courtyard hotels to stay in and key sights scattered around too, it's the most visitor-friendly neighbourhood in all Běijīng and makes a great base.

❸ Temple of Heaven Park & Dōngchéng South p106

Encompassing the former district of Chóngwén, this is an area both grand – dominated by the magnificent Temple of Heaven Park – and down-at-heel, a place where ordinary Beijingers have long resided. Now, it houses some of the finest Peking duck restaurants in the capital, as well as an increasing number of excellent Western eateries, and the restored shopping street of Qianmen Dajie.

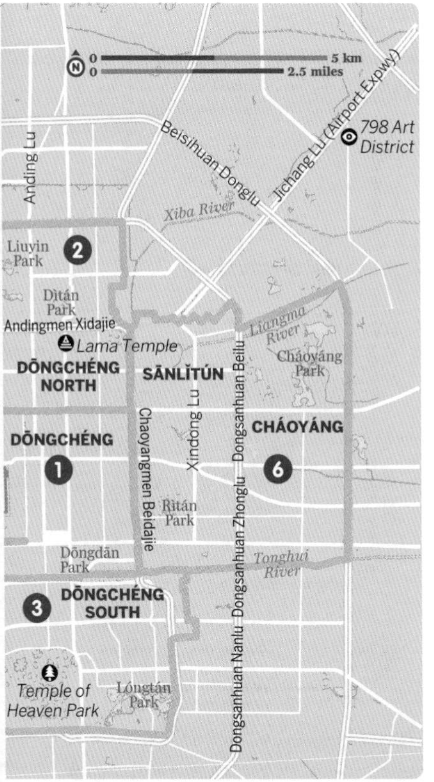

❹ Běihǎi Park & Xīchéng North p116

Northwest of the Forbidden City, Běihǎi Park and the adjacent Hòuhǎi Lakes act as one big playground for Beijingers. During the day, they are a great spot to kick back, while at night locals carouse at the bars and restaurants that surround them. Also a temple- and *hútòng*-rich neighbourhood, Xīchéng North has some fun accommodation hidden away in its alleyways. It's also where you'll find the Capital Museum, Běijīng's finest.

❺ Dashilar & Xīchéng South p130

With the historic shopping street of Dashilar providing a focus, and the many hostels in the nearby *hútòng* making it Běijīng's backpacker central, this neighbourhood southwest of Tiān'ānmén Sq is handy for the major sights and has plenty of character. Formerly known as Xuanwu district, it's also home to the best acrobatics and opera shows in town.

❻ Sānlǐtún & Cháoyáng p138

Big and brash and a key nightlife zone, with many of the most popular bars, clubs and restaurants clustered in the Sānlǐtún area. While Cháoyáng lacks the history of other districts, most of the city's top-end hotels and shops are also located here. Further out, the 798 Art District is the centre of the Chinese contemporary art scene.

❼ Summer Palace & Hǎidiàn p157

Home to many of Běijīng's universities, as well as museums and parks, the buzzing student district of Wǔdàokǒu makes for a fine contrast with the regal Summer Palace and the tranquil, rural delights of the Fragrant Hills, which occupy Hǎidiàn's northwestern edge.

Forbidden City & Dōngchéng Central

Neighbourhood Top Five

❶ Marvel at the might, splendour and sheer scale of the **Forbidden City** (p54), the world's largest palace complex and the place 24 consecutive emperors of China called home.

❷ Place yourself at the symbolic heart of the Chinese universe with a visit to iconic **Tiān'ānmén Square** (p62).

❸ Explore the area's **imperial hútòng** (p70) on our cycling tour of the historic alleyways surrounding the Forbidden City.

❹ Rise early to get the most out of this area's wonderful imperial parks; **Jǐngshān Park** (p65) is our favourite.

❺ Peruse some of the city's best museums and galleries. For starters, try the **National Museum of China** (p64).

For more detail of this area, see Maps on p284 and p286.

Explore Forbidden City & Dōngchéng Central

The most historically significant part of Běijīng, Dōngchéng Central comprises much of what was once the Imperial City, at the heart of which lay the Forbidden City: emperors ruled China from here for more than 500 years.

The *hútòng* (alleyways) fanning out to the north and east of the Forbidden City were where the members of the imperial court once lived, and are fascinating places to explore on foot or by bicycle. You can even base yourself here by settling in to one of this area's charming courtyard hotels.

You'll need at least a couple of days to visit all the best sights in this history-rich neighbourhood; figure on half a day for the Forbidden City alone.

Food options are strong, with cuisine from across China well represented, as well as street markets and some of the capital's more unusual fine-dining establishments. Nightlife is relatively thin on the ground, though.

Local Life

➡ **Food** Tuck into authentic Běijīng grub at Zuǒ Lín Yòu Shè (p71) or Yuèbīn Fànguǎn (p72). The street-food markets near Wángfǔjǐng (p73) may be fun, but locals find them touristy and overpriced. Enjoy your barbecued skewers from a hole-in-the-wall *hútòng* joint instead; spot the red neon 串 sign, and you're good to go.

➡ **Parks** Jǐngshān Park (p65) and Zhōngshān Park (p66) are two of Běijīng's most colourful – and locals, particularly the elderly, love to spend their mornings in them; dancing, singing and exercising with their friends. April and May are particularly popular as both parks burst into bloom during their annual flower fairs.

➡ **Formation Dancing** Join the legions of fitness-conscious ladies who meet at public squares (but not Tiān'ānmén) early evening, for a spot of line dancing. St Joseph's Church square (p67) is popular.

Getting There & Away

➡ **Subway** Tian'anmen West, Tian'anmen East, Wangfujing and Denghshikou are all useful subway stations, and the handy Line 8 extension south to the Chinese Museum of Art should be up and running by the time you read this.

➡ **Bus** The very handy buses 专1 and 专2 do clockwise circuits of the Forbidden City, looping south to Qiánmén, via Tiān'ānmén Sq. Bus 5 runs between Déshèngmén Gateway and Qiánmén, passing the Drum Tower, Jǐngshān Park, the Forbidden City and Tiān'ānmén Sq.

Lonely Planet's Top Tip

Be wary of rickshaw riders outside the north gate of the Forbidden City; they regularly trick tourists into paying over the odds (eg saying 'three', when they mean '300'!). As a rough indicator, you shouldn't be paying much more than ¥20 for a rickshaw from here to the Drum Tower or the Hòuhǎi Lakes.

Best Places for History

➡ Forbidden City (p54)

➡ National Museum of China (p64)

➡ Front Gate (p66)

➡ Gate of Heavenly Peace (p65)

➡ Workers Cultural Palace (p65)

➡ Zhìhuà Temple (p69)

For reviews, see p54.

Best Places to Eat

➡ Little Yúnnán (p73)

➡ Crescent Moon Muslim Restaurant (p71)

➡ Zuǒ Lín Yòu Shè (p71)

➡ Brian McKenna @ The Courtyard (p74)

➡ Temple Restaurant (p74)

For reviews, see p71.

Best Places to Shop

➡ Slow Lane (p77)

➡ Celadon Story (p76)

➡ Wangfujing Dajie (p76)

➡ Oriental Plaza (p76)

➡ Běijīng apm (p76)

For reviews, see p76. 

HUOGUANGLIANG / GETTY IMAGES ©

TOP SIGHT
FORBIDDEN CITY

Home to 24 Chinese emperors, spanning two complete dynasties (the Ming and the Qing) and more than 500 years, the astonishing Forbidden City (紫禁城; Zǐjìn Chéng; also known as, Gù Gōng (故宫), 'ancient palace') is the largest palace complex in the world and a must-see sight for most visitors to Běijīng.

Located at the geographical centre of China's capital, the palace occupies a primary position in the Chinese psyche. To communists, it's a contradictory symbol: a politically incorrect yarn from a pre-Revolutionary dark age, but also one spun from the very pinnacle of Chinese civilisation. Violent forces during the Cultural Revolution wanted to ruin the place. But Premier Zhou Enlai, perhaps hearing the distant tinkle of the tourist dollar, stepped in to calm down the Red Guards.

Although you can explore the Forbidden City in a few hours, a full day will keep you occupied and the enthusiast will make several trips. More than half of the complex is closed to the public, but a massive chunk remains open, mainly around the hugely impressive ceremonial halls, which line the central axis. Marvel at these by all means, but don't miss the delightful courtyards, pavilions and minimuseums within them on each side of the central axis. This is where the emperors actually lived, and it's fun to explore the passageways and courtyards that link them.

DON'T MISS

- Clock Exhibition Hall
- Ceramics Gallery
- Changyin Pavilion (opera house)
- Western Palaces

PRACTICALITIES

- Map p284
- ☎8500 7114
- www.dpm.org.cn
- admission Nov-Mar ¥40, Apr-Oct ¥60, Clock Exhibition Hall ¥10, Hall of Jewellery ¥10, audio tour ¥40
- 8.30am-4pm May-Sep, 8.30am-3.30pm Oct-Apr, closed Mon
- S Tian'anmen West or Tian'anmen East

Information & Warnings

As you approach the ticket office you may be encircled by a swarm of pushy guides. Note that their English levels vary and the spiel can often be tedious and formulaic. The better and cheaper alternative is to rent a funky automatically activated audio tour, which comes in 30 languages. Better still, just use this guidebook!

Don't confuse the Gate of Heavenly Peace with the Forbidden City entrance. Some visitors purchase a Gate of Heavenly Peace admission ticket by mistake, not realising that this admits you only to the upstairs portion of that gateway. The Forbidden City ticket booths are on the left and right of the wide pathway that leads north to Meridian Gate (the south entrance to the Forbidden City), and are about 100m before Meridian Gate.

Restaurants, cafes, ATMs and toilets can be found within the Forbidden City.

Wheelchairs (¥500 deposit) are free, as are pushchairs (¥300 deposit). Smoking is not permitted anywhere in the Forbidden City.

For the past couple of years, the Forbidden City has been closed for maintenance every Monday (apart from during national holidays, when it remains open).

History

Constructed on the site of a palace dating to Kublai Khan and the Mongol Yuan dynasty, the Ming emperor Yongle established the basic layout of the Forbidden City between 1406 and 1420, basing it on the now-ruined Ming-dynasty palace in Nánjīng. The grandiose emperor employed battalions of labourers and craftspeople – by some estimates there may have been up to a million of them – to build the Forbidden City. The palace once lay at the heart of the Imperial City, a much larger, now-vanished walled enclosure reserved for the use of the emperor and his personnel. The wall enclosing the Forbidden City – assembled from 12 million bricks – is the last intact surviving city wall in Běijīng.

This gargantuan palace complex – China's largest and best-preserved cluster of ancient buildings – sheltered two dynasties of emperors (the Ming and the Qing), who didn't stray from their pleasure dome unless they absolutely had to. So highly rarefied was the atmosphere that nourished its elitist community, it was as if a bell jar had been dropped over the whole spectacle. A stultifying code of rules, protocol and superstition deepened its otherworldliness, perhaps typified by its twittering band of eunuchs. From here the emperors governed China, often erratically and haphazardly, with authority occasionally drifting into the hands of opportunistic court officials and eunuchs. It wasn't until 1911 that revolution eventually came knocking at the huge doors, bringing with it the last orders for the Manchu Qing and dynastic rule.

ENTERING THE FORBIDDEN CITY

Tourists can only enter the Forbidden City via the south gate, known as Meridian Gate. It's a massive U-shaped portal that in former times was reserved for the use of the emperor. Gongs and bells would sound imperial comings and goings, while lesser mortals used lesser gates: the military used the west gate, civilians the east gate. The emperor also reviewed his armies from here, passed judgement on prisoners, announced the new year's calendar and oversaw the flogging of troublesome ministers.

Note that although tourists can only enter via Meridian Gate (the south gate), they are allowed to exit the Forbidden City via the south, north or east gates. There are places to lock bicycles by the south and northeast gates of nearby Zhōngshān Park.

CLOSED MONDAYS

The Forbidden City is usually closed on Mondays.

Forbidden City

WALKING TOUR

After entering through the imperious Meridian Gate, resist the temptation to dive straight into the star attractions and veer right for a peek at the excellent **Ceramics Gallery** ❶ housed inside the creaking Hall of Literary Glory.

Walk back to the central complex and head through the magnificent Gate of Supreme Harmony towards the Three Great Halls: first, the largest – the **Hall of Supreme Harmony** ❷, followed by the **Hall of Middle Harmony** ❸ and the **Hall of Preserving Harmony** ❹, behind which slopes the enormous Marble Imperial Carriageway.

Turn right here to visit the fascinating **Clock Exhibition Hall** ❺ before entering the **Complete Palace of Peace & Longevity** ❻, a mini Forbidden City constructed along the eastern axis of the main complex. It includes the beautiful **Nine Dragon Screen** ❼ and, to the north, a series of halls, housing some excellent exhibitions and known collectively as The Treasure Gallery. Don't miss the **Pavilion of Cheerful Melodies** ❽, a wonderful three-storey opera house.

Work your way to the far north of this section, then head west to the **Imperial Garden** ❾, with its ancient cypress trees and pretty pavilions, before exiting via the garden's West Gate (behind the Thousand Year Pavilion) to explore the **Western Palaces** ❿, an absorbing collection of courtyard homes where many of the emperors lived during their reign.

Exit this section at its southwest corner before turning back on yourself to walk north through the Gate of Heavenly Purity to see the three final Central Halls – the **Palace of Heavenly Purity** ⓫, the **Hall of Union** ⓬ and the **Palace of Earthly Tranquility** ⓭ – before leaving via the North Gate.

DANIEL MCCROHAN

Water Vats
More than 300 copper and brass water vats dot the palace complex. They were used for fighting fires and in winter were prevented from freezing over by using thick quilts.

ENTRANCE/EXIT

You must enter through the south gate (Meridian Gate), but you can exit via south, north or east.

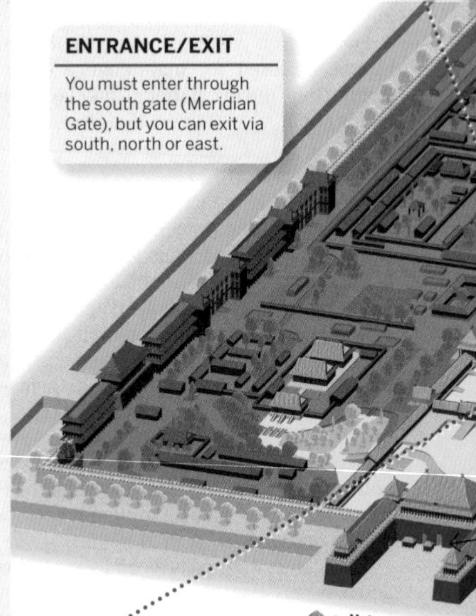

Guardian Lions
Pairs of lions guard important buildings. The male has a paw placed on a globe (representing the emperor's power over the world). The female has her paw on a baby lion (representing the emperor's fertility).

DANIEL MCCROHAN

DANIEL MCCROHAN

Kneeling Elephants

At the northern entrance of the Imperial Garden are two bronze elephants kneeling in an anatomically impossible fashion, which symbolise the power of the emperor; even elephants kowtowed before him.

DANIEL MCCROHAN

Nine Dragon Screen

One of only three of its type left in China, this beautiful glazed dragon screen served to protect the Hall of Imperial Supremacy from evil spirits.

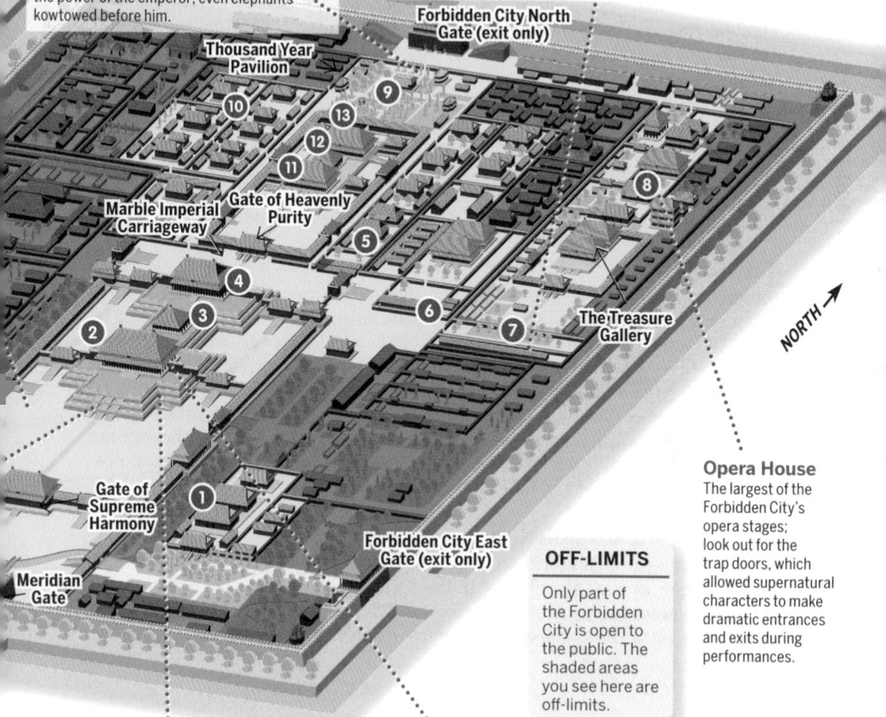

Forbidden City North Gate (exit only)

Thousand Year Pavilion

Marble Imperial Carriageway

Gate of Heavenly Purity

The Treasure Gallery

NORTH

Gate of Supreme Harmony

Meridian Gate

Forbidden City East Gate (exit only)

1 2 3 4 5 6 7 8 9 10 11 12 13

Opera House

The largest of the Forbidden City's opera stages; look out for the trap doors, which allowed supernatural characters to make dramatic entrances and exits during performances.

OFF-LIMITS

Only part of the Forbidden City is open to the public. The shaded areas you see here are off-limits.

Dragon-Head Spouts

More than a thousand dragon-head spouts encircle the raised marble platforms at the centre of the Forbidden City. They were – and still are – part of the drainage system.

DANIEL MCCROHAN

Roof Guardians

The imperial dragon is at the tail of the procession, which is led by a figure riding a phoenix followed by a number of mythical beasts. The more beasts, the more important the building.

DANIEL MCCROHAN

Its mystique diffused (the Běijīng authorities prosaically call the complex the Palace Museum, or Gùgōng Bówùguǎn; 故宫博物馆), the palace is no longer off limits. In former ages the price for uninvited admission would have been instant death; these days ¥40 to ¥60 will do.

Most of the buildings you see now are post-18th century. The largely wooden palace was a tinderbox and fire was a constant hazard – a lantern festival combined with a sudden gust of Gobi wind would easily send flames dancing in unexpected directions, as would a fireworks display. Fires were also deliberately lit by court eunuchs and officials who could get rich off the repair bills. It wasn't just buildings that burned, but also rare books, paintings and calligraphy. Libraries and other palace halls and buildings housing combustible contents were tiled in black; the colour represents water in the *wǔxíng* (five-element) theory, and its symbolic presence was thought to prevent conflagrations. Originally water was provided by 72 wells in the palace (only 30 have been preserved), while a complex system took care of drainage.

In the 20th century there were two major lootings of the palace by Japanese forces and the Kuomintang (KMT; Chiang Kaishek's Nationalist Party, the dominant political force after the fall of the Qing dynasty). Thousands of crates of relics were removed and carted off to Taiwan, where they remain on display in Taipei's National Palace Museum (worth seeing). Some say this was just as well, since the Cultural Revolution reduced much of China's precious artwork to confetti.

Layout

Ringed by a picturesque 52m-wide moat that freezes over in winter, the rectangular palace is laid out roughly symmetrically on a north–south axis, bisected by a line of grand gates and ceremonial halls that straddle the very axis that cleaves Běijīng in two. The palace is so unspeakably big (over 1 million sq metres, with 800 buildings and 9000 rooms) that restoration is a never-ending work in progress, and despite the attentions of restorers, some of the hall rooftops still sprout tufts of grass. Many halls have been repainted in a way that conceals the original pigment; other halls, such as the Hall of Mental Cultivation (p60), however, possess a more threadbare and faded authenticity.

Entering the Complex

After passing through **Meridian Gate** (午门; Wǔ Mén), the only one of the four gateways now used as an entrance to the Forbidden City, you enter an enormous courtyard. From here, you cross the Golden Stream (金水; Jīn Shuǐ) – shaped to resemble a Tartar bow and spanned by five marble bridges – on your way to the

BEWARE THE RICKSHAW HUSTLERS!

Pushy rickshaw and taxi touts wait at the north gate to take advantage of weary visitors exiting the complex. It's always fun to take a rickshaw ride, but be very clear when negotiating a fare with them. As a guide, it should cost about ¥20 per rickshaw to get from here to the Drum Tower.

A common trick is for them to say 'three'. You think they mean ¥3 (a bargain!). They insist later, they meant 300! It's perhaps best just to avoid them altogether by walking a few hundred metres in any direction, then hailing a passing cab.

Alternatively, turn left as you exit the north gate and walk to the nearby bus stop. From here, bus 124 goes to the Drum Tower, while buses 专1 and 专2 both do circuits of the Forbidden City, looping back south to Qiánmén, at the southern tip of Tiān'ānmén Sq.

Throne, Hall of Middle Harmony

magnificent **Gate of Supreme Harmony** (太和门; Tàihé Mén). This courtyard could hold an imperial audience of 100,000 people.

First Side Galleries

Before you pass through the Gate of Supreme Harmony to reach the Forbidden City's star attractions, veer off to the west and east of the huge courtyard to visit the **Calligraphy and Painting Gallery** inside the **Hall of Martial Valor** (武英殿; Wǔ Yīng Diàn) and the particularly good **Ceramics Gallery**, housed inside the creaking **Hall of Literary Glory** (文化殿; Wén Huà Dià).

Three Great Halls

Raised on a three-tier marble terrace with balustrades are the **Three Great Halls** (三大殿; Sān Dàdiàn), the glorious heart of the Forbidden City. The recently restored **Hall of Supreme Harmony** (太和殿; Tàihé Diàn) is the most important and largest structure in the Forbidden City. Built in the 15th century and restored in the 17th century, it was used for ceremonial occasions, such as the emperor's birthday, coronations and the nomination of military leaders. Inside the Hall of Supreme Harmony is a richly decorated **Dragon Throne** (龙椅; Lóngyǐ), from which the emperor would preside over trembling officials. The entire court had to touch the floor nine times with their foreheads (the custom known as kowtowing) in the emperor's presence. At

CLOCK EXHIBITION HALL

The Clock Exhibition Hall is one of the unmissable highlights of the Forbidden City. Located in the Hall for Ancestral Worship (Fèngxiàn Diàn), the exhibition contains an astonishing array of elaborate timepieces, many of which were gifts to the Qing emperors from overseas. Many of the 18th-century examples are crafted by James Cox or Joseph Williamson (both of London) and imported through Guǎngdōng from England; others are from Switzerland, America and Japan. Exquisitely wrought, fashioned with magnificently designed elephants and other creatures, they all display astonishing artfulness and attention to detail. Standout clocks include the Gilt Copper Astronomy Clock equipped with a working model of the solar system, and the automaton-equipped Gilt Copper Clock with a robot writing Chinese characters with a brush. The Qing-dynasty court must surely have been amazed by their ingenuity.

The **Clock Exhibition Hall** (钟表馆; Zhōngbiǎo Guǎn) is open from 8.30am to 4pm; clock performances are at 11am and 2pm. Admission costs ¥10.

the back of the throne is a carved Xumishan, the Buddhist paradise, signifying the throne's supremacy.

Behind the Hall of Supreme Harmony is the **Hall of Middle Harmony** (中和殿; Zhōnghé Diàn), which was used as the emperor's transit lounge. Here he would make last-minute preparations, rehearse speeches and receive ministers. On display are two Qing-dynasty sedan chairs, the emperor's mode of transport around the Forbidden City. The last of the Qing emperors, Puyi, used a bicycle and altered some features of the palace grounds to make it easier to get around.

The third of the Great Halls is the **Hall of Preserving Harmony** (保和殿; Bǎohé Diàn), used for banquets and later for imperial examinations. The hall has no support pillars, and to its rear is a 250-tonne marble imperial carriageway carved with dragons and clouds, which was transported into Běijīng on an ice path. The outer housing surrounding the Three Great Halls was used for storing gold, silver, silks, carpets and other treasures.

A string of side halls on the eastern and western flanks of the Three Great Halls usually, but not always, houses a series of excellent **exhibitions**, ranging from scientific instruments and articles of daily use to objects presented to the emperor by visiting dignitaries. One contains an interesting **diorama** of the whole complex.

Other Central Halls

The basic configuration of the Three Great Halls is echoed by the next group of buildings, which is accessed through **Heavenly Purity Gate**. Smaller in scale, these buildings were more important in terms of real power, which in China traditionally lies at the back door or, in this case, the back gate.

The first structure is the **Palace of Heavenly Purity** (乾清宫; Qiánqīng Gōng), a residence of Ming and early Qing emperors, and later an audience hall for receiving foreign envoys and high officials.

Immediately behind it is the **Hall of Union** (交泰殿; Jiāotài Diàn), which contains a clepsydra – a water clock made in 1745 with five bronze vessels and a calibrated scale. There's also a mechanical clock built in 1797, and a collection of imperial jade seals on display. The **Palace of Earthly Tranquillity** (坤宁宫; Kūnníng Gōng) was the imperial couple's bridal chamber and the centre of operations for the palace harem.

Imperial Garden

At the northern end of the Forbidden City is the **Imperial Garden** (御花园; Yù Huāyuán), a classical Chinese garden with 7000 sq metres of fine landscaping, including rockeries, walkways, pavilions and ancient, carbuncular cypresses. Before you reach the **Gate of Divine Prowess** (神武门; Shénwǔ Mén), note the pair of **bronze elephants** whose front knees bend in an anatomically impossible fashion just before you reach **Shùnzhēn Gate** (顺贞门; Shùnzhēn Mén). They signify the power of the emperor; even elephants kowtow before him!

Western & Eastern Palaces

About half-a-dozen smaller palace courtyards lie to the west and east of the three lesser central halls. They should all be open to the public, although at the time of research many of the eastern ones were closed for extensive renovation. It was in these smaller courtyard buildings that most of the emperors actually lived and many of the buildings, particularly those to the west, are decked out in imperial furniture. The **Hall of Mental Cultivation** (养心殿; Yǎng Xīn Diàn284) is a highlight, while the **Palace of Gathered Elegance** (储秀宫; Chǔ Xiù Gōng) contains some interesting photos of the last emperor, Puyi, who lived here as a child ruler at the turn of the 20th century.

Palace Quirks

Attached to buildings, or standing incongruously in the corners of courtyards, are quirky objects that can easily go unnoticed.

The huge **copper and brass vats** that dot the Forbidden City were once full of water for dousing fires. There are 308 in total, all in various states of disrepair. They used to be draped in quilts or warmed with fires in winter to keep them from freezing over.

Pairs of stone or bronze **guardian lions** protect important buildings, with two particularly fine specimens in front of the Gate of Supreme Harmony. The male always has a paw placed on a globe (representing the emperor's power over the world), while the female has a paw placed on a baby lion (representing the fertility of the emperor's court).

More than a thousand **dragon-head spouts** encircle the raised marble platforms at the centre of the Forbidden City. They were, and still are, part of the drainage system. If you are unlucky enough to visit on a day of torrential rain, you will at least get to see water spouting out of their mouths.

Roof guardians adorn many important historic buildings in Běijīng. Here too, on the upturned eaves of significant halls, you'll find processions of mythical creatures leading and protecting the imperial dragon, which lies at the tail end of the line. The more mythical beasts in the procession, the more important the building, with nine guardians being the maximum.

From the back of the Hall of Preserving Harmony slopes the largest of the city's **marble imperial carriageways**. This beautifully carved, 250-ton block of marble, transported to the palace in winter on sheets of ice, was one of a few that acted as VIP access ramps for the raised hallways. Sedan-chair bearers would walk up the steps on each side, while the emperor was carried over a celestial scene of marble-carved clouds and dragons.

Bronze turtles like the large one in front of the Hall of Supreme Harmony symbolise longevity and stability. It has a removable lid, and on special occasions incense was lit inside it so that smoke billowed from its mouth.

Sundials also dot the complex. You can find one to the east of the Hall of Supreme Harmony. To the west of the hall, on a raised terrace, is a small pavilion with a **bronze grain measure**; both objects are symbolic of imperial justice.

Also look out for the round, football-sized **tether stones** dotted around the weed-covered corners of the large central courtyards. It is assumed that these were used to tether horses.

COMPLETE PALACE OF PEACE & LONGEVITY

A mini Forbidden City, known as the Complete Palace of Peace and Longevity (宁寿全宫; Níng Shǒu Quán Gōng) was built in the northeastern corner of the complex. During the Ming dynasty, the Empress Dowager and the imperial concubines lived here. Now it houses quieter courtyard buildings, which contain a number of fine museum exhibitions, known collectively as the Treasure Gallery. Enter the complex from the south – not far from the Clock Exhibition Hall. Inside the entrance is the beautiful glazed Nine Dragon Screen, one of only three of its type left in China.

Visitors work their way north through the Complete Palace of Peace and Longevity, exploring a number of halls and courtyards before being popped out at the northern end of the Forbidden City. Don't miss the Pavilion of Cheerful Melodies, a three-storey wooden opera house, which was the palace's largest theatre.

TOP SIGHT
TIĀN'ĀNMÉN SQUARE

Flanked to the east and west by stern 1950s Soviet-style buildings and ringed by white perimeter fences that channel the hoi polloi towards periodic security checks and bag searches, the world's largest public square (440,000 sq metres) is a vast desert of paving stones at the heart of Běijīng. The square is also a poignant epitaph to China's hapless democracy movement, which got a drubbing from the People's Liberation Army (PLA) in June 1989. The stringent security and round-the-clock monitoring hardly make it the most relaxing of tourist sights, but such is its iconic status that few visitors leave Běijīng without seeing Tiān'ānmén Sq (天安门广场; Tiān'ānmén Guǎngchǎng). In any case, there's more than enough space to stretch a leg, and the view can be breathtaking, especially on a clear, blue day or at nightfall when the square is illuminated.

DON'T MISS

- ➡ Chairman Mao Memorial Hall
- ➡ Front Gate
- ➡ Flag-raising ceremony

PRACTICALITIES

- ➡ Map p284
- ➡ S Tian'anmen West, Tian'anmen East or Qianmen

History

Tiān'ānmén Sq as we see it today is a modern creation and there is precious little sense of history. During the Ming and Qing dynasties part of the Imperial City Wall (Huáng Chéng) called the Thousand Foot Corridor (Qiānbù Láng) poked deep into the space today occupied by the square, enclosing a section of the imperial domain. The wall took a 'T' shape, emerging from the two huge, now absent, gates that rose up south of the Gate of Heavenly Peace – Cháng'ān Zuǒ Gate and Cháng'ān Yòu Gate – before running south to the vanished Dàmíng Gate (Dàmíng Mén). Called Dàqīng Gate during the Qing dynasty and Zhōnghuá Gate during the Republic, the Dàmíng Gate had three watchtowers and upturned eaves and was guarded by a pair of stone lions. It was pulled down after 1949, a fate similarly reserved for Cháng'ān Zuǒ Gate and Cháng'ān Yòu Gate. East and west of the Thousand Foot Corridor stood official departments and temples, including the Ministry of Rites, the Ministry of Revenue, Honglu Temple and Taichang Temple.

Mao Zedong conceived the square to project the enormity of the Communist Party. During the Cultural Revolution, the chairman, wearing a Red Guard armband, reviewed parades of up to a million people here. The 'Tiān'ānmén Incident' is the term given to the near riot in the square that accompanied the death of Premier Zhou Enlai in 1976. Another million people jammed the square to pay their last respects to Mao in September that year.

Layout

The square is laid out on a north–south axis. Front Gate (p66), which can be climbed, lies to the south, while the Gate of Heavenly Peace (p65) – the gate that lends its name to the square – lies at the northern end, on the other side of the main road. Sitting innocuously in the middle of the square is the Chairman Mao Memorial Hall (p64), which thousands of domestic tourists visit each morning.

Standing in the square, you are in the symbolic centre of the Chinese universe. The rectangular arrangement, flanked by halls to both east and west, to some extent echoes the layout of the Forbidden City. As such, the square employs a conventional plan that pays obeisance to traditional Chinese culture, but its ornaments and buildings are largely Soviet-inspired.

Activities

Early risers can watch the **flag-raising ceremony** at sunrise, performed by a troop of PLA soldiers drilled to march at precisely 108 paces per minute, 75cm per pace. The soldiers emerge through the Gate of Heavenly Peace to goosestep faultlessly across Dongchang'an Jie as traffic is halted. The same ceremony in reverse is performed at sunset. Ask at your hotel for flag-raising and -lowering times so you can get there early, as crowds can be intense.

Bicycles can no longer be ridden, or even walked, across Tiān'ānmén Sq, although you can ride along the north–south avenues on either side of the square.

Kite-flying has also been banned.

Dangers & Annoyances

Unless you actually want a map you'll have to sidestep determined map sellers and their confederates – the incessant learners of English – and just say no to the 'poor' art students press-ganging tourists to view their exhibitions; fending them off can be draining. Avoid invitations to teahouses, unless you want to pay an exorbitant amount for the experience.

1989 PROTESTS

Tiān'ānmén Sq is best known in the West for the tragic events of 4 June 1989, when live television pictures showed the army forcing pro-democracy demonstrators out of the square. Although it is generally agreed that no one was actually killed within the square itself, it is likely that hundreds were killed in the surrounding streets as the military opened fire on protestors. During the 10th anniversary of the 1989 protests, the square was shut for renovations, and every year around 4 June, security is stepped up a notch.

Despite being a public place, the square remains more in the hands of the government than the people; it is monitored by closed-circuit TV cameras, Segway-riding policemen and plain-clothes officers who move like lightning at the first sign of any disruption.

SIGHTS

FORBIDDEN CITY HISTORIC SITE

See p54.

TIĀN'ĀNMÉN SQUARE SQUARE

See p62.

GATE OF HEAVENLY PEACE HISTORIC SITE

See p65.

FRONT GATE HISTORIC SITE

See p66.

NATIONAL MUSEUM OF CHINA MUSEUM

Map p284 (中国国际博物馆; Zhōngguó Guójì Bówùguǎn; en.chnmuseum.cn; Guangchangdongce Lu, Tiān'ānmén Sq; 天安门，广场东侧路; audio guide ¥30, cafe coffee from ¥20, tea from ¥10, pastries & sandwiches ¥10-20; ⏲9am-5pm Tue-Sun, last entry 4pm; **S** Tian'anmen East) **FREE** Běijīng's premier museum is housed in an immense 1950s building on the eastern side of Tiān'ānmén Sq, and is well worth visiting. The **Ancient China** exhibition on the basement floor is outstanding. You could easily spend a couple of hours in this exhibition alone. It contains dozens and dozens of stunning pieces, from prehistoric China through to the Qing Dynasty, all displayed beautifully in modern, spacious, low-lit exhibition halls.

Look out for the 2000-year-old jade burial suit, made for the clearly well-endowed Western Han Dynasty king Liu Xiu, and the life-sized bronze acupuncture statue, dating from the 15th century. The 2000-year-old rhino-shaped bronze *zūn* (wine vessel) is another standout piece. The Ancient Chinese Money exhibition on the top floor, and the Bronze Art and Buddhist Sculpture galleries, one floor below, are also worth seeing.

The museum, which is vast and energy-sapping, also has a ground-floor cafe (south end) and a teahouse (north end). Note, you must bring your passport along to gain museum entry.

CHAIRMAN MAO MEMORIAL HALL MAUSOLEUM

Map p284 (毛主席纪念堂; Máo Zhǔxí Jìniàntáng; Tiān'ānmén Sq; bag storage ¥2-10, camera storage ¥2-5; ⏲7.30am-1pm Tue-Sun; **S** Tian'anmen West, Tian'anmen East or Qianmen) **FREE** Mao Zedong died in September 1976 and his memorial hall was constructed on the southern side of Tiān'ānmén Sq soon afterwards. This squat, Soviet-inspired mausoleum lies on Běijīng's north–south axis of symmetry on the footprint of Zhōnghuá Gate (Zhōnghuá Mén), a vast and ancient portal flattened during the communist development of Tiān'ānmén Sq. Mao is still revered across much of China, and you'll see some people reduced to tears here at the sight of his mummified corpse.

It lies in a crystal cabinet, draped in an anachronistic red flag emblazoned with hammer and sickle, as guards in white gloves impatiently wave visitors on towards further rooms, where a riot of Mao kitsch – lighters, bracelets, statues, key rings, bottle openers, you name it – ensues.

Bags and cameras need to be deposited at the building east of the memorial hall

BĚIJĪNG MUSEUM PASS

If you're staying in the capital for a while, the **Běijīng Museum Pass** (博物馆通票; Bówùguǎn Tōngpiào; ☎6222 3793; www.bowuguan.bj.cn; ¥120) is a decent investment that will save you both money and queuing for tickets. For ¥120 you get either complimentary access or discounted admission (typically 50%) to 65 museums, temples and tourist sights in and around Běijīng. Attractions covered include the Great Wall at Bādálǐng, Front Gate, the Drum Tower, the Bell Tower, the Confucius Temple, the Botanic Gardens, the Railway Museum, Dōngyuè Temple, White Cloud Temple, Zhìhuà Temple and many others. Not all the sights are worth visiting, but you only have to visit a small selection to make it worth the money. The pass comes in the form of a booklet (Chinese with minimal English), valid from 1 January to 31 December in any one year. The pass, which is harder to obtain as the year goes on, can be picked up from participating museums and sights, from some post offices or, most easily, from the huge bookstore known as Běijīng Books Building (p129). Go to the service desk to your right as you enter the bookstore. Note the website and phone service are in Chinese only .

TOP SIGHT
GATE OF HEAVENLY PEACE

Hung with a vast likeness of Mao, and guarded by two pairs of Ming-dynasty stone lions, the double-eaved Gate of Heavenly Peace (天安门; Tiān'ānmén), north of Tiān'ānmén Sq, is a potent national symbol. Built in the 15th century and restored in the 17th century, the gate was formerly the largest of the four gates of the Imperial City Wall, and it was from this gate that Mao proclaimed the People's Republic of China on 1 October 1949. Today's political coterie watches mass troop parades from here.

Climb the gate for excellent views of the square, and peek inside at the impressive beams and overdone paintwork; in all there are 60 gargantuan wooden pillars and 17 vast lamps suspended from the ceiling. Within the gate tower there is also a fascinating photographic history of the gate (but only captioned in Chinese) and Tiān'ānmén Sq.

There's no fee for walking through the gate, en route to the Forbidden City, but if you climb it you'll have to pay. The ticket office is on the north side of the gate. For Forbidden City tickets, keep walking about 600m further north to the entrance at Meridian Gate.

DON'T MISS

- Mao's giant portrait
- Views of Tiān'ānmén Sq
- Impressive interior beams
- Photography exhibition

PRACTICALITIES

- Map p284
- admission ¥15, bag storage ¥2-6
- 8.30am-4.30pm
- S Tian'anmen West or Tian'anmen East

across the road from Tiān'ānmén Sq. And don't forget your passport. You won't be let into the hall without it. Note, the queues may seem impossibly long, but they are constantly moving (visitors aren't allowed to stop inside the hall), so go down relatively quickly.

JǏNGSHĀN PARK PARK

Map p284 (景山公园; Jǐngshān Gōngyuán; Jingshan Qianjie; admission ¥2, in summer ¥5; 6am-9.30pm; S Tian'anmen West, then bus 5) The dominating feature of Jǐngshān – one of the city's finest parks – is one of central Běijīng's few hills; a mound that was created from the earth excavated to make the Forbidden City moat. Called Coal Hill by Westerners during Legation days, Jǐngshān also serves as a feng shui shield, protecting the palace from evil spirits – or dust storms – from the north. Clamber to the top for a magnificent panorama of the capital and princely views over the russet roofing of the Forbidden City.

On the eastern side of the park a locust tree stands in the place where the last of the Ming emperors, Chongzhen, hung himself as rebels swarmed at the city walls. The rest of the park is one of the best places in Běijīng for people-watching. Come early to see (or join in with) elderly folk going about their morning routines of dancing, singing, performing taichi or playing keepie-uppies with oversized shuttlecocks. In April and May the park bursts into bloom with fabulously colourful peonies and tulips forming the focal point of a very popular flower fair (admission ¥10). The park has three gates: the south is directly opposite the Forbidden City's north gate (exit only), the west leads towards Běihǎi Park's east gate, while the east gate has a couple of nice cafes outside it.

WORKERS CULTURAL PALACE PARK

Map p284 (劳动人民文化宫, Láodòng Rénmín Wénhuà Gōng; park entrance ¥2; 6.30am-7.30pm; S Tian'anmen East) Despite the prosaic name and its location at the very heart of town, this reclusive park, between Tiān'ānmén Sq and the Forbidden City, is one of Běijīng's best-kept secrets. Few visitors divert to here from their course towards the main gate of the Forbidden City, but this was the emperor's premier place of worship and contains the **Supreme Temple** (太庙; Tài Miào; Map p284; admission ¥10), with its beautifully carved interior roofing.

If you find the Forbidden City either too colossal or crowded, the temple halls here are a cheaper, more tranquil and more manageable alternative. Enter the temple area of the park through the striking Glazed Gate (琉璃门; Liúli Mén). Then, rising up to the splendid Front Hall are three flights of steps. Only gods could traverse the central plinth; the emperor was consigned to the left-hand flight. Note how the plaque above the Front Hall is inscribed in both Chinese and Manchu. Sadly, this hall, as well as the Middle Hall and Rear Hall behind, is inaccessible. The northern perimeter of the park abuts the palace moat, where you can find a bench and park yourself in front of a fine view. For an offbeat experience, practise your backhand within a ball's bounce of the Forbidden City at the Royal Tennis Centre (p79), near the park's east gate. There's also a south gate, for Tiān'ānmén Sq, and a northwest gate, for the Forbidden City.

ZHŌNGSHĀN PARK — PARK

Map p284 (中山公园; Zhōngshān Gōngyuán; admission ¥3, Spring Flower & Tulips Show ¥10; ⌚6am-9pm; Ⓢ Tian'anmen West) Named after Sun Zhongshan (Sun Yatsen), the father of modern China, this peaceful park sits at the southwest corner of the Forbidden City and partly looks out onto the palace's moat (you can rent pedal-boats here) and towering walls. A refreshing prologue or conclusion to the magnificence of the Forbidden City, the park was formerly the sacred Ming-style Altar to the God of the Land and the God of Grain (Shèjìtán), where the emperor offered sacrifices. The **Square Altar** (Wǔsè Tǔ) remains, bordered on all sides by walls tiled in various colours

Near the park's south entrance stands a towering dark-blue-tiled *páilou* (traditional Chinese archway) with triple eaves that originally commemorated the German Foreign Minister Baron von Ketteler, killed by Boxers in 1900. Just off to the right (east) is the 100-year-old Láijīnyǔxuān Teahouse (p75). North of here, also in the eastern section of the park, is the Forbidden City Concert Hall (p76). As with Jǐngshān Park, April and May is a beautiful time to

TOP SIGHT FRONT GATE

Front Gate, or Qiánmén (前门), actually consists of two gates. The northernmost of the two gates is the 40m-high **Zhèngyáng Gate** (正阳门城楼; Zhèngyáng Mén Chénglóu), which dates from the Ming dynasty and was the largest of the nine gates of the Inner City Wall separating the inner, or Tartar (Manchu), city from the outer, or Chinese, city. Partially destroyed in the Boxer Rebellion around 1900, the gate was once flanked by two temples that have since vanished. With the disappearance of the city walls, the gate sits out of context, but it can be climbed for decent views of Tiān'ānmén Sq and Arrow Tower, immediately to the south.

Inside the upper levels are some fascinating historical photographs, showing the area as it was at the beginning of the last century, before the city walls and many of the surrounding gates and temples were demolished. Explanatory captions are in English as well as Chinese. **Zhèngyáng Gate Arrow Tower** (正阳门箭楼; Zhèngyángmén Jiànlóu), directly south, can't be climbed. It also dates from the Ming dynasty and was originally connected to Zhèngyáng Gate by a semicircular enceinte (enclosing wall), demolished last century.

DON'T MISS

- Fascinating historical photographs
- Views of Tiān'ānmén Sq

PRACTICALITIES

- Map p284
- admission ¥20, audio guide ¥20
- ⌚9am-4pm Tue-Sun
- Ⓢ Qianmen

visit thanks to the hugely colourful Spring Flower and Tulips Show. The northeast exit of the park brings you out by Meridian Gate, from where you can enter the Forbidden City. The south exit takes you out near Tiān'ānmén Sq. There is also a west gate.

MONUMENT TO THE PEOPLE'S HEROES — MONUMENT

Map p284 (人民英雄纪念碑; Rénmín Yīngxióng Jìniànbēi; Tiān'ānmén Sq; S Tian'anmen West, Tian'anmen East or Qianmen) North of Mao's mausoleum, and also in the centre of Tiān'ānmén Sq, the Monument to the People's Heroes was completed in 1958. The 37.9m-high obelisk, made of Qīngdǎo granite, bears bas-relief carvings of key patriotic and revolutionary events, as well as calligraphy from communist bigwigs Mao Zedong and Zhou Enlai.

FORMER FOREIGN LEGATION QUARTER — HISTORIC BUILDINGS

Map p284 (租界区; S Chongwenmen, Qianmen or Wangfujing) The former Foreign Legation Quarter, where the 19th-century foreign powers flung up their embassies, schools, post offices and banks, lies east of Tiān'ānmén Sq. Apart from the Běijīng Police Museum, the **former French Post Office** (Map p286), now a Sìchuān restaurant, and some of the Legation Quarter buildings (now high-end restaurants and members clubs), you can't enter any of the buildings, but a stroll along the streets here (Dongjiaomin Xiang, Taijichang Dajie and Zhengyi Lu) gives you a hint of the area's former European flavour. Try our walking tour for starters.

BĚIJĪNG POLICE MUSEUM — MUSEUM

Map p284 (北京警察博物馆; Běijīng Jǐngchá Bówùguǎn; ☎8522 5018; 36 Dongjiaomin Xiang; admission ¥5, through ticket ¥20; ⊙9am-4pm Tue-Sun; S Qianmen) Propaganda aside, riveting exhibits make this a fascinating exposé of Běijīng's *dà gài mào* (local slang for the constabulary). Learn how Běijīng's first Public Security Bureau (PSB) college operated from the **Dōngyuè Temple** in 1949 and find out how officers tackled the 'stragglers, disbanded soldiers, bandits, local ruffians, hoodlums and despots…' planted in Běijīng by the Kuomintang (KMT).

There are also eye-opening accounts of how KMT spies Li Andong and Yamaguchi Takachi planned to mortar the Gate of Heavenly Peace, and a welcome analysis of how the Běijīng PSB was destroyed during the 'national catastrophe' of the Cultural Revolution. For police weapons, head to the 4th floor. The through ticket includes some laser-shooting practice and a souvenir.

ST JOSEPH'S CHURCH — CHURCH

Map p286 (东堂; Dōng Táng; 74 Wangfujing Dajie; admission free; ⊙6.30am-5pm; S Dengshikou) A crowning edifice on Wangfujing Dajie, and one of Běijīng's four principal churches, St Joseph's is known locally as Dōng Táng (East Cathedral). Originally built during the reign of Shunzhi in 1655, it was damaged by an earthquake in 1720 and reconstructed. The luckless church also caught fire in 1807, was destroyed again in 1900 during the Boxer Rebellion and restored in 1904, only to be shut in 1966. Now fully repaired, the church is a testament to the long history of Christianity in China.

A large piazza in front swarms with kids skate-boarding, newlyweds posing for photographs and elderly folk meeting up in the early evening for formation dancing. Mass is held in English every Sunday at 4pm.

CHINA ART MUSEUM — MUSEUM

Map p286 (中国美术馆; Zhōngguó Měishùguǎn; 1 Wusi Dajie; ⊙9am-5pm, last entry 4pm; S National Art Museum) FREE This revamped museum has received a healthy shot of imagination and flair, with absorbing exhibitions from across China and abroad promising doses of colour and vibrancy. Běijīng's art-lovers have lapped up some top-notch presentations here, from the cream of Italian design to modern artworks from the Taipei Fine Arts Museum and exhibitions of paintings from some of China's ethnic minority groups.

Lifts allow for wheelchair access. There's a cafe on the ground floor. Bring your passport to gain entry.

DŌNG'ĀN MÉN REMAINS — RUIN

Map p286 (明皇城东安门遗址; Míng Huáng Chéng Dōng'ānmén Yízhǐ; Imperial Wall Foundation Ruins Park, cnr Donghuamen Dajie & Beiheyan Dajie; ⊙24hr; S Dengshikou or National Art Museum) FREE In two roadside pits, a couple of metres below the road surface on the north and south side of the crossroads here, are the remains of the once magnificent Dōng'ān Mén – the east gate of the Imperial City – as well as parts of the imperial city wall and parts of a bridge that used to cross the city canal (now a road).

Neighbourhood Walk
Tiān'ānmén Square & Foreign Legation Quarter

START TIĀN'ĀNMÉN SQ
END RAFFLES BĚIJĪNG HOTEL
LENGTH 2KM; ONE HOUR

From **1 Tiān'ānmén Square** (p62), cross the road and climb the steps into **2 Dongjiaomin Xiang** (东交民巷). The red-brick building on your left was the former **3 French Hospital**.

Through a sometimes-closed grey archway on your right stands the elegant former **4 Legation Quarter** (p67), now a collection of trendy restaurants facing onto a grass quadrangle, and accessed from the south.

Behind a wall a short walk east rises a green-roofed building at No 40, which was once the **5 Dutch Legation**.

Further along on your right stands a building with massive pillars, the erstwhile address of the First National City Bank of New York, now the quirky **6 Běijīng Police Museum** (p67).

Keep walking east to the domed building on the corner of Zhengyi Lu (正义路) and Dongjiaomin Xiang, once the **7 Yokohama Specie Bank**.

The grey building at No 19 is the **8 former French post office** (p67), now Jìngyuán Chuāncài Sichuanese restaurant and ideal for lunch before you reach the former **9 French Legation**, at No 15, with its large red entrance.

Backing onto a small school courtyard, the twin spires of the Gothic **10 St Michael's Church** rise ahead at No 11, facing the green roofs and ornate red brickwork of the old **11 Belgian Legation**.

Stroll north along Taijichang Dajie and hunt down the brick street sign embedded in the northern wall of Taijichang Toutiao (台基厂头条), carved with the old name of the road, **12 Rue Hart**. Along the north side of Rue Hart (at No 3) was the Austro-Hungarian Legation.

Reaching the north end of Taijichang Dajie, across busy Dongchang'an Jie, is the **13 Raffles Běijīng Hotel** (built 1900), which is just a stone's throw from the famous **14 Wangfujing Dajie** shopping strip.

The ruins are little more than small piles of bricks, but they are brought to life by a carved map fastened to one wall, showing what the area once looked like. Before being razed, the gate, Dōng'ān Mén, was a single-eaved, seven-bay-wide building with a hip-and-gable roof capped with yellow tiles. All that's left of it now are two layers of 18 bricks.

PŬDÙ TEMPLE BUDDHIST TEMPLE

Map p284 (普渡寺; Pǔdù Sì; Pudusi Dongxiang, off Nanheyan Dajie, 南河沿大街普渡寺东巷) This nonactive Ming-dynasty temple can't be entered, but the square in front of it, which forms part of a small park, is a peaceful place to rest up after a shopping spree on Wangfujing Dajie. The structure of the main hall is unusual in its Manchu style, and from the park's elevated position you get views of the surrounding *hútòng*.

ANCIENT OBSERVATORY OBSERVATORY

Map p286 (古观象台; Gǔ Guānxiàngtái; Jianguomen Bridge, East 2nd Ring Rd; Erhuandong Lu, Jianguomen Qiao, 二环东路建国门桥; admission ¥20; ⏰9am-4.30pm Tue-Sun; Ⓢ Jianguomen) This unusual former observatory is mounted on the battlements of a watchtower lying along the line of the old Ming City Wall and originally dates back to Kublai Khan's days, when it lay north of the present site. Kublai, like later Ming and Qing emperors, relied heavily on astrologers to plan military endeavours. The present observatory – the only surviving example of several constructed during the Jin, Yuan, Ming and Qing dynasties – was built between 1437 and 1446 to facilitate both astrological predictions and seafaring navigation.

At ground level is a pleasant courtyard flanked by halls housing displays (with limited English captions). Also within the courtyard is an armillary sphere dating to 1439, supported by four dragons.

Clamber the steps to the roof of the watchtower to admire a mind-boggling array of Jesuit-designed astronomical instruments, embellished with sculptured bronze dragons and other Chinese flourishes – a kind of East and West astronomical fusion.

POLY ART MUSEUM MUSEUM

Map p286 (保利艺术博物馆; Bǎolì Yìshù Bówùguǎn; ☎6500 8117; www.polymuseum.com; 9th fl, Poly Plaza, 14 Dongzhimen Nandajie; admission ¥20, audio guide ¥10; ⏰9.30am-5pm, closed Sun; Ⓢ Dongsi Shitiao) This small but exquisite museum displays a glorious array of ancient bronzes from the Shang and Zhou dynasties, a magnificent high-water mark for bronze production. Check out the intricate scaling on the *Zūn vessel in the shape of a Phoenix* (倗季凤鸟尊) or the *Yǒu with Divine Faces* (神面卣), with its elephant head on the side of the vessel. The detailed animist patterns on the *Gangbo You* (棡柏卣) are similarly vivid and fascinating.

In an attached room are four of the 12 Western-styled bronze animals that were plundered with the sacking of the Old Summer Palace and have been acquired by the museum; pig, monkey, tiger and ox. The last room is populated with a wonderful collection of standing Bodhisattva statues, dating from the Northern Qi, Northern Wei and Tang dynasties.

Those interested in Ming-dynasty architecture should check out the nearby **Imperial Granaries** (南新仓; Map p286; Nán Xīn Cāng). Nine of the storehouses, dating from 1409, have been lovingly restored. They once contained grain and rice for Běijīng's royalty; now they house posh wine bars and members-only clubs.

ZHÌHUÀ TEMPLE BUDDHIST TEMPLE

Map p286 (智化寺; Zhìhuà Sì; 5 Lumicang Hutong; admission ¥20, audio guide ¥10, Wed free; ⏰8.30am-4.30pm, closed Mon; Ⓢ Jianguomen or Chaoyangmen) Běijīng's surviving temple brood has endured casual restoration that often buried authenticity. But this rickety nonactive temple, hidden down a rarely visited *hútòng*, is thick with the flavours of old Peking, having eluded the Dulux treatment that invariably precedes entrance fee inflation and stomping tour groups.

You won't find the coffered ceiling of the **Zhìhuà Hall** (it's in the USA), and the Four Heavenly Kings have vanished from **Zhìhuà Gate** (智化门; Zhìhuà Mén), but the **Scriptures Hall**, off to one side of the central courtyard, encases a unique, eight-sided, Ming-dynasty wooden library topped with a seated Buddha and a magnificently unrestored ceiling. The highlight, the **Ten Thousand Buddhas Hall** (万佛殿; Wànfó Diàn), is right at the back of the complex, and is an enticing two floors of miniature niche-borne Buddhist effigies and cabinets for the storage of sutras. Its entrance is dominated by three stunning, wood-carved deities (a 20ft-tall Tathagata Buddha, flanked by Brahma and Indra). Unfortunately, visitors

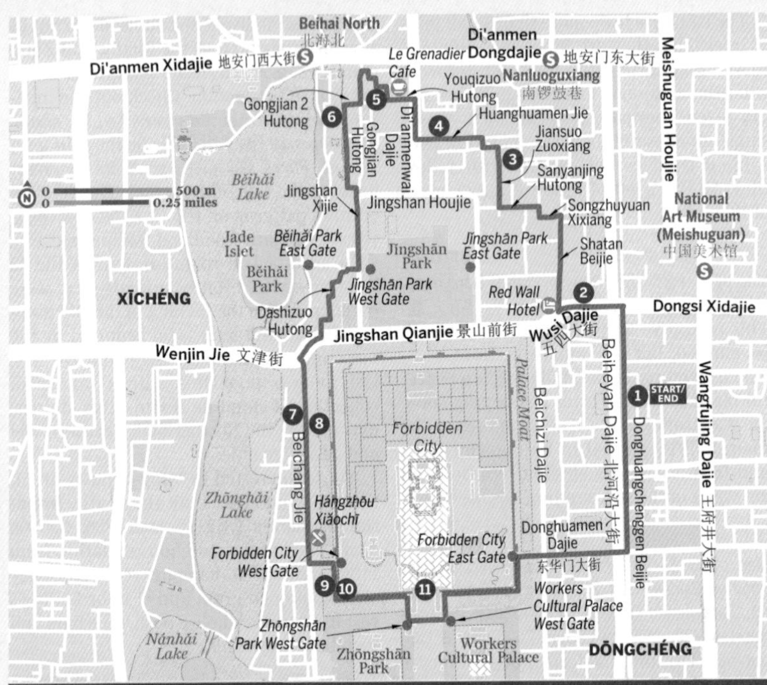

Neighbourhood Bike Tour
Imperial City Bike Tour

START BIKE BEIJING
END BIKE BEIJING
LENGTH 6KM; 1½ HOURS

Pick up a bike at ❶ **Bike Beijing** (p78) and head for the imperial *hútòng* east of Jǐngshān Park, passing the 1918 ❷ **Hóng Lóu**, where Mao Zedong once worked as a librarian.

Turn right into Shatan Beijie (沙滩北街) then left into Songzhuyuan Xixiang (嵩祝院西巷). Bear right, then turn left into Sanyanjing Hutong (三眼井胡同). Note the elaborately carved Qing-dynasty doorway on your right, now turned into a wall and window. Just before the end, turn right into Jiansuo Zuoxiang (吉安所左巷). No 8 was ❸ **Mao Zedong's former home**.

At the end, turn left, take the second right and turn left onto Huanghuamen Jie (黄花门街). No 43 is the ❹ **former courtyard home of imperial eunuch Li Lianyin**, a favourite of Empress Dowager Cixi.

At the end, turn right then left under an arch in part of the old imperial city wall, into Youqizuo Hutong (油漆作胡同).

Follow the wiggly ❺ **hútòng** to Gongjian Hutong (恭俭胡同). Soon after, turn right into Gongjian 2 Hutong (恭俭二胡同), a quiet residential alleyway, which hugs the ❻ **eastern wall of Běihǎi Park**.

Follow Jingshan Xijie (景山西街) to Jǐngshān Park west gate, turn right, then cycle under the car-park arch and into Dashizuo Hutong (大石作胡同), which wiggles its way to Jingshan Qianjie (景山前街), and the Forbidden City moat. Follow Beichang Jie (北长街), past the former entrance to the ❼ **Longevity and Prosperity Temple** (now houses) and the also-closed ❽ **Fúyòu Temple**.

Turn left to the west gate of the Forbidden City, and follow the ❾ **Forbidden City moat** and towering ❿ **palace walls** around to ⓫ **Meridian Gate**. Cross the square in front of the gate, and follow the moat eastward. Pass the palace's east gate before crossing onto Donghuamen Dajie (东华门大街), turning left into Donghuangchenggen Nanjie (东黄跟城南街) and returning to Bike Beijing.

are no longer allowed to climb to the 2nd floor of this hall.

Try to time your visit to coincide with the free, 15-minute, **musical performance** that takes place in Zhìhuà Hall at 10am and 3pm each day. Performers use traditional Chinese instruments associated with Buddhist worship.

Note the surreal juxtaposition of this 15th-century temple with the swirling, space-age curves of the Galaxy Soho buildings, which now loom over this historic *hútòng* neighbourhood.

SHǏJIĀ HÚTÒNG MUSEUM MUSEUM

Map p286 (史家胡同博物馆; Shǐjiā Hútòng Bówùguǎn; 24 Shijia Hutong; 史家胡同24号; ⌚9.30am-4.30pm Tue-Sun) FREE Housed in a pleasant, renovated double-courtyard, which used to be a local kindergarten, this small museum uses old photos, maps and artefacts, as well as some scale models, to explain the history of Shijia Hutong, and of Běijīng's *hútòng* districts in general. There are excellent English captions throughout, and the large-scale model of the whole local neighbourhood, with Shijia Hutong at its core, is particularly interesting to muse over.

LAO SHE MUSEUM HISTORIC BUILDING

Map p286 (老舍纪念馆, Lǎo Shě Jìniànguǎn; 19 Fengfu Hutong; ⌚9am-3.40pm, closed Mon; S Dengshikou) FREE Brimful of uncomplicated charm, this renovated courtyard house off Dengshikou Xijie was the home of Lao She (1899–1966), one of Běijīng's best-loved 20th-century writers. The life of Lao She – author of *Rickshaw Boy* and *Tea House*, and former teacher at London's School of Oriental and African Studies – is detailed in a modest collection of halls, via newspaper cuttings, first-edition books, photographs and personal effects.

The exhibition falls at the final hurdle, giving perfunctory mention to perhaps the most significant aspect of Lao She's life: his death by drowning in Taiping Lake on 24 August 1966 after a nasty beating by vituperative Red Guards the day before. Captions are largely in Chinese.

TEN FU'S TEA CULTURE HOUSE MUSEUM

Map p286 (天福茶文化馆; Tiānfú Chá Wénhuàguǎn; 3 Jinyu Hutong; 金鱼胡同3号; ⌚9am-10pm) It's a blatant attempt to promote the already hugely successful Ten Fu tea brand, but this teashop-cum-museum is interesting nevertheless. Sidestep the teas and tea sets for sale on the ground floor (unless you're in the buying mood, of course), and head upstairs to the 'tea corridor' for a brief introduction to the history and processes involved in Chinese tea production, including some miniature moving models of tea-making machinery.

Downstairs you can sample, and buy, teas from across China. It sells neat, slim, gift packs of tea (¥20 to ¥30), or else buy it by the *liǎng* (50g). Some English spoken. Look for the giant, gravity-defying tea pot outside.

SHÈNG XĪ FÚ HAT MUSEUM MUSEUM

Map p286 (368 Dongsi Beidajie; 东四北大街368号; ⌚8.45am-7pm) FREE This branch of the famous Shèng Xī Fú Hat Store (p78) has a quirky, free-to-visit hat museum out the back, detailing the history of the company and of hats in China.

EATING

★CRESCENT MOON MUSLIM RESTAURANT XINJIANG $

Map p286 (新疆弯弯月亮维吾尔穆斯林餐厅; Xīnjiāng Wānwānyuèliàng Wéiwú'ěr Mùsīlín Cāntīng; 16 Dongsi Liutiao Hutong, 东四六条胡同16号, 东四北大街; dishes from ¥18; ⌚11am-11pm; 📋; S Dongsi Shitiao) You can find a Chinese Muslim restaurant on almost every street in Běijīng. Most are run by Huí Muslims, who are Hàn Chinese, rather than ethnic-minority Uighurs from the remote western province of Xīnjiāng. Crescent Moon is the real deal – owned and staffed by Uighurs, it attracts many Běijīng-based Uighurs and people from Central Asia, as well as a lot of Western expats.

It's more expensive than most other Xīnjiāng restaurants in Běijīng, but the food is consistently good, and it has an English menu. The speciality is the barbecued leg of lamb (¥128). The lamb skewers (¥6) are also delicious, and there's naan bread (¥5), homemade yoghurt (¥12) and plenty of noodle options (¥18 to¥25). You can also get Xīnjiāng tea (¥30 per pot), beer (¥15) and wine (¥95).

ZUǑ LÍN YÒU SHÈ BEIJING $

Map p286 (左邻右舍褡裢火烧; 50 Meishuguan Houjie; 美术馆后街50号; dumplings per liang ¥6-7, dishes ¥10-30; ⌚11am-9.30pm; 📋; S National

Art Museum) This small, no-frills restaurant focuses on Běijīng cuisine. The speciality is *dālian huǒshāo* (褡裢火烧), golden-fried finger-shaped dumplings stuffed with all manner of savoury fillings; we prefer the pork ones, but there are lamb, beef and veggie choices too. They are served by the *liǎng* (两), with one *liǎng* equal to three dumplings, and they prefer you to order at least two *liǎng* (二两; *èr liǎng*) of each filling to make it worth their while cooking a batch.

Other specialities include the pickled fish (酥鲫鱼; *sū jì yú*), the spicy tofu paste (麻豆腐; *má dòufu*) and the deep-fried pork balls (干炸丸子; *gān zhá wánzi*), while filling bowls of millet porridge (小米粥; *xiǎo mǐ zhōu*) are served up for free. No English sign (look for the wooden signboard), and no English spoken, but most parts of the menu have been translated into English.

GRANDMA'S HANGZHOU **$**

Map p286 (外婆家; Wàipó Jiā; 6th fl, Beijing apm shopping mall, 138 Wangfujing Dajie; 王府井大街138号apm6楼; mains ¥10-45; ⏰10am-2.30pm & 4-9pm; 📋) Handy for shoppers on Wangfujing Dajie, but worth making the trip to from any part of the city, the Běijīng branch of this hugely successful Hángzhōu chain is a big hit in the capital. It's excellent value and is clean and bright, with comfy booth seating, so very popular with families. The menu is in English, although you might need a magnifying glass to read it.

Dishes we heartily recommend include Grandma's Pork (a juicy, braised pork dish, known in Hángzhōu as *Dōngpō ròu*; 东坡肉), Tea Flavoured Chicken (cooked with Hángzhōu's famous Lóngjǐng green tea), Potatoes on a Sizzling Iron Plate, the Grilled Eggplant and the Organic Cauliflour. But anything with a red thumbs-up icon next to it on the menu is a safe bet.

This place is so popular you usually have to wait at least an hour for a table. You can't reserve in advance; you have to come to the entrance and take a ticket (like in a bank). As you do so, you need to enter your details on the touch screen. In the first box, enter your mobile telephone number. In the second box, enter the number of people there are in your group. Then click on the left-hand red button that reads 领号 (meaning, 'receive a number'), and take your ticket. Armed with your mobile number, the restaurant will then text you about five minutes before your table is ready. If you don't have a local phone, you'll have to keep coming back to check what number they're up to. Expect to wait an hour on midweek evenings; two hours at weekends. Lunchtimes are less busy. Grandma's is on the 6th floor of the modern shopping mall known in English as 'Beijing apm'; the one with the massive Apple store on the ground floor.

CHUĀN BÀN SICHUAN **$**

Map p286 (川办餐厅; 28 Dongzongbu Hutong, off Chaoyangmen Nanxiaojie; 朝阳门南小街东总部胡同28号; dishes from ¥20; ⏰11am-2pm & 5-9pm Mon-Fri, 11am-11pm Sat & Sun; 📋; Ⓢ Jianguomen) Every Chinese province has its own official building in Běijīng, complete with a restaurant for cadres and locals working in the capital who are pining for a taste of home. Often they're the most authentic places for regional cuisines. This restaurant in the Sìchuān Government Offices is always crowded and serves up just about every variety of Sìchuān food you could want.

It's very much a place for fire fiends: almost every dish comes loaded with chillies and mouth-numbing Sìchuān peppercorns, whether it's bamboo shoots, Sìchuān specials such as *làzi jī* (here called 'young chicken Chongqing style'), or steamed fish with pepper and taro (here called 'boiled fish in spicy and hot pepper'). There are also dishes with rabbit and frog, both regional delicacies. There's an English menu with photos, but no English sign; it's housed in an office-block of a building, with the entrance round the back.

YUÈBĪN FÀNGUǍN BEIJING **$**

Map p286 (悦宾饭馆; 43 Cuihua Hutong, off Wusi Dajie; 五四大街翠花胡同43号; mains ¥20-50; ⏰11am-9pm) Post-1949, this was the first privately owned restaurant to open in Běijīng. It's so minimalist that it still has an old canteen-like feel to it, but the focus here, as with many of China's best restaurants, is on the food, not the decor. This is a proper locals joint, so ignore the cigarette smoking and the fish-bone spitting, pull up a chair, order a bottle of Yanjing beer (燕京啤酒; Yānjīng *píjiǔ*), and tuck in.

The menu, naturally, is in Chinese only. House specialities include: *guōshāo yā* (锅烧鸭; fried duck – the first dish ever served here, apparently), *suànní zhǒuzi* (蒜泥肘子; pork shoulder in garlic and vinegar), *miànjīn pá báicài* (面筋扒白菜; glutinous braised cabbage), *qīngchǎo xiārén* (清炒虾仁; stir-fried shrimp) and *wǔ sī tǒng* (五丝筒; chicken-and-veg egg rolls, served with pancakes, leeks and hoisin sauce). Note, check how much your beer costs before they open it for you. Some are cheap, but some cost almost ¥20 a bottle.

DŌNGZI LŮRÒU HUǑSHĀO HEBEI $

Map p286 (冬子驴肉火烧; 193 Chaoyangmen Nanxiaojie, 朝阳门南小街193号; mains ¥5-6; ⏲7.30am-11pm; Ⓢ Dengshikou) Small, no-nonsense, but clean restaurant serving some of the best *lǘròu huǒshāo* (驴肉火烧; donkey-meat pastry pockets; ¥6) in Běijīng. Bowls of *xiǎomǐ zhōu* (小米粥; millet porridge; ¥2) make an ideal accompaniment, or else just grab a beer (啤酒; *píjiǔ;* ¥4). No English sign or menu, and no English spoken.

WǓGĒ JĪCHÌ BARBECUE $

Map p286 (五哥鸡翅; 5 Nanbanqiao Hutong, off Dongsi Batiao, 东四八条,南板桥胡同5号; chicken wings ¥6; ⏲3pm-midnight) Not the friendliest place, but the fabulously tasty chicken wings in this tiny hole-in-the-wall joint are worth the grumpy reception. No menu and no English spoken, but it doesn't matter; all they usually do here are chicken wings (鸡翅; *jī chì;* ¥6 each), so you only have to convey how many you want, and whether you want them spicy (辣; *là*) or not (不辣; *bù là*).

To find it, head east along Dongsi Batiao then turn left at the tiny *hútòng* crossroads and the unmarked restaurant will be on your left. If, when walking along Dongsi Batiao, you reach Slow Boat Brewery (at No 56), you've gone slightly too far.

DŌNGHUÁMÉN NIGHT MARKET STREET FOOD $

Map p286 (东华门夜市; Dōnghuámén Yèshì; Dong'anmen Dajie, 东安门大街; snacks ¥5-15; ⏲4-10pm; Ⓢ Wangfujing) A sight in itself, the bustling night market near Wangfujing Dajie is a veritable food zoo: lamb, beef and chicken skewers, corn on the cob, smelly *dòufu* (tofu), cicadas, grasshoppers, kidneys, quail eggs, snake, squid, fruit, porridge, fried pancakes, strawberry kebabs, bananas, Inner Mongolian cheese, stuffed eggplants, chicken hearts, pita bread stuffed with meat, shrimps – and that's just the start.

It's not a very authentic Běijīng experience, but the vendors take great glee in persuading foreigners to try such delicacies as scorpion on a stick. Expect to pay ¥5 for a lamb skewer; more than you would pay for the same snack from a *hútòng* vendor. More exotic skewers cost up to ¥50. Noodles or savoury pancakes *(jiānbing)* will set you back about ¥10. Prices are all marked and in English.

HÁNGZHŌU XIǍOCHĪ DUMPLINGS $

Map p284 (杭州小吃; Hángzhōu Xiǎochī; 76 Beichang Jie, 北长街76号; mains ¥5-10; ⏲6.30am-8pm; Ⓢ Tian'anmen West, then Bus 5) Lao Li, the eccentric manager of What? Bar, two doors from here, swears by the boiled dumplings (蒸饺; *zhēng jiǎo*) in this simple restaurant. They come by the basket and are perfect for lining your stomach before you delve into the cheap beer at What? Bar.

You can also get fluffier, steamed dumplings (小笼包; *xiǎolóng bāo*) for the same price (¥6 per basket), as well as soups – seaweed (紫菜汤; *zǐcài tāng),* wonton (馄沌; *hún dùn*) and egg (鸡蛋汤, *jīdàn tāng*) – and noodles – beef (牛肉面, *niúròu miàn*) and spicy glass noodles (酸辣粉, *suān là fěn*). No English sign or menu.

WÁNGFǓJǏNG SNACK STREET STREET FOOD $

Map p286 (王府井小吃街, Wángfǔjǐng Xiǎochījiē; west off Wangfujing Dajie, 王府井大街西侧; dishes & snacks ¥10; ⏲9.30am-10pm; Ⓢ Wangfujing) Fronted by an ornate archway, this pedestrianised lane is lined with cheap-and-cheerful food stalls that are always busy. There are dishes from all over China, including *málà tàng* (a spicy soup from Sìchuān) and *zhájiàngmiàn* (Běijīng noodles in fried bean sauce), as well as skewers, savoury pancakes and oodles of noodles. Not all stalls have prices listed, but most things cost around ¥10 for a portion.

XĪN TIĀN YUÀN CHINESE FAST FOOD $

Map p292 (新天苑; Tiān'ānmén Sq, east side; 天安门广场东边; meals ¥20-40; ⏲5am-8.30pm) Tiān'ānmén Sq is one of the few remaining places in Běijīng where foreigners still have to put up with dual pricing in cheap restaurants. This branch of Xīn Tiān Yuàn, a Chinese fast-food chain, is one place you can avoid it. So if you don't have the time or the energy to go further afield, pop in here for a cheap bowl of noodles or a rice meal. They even serve cans of beer (¥8).

★LITTLE YÚNNÁN YUNNAN $$

Map p286 (小云南; Xiǎo Yúnnán; ☎6401 9498; 28 Donghuang Chenggen Beijie, 东皇城根北街28号; mains ¥20-60; ⏲10am-10pm; 📋) Run by young, friendly staff and housed in a cute courtyard conversion, Little Yúnnán is one of the more down-to-earth Yúnnán restaurants in Běijīng. The main room has a rustic feel to it, with wooden beams, flooring and furniture. The tables up in the eaves are fun, and there's also some seating in the small open-air courtyard by the entrance.

Dishes include some classic southwest China ingredients, with some tea-infused creations as well as river fish, mushroom dishes and *là ròu* (腊肉; cured pork – south China's answer to bacon). They also serve Yúnnán rice wine and the province's local Dali Beer. Has an English sign and a well-translated English menu.

MĂN FÚ LÓU HOTPOT **$$**

Map p286 (满福楼; 38 Di'anmennei Dajie; 地安门内大街38号; raw ingredients ¥10-50; ⏰11am-10pm) This grand-looking but inexpensive 20-year-old hotpot restaurant serves up Mongolian hotpot – the nonspicy, lamb-based version that hails from the steppes, but has been adopted as a Běijīng speciality. Here each diner gets their own, mini, conical brass pot in which to boil their food. Choose the clear broth (*qīng tāng;* 清汤; ¥12), which isn't spicy, then pick portions of raw ingredients from the menu (in English and with photos).

Each person should also order a small bowl of sesame-paste dipping sauce (小料; *xiǎo liào*), which you dip your cooked food into before eating it. There should be a pot of chilli oil (辣椒油; *làjiāo yóu*) on your table (if not, ask for it), which can be mixed into the sesame paste to spice things up a bit.

BRIAN MCKENNA @ THE COURTYARD FUSION **$$$**

Map p286 (马克南四合轩; Mǎkènán Sìhéxuān; ☎6526 8883; www.bmktc.com; 95 Donghuamen Dajie, 东华门大街95号; set menus from ¥588; ⏰11.30am-2.30pm & 6-10pm; 🚭📄; Ⓢ Tian'anmen East or Dengshikou) This 10-year-old classic of the Běijīng fine-dining scene has been given a new lease of life by UK-born chef Brian McKenna. Courtyard still enjoys its peerless location, housed in a Qing-dynasty building beside the Forbidden City moat, but McKenna has revamped the interior (there are more tables with a view of the moat now) and the menu (with some innovative new creations, such as his chocolate terracotta warrior).

The basement art gallery has been transformed into a classy cigar bar – head down here for an aperitif before your meal. Reservations are recommended, especially if you want a table overlooking the moat (the walls beside it are lit up in the evening). There are a number of set menus (ranging from ¥588 to ¥1488), including a five-course vegetarian set menu, but à la carte is also available, as are wine pairings.

TEMPLE RESTAURANT EUROPEAN **$$$**

Map p286 (嵩祝寺餐厅; Sōngzhù Sì Cāntīng; ☎8400 2232; www.trb-cn.com; Sōngzhù Temple, 23 Shatanbei Jie, off Wusi Dajie, 五四大街沙滩北街23号, 嵩祝寺; mains ¥200-300, set menus ¥300-900; ⏰11am-2pm & 5pm-midnight; 🚭📄; Ⓢ National Art Museum) Housed, along with its namesake hotel, in the beautifully renovated grounds of a disused, 600-year-old temple, and opened by celebrated chef Ignace Lecleir, this place is exquisite. The service is flawless, the food – salmon, lobster, pigeon, veal – is sheer quality (although some moan about the small portions) and the ambience is certainly unique.

It also has one of the best wine lists in town. The whole menu, including the ¥135 lunchtime set menu, can be viewed on its website. Reservations recommended.

BĚIJĪNG DÀDǑNG ROAST DUCK RESTAURANT PEKING DUCK **$$$**

Map p286 (北京大董烤鸭店; Běijīng Dàdǒng Kǎoyādiàn; ☎8522 1111; 5th fl Jinbao Place, 88 Jinbao Jie, 东城区金宝街88号金宝汇购物中心5层; roast duck ¥268; ⏰10am-11pm; 📄; Ⓢ Dengshikou) Ultramodern Dàdǒng sells itself on being the only restaurant that serves Peking duck with all the flavour of the classic imperial dish, but none of the fat – the leanest roast duck in the capital. For some it's hideously overpriced and far from authentic. For others it's the best roast duck restaurant in China.

There are seven branches in Běijīng (and one in Shànghǎi): this one, by the Regent hotel, and another housed in part of the former Imperial Granaries, are the most central. All are equally classy establishments. Note, it's not the roast duck that will neccessarily break the bank; it's the other dishes, delicious though they are. You'll pay ¥102, for example, for a medium portion of sauteed bean sprouts. Order wisely.

🍷 DRINKING & NIGHTLIFE

If you're shopping on Wángfǔjǐng, there are four or five drinks stalls (open 8.30am to midnight) on the main

AIRPOCALYPSE

Běijīng's smog has become notorious worldwide, but air pollution counts hit record levels in January 2013. The month was dubbed 'Airpocalypse' by the world's media as measures of fine particulate matter (known as PM2.5) reached an incredible 750 micrograms per cubic meter (and 900 by some measurements). According to the US Environmental Protection Agency (EPA), only PM2.5 readings of less than 50 are considered to be 'good', while the World Health Organization deems 25 to be a safe level.

Běijīng's air isn't always terribly polluted, and travellers who arrive during spells of beautiful blue skies may well wonder what all the fuss is about, but the long-term stats do not bode well. Between April 2008 and March 2014, Běijīng experienced just 25 'good' days.

Travellers, particularly those who are sensitive to air pollution, might want to consider buying a smog mask for their visit. You can find advice on which masks to buy on the excellent website **Air Quality Index China** (www.aqicn.org), which also publishes real-time pollution readings for Běijīng and other cities.

Places in Běijīng that stock good quality masks include Natooke (p251), Plastered 8 (p103) and **Torana Clean Air** (www.toranacleanair.com), which has two branches in the city. If you have kids in tow, you might want to buy their masks from home, as good-quality children's masks, which fit properly, are harder to find over here.

pedestrianised shopping strip that have shaded seating areas and serve cheap soft drinks and beer (from ¥10). There are also plenty of coffee shops inside the main two shopping centres: Oriental Plaza and Běijīng apm.

SLOW BOAT BREWERY TAPROOM — BAR

Map p286 (悠航鲜啤; Yōuháng Xiānpí; www.slowboatbrewery.com; 56-2 Dongsi Batiao; 东四八条56一2号; draft beer ¥25-55; ⌚Tue-Thu 5pm-midnight, Fri 5pm-late, Sat 2pm-late, Sun 2-10pm) Battling toe-to-toe with Great Leap Brewing for the title of Běijīng's best-loved craft-beer bar, Slow Boat comes out second best in the end, but knocks out some terrific ales nonetheless. They usually have around a dozen craft beers on tap here – see the website for the lowdown on each of them – and you'll often see their label sold in bottles at other bars around the city.

Struggling to decide which beer to choose first? Order the five- or 10-glass 'flights' instead, which allow you to sample a selection of ales in half-sized glasses. They also do mixers and soft drinks, as well as some bar food. The downside of this is that the place sometimes smells of ketchup and fries.

WHAT? BAR — BAR, LIVE MUSIC

Map p286 (什么酒吧; Shénme? Jiǔbā; ☎133 4112 2757; 72 Beichang Jie, 北长街72号, 故宫西门往北; beers from ¥20; ⌚3pm-midnight; Ⓢ Tian'anmen West, then Bus 5) If you like to get up close and personal with the bands you go and see, then visit this easy-to-miss venue. That doesn't mean it is groupie heaven here; rather, it's so small that the audience might as well be on stage with the musicians. There are gigs on Fridays and Saturdays (sometimes Thursdays and Sundays too), and it's a good place to hear up-and-coming local talent.

You could also just come here for a low-key, late-afternoon, street-side drink. If there's a cover charge, it's usually around ¥30, but that includes a drink.

ALLEY COFFEE — CAFE

Map p286 (寻常巷陌咖啡厅; Xúncháng Xiàngmò Kāfēi Tīng; cnr Jingshan Dongjie & Shatan Houjie, 景山东街，沙滩后街61号; ⌚8.30am-11pm; 📶; Ⓢ Nanluoguxiang or National Art Museum) Perfect for a coffee break after a visit to the Forbidden City or Jǐngshān Park, this cute, traveller-friendly courtyard cafe, diagonally opposite Jǐngshān Park's east gate, has friendly English-speaking staff and does fresh coffee (from ¥25), cold beer and a mix of Chinese and Western food, including breakfast fry-ups (until 11am). Also rents bikes (¥50 per day, deposit ¥600) and has free wi-fi.

★LÁIJĪNYǓXUĀN TEAHOUSE — TEAHOUSE

Map p284 (来今雨轩茶社; Láijīnyǔxuān Cháshè; inside Zhongshan Park; 中山公园, Zhōngshān Gōngyuán; tea per cup from ¥38, biscuit-cakes per serving ¥20; ⌚9am-9pm) This 100-year-old teahouse, set inside the grounds of Zhōngshān Park, has a large terrace in the east corner of the park and is a pleasant place to sample a cup of China's finest tea. A number of well-known writers, intellectuals and revolutionaries were known to hang out here. These days it's mostly tourists, of course.

You'll pay around ¥180 to ¥380 for a pot, but you can get a cup for less than ¥40, which, as always, can be topped up with hot water as many times as you wish. The traditional Chinese biscuit-cakes (¥20 for four) are tasty accompaniments. English tea menu.

OASIS CAFE — CAFE

Map p284 (绿洲咖啡; Lǜzhōu Kāfēi; 1 Jingshan Qianjie, 景山前街1号; coffee ¥20, tea ¥30, beer ¥18, sandwiches ¥25; 8am-9pm) This is a nice option for a break after visiting the Forbidden City. Oasis doesn't have a courtyard (although there is some street-side seating), but it does good coffee and Chinese tea (plus cheesecake) and is run by friendly management who speak English.

ENTERTAINMENT

FORBIDDEN CITY CONCERT HALL — CLASSICAL MUSIC

Map p284 (中山公园音乐堂; Zhōngshān Gōngyuán Yīnyuè Táng; 6559 8285; Zhongshan Park, 中山公园内; tickets ¥30-880; performances 7.30pm; S Tian'anmen West) Located on the eastern side of Zhōngshān Park, this is a wonderfully romantic venue for performances of classical and traditional Chinese music. It's also the best acoustically.

CHÁNG'ĀN GRAND THEATRE — PEKING OPERA

Map p286 (长安大戏院; Cháng'ān Dàxìyuàn; 5166 4621; Chang'an Bldg, 7 Jianguomennei Dajie, 建国门内大街7号; tickets ¥50-800; performances 7.30pm; S Jianguomen) This large theatre, with its distinctive model of a Peking-opera mask standing outside, offers a genuine experience, with the erudite audience chatting away knowledgably among themselves during the daily performances of Peking opera classics – this is a place for connoisseurs, although they do usually have English captions on a screen to one side of the stage.

Matinees, when they have them, usually start at 2pm; evening shows at 7.30pm. Most shows last for around two hours. Buy tickets in person from the ticket office here. Shows rarely sell out, but the cheaper seats sometimes do. Note, there are sometimes days, between a change of shows, when there are no performances.

STAR CITY — CINEMA

Map p286 (新世纪影城; Xīnshìjì Yǐngchéng; 8518 5399; Basement, Oriental Plaza,1 Dongchang'an Jie, 东长安街1号东方广场地下一层; English-language films from ¥80; S Wangfujing) This six-screen cinema, inside Wángfǔjǐng's Oriental Plaza, always has at least one English-language option being screened.

SHOPPING

Locals, out-of-towners and tourists haunt Wangfujing Dajie, a prestigious, partly pedestrianised shopping street that's been given a much-needed makeover in recent years and now sports some slick shopping malls and top-name brands. as well as plenty of tacky souvenir outlets.

ORIENTAL PLAZA — SHOPPING MALL

Map p286 (东方广场; Dōngfāng Guǎngchǎng; 8518 6363; 1 Dongchang'an Jie, 东长安街1号; 10am-10.30pm; S Wangfujing) Vast, modern, hugely popular shopping mall filled with midrange and high-end clothing brands from Asia and the West, plus a range of food outlets and Western coffee shops.

BĚIJĪNG APM — SHOPPING MALL

Map p286 (新东安广场; Xīndōng'ān Guǎngchǎng; 9am-10pm) Dominated at street level by its large two-storey Apple store, this modern, six-floor shopping centre is filled with well-known clothing shops (Zara, H&M, Gap), watch shops, supermarkets, restaurants and cafes.

★CELADON STORY — PORCELAIN

Map p284 (青瓷故事馆; Qīngcí Gùshi Guǎn; 49 Donghuamen Dajie; 东华门大街49号; 10am-7pm) This lovely little porcelain shop sells exquisite examples of China's famous, jade-like, pale-green celadon porcelain. You can pick up small tea cups for ¥30. Whole tea sets start from around ¥300. Staff speak English and are unobtrusive. There are a couple of other tea shops along this stretch

ALL THE TEA IN CHINA

Although most Chinese tea is produced thousands of miles away in south China, there are still plenty of opportunities for you to sample and buy tea here in Běijīng. In case you don't know your oolong from your Pu'erh, here's a quick-look guide to all the tea in China.

Tea Types

- **Green tea** (绿茶; *lǜ chá*) The most common tea in China, this tea undergoes the least amount of oxidation.
- **Black tea** (红茶; *hóng chá*) More commonly drunk outside China, the tea leaves are allowed to completely oxidise, resulting in a stronger tasting tea.
- **Oolong tea** (乌龙; *wū lóng*) This tea's oxidation is stopped somewhere between the standards for green tea and black tea. Tea leaves are often individually curled into tiny balls after processing.
- **Post-fermented tea** (黑茶; *hēi chá*) These teas are allowed to undergo a second oxidation after the fixation of the tea leaves, in a process not disimilar to composting. The most famous type by far is Pu'erh, which is often compressed into 'bricks' or 'cakes' of tea.
- **White tea** (白茶; *bái chá*) Young leaves or new-growth buds that have undergone minimal oxidation through a slight amount of withering before halting the oxidative processes by being baked dry.
- **Yellow tea** (黄茶; *huáng chá*) Usually implies a special tea processed similarly to green tea, but with a slower drying phase, where the damp tea leaves are allowed to sit and yellow.
- **Scented tea** (香片; *xiāng piàn*) Tea (usually green, but sometimes Oolong) scented with flowers, the most common being jasmine (茉莉花; *mòli huā*). Sometimes the tea leaves are bundled together with the flower into large balls (sold individually) which then 'bloom' in your tea cup.
- **Flower tea** (花茶; *huā chá*) These don't contain any actual tea leaves, and are therefore caffeine-free. Instead parts of flowers, such as chrysanthemum (菊花; *jú huā*), are used. Note, Jasmine tea is not flower tea so does contain caffeine.

Where to Drink Tea in Běijīng

- Láijīnyǔxuān Teahouse (p75)
- Tang Ren Teahouse (p128)
- Black-tea Tea Room (p101)
- Qi Baishi's Former Residence (p92)
- Bell Tower Tea House (p87)

Tea Tips

When buying tea, be aware that prices are usually marked by the *jīn* (斤; 500g), but that most people buy it by the *liǎng* (两; 50g); ask for *yī liǎng* (one *liǎng*).

When drinking tea in a teahouse, remember that you can fill up your cup or pot with hot water as many times as you wish for no extra cost. If you're not given a hot-water flash, ask them to help you '*jiā rè shuǐ*' (加热水; add hot water).

of road, selling tea, tea sets and other tea paraphernalia.

★SLOW LANE TEA, CLOTHING

Map p286 (细活裡; Xì Huó Lǐ; 13 Shijia Hutong; 史家胡同13号; ⊙10am-8pm) Secreted away down historic Shijia Hutong, this quietly seductive shop sells beautiful, handmade teaware and quality tea as well as elegant clothing, much of which is made from Tibetan yak wool. Tea sets starts from around ¥500.

FOREIGN LANGUAGES BOOKSTORE BOOKS

Map p286 (外文书店; Wàiwén Shūdiàn; 235 Wangfujing Dajie, 王府井大街235号; ⊙9.30am-9.30pm; SWangfujing) Stocks a good selection of English-language novels (ground floor) as well as lots of books on Chinese history, art and architecture. The kids' section (upstairs) is also decent. Has hundreds of Lonely Planet guides (although no China ones), and this is also a good place to pick up cards, postcards and maps of Běijīng,

SHÈNG XĪ FÚ HAT STORE HATS

Map p286 (盛锡福; Shèng Xī Fú; 196 Wangfujing Dajie; 王府井大街196号; ⏰8.30am-9pm) They used to say that a truly dignified person would only wear shoes made by Nèiliánshēng (p137), silk made by Ruìfúxiáng (p136) and hats made by Shèng Xī Fú. This is China's most famous hat producer. It was first established in the city of Qīngdǎo in 1911, and its hats have been warming the noggins of Chinese people ever since.

Chairman Mao used to get his famous berets from here, and you can pick up a good-quality replica for around ¥70. There are thick winter caps (from ¥150) – perfect for mid-January Běijīng – as well as Russian-style fur hats, some of which will set you back thousands of *yuán*. This Wangfujing branch is one of many. A branch further north has a small, free-to-enter hat museum (p71).

HÁOYUÁN MARKET SOUVENIRS

Map p286 (豪园市场, Háoyuán Shìchǎng; west off Wangfujing Dajie, 王府井大街西侧; Ⓢ Wangfujing) Branching off from Wangfujing Snack St is this small, bustling souvenir market. It has lots of Mao memorabilia, pandas and Buddhas, as well as other tacky tourist tat, but if you're pushed for time and need a last-minute present, you might find something. Haggling is imperative.

SPORTS & ACTIVITIES

BIKE BEIJING CYCLING

Map p286 (康多自行车租赁; Kāngduō Zìxíngchē Zūlìn; ☎6526 5857; www.bikebeijing.com; 34 Donghuangchenggen Nanjie, 东皇城根南街34号; ⏰9am-6pm; Ⓢ China Museum of Art) Rents a range of good-quality bikes, including mountain bikes (¥200), road bikes (¥400) and ordinary city bikes (¥100), and runs guided bike tours around the city (half-day tours from ¥300 per person) and beyond, including trips to the Great Wall (¥900 to ¥1800 per person).

Guides and shop assistants speak English. And they can also provide you with helmets (¥20), baby seats (¥50), children's trailers (¥100) and strong bike locks (free). Rental prices are for the first day, with prices halving for any subsequent days. Deposits range from ¥500 to ¥2000, depending on the bike. Alternatively, give staff a copy of your passport and details of where you are staying.

MÍLÚN KUNGFU SCHOOL MARTIAL ARTS

Map p286 (北京弥纶传统武术学校, Běijīng Mílún Chuántǒng Wǔshù Xuéxiào; ☎138 1170 6568; www.kungfuinchina.com; 33 Xitangzi Hutong, 西堂子胡同33号; drop-in per class ¥100, 8-class card ¥600; ⏰7-8.30pm Mon & Thu, 5-6.30pm Sat & Sun; Ⓢ Dengshikou) Runs classes in various forms of traditional Chinese martial arts from a historic courtyard near Wángfǔjǐng shopping district. In summer, typically in August, classes are held in Rìtán Park. Has set-time drop-in classes, but can arrange individual schedules too. Instruction is in Chinese, but with an English translator.

CON 'ARTISTS' & THE TEAHOUSE SCAM

We receive a number of emails from those unfortunate enough to be scammed in Běijīng. By far the most notorious is the tea-ceremony scam: tourists are invited (often by young ladies, and sometimes under the guise of an on-the-spot guided tour) to drink tea at a teahouse, after which the traveller is hit with a bill for hundreds of dollars. Many travellers pay up and only realise later that they have been massively conned. Tiān'ānmén Sq and Wangfujing Dajie are the two most notorious locations where foreigners are targeted. As a guide, a pot of tea (for at least four people) will normally cost between ¥100 and ¥400, depending on the grade of tea. As a rule, always double-check the price of anything you eat or drink before you order it.

Foreigners at Tiān'ānmén Sq and Wangfujing Dajie are also routinely hounded by 'art students' who rope visitors into going to exhibitions of overpriced art. Be suspicious if you are approached by anyone who speaks good English on the street, until you are sure all they want to do is chat.

LOCAL KNOWLEDGE

FALLING INTO LINE

Fitness dancing is as popular an activity in Běijīng as it is throughout China. Various forms exist, but the most common is a kind of line dance, which consists of a large number of people (usually middle-aged women) dancing in synchronicity to patriotic music played over a loudspeaker. The main purpose is fitness, but it is also done to continue and perform traditional dance moves, and to strengthen community spirit.

Groups congregate in parks or public squares, or even just on wide sections of pavement, either in the early morning or, more commonly, in the early evening. The dancers usually organise themselves into rank and file, with the most proficient at the front, while beginners (and foreign tourists) line up at the back, trying to copy their moves. Regulars are always happy for visitors to join in – just fall into line (at the back), and tag along.

Prime spots for formation dancing in central Běijīng include the square outside St Joseph's Church (p67), the small roadside square known as the **Imperial City Ruins Park** (皇城根遗址公园; Huángchénggēn Yízhǐ Gōngyuán; Map p286), and the large **square** (Map p290) situated between the Drum Tower and the Bell Tower (although this was undergoing renovations at the time of research).

Note, the courtyard was undergoing extensive renovations at the time of research, but should have reopened again by the time you read this. Hopefully, none of its old-Běijīng charm will have been lost.

DRAGONFLY THERAPEUTIC RETREAT MASSAGE TREATMENTS

Map p286 (悠庭保健会所; Yōutíng Bǎojiàn Huìsuǒ; ☎6527 9368; www.dragonfly.net.cn; 60 Donghuamen Dajie, 东华门大街60号; ⊙11am-11pm; Ⓢ Tian'anmen East) Ideal for a foot massage after hours of walking around the Forbidden City, this popular boutique has a variety of treatments designed to help you de-stress. The two-hour Hangover Relief Massage (¥358) is self-explanatory, but for real pampering go for the Royal Delight (¥538), in which two masseurs get to work at the same time. A standard, hour-long body or foot massage costs ¥188.

JǏNGSHĀN TABLE TENNIS PARK TABLE TENNIS

Map p286 (东城全民健身第一园; Dōngchéng Quánmín Jiànshēn Dìyī Yuán; Jingshan Houjie, 景山后街; ⊙6am-10pm; Ⓢ Nanluoguxiang or Beihai North) This small exercise park has five free-to-use outdoor table tennis tables, which attract some pretty hot ping-pong. Only the tables are provided. Players need to bring their own net, bats and ball. Regulars – all too keen to show foreigners who rules the world when it comes to table tennis – will almost certainly let you join in using their equipment, but if you fancy a proper session, head to the 2nd floor of nearby Tiān Yì Goods Market (p104) to buy a cheap table-tennis set.

ROYAL TENNIS CENTRE TENNIS

Map p284 (皇家网球场; Huángjiā Wǎngqiúchǎng; ☎6512 2856; Workers Cultural Palace, east gate; 劳动人民文化宫东门, Láodòng Rénmín Wénhuà Gōng Dōngmén; 6am-5pm Mon-Fri per hr ¥80, Sat & Sun ¥100, 5pm-midnight Mon-Fri ¥100, Sat & Sun ¥120; ⊙6am-midnight) Practise your ground strokes just a couple of bounces away from the Forbidden City at this small, uniquely located outdoor tennis centre. The two courts are inside the grounds of the Supreme Temple, which is in a park known as the Workers Cultural Palace. There are changing rooms, but you'll have to bring all your gear.

Enter the park through the east gate, and the tennis centre is in front of you. The east gate of the park remains open late for tennis players.

1

2

ALAN COPSON / GETTY IMAGES ©

3

MATT MUNRO / LONELY PLANET ©

1. Zhōngshān Park (p66)
Brightly painted corridor in the park named after Sun Yatsen

2. Tiān'ānmén Square (p62)
View of the Gate of Heavenly Peace from the iconic square

3. Hútòng (p222)
Be sure to tour these fast-disappearing remnants of old Běijīng.

Drum Tower & Dōngchéng North

Neighbourhood Top Five

❶ Lose yourself in the mazelike network of historic **hútòng** (alleyways), or follow our *hútòng* walking tour (p89).

❷ Stroll the incense-filled halls and courtyards of the **Lama Temple** (p84), Běijīng's largest and most impressive Buddhist temple.

❸ Listen to a drumming performance inside the magnificent ancient **Drum Tower** (p86) before climbing its equally impressive neighbour, the **Bell Tower** (p87).

❹ Browse the cutesy boutique shops on **Nanluogu Xiang** (p88), before sneaking into a courtyard cafe for coffee break.

❺ Catch a local band at one of the many excellent live-music venues in this part of town: **Jiāng Hú** (p101) is a good place to start.

For more detail of this area, see Map p290. ➡

Explore Drum Tower & Dōngchéng North

This *hútòng*-rich neighbourhood incorporates the northern section of Běijīng's historic Dōngchéng (东城) District and is the most pleasant area in which to base yourself during your stay in the capital. Book yourself into a *hútòng* hostel or a beautifully converted courtyard hotel, and make this most charming of neighbourhoods your new temporary home.

While there are less top-name sights here than in Dōngchéng Central, there is still some sightseeing to be done, although the main attraction is the chance to simply wander around the lanes getting lost.

You can shop till you drop in the cute alleyway boutiques of Nanluogu Xiang before putting your feet up in a *hútòng* cafe or settling down for a meal in a converted courtyard.

At night, this neighbourhood is the city's most enjoyable place to drink. Bars here are cool rather than brash and are often tucked away in hard-to-find *hútòng* locations. Some of them double as live-music venues where you can catch the latest local bands.

Local Life

- **Food** To sample some authentic Běijīng tucker, first check our Běijīng Menu (p95) then head to Yáojì Chǎogān (p93) for some dumplings and pig's liver stew, or to Róng Tiān (p94) for a succulent sheep-spine hotpot.
- **Music** See what the city's youth are listening to, and playing, at live-music venues such as Jiāng Hú (p101) or Jiāng Jìn Jiǔ (p101).
- **Parks** Head to Dìtán Park (p88) for a spot of kite-flying, before cooling off with the masses at the outdoor swimming complex in Qīngnián Hú Park (p105).

Getting There & Away

- **Subway** Lines 8, 2, 6 and 5 all serve this neighbourhood well.
- **Bus** Bus 107 links the Drum Tower with Dongzhimen Transport Hub. Bus 5 runs south from the Drum Tower, past Běihǎi and Jǐngshān Parks, along the west side of the Forbidden City and on to Qiánmén at the south end of Tiān'ānmén Sq. Bus 113 runs south from Andingmennei Dajie then east to the Workers Stadium and Sānlǐtún.

Lonely Planet's Top Tip

Rent a bike while you're here, or even buy a cheap secondhand one; you can give it away when you leave. Cycling is the best way to see the city, and is especially good for exploring this area's *hútòng*.

Best Places to Eat

- Bǎihé Vegetarian Restaurant (p96)
- Yáojì Chǎogān (p93)
- Zhāng Māma (p93)
- Yī Lóng Zhāi (p94)
- Róng Tiān Sheep Spine (p94)
- Dàlǐ Courtyard (p98)
- Ghost Street (p92)

For reviews, see p93.

Best Places to Drink

- Great Leap Brewing (p99)
- El Nido (p99)
- Zá Jiā (p99)
- Irresistible Cafe (p100)
- Other Place (p96)
- Mài (p100)

For reviews, see p98.

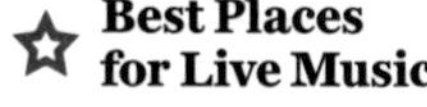

Best Places for Live Music

- Jiāng Hú (p101)
- Jiāng Jìn Jiǔ (p101)
- Yúgōng Yíshān (p101)
- Temple Bar (p101)
- Mao Livehouse (p101)

For reviews, see p101. 

CHRISTIAN KOBER / GETTY IMAGES ©

TOP SIGHT
LAMA TEMPLE

Běijīng's foremost Buddhist temple, the Lama Temple (雍和宫; Yōnghé Gōng) is one of the most magnificent Tibetan Buddhist temples outside Tibet itself. With three richly worked archways and five main halls (each one taller than the preceding one), revolving prayer wheels (propel them clockwise), multicoloured glaze tiles, magnificent Chinese lions, tantric statuettes and hall boards decorated with Mongolian, Manchu, Tibetan and Chinese, the sumptuous temple is a profound introduction to Tibetan Buddhist lore.

DON'T MISS

- 18m-tall Sandalwood Buddha
- Exhibition in Jiètái Lóu
- Exhibition in Bānchán Lóu

PRACTICALITIES

- Map p290
- 28 Yonghegong Dajie
- admission ¥25, English audioguide ¥50
- 9am-4.30pm
- S Yonghegong-Lama Temple

History

The temple was once the official residence of Count Yin Zhen, who became emperor in 1723 and traded up to the Forbidden City. His name changed to Yongzheng, and his former residence became Yōnghé Palace (Yōnghé Gōng). In 1744 it was converted into a lamasery (a monastery of lamas) and became home to legions of monks from Mongolia and Tibet.

In 1792 the Emperor Qianlong, having quelled an uprising in Tibet, instituted a new administrative system involving two golden vases. One was kept at the renowned Jokhang Temple in Lhasa, to be employed for determining the reincarnation of the Dalai Lama, and the other was kept at the Lama Temple for choosing the Panchen Lama. The Lama Temple thus assumed a new importance in ethnic minority control.

Premier Zhou Enlai stepped in when the Red Guards focused their iconoclastic attentions on the temple. Today the temple is an active place of worship, attracting pilgrims from across the land and thronging with worshippers, some of whom prostrate themselves at full length within its halls.

Yōnghé Gate

The first hall, Yōnghé Gate (雍和门; Yōnghé Mén), houses a statue of Maitreya, the future Buddha, flanked by celestial guardians. Above it is a board inscribed with the characters 心明妙现: 'If the heart is bright, the wonderful will appear'.

In the courtyard beyond is a pond with a bronze mandala depicting the Buddhist paradise. Glimpses of the more abstruse nature of the temple can be seen in the hall on the right after Yōnghé Gate: the **Esoteric Hall** (密宗殿; Mìzōng Diàn) contains the fierce, multi-armed deity Deweidejingang. Opposite is the **Exoteric Hall** (讲经殿; Jiǎngjīng Diàn), where sutras were studied and recited.

Yōnghé Hall

With its air of peaceful reverence, the second hall, Yōnghé Hall (雍和殿; Yōnghé Diàn), contains a trinity of gilded effigies representing the past, present and future Buddhas.

Yǒngyòu Hall

The third hall, Yǒngyòu Hall (永佑殿; Yǒngyòu Diàn), contains statues of the Buddhas of Longevity and Medicine (to the left). Peek into the **East Side Hall** (东配殿; Dōngpèi Dian) for its cobalt-blue Buddhas and huge dog-like creatures. The tantric statues have been partially draped to disguise their couplings.

Hall of the Wheel of the Law

The fourth hall, Hall of the Wheel of the Law (法轮殿; Fǎlún Diàn), houses a large bronze statue of Tsong Khapa (1357–1419), founder of the Gelukpa (Yellow Hat) sect, robed in yellow and illuminated from a skylight above. Also within the hall is a throne that seated the Dalai Lama when he lectured here.

Wànfú Pavilion

The final main hall, Wànfú Pavilion (万福阁; Wànfú Gé), has a stupendous 18m-tall **statue** of the Maitreya Buddha in his Tibetan form, reputedly sculpted from a single block of sandalwood.

Behind the statue is the **Vault of Avalokiteshvara** (观音洞; Guānyīn Dòng), from where a diminutive blue-faced statue of Guanyin peeks out. The Wànfú Pavilion is linked by an overhead walkway to the **Yánsuí Pavilion** (延绥阁; Yánsuí Gé), which encloses a huge lotus flower that revolves to reveal an effigy of the longevity Buddha.

Behind Wànfú Pavilion, worshippers gather to worship White Tara and Green Tara in the **Suíchéng Hall** (绥成殿; Suíchéng Diàn).

SIDE-HALL EXHIBITIONS

Don't miss the collection of bronze Tibetan Buddhist statues within **Jiètái Lóu** (戒台楼). Most effigies date from the Qing dynasty, from languorous renditions of Green Tara and White Tara to exotic tantric pieces (such as Samvara) and figurines of the fierce-looking Mahakala. Also peruse the collection of Tibetan Buddhist ornaments within the **Bānchán Lóu** (班禅楼): there's a fantastic array of *dorje* (Tibetan ritual sceptres), mandalas, tantric figures, and an impressive selection of ceremonial robes in silk and satin.

Photography is not permitted inside temple buildings, although you can snap away freely around the rest of the complex. English-speaking guides (¥80) can be found in the office to the left of the entrance gate, or loitering near the entrance to the complex.

TOP SIGHT
DRUM TOWER

Along with the older-looking Bell Tower, which stands behind it, the magnificent red-painted Drum Tower (鼓楼; Gŭlóu) used to be the city's official timekeeper, with drums and bells beaten and rung to mark the times of the day; effectively the Big Ben of Běijīng.

Originally built in 1272, the Drum Tower was once the heart of the Mongol capital of Dàdū, as Běijīng was then known. That structure was destroyed in a fire before a replacement was built, slightly to the east of the original location, in 1420. The current structure is a later Qing-dynasty version of that 1420 tower.

You can climb the incredibly steep inner staircase for views of the grey-tiled rooftops in the surrounding *hútòng* (alleys). Arguably the best view of the Drum Tower is from the top of the Bell Tower. Annoyingly, though, the view isn't reciprocated because visitors aren't allowed to walk round to the north-facing side of the Drum Tower's viewing balcony.

It's still well worth climbing the tower, though, especially if you can time it to coincide with one of the regular drumming performances, which are played out on reproductions of the 25 Ming-dynasty watch drums, that used to sound out across this part of the city. One of the original 25 drums – the Night Watchman's Drum (更鼓; Gēnggŭ) – is on display; now dusty, battered and worn. Also on display is a replica of a Song-dynasty water clock, which was never actually used in the tower, but is interesting nonetheless.

The times of the drumming performances, which only last for a couple of minutes, are posted by the ticket office. At the time of research they were as follows: 9.30am, 10.30am, 11.30am, 1.30pm, 2.30pm, 3.30pm and 4.45pm.

DON'T MISS

- ➡ Drumming Performance
- ➡ Night Watchman's Drum

PRACTICALITIES

- ➡ Map p290
- ➡ Gulou Dongdajie
- ➡ admission ¥20, both towers through ticket ¥30
- ➡ ⌚ 9am-5pm, last tickets 4.40pm
- ➡ S Shichahai or Gulou Dajie

TOP SIGHT
BELL TOWER

MAREMAGNUM / GETTY IMAGES ©

The more modest, grey-stone structure of the Bell Tower (钟楼; Zhōnglóu) is arguably more charming than its resplendent other half, the Drum Tower, after which this area of Běijīng is named. It also has the added advantage of being able to view its sister tower from a balcony.

Along with the drums in the Drum Tower, the bells in the Bell Tower were used as Běijīng's official timekeepers throughout the Yuan, Ming and Qing dynasties, and on until 1924. The Bell Tower looks the older of the two, perhaps because it isn't painted. In fact both are of similar age. The Bell Tower was also built during the Mongol Yuan Dynasty, in 1272, and was rebuilt in the 1440s after being destroyed in a fire. This current structure was built in 1745.

Like the Drum Tower, the Bell Tower can be climbed up an incredibly steep inner staircase. But the views from the top are even better here, partly because the structure is set back more deeply into the surrounding *hútòng,* and partly because you can get great photos of the Drum Tower from its viewing balcony. Marvel too at the huge, 600-year-old, 63-tonne bell suspended in the pleasantly unrestored interior. Note how Chinese bells have no clappers but are instead struck with a stout pole.

Inside the tower, on the ground floor (south side), is the **Bell Tower Tea House**, where you can sample a selection of Chinese teas (per person per hour ¥50) as well as buy tea and tea sets.

The Drum & Bell Sq, between the two towers, is a great people-watching area in which to while away some time even if you don't climb either of the two towers. There are a handful of excellent bars and cafes here too, some with rooftop views over the square. Both towers are lit up beautifully come evening. Note, the square was undergoing wholesale renovations at the time of research.

DON'T MISS

- 63-tonne bell
- View of the Drum Tower

PRACTICALITIES

- Map p290
- Gulou Dongdajie
- admission ¥20, both towers through ticket ¥30
- 9am-5pm, last tickets 4.40pm
- S Shichahai or Gulou Dajie

SIGHTS

LAMA TEMPLE BUDDHIST TEMPLE

See p84.

DRUM TOWER HISTORIC SITE

See p86.

BELL TOWER HISTORIC SITE

See p87.

CONFUCIUS TEMPLE & IMPERIAL COLLEGE CONFUCIAN TEMPLE

Map p290 (孔庙、国子监; Kǒng Miào & Guózǐjiàn; 13 Guozijian Jie; admission ¥30, audio guide ¥30; ⌚8.30am-5.30pm; Ⓢ Yonghegong-Lama Temple) An incense stick's toss away from the Lama Temple, China's second-largest Confucian temple had a refit in recent years, but the almost otherworldly sense of detachment is seemingly impossible to shift. A mood of impassiveness reigns and the lack of worship reinforces a sensation that time has stood still. However, in its tranquillity and reserve, the temple can be a pleasant sanctuary from Běijīng's often congested streets – a haven of peace and quiet.

Antediluvian *bìxì* (mythical tortoiselike dragons) glare from repainted pavilions while lumpy and ossified ancient cypresses claw stiffly at the Běijīng air. There's a stone 'forest' of 190 stelae recording the 13 Confucian classics in 630,000 Chinese characters at the temple rear. Also inscribed on stelae are the names of successful candidates of the highest level of the official Confucian examination system.

Next to the Confucius Temple, but within the same grounds, stands the Imperial College, where the emperor expounded the Confucian classics to an audience of thousands of kneeling students, professors and court officials – an annual rite. Built by the grandson of Kublai Khan in 1306, the former college was the supreme academy during the Yuan, Ming and Qing dynasties. On the site is a marvellous, glazed, three-gate, single-eaved decorative archway called a *liúli páifāng* (glazed archway). The Biyong Hall beyond is a twin-roofed structure with yellow tiles surrounded by a moat and topped with a splendid gold knob. Its stupendous interior houses a vermillion and gold lectern.

Some of Běijīng's last remaining *páilou* (decorated archways) bravely survive in the tree-lined street outside (Guozijian Jie) and the entire area of *hútòng* here is now dotted with small cafes, cute restaurants and boutique shops, making it an ideal place to browse in low gear. At the western end of Guozijian Jie stands a diminutive **Fire God Temple** (Huǒshén Miào; Map p290), built in 1802 and now occupied by Běijīng residents.

DÌTÁN PARK PARK

Map p290 (地坛公园; Dìtán Gōngyuán; admission park ¥2, altar ¥5; ⌚6am-9pm; Ⓢ Yonghegong-Lama Temple) Directly north of the Lama Temple, but cosmologically juxtaposed with the **Temple of Heaven** (Tiāntán), the **Altar of the Moon** (Yuètán), the **Altar of the Sun** (Rìtán) and the **Altar to the God of the Land and the God of Grain** (Shèjìtán), Dìtán is the Temple of the Earth. The park, site of imperial sacrifices to the Earth God, lacks the splendour of Temple of Heaven Park but is certainly worth a stroll if you've just been to nearby Lama Temple.

You'll find locals flying kites, singing songs, strumming *èrhú* (two-stringed fiddles), practising taichi and keeping fit in the exercise park (northeast corner). The park's large, open-air altar *(fāngzé tán)* is square in shape, symbolising the earth. Sadly, recent renovation work has robbed it of some of its previous authenticity. During Lunar New Year a huge (though rather commercialised) temple fair is held here.

NANLUOGU XIANG STREET

Map p290 (南锣鼓巷; Ⓢ Nanluoguxiang) Once neglected and ramshackle, strewn with spent coal briquettes in winter and silent bar the hacking coughs of shuffling oldtimers and the jangling of bicycle bells, the funky north–south alleyway of Nanluogu Xiang (literally 'South Gong and Drum Alley', and roughly pronounced *'nan-law-goo-syang'*) has been undergoing evolution since 1999 when **Passby Bar** first threw open its doors, and was the subject of a complete makeover in 2006. Today, the alley is an insatiably bubbly strip of bars, wi-fi cafes, restaurants, hotels and trendy shops.

It is also a victim of its own success, though. Come here on a summer weekend to experience more people than you thought could possibly fit onto one street! With that in mind, don't miss exploring the quieter alleys, which fan out from the main

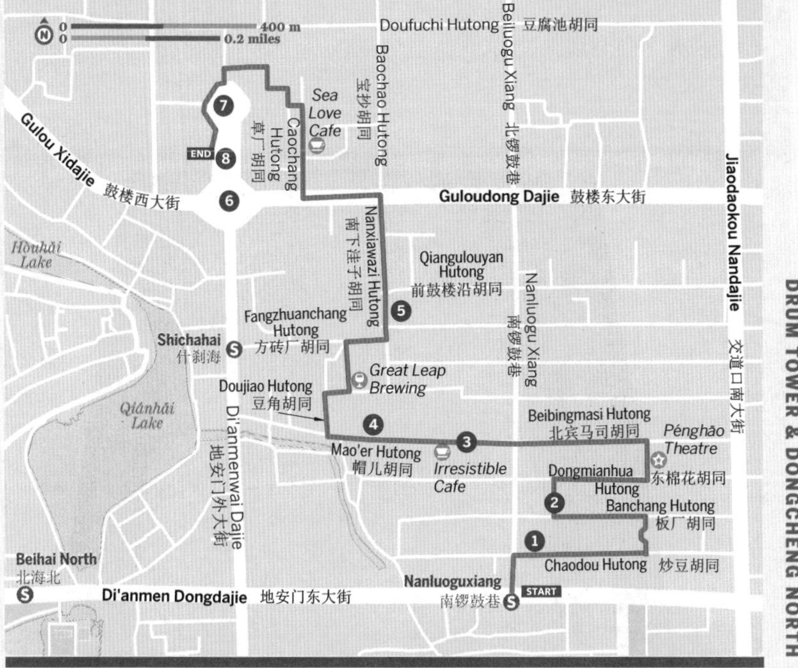

Neighbourhood Walk
Historic Hútòng Around Nanluogu Xiang

START NANLUOGUXIANG SUBWAY STATION
END DRUM & BELL TOWERS
LENGTH 2KM; ONE HOUR

Běijīng's *hútòng* are the heart and soul of the city.

Exit Nanluoguxiang subway station and turn right into Chaodou Hutong (炒豆胡同). Starting at No 77, the next few courtyards once made up the **1 former mansion of Seng Gelinqin**, a Qing-dynasty army general. Note the enormous *bǎogǔshí* (drum stones) at the entranceway to No 77, followed by more impressive gateways at Nos 75, 69, 67 and 63. After No 53 turn left up an unmarked winding alleyway then left onto Banchang Hutong (板厂胡同).

At No 19, turn right through an unusual **2 hallway gate**, a connecting passageway leading to Dongmianhua Hutong (东棉花胡同). Turn right here, then left down an unnamed alley signposted to Pénghāo Theatre.

Turn left onto Beibingmasi Hutong (北兵马司胡同) and cross Nanluogu Xiang into historic **3 Mao'er Hutong** (帽儿胡同). Stop for a drink at Irresistible Cafe, or just admire the entranceways, if the gates are open, to the charming courtyards at Nos 5 and 11. Further on, No 37 was the **4 former home of Wan Rong**, who would later marry China's last emperor, Puyi.

Next, turn right down Doujiao Hutong (豆角胡同) and wind your way (past Great Leap Brewing) to Fangzhuanchang Hutong (方砖厂胡同) then Nanxiawazi Hutong (南下洼子胡同), with its small **5 fruit & veg street-market**, and continue north to Gulou Dongdajie (鼓楼东大街). Turn left here and then, just before you reach the imperious red-painted **6 Drum Tower** (p86), turn right into Caochang Hutong (草厂胡同). Continue down the lane beside Sea Love Cafe, then take the second left: you'll see the magnificent grey-brick **7 Bell Tower** (p87) in front of you. Follow this wonderfully winding alley to the back of the Bell Tower, then walk around the tower to see how far the local government has got with its controversial plans to redevelop the **8 Drum & Bell Square**.

1

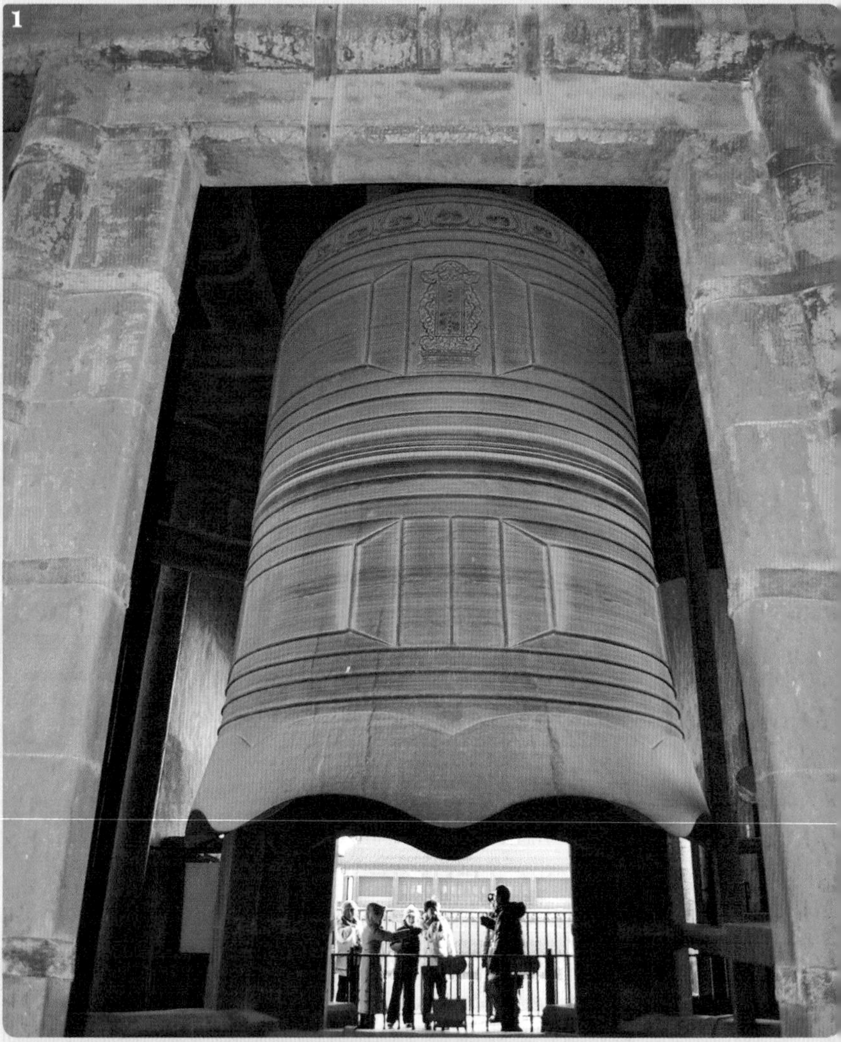

3

KYLIE MCLAUGHLIN / GETTY IMAGES ©

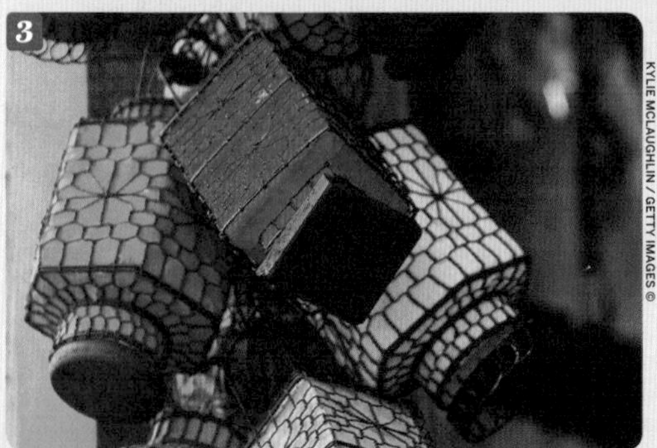

1. Bell Tower (p87)
The huge bell weighs 63 tonnes

2. Nanluogu Xiang (p88)
Lanterns for sale in this popular shopping street

3. Eating out (p93)
Yunnanese dishes at Dàlǐ Courtyard restaurant

2

MATT MUNRO / LONELY PLANET ©

DELVING DEEPER INTO CHINESE CULTURE

Hidden down a maze of narrow alleys, **The Hutong** (Map p290; ☎159 0104 6127; www.thehutong.com; 1 Jiudaowan Zhongxiang Hutong, off Shique Hutong, 北新桥石雀胡同九道弯中巷胡同1号; ⊙9am-9pm; Ⓢ Beixinqiao) is a highly recommended Chinese-culture centre, run by a group of extremely knowledgeable expats and skilled locals. Classes are held in a peaceful converted courtyard, and focus on three main areas:

➡ **Cookery Classes** Hugely popular, the focus is on cuisine from around China, but other Asian-cuisine classes are also run.

➡ **City Tours** Guided tours include the two-hour '*Hútòng* Tour' (¥120) around the city's network of alleyways, the five-hour 'Tea Tour' (¥280), which includes a trip to Mǎliándào Tea Market, and the 90-minute 'Culinary Market Tour' (¥100).

➡ **Traditional Chinese Medicine** Run by Alex Tan, an Australian-Chinese TCM expert, classes range from introductions to Qi Gong, yoga and Taoism as well as to Chinese medicine itself.

How to Find the Hutong

Come out of Exit C of Beixinqiao subway station and turn left onto Shique Hutong. Take the second right down the unmarked Jiudaowanxi Xiang (九道弯西巷), then take the first left followed by the first right and you'll see The Hutong on your right.

lane and house Qing-dynasty courtyards as well as hidden cafes, shops, restaurants and bars.

MAO DUN'S FORMER RESIDENCE — HISTORIC BUILDING

Map p290 (茅盾故居; Máo Dùn Gùjū; 13 Houyuan Ensi Hutong; ⊙9am-4pm Tue-Sun; Ⓢ Beixinqiao) FREE The lack of English captions is frustrating, but this small and unassuming museum does at least give visitors the chance to stroll around a trapped-in-time courtyard residence. Mao Dun was the pen name of Shen Yanbing (1896–1981), who was born into an elite family in Zhèjiāng province but educated in Běijīng. He lived at the back courtyard here from 1974 until his death.

In 1920 he helped found the Literary Study Society, an association promoting literary realism. Mao Dun joined the League of Left Wing Writers in 1930, becoming solidly entrenched in the bureaucracy after the communists came to power. He lay low during the Cultural Revolution, but briefly returned to writing in the 1970s. His best-known works are *Spring Silkworms* (1932) and *Midnight* (1934). Look for the well-used 1940s fridge, standing in a glass case in the back courtyard.

QI BAISHI'S FORMER RESIDENCE — MUSEUM

Map p290 (齐白石旧居纪念馆; Qí Báishí Jiùjū Jìniànguǎn; 13 Yu'er Hutong, off Nanluogu Xiang, 南锣鼓巷，雨儿胡同 13 号; admission ¥5; ⊙9am-4pm, closed Mon; Ⓢ Nanluoguxiang or Shichahai) Known for the whimsical, often playful style of his watercolors, Qi Baishi (1864–1957) was an influential Chinese painter who lived in Běijīng from 1917 onwards. This particular courtyard residence – built on the site of the Qing-dynasty home of Emperor Hong Taiji's fourth son, Ye Bushu (1627–1690) – was his home for just the final two years of his life. Rooms here contain numerous examples of his scroll paintings, and one includes a detailed introduction (with English translations) to his life story.

The courtyard also makes a pleasant spot for a cuppa. There's no cafe as such, but there are tables and chairs scattered around, and the drinks menu (also in English) includes good-value tea (¥10 to ¥20) and coffee (¥15).

ARROW FACTORY — GALLERY

Map p290 (箭厂空间; Jiànchǎng Kōngjiān; 38 Jianchang Hutong, off Guozijian Jie, 国子监街，箭厂胡同 38 号) This tiny, 15-sq-metre, one-room gallery occupies a former vegetable shop and is now an independently run art space for funky installations and modern-art projects designed to be viewed from the street, 24 hours a day, seven days a week. You can't enter the room, but its all-glass front means you can peer in whenever you walk past.

DADU MUSEUM OF ART GALLERY

Map p290 (大都美术馆; Dàdū Měishùguǎn; www.dadumuseum.org/en; 28 Guozijian Jie, 国子监街 28 号; ⏲9am-5pm, closed Mon) This enormous art gallery took more than four years to build, and was just about to open its doors to the public at the time of research. The intention is for this to become the capital's primary location for exhibiting contemporary Chinese oil paintings. Sadly, the building itself is no oil painting: while attempts have been made to include traditional design into its architecture, its sheer vastness weighs heavily on its small-scale *hútòng* surrounds.

EATING

This historic part of Běijīng has a huge range of dining options covering every type of Chinese cuisine, as well as plenty of international places. It's also home to some of the capital's most atmospheric restaurants, from beautifully converted courtyards, to the many hole-in-the-wall establishments scattered throughout the local *hútòng*. Locals also head to the very popular so-called Ghost Street (簋街; Gui Jie) for hotpot and seafood at all hours.

YÁOJÌ CHĂOGĀN BEIJING $

Map p290 (姚记炒肝店; 311 Gulou Dongdajie, 鼓楼东大街 311 号; mains ¥8-20; ⏲ 6am-10.30pm; Ⓢ Shichahai) Proper locals' joint, serving Běijīng dishes in a noisy, no-nonsense atmosphere. The house speciality is *chǎogān* (炒肝; pig's-liver stew; ¥6 to ¥9). This is also a good place to try *zhá guànchang* (炸灌肠; garlic-topped deep-fried crackers; ¥6) and *má dòufu* (麻豆腐; spicy tofu paste; ¥10).

Its steamed pork dumplings (包子; *bāozi;* ¥3 for two) are excellent, and are perfect for breakfast with a bowl of *xiǎomǐ zhōu* (小米粥; millet porridge; ¥2) or locals' favourite *dòuzhī* (豆汁; soy milk; ¥2). It also does a decent bowl of Běijīng's best-known noodle dish, *zhájiàng miàn* (炸酱面; ¥12). No English menu or English sign.

ZHĀNG MĀMA SICHUAN $

Map p290 (张妈妈特色川味馆; Zhāng Māma Tèsè Chuānwèiguǎn; 76 Jiaodaokou Nandajie, 交道口南大街 76 号; mains ¥10-20; ⏲10.30am-10.30pm; Ⓢ Beixinqiao) The original Zhāng Māma, on nearby Fensiting Hutong, was such a hit with Beijingers they were forced to also open this new, larger branch with two floors. At the smaller, original branch you have to wait up to an hour for a table. Here, they've cut that down to about 15 minutes. It's worth the wait. This is arguably Běijīng's best-value Sichuanese restaurant.

The speciality is *málà xiāngguō* (麻辣香锅; ¥48 to ¥58), a fiery, chilli-laced broth with either chicken (香锅鸡; *xiāngguō jī*), prawns (香锅虾; *xiāngguō xiā*) or ribs (香锅排骨; *xiāngguō páigǔ*) simmering away inside, and with a variety of vegetables added into the mix. One pot is enough for two or three people. Also worth trying here is the *dàndàn miàn* (担担面; spicy dry noodles; ¥8) and the rice meals; the classic being the *gōngbào jīdīng gàifàn* (宫爆鸡丁盖饭; spicy chicken with peanuts; ¥12), which is

BARBECUE SKEWERS

The red neon 串 signs that you see hanging outside restaurants come evening, are actually shaped as the Chinese character for *chuàn* (串; skewers) and signify that the restaurant serves barbecue skewers. They are often, but not always, Muslim-food restaurants, and sometimes they are simply a hole-in-the-wall outfit, which only serves skewers. Either way, they're a favourite snack spot for locals; pull up a stool, order a bottle of local beer (啤酒; *píjiǔ;* ¥3 to ¥5) and join them for a barbecue pit-stop.

Chances are the staff won't speak a word of English, so to help you order, here's a list of the most common skewers and their usual prices:

- **lamb skewers** 羊肉串; *yángròu chuàn;* ¥1 to ¥2
- **steamed buns** 馒头片; *mántou piàn;* ¥1
- **chicken wings** 鸡翅; *jī chì;* ¥4 to ¥6
- **lamb tendon** 肉筋; *ròu jīn,* ¥1
- **roasted garlic** 大蒜; *dà suàn;* ¥1

LOCAL KNOWLEDGE

TRADITIONAL BĚIJĪNG YOGHURT

On your shopping wanders through the *hútòng* (alleys), you may notice intriguing rows of little clay pots, sealed with thin, white and blue paper tops, and lined up outside small corner shops. The pots contain *lǎo Běijīng suānnǎi* (老北京酸奶), traditional Běijīng yoghurt, and make a perfect slurp-on-the-go street-side refreshment.

Prices vary slightly, but they tend to cost ¥3 or ¥4 if you drink them on the spot and return your pot, and ¥1 extra if you take them away.

lip-tinglingly delicious, thanks to the generous sprinkling of Sìchuān peppercorns. No English menu, so don't be shy about pointing to what fellow diners are eating. Chances are it'll be spicy, but delicious.

YĪ LÓNG ZHĀI XINJIANG $

Map p290 (伊隆斋; cnr Mao'er Hutong & Doujiao Hutong, 帽儿胡同和豆角胡同的路口; mains ¥15-30; ⏲11am-midnight; Ⓢ Shichahai) Bright and boisterous, this no-frills restaurant specialises in the Turkic-influenced cuisine of Xīnjiāng province, in west China. So expect lots of tasty lamb dishes. The *kǎo yáng tuǐ* (烤羊腿; grilled leg of lamb; ¥25) is excellent, as are the *yáng ròu chuàn* (羊肉串; lamb skewers; ¥3). There's also a good selection of noodle dishes (¥12 to ¥18) in the photo menu.

Another signature dish here is the *dà pán jī* (大盘鸡; literally, 'big plate chicken'; ¥70), which is enough to feed four or five hungry mouths, especially when the sauce is mopped up with some *kǎo náng* (烤馕; naan bread; ¥5). If there's only two or three of you, go for the small portion (小盘鸡; *xiǎo pán jī;* ¥40), which is still massive. There's patio seating out front in summer.

RÓNG TIĀN SHEEP SPINE HOTPOT $

Map p290 (容天土锅羊羯子馆; Róngtiān Tǔguō Yángjiézi Guǎn; 8 Jingtu Hutong, off Beiluogu Xiang, 北锣鼓巷净土胡同 8 号; sheep spine per jīn ¥35, other ingredients ¥8-12; ⏲10.30am-10pm; Ⓢ Guloudajie) Rough-and-ready locals' favourite serving mouthwateringly good sheep-spine hotpot. Order your sheep-spine chunks (普通羊蝎子; *pǔtōng yángxiēzi*) by the *jīn* (500g). Two *jins'* worth (二斤; *èr jīn*) is normally about right. They will come ready-cooked in a boiling broth – the longer you leave them to simmer, the juicier they get. You then add other raw ingredients to cook in the broth like a standard Chinese hotpot.

Our favourite extras include sweet potato (红薯; *hóng shǔ*), tofu blocks (鲜豆腐; *xiān dòufu*), mushrooms (木耳; *mù'ěr*), Oriental raddish (白萝卜; *bái luóbo*) and Chinese spinach (油麦菜; *yóu mài cài*). Complimentary fresh noodles are thrown in at the end, to soak up the juices. When you're ready for them, say *'fàng miàn'* (put the noodles in). No English sign or menu, and no English spoken.

YÁNG FĀNG LAMB HOTPOT HOTPOT $

Map p290 (羊坊涮肉; Yáng Fāng Shuàn Ròu; 270 Gulou Dongdajie, 鼓楼东大街 270 号; broth ¥8-15, dips & sauces ¥2-5, raw ingredients ¥6-25; ⏲11am-11pm; Ⓢ Shichahai) There are two main types of hotpot in China: the ridiculously spicy one that comes from the fire-breathing southwestern city of Chóngqìng, and the milder version which is cooked in an unusual conical brass pot and which originally hails from Mongolia, but has been adopted as a Běijīng speciality. Yáng Fāng is a salt-of-the-earth version of the latter, and is a real favourite with the locals round here.

First order the broth you want in your pot – clear (清汤锅底; *qīng tāng guōde;* ¥8), or spicy (辣锅底; *là guōde;* ¥15); clear is more common. Then ask for some sesame-paste dipping sauce (小料; *xiǎo liào;* ¥5); each person should have one. And, if you fancy it, order some freshly prepared chilli oil (鲜榨辣椒油; *xiān zhá là jiāo yóu;* ¥2) to mix into your dipping sauce; one bowl is enough for everyone to share.

Finally, select the raw ingredients you want to cook in your broth. Our favourites include wafer-thin lamb slices (鲜羊肉; *xiān yáng ròu;* ¥26), lotus root slices (藕片; *ǒu piàn;* ¥6), tofu slabs (鲜豆腐; *xiān dòufu;* ¥6), sweet potato (红薯; *hóng shǔ;* ¥6) and spinach (菠菜; *bō cài;* ¥6). No English sign; no English menu; no English spoken.

WŬ JĪN CAFE

WESTERN BREAKFAST $

Map p290 (五金; Wǔjīn Kāfēi; 38 Jianchang Hutong, off Guozijian Jie, 国子监街、 箭厂胡同 38 号; breakfasts incl tea or coffee ¥10-30; ⏲8.30am-12.30pm, closed Mon; 📵; Ⓢ Andingmen) This simple-as-it-gets, two-table minicafe serves thick-cut toast, homemade jam, eggs, yoghurt granola and Yúnnán coffee. That's it. We told you it was simple. In summer, it opens up again early evening (5.30pm to 9.30pm) for a spot of cheese and wine. There's no sign.

TÀN HUĀ LAMB BBQ

BARBECUE $

Map p290 (碳花烤羊腿; Tàn Huā Kǎo Yángtuǐ; 63 Beixinqiao Santiao, 北新桥三条 63 号; lamb per jīn ¥52, side dishes ¥2-18; ⏲11am-midnight; Ⓢ Beixinqiao) Meat-loving Beijingers flock to this raucous joint where you roast a leg of lamb on a your own personal table-top barbecue spit before hacking away at the meatiest bits with a rudimentary, long-handled knife and fork. Tables spill out onto the lively *hútòng*, creating a party atmosphere of multibarbecue revelry.

Order your leg of lamb (羊腿; *yáng tuǐ*) by the *jīn* (500g). Three *jīn* (三斤; *sān jīn*) is enough for two or three people. You'll then be given a selection of free cold dishes as accompaniments, plus a cumin-based dry dip to roll your lamb slices in. Other popular side dishes include barbecued naan bread (烤馕; *kǎo náng;* ¥6), soy fried rice (酱油炒饭; *jiàng yóu chǎo fàn;* ¥10) and noodle-drop soup (疙瘩汤; *gēda tāng;* ¥12).

BĀOZI PÙ

DUMPLINGS $

Map p290 (包子铺; 108 Gulou Dongdajie, 鼓楼东大街 108 号; dumplings per basket ¥5-6, noodles ¥10-12, rice meals ¥13-18; ⏲6am-9pm; Ⓢ Shichahai) A local favourite, especially for breakfast, Bāozi Pù – literally 'dumplings shop' – has been on this corner for years. Steamed pork dumplings (包子; *bāozi;* ¥6 per basket) are the speciality; say *'sù bāozi'* if you want vegetable ones (¥5). The boiled dumplings (蒸饺; *zhēng jiǎo*) are also good. Wash them down either with a traditional soy milk drink (豆浆; *dòu jiāng*) or rice porridge (紫米粥; *zǐ mǐ zhōu*).

LOCAL KNOWLEDGE

BĚIJĪNG MENU

The following are all classic Běijīng dishes, many of which you'll only find at places specialising in Běijīng cuisine. Try Zuǒ Lín Yòu Shè (p71), Yáojì Chǎogān (p93) or Bàodǔ Huáng (p144). Many roast duck restaurants will have some of the other Běijīng specialities as well as roast duck.

➡ **Peking Duck** (烤鸭; *kǎoyā*) Roast duck, known in the West as Peking duck, is Běijīng's most famous dish. The duck here is fattier but much more flavoursome than the 'crispy duck' typically served in Chinese restaurants in the West. Like back home, though, it also comes with pancakes, cucumber slices and plum sauce.

➡ **Zhá Jiàng Miàn** (炸酱面) Běijīng's most famous noodle dish; thick wheat noodles with ground pork and cucumber shreds mixed together in a salty fermented soybean paste. Chilly oil (辣椒油; *là jiāo yóu*) is a popular optional extra.

➡ **Dālian Huǒshāo** (褡裢火烧) Finger-shaped fried dumplings with a savoury filling.

➡ **Má Dòufu** (麻豆腐) Spicy tofu paste.

➡ **Zhá Guànchang** (炸灌肠) Deep-fried crispy crackers served with a very strong garlic dip.

➡ **Chǎo Gānr** (炒肝) Sauteed liver served in a gloopy soup.

➡ **Bào Dǔ** (爆肚) Boiled tripe, usually lamb. Sometimes served in a seasoned broth.

➡ **Yáng Zá** (羊杂) Similar to *bào dǔ,* but includes an assortment of sheep's innards, not just tripe, and is always served in a broth.

➡ **Ròu Bǐng** (肉饼) Meat patty, usually filled with pork or beef before being lightly fried.

➡ **Jiāo Quān** (焦圈) Deep-fried dough rings, usually accompanied with a cup of *dòu zhī.*

➡ **Dòu Zhī** (豆汁) Sour-tasting soy milk drink.

At lunchtimes, try the knife-sliced pork noodles (刀削面; *dāo xiāo miàn*), the spicy dry mincemeat noodles (担担面; *dàndàn miàn*), or one of the many rice meals (盖饭; *gài fàn*). There's no English sign or English menu, although the menu does have some small photos.

CHEZ GÉRARD DELICATESSEN **$**

Map p290 (40 Jianchang Hutong, off Guozijian Jie, 国子监街，箭厂胡同 40 号; ⏲10am-10.30pm) This small French boucherie, located inside two adjacent shop fronts, is a decent place to grab picnic supplies. It stocks freshly baked breads, imported cheeses, a selection of cold meats and some well-priced imported wines.

XĪNMÍN FOOD MARKET MARKET **$**

Map p290 (新民菜市场; Xīnmín Càishìchǎng; Jiugulou Waidajie, 就鼓楼外大街; ⏲5am-noon) Large, covered market selling all manner of foodstuffs – perfect for picnic supplies, and photo opportunities.

★BǍIHÉ VEGETARIAN RESTAURANT CHINESE, VEGETARIAN **$$**

Map p290 (百合素食; Bǎihé Sùshí; 23 Caoyuan Hutong, 东直门内北小街草园胡同甲 23 号; mains ¥25-60, tea per cup/pot from ¥16/45; ⏲11am-10pm; 🚭 📖; Ⓢ Dongzhimen or Beixinqiao) This peaceful, tastefully furnished, courtyard restaurant, which also serves as a delightful teahouse, has a wonderful air of serenity – it's not uncommon to see monks from nearby Lama Temple coming here for a pot of tea. The all-vegetarian menu (with English translations) includes imaginative mock-meat dishes as well as more conventional vegetable dishes and a range of tasty noodles.

With courteous service, this is one of Běijīng's more soothing dining experiences; and it's nonsmoking throughout. There's also a separate and extensive tea menu – customers are welcome to come here just to sample the tea. To get here, walk north on Dongzhimen Beixiaojie from the junction with Ghost Street for 100m, then turn left

GHOST STREET

For a close-up look at how Beijingers treat their restaurants as party venues and not just places for a meal, take a trip to **Ghost Street** (簋街, Gui Jie; Map p290; Ⓢ Beixinqiao). This 1.4km strip of Dongzhimennei Dajie is home to over 150 restaurants that attract everyone from hipsters to office workers, man-bag-toting businessmen and families, as well as the odd celebrity.

It never closes, making it one of Běijīng's most buzzing streets, and it's especially fun on Friday and Saturday nights. Traffic slows to a crawl as the restaurant workers line the side of the road trying to entice passing cars to stop at their joint. Crowds of people spill out onto the pavement waiting for a free table, while inside the packed restaurants the sweating staff rush around delivering food and beers to people celebrating the end of the week.

Most styles of Chinese cuisine are represented on Ghost Street, but it's best known for its hotpot and spicy seafood restaurants.

The giant **Xiǎo Yú Shān** (小渔山; Map p290; 195 Dongzhimennei Dajie, 东直门内大街 195 号; ⏲ 10.30am-6am) is always jammed with people cracking open crayfish and shrimp. For classic Mongolian hotpot, try **Little Sheep** (小肥羊; Xiǎo Féi Yáng; Map p290; 209 Dongzhimennei Dajie, 东直门内大街 209 号; ⏲ 9am-4am), which sources its mutton from Inner Mongolia. For the spicier, Sìchuān version of hotpot, cross the road to **Chóngqìng Kǒngliàng Huǒguō** (重庆孔亮火锅; Map p290; 218 Dongzhimennei Dajie, 东直门内大街 218; pot from ¥35, dipping ingredients ¥7-20; ⏲ 9.30am-3am).

Ghost Street gets its English name from a mistranslation of the Chinese nickname of the street, *Guǐ Jiē* (簋街 簋), an ancient bronze food vessel, a statue of which you can find at the far eastern end of Dongzhimennei Dajie, by the 2nd Ring Rd, but it's pronounced the same as 鬼 – Chinese for 'ghost'.

Sadly its signature red lanterns, which for years lined both sides of the street, lending it a unique look, were torn down by overzealous local officials in 2014 – they were a fire risk, apparently.

LOCAL KNOWLEDGE

CYCLE RICKSHAW PANCAKES

One of the tastiest street-food snacks to be found in Běijīng is the *jiānbing* (煎饼), a savoury pancake sprinkled with chives and spring onion and rubbed in chilli sauce before being wrapped around a crunchy slice of fried dough. They're either sold from a hole-in-the-wall stall, or simply off the back of a cycle rickshaw. Ordering is easy, as the vendor generally only sells one type; all you have to decide is whether you want chilli *(yào làjiāo)* or not *(bú yào làjiāo)*, and then hand over your ¥5.

Jiānbing vendors come and go (especially those working off cycle rickshaws), but you often find them outside subway stations. One sometimes hangs out on Gulou Dongdajie, near the junction with Baochao Hutong.

Failing that, head to 153 Yonghegong Dajie to find a the permanent hole-in-the-wall **jiānbing stall** (煎饼; Map p290; 153 Yonghegong Dajie; 雍和宫大街153号; ¥5 to ¥6; ⏲7am-7pm). About 500m south of the Lama Temple, and operating from a window at the front of a restaurant called Chūnbǐng Jīngwèi Cài (春饼京味菜), this pancake stall is one of the few that offers a variety of pancake mixes. Choose from millet (小米; *xiǎo mǐ* – the most popular), mung bean (绿豆; *lǜ dòu*), glutinous rice (糯米; *nuò mǐ*) or purple glutinous rice (紫米; *zǐ mǐ*).

And while you're here, the window to the left sells damn good *bāozi* (steamed dumplings; ¥1.50 each).

into the first *hútòng* . The restaurant is on the right, although the sign is in Chinese only.

JĪN DǏNG XUĀN — CANTONESE $$

Map p290 (金鼎轩; 77 Hepingli Xijie, 地坛南门和平里西街77号; dim sum ¥10-20, mains ¥30-100; ⏲24hr; 📋; Ⓢ Yonghegong-Lama Temple) By the south gate of Dìtán Park, this giant, busy, neon-lit, 24-hour restaurant on three floors serves up good-value dim sum, as well as a selection of other mostly Cantonese dishes. Note, the dim sum (点心; *diǎn xin*) is in the second half of the menu, entitled 'North & South Snacks'.

STUFF'D — WESTERN $$

Map p290 (塞; Sāi; 9 Jianchang Hutong, off Guozijian Jie, 国子监街，箭厂胡同 9 号; sausages ¥50, pies ¥60, pizza ¥60, home-brewed ale ¥40; ⏲11.30am-2.30pm & 6-10pm, closed Tue; 📋) Handmade sausages and home-brewed beer. What more could you want? This cute little sister branch of nearby Vineyard Cafe has a more rustic feel to it; almost like an English pub, only housed in a restored Chinese *píngfáng* (bungalow). Lunchtimes are all about the sausages and ale, but the evening menu also includes pies and pizza.

XÙ XIĀNG ZHĀI VEGETARIAN RESTAURANT — VEGETARIAN $$

Map p290 (叙香斋; Xù Xiāng Zhāi; 26 Guozijian Jie, 国子监街 26 号; buffet ¥68, mains ¥30-80; ⏲buffet 11.30am-2pm & 5.30-9pm, a la carte 1.30-3.30pm & 7.30-9pm; 📋; Ⓢ Yonghegong Lama Temple) The lunchtime and early-evening set-price buffet is very popular here, and good value. There's an eleborate selection of beautifully presented mock-meat creations, plus other standard vegetable dishes, representing vegetarian cuisine from across China. And it's all served in an elegant dining hall on the historic *hútòng* Guozijian Jie. The à la carte menu is in English and is also decent value.

CAFÉ SAMBAL — MALAYSIAN $$

Map p290 (☎6400 4875; 43 Doufuchi Hutong, 旧鼓楼大街豆腐池胡同 43 号; mains ¥60-90; ⏲11am-11pm; 🚭 📋; Ⓢ Guloudajie) This cool Malaysian restaurant located off Jiugulou Dajie is in a cleverly converted courtyard house at the entrance to Doufuchi Hutong. The minimalist bar opens into a narrow dining area that has a temporary roof during winter, but is open in summer. The food is classic Malaysian. Try the beef rendang (¥78), or the various sambals (from ¥90). The wine list is decent, as are the mojitos (¥55).

CAFÉ DE LA POSTE — FRENCH $$

Map p290 (云游驿; Yúnyóu Yì; 58 Yonghegong Dajie, 雍和宫大街 58 号; mains ¥80-100; ⏲12.30-3pm & 6pm-midnight, kitchen closes at 10.30pm; 📋; Ⓢ Yonghegong-Lama Temple) Just down the street from the Lama Temple, this long-time expat favourite, with a relaxed vibe and friendly service, is Běijīng's original French bistro. A small bar area opens into an intimate, nicely lit dining space, and the food is unpretentious and hearty.

The steaks (from ¥90) are impressive cuts of meat, but it does a decent Salade Lyonnais (¥52) too, while the desserts include the renowned Death by Chocolate (¥52). There's a set lunch during the week, brunch at weekends, and an impressive wine list. The bar stays open late, has clientele spilling out onto the pavement in summer and, if you side-step the wine and go for the draft beer or the pastis, it's one of the cheapest places for a drink.

VINEYARD CAFÉ WESTERN **$$**

Map p290 (葡萄院儿, Pútáo Yuànr; www.vineyardcafe.cn; 31 Wudaoying Hutong, 五道营胡同 31 号; mains ¥60-90; 11am-3pm & 6-10pm, closed Mon; ; ; Yonghegong-Lama Temple) A huge hit with expats, this laid-back, family-friendly cafe-restaurant was the first place to open its doors on the increasingly popular Wudaoying Hutong. The menu, which can be viewed in full on the website, serves up Western standards such as pastas, pies, good cuts of steak and decent pizza. There's a strong wine list, and imported beers.

Has a nice conservatory, a nonsmoking area and lots of sofas to sink into. Particularly popular for brunch or lunch.

NOODLE IN PAN-ASIAN **$$**

Map p290 (吃面; Chī Miàn; Xiaojingchang Hutong, off Gulou Dongdajie, 鼓楼东大街 81 号小经厂胡同; mains ¥28-78; noon-10pm; ; Andingmen) Run partly by members of a local punk band, this tiny place comes with retro decor, upholstered dining chairs and, as you'd expect, energetic music. The pan-Asian menu – mostly stews, curries and, of course, noodles – is quite limited, but it adds to the home-cooked feel. English spoken. English menu.

TASTE CHINESE **$$**

Map p290 (咂摸; Zāmo; 106 Nanluogu Xiang, 南锣鼓巷 106 号; mains ¥30-80; 11am-2am, kitchen closes around 10pm;) There's nothing outstanding about the food here, although it's tasty enough. But the heritage building and the roof terrace seating overlooking the shopping frenzy below make it stand out from the crowd on Nanluogu Xiang. The European-influenced two-storey building is unusual in these parts and dates from the early 1900s. You can eat inside the central building on either floor, or outside on the 1st-floor terrace.

The food is pan-Chinese, plus some questionable Chinese-Western combos, such as Peking duck pizza. There's an English menu and the place doubles up as a bar in the evening.

DÀLǏ COURTYARD YUNNAN **$$$**

Map p290 (大理; Dàlǐ; 8404 1430; 67 Xiaojingchang Hutong, Gulou Dongdajie, 鼓楼东大街小经厂胡同 67 号; set menu ¥150; noon-2pm & 6-10.30pm; Andingmen) The charming *hútòng* setting in a restored courtyard makes this one of Běijīng's more pleasant places to eat, especially in summer (in winter they cover the courtyard with an unattractive temporary roof). It specialises in the subtle flavours of Yúnnán cuisine. There's no menu. Instead, you pay ¥150 (drinks are extra), and enjoy whatever inspires the chef that day. He rarely disappoints.

From Gulou Dongdajie, turn north onto Xiaojingchang Hutong and look for the red lanterns down the first alley on the left.

SOURCE SICHUAN **$$$**

Map p290 (都江园; Dūjiāngyuán; 6400 3736; 14 Banchang Hutong, 板厂胡同 14 号; set menu ¥188 & 268; 11am-2pm & 5-10pm; ; Nanluoguxiang) Swish Sìchuān with a twist, served up in a courtyard that was once the home of a famous Qing-dynasty general. Source is an amenable place to sample the delights of some of China's hottest dishes, as the chefs here tend to go easy on the chillies. You choose from a selection of set menus, which changes every month, and there's an extensive wine list.

DRINKING & NIGHTLIFE

This neighbourhood, and its network of historic *hútòng*, is our favourite place to drink in Běijīng. New bars are popping up (and closing) all the time, so take a wander and see what you stumble across. Top drinking strips include Nanluogu Xiang and its quieter,

northern extension Beiluogu Xiang; Baochao Hutong (just west of Beiluogu Xiang); the area surrounding the Drum and Bell Towers; and Fangjia Hutong (towards the Lama Temple). Don't forget that the Hòuhǎi Lakes area has dozens of bars too, and is a short walk from here.

★GREAT LEAP BREWING BAR

Map p290 (大跃啤酒; Dàyuè Píjiǔ; www.greatleapbrewing.com; 6 Doujiao Hutong, 豆角胡同 6 号; beer per pint ¥25-50; ⏲2pm-midnight; ⓈShichahai) Běijīng's original microbrewery, this refreshingly simple courtyard bar, run by American beer enthusiast Carl Setzer, is housed in a hard-to-find, but beautifully renovated, 100-year-old Qing-dynasty courtyard and serves up a wonderful selection of unique ales made largely from locally sourced ingredients. Sip on familiar favourites such as pale ales and porters or choose from China-inspired tipples like Honey Ma, a brew made with lip-tingling Sìchuān peppercorns.

All they serve here is ale (although they do hand out bottled water and spicy peanuts for free). If you want other drinks and bar food too, head to their newer, larger branch (p149) out in Sānlǐtún. To get here, walk south out of Shichahai subway station, then left down Mao'er Hutong, then left down Doujiao Hutong, and you'll soon wind your way to the bar. From Nanluogu Xiang, walk west down Jingyang Hutong (景阳胡同), bearing right, then left, then right again before turning left down Doujiao Hutong.

EL NIDO BAR

Map p290 (59 号酒吧; Wǔshíjiǔ Hào Jiǔbā; 59 Fangjia Hutong, 方家胡同 59 号; beers from ¥10; ⏲6pm-late; ⓈAndingmen) Friendly pint-sized bar, with more than 100 types of imported beer. There's no drinks menu; just dive into the fridge and pick out whichever bottles take your fancy. Prices for the foreign beers start at ¥30, while Harbin beer costs just ¥10 a bottle. There's also some imported liquor, including a number of different types of absinthe.

There's some street-side seating out the front, but if it gets too packed (it really is tiny) then try walking up the road to No 46, where there's a bunch of bars and cafes in a small cul-de-sac.

ZÁ JIĀ BAR

Map p290 (杂家; www.zajia.cc; Hóng Ēn Temple, Doufuchi Hutong, 豆腐池胡同宏恩观; ⏲1pm-2am; ⓈGuloudajie) Built into the entrance gate of Hóng Ēn Guàn (宏恩观), a 600-year-old former Taoist temple – most of which is now a household goods market – beautiful Zá Jiā is a cafe by day (coffee from ¥25), bar by night (beer from ¥20). The interior is as cool as it is unique, with split-level seating reaching up into the eaves, and the atmosphere is friendly and relaxed.

It sometimes holds free film screenings and art exhibitions, but if there's live music at the weekends, there's a cover charge (¥30 to ¥50).

BALL HOUSE BAR

Map p290 (波楼酒吧; Bōlóu Jiǔbā, Lǎo Mó; 40 Zhonglouwan Hutong, 钟楼湾胡同 40 号; ⏲2pm-2am; ⓈGuloudajie) A bar for those in the know, Ball House is impossible to stumble across; there's no sign and it's set back from the main *hútòng* (which circumnavigates the Bell Tower) at the end of a narrow pathway which looks like it leads to ordinary housing. There's washing hanging outside and bikes leant up against the wall, but if you push the door open at the end of the pathway, you enter an enormous, beautifully restored split-level room and one of the capital's most unusual drinking spaces.

There are pool tables (¥30 per hour) and table football tables (free) dotted around the place – hence the name – but there are enough nooks and crannies to find your own quiet spot if you don't fancy the ball games. Beers from ¥15. Cocktails from ¥40.

MAO MAO CHONG BAR BAR

Map p290 (毛毛虫; Máo Máo Chóng; 12 Banchang Hutong, 板厂胡同 12 号; beers from ¥35, cocktails ¥40-50; ⏲7pm-midnight, closed Mon & Tue; 🚭; ⓈNanluoguxiang) This small but lively expat favourite has a rustic interior, good-value cocktails and a no-smoking policy. Its pizzas (¥40 to ¥65) also get rave reviews.

IF BAR

Map p290 (如果酒吧; Rúguǒ Jiǔbā; 67 Beiluogu Xiang, 北锣鼓巷 67 号; beers from ¥20; ⏲1pm-2am; Guloudajie) The first bar to open on Beiluogu Xiang, quirky If (or Siif, as some people call it because of its sign out front, which incorporates the Spanish and the English for the word 'if') is housed on three

LOCAL KNOWLEDGE

HÚTÒNG CAFES

Cute wi-fi cafes have been all the rage in Běijīng for some time now and these days there are dozens of excellent ones, particularly in and around the *hútòng* (alleys) of Dōngchéng North. Some are housed in converted courtyards, most have free wi-fi, fresh coffee (from ¥20), well-priced local beer (from ¥15) and a limited choice of mostly Western food (dishes from ¥30). They are also among the cheapest places in Běijīng to sample Chinese tea (from ¥30 per cup, with unlimited refills). Here are our current favourites.

Irresistible Cafe (诱惑咖啡厅; Yòu Huò Kāfēitīng; Map p290; 14 Mao'er Hutong, 帽儿胡同 14 号; ⊙11am-midnight, closed Mon & Tue;) Large courtyard. Czech beers. Good, healthy food.

Cafe Confucius (秀冠咖啡; Xiù Guàn Kāfēi; Map p290; 25 Guozijian Jie, 国子监街 25 号; ⊙8.30am-8.30pm;) Buddhist themed. Very friendly.

Other Place (Map p290; 1 Langjia Hutong, 朗家胡同 1 号; ⊙ noon-midnight;) Cool staff. Cool tunes. Cool courtyard. No food.

Essence (萃饮咖啡; Cuìyǐn Kāfēi; Map p290; 47 Zhonglouwan Hutong, off Drum & Bell Square; 钟鼓楼广场，钟楼湾胡同 47 号; ⊙10am-10pm) Top-quality coffee. Small roof terrace with Drum Tower views.

Le Grenadier (石榴树下; Shíliushù Xià; Map p294; 7 Youqizuo Hutong, off Di'anmen Neidajie; 地安门内大街，油漆作胡同 7 号; ⊙ 11am-9pm, closed Wed) Quiet location. Cheap coffee. Rooftop seating. French cuisine.

Three Trees Coffee (三棵树; Sān Kē Shù; Map p290; 89 Nanluogu Xiang; 南锣鼓巷 89 号; ⊙ 9.30am-10pm) Cosy Bohemian retreat from Nanluogu Xiang's shopping frenzy.

small levels fitted with strange-shaped furniture, cheeselike wall panelling punctured with holes, and floors with rather disconcerting glass sections that allow you to view the level below.

There's a free pool table and table football (¥5) as well as a neat little roof terrace, which looks out over the *hútòng*. The basement has a small dance floor.

MÀI — BAR

Map p290 (麦; 40 Beiluogu Xiang, 北锣鼓巷 40 号; cocktails from ¥45, beers from ¥30; ⊙6pm-2am; S Guloudajie) This area's first proper cocktail bar, Mài is funky, friendly and housed in a beautifully renovated part of an old courtyard building. Most importantly, though, the manager mixes very good cocktails.

MODERNISTA — BAR

Map p290 (老摩; Lǎo Mó; 44 Baochao Hutong, 宝钞胡同 44 号; ⊙ 4pm-2am, closed Mon; S Guloudajie) Styled on a European tapas bar, this small place reels in well-dressed, artsy types with its live music (mostly jazz) and cultural events such a film screenings, dance classes and mah jong evenings. The drinks are well priced, with beers and pastis from ¥15 and imported wines from ¥30. An upstairs section overlooks the small stage. Has a small tapas menu (¥30 to ¥50).

SALUD — BAR

Map p290 (老伍; lǎowǔ; ☎6402 5086; 66 Nanluogu Xiang, 南锣鼓巷 66 号; beers from ¥20, cocktails from ¥30; ⊙3pm-late; S Andingmen) The biggest and liveliest bar on Nanluogu Xiang, Salud is expat-centric, but gets very busy on weekends with a mixed crowd of locals and foreigners who party well into the early hours. Its house-special flavoured rums (¥20) come in test-tube-like vessels and are lethal.

MADO — BAR

Map p290 (麻朵; Má Duǒ; 60 Baochao Hutong; 宝抄胡同 60 号; beers from ¥15; ⊙summer 2pm-2am, winter 7pm-2am; S Shichai or Gulou Dajie) Friendly, no-frills bar with good-priced drinks and a large roof terrace.

HIPPO — BAR

Map p290 (河马啤酒; Hémǎ Píjiǔ; 19 Beixinqiao Santiao; 北新桥三条 19 号; ⊙3pm-2am; S Beixinqiao) Tiny, hole-in-the-wall bar with a fridge full of imported beers (from ¥20) and dangerously cheap shots (¥10).

NIǍN BAR BAR

Map p290 (辇酒吧; Niǎn Jiǔbā; 21 Cheniandian Hutong, off Andingmennei Dajie; 安定门内大街, 车辇店胡同 21 号; ⌚6pm-midnight, weekends 6pm-2am) Probably the cheapest bar in this neighbourhood; shots cost ¥10, as do small glasses of beer, while on Fridays it's drink as much as you like for ¥50.

BLACK-TEA TEA ROOM TEAHOUSE

Map p290 (巷口红茶馆; Xiàngkǒu Hóngcháguǎn; 65 Beiluogu Xiang; 北锣鼓巷 65 号; tea from ¥28 per cup; ⌚10am-10pm, closed Mon) Despite the name, this place does plenty of other Chinese teas besides black tea and is a welcoming little teahouse. The tea menu is translated into English, but one half of the couple who runs the place speaks some English so can talk you through things too. They also sell a small selection of teas and are happy for you to taste before you buy.

☆ ENTERTAINMENT

★JIĀNG HÚ LIVE MUSIC

Map p290 (江湖酒吧; Jiāng Hú Jiǔbā; 7 Dongmianhua Hutong, 东棉花胡同 7 号; admission ¥30-50; ⌚7pm-2am, closed Mon; Ⓢ Nanluoguxiang) One of the coolest places to hear Chinese indie and rock bands, Jiāng Hú, run by a trombone-playing, music-loving manager, is housed in a small courtyard and packs in the punters on a good night. Intimate, cool, and a decent spot for a drink in a courtyard, even when no bands are playing. Beers from ¥25.

★JIĀNG JÌN JIǓ LIVE MUSIC

Map p290 (疆进酒吧; Jiāngjìnjiǔ Jiǔbā; 2 Zhongku Hutong, 钟库胡同 2 号 (鼓楼北门; admission from ¥20, beers from ¥15, cocktails from ¥25; ⌚1pm-2am; Ⓢ Guloudajie, Shichahai) This tiny, laid-back venue is one of the best places to hear Chinese folk music from the country's ethnic minorities, particularly Uighur and Mongolian. Live music is Thursday to Sunday only and is usually free, although there's sometimes a cover charge on Fridays and Saturdays if a more popular act is playing. Fingers crossed this one escapes the Drum Tower redevelopment wrecking ball.

YÚGŌNG YÍSHĀN LIVE MUSIC

Map p290 (愚公移山; ☎6404 2711; www.yugongyishan.com; 3-2 Zhangzizhong Lu, West Courtyard, 张自忠路 3-2, 号段祺瑞执政府旧址西院; admission from ¥50; ⌚7pm-2am; Ⓢ Zhangzizhonglu) Reputedly one of the most haunted places in Běijīng, this historic building has been home to Qing-dynasty royalty, warlords and the occupying Japanese army in the 1930s. You could probably hear the ghosts screaming if it wasn't for the array of local and foreign bands, solo artists and DJs who take to the stage here every week.

With a very sound booking policy and a decent space to play with, this is one of the best places in town to listen to live music.

TEMPLE BAR LIVE MUSIC

Map p290 (坛酒吧; Tán Jiǔbā; Bldg B, 206 Gulou Dongdajie, 鼓楼东大街 206 号; beers from ¥25, cocktails from ¥30; ⌚5pm-late; Ⓢ Shichahai) Large single-room space above a 24-hour internet cafe, with a long bar in one corner, a low stage in another and tables, chairs and sofas strewn across the rest of the floor. The three music-loving managers ensure decent billing from local bands, and gigs are often free. Nightly Happy Hour (5pm to 10pm) has a buy-one-get-one-free deal on local beers.

No sign; walk under the decorative archway by 206 Gulou Dongdajie, continue to Building B, right at the back of the small car park, then walk up the stairs to your right.

MAO LIVEHOUSE LIVE MUSIC

Map p290 (光芒; Guāngmáng; 111 Gulou Dongdajie, 鼓楼东大街 111 号; admission from ¥60, beers from ¥20; ⌚8pm-late; Ⓢ Shichahai) This midsized venue, opposite the northern entrance to Nanluogu Xiang, is large enough to give the many gigs it hosts a sense of occasion, but small enough to feel intimate. The decor is functional and the sound tight. All sorts of bands play here, but if they're from overseas, the entrance price can be sky-high.

PÉNGHĀO THEATRE THEATRE

Map p290 (蓬蒿剧场; Pénghāo Jùchǎng; ☎6400 6452; www.penghaotheatre.com; in an alley beside 35 Dongmianhua Hutong, 东棉花胡同 35 号; tickets from ¥50; Ⓢ Nanluoguxiang) Students from the nearby drama academy sometimes

LOCAL KNOWLEDGE

TIME WILL TELL FOR THE DRUM & BELL

Despite five years of opposition from local residents and heritage-preservation campaigners, controversial plans to redevelop the *hútòng*-rich neighbourhood surrounding the Drum and Bell Towers looked to be finally going ahead at the time of research.

The original plan to transform the area into the 'Běijīng Time Cultural City', complete with an underground mall, was, thankfully, scrapped. At the time of research, it was still unclear what the precise development plans were, but demolition had already begun.

The local district government was saying it wanted to restore the Drum & Bell Square to its 'original appearance' by using maps of the Qianlong period (18th century), though details remained vague.

Although none of the buildings slated for demolition was more than 70 or 80 years old, critics argue that gentrifying the area to look like it did during its prosperous Qing-dynasty heyday would smack of inauthenticity. Certainly, if the 2007 redevelopment of the Qiánmén area – once the city's largest block of *hútòng* and now a Disneyfied 'Qing-style' shopping zone – is anything to go by, then fears of tearing the heart and soul out of a community would seem not to be the primary concern of the authorities.

perform here, in this small informal non-profit theatre, tucked away down a narrow, unnamed alleyway between Dongmianhua Hutong and Beibinmasi Hutong. The venue, which doubles as a cafe (drinks only), is enchanting, and has some lovely rooftop seating areas, shaded by a 200-year-old tree which slices through part of the building.

Performances are mostly modern drama, and are sometimes (but not always) held in English as well as Chinese. Check the website for details. Some English spoken.

CHINA PUPPET THEATRE THEATRE

(中国木偶剧院; Zhōngguó Mù'ǒu Jùyuàn; ☎6425 4847; www.puppetchina.com; cnr Anhua Xili & North 3rd Ring Rd, 北三环中路安华西里; SAnhuaqiao) Aimed at families, this theatre puts on shadow play, puppetry, music and dance events on Saturdays and Sundays only. There are two theatres. The larger one (大剧场; *dà jùchǎng;* tickets ¥180 to ¥380, shows at 10.30am and 2.30pm) hosts music and dance shows. The puppet shows are in the small theatre (小剧场; *xiǎo jùchǎng;* tickets ¥100, shows at 10am, 11am, 12pm, 1.30pm and 2.30pm). No English.

The theatre is just inside the North 3rd Ring Rd. Come out of Exit D1 of Anhuaqiao subway station (Line 8) and walk east along the main road for about 500m until you see the fairy-tale castlelike theatre building.

STAR LIVE LIVE MUSIC

Map p290 (星光现场; Xīngguāng Xiànchǎng; www.clubtango.cn; 3rd fl, Tango nightclub, 79 Hepingli Xijie, 糖果 3 层, 和平西街 79 号; admission from ¥50; ⏲6.30pm-late; 🚻; SYonghegong Lama Temple) It's a great space and as the only medium-sized venue in Běijīng, it hosts a fair few international bands. The venue hosts occasional dance parties, too. Shares a building with the 24-hour KTV (karaoke) joint, Tango.

SHOPPING

The wildly popular *hútòng* of Nanluogu Xiang contains an eclectic mix of clothes and gifts, sold in trendy boutique shops. It can be a pleasant place to shop for souvenirs, but avoid summer weekends when the shopping frenzy reaches fever pitch and you can hardly walk down the street for the crowds. At its northern end, Gulou Dongdajie has for a while now been a popular place for young Beijingers to shop for vintage clothing, skater fashion and music gear.

Yonghegong Dajie, the road the Lama Temple is on, is chock-full of Buddhist-themed shops, selling prayer flags, incense sticks and Buddha figurines to a backdrop of Tibetan-mantra music.

RUÌFÚXIÁNG — CLOTHING

Map p290 (瑞蚨祥; Ruìfúxiáng; 50 Di'anmen Waidajie, 地安门外大街 50 号; ⏲10am-8.30pm; S Shichahai) Relatively new branch of the 150-year-old Ruìfúxiáng silk store, this place does all manner of silk items, from scarves and shawls (from ¥150) to slippers and hats (from ¥50). It's a great place to come for Chinese-style clothing (women's *qípáo* dresses start at around ¥500), including very cute children's outfits (from ¥100). The quality is good, and the prices, which are marked, are all very reasonable considering how famous the brand is.

JĪNGCHÉNG BĂIXÌNG — CLAY MODELS

Map p290 (京城百姓 （泥塑陶艺); 44 Guozijian Jie; 国子监街 44 号; ⏲ 9am-9pm; S Yonghegong Lama Temple, Andingmen) This small shop on historic Guozijian Jie sells beautifully painted traditional clay figurines, which make wonderfully affordable China souvenirs. What makes this place stand out from other, similar shops, though, is that they also set up tables and chairs outside so customers can paint, and even mold, their own figurines. Young kids love it, although you'll often see adults mucking in too.

If you want make your own figurine, say: *'néng ní sù ma?'* (能泥塑吗? – can I do some clay modeling?). If you just want to paint a figurine, say: *'néng cǎi huì ma?'* (能彩绘吗? – can I do some painting?). It's completely free of charge to do either, but if you want to take away your creations, you'll have to pay ¥10 (more for larger figures).

The professionally painted figurines, which also cost from just ¥10 upwards, come in all sorts of shapes and sizes, but the main three types are the Běijīng Rabbit Lord (兔儿爷; *tù ér yé*), the Shāndōng Roaring Tiger (山东泥叫虎; *Shāndōng ní jiào hǔ*) and Tiānjīn Clay People (天津泥人; *Tiānjīn ní rén*).

ESY DRAGON GIFT SHOP — SOUVENIRS

Map p290 (石怡集; Shí Yí Jí; 19 Nanluogu Xiang, 南锣鼓巷 19 号; ⏲ 9.30am-9.30pm; S Nanluoguxiang) Stocks a good range of souvenirs that are of decent quality, but small in size, and therefore cheap. You'll find pens, bookmarks and decorative Chinese knots for less than ¥15, while key rings emblazoned with Chinese motifs start at ¥20. Sets of coasters or Chinese cloth slippers for kids can be had for less than ¥80.

If you're after something a bit fancier, there's a range of attractive hand-painted porcelain cups at the back of the shop that go for around ¥200 each.

PLASTERED 8 — CLOTHING

Map p290 (创可贴 T- 恤; Chuàngkětiē Tìxù; www.plasteredtshirts.com; 61 Nanluogu Xiang, 南锣鼓巷 61 号; ⏲10am-10pm; S Nanluoguxiang) British-owned, this iconic Nanluogu Xiang T-shirt shop prints ironic takes on Chinese culture onto its good-quality T-shirts and tops (from ¥158). Also stocks decent smog masks (from ¥180). Opposite the entrance to the shop is a rare surviving slogan from the Cultural Revolution era, which exhorts the people to put their trust in the People's Liberation Army (PLA; China's armed forces).

LOCAL KNOWLEDGE

TRADITIONAL CLAY FIGURINES

Clay figurines are popular souvenirs in China, and you'll find them in gift shops across Běijīng. Try Jīngchéng Bǎixìng near the Lama Temple.

Here are the three best-known types of figures you'll find:

- **Běijīng Rabbit Lord** (兔儿爷; *tù ér yé*) These tall-eared rabbit figures have been around since the late Ming Dynasty (17th century) and are supposed to represent the Rabbit Lord who was sent down to Běijīng by Chang'e (the Moon God) to protect the city from a deadly plague. The figurines now represent good health.
- **Tiānjīn Clay People** (天津泥人; *Tiānjīn ní rén*) Characterised by plump, playful childlike figures, these originated in the city of Tiānjīn around 180 years ago, and were first created by a famous sculpturer named Zhang Mingshen (1826–1906).
- **Shāndōng Roaring Tiger** (山东泥叫虎; *Shāndōng ní jiào hǔ*) Originating from the town of Gāomì in Shāndōng province, these clay tigers have a piece of sheep skin connecting their front and hind legs, which makes a roaring sound when squeezed (young kids love these).

FAMOUS TEA OF CHINA — TEA

Map p290 (福建茶行; Fújiàn Cháháng; 123 Gulou Dongdajie; 鼓楼东大街 123 号; ⌚8am-10pm) This small tea shop is run by a friendly couple who speak almost no English but are as accommodating as they can be towards foreign tourists. Most of the tea is sold by weight; priced by the *jīn* (500g), but more commonly sold by the *liǎng* (50g). They have a few tea sets for sale too.

The shop also sells tea in small prewrapped parcels (perfect for gifts), and there are cute, tiny 'cakes' of Pu'erh tea, sold for ¥10 for 10 pieces; each piece is enough for one cup of tea. You can buy individual tea cups here (from as little as ¥3), as well as individual *gàiwǎn* (lidded cups, used as tea pots; from ¥20). Also look out for the smart little travel tea sets (旅行茶具; *lǚxíng chájù;* ¥60).

C ROCK — MUSIC

Map p290 (C Rock 音乐光盘店; C Rock yīnyuè guāngpán diàn; 99 Gulou Dongdajie, 鼓楼东大街 99 号; ⌚11am-10pm; Ⓢ Andingmen) This pocket-sized shop is the best place in the area to pick up albums produced by Chinese artists. The guy who runs it speaks enough English to help you decide and is happy to let you listen to an album that takes your fancy. There's music of all types from all over China (as well as some international stuff), but the focus is on local rock bands and folk music. CDs cost between ¥35 and ¥100.

TIĀN YÌ GOODS MARKET — MARKET

Map p290 (天意商场; Tiānyì Shāngchǎng; 158 Di'anmen Waidajie, 地安门外大街 158 号; ⌚9am-7.30pm; Ⓢ Shichahai) There's little in the way of conventional souvenirs here (although there are some), but the fact that tourists don't shop here means that whatever you buy is almost bound to be a bargain. This isn't so much the place to come to buy gifts for friends back home; it's where to come for that gadget you've lost, or that pair of gloves you didn't think you'd need.

Items for sale include electronics, stationery and toys (ground floor), jewellery and souvenirs (1st floor), tea sets and sports equipment, including kites and table-tennis sets (2nd floor), clothing (3rd floor) and shoes, including flip-flops and old-school Chinese plimsolls (4th floor).

JH 2ND-HAND BIKE SHOP — BICYCLES

Map p290 (金典新桥信托商行; Jīndiǎn Xīnqiáo Xìntuō Shàngháng; 43 Dongsi Beidajie, 东四北大街 43 号; ⌚9am-5pm; Ⓢ Beixinqiao) You can pick up all sorts here, from battered old Tiānjīn-made Flying Pigeons and Shànghǎi Forevers (sometimes starting as cheap as ¥100) to lovingly restored British-made Raleighs that go for up to ¥5000. There are also some new bikes on display, but the quality of them isn't as good as at the nearby Giant shop. Guys outside the shop also sell second-hand bikes. Bargain hard.

GIANT — BICYCLES

(捷安特; Jié'āntè; Map p290; 77 Jiaodaokou Dongdajie, 交道口东大街 77 号; ⌚9am-7pm; Ⓢ Beixinqiao) One of a string of decent bike shops on this stretch of road, Giant has the biggest range of new bicycles and bike equipment, such as helmets, locks and baby seats. Bikes start at around ¥600. Also rents good-as-new mountain bikes (per day ¥100 including helmet; deposit ¥1500). Chinese for bike rental is: 租车 *(zū chē)*, pronounced 'zoo chuh'.

SPORTS & ACTIVITIES

NATOOKE — CYCLING

Map p290 (耍 (自行车店), Shuǎ (Zìxíngchē Diàn); www.natooke.com; 19-1 Wudaoying Hutong, 五道营胡同 19 – 1 号; ⌚10am-7pm; Ⓢ Yonghegong Lama Temple) The coolest bike shop in Běijīng, Natooke sells fixed-gear bikes (from ¥2800), but also rents a small range of secondhand bikes (per day ¥50, deposit per day ¥500), including fixies. You can buy good-quality smog masks here too. It also organises cycling events in and around Běijīng – check the website.

BLACK SESAME KITCHEN — COOKING COURSES

Map p290 (☎136 9147 4408; www.blacksesamekitchen.com; 3 Heizhima Hutong, off Nanluogu Xiang; 南锣鼓巷黑芝麻胡同 3 号) Runs popular cooking classes with a variety of recipes from across China. No sign; walk-in guests are not encouraged as this is a residential courtyard. Pre-booking essential. You can also eat here (set menu ¥300 per person) – it gets rave reviews – but again you must prebook.

CULTURE YARD
LANGUAGE COURSES

Map p290 (天井越洋; Tiānjǐng Yuèyáng; ☎8404 4166; www.cultureyard.net; 10 Shique Hutong, 石雀胡同 10 号; ⊙10am-7pm, closed Sun; S Beixinqiao) Tucked away down a *hútòng,* this cultural centre focuses on Chinese-language classes. Its main program is a six-week course (¥3600), but you can tailor courses to suit your needs. Its 'Survival Chinese' course (four two-hour classes for ¥400) is ideal for tourists.

QĪNGNIÁN HÚ PARK
SWIMMING

Map p290 (青年湖公园; Qīngnián Hú Gōngyuán; Qingnianhu Lu, off Andingmenwai Dajie, 安定门外大街，青年湖路; adult/child ¥40/30; ⊙6am-10pm May-Sep; S Andingmen) In summer, locals flock to Qīngnián Hú Park where there's an outdoor swimming complex with water slides and a shallow pool for young'uns. It's floodlit in the evening. You can buy all the swimming gear you need, and there are stalls selling grilled kebabs, snacks and even beer.

MÀO'ÉR LǍOLǏ HEALTH CLUB
MASSAGE

Map p290 (帽儿老李足疗保健馆; Mào'ér Lǎolǐ Zúliáo Bǎojiàn Guǎn; 3 Mao'er Hutong, 帽儿胡同 3 号; ⊙11am-midnight) Located inside part of an old courtyard off historic Mao'er Hutong, this small massage parlour is great value. Half-hour foot massages are ¥49, one-hour full-body massages are from ¥89. There is also cupping therapy (¥39) and Tibetan 'fire-dragon' therapy (¥59) – actual flames are used. Not much English spoken, but the massage menu has English translations.

The sign outside is in Chinese, but has the word 'massage' on it. Walk through the gateway, and continue on through a beautiful old carved gateway into the back courtyard where you'll find the place on your left.

JĪNSÈ FĒILÚN BIKE SHOP
BICYCLE RENTAL

Map p290 (金色飞轮自行车商行; Jīnsè Fēilún Zìxíngchē Shānghháng; 35 Gulou Dongdajie; 鼓楼东大街 35 号; ⊙8am-10pm) This small bike shop rents out ordinary bicycles (per day ¥30) and electric scooters (¥60). No English spoken. No English sign.

Temple of Heaven Park & Dōngchéng South

Neighbourhood Top Five

❶ Absolutely unmissable, the **Temple of Heaven Park** (p108) is a unique, simply stunning collection of halls and altars where China's emperors came to seek divine guidance. The surrounding park is equally special.

❷ Gorge yourself on **Peking duck**, the capital's signature dish, in the **restaurants** (p113) where it originated.

❸ Step back in time to imperial China by strolling the sole remaining stretch of the old **City Walls** (p111).

❹ Hunt for pearls of all varieties in **Hóngqiáo (Pearl) Market** (p115).

❺ Browse with the locals on the restored shopping street of **Qianmen Dajie** (p112).

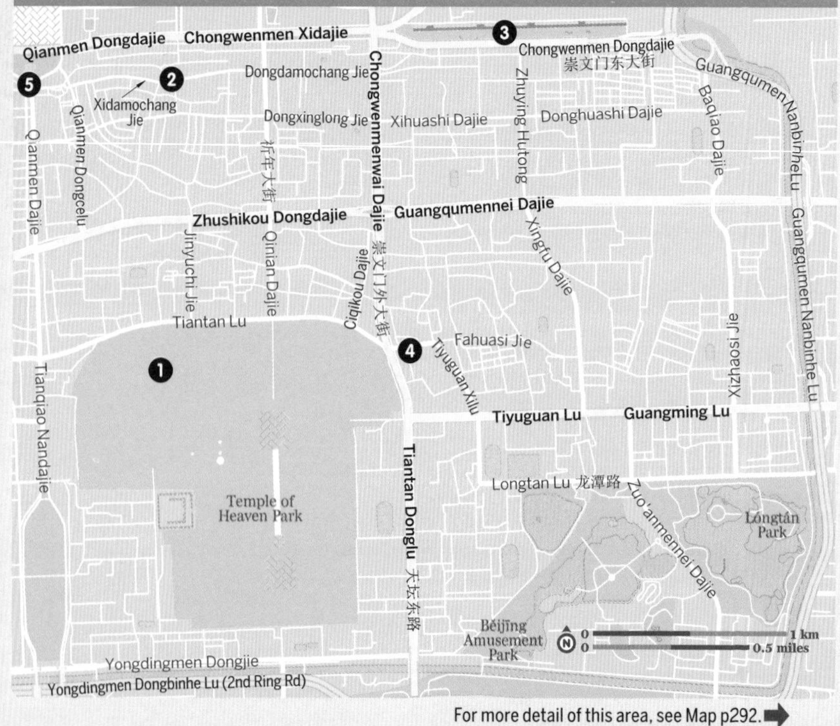

For more detail of this area, see Map p292.

Explore Temple of Heaven Park & Dōngchéng South

Ranging south and southeast of the Forbidden City, and encompassing the now defunct district of Chóngwén, this neighbourhood is far less fashionable than the rest of Dōngchéng (东城) – it's a nightlife desert – and has always been home to the *lǎobǎixìng* (common people).

Start at Temple of Heaven Park. After touring the sights, amble through the park itself before heading north to the Qiánmén area. Alternatively, shopaholics can hit the Hóngqiáo Market, a few hundred metres north of the park's east gate, where five floors of pearls, jewellery, jade and more await. The roof terrace offers fantastic views across the Temple of Heaven Park.

The last remaining stretch of Běijīng's city walls are a brief subway ride north of the Temple of Heaven. From there, wander west through the surviving *hútòng* (alleyways) of the neighbourhood towards Qiánmén, where museums and the popular pedestrian shopping street of Qianmen Dajie await you. Nearby are some of Běijīng's oldest and most traditional Peking duck restaurants, as well as an increasing number of Western fine-dining options. Be sure to check out 23 Qianmen Dongdajie, home to imposing, European-style buildings that formerly housed foreign embassies.

Local Life

- **Hútòng** Make sure to spend some time exploring the decaying alleyways and lanes to the east of Qianmen Dajie (p112), still home to many locals.
- **Peking duck** If you want to eat Peking duck where the locals do, try Biànyífāng (p115).
- **Park life** Serene Lóngtán Park, to the east of Temple of Heaven Park, is one of Běijīng's best-kept secrets.

Getting There & Away

- **Subway** Line 2 stops at Qianmen subway station and Chongwenmen subway station, where the north–south Line 5 intersects with it. For Temple of Heaven Park take Line 5 direct to the Tiantandongmen stop; get off at Chongwenmen for the Ming City Ruins Park and Southeast Corner Watchtower. Qianmen subway station serves Qianmen Dajie and the area around it.
- **Bus** Bus 20 journeys from Běijīng South Train Station via the Temple of Heaven and Qiánmén to Wángfǔjǐng, Dōngdān and Běijīng Train Station.

Lonely Planet's Top Tip

Do as the locals do and rise early to get to Temple of Heaven Park when it opens at sunrise. Not only will you see Běijīng's senior citizens at play – practising taichi and formation dancing – but the park is a superb, tranquil experience at this time and you'll have the jump on the crowds when the sights open at 8am.

Best Places to Eat

- Lost Heaven (p113)
- Capital M (p114)
- Dūyīchù (p113)

For reviews, see p113.

Best Peking Duck

- Lìqún Roast Duck Restaurant (p113)
- Biànyífāng (p115)
- Qiánmén Quánjùdé Roast Duck Restaurant (p114)

For reviews, see p113.

Best Places to Shop

- Hóngqiáo (Pearl) Market (p115)
- Qianmen Dajie (p112)
- Toys City (p115)

For reviews, see p115.

TOP SIGHT
TEMPLE OF HEAVEN PARK

Extraordinary to contemplate, the collection of halls and altars set within the delightful 276-hectare Temple of Heaven Park (天坛公园, Tiāntán Gōngyuán) is *the* most perfect example of Ming architectural design. Each year, the Chinese emperors – the sons of heaven – came here to seek divine clearance and good harvests and to atone for the sins of their people in an esoteric ceremony of prayers and ritual sacrifices.

Everything about the complex is unique, with shape, colour and sound combining to take on symbolic significance. The park itself is equally harmonious, a true oasis amid Běijīng's bedlam. Don't expect to see worshippers in prayer; this is not so much a temple as an altar. Essentially Confucian in function, the cosmic overtones of the Temple of Heaven will delight numerologists, necromancers and the superstitious – not to mention acoustic engineers and carpenters. Seen from above the structures are round and the bases square, a pattern deriving from the ancient Chinese belief that heaven is round and earth is square. Thus the northern end of the park is semicircular and the southern end is square. Temple of the Earth, also called Dìtán, in the north of Běijīng, is on the northern compass point and Temple of Heaven is on the southern point.

There are four gates to the park, one on each point of the compass, and you can enter through any of them. The imperial approach to the temple was via **Zhāohēng Gate** (昭亨门, Zhāohēng Mén) in the south, and that is reflected in our ordering of the principal sights following. You can enter either with just the basic park ticket (¥15), then buy a ¥20 ticket that includes each major sight later, or buy the through ticket (¥35) which gets you into the park and all the sights.

DON'T MISS

- Hall of Prayer for Good Harvests
- Echo Wall

PRACTICALITIES

- Map p292
- 6701 2483
- Tiantan Donglu
- admission park/through ticket high season ¥15/35, low season ¥10/30, audio tour ¥40 (deposit ¥100)
- park 6am-8pm, sights 8am-5.30pm Apr-Oct, park 6am-8pm, sights 8am-5pm Nov-Mar
- S Tiantandongmen

Round Altar

Constructed in 1530 and rebuilt in 1740, the 5m-high **Round Altar** (圜丘; Yuán Qiū) once looked very different: its first incarnation was in deep-blue glazed stone before being redone in light green. The current white marble structure is arrayed in three tiers; its geometry revolves around the imperial number nine. Odd numbers were considered heavenly, and nine is the largest single-digit odd number. The top tier, thought to symbolise heaven, contains nine rings of stones. Each ring has multiples of nine stones, so that the ninth ring has 81 stones. The middle tier (earth) has the 10th to 18th rings. The bottom tier (humanity) has the 19th to 27th rings. The numbers of stairs and balustrades are also multiples of nine. If you stand in the centre of the upper terrace and say something, the sound bounces off the marble balustrades, making your voice sound louder (by nine times?).

Echo Wall

Just north of the altar, surrounding the Imperial Vault of Heaven, is **Echo Wall** (回音壁; Huíyīn Bì), 65m in diameter. Its form has unusual acoustic properties, enabling a whisper to travel clearly from one end to the other (unless a tour group or a loudmouth with a mobile phone gets in the way). In the courtyard are the **Triple-Sounds Stones** (三音石; Sānyīn Shí). It is said that if you clap or shout while standing on the stones, the sound is echoed once from the first stone, twice from the second stone and thrice from the third stone. Queues can get long here.

Imperial Vault of Heaven

The octagonal **Imperial Vault of Heaven** (皇穹宇; Huáng Qióng Yǔ) was built at the same time as the Round Altar, and is structured along the same lines as the older Hall of Prayer for Good Harvests. The vault once contained spirit tablets used in the winter solstice ceremony. Behind the Imperial Vault of Heaven stands the Nine Dragon Juniper, a hoary tree with a trunk of sinewy and coiling knots. Proceeding north from the Imperial Vault is a walkway called the **Red Stairway Bridge** (丹陛桥; Dānbì Qiáo), leading to the Hall of Prayer for Good Harvests.

Hall of Prayer for Good Harvests

The crowning structure of the whole complex is the **Hall of Prayer for Good Harvests** (祈年殿, Qínián Diàn; admission ¥20), magnificently mounted on a three-tiered marble terrace and capped with a triple-eaved umbrella roof of purplish-blue tiles.

THE WINTER SOLSTICE CEREMONY

The emperor, the Son of Heaven (天子; Tiānzǐ), visited the Imperial Vault of Heaven twice a year, but the most important ceremony was performed just before the winter solstice.

The emperor and his enormous entourage passed down Qianmen Dajie in total silence to the Imperial Vault of Heaven. Commoners were not permitted to view the ceremony and remained cloistered indoors. The procession included elephant and horse chariots and long lines of lancers, nobles, officials and musicians dressed in their finest. The imperial 12m-long sedan was almost 3m wide and employed 10 bearers. The next day the emperor waited in a yellow silk tent at the southern gate while officials moved the sacred tablets to the Round Altar, where prayers and sacrificial rituals took place. It was thought that this ritual decided the nation's future; hence a hitch in any part of the proceedings was regarded as a bad omen.

The ritual was last attempted in 1914 by Yuan Shikai, who harboured unfulfilled ambitions of becoming emperor.

LOCATION, LOCATION, LOCATION

Building Běijīng's principal shrine in the heart of the former Chóngwén district, a traditionally down-at-heel, working-class neighbourhood outside the walls of the Imperial City, might seem unusual at first, especially as the vast majority of the capital's other major temples are located further north. But Chóngwén lies in the south, with an aspect facing the sun and indicative of *yáng* (the male and positive principle). Blessed with such positive feng shui (geomancy; literally 'wind and water'), it is not surprising that the Temple of Heaven was sited here.

Built in 1420, it was burnt to cinders in 1889 and heads rolled in apportioning blame (although lightning was the most likely cause). A faithful reproduction based on Ming architectural methods was erected the following year, the builders choosing Oregon fir for the support pillars.

The four central pillars symbolise the seasons, the 12 in the next ring denote the months of the year, and the 12 outer ones represent the day, broken into 12 'watches'. Embedded in the ceiling is a carved dragon, a symbol of royalty. The patterning, carving and gilt decoration of this ceiling and its swirl of colour are a dizzying sight.

All this is made more amazing by the fact that the wooden pillars ingeniously support the ceiling without nails or cement – quite an accomplishment for a building 38m high and 30m in diameter.

Other Buildings

With a green-tiled two-tier roof, the **Animal Killing Pavilion** (Zǎishēng Tíng) was the venue for the slaughter of sacrificial oxen, sheep, deer and other animals. Today it stands locked and passive but can be admired from the outside. Stretching out from here runs the **Long Corridor** (Cháng Láng) where Chinese crowds sit around card games, listen to the radio, play keyboards, and practise Peking opera, dance moves and hacky-sack. Sacrificial music was rehearsed at the **Divine Music Administration** (Shényuè Shǔ) in the west of the park, while wild cats live in the dry moat of the green-tiled **Fasting Palace** (Zhāi Gōng).

The Park

There are around 4000 ancient, knotted cypresses (some 800 years old, their branches propped up on poles) providing much-needed shade. The parkland itself is typical of Chinese parks, with the imperfections and wild irregularity of nature largely eliminated and the harmonising hand of humans accentuated in its obsessively straight lines and regular arrangements. The resulting order, balance and harmony has a haunting but slightly claustrophobic beauty.

SIGHTS

TEMPLE OF HEAVEN PARK — PARK

See p108.

BĚIJĪNG NATURAL HISTORY MUSEUM — MUSEUM

Map p292 (北京自然博物馆; Běijīng Zìrán Bówùguǎn; ☎6702 7702; 126 Tianqiao Nandajie; admission ¥10; ⏲9am-5pm Tue-Sun, last entry 4pm; S Qiánmén or Tiantandongmen) The main entrance to this overblown, creeper-laden museum is hung with portraits of the great natural historians, including Darwin and Linnaeus. The contents range from dinosaur fossils and skeletons, including a *Mamenchisaurus jingyanensis* (a vast sauropod that once roamed China) to creepy-crawlies, an aquarium with Nemo-esque clown fish and an exhibition on the origins of life on earth.

MING CITY WALL RUINS PARK — CITY WALLS

Map p292 (明城墙遗址公园; Míng Chéngqiáng Yízhǐ Gōngyuán; Chongwenmen Dongdajie; ⏲24hr; S Chongwenmen) This slice of restored Ming Inner City Wall runs along the length of the northern flank of Chongwenmen Dongdajie and is attached to a slender strip of park. It's all that is left of the original 24km-long city wall, which started being demolished in the 1960s to make room for new roads and the subway system.

The wall stretches from the former site of Chóngwén Mén (崇文门; Chóngwén Gate), one of the nine gates of the Inner City Wall, to the Southeast Corner Watchtower and then turns north for a short distance along Jianguomen Nandajie to Beijingzhan Dongjie. Chóngwén Mén was also called Shuì Mén (税门; Tax Gate) as the capital tax bureau lay just outside the gate. You can walk the park's length, taking in its higgledy-piggledy contours and the interior layers of stone in parts of the wall that have collapsed. The restored sections run for just over 2km, rising to a height of around 15m and interrupted every 80m with buttresses extending to a maximum depth of 39m. The most interesting sections of wall are those closer to their original and more dilapidated state and some of the bricks come complete with bullet holes.

SOUTHEAST CORNER WATCHTOWER & RED GATE GALLERY — WATCHTOWER, GALLERY

Map p292 (东南角楼、红门画廊; Dōngnán Jiǎolóu & Hóngmén Huàláng; ☎6527 0574; admission ¥10; ⏲8am-5.30pm; S Jianguomen, Chongwenmen) This splendid fortification, with a green-tiled, twin-eaved roof rising up imperiously south of the Ancient Observatory, dates back to the Ming dynasty. Mount the battlements for views alongside camera-wielding Chinese trainspotters eagerly awaiting rolling stock grinding in and out of Běijīng Train Station. Make sure to hunt out the **signatures** etched in the walls by allied forces during the Boxer Rebellion.

You can make out the name of a certain P Foot; 'USA' is also scrawled on the brickwork. The international composition of the eight-nation force that relieved Běijīng in 1900 is noted in names such as André, Stickel and what appears to be a name in Cyrillic. One brick records the date 'Dec 16 1900'. Allied forces overwhelmed the redoubt after a lengthy engagement. Note the drainage channels poking out of the wall along its length. You can reach the watchtower from the west through the Railway Arch, which was built for the first railway that ran around Běijīng.

The watchtower is punctured with 144 archers' windows, as well as two forlorn stumps of flag abutments and a cannon or two. Attached to it is a 100m section of the original Inner City Wall, beyond which stretches the restored Ming City Wall extending all the way to Chōngwénmén and north to Beijingzhan Dongjie. Inside the

LOCAL KNOWLEDGE

FROM CITY GATE TO SUBWAY STOP

The names of the subway stations of Qianmen, Chongwenmen and Jianguomen recall some of the Tartar City Wall's vast and imposing gates, which divided the Imperial City from the Chinese city beyond it. Today, Front Gate and the Southeast Corner Watchtower to the southeast are the only reminders of that wall. The road looping south from Jianguomen Station, following the line of the city moat, marks the outline of the levelled Chinese City Wall, whose gates *(mén)* survive only in street names, such as Guangqumen Nanbinhe Lu, Zuo'anmen Xibinhe Lu and Yongdingmen Dongbinhe Lu. Vestiges of this wall can still be seen at the Ming City Wall Ruins Park.

LOCAL KNOWLEDGE

THE LOST CITY WALLS OF BĚIJĪNG

As Běijīng develops relentlessly, it's increasingly hard to believe that as recently as 40-odd years ago the capital was still surrounded by the city walls that protected it from invaders for over 500 years.

Two walls once guarded Běijīng: an outer wall and an inner wall. Now, nothing is left of the original outer wall, while only a few remnants of the inner city wall remain, most notably the stretch now known as the Ming City Wall Ruins Park (p111). Their absence is perhaps the most conspicuous chunk of lost heritage in Běijīng.

The outer wall went first. Demolition started in the early 1950s and by 1961 half a millenia of history had vanished. The inner wall disappeared more slowly; as late as the mid-1970s sections of wall and their gates and watchtowers were being torn down.

It was Mao Zedong who ordered the removal of the walls. The justification was that they stood in the way of the new roads being built, as well as the subway system (Line 2 follows the route of the old inner wall). But blotting out the grandeur of earlier dynasties may also have inspired Mao's decision to erase such a vital part of Běijīng's identity.

Opposition to the scheme was unusually vigorous, given Mao's dislike of public criticism. It was led by the late Liang Sicheng, a famed architect known as the father of modern Chinese architecture. Liang argued that Běijīng could still develop into a modern city while keeping its walls. He was almost certainly right. Nánjīng and Xī'ān are examples of Chinese cities that have evolved while retaining their walls.

But Liang failed to convince Mao and in a horrible irony, Liang's own *sìhéyuàn* (traditional courtyard house) disappeared under the wrecking ball in 2012.

highly impressive interior is some staggering carpentry: huge red pillars that are topped with solid beams surge upwards. The 1st floor is the site of the **Red Gate Gallery**, one of Běijīng's long-established modern art galleries. The 3rd-floor gallery has a fascinating photographic exhibition on the old gates of Běijīng, while the 4th-floor gallery contains more paintings. Say you are visiting the Red Gate Gallery and the ¥10 entry fee to the watchtower is normally waived.

BĚIJĪNG RAILWAY MUSEUM — MUSEUM

Map p292 (北京铁路博物馆; Běijīng Tiělù Bówùguǎn; ☎6705 1638; 2a Qianmen Dongdajie, 前门东大街2a号; admission ¥20; ⏲9am-5pm Tue-Sun; Ⓢ Qianmen) Located in the historic former Qiánmén Railway Station, which once connected Běijīng to Tiānjīn, this museum offers an engaging history of the development of the capital and China's railway system, with plenty of photos and models. Its lack of space, though, means it doesn't have many actual trains, although there is a life-size model of the cab of one of China's high-speed trains to clamber into (¥10).

Hard-core trainspotters should make tracks to the **China Railway Museum** (中国铁道博物馆; Zhōngguó Tiědào Bówùguǎn; ☎6438 1519; 1 Jiuxianqiao Bei Lu, Chaoyang District; 朝阳区酒仙桥北路1号院北侧; admission ¥20; ⏲9am-4pm Tue-Sun; 🚌403) on the far northeastern outskirts of Běijīng, which is vast and has far more loco action.

BĚIJĪNG PLANNING EXHIBITION HALL — MUSEUM

Map p292 (北京市规划展览馆; Běijīngshì Guīhuà Zhǎnlǎnguǎn; ☎6701 7074; 20 Qianmen Dongdajie; admission ¥30; ⏲9am-5pm Tue-Sun; Ⓢ Qianmen) It doesn't see much foot traffic, but a lot of thought has gone into making this modern museum a visitor-friendly experience. True, it strains every sinew to present Běijīng's gut-wrenching, *hútòng*-felling metamorphosis in the best possible light but the 3rd floor houses a fantastic, giant scale model of the capital mounted on a series of even bigger satellite photos.

It's a great way to get a perspective on this ever-expanding city. There's also a scale model of the Forbidden City and 3D films touting the Běijīng of the future.

QIANMEN DAJIE — HISTORIC STREET

Map p292 (前门大街; Ⓢ Qianmen) Restored to resemble a late-Qing-dynasty street scene and wildly popular with domestic visitors, this ancient thoroughfare (once known as Zhengyangmen Dajie, or Facing the Sun

Gate Street) is something of a tourist theme park. That said, it is beginning to stir into life as more (overpriced) restaurants and shops open up, while the rebuilt Qiánmén Decorative Arch (the original was torn down in the 1950s) looks handsome.

EATING

OLD BĚIJĪNG ZHÁJIÀNG NOODLE KING — NOODLES $

Map p292 (老北京炸酱面大王; Lǎo Běijīng Zhájiàng Miàn; 56 Dongxinglong Jie, 东兴隆街56号; noodles from ¥18, other dishes from ¥28; ⏲10.45am-10pm; 📄; Ⓢ Chongwenmen) Faux old-school Běijīng style – look for the two rickshaws parked outside the entrance – but always busy (especially at lunchtime) with locals sampling the signature noodles with bean paste sauce on offer here. The sauce, scallions and your choice of meat or vegie options come on the side and you mix them with the noodles.

WEDOMÉ — CAFE $

Map p292 (味多美; Wèiduōměi; ☎6715 9205; 12 Tiyuguan Lu, 体育馆路12号; coffee & tea from ¥10; ⏲7.30am-9pm; 🚭; Ⓢ Tiantandongmen) If you're looking for a place to rest your legs after shopping or sightseeing in the area, then retreat to the 2nd floor of this cafe opposite the east gate of the Temple of Heaven Park. It offers a wide selection of coffee, tea and juices, as well as cakes and sandwiches.

DŪYĪCHÙ — DUMPLINGS $$

Map p292 (都一处; ☎6702 1671; 38 Qianmen Dajie, 前门大街38号; dishes from ¥32; ⏲6.30am-9.30pm; 📄; Ⓢ Qianmen) Now back on the street where it opened during the mid-Qing dynasty, Dūyīchù specialises in the delicate dumplings called *shāomài* (¥42 to ¥52). The shrimp-and-leek and vegie ones are especially good, and are presented very nicely, but it also does a nice line in seasonal variations, such as sweet corn and bean in the summer, or beef and yam in the winter.

There are other nondumpling dishes on the menu too. No-frills service here and be prepared to queue at weekends.

★LÌQÚN ROAST DUCK RESTAURANT — PEKING DUCK $$$

Map p292 (利群烤鸭店; Lìqún Kǎoyādiàn; ☎6702 5681, 6705 5578; 11 Beixiangfeng Hutong, 前门东大街正义路南口北翔凤胡同11号; roast duck for 2/3 people ¥255/275; ⏲10am-10pm; 🚭📄; Ⓢ Qianmen) As you walk in to this compact courtyard restaurant, you're greeted by the fine sight of rows of ducks on hooks glowing in the ovens. The delectable duck on offer is so in demand that it's essential to call ahead to reserve both a bird and a table (otherwise, turn up off-peak and be prepared to wait an hour).

Inside, it's a little tatty (no prizes for the toilets) and service can be chaotic, but the food more than makes up for it. Buried away in east Qiánmén, the approach to the restaurant is through a maze of crumbling *hútòng* that have somehow survived total demolition; look for the duck signs pointing the way.

★LOST HEAVEN — YUNNAN $$$

Map p292 (花马天堂; Huāmǎ Tiāntáng; ☎8516 2698; 23 Qianmen Dongdajie, 前门东大街23号; dishes from ¥68; ⏲11am-2pm & 5.30pm-10.30pm; 🚭📄; Ⓢ Qianmen) The Běijīng branch of the famed Shànghǎi restaurant,

LOCAL KNOWLEDGE

THE EVOLUTION OF 23 QIANMEN DONGDAJIE

Known today for its high-class restaurants and as the site of exclusive fashion shows, 23 Qianmen Dongdajie is host to far more than just top chefs and supermodels. The elegant buildings in a neoclassical style set around a quadrangle have a unique history, having been built in 1903 to house the US embassy. The original American legation was located on nearby Dongjiaomin Xiang and was badly damaged during the 1900 Boxer Rebellion when it, and other foreign embassies, came under siege for months.

The address stayed as the US embassy until 1949 and the communist takeover of China, when the American diplomats decamped to Taiwan. The next resident was the Dalai Lama; it was his official Běijīng home until he too fled China for India in 1959. Later, the buildings became part of the Chinese foreign ministry and were the venue for secret talks between the US and China in 1971 that led to President Nixon's historic visit to China the next year, and the beginning of the normalisation of relations between Běijīng and Washington.

LOCAL KNOWLEDGE

DUCK DEVOTION

Zhang Liqun, owner of the Lìqún Roast Duck Restaurant, is 65 years old and has spent 32 years of his life serving up duck in Běijīng.

How did you come to be a roast duck chef? Even though I'm a third-generation Beijinger, my first job was as a farmer. I left school in 1968, during the Cultural Revolution, and was sent to work on a farm in Shǎnxī. After I came back to Běijīng, I just felt an urge to cook delicious food. I had a friend who worked at Quánjùdé Roast Duck Restaurant and he helped me get a job there in 1982.

Does it take a long time to learn how to cook Peking duck? I started at the bottom in the kitchen. First you study everything about ducks: how they should be fed and slaughtered, although cooks don't kill the ducks themselves anymore. Then you learn about all the ingredients that go into making it taste so good. Finally, you learn how to cook the bird. It takes about three years to learn how to cook it properly. It's difficult to be a good roast duck chef. You have to be very nimble with your fingers.

Why did you open your own place? By 1992 I was in charge of opening new branches of Quánjùdé and wasn't cooking anymore, so I had a lot of free time and decided to open my own restaurant. Quánjùdé didn't mind; it's a much bigger company. Back then, we sold the duck for ¥30 each and it was the same quality as it is now.

What's the secret of your restaurant's success? It's because we cook the duck in the traditional way and after 22 years we won't change that. Normally, we cook 50 ducks a day. On public holidays and at Chinese New Year, we'll go through 100 ducks in a day.

Do you still cook the duck yourself? Not unless it's a very busy time. I sometimes cook at home, but not roast duck because I see enough of that in the restaurant.

Lost Heaven specialises in the folk cuisine of Yúnnán province. While the spices have been toned down, the flavours remain subtle and light and are guaranteed to transport you to China's balmy southwest. The location in the elegant former Legation Quarter is an added bonus, and there's an outside terrace for the summer.

Try the Dai-style roast pork in banana leaf (¥68), or one of the many splendid salads such as the marinated beef salad and peppers or the Burmese tea leaves salad. But all the dishes on the extensive menu are enticing, and the service is attentive. Book ahead in the evenings.

QIÁNMÉN QUÁNJÙDÉ ROAST DUCK RESTAURANT PEKING DUCK **$$$**

Map p292 (前门全聚德烤鸭店; Qiánmén Quánjùdé Kǎoyādiàn; ☎6701 1379; 30 Qianmen Dajie, 前门大街30号; roast duck ¥296; ⏰11am-1.30pm, 4.30-8pm; 📄; Ⓢ Qianmen) The most popular branch of Běijīng's most famous duck destination – check out the photos of everyone from Fidel Castro to Zhang Yimou. The duck, while not the best in town, is roasted in ovens fired by fruit-tree wood, which means the birds have a unique fragrance, as well as being juicy, if slightly fatty.

It's very much geared to the tourist hordes (both domestic and foreign) and the crowds mean it is wise to reserve ahead here. Service can be peremptory, while the huge, two-floor venue lacks atmosphere.

CAPITAL M MEDITERRANEAN **$$$**

Map p292 (M餐厅; M Cāntīng; ☎6702 2727; 3rd fl, 2 Qianmen Dajie, 前门步行街2号; mains from ¥198; ⏰11.30am-3pm & 5.30-10pm; 🚭📄; Ⓢ Qianmen) The terrace of this swish but relaxed restaurant, with its unfussy menu of Mediterranean favourites, offers fine views over Qiánmén Gate and Tiān'ānmén Sq. The weekday lunch menu is decent value (¥188). It's down the first turning on the left at the beginning of Qianmen Dajie; look for the 'M' hanging off the side of the building. Book ahead.

The menu ranges across France, Italy, Greece and north Africa. We like the tagines and Sicilian seafood stew, but the signature dishes of leg of lamb and suckling pig are equally as tasty. If you can't snaffle a table on the terrace, the large, light-filled dining room is almost as good a spot to enjoy your meal. There's a weekend brunch deal with two/three courses for ¥248/288.

BIÀNYÍFĀNG PEKING DUCK **$$$**

Map p292 (便宜坊烤鸭店; Biànyífāng Kǎoyādiàn; ☎6708 8680; 3rd fl, China New World Shopping Mall, 5 Chongwenmenwai Dajie, 崇文门外大街5号新世界商场二期三层; roast duck ¥198; ⊙11am-9.30pm; ⊜ 📋; Ⓢ Chongwenmen) Biànyífāng claims to be the original Peking duck restaurant – it cites a heritage that dates back to the reign of the Qing emperor Xianfeng. The birds here are roasted in the *mènlú* style (in a closed oven, as opposed to a half-open one where the duck hangs to cook) and the meat is nice and tender.

A half bird is ¥108 (trimmings are extra) and the menu also offers duck liver, heart and feet dishes. In fact, just about any part of the duck that is edible is available here. It's nonsmoking throughout and rather less touristy than the other duck options in the area.

ENTERTAINMENT

RED THEATRE ACROBATICS

Map p292 (红剧场; Hóng Jùchǎng; ☎6714 2473; 44 Xingfu Dajie, 幸福大街44号; tickets ¥200-680; ⊙performances 5.15pm & 7.30pm; Ⓢ Tiantandongmen) The daily show here is *The Legend of Kung Fu,* which follows one boy's journey to becoming a warrior monk. Slick, high-energy fight scenes are interspersed with more soulful dance sequences, as well as plenty of 'how do they do that' balancing on spears and other body-defying acts. To find the theatre, look for the all-red exterior set back from the road.

SHOPPING

HÓNGQIÁO (PEARL) MARKET MARKET

Map p292 (红桥市场; Hóngqiáo Shìchǎng; ☎6711 7429; 36 Hongqiao Lu, 红桥路36号; ⊙9.30am-7pm; Ⓢ Tiantandongmen) Besides a cosmos of clutter (shoes, clothing, cosmetics, electronics and bags), Hóngqiáo is home to more pearls than the South Sea. The range is huge (freshwater, seawater, white and black) and prices vary incredibly depending on quality. Behind the market is **Toys City** (红桥天乐玩具市场; Hóngqiáo Tiānlè Wánjù Shìchǎng; Map p292; ⊙8.30am-7pm), stuffed to the gills with soft toys, cars, model kits, Wii sets, X Boxes and computer games.

The 3rd floor has the cheaper pearls, mostly sourced from Zhèjiāng province, as well as other jewellery and jade. The better-quality, pricier pearls can be found on the far more hushed 4th and 5th floors, where there's a roof terrace that offers an excellent overview of the Temple of Heaven. Prices are generally high, while the vendors, who all speak some English, are canny bargainers.

SPORTS & ACTIVITIES

NTSC TENNIS CLUB TENNIS

Map p292 (国家体育总局训练局网球俱乐部; Guójiā Tǐyù Zǒngjú Xùnliànjú Wǎngqiú Jùlèbù; ☎8718 3401; 50 Tiantan Donglu, 天坛东路50号; nonmembers per hour ¥300; ⊙9am-9pm; Ⓢ Tiantandongmen) Tennis *(wǎng qiú)* is an increasingly popular sport in Běijīng, so phone in advance to book one of the courts here.

Běihǎi Park & Xīchéng North

For more detail of this area see Map p294.

Neighbourhood Top Five

❶ Once reserved for emperors only, **Běihǎi Park** (p118) is one of the capital's most striking imperial parks. Dominated by its namesake lake, dotted with temples and with a fascinating, 1000-year-long history, it's one of the city's premier spots to escape the urban sprawl.

❷ Sedate during the day, raucous at night, the **Hòuhǎi Lakes** (p120) are one of Běijīng's great playgrounds. They're also surrounded by some of the city's oldest and best-preserved *hútòng* (alleyways).

❸ Spend a morning at the impressive **Capital Museum** (p124) to understand the evolution of this great city.

❹ Enjoy a show at the **National Centre for the Performing Arts** (p128), or just stare open-mouthed at the building itself.

❺ Shop like a Beijinger at **77th Street** (p129), Xīdān's unique underground mall.

Explore Běihǎi Park & Xīchéng North

Most of the Imperial City was in this part of Xīchéng (西城; literally 'West City'), lending it a regal grandeur that survives to this day. Less visited than Dōngchéng to the east, but equally impregnated with ancient temples and charming *hútòng* (narrow alleyways), it's one of the most worthwhile neighbourhoods to visit in all Běijīng.

Any tour has to start at the lakes that dominate the eastern part of the district. Take in Běihǎi Park first, perhaps spending an hour or more floating around its lake, before striking out through the park's north gate to take in the sights and *hútòng* scattered around Qiánhǎi, Hòuhǎi and Xīhǎi Lakes, collectively known as either 'Shíchàhǎi' or more commonly just 'Hòuhǎi'. Once night falls, eat at one of the many restaurants close to the lakes and then join the crowds promenading around them, stopping in for a drink at the many bars and cafes that line their shores.

A second day here is more or less an imperative. Head to Fuchengmennei Dajie, a street lined with lesser-known temples; the most impressive being Miàoyīng Temple White Dagoba. Then dive into the *hútòng* behind them. The district's best temple, though, is southwest of here: the Taoist White Cloud Temple, which can be combined with a visit to nearby Capital Museum, one of Běijīng's finest museums. Come evening, there's a wealth of venues in which to catch everything from jazz to classical music and Peking opera.

Local Life

➡ **Fly a Kite** Běihǎi Park is prime kite-flying territory. Visit Three Stone Kite Shop (p129) to kit yourself out.

➡ **Hútòng** The alleyways and lanes here are far less commercial and are a great introduction to Běijīng's tremendous street life. The *hútòng* by Rùndélì Food Market (p127) are fascinating, as are those behind Miàoyīng Temple White Dagoba (p120).

➡ **Ice Skating** When winter freezes the Hòuhǎi Lakes, join the Beijingers and strap on some skates.

Getting There & Away

➡ **Subway** Beihai North (Line 6) and Shichahai (Line 8) subways stations best serve Běihǎi Park and the Hóuhǎi Lakes, although you can also reach them from Line 2 (which circles the district) and Line 4 (which runs north–south). Line 1 cuts across the south of this district.

➡ **Bus** Bus 1 runs along Xichang'an Jie, Fuxingmennei Dajie and Fuxingmenwai Dajie, taking you to Capital Museum. Bus 22 takes you from Tiān'ānmén West to Xīdān and then north to Xīnjiēkou.

Lonely Planet's Top Tip

Come nightfall, the Hòuhǎi Lakes become a madhouse of milling crowds and bar touts trying to entice you into their overpriced bars. If you want to experience a night out drinking, Chinese style: dive in. If you'd rather avoid the wailing karaoke, slip down the *hútòng* that run off the lakeshore, where you'll find quieter bars and cafes. The lanes on the southwest side of Silver Ingot Bridge are a good place to start.

Best Places to Eat

➡ Royal Icehouse (p127)

➡ Kǎo Ròu Jì (p127)

➡ Le Petit Saigon (p127)

For reviews, see p126.

Best Places for a Drink

➡ East Shore Jazz Café (p128)

➡ NBeer Pub (p128)

➡ Golden Sail Water Sports Club (p126)

➡ Tang Ren Teahouse (p128)

For reviews, see p128.

Best Places for People-Watching

➡ Běihǎi Park (p118)

➡ Hòuhǎi Exercise Park (p125)

➡ Hòuhǎi Park (p125)

For reviews, see p120.

TOP SIGHT
BĚIHǍI PARK

With an extraordinary history as the former palace of the great Mongol emperor Kublai Khan, and back garden for the subsequent Yuan dynasty emperors, Běihǎi Park (北海公园; Běihǎi Gōngyuán) is the principal oasis for Beijingers in this part of town. With the tranquil lake of Běhǎi (literally, 'North Sea') at its centre and temples, pavilions and spirit walls scattered around it, the park offers visitors a rare chance in Běijīng to combine sightseeing with fun, whether it's mucking around in a boat, having a picnic or just watching the dancing, taichi and the parade of humanity that passes through.

You can enter or leave the park by its **South Gate** on Wenjin Jie, its **North Gate** on Di'anmen Xidajie or its **East Gate**, hidden among the *hútòng* between this park and Jǐngshān Park. There's also a rarely used **West Gate** (also on Wenjin Jie), which you can use if you wish to walk a complete circuit of the lake – you'll have to leave the park (hang on to your ticket) then re-enter again through the South Gate.

If your legs are feeling weary, electric carts (¥10 per ride) can whizz you between sights. You can also catch a small ferry (¥10) across the lake.

DON'T MISS

- Yǒngān Temple
- Xītiān Fànjìng

PRACTICALITIES

- Map p294
- ☎6403 1102
- admission high/low season ¥10/5, through ticket high/low season ¥20/15
- park 6am-9pm, sights until 5pm
- Xisi or Nanluogu Xiang

Jade Islet

Made out of the heaped earth scooped out to create Běihǎi Lake itself, which some attribute to Kublai Khan, and dominated by the 36m-high **White Dagoba**, which was originally constructed in 1651 for a visit by the Dalai Lama and then rebuilt in 1741 after being destroyed in an earthquake, Jade Islet sits in the southeastern corner of the lake. You can reach it by a land bridge close to the South Gate and East Gate, or catch a boat (¥10) from the northwestern shore if you come in by the North Gate. You can also hire pedalos (¥80 per hour, ¥200 deposit) from here as well.

Yǒngān Temple

The principal site on **Jade Islet** is the impressive **Yǒngān Temple** (永安寺; Yǒngān Sì; Map p294; admission included in the through ticket), meaning Temple of Eternal Peace. Enter from the south, through the Hall of the Heavenly Kings (Tiānwáng Diàn), past the Drum and Bell Towers to the **Hall of the Wheel of the Law** (Fǎlún Diàn), with its central effigy of Sakyamuni and flanked by Bodhisattvas and 18 *luóhàn* (Buddhists, especially monks, who achieved enlightenment and passed to nirvana at death). At the rear of the temple you will find a bamboo grove and quite a steep flight of steps up through a decorative archway, which is emblazoned with the characters 'Lóng Guāng' (龙光) on one side and 'Zǐzhào' (紫照) on the other side. Head up more steps to the **Zhèngjué Hall** (Zhèngjué Diàn), which contains a statue of Milefo and Weituo.

Pǔ'ān Hall (Pǔ'ān Diàn) the next hall, houses a statue of Tsongkhapa, who was the founder of the Yellow Hat sect of Tibetan Buddhism, flanked by statues of the fifth Dalai Lama and the Panchen Lama. Eight golden effigies on either flank include tantric statues and the goddess Heinümu, adorned with a necklace of skulls. The final flight of steep steps brings you to the White Dagoba.

Xītiān Fànjìng

Located on the lake's northern shore, **Xītiān Fánjìng** (西天梵境; Western Paradise; Map p294) is one of the most interesting temples in Běijīng (admission is included in the through ticket). The first hall, the Hall of the Heavenly Kings, takes you past Milefo, Weituo and the four Heavenly Kings.

The **Dàcízhēnrú Hall** (Dàcízhēnrú Diàn) dates back to the Ming dynasty and contains three huge statues of Sakyamuni, the Amithaba Buddha and Yaoshi Fo (Medicine Buddha). Sadly, the golden statue of Guanyin at the rear is not accessible. The hall is supported by huge wooden pillars (which are called *nánmù*), and you can still make out where the original stone pillars once existed. At the very rear of the temple are a glazed pavilion and a huge hall that are both unfortunately out of bounds.

The nearby **Nine Dragon Screen** (Jiǔlóng Bì; Map p294; admission included in the through ticket), a 5m-high and 27m-long spirit wall, is a glimmering stretch of coloured glazed tiles.

THE PALACE OF THE GREAT KHAN

Kublai Khan, the grandson of the even more dominant Genghis Khan, conquered China and established the Yuan dynasty in 1271. He chose what is now Běihǎi Park as the site of his palace. All that remains of his former home is a large jar made of green jade dating from 1265 in the **Round City** (团城; Tuán Chéng) near the park's southern entrance. Sadly, the Round City, which also houses the **Chéngguāng Hall** (Chéngguāng Diàn), where a white jade statue of Sakyamuni from Myanmar (Burma) can be found, had been closed at the time of research since 2012, with no word on when it might re-open. The park in general, though, has been associated with the centre of power of China since the 10th century, when it was laid out as an imperial garden. Even now, it remains as close to the nerve centre of the country as you are likely to get.

Directly south of the park is Zhōngnánhǎi, the closely guarded lakeside compound where China's president and senior Chinese Communist Party (CCP) officials reside in cosy proximity to each other.

SIGHTS

BĚIHǍI PARK — PARK

See p118.

HÒUHǍI LAKES — LAKES

Map p294 (后海; Hòuhǎi; Ⓢ Shichahai, Nanluogu Xiang, Jishuitan) FREE Also known as Shíchàhǎi (什刹海) but mostly just referred to collectively as 'Hòuhǎi', the Hòuhǎi Lakes are compromised of three lakes: Qiánhǎi (Front Lake), Hòuhǎi (Back Lake) and Xīhǎi (West Lake). Together they are one of the capital's favourite outdoor spots, heaving with locals and out-of-towners in the summer especially, and providing great people-spotting action.

During the day, senior citizens meander along, use the exercise machines scattered along the lakeshore, fish, fly kites or just sit and chew the fat. At night, the area turns into one of the more popular nightlife areas, as the restaurants, bars and cafes that surround the lakes spring into life. This is a night out, Chinese style, so be prepared for neon lights galore, and plenty of karaoke being blasted out onto the surrounding lanes. Meanwhile, as the midday sun disappears, the lakes become a mass of pedalos circling round and round.

It's great fun, and it's easy enough to escape the crowds (Silver Ingot Bridge is a major bottleneck) by exploring the many *hútòng* that run both east and west of the lakes, or to just venture further northwest towards the quieter Xīhǎi Lake. It's particularly good to cycle around and numerous places by the lakeshores hire out bikes by the hour (¥10 per hour, ¥200 deposit). There are many spots to rent pedalos too (¥80 per hour, ¥300 deposit), if you want to take to the water. Some locals swim in the lakes, even in midwinter!

The lakes look majestic in winter, when they become the best place in Běijīng to ice skate (usually for around six weeks in January and February). Qiánhǎi Lake is most popular, although some people skate on Hòuhǎi Lake too; local vendors set themselves up with all the gear you need. You have to pay to enter the ice-skating area (weekday/weekend & evenings ¥15/¥20). If you want to rent ice skates and the like, you also have to buy a rental swipe card from kiosks by the entrance gates. The card will have a ¥200 deposit on it. You then get back any money you don't use. Skates (¥20 per day), chair sleds (¥20 per day), ice bikes ¥40 per hour) and even ice bumper cars (¥20 per 10 minutes) can all be rented. There is also a giant ice slide (¥5 per go).

PRINCE GONG'S RESIDENCE — HISTORIC BUILDING

Map p294 (恭王府; Gōngwáng Fǔ; ☎8328 8149; 14 Liuyin Jie; admission ¥40, tours incl short opera show & tea ceremony ¥70; ⏲7.30am-4.30pm Mar-Oct, 8am-4pm Nov-Mar; Ⓢ Ping'anli) Reputed to be the model for the mansion in Cáo Xuěqín's 18th-century classic *Dream of the Red Mansions*, the residence is one of Běijīng's largest private residential compounds. It remains one of the capital's more attractive retreats, decorated with rockeries, plants, pools, pavilions and elaborately carved gateways, although it can get crowded with tour groups.

SONG QINGLING FORMER RESIDENCE — MUSEUM

Map p294 (宋庆龄故居; Sòng Qìnglíng Gùjū; ☎6402 3195; 46 Beiheyan Lu; admission ¥20; ⏲9am-5pm; Ⓢ Jishuitan) Madam Song is lovingly venerated by the Chinese as the wife of Sun Yatsen, founder of the Republic of China. Set in a lovely garden, her house, the former home of the father of Puyi, is rather dormant, displaying personal items, pictures, clothing and books. But the building to the side houses an exhibition on Madam Song's fascinating life, including the car given to her by Stalin, which comes with good English captions.

MEI LANFANG FORMER RESIDENCE — MUSEUM

Map p294 (梅兰芳纪念馆; Méi Lánfāng Jìniàn Guǎn; ☎8322 3598; 9 Huguosi Jie; admission ¥10; ⏲9am-4pm Tue-Sun; Ⓢ Ping'anli) Place of pilgrimage for Peking opera aficionados, this former *sìhéyuàn* (traditional courtyard house) of actor Mei Lanfang (1894–1961) is on the corner of a *hútòng* that's named after the nearby remains of Hùguó Temple (护国寺; Hùguó Sì; only one hall remains, and it's not open to the public).

Peking opera was popularised in the West by Mei Lanfang, who played *dàn* (female roles) and is said to have influenced Charlie Chaplin. His former residence has been preserved as a museum, replete with costumes, furniture, opera programs and video presentations of his opera performances.

MIÀOYĪNG TEMPLE WHITE DAGOBA — BUDDHIST TEMPLE

Map p294 (妙应寺白塔; Miàoyīng Sì Báitǎ; ☎6616 0211; 171 Fuchengmennei Dajie; admission ¥20;

LOCAL KNOWLEDGE

TAICHI TIPS

Characterised by its lithe and graceful movements, *tàijíquán* (literally 'Fist of the Supreme Ultimate'), also known as taichi, is an ancient Chinese physical discipline practised by legions of Chinese throughout the land.

Considerable confusion exists about taichi – is it a martial art, a form of meditation, a qì gōng (exercise that helps channel *qì*, or energy) style or an exercise? In fact, taichi can be each and all of these, depending on what you seek from the art and how deep you dig into its mysteries.

In terms of health benefits, taichi strengthens the leg muscles, exercises the joints, gives the cardiovascular system a good workout and promotes flexibility. It also relaxes the body, dissolving stress, loosening the joints and helping to circulate *qì*.

As a system of meditation, taichi leaves practitioners feeling both centred and focused. Taichi introduces you to Taoist meditation techniques, as the art is closely allied to the philosophy of Taoism. And if you're adept at taichi, it is far easier to learn other martial arts, as you'll have learned a way of moving that is common to all of the fighting arts.

Useful Pointers

- When executing a movement, bodily motion and power are directed by the waist before moving to the hands (observe a skilled practitioner and see how the motion reaches the hands last). The hands never lead the movement.
- When performing a form (as the moving sets are called), keep your head level, neither rising nor dipping.
- Practise taichi as if suspended by an invisible thread from a point at the top of your head.
- Don't lean forward or back and keep your torso vertical.
- Relax your shoulders and let your weight sink downwards.

Where to Learn

Mílún Kungfu School (p78)

Jīnghuá Wǔshù Association (p156)

The Hutong (p92)

9am-5pm Tue-Sun; S Fuchengmen, then bus 13, 101, 102 or 103 to Baita Si) Originally built in 1271, the Miàoyīng Temple slumbers beneath its huge, distinctive, chalk-white Yuan-dynasty pagoda, which towers over the surrounding *hútòng*. It was, when it was built, the tallest structure in Dàdū (the Yuan-dynasty name for Běijīng), and even today it is the tallest Tibetan-style pagoda in China.

The temple has been under extensive renovation for some years, and was still closed at the time of research, but previous highlights of a visit here included the diverse collection of Buddhist statuary: the Hall of the Great Enlightened One (大觉宝殿; Dàjué Bǎodiàn), for example, glittered splendidly with hundreds of Tibetan Buddhist effigies. After you finish here, exit the temple and wander the tangle of local alleyways for street-market action and earthy shades of *hútòng* life.

TEMPLE OF ANCIENT MONARCHS TAOIST TEMPLE

Map p294 (历代帝王庙 Lìdài Dìwáng Miào; 131 Fuchengmennei Dajie, 阜成门内大街131号; admisssion ¥20) Constructed in 1530 as a twin of a temple built in Nánjīng in the 14th century, this rarely visited ancestral temple was reopened in 2004 after extensive renovations. It had spent the past 80-odd years housing various locals schools, having been abandoned after the fall of the Qing Dynasty.

The scale of the complex is vast – the main hall is the second largest of its kind in Běijīng (after the Forbidden City's Hall of Supreme Harmony) – and although the atmosphere is somewhat lifeless, the architecture is impressive enough to warrant a quick side trip from your visit to nearby Miàoyīng Temple. Look out for the huge marble stele turtles and the glazed furnaces, used to burn paper and silk offerings.

1

MAREMAGNUM / GETTY IMAGES ©

2

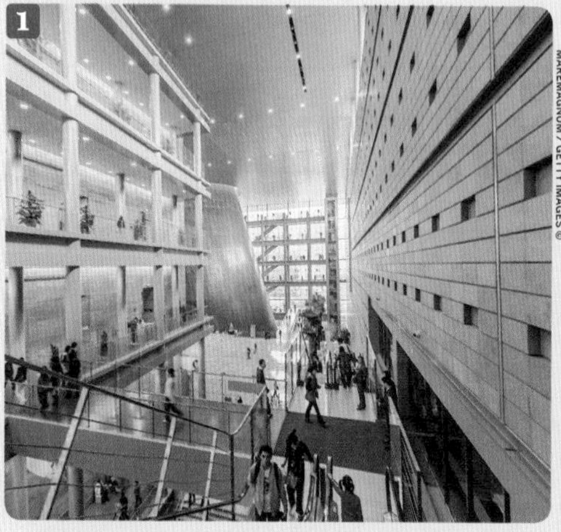

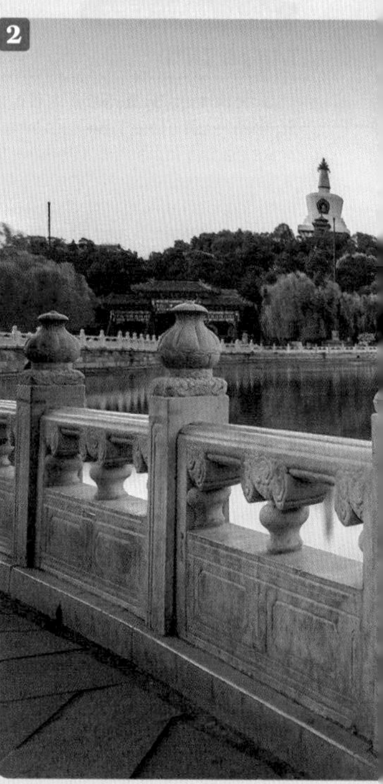

1. Capital Museum (p124)
The museum's bold good looks frame some wonderful exhibits (architect Cui Kai).

2. Běihǎi Park (p118)
Bridge leading over serene Běihǎi Lake to Jade Islet

3. White Cloud Temple (p124)
Once the Taoist centre of northern China, this is a huge, lively complex of shrines and courtyards.

4. National Centre for the Performing Arts (p124)
Known as the 'Egg', the NCPA is designed to embody China's global aspirations (architect Paul Andreu).

4

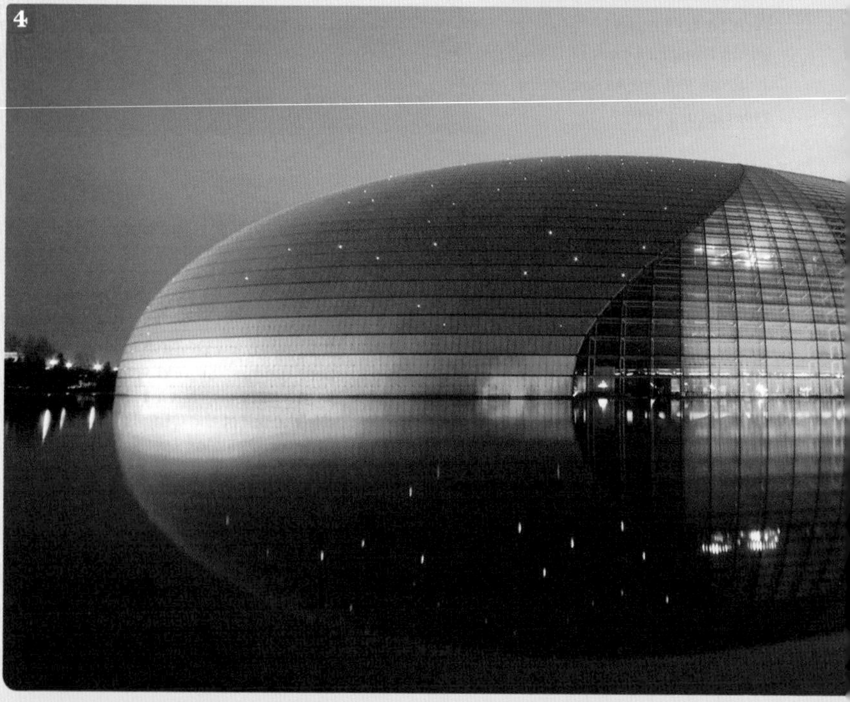

ZHAOLINGHE / GETTY IMAGES ©

ARCHITECT: PAUL ANDREU / CHRISTIAN KOBER / GETTY IMAGES ©

CHRISTIAN KOBER / GETTY IMAGES ©

GUǍNGJÌ TEMPLE BUDDHIST TEMPLE

Map p294 (广济寺; Guǎngjì Sì; 25 Fuchengmennei Dajie, 阜城门内大街25号) FREE Now the HQ of the Buddhist Association of China, this small, informal temple is a Ming rebuild of the original Jin-dynasty temple, and is often busy with worshippers.

LU XUN MUSEUM MUSEUM

Map p294 (鲁迅博物馆; Lǔ Xùn Bówùguǎn; ☎6616 4080; 19 Gongmenkou Ertiao; ⊙9am-4pm Tue-Sun; Ⓢ Fuchengmen) FREE Lu Xun (1881–1936) is regarded as the father of modern Chinese literature. Born in Shàoxīng in Zhèjiāng province and buried in Shànghǎi, he lived in Běijīng for over a decade. As a writer, Lu Xun, who first trained in medicine, articulated a deep yearning for reform by mercilessly exposing the foibles of the Chinese character in such tales as *Medicine* and *Diary of a Madman*. The modern two-storey museum here depicts his life in great detail.

The exhibits are well presented and come with English captions. Don't miss visiting Lu Xun's small former courtyard home, off to the left as you face the museum. The room round the back, overlooking the yard, was his study. Just by the entrance to his home is a small bookshop where you can buy English translations of some of his works (around ¥50 per book).

CAPITAL MUSEUM MUSEUM

(首都博物馆; Shǒudū Bówùguǎn; ☎6339 3339; www.capitalmuseum.org.cn; 16 Fuxingmenwai Dajie; ⊙9am-5pm Tue-Sun; Ⓢ Muxidi) FREE Behind the riveting good looks of the Capital Museum are some first-rate galleries, including a mesmerising collection of ancient Buddhist statues and a lavish exhibition of Chinese porcelain. There is also an interesting chronological history of Běijīng, an exhibition that is dedicated to cultural relics of Peking opera, a fascinating Běijīng Folk Customs exhibition, and displays of ancient bronzes, jade, calligraphy and paintings.

Bring your passport for free entry. The small teahouse on the 2nd floor sells tea sets (from ¥500) as well as serving tea (from ¥15 per cup).

Come out of Exit C1 of Muxidi subway station (Line 1), and you'll soon see the museum on your right (200m).

WHITE CLOUD TEMPLE TAOIST TEMPLE

(白云观; Báiyún Guàn; ☎6346 3887; 9 Baiyunguan Jie; admission ¥10; ⊙8.30am-4.30pm; Ⓢ Muxidi) White Cloud Temple, once the Taoist centre of northern China, was founded in AD 739, although most of the temple halls date from the Qing dynasty. It's a lively, huge and fascinating complex of shrines and courtyards, tended by Taoist monks with their hair gathered into topknots.

Near the temple entrance, worshippers rub a polished stone carving for good fortune. The halls at the temple, centre of operations for the Taoist Quanzhen School and abode of the China Taoist Association, are dedicated to a host of Taoist officials and marshals. The Hall of the Jade Emperor celebrates this most famous of Taoist deities, while Taoist housewives cluster earnestly at the Hall to the God of Wealth to divine their financial future. Depictions of the Taoist Hell festoon the walls of the Shrine Hall for the Saviour Worthy.

Drop by White Cloud Temple during the Spring Festival (Lunar New Year) and you will be rewarded with the spectacle of a magnificent temple fair *(miàohuì)*.

The temple is about a 1km-walk from Muxidi subway station (Line 1). Come out of Exit C1, walk past the Capital Museum, then turn right down Baiyun Lu. After crossing the canal, take the second left, down Baiyunguan Jie, and the temple will be on your left.

NATIONAL CENTRE FOR THE PERFORMING ARTS (NCPA) CONCERT HALL

Map p294 (国家大剧院; Guójiā Dàjùyuàn; ☎6655 0000; www.chncpa.org/ens; admission ¥30, concert tickets ¥100-400; ⊙9am-5pm Tue-Sun; Ⓢ Tian'anmen West) Critics have compared it to an egg (although it looks more like a massive mercury bead), while modernists love it to bits. The NCPA, also known as the National Grand Theatre, is a surreal location in which to catch a show.

Examine the bulbous interior, including the titanic steel ribbing of interior bolsters (each of the 148 bolsters weighs 8 tonnes), and tour the three halls. See the website for details on concerts.

GREAT HALL OF THE PEOPLE PARLIAMENT

Map p294 (人民大会堂; Rénmín Dàhuìtáng; admission ¥30, bag deposit ¥2-5; ⊙8.30am-3pm (times vary); Ⓢ Tian'anmen West) On the western side of Tiān'ānmén Sq, on a site previously occupied by Taichang Temple, the Jinyiwei (Ming-dynasty secret service) and the Ministry of Justice, the Great Hall of the People is the venue of the legislature, the National People's Congress (NPC). The 1959

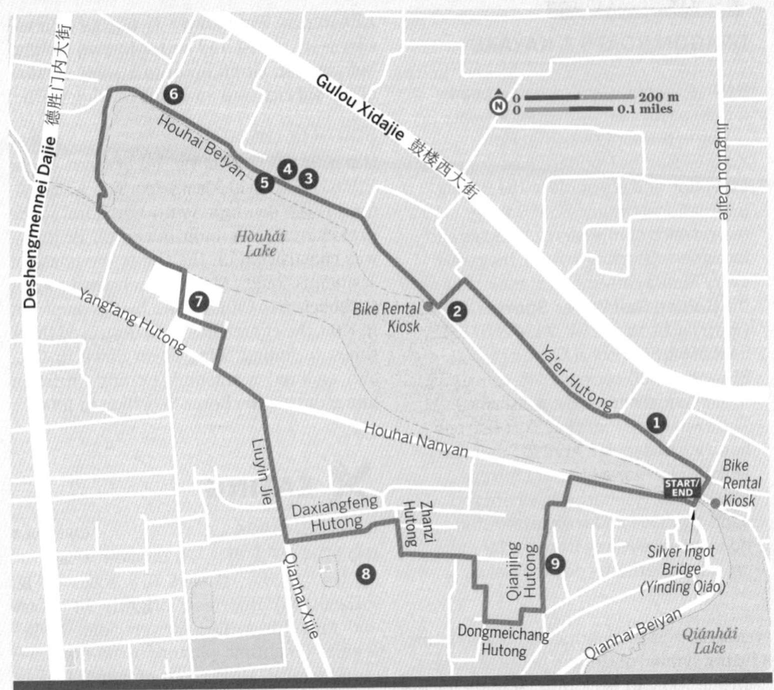

Neighbourhood Bike Tour
Hòuhǎi Lakes Bike Ride

START YÍNDÌNG QIÁO (SILVER INGOT BRIDGE)
END YÍNDÌNG QIÁO (SILVER INGOT BRIDGE)
LENGTH 3KM; ONE HOUR

There's a bike rental place beside Silver Ingot Bridge. You could easily walk this too.

Going north from the bridge, turn left down Ya'er Hutong, where you'll soon reach the serene Buddhist 1 **Guǎnghuā Temple**, dating from the far-off Yuan Dynasty, and open to the public. As the *hútòng* bears sharp right, turn left (at No 46) down a narrow alley, which will take you to the lakeside, past 2 **Dàzànglónghuá Temple** (on your left), built in 1719 and now a kindergarten.

Turn right at the lake and push on past 3 **Prince Zaifeng's former stables** (at No 43) and 4 **Prince Chun's Mansion** (at No 44), where China's last emperor, Puyi, was born. You may pass some locals on your left playing table tennis and swimming in the lake at 5 **Hòuhǎi Exercise Park** before you reach 6 **Song Qingliang's Former Residence**, now a museum.

Follow the lake anticlockwise until you reach a small public square called 7 **Hòuhǎi Park**, a popular spot for early morning and evening formation dancing. Go up the access ramp at the far right-hand corner of the square, then turn left into Yangfang Hutong, then right into Liuyin Jie and left into Daxiangfeng Hutong, following the huge grey-brick 8 **back wall of Prince Gong's Mansion**.

Now the wiggly-*hútòng* fun begins: turn right (still following the big wall) into Zhanzi Hutong, bear left, but then go straight on as the *hútòng* bears right, and turn right at the very end into the narrowest of alleys. Follow this alley before taking the first left (Dongmeichang Hutong). Bear left, then right, then turn left at the *hútòng* crossroads onto Qianjing Hutong. The small, unmarked courtyard at No 8, on your right, was the 9 **former residence of Emperor Puyi's sister**, Yunxin. Puyi lived here briefly in 1959.

Follow Qianjing Hutong back to the lakeside, where you can turn right towards Silver Ingot Bridge.

LOCAL KNOWLEDGE

DRAGON BOATS & KAYAKS

Běijīng's general lack of water means it's not associated with dragon boat racing in the same way that Hong Kong is. But the Hòuhǎi Lakes are an exception and are home to the Běijīng International Dragon Boat Racing team, which comprises both locals and foreigners. Starting in April, they train every Sunday afternoon at their base at the **Golden Sail Water Sports Club** (金饭, Jīnfān; Map p294; ☎134 2607 6511, 6401 2664; 81A Houhai Xiyan, 后海西沿81A号; beer ¥30, cocktails ¥45, coffee ¥35; ⏲1pm-1am, summer only; Ⓢ Jishuitan). The owner also rents kayaks (¥80 per hour, ¥200 deposit, April to Setember) and the club has a pleasant terrace overlooking Hòuhǎi Lake, where you can sit outside and enjoy a late afternoon beer well away from the far more crowded southern end of the lakes.

architecture is monolithic and intimidating, a fitting symbol of China's political powers.

Inside you can peek into 29 of its lifeless rooms named after the provinces of the Chinese universe. Also here is the banquet room where US president Richard Nixon dined in 1972, and the 10,000-seat auditorium with the familiar red star embedded in a galaxy of ceiling lights. The ticket office is down the south side of the building. Bags must be checked in but cameras are admitted.

CHINA NUMISMATIC MUSEUM — MUSEUM

Map p294 (中国钱币博物馆; Zhōngguó Qiánbì Bówùguǎn; ☎6608 4178; 17 Xijiaomin Xiang; admission ¥10; ⏲9am-4pm Tue-Sun, closed when NPC in session; Ⓢ Tian'anmen West) This intriguing three-floor museum follows the technology of money production in China from the spade-shaped coins of the Spring and Autumn period to modern coinage and paper currency. You'll find chunky gold-nugget coins, coins inscribed with beautiful Chinese characters, 'money necklaces' containing strings of small bronze knives, and all five sets of the modern-day rénmínbì, only two of which are still in circulation.

XĪBIÀNMÉN WATCHTOWER — WATCHTOWER

Map p294 (西便门角楼; Xībiànmén Jiǎolóu; Ⓢ Changchunjie) FREE The counterpart of the Southeast Corner Watchtower, the Xībiànmén Watchtower is not as impressive as its robust and better-known sibling, but you can climb up onto a short section of the old city wall amid the roaring traffic.

SOUTH CATHEDRAL — CHURCH

Map p294 (南堂; Nántáng; 141 Qianmen Xidajie; ⏲Mass in English 10.30am & 3pm Sun; Ⓢ Xuanwumen) FREE Běijīng's South Cathedral – the first church to be built in central Běijīng – was constructed on the site of the house of Jesuit missionary Matteo Ricci, who brought Catholicism to China. Since being completed in 1703, the church has been destroyed three times, including being burnt down in 1775, and endured a trashing by anti-Christian forces during the Boxer Rebellion in 1900.

EATING

GUǍNSHÌ CHÌBĀ — BARBECUE $

Map p294 (管氏翅吧; 20 Di'anmen Xidajie; 地安门西大街20号; skewers ¥2-8, soups ¥10-12; ⏲11am-11pm) Informal, brightly lit, noisy and fun, this grilled-skewers joint makes a great lunchtime pitstop, or no-nonsense evening meal, after a tour of Běihǎi Park or the Hóuhǎi Lakes.

The house speciality is chicken wings (鸡翅; *jī chì*), which are cooked using a secret recipe. The lamb skewers (羊肉串; *yángròuchuàn*) are also delicious and the lightly grilled baked-bread slices (馒头片; *mántou piàn*) are perfect for dipping into one of the soups; the noodle-drop soup (疙瘩汤; *gēda tāng*) is our favourite, and is enough for four people to share. No English menu. Instead you'll have to fill in the Chinese tick-box menu. Other grilled skewers to look for include: 烤尖椒 (*kǎo jiānjiāo;* green chilli peppers), 烤茄子 (*kǎo qiézi;* aubergine) and 烤大蒜 (*kǎo dàsuàn;* garlic). Don't forget to tick what spice level you want: 不辣 (*bù là;* low spice) or 微辣 (*wēi là;* medium spice).

WANG PANG ZI DONKEY BURGER — HEBEI $

Map p294 (王胖子驴肉火烧; Wáng Pàngzi Lǘròu Huǒshāo; 80 Gulou Xidajie; 鼓楼西大街80号; pastry pockets ¥9, soups ¥2-10; ⏲24hr) Lauded by many as the best donkey-meat place in town, this small 24-hour restaurant specialises in flaky pastry pockets, stuffed with lightly spiced shreds of donkey meat, known in Chinese as 驴肉火烧 (*lǘròu huǒshāo;* pronounced 'loo row hwore shaow').

Two per person, plus a soup, is plenty for lunch. Soups include 西红柿鸡蛋汤 (*xīhóngshì jīdàn tāng;* egg and tomato), 紫菜鸡蛋汤 (*zǐcài jīdàn tāng;* egg and seaweed), 小米粥 (*xiǎomǐ zhōu;* millet porridge) and, of course, 驴肉汤 (*lǘròu tāng;* donkey-meat soup). English sign, but no English menu.

LǏJÌ FĒNGWÈI MĚISHÍ CĀNTĪNG CHINESE MUSLIM $

Map p294 (李记风味美食餐厅; Ya'er Hutong; 鸦儿胡同 (烟袋斜街西口); mains ¥20-40, snacks ¥1-10; ⏰breakfast dumplings 5am-9am, main restaurant 10am-11pm) Known simply as Lǐjì (pronounced 'lee jee'), this popular place has two outlets close to each other on Ya'er Hutong, both of which serve great-value Chinese Muslim dishes and snacks.

The first one you come to, if walking from Silver Ingot Bridge, is the main sit-down restaurant (look for the long, green-and-yellow sign). It has an English menu, including grilled skewers, lamb dishes and noodles, and is basic but clean. Further on is a smaller, older branch, which specialises in boiled tripe (爆肚; *bàodǔ*) and has an adjacent takeaway-dumplings stall, which is very popular at breakfast time: try the beef and onion dumplings (牛肉大葱包子; *niúròu dàcōng bāozi;* ¥2 each). It also roasts very good sesame-seed buns (烧饼; *shāobing;* ¥1 each), which you can have filled with lamb (烧饼夹肉; *shāobing jiā ròu;* ¥7 each).

RÙNDÉLÌ FOOD MARKET MARKET $

Map p294 (润得立菜市场; Rùndélì Càishìchǎng; 4 Sihuan Hutong, off Deshengmennei Dajie; 德胜门内大街四环胡同; ⏰7am-7pm) Also known as Sìhuán Market (四环市场; Sìhuán Shìchǎng), this huge open-air food market is filled with fresh fruit and snacks – perfect for a pedal-boat picnic on the Hòuhǎi Lakes – as well as fish, frogs, crabs and lobsters. You can also buy Chinese teas here. Prices for things such as fruit tend to be marked per *jīn* (500g).

★ROYAL ICEHOUSE SHANDONG $$

Map p294 (皇家冰窖小院; Huángjiā Bīngjiào Xiǎoyuàn; ☎6401 1358; 5 Gongjian Wuxiang, Gongjian Hutong; 恭俭胡同5巷5号; mains ¥30-60; ⏰11.30am-2pm & 5.30-9.30pm; 📖) Tucked away in the *hútòng* running alongside the east wall of Běihǎi Park, this intriguing restaurant is located inside one of the city's former royal ice houses – where, before the days of refrigeration, massive blocks of ice were stored for use in the imperial court during summer.

You can walk down into the underground ice cellars (which now keep the wine cool); look for the red arched door.

The main restaurant is decked out in old-Běijīng paraphernalia; look for the home-made *báijiǔ* (sorghum liquor) hanging in pig's bladders. The food is imperial cuisine, but with a heavy Shāndōng influence (the original chef was from Shāndōng province), so there is some crossover in dishes. All are very well done, though. The menu is in English. Specialities include: sauteed tofu with ham and pea, braised chicken in chilli sauce, and a dish called 'the fifth pot', which is a pork and vegetable stew. To find the restaurant, walk south down Gongjian Hutong from Di'anmen Xidajie, turn right into 5 Gongjian Wuxiang and you'll see it straight ahead of you.

LE PETIT SAIGON FRENCH, VIETNAMESE $$

Map p294 (西贡在巴黎; Xīgòng Zài Bālí; ☎6401 8465; 141 Jiugulou Dajie, 旧鼓楼大街141号; mains ¥40-80; ⏰10.30am-11pm; 📶📖; Ⓢ Shichahai) The menu at this stylish bistro – with a nice roof terrace in summer – is a mix of classic Vietnamese – *pho* (Vietnamese soup), lemon chicken, shrimps in tamarind sauce – and French – beef bourguignon and foie gras. The desserts are especially good. The decor and decent wine list are decidedly Gallic, making it popular with French expats and anyone in search of a lovingly prepared cup of coffee, whether it's the European or Vietnamese variety.

KǍO RÒU JÌ CHINESE MUSLIM $$

Map p294 (烤肉季; Qianhai Dongyan; 前海东沿银锭桥; mains ¥40-80; ⏰1st fl 11am-10pm, 2nd fl 11am-2pm & 5-8.30pm; 📖) There's good-value roast duck (¥118), and a range of China-wide dishes, but it's the mutton that everyone comes for – and the lake views from the 2nd floor.

This place has been around for years (it featured in our very first edition of Lonely Planet *China*, in 1984), and its choice location, overlooking Qiánhǎi Lake, makes it as popular as ever. It's pricier than it should be, but the atmosphere is fun, and the English menu with photos makes ordering easy. Bag a table by the window on the 2nd floor (only open until 8.30pm), and order the roast mutton (¥98), a hot plate from heaven. If you're stuck for cash, fill up on freshly roasted sesame-seed buns (¥2 each), called 'sesame cakes' on the menu.

DRINKING & ENTERTAINMENT

NBEER PUB

BAR

Map p294 (牛啤堂; Niú Pí Táng; Huguo Xintiandi, 85 Huguosi Dajie; 护国寺大街85号护国新天地一层; bottles from ¥25, draft ¥35-50; ⏱3pm-2am) Boasting the biggest fridge of beers in Běijīng, this relative newcomer to the craft-brew scene stocks hundreds of imported real ales and has about a dozen local brews on tap (behind a bar made from Lonely Planet guidebooks!). Ask for the six-glass 'flight' (¥68), so you can taste a selection of locally brewed beers in small glasses, or else just dive into the fridge. Don't miss sampling the enormous, juicy kebabs they do as part of their small food menu.

NBeer is located on the ground floor of a recently built multifloor complex known as Xīntiāndì, at the western end of Huguosi Dajie. You can sometimes sit on the patio out the back in summer and spy Jīngāng Hall (金刚殿; Jīngāng Diàn), originally built in 1284 and the only surviving feature of Hùguó Temple, which this *hútòng* is named after.

HÒUHǍI BAR STRIP

BAR

Map p294 (后海银锭桥; Silver Ingot Bridge; ⏱noon-late) For a peek at how moneyed Beijingers party the night away, take a stroll around the neon-lit bars lining the lakes either side of Silver Ingot Bridge (银锭桥; Yíndìng Qiáo).

Fabulously located, and with roof terraces overlooking the lakes, these potentially peaceful drinking holes are transformed into noisy guitar bars and karaoke joints come evening, and fitted with speakers facing out onto the lakeshore. Inside, punters sing songs, play dice games or just down shots until they have to be carried home. All the bars are similar, so it's best just to walk around and see which one takes your fancy. Drinks prices start high, but can be negotiated. The further you walk away from Silver Ingot Bridge, the quieter the bars become.

TÁNGRÉN TEAHOUSE

TEAHOUSE

Map p294 (唐人茶道听茶轩; Tángrén Chádàoyīn Cháxuān; 15 Qianhai Nanyan, 前海南沿15号; tea per cup from ¥40; ⏱9.30am-1am) Commanding fine views across Qiànhǎi Lake from its rooftop terrace, this cute teahouse is on a quieter stretch of the lake, away from the noisier bars, and is a delightful spot in which to sample Chinese tea.

Prices are high – you even have to pay extra for the spring water your tea is brewed in (from ¥10 per cup) – but the location, service and ambience compensate. The wooden decor is attractive, as is the tea menu – a bamboo scroll – which is translated into English. Teas are listed to the left of the tea type (oolong, green, black etc) they belong to.

AWAIT CAFE

CAFE

Map p294 (那间咖啡; Nàjiā Kāfēi; 59 Xisi Nandajie, 西四南大街59号; coffee ¥20, beer ¥15, mains ¥35-65; ⏱9am-midnight; 📶) One of the loveliest cafes in this part of Běijīng, Await stands next to a church and its main room has the feeling of a small nave, with its high ceilings and cool, calm atmosphere. The coffee is heavenly, the homemade cheesecakes are divine, and they do a range of Western main courses too (pastas, pizzas, salads, soups).

There are three rooms spread over two floors, plus a small 3rd-floor terrace which is open in summer. The only downside is the spotty wi-fi connection.

★EAST SHORE JAZZ CAFÉ

JAZZ

Map p294 (东岸; Dōng'àn; ☎8403 2131; 2nd fl Shichahai Nanyan, 地安门外大街 什刹海南沿2号楼2层, 地安门邮局西侧; beers from ¥30, cocktails from ¥45; ⏱3pm-2am; Ⓢ Shichahai) Cui Jian's saxophonist, whose quartet play here, opened this chilled venue just off Di'anmen Waidajie and next to Qiánhǎi Lake. It's a place to hear the best local jazz bands, with live performances from Wednesdays to Sundays (from 10pm), in a laid-back, comfortable atmosphere. There's a small roof terrace open in summer with a nice view of the lake. No cover charge.

NATIONAL CENTRE FOR THE PERFORMING ARTS

CLASSICAL MUSIC

Map p294 (国家大剧院; Guójiā Dàjùyuàn; ☎6655 0000; www.chncpa.org/ens; 2 Xichang'an Jie, 西长安街2号; tickets ¥80-880; ⏱performances 7.30pm; Ⓢ Tian'anmen West) Sometimes called the National Grand Theatre, this spectacular Paul Andreu–designed dome, known to Beijingers as the 'Alien Egg', attracts as many architectural tourists as it does music fans. But it's *the* place to listen to classical music from home and abroad. You can also watch ballet, opera and classical Chinese dance here.

MEI LANFANG GRAND THEATRE

PEKING OPERA, THEATRE

Map p294 (梅兰芳大戏院; Méi Lánfāng Dàxìyuàn; ☎5833 1288; 32 Ping'anli Xidajie, 平安里

LOCAL KNOWLEDGE

GOING UNDERGROUND

The hordes of teens and 20-somethings who crowd out 77th Street might not know it, but their favourite shopping mall was once part of what was possibly the world's largest bomb shelter. In 1969, alarmed at the prospect of possible nuclear war with either the Soviet Union or the US, Mao Zedong ordered that a huge warren of underground tunnels be burrowed underneath Běijīng. The task was completed Cultural Revolution–style – by hand – with the finishing touches made in 1979, just as the US reopened its embassy in the capital and the Russians were marching into Afghanistan.

Legend has it that one tunnel stretched all the way to Tiānjīn (a mere 130km away), while another runs to the Summer Palace. Nowadays it is believed that some tunnels are still used for clandestine official purposes, while the rest of the underground city has been rendered unsafe by the construction boom that has gone on above it since the 1990s. But a few portions of the complex have been turned over for commercial use, like the 77th Street mall, a fitting metaphor for the way China has embraced consumerism and left Maoism far behind.

西大街32号; tickets ¥30-380; ⊙performances 7.30pm; ⓈChegongzhuang) Named after China's most famous practitioner of Peking opera, this theatre opened its doors in 2007 and has since become one of the most popular and versatile venues in town. As well as traditional opera, you can see Shakespeare productions and modern theatre. Performances start at 7.30pm daily. Tickets have to be bought from the ticket office in the lobby between 10am and 7.30pm.

SHOPPING

THREE STONE KITE SHOP KITES

Map p294 (三石斋风筝; Sānshízhāi Fēngzhēng; ☎8404 4505; 25 Di'anmen Xidajie, 地安门西大街甲25号; ⊙9am-9pm; ⓈNanluogu Xiang) Kites by appointment to the former Qing emperors; the great-grandfather of the owner of this friendly store used to make the kites for the Chinese royal family. Most of the kites here are handmade and hand-painted, although the selection is limited these days, now that the owner uses half his shop to display other, admittedly attractive, souvenirs.

Kites start from around ¥180. You can also find all the gear you'll need to fly your new kite, as well as miniature framed kites, which make pretty gifts.

YANDAI XIEJIE SHOPPING STREET

Map p294 (烟袋斜街; Yandai Xiejie, off Di'anmen Neidajie, 地安门内大街烟袋斜街) If nearby Nanluogu Xiang is too hectic for you, you can find some of the same here, on a smaller scale. It's still busy at weekends, but more manageable. Shops on this re-built 'old-Běijīng' *hútòng*, which leads down to the lakes, are almost exclusively souvenir shops – T-shirts, silk shawls, fabric slippers, paper fans, fake antiques etc, etc – but it's more fun shopping for them here than in one of the city's big, multifloor souvenir markets. Walk south from the Drum Tower, along Di'anmenwai Dajie, and it's the first *hútòng* on the right.

77TH STREET SHOPPING MALL

Map p294 (77街; Qīshíqī Jiē; ☎6608 7177; B2-3F, 180 Xidan Beidajie, 西单北大街180号地下2-3层; ⊙10am-10pm; ⓈXidan) Descend the stairs into this unique underground mall and see where ordinary teen and 20-something Beijingers go for their clothes and accessories. It opens out into a huge, circular, three-storey collection of hundreds of stores. As well as funky T-shirts, belts and bags, there are shoe shops galore, a food court, a cinema and even an ice rink. It's lots of fun, but a madhouse at weekends.

To get here, come out of Exit A of Xidan subway station then turn right immediately, keeping an eye out for the orange '77th Street Plaza' signs. If you're already above ground, the mall is underneath Xidan Culture Sq.

BĚIJĪNG BOOKS BUILDING BOOKS

Map p294 (北京图书大厦, Běijīng Túshū Dàshà; ☎6607 8477; 17 Xichang'an Jie, 西长安街17号; ⊙9am-9pm; ⓈXidan) Massive emporium crammed with tomes of all descriptions. The ones in English, and some other foreign languages too, are in the basement. There's a decent range of Lonely Planet guides as well, plus plenty of children's books.

Dashilar & Xīchéng South

Neighbourhood Top Five

❶ Peruse the historic shopping street of **Dashilar** (p132), still home to some of the oldest and most prestigious emporiums in the city. Whether it's silk or ancient aphrodisiacs, you'll find it here.

❷ Wind your way through the fascinating *hútòng* (alleyways) west of Meishi Jie, once infamous as old Peking's **red-light district**.

❸ Check out the capital's largest Muslim neighbourhood around **Niújiē Mosque** (p132).

❹ Visit the **Běijīng Ancient Architecture Museum** (p132) to discover how imperial Běijīng was built.

❺ Pop into the little-visited **Fǎyuán Temple** (p132), one of the city's oldest and most peaceful Buddhist shrines.

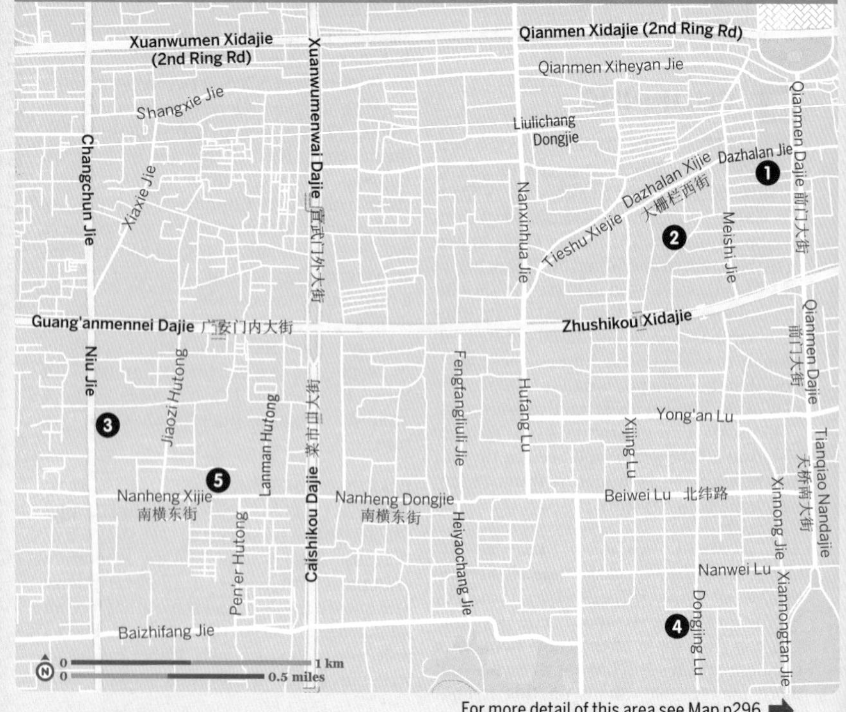

For more detail of this area see Map p296.

Explore Dashilar & Xīchéng South

Divided from neighbouring Dōngchéng by Qianmen Dajie, Dashilar (大栅栏) and Xīchéng South (南西城) take in the former district of Xuānwǔ. Its major sights are concentrated in two distinct areas: Dashilar and the Muslim district around Niu Jie, with nearby *hútòng* to explore as well.

Spend a morning visiting Dashilar's shops, before lunch at one of the small restaurants on Dazhalan Xijie. The *hútòng* off Dazhalan Xijie were once the red-light district of old Peking and are well worth diving into.

From the western end of Dazhalan Xijie, it's a short stroll to Liulichang, the capital's premier shopping street for antiques, calligraphy and traditional Chinese art and a must for curio-hunters. In the evening, catch a show at one of the acrobatics or Peking opera theatres in the neighbourhood.

Begin a second day in the area with a trip to the Běijīng Ancient Architecture Museum. Then, hop a taxi to Niu Jie, the main drag of Běijīng's Muslim Huí neighbourhood. Visit the mosque, a blend of Chinese and Arabic styles, and eat at a local Muslim restaurant. Nearby Fǎyuán Temple is a serene shrine surrounded by intriguing *hútòng*.

Local Life

- **Táorántíng Park** North of Běijīng South Railway Station, this is the lungs of the neighbourhood and a great escape from the surrounding urban madness.
- **Hútòng** Visit the alleyways sandwiched between Dazhalan Xijie and Qianmen Xidajie; they see far fewer foreigners than others in the area.
- **Market** Locals head to the streets around Mǎliándào Tea Market (p137) for both tea and reasonably priced tea sets.

Getting There & Away

- **Subway** For Dashilar, get off at the Qianmen stop on Line 2. Go to Hepingmen on the same line for Liulichang. Line 4 runs north–south through the neighbourhood towards Běijīng South Railway Station, with the stop at Caishikou walking distance from both Nui Jie and Fǎyuán Temple.
- **Bus** Niu Jie is connected with Wangfujing Dajie by bus 10, running through Tiān'ānmén, Xīdān and Changchun Jie.

Lonely Planet's Top Tip

Avoid the restaurants off the south end of Dashilar; many still try to charge foreigners more than locals by offering them a special English menu. Instead, head down Dazhalan Xijie for cheaper options. Look for the places which have plenty of locals eating in them. Be wary of anyone in the Dashilar area offering to take you to a tea ceremony; it's a very expensive scam.

Best Places to Eat & Drink

- Turpan Restaurant (p134)
- Gǒubùlǐ (p134)
- Liu Family Noodles (p134)

For reviews, see p134.

Best Entertainment

- Tiānqiáo Acrobatics Theatre (p134)
- Húguǎng Guild Hall (p135)
- Lao She Teahouse (p135)

For reviews, see p134.

Best Places to Shop

- Yuèhǎixuān Musical Instrument Store (p136)
- Ruìfúxiáng (p136)
- Mǎliándào Tea Market (p137)

For reviews, see p135.

SIGHTS

DASHILAR — SHOPPING STREET

Map p296 (大栅栏; Dàzhàlan; **S** Qianmen) This centuries-old shopping street, also known as Dazhalan Jie, is just west of Qianmen Dajie. While a misjudged makeover has sadly robbed it of much of its charm, many of the shops have been in business here for hundreds of years and still draw many locals. Some specialise in esoteric goods – ancient herbal remedies, handmade cloth shoes; most make for intriguing window shopping.

FǍYUÁN TEMPLE — BUDDHIST TEMPLE

Map p296 (法源寺; Fǎyuán Sì; 7 Fayuansi Qianjie; admission ¥5; ⏲8.30-4pm; **S** Caishikou) Infused with an air of reverence and devotion, this lovely temple dates back to the 7th century. The temple follows the typical Buddhist layout, with drum and bell towers. Do hunt out the unusual **copper-cast Buddha**, seated atop four further Buddhas ensconced on a huge bulb of myriad effigies in the Pilu Hall (the fourth hall).

Within the Guanyin Hall is a Ming-dynasty **Thousand Hand and Thousand Eye Guanyin**, while a huge **reclining Buddha** lies in the rear hall. Originally built to honour Tang-dynasty soldiers who had fallen during combat against the northern tribes, Fǎyuán is still a working temple, as well as home to the **China Buddhism College**, and you'll see plenty of monks about. To find it from the entrance of Niújiē Mosque, walk left 100m and then turn left into the first *hútòng*. Follow this for about 10 minutes and you'll arrive at the temple.

NIÚJIĒ MOSQUE — MOSQUE

(牛街礼拜寺; Niújiē Lǐbài Sì; ☎6353 2564; 88 Niu Jie; admission ¥10, for Muslims free; ⏲8.30am-sunset; **S** Caishikou) Dating back to the 10th century and lively with worshippers on Fridays (it's closed to non-Muslims at prayer times), Běijīng's largest mosque is the centre of the community for the 10,000 or so Huí Chinese Muslims who live nearby. Look out for the **Building for Observing the Moon** (望月楼; Wàngyuèlóu), from where the lunar calendar was calculated.

The mosque blends traditional Chinese temple design with Middle Eastern flourishes – note the spirit wall on Nui Jie that guards the entrance, a feature of all Chinese temples regardless of denomination. The main prayer hall is out of bounds for non-Muslims. Remember to dress appropriately for a mosque (no shorts or short skirts).

XIĀNNÓNG ALTAR & BĚIJĪNG ANCIENT ARCHITECTURE MUSEUM — MUSEUM

Map p296 (先农坛、北京古代建筑博物馆; Xiānnóngtán & Běijīng Gǔdài Jiànzhù Bówùguǎn; ☎6304 5608; 21 Dongjing Lu; admission ¥15; ⏲9am-4pm; **S** Taoranting) This altar – to the west of the Temple of Heaven – was the site of solemn imperial ceremonies and sacrificial offerings. Located within what is called the **Hall of Jupiter** (太岁殿; Tàisuì Diàn) – the most magnificent surviving hall – is the excellent Běijīng Ancient Architecture Museum, which informatively narrates the elements of traditional Chinese building techniques.

Glance at any pre-1949 map of Běijīng and you can gauge the massive scale of the

LOCAL KNOWLEDGE

THE HUÍ

China's 25-million-odd Muslims are divided into two distinct groups. One is comprised of the Uighurs, a rebellious, Turkic-speaking minority from the far west of China whose roots lie in Central Asia. The other are the Huí. You can find both in the Niu Jie area but it is predominantly a district associated with the Huí.

The descendants of Arab traders who came down the Silk Road well over a thousand years ago, the 10 million or so Huí are technically an ethnic minority. But they are spread all over China and have intermarried so much with the Han Chinese over the centuries that they are indistinguishable from them ethnically. Nor do they have their own language, speaking only Mandarin.

Yet, they are easily spotted. Many Huí women wear a headscarf, while the men sport white skullcaps. They are most associated with running restaurants; you can find a Huí eatery in even the smallest Chinese towns. Don't expect to find pork on the menu and some don't serve alcohol. Apart from the Niu Jie area, you're most likely to encounter the Huí serving up *yáng'ròu chuàn* (lamb skewers) from streetside stalls and hole-in-the-wall restaurants all over Běijīng.

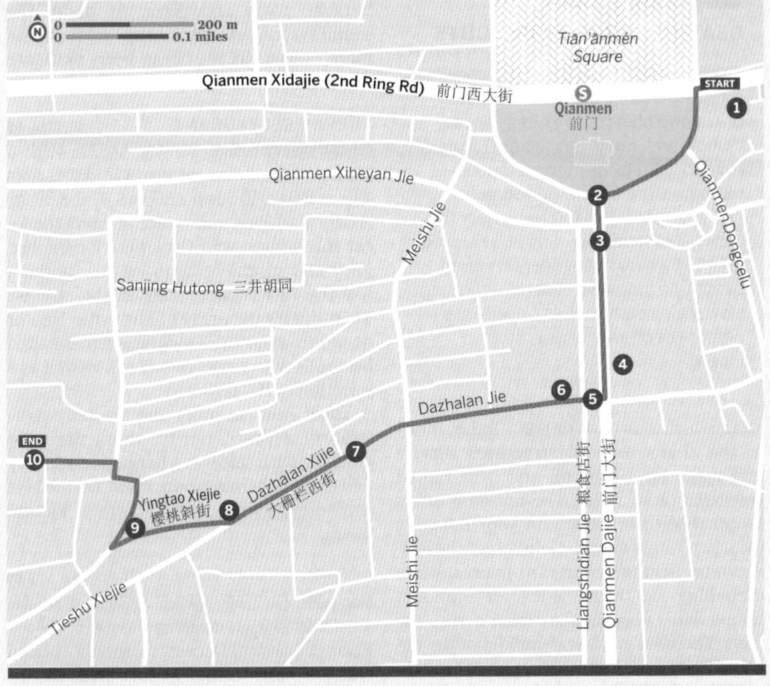

Neighbourhood Walk
Qiánmén to Liulichang

START BĚIJĪNG RAILWAY MUSEUM
END LIULICHANG DONGJIE
LENGTH 2.5KM; ONE HOUR

Start at the ❶ **Běijīng Railway Museum**, housed in the historic Qiánmén Railway Station building. Walk south to the ❷ **Qiánmén Decorative Arch**, a rebuilt Five-Bay Decorative Arch (Wǔpáilóu) that was originally felled in the 1950s and reconstructed prior to the 2008 Olympics. The arch stands at the head of ❸ **Qianmen Dajie**, a street completely revamped in the style of old Peking.

Look at some of the ❹ **restored old shop buildings** along Qianmen Dajie, then turn right onto the historic shopping street of ❺ **Dashilar** (aka Dazhalan Jie). Down the first alley on the left is Liubiju, a traditional Běijīng *lǎozìhào* (old, established shop) famous for its pickled condiments.

Push on through the crowds on Dazhalan Jie. On your right at No 5 is ❻ **Ruìfúxiáng** (p136), a famous old Běijīng silk store dating to 1893. Pop in and view the grey brickwork and carved decorative flourishes of the entrance hall.

Cross Meishi Jie and enter ❼ **Dazhalan Xijie**, once known as Guanyin Temple Street. If you're peckish, stop at any of the many food vendors here, then turn right at the fork with Yingtao Xiejie (樱桃斜街) to see the ❽ **plaque** marking the site of the former Guanyin Temple (Nos 6 to 8 Yingtao Xiejie) that stood here.

Continue along Yingtao Xiejie past the narrow and pinched Taitou Xiang (抬头巷; Raise Head Alley) for around 100m and examine the house at ❾ **27 Yingtao Xiejie**. Look out for the red characters 'Long Live the Revolution' (革命万岁), a fading legacy of a Cultural Revolution slogan.

Loop round to the right and at the end of Yingtao Xiejie, turn sharp left and the road will bend round to ❿ **Liulichang Dongjie**, Běijīng's premier antique street.

LOCAL KNOWLEDGE

DEATH BY A THOUSAND CUTS

The now-abolished district of Xuānwǔ owed its name to the grand old gate of Xuānwǔ Mén (宣武门), long since demolished. But the irreverent locals used to call it by its more nefarious nickname, the Gate of Punishment (刑门; Xíng Mén), as it rose up near the imperial execution ground at Càishìkǒu (菜市口), where wrongdoers endured death by a thousand cuts (an agonising slow slicing of the body). Càishìkǒu's name lives on as a subway stop on Line 4.

altar, which was built in 1420. Today, many of the altar's original structures survive and make up a tranquil and little-visited constellation of relics. The museum offers the chance to brush up on your *dǒugǒng* (brackets) and *sǔnmǎo* (joints), get the low-down on Běijīng's courtyard houses, while eyeballing detailed models of standout temple halls and pagodas from across the land. There's a great scale model of the old walled city and English captions throughout. On Wednesdays the first 200 visitors get in free.

EATING

LIÚ FAMILY NOODLES NOODLES $

Map p296 (刘家人刀削面; Liú Jiārén Dāoxiāomiàn; 6 Tieshuxie Jie, 铁树斜街6号; noodles from ¥8; 11am-3pm & 5-10pm; ; Qianmen) A rarity in this area: a restaurant that welcomes foreigners without trying to overcharge them. On the contrary, the prices couldn't be much lower, while the friendly owner is keen to practise her (limited) English. Choose from a selection of tasty noodle and cold dishes. To find it, look for the black sign with 'Best Noodles in China' written in English.

LONG TABLE WESTERN $

Map p296 (长桌; Chángzhuō; 6302 8699; 55 Dazhalan Xijie, 大栅栏西街55号; dishes from ¥29; 8am-1am; ; Qianmen) With its graffiti-covered walls and wooden benches, this is a backpacker hang-out a (long-ish) stone's throw from Tiān'ānmén Sq. During the day it functions as a cafe serving up Western standards: all-day breakfasts, burgers, pasta and pizza. At night, the sound system gets cranked up and it all gets more raucous as the cheap beers (¥10) are downed at pace.

TURPAN RESTAURANT XINJIANG $$

(吐鲁番餐厅; Tǔlǔfān Cāntīng; 8316 4691; 6 Niu Jie, 牛街6号; kebabs from ¥12, dishes from ¥35; 6-9am, 10.30am-2.30pm & 4.30-8.30pm; Caishikou) This huge place attracts the local Huí hordes, who flock here for the big, juicy and succulent lamb kebabs (nothing like the tiny skewers sold on the streets). Then there's the array of authentic Uighur dishes from far-off Xīnjiāng, such as salted beef rolls with sweet yam (¥46), as well as a selection of Halal choices.

You'll need to order the roasted whole lamb in advance, but we think the roast lamb leg with spices is a bargain at ¥58. Try and come here in a group; it's by far the best way to experience this restaurant. Picture menu.

GǑUBÙLǏ DUMPLINGS $$

Map p296 (狗不理; 6353 3338; 31 Dazhalan Jie, 大栅栏街31号; dumplings from ¥56; 8am-10pm; Qianmen) Decent, reasonably priced eats are hard to find in this area, so this outpost of the renowned Tiānjīn restaurant will delight dumpling devotees. True, they are more pricey here than at your average hole-in-the-wall joint, but there are eight different types to pick from, including meat, prawn, crab and vegie options, and each serving includes eight dumplings.

There's a picture menu, and plenty of cold dishes to accompany your dumplings.

ENTERTAINMENT

TIĀNQIÁO ACROBATICS THEATRE ACROBATICS

Map p296 (天桥杂技剧场; Tiānqiáo Zájì Jùchǎng; 6303 7449; 95 Tianqiao Shichang Lu Jie, 天桥市场街95号; tickets ¥180-380; performances 5.30pm & 7.15pm; Taranting) West of the Temple of Heaven Park, this 100-year-old theatre offers one of Běijīng's best acrobatic displays, a one-hour show performed by the Běijīng Acrobatic Troupe. Less touristy than the other venues, the theatre's small size means you can get very close to the action. The high-wire display is awesome. The entrance is down the eastern side of the building.

LOCAL KNOWLEDGE

CHINA'S OLDEST CINEMA

Shànghǎi might have been where the movies first arrived in China – courtesy of a Spanish showman who set up a projector in a teahouse in 1896 – but Dashilar and Běijīng was the site of China's first proper movie theatre. **Dàguānlóu Cinema** (大观楼影城; Dàguānlóu Yǐngchéng; Map p296; 36 Dazhalan Jie, 大栅栏街36号; tickets ¥40-50; 9am-11.30pm; Qianmen) started screening films way back in 1903. Amazingly, considering how much of China's architectural heritage has disappeared, it's not only still standing but continues to show movies, including a few Western releases.

The cinema was opened by Ren Qingtai, a pioneer photographer before he discovered moving pictures. Ren would go on to direct China's first film in 1905 – an excerpt of Peking opera – as well as founding the country's first movie studio in southwest Běijīng's Fēngtái District. Appropriately, given the significant role he played in China's cinematic history, he was the inspiration for the 2000 Chinese film *Shadow Magic*, which chronicles the early days of cinema in the capital.

The **Old Cinema Cafe** on the ground floor has a small exhibition on the cinema's history, alongside photos of old-time Chinese movie stars and a few ancient cameras and projectors. It makes a good pit stop for a coffee (¥25), if you need a break from shopping on Dashilar. And the cinema, despite its illustrious past, remains one of the cheapest places in town to catch a flick.

HÚGUǍNG GUILD HALL — PEKING OPERA

Map p296 (湖广会馆; Húguǎng Huìguǎn; 6351 8284; 3 Hufang Lu, 虎坊桥路3号; tickets ¥180-680, opera museum ¥10; performances 8pm, opera museum 9am-5pm; Caishikou) The most historic and atmospheric place in town for a night of Peking opera. The interior is magnificent, coloured in red, green and gold, and decked out with tables and a stone floor, while balconies surround the canopied stage. Opposite the theatre there's a very small opera museum displaying operatic scores, old catalogues and other paraphernalia.

There are also colour illustrations of the *liǎnpǔ* (types of Peking opera facial makeup) – examples include the *hóu liǎnpǔ* (monkey face) and the *chǒujué liǎnpǔ* (clown face). The theatre dates back to 1807 and, in 1912, was where the Kuomintang (KMT), led by Dr Sun Yatsen, was founded. Shows here attract a lot of domestic tour groups. There are few English captions, but it's not hard to follow what's going on.

LAO SHE TEAHOUSE — PERFORMING ARTS

Map p296 (老舍茶馆; Lǎoshě Cháguǎn; 6303 6830; www.laosheteahouse.com; 3rd fl, 3 Qianmen Xidajie, 前门西大街3号3层; evening tickets ¥180-380; performances 7.50pm; Qianmen) Lao She Teahouse, named after the celebrated writer, has daily and nightly shows, mostly in Chinese, which blend any number of traditional Chinese performing arts. The evening performances of Peking opera, folk art and music, acrobatics and magic (7.50pm to 9.20pm) are the most popular. But there are also tea ceremonies, frequent folk-music performances and daily shadow-puppet shows.

Prices depend on the type of show and your seat. Phone ahead or check the schedule online. Look for two stone lions guarding the front of the building.

LÍYUÁN THEATRE — PEKING OPERA

Map p296 (梨园剧场; Líyuán Jùchǎng; 6301 6688; Qianmen Jianguo Hotel, 175 Yong'an Lu, 永安路175号前门建国饭店; tickets without tea ¥200-280, with tea ¥580; performances 7.30pm; Caishikou) This touristy theatre, in the lobby of the Qiánmén Jiànguó Hotel (p199), has daily performances for Peking opera newbies. If you want to, you can enjoy an overpriced tea ceremony while watching. The setting isn't traditional: it resembles a cinema auditorium (the stage facade is the only authentic touch), but it's a gentle introduction to the art form.

SHOPPING

Dashilar and Xīchéng South are two of the capital's finest neighbourhoods for shopping. Apart from Dashilar (p132) itself, Liulichang (meaning 'glazed-tile factory') is Běijīng's best-known antiques street, even if the goods on sale are largely fake. The street is

LOCAL KNOWLEDGE

RED-LIGHT PEKING

These days, Dazhalan Xijie and the surrounding *hútòng* are Běijīng's backpacker central. But for hundreds of years, these innocuous-looking alleys were infamous for being old Peking's red-light district (红灯区; *hóngdēngqū*).

Centered on Bada Hutong, a collection of eight alleys, the area had already acquired a raunchy reputation in the 18th century. By the time of the fall of the Qing dynasty in 1912, there were over 300 brothels lining the lanes. The working girls ranged from cultivated courtesans who could recite poetry and dance gracefully and whose clients were aristocrats and court officials, to more mundane types who served the masses. It was very much an area for the locals; the small foreign community had its own little zone of brothels, dive bars and opium dens in still surviving Chuanban Hutong, close to the Chongwenmen subway stop.

Bada Hutong owed its dubious fame to the fact that it was outside the city walls (the emperors didn't want houses of ill repute near the royal palace), yet close enough to the Imperial City for customers to get there easily. But the fall of the emperors signalled the beginning of the end for Bada Hutong. Just over a month after the founding of the PRC in October 1949, soldiers marched into the area, closed down the brothels and 'liberated' the prostitutes working there.

Many of the eight alleys that made up Bada Hutong have been demolished and/or rebuilt. Shanxi Xiang, though, is still standing and the historic building that is now the hostel Leo Courtyard (p199) was once one of the most upmarket knocking shops in the capital. But it didn't do dorm beds back then.

something of an oasis in the area and worth delving into for its quaint, albeit dressed-up, villagelike atmosphere. Alongside ersatz Qing monochrome bowls and Cultural Revolution kitsch, you can rummage through old Chinese books, paintings, brushes, ink and paper. Prepare yourself for pushy sales staff and overly optimistic prices. If you want a name *chop* (seal) made, this is a good place to do it.

At the western end of Liulichang Xijie, a collection of more informal shops flog bric-a-brac, Buddhist statuary, Cultural Revolution pamphlets and posters, shoes for bound feet, silks, handicrafts and so on. Further west, Mǎliándào Tea Market is an essential stop for tea lovers.

★YUÈHǍIXUĀN MUSICAL INSTRUMENT STORE — MUSICAL INSTRUMENTS

Map p296 (乐海轩门市部; Yuèhǎixuān Ménshìbù; ☎6303 1472; 97 Liliuchang Dongjie, 琉璃厂东街97号; ⏰9.30am-6pm; Ⓢ Hepingmen) Fantastic, friendly emporium that specialises in traditional Chinese musical instruments, such as the zitherlike *gǔzhēng* (some of which come with elaborate carvings on them), the *èrhú* and *bǎnhú* (two-string Chinese violins), and *gǔ* (drums). It does great gongs and has many esoteric instruments from Tibet and Mongolia, too. It's on the eastern side of Liliuchang Dongjie.

XÍAN YÀN TĀNG — SHADOW PUPPETS

Map p296 (贤燕堂; ☎136 931 33759; 102 Liliuchang Dongjie, 琉璃厂东街102号; ⏰9am-6pm; Ⓢ Hepingmen) Tucked down a tiny alley lined with examples of its handmade wares, this cubbyhole of a shop turns out traditional shadow puppets. They come in all shapes and sizes, and you can get them framed (they make good gifts) if you don't fancy using them to put on your own shadow play back home.

The shop is opposite the Yuèhǎixuān Musical Instrument Store on the east side of Liliuchang Dongjie.

RUÌFÚXIÁNG — SILK

Map p296 (瑞蚨祥丝绸店; Ruìfúxiáng Sīchóudiàn; ☎6303 5313; 5 Dazhalan Jie, 大栅栏街5号; ⏰9.30am-8pm; Ⓢ Qianmen) Housed in a historic building on Dashilar, this is one of the best places in town to browse for silk. There's an incredible selection of Shāndōng silk, brocade and satin-silk. The silk starts at ¥168 a metre, although most of the fabric is more expensive. Ready-made, traditional Chinese clothing is sold on the 2nd floor.

Ruìfúxiáng also has an outlet at Dianmenwai Dajie (p103).

MĂLIÁNDÀO TEA MARKET TEA

(马连道茶城; Măliándào Cháchéng; ☎6334 3963; 11 Maliandao Lu, 马连道路11号; ⏲8.30am-6pm; ⓈBěijīng West Railway Station) Măliándào is the largest tea market in northern China and home to if not all the tea in China, then an awful lot of it. There are brews from all over the country here, including Pu'erh and oolong. Maliandao Lu has hundreds of tea shops, where prices for tea and tea sets are lower than in tourist areas.

Although it's mostly for wholesalers, the market is a great place to wander for anyone interested in tea and the vendors will happily invite you in to sample some. They also sell tea sets here, with prices ranging dramatically depending on the design, glaze and porcelain used. A single tea cup can cost upwards of ¥150, or you can pick up a basic tea set in the market and the nearby shops for ¥450. Maliandao Lu is south of Běijīng West Train Station. To find the tea market, look for the statue of Lu Yu, the 8th-century sage who wrote the first book on growing, preparing and drinking tea, which stands outside it.

RÓNGBĂOZHĀI ARTWORK

Map p296 (荣宝斋; ☎6303 6090; 19 Liulichang Xijie, 琉璃厂西街19号; ⏲9am-5.30pm; ⓈHepingmen) Spread over two floors and sprawling down a length of the road, this place contains scroll paintings, woodblock prints, paper, ink and brushes presented in a rather flat, uninspired way by bored staff – a consequence of it being state run – and not much English is spoken. Prices are generally fixed, although you can usually get 10% off.

The ground floor has ceramics and art and calligraphy supplies. Head to the 2nd floor for traditional Chinese ink and scroll paintings.

CATHAY BOOKSHOP BOOKS, ARTWORK

Map p296 (中国书店; Zhōngguó Shūdiàn; ☎6303 2104; 34 Liulichang Xijie, 琉璃厂西街34号; ⏲9am-6pm; ⓈHepingmen) This is the larger of the two branches of the Cathay Bookshop on the south side of Liulichang Xijie and is worth checking out for its wide variety of colour books on Chinese painting, ceramics and furniture, as well as tomes on religion (most are in Chinese). Upstairs has more art books, stone rubbings and antiquarian books.

There's another, smaller branch close by on Liulichang that sells art supplies, paper cuts and bookmarks, some of which feature photographs of the old Qing imperial household, including snapshots of Reginald Fleming Johnson (last emperor Puyi's Scottish tutor), Puyi practising shadow boxing, eunuchs and Cixi dressed as Avalokiteshvara (Guanyin). Both stores take credit cards.

TÓNGRÉNTÁNG CHINESE MEDICINE

Map p296 (同仁堂; ☎6303 1155; 24 Dazhalan Jie, 大栅栏街24号; ⏲8am-7.30pm; ⓈQianmen) This famous, now international, herbal medicine shop has been peddling pills and potions since 1669. It was a royal dispensary in the Qing dynasty and its medicines are based on secret prescriptions used by royalty. You can be cured of anything from fright to encephalitis, or so the shop claims. Traditional doctors are available on the spot for consultations.

Look for the pair of *qílín* (hybrid animals that appear on earth in times of harmony) standing guard outside.

NÈILIÁNSHĒNG SHOE SHOP SHOES

Map p296 (内联升鞋店; Nèiliánshēng Xiédiàn; ☎6301 4863; 34 Dazhalan Jie, 大栅栏街34号; ⏲9am-8pm; ⓈQianmen) They say this is the oldest existing cloth shoe shop in China (opened in 1853) and Mao Zedong and other luminaries had their footwear made here. You too can pick up ornately embroidered shoes, or the simply styled cloth slippers frequently modelled by Běijīng's senior citizens (from ¥215). It does cute, patterned kid's slippers (from ¥58) too.

All are made in a factory that employs more than 100 workers. But despite upgrading the soles of their slippers to cope with modern-day street pounding, both the shop and staff remain defiantly old-school.

Sānlǐtún & Cháoyáng

Neighbourhood Top Five

❶ Discover China's vibrant contemporary art scene at **798 Art District** (p140).

❷ Hunt for arts, crafts and antique treasures at the wonderfully chaotic **Pānjiāyuán Market** (p154).

❸ Sip cocktails at **Apothecary** (p149), just one of an ever-increasing number of hip Sānlǐtún bars.

❹ Enjoy the best of Běijīng's fine dining at restaurants like **Duck de Chine** (p147).

❺ Muse on life's finalities at the fascinatingly morbid Taoist shrine that is **Dōngyuè Temple** (p141).

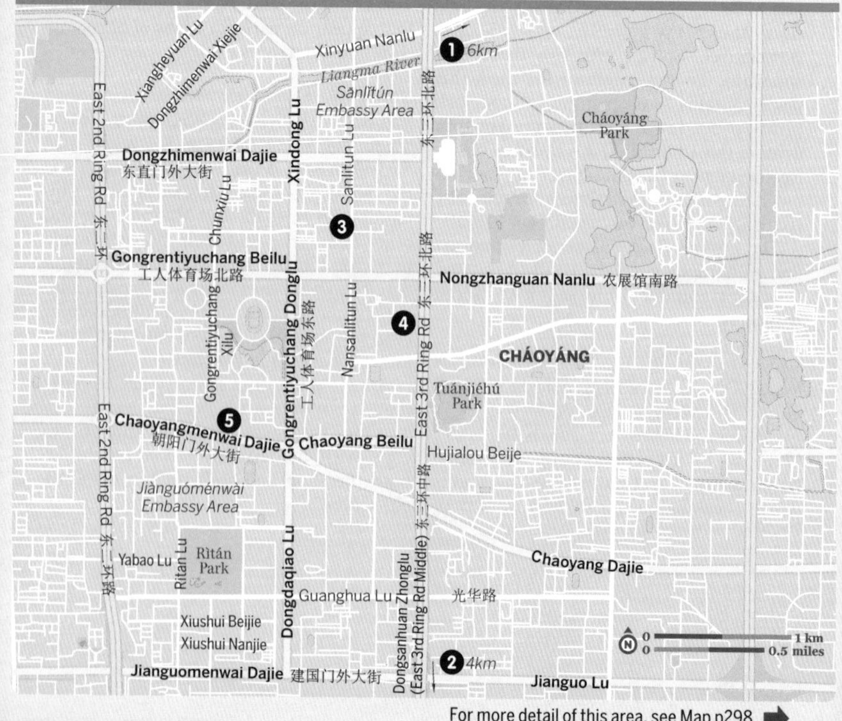

For more detail of this area, see Map p298.

Explore Sānlǐtún & Cháoyáng

The only sights of real interest in the spread-out district of Cháoyáng (朝阳) are Dōngyuè Temple and the oasis that is Rìtán Park, although spending at least half a day at the 798 Arts District is more or less essential. Once your sightseeing is done, it's time to focus on Cháoyáng's more hedonistic pleasures: shopping, eating and partying.

You'll find many of Běijīng's best and most eye-catching shopping malls here, as well as some of the city's finest markets. You could easily put aside a day for shopping, including a lazy brunch or lunch stop.

Come evening, the choice of restaurants is staggering. Whether you fancy keeping it real with dumplings, dressing up for posh nosh or sampling international cuisine from African to Thai, you can find it in Cháoyáng.

Once you've satisfied your hunger cravings, hop in a cab to one of the many bars in the area, where you can discuss where best to dance the night away over a cocktail or three.

Local Life

➡ **Food** If you want to sidestep the expats and moneyed out-of-towners and eat like a real Beijinger, head for Bàodǔ Huáng (p144).

➡ **Art** 798 Art District is well worth a trip, but true art-lovers should also head slightly further northeast, to the less-touristy galleries at Cǎochǎngdì (p140).

➡ **Parklife** Rìtán Park (p141) is a favourite spot for locals who come here to fly kites, play cards and do their daily exercises. Other outdoor spaces include Cháoyáng and Tuánjiéhú Parks, which both have popular swimming complexes.

Getting There & Away

➡ **Subway** The main bar, restaurant and clubbing areas in Sānlǐtún are between Dongsi Shitiao and Tuanjiehu stations. Whichever way you're heading, you're faced with a 10- to 15-minute walk.

➡ **Dōngzhímén Transport Hub** The Airport Express terminates here, two subway lines meet here, and there are buses to every corner of the city, including ones to the Great Wall.

➡ **Bus** Bus 113 runs past Sānlǐtún and the Workers Stadium before turning north up Jiaodaokou Nandajie (for Nanluogu Xiang). Bus 120 goes from the east gate of the Workers Stadium to Wángfǔjǐng and Qiánmén. Bus 701 runs the length of Gongrentiyuchang Beilu and continues west to Běihǎi Park.

Lonely Planet's Top Tip

Market vendors in this area are very accustomed to foreign tourists, so prepare yourself for some serious bargaining. There are no fixed rules as to how much to cut the starting price by. The best way to see how low vendors will go is simply to walk away, hopefully prompting a genuine 'last price'.

Best Places to Eat

➡ Nàjiā Xiǎoguǎn (p145)
➡ Jīngzūn Peking Duck (p145)
➡ Bǎoyuán Dumpling Restaurant (p144)
➡ Bàodǔ Huáng (p144)
➡ In & Out (p145)

For reviews, see p144. ➡

Best Places to Drink

➡ Migas Bar (p149)
➡ Apothecary (p149)
➡ Great Leap Brewing (p149)
➡ Revolution (p149)
➡ Janes and Hooch (p149)

➡ For reviews, see p148. ➡

Best Places to Shop

➡ Pānjiāyuán Market (p154)
➡ Sānlǐtún Village (p153)
➡ Silk Market (p153)
➡ Sānlǐtún Yashow Clothing Market (p154)
➡ Shard Box Store (p154)

For reviews, see p153. ➡

MATT MUNRO / LONELY PLANET ©

TOP SIGHT
798 ART DISTRICT

A vast area of disused factories built by the East Germans, 798 Art District (798 艺术区; Qī Jiǔ Bā Yìshù Qū), also known as Dà Shānzi (大山子), is Běijīng's main concentration of contemporary art galleries. The industrial complex celebrates its proletarian roots in the communist heyday of the 1950s via retouched red Maoist slogans decorating gallery interiors and statues of burly, lantern-jawed workers dotting the lanes. The giant former factory workshops are ideally suited to multimedia installations and other ambitious projects.

Visiting

From Exit C of Dongzhimen subway station, take bus 909 (¥2) for about 6km northeast to Dashanzi Lukou Nan (大山子路口南), where you'll see the big red 798 sign. Buses run until 8.30pm. Signboards with English-language maps on them dot the lanes. There are many cafes scattered throughout 798, all serving coffee, alcohol and a selection of Chinese and Western dishes.

Galleries

Highlights include **BTAP** (Ceramics Third St; ⏲10am-6pm, Tue-Sun), one of 798's original galleries; **UCCA** (798 Rd; ⏲10am-7pm Tue-Sun), a big-money gallery with exhibition halls, a funky shop and a cinema screening ¥15 films most days; **Pace** (797 Rd; ⏲10am-6pm Tue-Sun), a wonderfully large space holding some top-quality exhibitions; and **Galleria Continua** (just south of 797 Rd; ⏲11am-6pm, Tue-Sun), another large space, below a towering, hard-to-miss brick chimney.

Cǎochǎngdì

A further extensive colony of art galleries can be found 3km northeast of 798 Art District at Cǎochǎngdì (草场地). Bus 909 continues here.

DON'T MISS

- UCCA
- Timezone 8 (p152)

PRACTICALITIES

- cnr Jiuxianqiao Lu & Jiuxianqiao Beilu, 酒仙桥路
- ⏲ galleries 10am-6pm, most closed Mon
- 🚌 403 or 909

SIGHTS

798 ART DISTRICT GALLERY

See p 140.

DŌNGYUÈ TEMPLE TAOIST TEMPLE

Map p298 (东岳庙; Dōngyuè Miào; 141 Chaoyangmenwai Dajie; admission ¥10, with guide ¥40; ⌚7.30am-5.30pm Apr-Oct, 8.30am-4.30pm Nov-Mar, closed Mon year-round; Ⓢ Chaoyangmen, Dongdaqiao) Dedicated to the Eastern Peak (Tài Shān) of China's five Taoist mountains, the morbid Taoist shrine of Dōngyuè Temple is an unsettling, albeit fascinating, experience and one of the capital's most unique temples. An active place of worship tended by top-knotted Taoist monks, the temple's roots go all the way back to the Yuan dynasty. A visit here takes you into a world entirely at odds with the surrounding glass and steel high-rises.

Before going in, note the temple's fabulous **Páifāng** (memorial archway) lying to the south, divorced from its shrine by the intervention of the busy main road, Chaoyangmenwai Dajie.

Stepping through the entrance pops you into a Taoist Hades, where tormented spirits reflect on their wrongdoing and elusive atonement. You can muse on life's finalities in the **Life and Death Department** or the **Final Indictment Department**. Otherwise get spooked at the **Department for Wandering Ghosts** or the **Department for Implementing 15 Kinds of Violent Death**.

It's not all doom and gloom: the luckless can check in at the **Department for Increasing Good Fortune and Longevity**. Ornithologists will be birds of a feather with the **Flying Birds Department**, while the infirm can seek cures at the **Deep-Rooted Disease Department**. The **Animal Department** has colourful and lively fauna. English explanations detail department functions.

Other halls are no less fascinating. The huge **Dàiyuè Hall** (Dàiyuè Diàn) is consecrated to the God of Tàishān, who manages the 18 layers of hell. Visit during festival time, especially during the Lunar New Year and the Mid-Autumn Festival, and you'll see the temple at its most vibrant.

Just outside the complex, in a small car park to the east, stands the handsome, but rather lonely **Jiǔtiān Pǔhuā Gōng** (九天普化宫), a small temple hall which is the only remaining structure of two other Taoist temples that once stood in this area. Built in 1647, the hall, which we think is now empty, once contained more than 70 clay and wooden statues dedicated to Leizu (雷祖), Taoism's God of Thunder. Unfortunately, it's not open to the public. Note the two impressive stone tablets that rise up from the platform at the front.

RÌTÁN PARK PARK

(日坛公园; Rìtán Gōngyuán; Ritan Lu; admission free; ⌚6am-9pm; Ⓢ Chaoyangmen, Jianguomen) Meaning 'Altar of the Sun', Rìtán (pronounced 'rer-tan') is a real oasis in the heart of Běijīng's business district. Dating back to 1530 and one of a set of imperial parks which covered each compass point – others include the Temple of Heaven and Temple of Earth (Dìtán Park) – the altar is now little more than a raised platform. But the surrounding park is beautifully landscaped and a great place to tune out from the surrounding mayhem.

Activities include dancing, singing, kite flying, rock climbing (¥25 per hour or ¥60 per day), table tennis and pond fishing (¥5 per hour). Otherwise, just stroll around and enjoy the flora, or head to one of the park's cafes; the standout one is **Stone Boat** (石舫咖啡; Shífǎng Kāfēi; Map p298; ☎6501 9986; beers & coffee from ¥25, cocktails from ¥40; ⌚10am-10pm Apr-Oct, 10am-6pm Nov-Mar; Ⓢ Jianguomen), located by a large pond artfully strewn with rocks.

CCTV BUILDING ARCHITECTURE

Map p298 (央视大楼; Yāngshì Dàlóu; 32 Dongsanhuan Zhonglu; Ⓢ Jintaixizhao) Shaped like an enormous pair of trousers, and known locally as Dà Kùchǎ (大裤衩), or Big Underpants, the astonishing CCTV Tower is an architectural fantasy that appears to defy gravity. It's made possible by an unusual engineering design which creates a three-dimensional cranked loop, supported by an irregular grid on its surface. Designed by Rem Koolhaas and Ole Scheeren, the building is an audacious statement of modernity (despite its nickname) and a unique addition to the Běijīng skyline.

Unfortunately, there's no access to the site, unless you can score a visitors pass from someone who works there, and the armed police who guard the gates lack a sense of humour. The strict security is partly a result of a February 2008 fire caused by stray fireworks from CCTV's own Lantern Festival celebration, which sent the costly Television Cultural Center in the north of the complex up in flames. Despite burning for five hours

1

LUIS CASTANEDA INC. / GETTY IMAGES ©

2

4

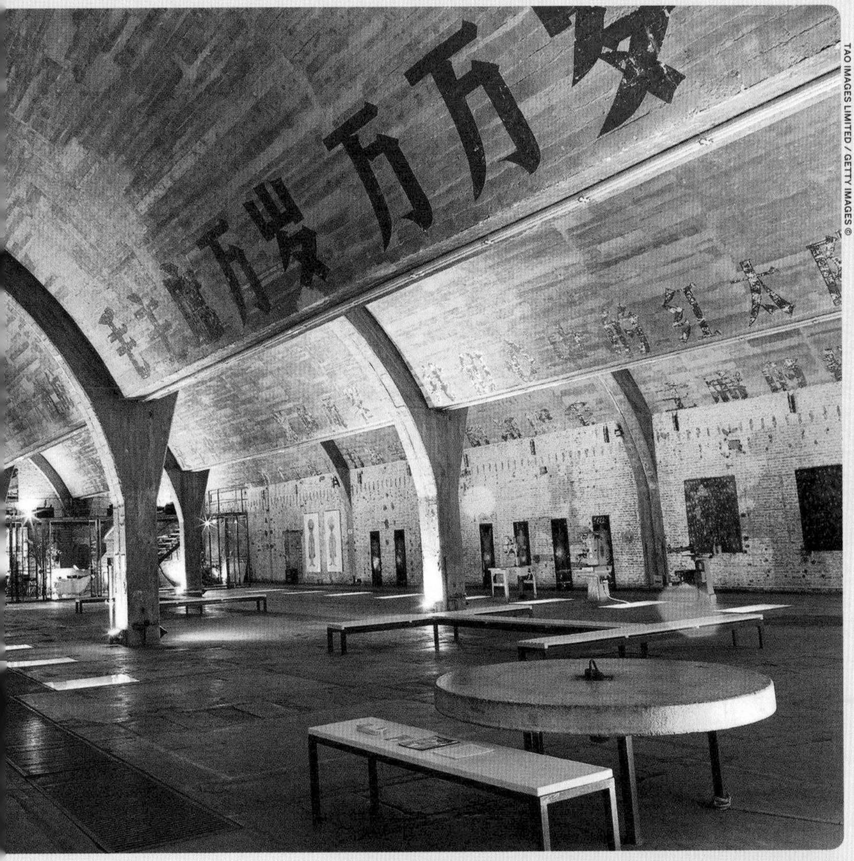

TAO IMAGES LIMITED / GETTY IMAGES ©

1. 'Bird's Nest' (National Stadium) (p144)
This iconic piece of architecture has quietened down after the heady days of the 2008 Olympics.

2. 798 Art District (p140)
A slogan from the Cultural Revolution decorates this space from the art district.

3. Dōngyuè Temple (p141)
Red 'wishing cards' at this disturbing and fascinatingTaoist temple

4. Pānjiāyuán Market (p154)
Hands down the best place to buy arts and crafts in Běijīng. Open every day, but weekends are the busiest.

3

ANTON HAZEWINKEL / GETTY IMAGES ©

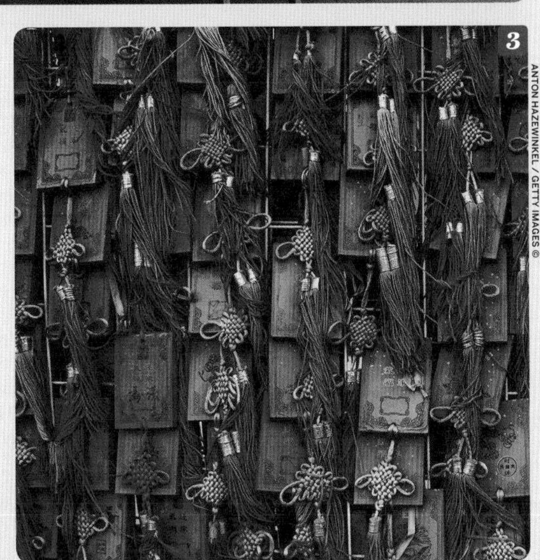

with spectacular ferocity, none of this was shown on TV, with CCTV famously censoring its reporting of the huge conflagration (Běijīng netizens dryly noted how CCTV created one of the year's biggest stories only to not cover it). The Běijīng Mandarin Oriental, a visitors centre and theatre were also destroyed in the blaze, but Big Underpants itself escaped unsinged.

BIRD'S NEST & WATER CUBE ARCHITECTURE

(国家体育场、国家游泳中心; Guójiā Tǐyùchǎng & Guójiā Yóuyǒng Zhōngxīn; Bird's Nest ¥50, Water Cube ¥30; 9am-5pm Nov-Mar, 9am-6.30pm Apr-Oct; S Olympic Sports Centre) Seven years after the 2008 Olympics, walking around the Olympic Sports Centre midweek is rather like being stuck in a district of Brasilia or one of those zombie movies where humans have all but been wiped out. A few events are staged at the signature National Stadium, known colloquially as the Bird's Nest (鸟巢; Niǎocháo), but it mostly stands empty and security staff and optimistic street vendors outnumber visitors. Nevertheless, it remains an iconic, if forlorn, piece of architecture.

Such, though, is the fate of most Olympics projects after the event and the Bird's Nest has fared better than many of the other venues for the 2008 Olympics, some of which are now no more than decaying structures surrounded by wasteland. The neighbouring, bubble-covered Water Cube is worth a look too, and now houses the Happy Magic Water Park (p156). The site is around 7km north of the city centre.

CHINA SCIENCE & TECHNOLOGY MUSEUM MUSEUM

(中国科技馆; Zhōngguó Kējìguǎn; 5 Beichendong Lu, 北辰东路 5 号; ¥30, 1 child gets in free; 9.30am-5pm Tue-Sun; S South Gate of Forest Park) About 8km north of the city centre and a big favourite with kids, this imposing facility has an array of hands-on scientific exhibitions, a kids' science playground and state-of-the-art 3D and '4D' cinemas. Walk east from South Gate of Forest Park subway station, then take the second right (10 minutes).

EATING

The presence of embassies and many foreign companies, as well as the Sānlǐtún bar and entertainment district, means Cháoyáng has the greatest concentration of international restaurants, foreign-friendly Chinese restaurants and fine-dining options in all Běijīng.

BǍOYUÁN DUMPLING RESTAURANT DUMPLINGS $

Map p298 (宝源饺子屋; Bǎoyuán Jiǎozi Wū; 6586 4967; 6 Maizidian Jie, 麦子店街 6 号; mains from ¥28, dumplings from ¥13; 11.15am-10.15pm; ; ; S Liangmaqiao, Agricultural Exhibition Centre) Fun for the kids – but also tasty enough for parents – this excellent dumplings restaurant dazzles diners with a huge selection of multicoloured *jiǎozi* (饺子; boiled dumplings), including many vegetarian options. The dough dyes are all natural (carrots make the orange; spinach the green) and only add to the flavour of the fillings; as good as any in Běijīng.

Dumplings are ordered and priced by the *liǎng* (about 50g). One *liǎng* gets you six dumplings. Not much English spoken, but there's an English sign and menu, and it's nonsmoking.

BÀODǓ HUÁNG BEIJING $

Map p298 (爆肚皇; 15 Dongzhimenwai Dajie, 东直门外大街 15 号; mains ¥18-35; 11am-2pm & 5-9pm; S Dongzhimen) Be prepared to queue at this no-nonsense apartment-block restaurant (look for the green sign with four yellow characters), where locals gobble and slurp their way through the authentic Běijīng-grub menu. The speciality is *bàodǔ* (爆肚; boiled lamb tripe; ¥18 or ¥35 depending on portion size). If you can't stomach that, then plump instead for a delicious *niúròu dàcōng ròubǐng* (牛肉大葱肉饼; beef and onion fried patty; ¥8).

The blanched vegetables are popular side dishes; choose from *chāo báicài* (焯白菜; blanched cabbage; ¥6), *chāo fěnsī* (焯粉丝; blanched glass noodles; ¥6) or *chāo dòng dòufu* (焯冻豆腐; blanched tofu; ¥6). And if you haven't ordered a meat patty, grab a *zhīma shāobing* (芝麻烧饼; roasted sesame-seed bun; ¥1.5) instead. True Beijingers will also nibble on *jiāo quān* (焦圈; deep-fried dough rings; ¥1), washed down with gulps of *dòu zhī* (豆汁; sour soy milk). But you may prefer to go for a bottle of *píjiǔ* (啤酒; local beer; ¥5). No English spoken, no English menu, no English sign.

YÀN LÁN LÓU GANSU $

Map p298 (燕兰楼; 6599 1668; 4/F, 12 Chaoyangmenwai Dajie, 朝阳门外大街 12 号昆泰

商厦 4 楼; noodles ¥18-38; ⏲9.30am-2pm & 4.30-9.30pm; Ⓢ Dongdaqiao) Famous for its hand-pulled noodles, a speciality of Gānsù Province in China's northwest, Yàn Lán Lóu is especially popular with Běijīng's Huí community (Muslims originally from the northwest); don't expect to find any pork here. It's on the 4th floor of a building opposite the Bǎinǎohuì Computer Mall (p155). Little English is spoken, but there is a picture menu.

Noodle options aside, the other dishes on the menu reveal the influence of the Muslim cuisine of Níngxià and Xīnjiāng. They're more expensive than the noodle choices, but the charcoal roasted lamb leg (¥48) is definitely worth trying. This is also one of the few places in the capital where you'll find yak meat.

BOCATA — CAFE $

Map p298 (☎6417 5291; 3 Sanlitun Lu, 三里屯北路 3 号; sandwiches from ¥28, coffee from ¥22; ⏲11.30am-midnight; 📶📋; Ⓢ Tuanjiehu) Great spot for lunch, especially in summer, located slap-bang in the middle of Sānlǐtún's bar street and opposite Běijīng's trendiest shopping area. As the name suggests, there's a Spanish/Mediterranean theme to the food, with Iberian ham and cheeses and decent salads (from ¥28), as well as great chips, but most punters go for the fine sandwiches on ciabatta.

The coffee, juices and smoothies go down a treat, too, and the large, tree-shaded terrace is very popular when the sun is out.

UIGHUR WILLOW — XINJIANG $

Map p298 (新疆红柳餐厅; Xīnjiāng Hóngliǔ Cāntīng; ☎5622 1508; 39 Shenlu Jie, 神路街 39 号日坛国际贸易中心; mains from ¥22, kebabs ¥10; ⏲10am-11pm; 📋; Ⓢ Chaoyangmen) Down a lane of restaurants, almost directly opposite the north gate of Rìtán Park, that come alive at night, this is a friendly and comfortable establishment catering almost exclusively to Uighurs, the people native to Xīnjiāng in China's far west. It's alcohol-free and offers Uighur classics such as polo, *laghman* noodles and the inevitable kebabs.

There's a small English menu, but if you're feeling adventurous you may do better pointing at what other people are eating.

NÀJIĀ XIǍOGUǍN — MANCHU $$

Map p298 (那家小馆; ☎6567 3663; 10 Yong'an Xili, off Jianguomenwai Dajie, Chunxiu Lu, 建国门外大街永安西里 10 号; mains ¥40-90; ⏲11.30am-9pm; 📋; Ⓢ Yong'anli) There's a touch of the traditional Chinese teahouse to this excellent restaurant, housed in a reconstructed two-storey interior courtyard, and bubbling with old-Peking atmosphere. The menu is based on an old imperial recipe book known as the *Golden Soup Bible,* and the dishes are consistently good (and fairly priced considering the quality).

The imperial Manchu theme could be tacky, but it's carried off in a fun but tasteful way that doesn't give you the feeling you're in a tourists-only restaurant. You don't need to book (in fact, at peak times you can't), but be prepared to hang around for at least half an hour for a table. It's worth the wait. No English sign and not much English spoken, but the menu is in English.

JĪNGZŪN PEKING DUCK — PEKING DUCK $$

Map p298 (京尊烤鸭; Jīngzūn Kǎoyā; ☎6417 4075; 6 Chunxiu Lu, 春秀路 6 号; mains ¥36-96; ⏲11am-10pm; 📋; Ⓢ Dongzhimen, Dongsi Shitiao) Very popular place to sample Běijīng's signature dish. Not only is the bird here extremely good value at ¥128 including all the trimmings but, unusually for a roast duck restaurant, you can also sit outside on a wooden-decked terrace. There's also a big choice of dishes from across China, all decent, if you're not in the mood for duck.

During the summer, book ahead if you want a spot on the terrace. Some English spoken.

IN & OUT — YUNNAN $$

Map p298 (一坐一忘; Yī Zuò Yī Wàng; ☎8454 0086; 1 Sanlitun Beixiaojie, 三里屯北小街 1 号; mains from ¥28; ⏲11am-10pm; 📋; Ⓢ Agricultural Exhibition Centre) Fashionable but friendly restaurant specialising in the many cuisines of the ethnic minority groups in southwestern Yúnnán province. The flavours are authentic and, given its popularity, the prices are surprisingly reasonable unless you go for the mushroom dishes (Yúnnán mushrooms are prized across Asia). Try the classic Over the Bridge Noodles (¥45), or the excellent Dongba beef ribs (¥56).

It's worth booking ahead here, especially if you're in a group.

DIN TAI FUNG — DUMPLINGS $$

Map p298 (鼎泰丰; Dǐng Tài Fēng; ☎6553 1536; 6f Shin Kong Place, 87 Jianguo Lu, 建国路 87 号新光天地店 6 楼; dumplings from ¥23, noodles

¥28-55; ⊙11.30am-9.30pm; ⊜; Ⓢ Dawanglu) The *New York Times* once picked the original Taipei branch of this upmarket dumplings chain as one of the 10 best restaurants in the world. That's no longer true, but the dumplings here are certainly special. The *xiǎolóngbāo* – thin-skinned packages with meat or vegie fillings that are surrounded by a superb, scalding soup – are especially fine.

Din Tai Fung also does Shànghǎi hairy crabmeat *jiǎozi* (stuffed dumplings) and *shāomài,* as well as excellent soups and noodle dishes. Completely nonsmoking, it prides itself on being kid-friendly and is packed out with families at weekends. It's on the top floor of the posh Shin Kong Place Mall, along with a host of other restaurants.

HÓNG LÚ BEIJING $$

Map p298 (红炉; ☎6595 9872; 60 Sanlitun Nanlu, 三里屯南路 6 号楼南侧 60 米; dishes from ¥28; ⊙11am-10pm; ⊜; Ⓢ Tuanjiehu) A great place to sample authentic Běijīng dishes in a clean environment (it's nonsmoking). The braised beef (¥56) is wonderfully tender, the Manchu Bannerman lamb (¥56) is packed with flavour, while you can get half a duck here for ¥88. The plum juice makes a healthy accompaniment to the meal. There's no English sign: look for the bright red door.

There are many intestine-based dishes here – testimony to Beijingers love of internal organs – but the English menu will help you avoid choosing dishes that might be too local for your tastes.

JÍXIÁNGNIĂO XIĀNGCÀI HUNAN $$

Map p298 (吉祥鸟湘菜; ☎6552 2856; Jishikou Donglu, 吉市口东路; dishes from ¥28; ⊙11am-9.30pm; Ⓢ Chaoyangmen) Not enough places in Běijīng serve *xiāng cài* (湘菜), the notoriously spicy cuisine of Húnán province, but this large, fiery restaurant is arguably the best of them. The braised pork with brown sauce (¥42), known in China as *hóngshāo ròu* (红烧肉), is the house speciality: it was the favourite dish of Mao Zedong, who hailed from Húnán,

But the fish head with chopped pepper (¥78) and the ribs (¥128) are not be missed, while the dry hotpots are also popular. You won't hear much English spoken, but there's a picture menu in English. It gets busy at lunchtimes especially. No English sign; look for the red neon Chinese characters.

NÁNJĪNG IMPRESSIONS NANJING $$

Map p298 (南京大牌档; Nánjīng Dàpáidàng; ☎8405 9777; 4th fl Shimao Shopping Centre, 13 Gongrentiyuchang Beilu, 工体北路 13 号世茂百货 4 层; mains from ¥28; ⊙11am-2pm & 5-10pm; Ⓢ Tuanjiehu) This place attempts to give diners an impression of a traditional street-side restaurant, which is hard as it's located on the 4th floor of a shopping mall. But the atmosphere is fun and the food is both authentic and good value. The dishes are sized to encourage you to sample a few and most are very tasty.

Either tick dishes off the menu, or browse the in-restaurant snack stalls and point at what you fancy. Duck dishes are a speciality – try the duck dumplings – as are the various sticky-rice dishes such as *jiāngmǐ kòuroù* (江米扣肉; a dome of sticky rice with pork belly strips; ¥32).

RUMI PERSIAN $$

Map p298 (入迷; ☎8454 3838; 1a Gongrentiyuchang Beilu, 工体北路 1-1 号; mains from ¥69; ⊙11am-midnight; Ⓢ Tuanjiehu) Běijīng's only Persian restaurant features cool white walls and furniture, but the food is the real deal. Check out dishes such as *ghormeh sabzi,* a beef or vegetarian stew, the fine shish kebabs (from ¥99), including a vegetarian option, and decent hummus. No alcohol is served, but you can bring your own and there's no corkage fee.

Shishas are also available to smoke (from ¥58) and there's a large street-side terrace for the summer.

XIĂO WÁNG'S HOME RESTAURANT CHINESE $$

Map p298 (小王府; Xiǎo Wángfǔ; ☎6591 3255; 2 Guanghua Dongli, 光华东里 2 号; mains ¥28-88; ⊙11am-10.30pm; Ⓢ Jintaixizhao) This clean and well-run restaurant has been serving customers for almost 20 years and has grown over time to occupy part of three floors of an old-fashioned, low-rise housing block. The menu is a medley of Chinese cuisine, but make sure to try the deservedly famous pork ribs with pepper and salt. The Peking duck (¥158) is good value here.

The restaurant has some balcony seating and an English sign, but is tucked away down an alley and can be hard to find. It's best accessed from Guanghua Lu.

CARMEN SPANISH $$

Map p298 (卡门; Kămén; ☎6417 8038; Nali Patio north side, 81 Sanlitun Lu, 三里屯路那里花园北

外1层; mains from ¥70; ⏲noon-1am; 📄; ⓈTuanjiehu) Běijīng's busiest tapas joint is a long, narrow space with tables hugging the walls. It's not the place for an intimate meal, but there's a great range of tapas, Spanish ham and cheeses and Mediterranean-inspired mains, including the huge paella (¥199), which can easily feed four. Strong wine list. It's around the corner from the popular terrace courtyard Nali Patio. There's live music from 7.30pm every night.

DESERT ROSE
CENTRAL ASIAN $$

Map p298 (沙漠玫瑰, Shāmò Méiguī; ☎8569 3576; 1-07, 39 Shenlu Jie, 神路街 39 号院 1 号楼 1-07; mains from ¥45; ⏲9am-1am; 🚭📄; ⓈChaoyangmen) The finest Central Asian restaurant in the capital, this Azerbaijan-run place takes the cuisine of the region and mixes it with Turkish and Russian influences. There's a huge range of superb kebabs (from ¥50), as well as different versions of pilaf, a rice and meat dish that is a Central Asian staple. It's nonsmoking and no alcohol is served.

Tobacco fiends can head to the outside terrace, although you are allowed to smoke a shisha inside. Make sure to try the different teas and sweet pastries.

MÉIZHŌU DŌNGPŌ JIǓLÓU
SICHUAN $$

Map p298 (眉州东坡酒楼; ☎5968 3370; Chunxiu Lu, 春秀路; mains from ¥26; ⏲6.30-9am, 10.30am-2pm & 5-10pm; 📄; Ⓢ Dongzhimen, Dongsi Shitiao) This good-value Sichuanese restaurant chain is one of the cheaper places to eat in this relatively expensive end of town. Despite the low prices, it still serves up good-quality, typically mouth-numbing Sìchuān dishes in a clean, comfortable setting. The menu is in English and has photos as well as very handy chilli-logo spice indicators. Beer is ¥12 a bottle.

INDIAN KITCHEN
INDIAN $$

Map p298 (北京印度小厨餐厅; Běijīng Yìndù Xiǎo Chú Cāntīng; ☎6462 7255; 2f, 2 Sanlitun Beixiaojie, 三里屯北小街 2 号二楼; mains ¥45-88; ⏲11am-2.30pm & 5.30-11pm; 📄; ⓈAgricultural Exhibition Center) Still the most reliable place in town for Indian food, attracting expats and locals in equal numbers. Solid service too.

PURPLE HAZE
THAI $$

Map p298 (紫苏庭; Zǐsū Tíng; ☎6413 0899; 55 Xingfu Yicun, off Gongrentiyuchang Beilu, 工人体育场北路幸福一村 55 号; mains from ¥48; ⏲11.30am-10.30pm; 🚭📶📄; ⓈDongsi Shitiao) This is the trendiest and most congenial Thai restaurant in town, as well as being the most authentic thanks to its 'keep it spicy' policy. The excellent cocktails will help soothe your tongue. Book ahead at weekends.

ELEPHANT
RUSSIAN $$

Map p298 (大笨象; Dàbèn Xiàng; ☎8561 4013; Ritan Beilu, 日坛北路; mains from ¥42; ⏲9am-4am; 📄; ⓈChaoyangmen) Fun Russian restaurant that stays busy into the early hours, thanks to its huge menu of Russian standards and cheap vodka (from ¥10 a shot). It serves food until 1am and has a large terrace for the summer.

BELLAGIO
TAIWANESE $$

Map p298 (鹿港小镇; Lùgǎng Xiǎozhèn; ☎6551 3533; 6 Gongrentiyuchang Xilu, 工体西路 6 号; mains ¥30-85; ⏲11am-5am; 📄; ⓈChaoyangmen) Despite the Italian name, this is a slick, late-opening Taiwanese restaurant conveniently located next to the strip of nightclubs on Gongrentiyuchang Xilu (Gongti Xilu). The large menu includes Taiwanese favourites such as three cup chicken (¥54), as well as a wide range of vegetarian options. But the real reason to come here is for the renowned shaved-ice puddings.

Try the red beans with condensed milk on shaved ice (¥27) and the fresh mango cubes on shaved ice (¥36). Top-notch coffee too. During the day and the evening, it attracts cashed-up locals and foreigners. After midnight, the club crowd moves in.

BITEAPITTA
MIDDLE EASTERN $$

Map p298 (吧嗒饼; Bāda Bǐng; unit 201, 2nd fl, Tongli Bldg, 43 Sanlitunbei Lu, 三里屯北路 43 号同里花园 201 号; mains ¥50-100; ⏲11am-1am; 📄; ⓈTuanjiehu) This unpretentious Middle Eastern restaurant-cafe is a decent spot for lunch or a late-night filler (stays open till 1am at weekends when it gets busy). Has a range of pitta-bread sandwiches, plus hummus, falafel, shawarma and salads. Also does a variety of kebabs, as well as Middle Eastern–style coffee.

DUCK DE CHINE
PEKING DUCK $$$

Map p298 (全鸭季; Quányājì; ☎6521 2221; Courtyard 4, 1949, near Gongrentiyuchang Beilu, 工体北路四号院; mains ¥78-488; ⏲11am-2pm & 5.30-10.30pm; 📄; ⓈTuanjiehu) Housed in a reconstructed industrial-style courtyard

BĚIJĪNG'S BEST LIBRARY

A combination of a bar, cafe, restaurant and library, the **Bookworm** (书虫; Shūchóng; Map p298; ☎6586 9507; www.beijingbookworm.com; Bldg 4, Nansanlitun Lu, 南三里屯路 4 号楼; mains from ¥60; ⏰9am-midnight; ⊖ 📶 📋; Ⓢ Tuanjiehu) is a Běijīng institution and one of the epicentres of the capital's cultural life. Much more than just an upmarket cafe, there are 16,000-plus books here you can browse while sipping your coffee. The food is reasonably priced, if uninspired, but there's a decent wine list.

The 'Worm also hosts lectures, poetry readings, a Monday-night quiz and a very well regarded annual book festival. Any author of note passing through town gives a talk here. Check the website for upcoming events. There's a roof terrace in summer and a nonsmoking area.

complex known as 1949, this very slick and stylish operation incorporates both Chinese and French duck-roasting methods to produce some stand-out duck dishes, including a leaner version of the classic Peking roast duck (¥238). The mix of expats and moneyed locals who flock here argue it's the best bird in town.

The service is as good as it gets in Běijīng, while the wine list is lengthy and expensive. The pumpkin infused with sour plums makes a delicious accompaniment. Book ahead.

MOSTO EUROPEAN $$$

Map p298 (摸石头, Mō Shítou; ☎5208 6030; 81 3rd fl, Nali Patio, Sanlitun Lu, 三里屯路 81 号 D308 那里花园 3F; mains from ¥135; ⏰ noon-2.30pm, 6-10pm; ⊖ 📋; Ⓢ Tuanjiehu) Consistently popular, especially at lunchtimes thanks to its attractive set lunch deal (two courses for ¥95), Mosto serves up solid, well-presented dishes with a vaguely Mediterranean theme. You can sit outside on the terrace, or inside around the open kitchen. There's a good wine list, excellent desserts and attentive service, and it's nonsmoking inside. Reserve on weekends.

O'STEAK FRENCH $$$

Map p298 (欧牛排法式餐厅; Ōu Niúpái Fàshì Cāntīng; ☎8448 8250; 55-7 Xingfucun Zhonglu, 幸福村中路 55-7 杰座大厦底层; steaks from ¥88; ⏰11am-11pm; 📋; Ⓢ Dongsi Shitiao) Superior steaks in a relaxed atmosphere at this French-run newcomer that will delight meat-lovers searching for a decently priced chunk of beef. There's a selection of sauces to accompany the steak of your choice, as well as salads and starters such as snails in a Burgundy style (¥69), and some very tempting puddings if you can find room for one.

Unsurprisingly, considering its popularity with Běijīng's French community, the wine list is extensive. Downstairs is nonsmoking.

OKRA JAPANESE $$$

Map p298 (☎6593 5087; Courtyard 4, 1949, near Gongrentiyuchang Beilu, 工人体育场北路 4 号院 1949 内（盈科中心南面）; mains from ¥120, sushi per piece from ¥30; ⏰6pm-10.30pm Tue-Sun; ⊖📋; Ⓢ Tuanjiehu) The sleek, minimalist design can feel a little cold at first, but the chef here knows his fish and the sushi and sashimi are as fresh as you'll find in Běijīng. You can watch him at work while you sip a cocktail or some sake. The tasting menu (¥450 to ¥850, six or 10 dishes) is perhaps the best option here.

DRINKING & NIGHTLIFE

The days when Sānlǐtún was the be-all and end-all of Běijīng nightlife are long gone. These days, the main drag of Sanlitun Lu is rather tawdry – at night the touts for massage parlours and hookers emerge – and the bars are strictly for the undiscerning. But hidden within the new, ultramodern shopping precincts of the Village is the area's hotspot: Nali Patio (Map p298), a small, modern courtyard space surrounded by popular bars, cafes and restaurants. Other jumping areas include Courtyard 4 (just south of Gongrentiyuchang Beilu) and the Workers Stadium, which contains most of Běijīng's busiest nightclubs. The area around Jianguomenwai Dajie is home to upmarket cocktail bars for the CBD crowd.

MIGAS BAR
BAR

Map p298 (米家思; Mǐ Jiā Sī; ☎5208 6061; 6th fl, Nali Patio, 81 Sanlitunbei Lu, 三里屯北路 81 号那里花园 6 层; beer from ¥30, cocktails from ¥60, mains from ¥98; ⏰noon-2.30pm & 6-10.30pm, bar 6pm-late; 📶; ⓈTuanjiehu) A good-quality Spanish restaurant, cosy bar and enticing rooftop terrace are three reasons why Migas remains one of the most popular venues in the area. During the summer, the terrace offers cocktails and city views and is jammed at weekends. There are DJs on Fridays and live music on Tuesdays, and the separate restaurant is almost as busy most evenings.

The tapas are excellent, if not as good value as nearby Carmen, and the three-course set lunch (¥95) is a solid deal. There's an extensive wine list, reasonably priced for Sānlǐtún, while the service is better than it was, although the crowds who gather here mean waiting for a drink is unavoidable.

APOTHECARY
COCKTAIL BAR

Map p298 (酒术; Jiǔ Shù; ☎5208 6040; www.apothecarychina.com; 3rd fl, Nali Patio, 81 Sanlitunbei Lu, 三里屯北路 81 号那里花园 3 层; cocktails from ¥65; ⏰6pm-late; 📶; ⓈTuanjiehu) A candidate for the city's best cocktail bar, Apothecary's blend of lovingly mixed drinks – including ingenious in-house creations – and a sophisticated but laid-back atmosphere has spawned an increasing number of imitators around town. Few, though, can match Apothecary's attention to detail – the history of each drink is detailed on the menu – or the quality of the cocktails.

Service can be slow, and there's a rather bizarre 'no standing at the bar' policy, but decent food is available as well and, best of all, it's far less stuffy than its five-star hotel bar competitors.

GREAT LEAP BREWING
BAR

Map p298 (大跃啤酒, Dàyuè Píjiǔ; ☎6416 6887; Ziming Mansion Unit 101, 12 Xinzhong Jie, 新中街乙 12 号紫铭大厦 101 室; beers from ¥25, burgers from ¥40; ⏰11.30am-1am Sun-Thu, 11.30am-2am Fri & Sat; 🚭📶; ⓈDongsi Shitiao) A hotspot for hipsters and anyone in search of a decent beer, Great Leap's wooden benches and long bar are rammed most nights. The original Běijīng craft brewery, there are normally 12 beers on tap here, changing depending on the season, as well as sandwiches and burgers to accompany them. There's another branch off Nanluogu Xiang (p99).

REVOLUTION
BAR

Map p298 (革命酒吧; Gémìng Jiǔbā; ☎6415 8776; West side of Yashow Market, Gongti Beilu, 工体北路雅秀市场西侧; beers from ¥35, cocktails from ¥45; ⏰Sun-Tue 5pm-1am, Wed-Sat 5pm-2am; ⓈTuanjiehu) Amenable and cute cubbyhole of a bar with a Cultural Revolution theme: photos of Mao adorn the walls and patriotic Chinese movies from the 1960s play on the TV. But the strong selection of cocktails and single malt whiskies, all reasonably priced, are a bigger draw than the Chairman. Happy hour is 5pm to 8pm.

JANES AND HOOCH
COCKTAIL BAR

Map p298 (☎6503 2757; Lot 10, Courtyard 4, Gongti Beilu, 工体北路 4 号机电院; cocktails from ¥65; ⏰7pm-2am; ⓈTuanjiehu) The bar of the moment, and as popular with locals as it is with Westerners. Sip your drink at the stylish long bar on the ground floor, or head upstairs and grab a table. The drinks are decent without being outstanding, the service efficient. It gets very busy on weekends.

PARLOR
COCKTAIL BAR

Map p298 (香; Xiāng; ☎8444 4135; 39-9 Xingfu'ercun, Xindong Lu, 新东路幸福二村 39-9 号; cocktails from ¥60; ⏰ 6pm-late; ⓈDongsi Shitiao) Deliberately hidden away, Parlor aims to recreate the atmosphere of an old-school Shànghǎi speakeasy. It mostly succeeds, with bartenders in bow ties, a solid wooden bar counter and the roaring 1920s decor. To find it, walk to the end of an alley leading into a car park just before the Bank of China on Xingfuercun and look for the wooden door.

Upstairs is another world of private rooms that are strictly for high-rollers; you'll need to drop a minimum of ¥50,000 to gain access.

FIRST FLOOR
BAR

Map p298 (壹楼; Yī Lóu; ☎6413 0587; ground fl Tongli Studios, Sanlitun Houjie, 三里屯后街同里 1 层; beer from ¥20, cocktails from ¥40; ⏰ 10am-2am; ⓈTuanjiehu) Solid bar with a publike vibe that attracts an older, expat crowd as well as increasing numbers of locals. Stocks a big selection of foreign beers and the outside terrace means it doesn't get as smoky as its upstairs sister bar, **Second Floor** (Map p298). There's a daily happy hour from 5pm to 9pm and it's open till 4am at weekends.

LOCAL KNOWLEDGE

CRAFT BEERS & BARBECUE

A revolution began in Běijīng in 2010. For once, it didn't concern politics. Instead, it was all about beer. When Great Leap Brewing (p149) started making its own ales from 100% local ingredients, it marked the emergence of the capital's very own craft breweries. Now, at least five microbreweries are operating in Běijīng.

Great Leap, Slow Boat Brewery (p75) and 京 A Brewing (Jīng A, or Capital A Brewing) are by the far the best of them. And with craft beers increasingly popular with both locals and foreigners, there are more and more places around town where you can sample their ales. The venues below offer the added bonus of serving up old-fashioned American-style barbecue.

Big Smoke (Map p298; ☎6416 5195; 1/F, Lee World Bldg, 57 Xingfucun Zhong Lu, 幸福村中路57号利世商务楼一层; beer from ¥35; ⏰11am-midnight; 📶; Ⓢ Dongsi Shitiao) Home base of Jīng A brewing, perhaps Běijīng's finest brew masters, this is the place to sample its superb Flying Fist IPA or a Workers Pale Ale. Accompany them with some Southern US–inspired barbecue.

Home Plate Bar B-Que (本垒美式烤肉; Běnlěi Měishì Kǎoròu; Map p298; ☎400 096 7670; Lot 10, Courtyard 4, 三里屯机电院 10 号; beers from ¥30, dishes from ¥30; ⏰11am-1am; Ⓢ Tuanjiehu) Hefty dishes are on offer here – slobbery burgers, fries covered in cheese and chilli – but it's the beer that's the main draw. Draft Slow Boat ales start at ¥45. Try the First Immortal Double IPA.

Local (Map p298; ☎6591 9525; Courtyard 4, 工体北路4号机电院; beers from ¥20, mixed drinks from ¥40; ⏰noon-1am Sun & Mon, noon-3am Tue-Thu, noon-4am Fri & Sat; 📶; Ⓢ Tuanjiehu) Jīng A and Slow Boat beers on tap and in bottles, as well as buffalo wings, Tex-Mex offerings and good-value steaks. There's a daily happy hour until 9pm.

ICHIKURA — COCKTAIL BAR

Map p298 (☎6507 1107; 36 Dongsanhuan Beilu, 东三环北路 36 号; whiskies & cocktails from ¥60; ⏰6pm-1.30am; ⓈHujialou) For those in the know, this tiny Japanese-style bar is the best place for a whisky in all Běijīng. Only the drinks matter here, with a vast selection of single malt and Japanese whiskies, while the silent barman can concoct any cocktail you can think of. It's up a staircase by the northern side of the Cháoyáng Theatre (p153).

LANTERN — CLUB

Map p298 (灯笼俱乐部; Dēnglóng Jùlèbù; Gongrentiyuchang Xilu, 工人体育场西门向北100 米; entry ¥30-100; ⏰9pm-late; ⓈDongsi Shitiao) The closest thing to an underground dance club in the capital, with a roster of the best local DJs (and occasional foreign guests) spinning a more eclectic mix of techno and house than you'll hear anywhere else. The ticket price varies depending on who's playing.

SPARK — CLUB

Map p298 (☎6587 1501; B108, The Place, Guanghua Lu, 光华路9号世贸天阶 B108; entry ¥100-200; ⏰10pm-late Fri & Sat, 10pm-2.30am Sun-Tue, 10pm-3.30am Wed & Thu; ⓈDongdaqiao, Yonganli) A branch of a Taiwanese club chain, Spark has stormed the Běijīng club scene leaving its competitors trailing in its wake. This is where the beautiful people come to groove to mainstream house and electro, often spun by overseas DJs, despite the club's incongruous location in the basement of the Place shopping mall. The entry fee drops during the week.

TREE — BAR

Map p298 (树酒吧; Shù Jiǔbā; ☎6415 1954; 43 Sanlitun Beijie, 三里屯北街 43 号; beers from ¥20; ⏰10am-2am; ⓈTuanjiehu) A low-key, long-term favourite, the Tree attracts a mix of locals, expats and tourists. There's a fine selection of Belgian beers (from ¥45) and the thin-crust pizzas (from ¥55), cooked in a wood-fired oven, are some of the best in town. Around the corner is its close relative **Nearby the Tree** (树旁边酒吧; Shù Pángbiān Jiǔbā; Map p298; Xingfu Sancun Yixiang, off Sanlitunbei Lu, 三里屯北路幸福三村一巷; beers from ¥20; ⏰10am-2am; ⓈTuanjiehu), which has a happy hour 6pm to 9pm.

CHOCOLATE — CLUB

Map p298 (巧克力; Qiǎokèlì; ☎8561 3988; 19 Ritan Beilu, 日坛北路 19 号; ⏰9pm-6am;

ⓈChaoyangmen) There are a number of Russian-style bars around the Rìtán Park area, but with its over-the-top, gold-themed decor, cheesy dance shows (10pm and midnight) and party techno tunes this is the closest you will come to a genuine Moscow nightlife experience in Běijīng. A shot of vodka starts at ¥20, beers at ¥30. It gets going after midnight.

If you're in a group, do as as the Russians do and order a bottle of vodka (from ¥180).

PADDY O'SHEA'S — SPORTS BAR

Map p298 (爱尔兰酒吧; Ài'érlán Jiǔbā; ☎6415 6389; 28 Dongzhimenwai Dajie, 东直门外大街 28 号; beers from ¥25; ⏲10am-2am; 📶; ⓈDongzhimen) One of the top spots in Běijīng for watching sport on TV (Premiership football especially, but also rugby, tennis and Formula 1), Paddy's has a large number of screens, allowing for multichannel viewing. It's about as Irish as a Guinness poster, but there's a proper bar to sit at, the service is warm and efficient and it does pub grub.

Kilkenny and Guinness are on tap and there's a sound selection of whiskies (from ¥35). Happy hour is 3pm to 8pm Monday to Friday. There's a handy Indian restaurant upstairs to order from too.

DESTINATION — CLUB

Map p298 (目的地; Mùdìdì; 7 Gongrentiyuchang Xilu, 工体西路 7 号; entry ¥60; ⏲8pm-late; ⓈChaoyangmen) A club for boys who like boys and girls who want a night off from them; check out the teddy bears behind the bar. The rough-hewn and concrete-walled interior doesn't stop Destination being packed on weekends. But then, as Běijīng's only genuine gay club, it doesn't have to worry about any competition.

MESH — COCKTAIL BAR

Map p298 (Bldg 1, Village, 11 Sanlitun Lu, 三里屯路 11 号院 1 号楼; cocktails from ¥70; ⏲5pm-2am; ⓈTuanjiehu) Located inside the achingly trendy Opposite House Hotel, Mesh has been designed to within an inch of its life – with white bar, mirrors, fancy light fittings and mesh screens separating its different areas – but the effect isn't overpowering and it can be fun on the right night. The lychee martinis here are justly popular. Thursday is gay night.

XIÙ — BAR

Map p298 (秀酒吧; Xiù Jiǔbā; 6th fl Park Life, Yintai Centre, 2 Jianguomenwai Dajie, 建国门外大街 2 银泰中心柏悦酒店 6 层; cocktails from ¥80; ⏲6pm-2am; ⓈGuomao) With its large wood-decked open terrace, pavilion and water features, the Park Hyatt's 6th-floor drinking spot beats other swish hotel bars come summer. It would be a calm, almost serene, space were it not for the crowd of flush locals and expats who assemble here. The cocktails are decent without being Běijīng's best and there's live music and DJs.

D LOUNGE — BAR

Map p298 (酒术; Jiǔ Shù; Courytard 4, Gongrentiyuchang Beilu, 工体北路 4 号院; cocktails from ¥60; ⏲7pm-late; ⓈTuanjiehu) High ceilings and exposed brick walls give this cool venue a converted factory feel. The bright white bar adds some futuristic flavour, while the drinks are well made and the atmosphere is trendy without being overly swanky (although some complain of slightly obnoxious staff). Can be hard to find because of a lack of signage; look for the lower-case 'd'.

MIX — CLUB

Map p298 (密克斯; Mìkèsī; ☎6530 2889; Workers Stadium, North Gate, Gongrentiyuchang Beilu, 工人体育场北路， 工人体育场北门; admission Sun-Thu ¥30, Fri & Sat ¥50; ⏲8pm-6am; ⓈDongsi Shitiao) Mainstream hip-hop and R&B are the drawcards at this ever-popular nightclub with big-name DJs making occasional guest appearances and a packed dance floor. It attracts a younger clientele than nearby Vics and the music is generally better.

VICS — CLUB

Map p298 (威克斯; Wēikèsī; ☎5293 0333; Workers Stadium, North Gate, Gongrentiyuchang Beilu, 工人体育场北路， 工人体育场北门; admission Sun-Thu ¥50, Fri & Sat ¥100; ⏲8.30pm-5am; ⓈDongsi Shitiao) Not the most sophisticated nightclub, but a favourite with the young (and older and sleazy) crowd for many years now, which makes it some sort of an institution. The tunes are mostly standard R&B and hip-hop and there's an infamous ladies night on Wednesdays (free drinks for women before midnight). If you can't score here, you never will.

It's located inside the north gate of the Workers Stadium. The attached **V Sports Bar** (Workers Stadium, North Gate, Gongrentiyuchang Beilu, 工人体育场北路， 工人体育场北门; beer from ¥30, cocktails from ¥50; ⏲5pm-5am; ⓈDongsi Shitiao) has pool and darts and

KTV

Karaoke, or as it's known here, KTV, is the number one leisure pastime for most Chinese people. There are hundreds of KTV venues in Běijīng and if you get the chance to go to one with some Chinese friends, take it. The enthusiasm the locals show for belting out their favourite pop classics across a small room filled with their mates, is astonishing.

If you speak Mandarin, you can sing along to the latest Mando-pop hits. English speakers will have to content themselves with a smaller and older selection of tunes, but you'll always find something you can sing. Prices depend on the size of the room you want and the time of day. It's always advisable to book ahead at weekends.

Tango KTV (糖果; Tángguǒ; Map p290; ☎6428 2288; 79 Hepinglixi Jie, 和平里西街 79 号, 地坛公园南门; small room for 5 to 6 people per 1hr weekday/weekend evenings ¥120/180, after midnight ¥90/110; ⏲ 24hr) By the south gate of Dìtán Park.

Melody KTV (麦乐迪; Màilèdí; Map p298; ☎6551 0808; A-77 Chaoyangmenwai Dajie, 朝阳门外大街 A-77 号; small room for 5 to 6 people per 1hr weekday/weekend evenings from ¥160/260; ⏲ 11am-6am) South of the Workers Stadium.

Partyworld KTV (钱柜; Qiánguì; Map p298; ☎6588 3333; Fanli Bldg, 22 Chaoyangmenwai Dajie, 朝阳门外大街 22 号泛利大夏; small room for 5-6 people per 3hr weekday/weekend evenings ¥200/400; ⏲ midday-5.30am) Walking distance from Chaoyangmen subway station;accessed viaChaowaishichang Jie.

is a good place to catch live football on one if its many screens.

ALFA — CLUB

Map p298 (阿尔法; Ā'ěrfǎ; 6 Xingfu Yicun, 幸福一村 6 号, 工体北门对面; beers from ¥25, cocktails from ¥45; ⏲5pm-2am; Ⓢ Dongsi Shitiao) Now one of the longest-running bar-clubs in Běijīng. Has a pleasant, enclosed terrace where you can smoke a shisha (¥120). Popular gay night on Fridays.

Q BAR — BAR

Map p298 (Q 吧; top fl, Eastern Inn Hotel, Nansanlitun Lu, 三里屯南路麦霓啤酒吧南 100 米; cocktails from ¥60; ⏲6pm-late; Ⓢ Tuanjiehu) Newly refurbished and friendly cocktail bar with large roof terrace. Accessed through Eastern Inn Hotel.

AT CAFE — CAFE

(☎5978 9943; 798 Rd; mains from ¥38; ⏲10am-midnight) This is 798's first cafe and still a popular hang-out for both artists and visitors. It serves Western standards like pasta and pizza, as well as good coffee (from ¥28). The outside terrace is fine for a drink in the evening.

TIMEZONE 8 — CAFE

(☎5978 9917; 798 Road; mains from ¥55, sushi from ¥32; ⏲7am-2am) Cool cafe and the best spot to eat in 798, Timezone no longer has its attached bookshop but continues to pack people in with its huge sandwiches, burgers and all-day breakfasts, as well as a sushi bar. In the summer, the outside terrace gets jammed.

☆ ENTERTAINMENT

★DOS KOLEGAS — LIVE MUSIC

(两个好朋友; Liǎnggè Hǎo Péngyou; 21 Liangmaqiao Lu, 亮马桥路 21 号（汽车电影院内）; admission ¥30, beer from ¥15; ⏲8pm-2am Mon-Sat, 10am-9pm Sun; Ⓢ Liangmaqiao then 🚌909) Tucked away to the side of Běijīng's drive-in cinema, a couple of kilometres northeast of Sānlǐtún, this fabulously bohemian venue has a large garden with patio seating and offers evening barbecues alongside some excellent live music. This is a great place to hear local bands (punk, rock, metal), especially in the summer when the whole gig moves outdoors.

UNIVERSAL THEATRE (HEAVEN & EARTH THEATRE) — ACROBATICS

Map p298 (天地剧场; Tiāndì Jùchǎng; ☎6416 0757; 10 Dongzhimen Nandajie, 东直门南大街 10 号; tickets ¥180-680; ⏲performances 7.15pm; Ⓢ Dongsi Shitiao) Young performers from the China National Acrobatic Troupe perform their mind-bending, joint-popping contortions. A favourite with tour groups, so best to book ahead. Tickets are pricier the further from the stage you sit. Keep an eye out for the dismal white structure that looks like an airport control tower – that's where you buy your tickets.

POLY PLAZA INTERNATIONAL THEATRE CLASSICAL MUSIC

Map p298 (保利大厦国际剧院; Bǎolì Dàshà Guójì Jùyuàn; ☎6500 1188, ext 5621, 6506 5343; 14 Dongzhimen Nandajie, 东直门南大街 14 号; tickets ¥180-880; ⊙performances 7.30pm; Ⓢ Dongsi Shitiao) Right by Dongsi Shitiao subway station, this venue hosts a range of performances, including ballet, classical music, opera and traditional Chinese folk music. It also puts on an increasing number of works by foreign playwrights.

CHÁOYÁNG THEATRE ACROBATICS

Map p298 (朝阳剧场; Cháoyáng Jùchǎng; ☎6507 2421; 36 Dongsanhuan Beilu, 东三环北路 36 号; tickets ¥280-880; ⊙performances 5.15pm & 7.15pm; Ⓢ Hujialou) An accessible place for foreign visitors, and often bookable through your hotel, this theatre hosts visiting acrobatic troupes from around China who fill the stage with plate spinning and hoop jumping.

MEGABOX CINEMA

Map p298 (美嘉欢乐影城; Měijiā Huānlè Yǐngchéng; ☎6417 6118; B1 Fl Sanlitun Village South, 19 Sanlitun Lu, 三里屯路 19 号三里屯 Village 南区地下 1 层; tickets ¥80-120; ⊙performances noon-midnight; Ⓢ Tuanjiehu) The most convenient place to catch English-language Hollywood blockbusters, MegaBox is a multiplex cinema in the basement of the trendy Sānlǐtún Village shopping mall. It always shows at least one or two English-language films and offers an experience almost identical to cinemas in the West (although don't expect much English from the attendants who work here).

EAST GATE CINEMA CINEMA

Map p298 (东环影城; Dōnghuán Yǐngchéng; ☎6418 5935; Bldg B, Basement, East Gate Plaza, Dongzhong Jie, 东中街东环广场 B 座地下一层; tickets ¥80-120; Ⓢ Dongsi Shitiao) Shows the latest big releases, both domestic and foreign. Foreign films are shown with their original audio, but with Chinese subtitles.

SHOPPING

The Cháoyáng District has some of the swankiest malls in town, as well as many of the most popular markets for visitors, including the Silk Market and Yashow, two multifloor indoor clothes and souvenir markets which are heaving at weekends. Key areas for purchases are Sānlǐtún and Guómào, but there are shops of all descriptions spread across the district. Pānjiāyuán Market is on the edge of Cháoyáng and is the city's premier souvenir market.

SĀNLǏTÚN VILLAGE SHOPPING MALL

Map p298 (19 Sanlitun Lu, 三里屯路 19 号; ⊙10am-10pm; Ⓢ Tuanjiehu) This eye-catching collection of midsized malls is a shopping and architectural highlight of this part of the city. The Village (known officially as Taikooli; Tàigǔlǐ; 太古里) looms over what was once a seedy strip of dive bars and has transformed the area into a hotspot for locals and foreigners alike. There are two parts to the complex, **South Village** (Map p298) and **North Village** (Map p298).

The South Village was completed a few years back and is home to Běijīng's first Apple store, the world's largest Adidas shop and a number of midrange Western clothing stores, as well as cafes, restaurants and the multiplex cinema MegaBox. Nearby North Village is home to more high-end labels and local designer boutiques, including Emporio Armani, Comme des Garçons, Balenciaga and Shanghai Trio, and is set beside Běijīng's fancy-pants boutique hotel Opposite House.

SILK MARKET CLOTHING, SOUVENIRS

Map p298 (秀水市场, Xiùshuǐ Shìchǎng; 14 Dongdaqiao Lu, 东大桥路 14 号; ⊙9.30am-9pm; Ⓢ Yong'anli) The six-storey Silk Market is more upmarket than it once was, but remains jammed with fake clothing, bags, electronics and jewellery, despite some vendors being hit by lawsuits from top-name brands tired of being counterfeited on such a huge scale. The silk, which you'll find on the 3rd floor, is one of the few genuine items on sale here.

With coach loads of tourists descending on the market daily, effective bargaining is difficult. But this is a good place for cashmere, T-shirts, jeans, shirts, skirts and, of course, silk. There's a food court on the top floor.

LOCAL KNOWLEDGE

ARTS, CRAFTS & ANTIQUES

Pānjiāyuán Market (潘家园古玩市场; Pānjiāyuán Gǔwán Shìchǎng; West of Panjiayuan Qiao, 潘家园桥西侧; ⏲ 8.30am-6pm Mon-Fri, 4.30am-6pm Sat & Sun; Ⓢ Panjiayuan) is hands down the best place in Běijīng to shop for *yìshù* (arts), *gōngyì* (crafts) and *gǔwán* (antiques). Some stalls open every day, but the market is at its biggest and most lively on weekends, when you can find everything from calligraphy, Cultural Revolution memorabilia and cigarette ad posters, to Buddha heads, ceramics, Qing dynasty–style furniture and Tibetan carpets.

Pānjiāyuán hosts around 3000 dealers and up to 50,000 visitors a day, all scoping for treasures. The serious collectors are early birds, swooping here at dawn to snare precious relics. If you want to join them, an early start is essential. You might not find that rare Qianlong *dòucǎi* stem cup or late Yuan dynasty *qīnghuā* vase, but what's on view is nothing less than a compendium of Chinese curios and an A to Z of Middle Kingdom knick-knacks. The market is chaotic and can be difficult if you find crowds or hard bargaining intimidating. Ignore the 'don't pay more than half' rule here – some vendors might start at 10 times the real price. Make a few rounds to compare prices and weigh it up before forking out for something. To get here, come out of Exit B at Panjiayuan subway station, then walk west for 200m to find the main entrance to the market.

SĀNLǏTÚN YASHOW CLOTHING MARKET — CLOTHING, SOUVENIRS

Map p298 (三里屯雅秀服装市场; Sānlǐtún Yǎxiù Fúzhuāng Shìchǎng; 58 Gongrentiyuchang Beilu, 工体北路 58 号; ⏲10am-8.30pm; ⓈTuanjiehu) Five floors of anything you might need and a favourite with expats and visitors. Basement: shoes, handbags and suitcases. Big Shoes is useful if you're struggling to find suitably sized footwear. First floor: coats and jackets. Second floor: shirts, suits and ladies wear. Third floor: silk, clothes. Fourth floor: carpets, fabrics, jewellery, souvenirs and toys. Bargain hard here.

If you need to fashion your newly bought silk or fabrics into something wearable, head for the tailors on the 3rd floor. DVD stores surround the market.

SHARD BOX STORE — JEWELLERY

Map p298 (慎德阁; Shèndégé; ☎8561 8358; 4 Ritan Beilu, 日坛北路 4 号; ⏲9am-7pm; ⓈDongdaqiao) Using porcelain fragments from Ming- and Qing-dynasty vases that were destroyed during the Cultural Revolution, this fascinating family-run store creates beautiful and unique shard boxes, bottles and jewellery. The boxes range from the tiny (¥25), for storing rings or cufflinks, to the large (¥780). It also repairs and sells jewellery, mostly sourced from Tibet and Mongolia.

UCCA DESIGN STORE — CLOTHING, SOUVENIRS

(尤伦斯当代艺术中心; Yóulúnsī Dāngdài Yìshù Zhōngxīn; ☎5780 0224; 4 Jiuxianqiao Lu, 酒仙桥路 4 号 798 艺术区; ⏲10am-7pm Tue-Sun; 🚌909) A haven for style mavens, UCCA is the place to come for limited-edition prints and lithographs by famous local artists, as well as stylish clothes (including kids wear), jewellery, books on art and design and all manner of quirky potential gifts and mementos. It's next door to the UCCA gallery (p140) in the 798 Art District.

ALIEN'S STREET MARKET — CLOTHING

Map p298 (老番街市场; Lǎo Fān Jiē Shìchǎng; Chaowaishichang Jie, 朝外市场街; ⏲9.30am-7pm; ⓈChaoyangmen) This somewhat cramped market, just north of Rìtán Park, is packed with a huge variety of clothing, as well as tons of accessories. You can find most things here and it's popular with visiting Russian traders, which means the clothes come in bigger sizes than usual and the vendors will greet you in Russian. Haggling is essential.

3.3 SHOPPING CENTRE — SHOPPING MALL

Map p298 (服饰大厦; Fúshì Dàshà; 33 Sanlitun Beijie, 三里屯北街 33 号; ⏲11am-11pm; ⓈTuanjiehu) With its collection of trendy boutiques and accessories stores, as well as massage and manicure salons, this mall, sandwiched between the North and South blocks of the even trendier Sānlǐtún Village, caters for

Běijīng's bright young things. Prices are accordingly high. But with 300 shops here, it's good window-shopping territory.

CHINA WORLD SHOPPING MALL SHOPPING MALL

Map p298 (国贸商城; Guómào Shāngchéng; 1 Jianguomenwai Dajie; 建国门外大街 1 号; ⏲10am-9.30pm; Ⓢ Guomao) Adjacent to the first-rate China World Hotel, this is a popular, if soulless, mall packed with top-name brands, including Burberry, Marc Jacobs and Prada, as well as boutiques, jewellery stores and fast-food restaurants. Le Cool Ice Rink (p156) is in the basement.

BǍINǍOHUÌ COMPUTER MALL ELECTRONICS

Map p298 (百脑汇电脑市场; Bǎinǎohuì Diànnǎo Shìchǎng; 10 Chaoyangmenwai Dajie, 朝阳门外大街 10 号; ⏲9am-8pm; Ⓢ Dongdaqiao) Four floors of gadgetry, including computers, iPods, MP3 players, blank CDs, DVDs, gaming gear, software and other accessories. The prices are fairly competitive and you can bargain here, but don't expect too much of a reduction. Next to this mall there are a number of shops that are good places to pick up mobile phones and local SIM cards.

There's another Bǎinǎohuì mall across the road by Dōngyuè Temple.

PLACE SHOPPING MALL

Map p298 (世贸天阶; Shìmào Tiānjiē; 9a Guanghua Lu, 光华路甲 9 号; ⏲10am-10pm; Ⓢ Yong'anli) Dominated by its spectacular giant outdoor video screen, an object of fascination for kids, the Place has an extremely popular branch of Zara, as well as French Connection, Miss Sixty and a number of coffee shops. Also accessed from Dongdaqiao Lu and Jintong Xilu.

SPORTS, ACTIVITIES & COURSES

BODHI THERAPEUTIC RETREAT MASSAGE

Map p298 (菩提会所; Pútí Huìsuǒ; ☎6417 9595; 17 Gongrentiyuchang Beilu, 工体北路 17 号; ⏲11am-12.30am; Ⓢ Dongsi Shitiao) The serene setting, just moments away from the madness of Běijīng's traffic, helps you shift gears straightaway, and that's before one of the many massage therapists here gets to work in a comfy, private room. Bodhi offers aromatherapy, ayurvedic, Thai- and Chinese-style massage, as well as great foot reflexology massages and a wide range of facial treatments.

There's free snacks and drinks, and with TVs in all the rooms you can lie back

LOCAL KNOWLEDGE

'GUÓ'ĀN, GUÓ'ĀN, BĚIJĪNG GUÓ'ĀN!'

While you'll rarely see kids playing football (soccer) on the streets of Běijīng (basketball being the main game of choice), watching it is far more popular. Until recently, Chinese football fans contented themselves with viewing the big European leagues on TV. Now, though, increasing numbers of people are going to see a live game in the Chinese Super League, China's premier competition. In Běijīng, that means following **Běijīng Guó'ān** (www.fcguoan.com), the capital's sole team. Although it lacks the cash and star names of Guǎngzhōu Evergrande and Shànghǎi Shēnhuā, it is still one of China's most successful teams. Best of all, it has a passionate fan base and draws large crowds for its home games at the **Workers Stadium** (工人体育场; Gongren Tiyuchang). It's not unusual for over 30,000 spectators to attend big games. Going to see one before hitting the bars and clubs in the area makes a fun night out for footie fans, even if the standard of football isn't that high.

The season runs from March until November. Match days can be Thursday, Friday, Saturday or Sunday; kick-offs are usually 7.30pm. You can find Guó'ān's fixtures in English on www.worldfootball.net. Tickets are sold online through Chinese-language websites, or over the phone (Chinese only), but are sold out so quickly it's not worth bothering trying to go through these official channels. Standard practise is to just go to the stadium an hour or so before kick-off and buy your tickets off ticket touts. Expect to pay at least double or triple the face value of the ticket, meaning you'll probably have to fork out around ¥100 to ¥150 per ticket.

If you're interested in playing football while you're in Běijīng, contact the guys who run **China ClubFootball** (www.clubfootball.com.cn).

and watch a DVD while being pummelled into shape. Prices start at ¥188 for a basic full-body massage, although Thai and ayurvedic massages cost ¥328. Massages are sometimes discounted during weekday afternoons.

DRAGONFLY THERAPEUTIC RETREAT — MASSAGE

Map p298 (☎8529 6331; Kerry Centre, 1 Guanghua Lu; 嘉里中心光华路 1 号; ⊙10am-11pm) Swish, professional operation located in the basement of the Kerry Centre.

YOGA YARD — YOGA

Map p298 (瑜珈苑; Yújiā Yuàn; ☎6413 0774; www.yogayard.com; 6th fl, 17 Gongrentiyuchang Beilu, 工体北路 17 号 6 层; ⊙7am-7.45pm; S Dongsi Shitiao) This friendly English-speaking centre has traditional hatha yoga classes, for everyone from beginners to advanced. Ninety-minute lessons are ¥150; lunchtime classes ¥100.

JĪNGHUÁ WŪSHÙ ASSOCIATION — MARTIAL ARTS

Map p298 (京华武术协会; Jīnghuá Wǔshù Xiéhuì; ☎135 2228 3751; Basement, Pulse Club, Kempinski Hotel, Liangmaqiao Lu, 亮马桥路凯宾斯基地下一层脉搏俱乐部; ⊙ 5.30-7pm Sat & Sun; S Liangmaqiao) Run from the gym at Pulse Club in the basement of the building next to Kempinski Hotel, classes here are held in English and are given by teachers trained in traditional Shàolín forms. *Wǔshù, qìgōng* and taichi are all taught here. Ten classes costs ¥1200; a single class is ¥150. There are classes for kids (five years and over), too

If you're not staying at the Kempinski, you can use the Pulse Health Club for ¥300 a day. Aerobics, yoga and belly-dancing classes are available, as are squash courts.

HAPPY MAGIC WATER PARK — SWIMMING

(水立方嬉水乐园; Shuǐlìfāng Xīshuǐ Lèyuán; Olympic Green, off Beichen Lu, 北辰路奥林匹克公园内; water park entrance adult/child ¥200/160, swimming only ¥50; ⊙10am-8pm; S Olympic Green) Unlike most of the 2008 Olympics venues, Běijīng's National Aquatics Centre, aka the Water Cube, has found a new lease of life post-Olympics. The otherworldly, bubblelike structure now houses Běijīng's largest indoor water park. It's a fave with children, who can negotiate neon plastic slides, tunnels, water jets and pools, all set alongside elaborate, surreal underwater styling.

There's a lazy river, a 12m freefall drop inside a plastic tube, and a wave pool designed to mimic the ocean. You can pay ¥50 for a two-hour swimming session in the ordinary pool, but for full-on water-slide action, you need the ¥200 ticket. The park is about 7km north of the city centre.

LE COOL ICE RINK — ICE SKATING

Map p298 (国贸溜冰场; Guómào Liūbīngchǎng; ☎6505 5776; Basement 2, China World Shopping Mall, 1 Jianguomenwai Dajie, 建国门外大街 1 号; per 90min ¥30-50; ⊙10am-10pm; S Guomao) Like many of the rinks in Běijīng, Le Cool is not very big. But it's easily accessible and perfect for kids. Visit in the morning or evening if you want to avoid the crowds. Skate hire is included in the price, which varies depending on the time of day. Individual, 30-minute lessons are ¥120.

BERLITZ — LANGUAGE COURSES

Map p298 (北立兹; Běilìzi; ☎6593 0478; www.berlitz.com; Room 801, Sunjoy Mansion, 6 Ritan Lu, 日坛路 6 号新旅大夏 8 层; S Jianguomen, Yong'anli) Berlitz runs group and one-on-one classes in Chinese, although you'll likely have to form your own group beforehand.

BRIDGE SCHOOL — LANGUAGE COURSES

Map p298 (桥学校; Qiáo Xuéxiào; ☎6506 4409; www.bridgeschoolchina.com; Room 903, e-Tower, Guanghua Lu, 光华路内 12 号楼吗 01 大夏 9 层; per hour from ¥90; S Jintaixizhao) Group and one-on-one classes. Has set-time classes you can join at various language levels.

Summer Palace & Hǎidiàn

Neighbourhood Top Five

❶ Enjoy a taste of imperial high-life by wandering the glorious **Summer Palace** (p159).

❷ Commune with nature in **Fragrant Hills Park** (p161).

❸ Spend a night exploring the buzzing restaurants and clubs of **Wǔdàokǒu** (p168), Běijīng's student heartland.

❹ Push through the bamboo fronds in the **Běijīng Botanic Gardens** (p163), China's top collection of flora.

❺ Temple-hop your way around the district, starting at the fascinating **Wǔtǎ Temple** (p163).

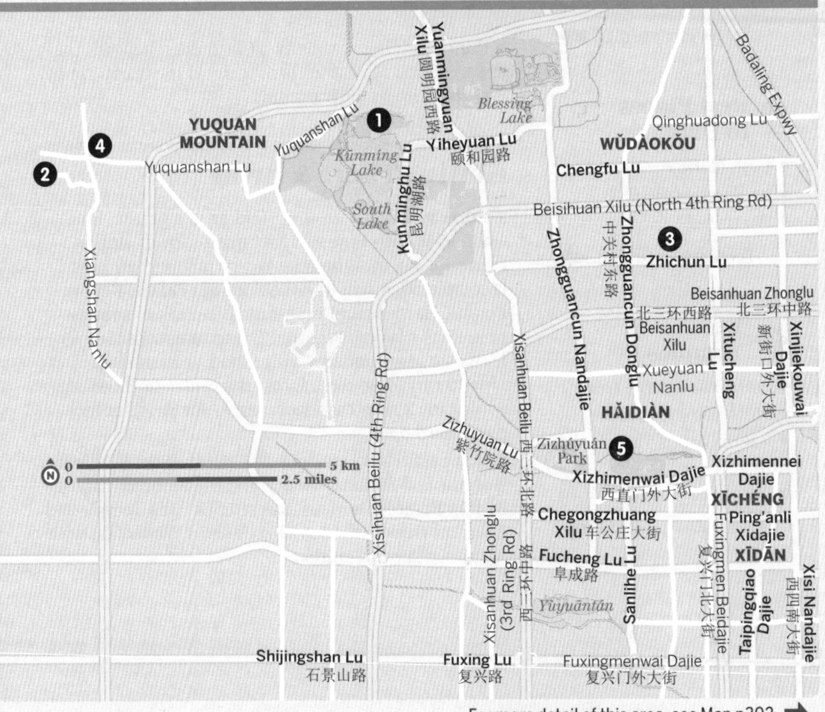

For more detail of this area, see Map p302. ➡

Lonely Planet's Top Tip

China has a special university (民族大学; Mínzú Dàxué) for its many ethnic minorities and the area around it is where you'll find some of the most authentic restaurants serving up their local cuisines. The hub is Weigong Jie, where you can find fantastic Dai (a minority from the far south of Yúnnán Province) food, as well great Uighur and Mongolian eateries. To get there, jump on Line 4 to Weigongcun and then walk south 400m.

Best Places to Eat

- Isshin Japanese Restaurant (p167)
- Salang-Bang (p167)
- Golden Peacock (p167)
- Lǎo Chē Jì (p167)

For reviews, see p167. 

Best Places to Drink

- Lush (p168)
- La Bamba (p167)
- Wu (p168)

For reviews, see p168.

Best Temples

- Wànshòu Temple (p161)
- Wǔtǎ Temple (p163)
- Azure Clouds Temple (p161)
- Great Bell Temple (p166)

For reviews, see p161.

Explore Summer Palace & Hǎidiàn

Hǎidiàn sprawls across a huge mass of west and northwest Běijīng, so you'll need to attack it in chunks.

You could easily spend a day exploring the Summer Palace's sumptuous gardens, temples, pavilions and corridors. Don't miss climbing Longevity Hill for fine views over Běijīng. From the palace, it's a short bus or taxi ride to the Fragrant Hills Park, especially beautiful in the autumn. Nature buffs will also want to visit the nearby Botanic Gardens.

In the evening head to Wǔdàokǒu, one of Běijīng's most happening areas. Surrounded by universities, it's the capital's student heartland and home to many cafes and bars, as well as some of the best Korean and Japanese restaurants in town.

Hǎidiàn is one of Běijīng's best neighbourhoods for temple-hopping. Begin at the Indian-inspired Wǔtǎ Temple. From there, walk due west to Wànshòu Temple and then northeast towards the Great Bell Temple. End the day in quiet contemplation at the superb Azure Clouds Temple inside Fragrant Hills Park.

Local Life

- **Hang-outs** Lush (p168) and the Bridge Café (p167) are busy around the clock.
- **Shopping** Wǔdàokǒu has stacks of quirky clothes shops for hipster students.
- **Parks** Hǎidiàn has many parks hidden beneath the tower blocks; retreat to them to avoid the urban sprawl, especially in the early evening.

Getting There & Away

- **Subway** Getting around Hǎidiàn is a breeze. Line 4 connects with Line 2 at Xizhimen subway station, then runs north. When the Western Suburban Line is completed, it will link the Summer Palace, Běijīng Botanic Gardens and Fragrant Hills Park to subway Line 10. For Wǔdàokǒu, and Dazhongsi, take Line 13, which also connects with Line 2 at Xizhimen. Line 10 runs east–west across the centre of Hǎidiàn, while Line 2 runs east–west across the south of the neighbourhood.
- **Bus** Useful buses include 331, which links Wǔdàokǒu with the Old Summer Palace and the Summer Palace, Běijīng Botanic Gardens, Sleeping Buddha Temple and Fragrant Hills Park. Bus 375 connects Wǔdàokǒu with Xizhimen subway station.

ZHAOLINGHE / GETTY IMAGES ©

TOP SIGHT
SUMMER PALACE

The splendid regal encampment of the Summer Palace (颐和园; Yíhé Yuán) in the northwest of town is one of Běijīng's must-see sights. This former playground for the imperial court fleeing the insufferable summer torpor of the old Imperial City is a marvel of landscaping: a wonderful, over-the-top mix of temples, gardens, pavilions, lakes, bridges, gate towers and corridors. It's a fine place just to amble around in the sunshine, but is also packed with stunning individual sights.

DON'T MISS

- Longevity Hill
- Long Corridor

PRACTICALITIES

- Map p302
- 19 Xinjian Gongmen
- ticket ¥20, through ticket ¥50, audio guide ¥40
- 7am-7pm, sights 8am-5pm summer, 8.30am-4.30pm winter
- S Xiyuan, Beigongmen

Hall of Benevolence & Longevity

The main building at ground level, this **hall** (Rénshòu Diàn) sits by the east gate and houses a hardwood throne. Look for the bronze animals that decorate the courtyard in front, including the mythical *qílín* (a hybrid animal that appeared on earth only at times of harmony).

Kūnmíng Lake

Three-quarters of the parkland in the palace is water, made up of Kūnmíng Lake (Kūnmíng Hú). Check out the extravagant **Marble Boat** (清晏船; Qīngyuàn Chuán) moored on the northwestern shore. First built in 1755, it was restored in 1893 on the orders of Empress Cixi (using money meant to go towards building ships for the Chinese Navy). Much of it is actually wood painted to look like marble. Nearby are fine Qing-dynasty boathouses and the **Gate Tower of the Cloud-Retaining Eves** (Sùyún Yán), which once housed an ancient silver statue of Guanyu (God of War).

Boats ply the lake (¥15), running from the northern shore to South Lake Island, home to the **Dragon King Temple** (龙王庙; Lóngwáng Miào), where royalty came to pray to the Dragon King's fearsome statue for rain in times of drought. But you can also hire your own pedalo (four/six people ¥60/80 per hour, ¥300 deposit) or electric-powered boat (¥100 per hour, ¥400 deposit) to sail around at your own pace.

Long Corridor

Awesome in its conception and execution, the **Long Corridor** (长廊; Cháng Láng) is absolutely unmissable. Open at the sides but covered with a roof to shield the emperors from the elements, and with four pavilions along the way, it stretches for over 700m towards the foot of Longevity Hill. Its beams, the pavilion walls and some of the ceiling are decorated with 14,000 intricate paintings depicting scenes from Chinese history and myths, as well as classic literary texts. Your neck will ache from all that staring upwards, but the pain is worth it.

Longevity Hill

Rearing up by the side of Kūnmíng Lake and at the far end of the Long Corridor, the slopes of this 60m-high hill are covered in temples and pavilions, all arranged on a north–south axis. The most prominent and important are the **Buddhist Fragrance Pavilion** (佛香阁; Fóxiāng Gé) and the **Cloud Dispelling Hall** (排云殿; Páiyún Diàn), which are connected by corridors. Awaiting you at the peak of the hill is the **Buddhist Temple of the Sea of Wisdom** (智慧海; Zhìhuì Hǎi), featuring glazed tiles (many sadly damaged) depicting Buddha. On a clear day there are splendid views of Běijīng from here.

West Causeway

A great way to escape the crowds who converge here is to strike out along the **West Causeway** (西堤, Xīdī) and then do a circuit of the lake by returning along the east shore. The causeway is lined with delightful willow and mulberry trees, and along the way you'll come across the grey and white marble **Jade Belt Bridge** (玉带桥; Yùdài Qiáo), which dates from the 18th century. There's also the graceful **17-Arch Bridge** (十七孔桥; Shíqīkǒng Qiáo), which links the east shore to South Lake Island.

Wénchāng Gallery

South of the main entrance, come to the **Wénchāng Gallery** (文昌阁; Wénchāng Gé) to take a look at Empress Cixi's handwriting (some of her calligraphy is on display), as well as porcelain, bronzes and a jade gallery. Various other Qing-era artefacts are on show as well.

THE RISE & FALL & RISE OF THE SUMMER PALACE

It was Emperor Qianlong who created the Summer Palace, on the site of what had long been a royal garden. With the same determination he displayed in expanding China's borders, Qianlong enlisted 100,000 workers in 1749 to enlarge the gardens and deepen Kūnmíng Lake, while giving Longevity Hill its name in honour of his mother's 60th birthday. Thankfully, Qianlong was long dead by the time British and French soldiers rampaged through the palace in 1860 at the end of the Second Opium War. Apart from pillaging anything not nailed down, they trashed many of the temples and pavilions. That left Empress Cixi to restore it to its former glory, only for foreign soldiers to return in 1900 in the wake of the Boxer Rebellion. Not until after 1949 and the communist takeover was work begun to repair it.

The original name of the Summer Palace was the romantic, but not very regal, Garden of Clear Ripples. It was Empress Cixi who redubbed it in 1888.

SIGHTS

SUMMER PALACE HISTORIC SITE

See p159.

WÀNSHÒU TEMPLE BUDDHIST TEMPLE

Map p297 (万寿寺; Wànshòu Sì; Suzhou Jie; admission ¥20; ⊙9am-4.30pm Tue-Sun; S National Library, or Gongzhufen, then 🚌944) Ringed by a red wall on the southeastern corner of Suzhou Jie (off the 3rd Ring Rd), the tranquil, little-visited Ming-dynasty Wànshòu Temple (Longevity Temple) was originally consecrated for the storage of Buddhist texts. Its name echoes the Summer Palace's Longevity Hill (Wànshòu Shān), and the imperial entourage would stop here to quaff tea en route to and from the palace.

The temple was one of almost 50 that once lined the canal route from the western edge of the Imperial City walls (at Xīzhímén) to the Summer Palace. Now it is pretty much the only one that remains (Wǔtǎ Temple being another notable survivor). The temple fell into disrepair after the fall of the Qing dynasty in 1912, with the Wànshòu Hall burning down. Things went from bad to worse, and during the Cultural Revolution the temple served as an army barracks.

There's an interesting introduction to the history of the temple in the small hall (once the temple's Drum Tower) immediately to your left as you enter the complex. And as you walk through the Hall of the Deva Kings, which leads to the second courtyard, notice the illustration on your right that shows all the temples that once lined the canal. The names are in Chinese only, but see if you can spot the temple you're in (万寿寺) as well as neighbouring Yánqìng Temple (延庆寺; Yánqìng Sì), nearby Dragon King Temple (龙王庙; Lóngwáng Sì) and the magnificent Wǔtǎ

WORTH A DETOUR

FRAGRANT HILLS PARK

Easily within striking distance of the Summer Palace are Běijīng's Western Hills (西山; Xī Shān), another former villa-resort of the emperors. The part of Xī Shān closest to Běijīng is known as **Fragrant Hills Park** (香山公园; Xiāng Shān Gōngyuán; summer/winter ¥10/5, through ticket ¥15; ⊙6am-7pm; S Xiyuan, Yuanmingyuan, then 🚌331). Beijingers flock here in autumn when the maple leaves saturate the hillsides in great splashes of red.

Scramble up the slopes to the top of **Incense-Burner Peak** (Xiānglú Fēng), or take the **chairlift** (one way/return ¥60/120, 9.30am to 3.30pm). From the peak you get an all-embracing view of the countryside, and you can leave the crowds behind by hiking further into the Western Hills.

Near the north gate of Fragrant Hills Park, but still within the park, is the excellent **Azure Clouds Temple** (Bìyún Sì; admission ¥10; ⊙8am-4.30pm), which dates back to the Yuán dynasty. The **Mountain Gate Hall** (Shānmén) contains two vast protective deities: Heng and Ha, beyond which is a small courtyard and the drum and bell towers, leading to a hall with a wonderful statue of Milefo – it's bronze, but coal-black with age. Only his big toe shines from numerous inquisitive fingers.

The **Sun Yatsen Memorial Hall** (Sūn Zhōngshān Jìniàn Tāng) contains a statue and a glass coffin donated by the USSR on the death of Mr Sun (the Republic of China's first president) in 1925. At the very back is the marble **Vajra Throne Pagoda** (Jīngāng Bǎozuò Tǎ), where Sun Yatsen was interred after he died, before his body was moved to its final resting place in Nánjīng. The **Hall of Arhats** (Luóhán Tāng) is well worth visiting; it contains 500 statues of *luóhàn* (those freed from the cycle of rebirth), each crafted with an individual personality.

Southwest of the Azure Clouds Temple is the Tibetan-style **Temple of Brilliance** (Zhāo Miào), and not far away is a glazed-tile pagoda. Both survived visits by foreign troops intent on sacking the area in 1860, and then in 1900.

There are dozens of cheap restaurants and snack stalls on the approach road to the north gate of the park, making this your best bet for lunch out of any of the sights in this part of the city.

At the time of writing it was expected that sometime after 2015 the subway will extend here via the Summer Palace and Botanic Gardens.

WORTH A DETOUR

OLD SUMMER PALACE

Located northwest of the city centre, the **Old Summer Palace** (圆明园; Yuánmíng Yuán; 28 Qinghua Xilu; admission ¥10, through ticket ¥25, map ¥6; ⏲ 7am-6pm; Ⓢ Yuanmingyuan) was laid out in the 12th century. The ever-capable Jesuits were later employed by Emperor Qianlong to fashion European-style palaces for the gardens, incorporating elaborate fountains and baroque statuary. In 1860, during the Second Opium War, British and French troops torched and looted the palace, an event forever inscribed in Chinese history books as a low point in China's humiliation by foreign powers.

Most of the wooden palace buildings were burned down in the process and little remains, but the hardier Jesuit-designed European Palace buildings were made of stone, and a melancholic tangle of broken columns and marble chunks survives. Note: to see these remains, you need to buy the more expensive through ticket.

The subdued marble ruins of the **Palace Buildings Scenic Area** (Xīyánglóu Jǐngqū) can be mulled over in the **Eternal Spring Garden** (Chángchūn Yuán) in the northeast of the park, near the east gate. There were once more than 10 buildings here, designed by Giuseppe Castiglione and Michael Benoist. The buildings were only partially destroyed during the 1860 Anglo-French looting and the structures apparently remained usable for quite some time afterwards. However, the ruins were gradually picked over and carted away by local people all the way up to the 1970s.

The **Great Fountain Ruins** (Dàshuǐfǎ) themselves are considered the best-preserved relics. Built in 1759, the main building was fronted by a lion-head fountain. Standing opposite is the **Guānshuǐfǎ**, five large stone screens embellished with European carvings of military flags, armour, swords and guns. The screens were discovered in the grounds of Peking University in the 1970s and later restored to their original positions. Just east of the Great Fountain Ruins stood a four-pillar archway, chunks of which remain.

West of the Great Fountain Ruins are the vestiges of the **Hǎiyàntáng Reservoir** (Hǎiyàntáng Xùshuǐchí Táijī), where the water for the impressive fountains was stored in a tower and huge water-lifting devices were employed. The metal reservoir was commonly called the Tin Sea (Xīhǎi). Also known as the Water Clock, the **Hǎiyàntáng**, where 12 bronze human statues with animal heads jetted water for two hours in a 12-hour sequence, was constructed in 1759. The 12 animal heads from this apparatus ended up in collections abroad and Běijīng is attempting to retrieve them (four can now be seen at the Poly Art Museum). Just west of here is the **Fāngwàiguàn**, a building that was turned into a mosque for an imperial concubine. An artful reproduction of a former labyrinth called the **Garden of Yellow Flowers** is also nearby.

The palace gardens cover a huge area – 2.5km from east to west – so be prepared for some walking. Besides the ruins, there's the western section, the **Perfection & Brightness Garden** (Yuánmíng Yuán) and, in the southern compound, the **10,000 Springs Garden** (Wànchūn Yuán).

Bus 331 goes from the south gate (which is by Exit B of Yuanmingyuan subway station) to the east gate of the Summer Palace before continuing to the Botanic Gardens and eventually terminating at Fragrant Hills Park.

Temple (marked on the map with its former name, 真觉寺), all of which still stand, at least in part.

The highlight of a visit here, though, is to view the prized collection of bronze Buddhist statuary in the Buddhist Art Exhibition of Ming and Qing dynasties, housed in two small halls on either side of the second courtyard. The displays guide you through the Buddhist pantheon with statues of Sakyamuni, Manjusri, Amitabha, Guanyin (in bronze and *déhuà*, or white-glazed porcelain) and exotic tantric pieces. Also look out for the *kapala* bowl made from a human skull, *dorje* and *purbhas* (Tibetan ritual daggers). Further halls contain museum exhibitions devoted to Ming and Qing porcelain and jade.

Also worth checking out are the Buddhist stone and clay sculptures housed in the large unnamed central hall at the back of the second courtyard. There are four magnificent central pieces, plus a dozen or so *arhats* (Buddhist disciples) lining the flanks. The pavilion at the rear of the whole complex once housed a 5m-high gold-lacquered brass statue that's now long gone; in its place is a miniature Ming-dynasty pagoda alloyed from gold, silver, zinc and lead.

Note that on Wednesdays the first 200 visitors get in for free.

As you exit the temple, see if you can track down the nearby remains of Yánqìng Temple and Dragon King Temple, further east along the canal. To walk from here to Wǔtǎ Temple takes around 20 minutes.

WǓTǍ TEMPLE BUDDHIST TEMPLE

Map p297 (五塔寺; Wǔtǎ Sì; 24 Wutasi Cun, 五塔寺村 24 号; admission ¥20, audio guide ¥10; ⏲9am-4pm; Ⓢ National Library) Undergoing renovations at the time of writing, the distinctive Indian-styled Wǔtǎ Temple (Five Pagoda Temple) is a hugely rewarding place to visit. That's not just because of its unusual architectural style – the temple is topped by its five attractive namesake pagodas – but also because of the magnificent collection of stone carvings contained within its grounds.

Previously known as Zhēnjué Temple (真觉寺; Zhēnjué Sì), the exterior of the main hall is decorated with *dorje*, hundreds of images of Buddha and legions of beasts, amid traces of red pigment. During Ming times the temple ranged to at least six halls, all later tiled in yellow during Qing times; the terrace where the Big Treasure Hall once stood can still be seen. The temple, dating from 1473, is highly unusual for Běijīng, and well worth a visit in itself, but the highlight here is the extraordinary collection of stone carvings, some housed carefully in buildings at the back of the complex but many just scattered around the temple grounds. Pieces you might stumble across include gravestones, animal statues, carved human figures, stone stele and some enormous *bìxì* (mythical tortoiselike dragons often seen in Confucian temples). The pieces were all recovered from various places in Běijīng and put here for their protection during the latter end of the last century. Most are Qing and Ming dynasty, but there are a number of Yuan-, Tang-, Jin- and even Eastern Han-dynasty pieces, some of which are almost 2000 years old. Many, although not all, have explanatory captions in English; those captioned in Chinese only do at least have the date of origin written in numerals.

WORTH A DETOUR

BĚIJĪNG BOTANIC GARDENS

Exploding with blossom in spring, the well-tended **Běijīng Botanic Gardens** (北京植物园; Běijīng Zhíwùyuán; admission ¥5, through ticket ¥50; ⏲6am-8pm summer, last entry 7pm, 7.30am-5pm winter, last entry 4pm; Ⓢ Xiyuan or Yuanmingyuan, then 🚌 331), set against the backdrop of the Western Hills and about 1km northeast of Fragrant Hills Park, makes for a pleasant outing among bamboo fronds, pines, orchids, lilacs and China's most extensive botanic collection. Containing a rainforest house, the standout **Běijīng Botanical Gardens Conservatory** (Běijīng Zhíwùyuán Wēnshì; admission with through ticket; ⏲8am-4.30pm) bursts with 3000 different varieties of plants.

About a 15-minute walk from the front gate (follow the signs), but still within the grounds of the gardens, is **Sleeping Buddha Temple** (Wòfó Sì; admission ¥5, or entry with through ticket; ⏲8am-4.30pm summer, 8.30am-4pm winter). The temple, first built during the Tang dynasty, houses a huge reclining effigy of Sakyamuni weighing 54 tonnes; it's said to have 'enslaved 7000 people' in its casting. Sakyamuni is depicted on the cusp of death, before his entry into nirvana. On each side of Buddha are arrayed some sets of gargantuan shoes, gifts to Sakyamuni from various emperors in case he went for a stroll.

On the eastern side of the gardens is the **Cao Xueqin Memorial** (Cáo Xuěqín Jìniànguǎn; 39 Zhengbaiqi; ⏲8.30am-4.30pm summer, 9am-4pm winter), where Cao Xueqin lived in his latter years. Cao (1715–63) is credited with penning the classic *Dream of the Red Mansions*, a vast and prolix family saga set in the Qing period. Making a small buzz in the west of the gardens is the little **China Honey Bee Museum** (中国蜜蜂博物馆; Zhōngguó Mìfēng Bówùguǎn; ⏲8.30am-4.30pm Mar-Oct).

MING TANG-EVANS / GETTY IMAGES ©

1. Běijīng Botanic Gardens (p163)
Tropical Conservatory at the Botanic Gradens, just north of Fragrant Hills

2. Summer Palace (p159)
View of the splendid Summer Palace over Kūnmíng Lake and giant water lillies

3. Wǔtǎ Temple (p163)
Carved Buddha footprints at this distinctive Indian-styled temple.

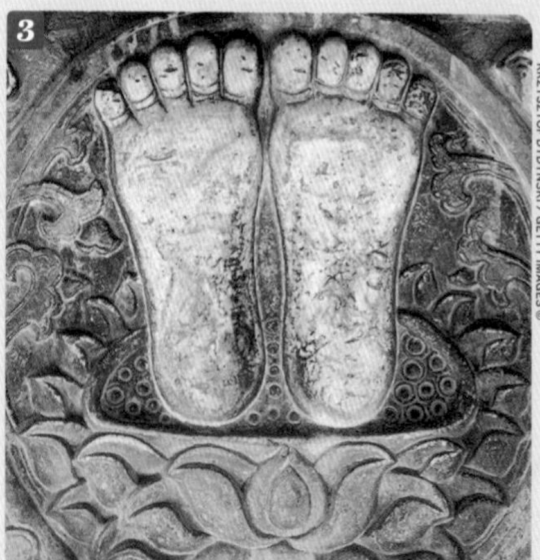

KRZYSZTOF DYDYNSKI / GETTY IMAGES ©

LOVEGULI / GETTY IMAGES ©

As with Wànshòu Temple, on Wednesdays the first 200 visitors get in for free. Take Exit C at the National Library subway stop and then take the first left to get here.

Note, you can enter the north gate of Běijīng Zoo from here. Cross the canal over the decorative arched bridge.

GREAT BELL TEMPLE BUDDHIST TEMPLE

Map p303 (大钟寺; Dàzhōng Sì; ☎6255 0819; 31a Beisanhuan Xilu; ticket ¥20; ⏲9am-4.30pm Tue-Sun; Ⓢ Dazhongsi) Newly refurbished, this famous shrine (originally called Juéshēng Temple) was once a pit stop for Qing emperors who came here to pray for rain. Today the temple is named after its massive Ming-dynasty bell (6.75m tall and weighing a hefty 46.5 tonnes), which is inscribed with Buddhist sutras, comprising more than 227,000 Chinese characters, and decorated with Sanskrit incantations.

The bell was cast during the reign of Emperor Yongle in 1406, with the tower built in 1733. To transport the bell from the foundry to the temple, a shallow canal was dug, and when it froze over in winter the bell was shunted across the ice by sled. Nowadays, the bell is rung just once a year, on Lunar New Year's Eve.

If you're bell crazy, you'll be spellbound by the exhibitions on bell casting, and the collection of bells from France, Russia, Japan, Korea and other nations. Also on view are copies of the bells and chimes of the Marquis of Zeng and a collection of Buddhist and Taoist bells, including *vajra* bells and the wind chimes hung from temple roofs and pagodas

ARTHUR M SACKLER MUSEUM OF ART & ARCHAEOLOGY MUSEUM

Map p303 (赛克勒考古与艺术博物馆; Sàikèlè Kǎogǔ Yǔ Yìshù Bówùguǎn; Peking University; ⏲9am-4.30pm; ⓈEast Gate of Peking University) FREE Excellent collection of relics brought together on the campus of Peking University (enter via west gate), although some English captions would be nice given the significance of this collection. Exhibits include the skeleton of the Jīnniúshān Man, thought to be over 250,000 years old, bronze artefacts, jade pieces and a host of other relics from primordial China. Bring your passport for free entry.

Afterwards, make sure to wander the pleasant, historic campus, a great way to tune out from Běijīng's frantic mayhem.

MILITARY MUSEUM MUSEUM

Map p297 (军事博物馆; Jūnshì Bówùguǎn; 9 Fuxing Lu; admission ¥20; ⏲8.30am-5.30pm Apr-Oct, 8.30am-5pm Nov-Mar, closed Mon year-round; ⓈMilitary Museum) Military enthusiasts may get a rush at this hulking monolith of a building topped with a communist star. Cold War–era fighters, tanks and surface-to-air missiles are mustered below, while upstairs bristles with more weaponry. The Hall of Agrarian Revolutionary War and the Hall of the War to Resist US Aggression and Aid Korea are tours de force of communist spin.

LOCAL KNOWLEDGE

BRAINY BĚIJĪNG

Hǎidiàn's residents are some of the cleverest in all China. Not only are there over 60 universities in the district, but Hǎidiàn is also home to Zhōngguāncūn, the Chinese equivalent of California's Silicon Valley.

With so many tech heads, students and academics working and living in Hǎidiàn, it's no wonder that the area has long been associated with brain power. As far back as 1937, Lao She – the father of modern Chinese literature – described the neighbourhood as an 'academic village' in his classic novel *Rickshaw Boy*.

It was the founding of **Peking University** (Map p303) and **Qīnghuá University** (Map p303) in 1908 and 1911 respectively that set Hǎidiàn on the road to academic stardom. Still China's two most prestigious colleges, they were joined in the area by newer universities who thought they could attract students by being in the same location as their more famous counterparts. After 1949 and the founding of the People's Republic of China, government institutions were established here too.

You'll find many of Běijīng's brightest young things (and a few old ones) in the cafes and restaurants of Wǔdàokǒu. Alternatively, combine a trip to the Arthur M Sackler Museum of Art & Archaeology with strolling the attractive Peking University campus, where the museum is located.

At the time of research, the main building was closed as part of a massive renovation project. But a large collection of tanks, aircraft, artillery and military vehicles are on view in the forecourt, which is free to enter (bring your passport).

YUAN-DYNASTY WALLS RELICS PARK PARK

Map p303 (元大都城垣遗址公园; Yuán Dàdū Chéngyuán Yízhǐ Gōngyuán; S Xitucheng) FREE The name is an ambitious misnomer as there are not many genuine Yuan-dynasty relics here, but this slender strip of parkland, running alongside the Little Moon River (Xiǎoyuè Hé), commemorates a strip of the long-vanished Mongol city wall. At 9km in length, this is Běijīng's longest parkland and a relaxing place for a stroll.

EATING

LA BAMBA MEXICAN $

Map p303 (☎8286 6755; Wudaokou, Huaqing Jiayuan East Gate, 五道口华清嘉园东门北侧 12-3; dishes from ¥18; ⏱10.30am-5am;) Heaving on the weekend, and busy most nights thanks to the daily food and drink specials, La Bamba is a key student hang-out. It's not the most authentic Mexican food you'll ever taste, but the cheap beer (from ¥20) and pool table are as big an attraction as the burritos. The menu also features a wide selection of Western classics.

BRIDGE CAFÉ CAFE $

Map p303 (桥咖啡; Qiáo Kāfēi; ☎8286 7026; 12-8 Huaqing Jiayuan, 华清嘉园 12-8; dishes from ¥33; ⏱24hr; ; S Wudaokou) Friendly, lively and light-filled place that's a top spot for Western breakfasts and panini, as well as homemade pasta and tasty pizzas, or coffee and drinks at any time of day or night. It's on the 2nd floor; enter through the door to the side of a gift shop and climb the stairs.

ISSHIN JAPANESE RESTAURANT JAPANESE $$

Map p303 (日本料理一心; Rìběn Liàolǐ Yī Xīn; ☎6119 3606; Room 403, West Bldg, 35 Chengfu Lu, 成府路 35 号院内西楼 403 室; sushi from ¥14, dishes from ¥36; ⏱11am-10pm; ; S Wudaokou) A long-time local favourite, Isshin is well worth tracking down if you're in the area. With its thoughtful design, laid-back atmosphere and reasonable prices, it's a place where business types, expat Japanese and students can all feel at home. The sushi bar is made for solo travellers, while the sushi bowls (¥48), including salad, are a great deal.

The extensive menu includes hotpots, udon noodles and teriyaki dishes. You'll find the restaurant set back from the road, about 50m north of the traffic lights at the intersection of Chengfu Lu and Wudaokou station.

GOLDEN PEACOCK DAI $$

Map p303 (金孔雀德宏傣味餐厅; Jīn Kǒngquè Déhóng Dǎiwèi Cāntīng; ☎6893 2030; Weigongcun, 魏公村韦伯豪家园南门 对 面; dishes from ¥18; ⏱11am-10pm; ; S Weigongcun) Make sure you try the pineapple rice and the tangy dried beef at this unpretentious and popular restaurant (get here early or reserve). It specialises in the cuisine of the Dǎi people, an ethnic minority from southwest China, who use a lot of flavourings, like lemongrass, common to Southeast Asian food. The rice wine makes a fine accompaniment to a meal.

Thanks to its proximity to the Mínzú Dàxué (民族大学), China's university for its 55 official ethnic minorities, Weigoncun is a great place to try other minority cuisines, especially Korean, Mongolian and Xinjiang food, too.

SALANG-BANG KOREAN $$

Map p303 (舍廊房; Shèláng Fáng; ☎8261 8201; 3rd fl, Dōngyuán Plaza, 35 Chengfu Lu, 成府路 35 号东源大厦 3 层; dishes from ¥30; ⏱11am-2.30am; S Wudaokou) Always busy with expat Korean students looking for a taste of home, this is one of the most popular of the many Korean eateries in Wǔdàokǒu. The various hotpots, including the classic *shíguō bànfàn* (rice, vegetables, meat and an egg served in a claypot), start at ¥30. Alternatively, grill your choice of seafood and meat at your table. Picture menu.

LǍO CHĒ JÌ SICHUAN $$

Map p303 (老车记; ☎6266 6180; 5th fl, Wǔdàokǒu U-Centre, 36 Chengfu Lu, 成府路 36 号五道口购物中心 5 层; meals for 2 from ¥85; ⏱11am-10pm; ; S Wudaokou) The speciality here is *Málàxiāngguō* (麻辣香锅), a kind of dry hotpot where you add your own meat, fish and veggies, but it comes without the bubbling broth you get with standard hotpot. Choose from three different levels of spice; go for the lowest if

LOCAL KNOWLEDGE

WŬDÀOKŎU BEER GARDEN

When Běijīng emerges from the deep freeze of its winter, so do its residents. Come summer in Wŭdàokŏu, the area just west of the subway stop turns into a hugely popular open-air beer garden. Locals congregate at the tables, sipping draught beers and snacking on *shāokăo* (barbecue) from the food stalls surrounding them.

The party starts in the late afternoon and continues late, getting louder and louder as those ¥10 beers disappear down thirsty throats.

you can't handle the heat. You can also pick up a bowl of noodles here from ¥10. Picture menu.

DRINKING & NIGHTLIFE

LUSH BAR

Map p303 (☎8286 3566; 1 Huaqing Jiayuan, Chengfu Lu, 华清嘉园 1 号楼 2 层; beers from ¥20, cocktails from ¥35; ⏱8am-4am; 📶; Ⓢ Wudaokou) For the hordes of students in Wŭdàokŏu, both foreign and local, all roads lead to Lush. During the day it functions as a cafe with a Western menu, including breakfast (¥40) and sandwiches and salads (from ¥45). After dark, it offers something different every night, including live music, a pub quiz and an open-mic night for aspiring poets and singers.

There's a daily happy hour from 8pm to 10pm and Monday is martini night. It's above the Meet Fresh Café.

WŬ CLUB

Map p303 (五; 1/F, NW Corner, Wudaokou U-Centre, Chengfu Lu, 成府路 36 号五道口购物中心一层西北角; beers from ¥20; ⏱8pm-5am; Ⓢ Wudaokou) Firmly aimed at the college crowd, with daily drink specials and party tunes, Wu is nevertheless rather more upmarket than the other clubs in the area. Its clean and modern design is the opposite of the grungy look that characterises most Wŭdàokŏu venues. It's located on the ground floor of the U-Centre shopping mall, very close to the subway station.

PROPAGANDA CLUB

Map p303 (☎8286 3991; Huaqing Jiayuan, 华清嘉园; ⏱ 8.30pm-5.30am; Ⓢ Wudaokou) Wŭdàokŏu's student crew are drawn to this unprepossessing but long-running club for its cheap drinks, hip-hop sounds and the chance for cultural exchange with the locals. Entry is free. It's 100m north of the east gate of Huaqing Jiayuan.

☆ ENTERTAINMENT

NATIONAL LIBRARY CONCERT HALL CLASSICAL MUSIC, DANCE

Map p297 (国家图书馆音乐厅; Guójiā Túshūguăn Yīnyuètīng; ☎8854 5531; 33 Zhongguangcun Nandajie, 中关村南大街 33 号; tickets ¥80-580; Ⓢ National Library) Undergoing a massive refit at the time of writing, this impressive venue doesn't just put on recitals and concerts (many by overseas musicians); it's also a good place to catch Chinese classical dance, which blends martial arts styles with traditional dance choreography performances.

13 CLUB LIVE MUSIC

Map p303 (13 俱乐部; 13 Jùlèbù; ☎8668 7151; 161 Chengfu Lu, 成府路 161 号; admission from ¥30; ⏱6pm-late; Ⓢ Wudaokou) A dark and forbidding venue down a suitably grimy alley. A lot of metal acts play here, so if you're a fan of guitar solos and making the sign of the horns, this is the place for you. Look for the red sign.

UME INTERNATIONAL CINEPLEX CINEMA

Map p303 (☎8211 5566; 44 Kexueyuan Nanlu, 科学院南路 44 号; tickets ¥65-100; Ⓢ Renmin University) Posh multiplex that shows the latest Western movie releases (the ones that pass muster with the Chinese censors), but check they haven't been dubbed into Chinese.

SHOPPING

CENTERGATE COMO ELECTRONICS

Map p303 (科贸电子城; Kēmào Diànzĭchéng; 18 Zhongguancun Dajie, 中关村大街 18 号; ⏱9am-7pm; Ⓢ Zhongguancun) Zhōngguāncūn is China's Silicon Valley and Zhongguancun Dajie and the streets around it are home to many malls selling digital and electronic products. This is one of the biggest of them, a 10-floor space full of vendors selling reasonably priced computer software and hardware, games, cell phones, MP3 players and iPods.

Not all of it is the genuine article, but you can bargain here. Go to the 2nd floor for laptop repairs. There's a food court on the 8th floor.

SPORTS & ACTIVITIES

FRIENDSHIP HOTEL SWIMMING, TENNIS

Map p303 (☎6849 8888, ext 32; 1 Zhongguancun Nandajie, 友谊宾馆 中关村南大街1号; ⏰7am-10.30pm; S Renmin University) The venerable Friendship Hotel has a great Olympic-sized pool, once outdoor but now sadly enclosed, costing ¥150 for a day or however long you stay. There are also tennis courts for hire (¥400 per hour) and a gym and sauna.

CHINA STUDY ABROAD LANGUAGE COURSES

Map p303 (☎8286 3166; www.chinastudyabroad.org; Huaqing Jiayuan, Bldg 7, 803B, 成府路华清嘉园 7 号楼 803B 室; S Wudaokou) This professionally run organisation offers the whole spectrum of Chinese-language programs, ranging from summer camps and private tuition to long-term university placements.

The Great Wall

History

The Great Wall (长城; Chángchéng), one of the most iconic monuments on earth, stands as an awe-inspiring symbol of the grandeur of China's ancient history. Dating back 2000-odd years, the Wall – or to be more accurate, Walls, for it has never been one continuous structure – snakes its way through 17 provinces, principalities and autonomous regions. But nowhere is better than Běijīng for mounting your assault of this most famous of bastions.

Official Chinese history likes to stress the unity of the Wall through the ages. In fact, there are at least four distinct Walls. Work on the 'original' was begun during the Qin dynasty (221–207 BC), when China was unified for the first time under Emperor Qin Shihuang. Hundreds of thousands of workers, many political prisoners, laboured for 10 years to construct it. An estimated 180 million cu metres of rammed earth was used to form the core of this Wall, and legend has it that the bones of dead workers were used as building materials, too.

After the Qin fell, work on the Wall continued during the Han dynasty (206 BC–AD 220). Little more was done until almost 1000 years later, during the Jin dynasty (1115–1234), when the impending threat of Genghis Khan spurred further construction. The Wall's final incarnation, and the one most visitors see today, came during the Ming dynasty (1368–1644), when it was reinforced with stone, brick and battlements over a period of 100 years and at great human cost to the two to three million people who toiled on it. During this period it was home to around one million soldiers.

The great irony of the Wall is that it rarely stopped China's enemies from invading. It was never one continuous structure; there were inevitable gaps and it was through those that Genghis Khan rode in to take Běijīng in 1215.

While the Wall was less than effective militarily, it was very useful as a kind of elevated highway for transporting people and equipment across mountainous terrain. Its beacon tower system, using smoke signals generated by burning wolves' dung, quickly transmitted news of enemy movements back to the capital. But with the Manchus installed in Běijīng as the Qing dynasty (1644–1911) and the Mongol threat long gone, there was little need to maintain the Wall, and it fell into disrepair.

Ruin & Restoration

The Wall's degeneration accelerated during the war with Japan and then the civil war that preceded the founding of the new China in 1949. Compounding the problem, the communists didn't initially have much interest in the Wall. In fact, Mao Zedong encouraged people living near it to use it as a source of free building materials, something that still goes on unofficially today. It wasn't until 1984 that Mao's successor Deng Xiaoping ordered that the Wall be restored in places and placed under government protection.

But classic postcard images of the Wall – flawlessly clad in bricks and stoutly undulating over hills into the distance – do not reflect the truth of the bastion today. While the sections closest to Běijīng and a few elsewhere have been restored to something approaching their former glory, huge parts of the Wall are either rubble or, especially in the west, simply mounds of earth that could be anything.

Visiting the Wall

The heavily reconstructed section at Bādálǐng is the most touristy part of the Wall. Mùtiányù and Jīnshānlǐng are also restored sections. These can feel less than authentic, but have the advantage of being much more accessible (with cable cars, handrails etc). Huánghuā Chéng and Zhuàngdàokǒu are part-restored, part-'wild' and offer some short but challenging hikes. Unrestored sections of 'wild Wall' include Gǔběikǒu and Jiànkòu, but there are many others. All of these can be reached using public transport (you can even get to Bādálǐng by train!), although some people choose to hire a car to speed things up. Staying overnight by the Wall is recommended.

Tours run by hostels, or by specialist tour companies, are far preferable to those run by ordinary hotels or general travel companies, as they tend to cater more to the needs of adventurous Western travellers and don't come with any hidden extras, such as a side trip to the Ming Tombs (a common add-on) or a tiresome diversion to a gem factory or traditional Chinese medicine centre. The following reputable companies and associations run trips to the Wall that we like:

The Great Wall

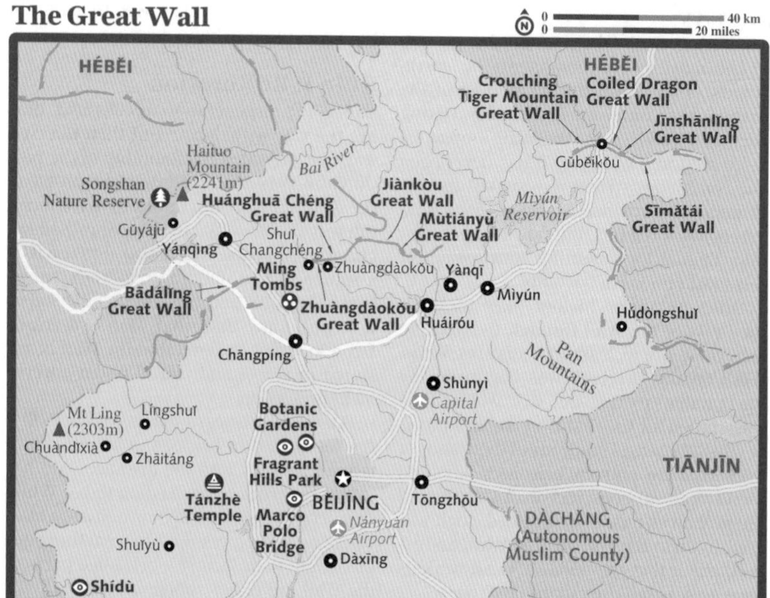

Bespoke Beijing (www.bespokebeijing.com) High-end trips and tours.

Great Wall Hiking (www.greatwallhiking.com) Locally run hiking trips.

China Hiking (www.chinahiking.cn) Affordable hiking and camping trips run by a Chinese-Belgian couple.

Beijing Hikers (www.beijinghikers.com) Social group offering good-value hiking trips.

Bike Beijing (www.bikebeijing.com) For cycling trips.

Beijing Sideways (www.beijingsideways.com) For trips in a motorbike sidecar.

Mùtiányù

Mùtiányù (慕田峪) is a recently renovated stretch of Wall that sees a lot of tourists and is fairly easy to reach from Běijīng. It's also well set up for families, with a cable car, a chairlift and a hugely popular toboggan ride. Far fewer tour groups come here than go to Bādálǐng, so the crowds are much more manageable.

Exploring the Wall

Famed for its Ming-era guard towers and excellent views, this 3km-long section of wall is largely a recently restored Ming-dynasty structure that was built upon an earlier Northern Qi–dynasty edifice. With 26 watchtowers, the wall is impressive and manageable and, although it's popular, most souvenir hawking is reserved to the lower levels.

From the ticket office at Mùtiányù, there are three or four stepped pathways leading up to the wall, plus a **cable car** (缆车; lǎn chē; 1 way/return ¥60/80, children half price), a **chairlift** (索道; suǒdào; combined ticket with toboggan ¥80), called a 'ropeway'on the signs here, and a **toboggan ride** (滑道; huá dào; 1 way ¥60), making this ideal for those who can't manage too many steps, or who have kids in tow.

Top Tip

If taking bus 916快 to Huáiróu, ignore the tout who almost always gets on this bus at Nanhua Shichang bus stop and tries to lure foreign tourists onto an expensive minibus tour to the Great Wall. He sometimes wears a bus-driver shirt to aid the scam.

JUST HOW GREAT IS IT?

The Chinese call the Great Wall the '10,000 Lǐ Wall' (万里长城; Wànlǐ Chángchéng). With one 'Lǐ' equivalent to around 500m this makes the Wall around 5000km long. More modern calculations, though, put the figure at far longer than that. A report by China's State Administration of Cultural Heritage in April 2009 estimated the non-continuous length of the Ming-dynasty wall at 8851km. But the Ming dynasty was just one (albeit the most significant) of 13 dynasties to have contributed to the Wall over the course of history. A more recent, more thorough, survey has calculated the total length of all fragments of the Great Wall that have ever stood, including sections that run parallel with others, and sections that have weathered away to nothing, to be 21,119km.

Getting There & Away

- **Bus** From Dongzhimen Wai bus stand, bus 867 makes a special detour to Mùtiányù twice every morning (¥16, 2½ hours, 7am and 8.30am, 15 March to 15 November only) and returns from Mùtiányù twice each afternoon (2pm and 4pm). Otherwise, go via Huáiróu: from Dongzhimen Transport Hub (Dōngzhímén Shūniǔzhàn) take bus 916快 (the character is *'kuài'*, and means 'fast') to Huáiróu (¥12, one hour, 6.30am to 7.30pm). Get off at Mingzhu Guangchang (明珠广场) bus stop, then take the first right to find a bunch of minivans waiting to take passengers to Mùtiányù (per person ¥10 to ¥20, 30 minutes). Note, after around 1pm, you'll probably have to charter your own van (¥60 one way). Return minivans start drying up around 6pm. The last 916快 back to Běijīng leaves Huáiróu at around 7pm. If you miss that, catch a taxi from Huáiróu to Shunyi subway station (顺义地铁站; Shùnyì Dìtiě Zhàn; about ¥100) on Line 15, or all the way back to Dōngzhímén (¥220).
- **Taxi** Around ¥600 to ¥700 return day trip from Běijīng.

Need to Know

- **Location** 90km from Běijīng
- **Price** adult/student ¥45/25
- **Opening hours** 7am to 6.30pm summer, 7.30am to 5.30pm winter

EATING

Mùtiányù has a branch of Subway (just down from the car park). There are also lots of fruit and snacks stalls.

YÌ SŌNG LÓU RESTAURANT CHINESE **$$**
(翼松楼餐厅; Yì Sōng Lóu Cāntīng; mains ¥20-60; ⌚8.30am-5pm; 📋) Up by the main entrance. Does OK Chinese food.

SLEEPING

There are half a dozen village guesthouses about 500m downhill from the Mùtiányù entrance. All have English signage and have been recently renovated. Expect to pay around ¥100 for a room.

BRICKYARD ECO RETREAT GUESTHOUSE **$$$**
(瓦厂; Wǎ Chǎng; ☎6162 6506; www.brickyardatmutianyu.com; Běigōu Village, Huáiróu District 怀柔区渤海镇北沟村; r ¥1480-1980, ste ¥3990; ❄📶) 🍃 A 1960s glazed-tile factory renovated into a beautiful guesthouse, sporting five lovingly restored rooms, each with views of the Great Wall. Rates include breakfast, use of a spa, and shuttle services to the Wall and surrounding villages. Brickyard is in Běigōu village (北沟村; Běigōu Cūn), about 2km from the Mùtiányù Great Wall. Reservations essential.

Gǔběikǒu

The historic, far-flung town of Gǔběikǒu (古北口) is no more than a village these days, but was once an important, heavily guarded gateway into Běijīng from northeast China. The village, split into two sections by a ridge, with the Great Wall running along it and a small tunnel running through it, contains plenty of old courtyard homes (plus lots of rebuilt ones) and half a dozen small temples (¥20 combined ticket). Various stretches of

1

3

1. Jiànkòu (p177)
Snaking along a mountain ridge, this unrestored section of the Wall is wildly picturesque.

2. Bādálǐng (p180)
This busy section is the easiest part of the Wall to get to.

3. Great Wall (p170)
Restored and child-friendly or wild and dilapidated? The question isn't whether to see the Great Wall, it's how.

PANORAMA MEDIA / GETTY IMAGES ©

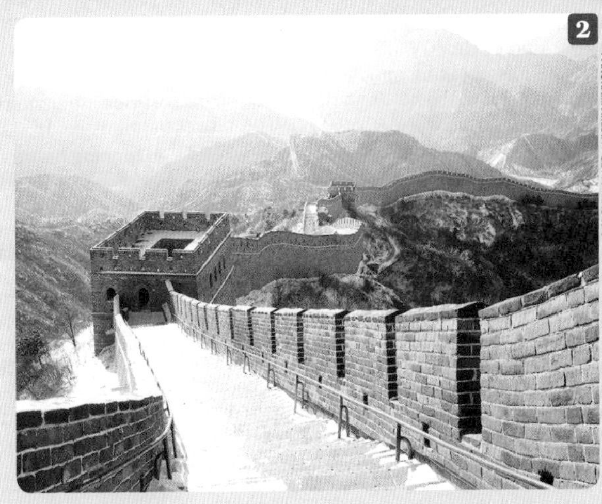

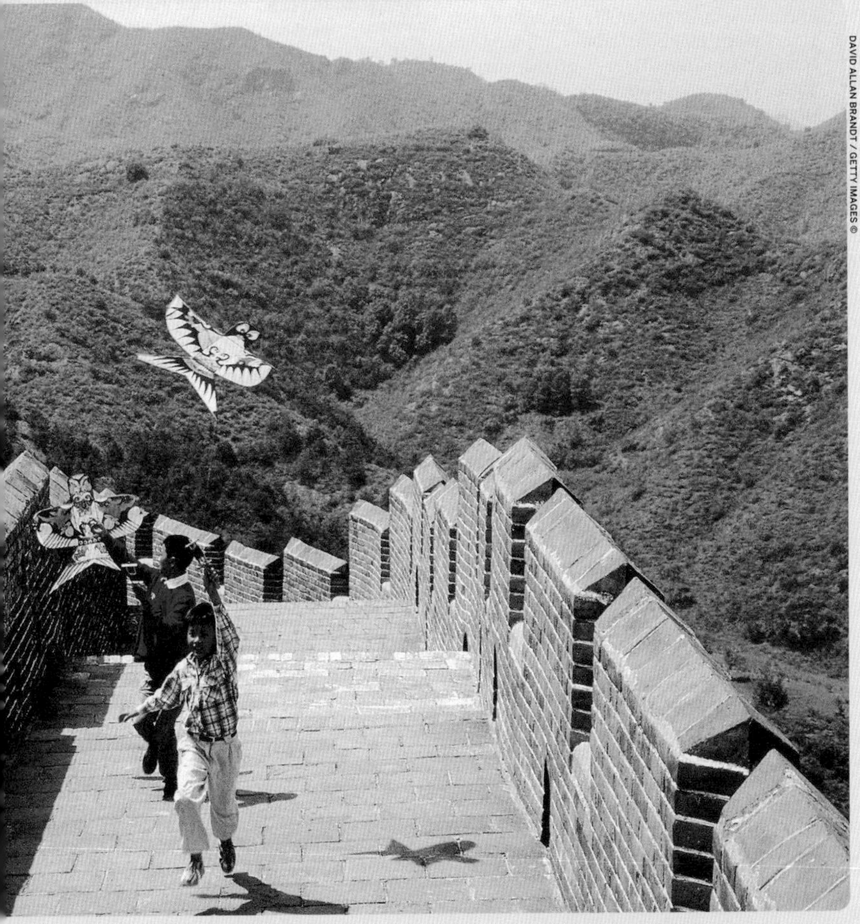

DAVID ALLAN BRANDT / GETTY IMAGES ©

the Wall meet in and around the village, in a kind of Great Wall crossroads that gives you lots of hiking options. One short stony stretch of wall dates from the far-off Northern Qi dynasty (AD 550–577). The other stretches are Ming. There are well-worn dirt pathways on or beside them, so hiking here isn't as dangerous as it can be at other unrestored sections of the Wall. You should still take great care, though.

Exploring the Wall

There are two main sections of Wall here: the **Coiled Dragon** (蟠龙; Pán Lóng), which runs along the ridge that cuts Gǔběikǒu village in two and which eventually leads to Jīnshānlǐng Great Wall, and **Crouching Tiger Mountain** (卧虎山; Wò Hǔ Shān), on the other side of the Cháo Hé River (walk through the tunnel, cross the river bridge, and follow the steps you'll soon see on your right). Both make for fabulous hiking, although Crouching Tiger is extraordinarily steep. There are other short splintered sections of Wall, like the one that runs down from Coiled Dragon, past Great Wall Box House. The Wall here is less well defined than at other locations across Běijīng, but the scenery is lush, making for pleasant hiking. Pathways along the Coiled Dragon section have yellow spray-paint markers left over from a Great Wall marathon that was run here a few years back, so navigation is less confusing than it might otherwise be.

Top Tip

Even if you don't stay at Great Wall Box House, pop in for a drink or a bowl of noodles, so you can ask Joe or Sophie about hiking routes.

Getting There & Away

➡**Bus** Take bus 980快 from Dongzhimen Transport Hub (Dōngzhímén Shūniǔzhàn) to its terminus at Mìyún Bus Station (密云汽车站; Mìyún qìchēzhàn; ¥15, 90 minutes, 6am to 7pm). The 快 (*kuài*) means fast. Come out of the bus station, cross the road and turn right to find the bus stop for bus 密25. The 密 (Mì) sands for Mìyún. Then take bus 密25 to Gǔběikǒu (¥9, 70 minutes). The last 密25 back to Mìyún leaves at 5.30pm. The last 980 back to Dongzhimen is at 7pm.

➡**Taxi** Around ¥1000 to ¥1200 return day trip from Běijīng.

Need to Know

➡**Location** 130km from Běijīng

➡**Price** admission ¥25 (though rarely administered)

➡**Opening hours** no official hours

EATING & SLEEPING

All the tourist accommodation is in the recently redeveloped southern half of the village (before the Gǔběikǒu Tunnel), now called the **Folk Customs Village** (it's less twee than it sounds). Get off the bus immediately before the tunnel (if you miss the stop, you can walk back through the tunnel from the next stop), and walk through the archway on the right. There are dozens of *nóngjiāyuàn* (农家院; village guesthouses), so there's no need to book anything. Just turn up and look for one you like. They all have English signage, but very little English is spoken. Expect to pay ¥80/120/150 for a single/double/triple occupancy in a simple room with bathroom. All guesthouses also do food (mains ¥20 to ¥40).

★**GREAT WALL BOX HOUSE** GUESTHOUSE **$$**
(团园客栈; Tuán Yuán Kèzhàn; ☎8105 1123; http://en.greatwallbox.com; No 18 Dongguan, Gǔběikǒu Village; 古北口镇东关甲18号; weekday/weekend, incl dinner dm ¥180/200, s ¥200/220, tw ¥500/550) Run by a young, friendly, English-speaking Chinese couple called Joe and Sophie, this wonderful place is housed in a 100-year-old courtyard building that was an abandoned chessboard factory before being lovingly renovated by Joe. Rooms surround a long, well-tended garden-courtyard, and are large (the dorm is enormous), bright and spotlessly clean. Incredibly, a small, overgrown section of the Great Wall runs along one side of the property.

The shared bathroom is modern (with sit-down toilets), there's a small kitchen-dining area, and 12 adorable cats. Joe and Sophie dish out reliable hiking advice and rent mountain bikes (per hour/day ¥10/40). They also do tasty vegetarian meals. Get off the bus just before the Gǔběikǒu Tunnel and, instead of walking through the archway, walk along the lane to the south of the village stream. You'll see the Box House sign after about 500m.

Jiànkòu

For stupefying hikes along perhaps Běijīng's most incomparable section of 'wild Wall', head to the rear section of the Jiànkòu Great Wall (后箭扣长城; Hòu Jiànkòu Chángchéng), accessible from Xīzhàzi village (西栅子村; Xīzhàzi Cūn), via the town of Huáiróu. Tantalising panoramic views of the Great Wall spread out in either direction from here, as the crumbling brickwork meanders dramatically along a mountain ridge; the setting is truly sublime. But this is completely unrestored wall, so it is both dangerous and, strictly speaking, illegal to hike along it. Make sure you wear footwear with very good grip, and never attempt to traverse this section in the rain, particularly during thunderstorms. When the weather is fine, the Jiànkòu (箭扣) area offers fabulous opportunities to hike and camp along the Wall.

Exploring the Wall

Xīzhàzi village is actually a collection of five hamlets, or *duì* (队), strung out along a valley, to the left of which is a forested ridge, along the top of which runs the Great Wall. You can access the Wall from a number of points along this valley. If you're aiming to hike all the way to Mùtiányù Great Wall, turn left when you hit the Wall. The Wall here has various features that have been given names according to their appearance. They include the **Ox Horn** (牛角边; Niú Jiǎo Biān; 90 minutes walk to Mùtiányù), which performs a great sweeping, 180-degree u-turn; the **Sharp North Tower** (正北楼; Zheng Bei Lou; 3½ hours to Mùtiányù), which is the highest tower you can view to your left when standing in hamlet No 5; the **Arrow Nock** (剪扣; Jiànkòu; six hours), a low pass in the ridge; and **Upward Flying Eagle** (鹰飞到仰; Ying Fei Dao Yang; nine hours), consisting of three beacon towers, two of which (the wings) stand on the highest point of the mountain above the lower, middle one (the eagle's head).

The H25 bus terminates at the end of the valley road, at hamlet No 5 (五队, *wǔ duì*). From here you can access pathways to Upward Flying Eagle (beyond the village) and Arrow Nock (back towards hamlet No 4). Before the bus gets that far, though, it passes through a decorative archway at the entrance to the valley. Here you'll have to get out to buy an entrance ticket to the scenic area (¥25). Hamlet No 1 (一队; *yī duì*) is just through this archway, to your left. You can walk from here to the Ox Horn in about 90 minutes.

Top Tip

If you don't plan on staying the night or aren't hiking to another section of the wall, make sure you get your taxi driver to wait for you (don't pay until afterwards!) because it's tough to find taxis at Xīzhàzi village.

Getting There & Away

➡**Bus** Take bus 916快 from the Dongzhimen Transport Hub to its teminus at Huáiróu Bus Station (怀柔汽车站; Huáiróu qìchēzhàn, ¥12, 90 minutes, 6.30am to 7.30pm). Turn left out of the station, right at the crossroads and take bus 862 from the first bus stop to Yújiāyuán (于家园; ¥2; five stops), then take the H25 to Xīzhàzi (西栅子; ¥8, 70 minutes). Note, the H25 only runs twice a day; at 11.30am and 4.30pm. The return H25 bus leaves Xīzhàzi at 6.30am and 1.15pm, so you can't do this in a day trip on public transport alone.

➡**Taxi** Around ¥700 to ¥900 return day trip from Běijīng. From Huáiróu to Xīzhàzi village, expect to pay at least ¥120 one way.

Need to Know

➡**Location** 100km from Běijīng

➡**Price** admission ¥20

➡**Opening hours** no official hours

EATING & SLEEPING

YÁNG ÈR GUESTHOUSE $

(杨二; ☎136 9307 0117, 6161 1794; Xīzhàzi Village No 1; 西栅子村一队; r ¥100; ❄📶) The first *nóngjiāyuàn* (农家院; farmers-style courtyard) you come to as you enter hamlet No 1 of Xīzhàzi village. Rooms are set around a vegetable-patch courtyard, and are simple, with private bathrooms. Food menu (mains ¥25 to ¥50) includes some photos. No English.

ZHÀO SHÌ SHĀN JŪ GUESTHOUSE $

(赵氏山居; ☎135 2054 9638, 6161 1762; www.jkwall.com – Chinese only ; r ¥100-220; ❄📶) The last property in the valley (in hamlet No 5 of Xīzhàzi village), this place is a favourite for Chinese hikers (not much English is spoken here). Has a large shaded terrace dining area with fine Great Wall views. Rooms are neat and clean and sleep two to four people. Most have attached bathrooms. Keep walking along the main road beyond where the bus terminates, and you'll see it up to your right. Food menu (mains ¥20 to ¥40) has photos.

Huánghuā Chéng

Less touristy than other parts of the Great Wall close to Běijīng, Huánghuā Chéng (黄花城) is an extremely rewarding, and impossibly steep, section of the Wall. Undulating across the hillsides east and west of a small reservoir and offering spectacular views of the surrounding countryside, it has undergone only partial restoration and is refreshingly free of the hawkers who can make visits to other sections a trying experience. There are good opportunities for hikes too.

Exploring the Wall

Strikingly free of crowds, Huánghuā Chéng allows visitors to admire this classic and well-preserved example of Ming defence, with its high and wide ramparts, intact parapets and sturdy beacon towers, in relative isolation. The patchy and periodic restoration work on the Wall here has left its crumbling nobility and striking authenticity largely intact, with the ramparts occasionally dissolving into rubble and some of the steps in ruins.

From the road, you can go either west (left) towards Zhuàngdàokǒu or east (right) up the stupidly steep section which rises up from the reservoir and eventually leads to Jiànkòu (after about two days). For the eastern route, cross the small dam, pay the enterprising local who sells unofficial ¥3 entrance tickets, and follow the path beside the reservoir. Walk up the steps just after the small shop-cum-cafe until you reach a metal ladder which is used to access the Wall. The Wall climbs abruptly uphill through a series of further watchtowers before going over, dipping down, then climbing again, even more steeply than before.

To head west, it's easiest to climb the path that leads up to the Wall from behind Ténglóng Hotel. The wall on this side of the road is almost as steep and, in places, equally smooth and slippery. The views from the top are stunning, and you can continue from here to Zhuàngdàokǒu village (30 minutes); turn left off the Wall at its lowest point.

Getting There & Away

➡**Bus** From Dongzhimen Transport Hub (Dōngzhímén Shūniǔzhàn) take bus 916 快 to Huáiróu (¥11, one hour, 6.30am to 7.30pm). Get off at Nanhuayuan Sanqu (南花园三区) bus stop, then walk straight ahead about 200m (crossing one road), to the next bus stop, Nanhuayuan Siqu (南花园四区). From here take the H14 bound for Èr Dào Guān (二道关) and get off at Huánghuā Chéng (¥8, one hour, until 6.30pm). It only runs about once an hour; taxi drivers hover by the bus stop (¥100 one way). The last 916快 from Huáiróu back to Běijīng leaves Huáiróu at around 7pm.

➡**Taxi** Around ¥700 to ¥800 return day trip from Běijīng.

Need to Know

➡**Location** 77km from Běijīng

➡**Price** ¥3 (unofficial)

➡**Opening hours** no official hours

EATING & SLEEPING

TÉNGLÓNG HOTEL GUESTHOUSE $

(滕龙饭店; Ténglóng Fàndiàn; ☎6165 1929; r with/without attached bathroom ¥100/60) One of a number of small guesthouses here. Most are on the river side of the road, but this friendly place, accessed via steps on your left just before the wall, clings to the hillside on the other side of the road and sports fine views of the Wall. Rooms are basic but clean and sleep two to three people. No English spoken, but the restaurant has an English menu (mains ¥15 to ¥40).

Zhuàngdàokǒu

Zhuàngdàokǒu (撞道口), a small village just over the hill to the east of Huánghuā Chéng, has access to a rarely visited and completely unrestored section of 'wild Wall'. It's also possible to hike over to Huánghuā Chéng on a restored section from here, although few people do this – surprising, considering how straightforward it is. The 'wild' section, towards the reservoir at Shuǐ Chángchéng, is crumbling away and overgrown with small trees and shrubs, but it is still possible to hike along. Just take extreme care.

Exploring the Wall

The bus should drop you off at the far end of Zhuàngdàokǒu village, where the road crosses a small stream. Pick up some water and snacks at the nearby shop, then turn right and follow the lane along the stream and up behind the houses until it meets a rocky pathway leading up the Wall. Once at the Wall (20 minutes), turn right for the one-hour walk along a restored but very steep section of Wall, which eventually leads down to the road at Huánghuā Chéng, from where you can catch the H14 back to Huáiróu. Or turn left to commence a two-hour hike along a crumbling stretch of shrub-covered Wall towards the **Huánghuāchéng Great Wall Lakeside Reserve** (黄花城水长城旅游区; Huánghuāchéng Shuǐchángchéng Lǚyóuqū; admission ¥45; ⌚8am-5.30pm), known simply as Shuǐ Chángchéng (水长城), from where you can catch the H21 bus back to Huáiróu. The latter route is extremely tough under foot. Take care.

Getting There & Away

➡ **Bus** From Dongzhimen Transport Hub (Dōngzhímén Shūniǔzhàn) take bus 916快 to Huáiróu (¥11, one hour, 6.30am to 7.30pm). Get off at Nanhuayuan Sanqu (南花园三区) bus stop, then walk straight ahead about 200m (crossing one road), until you get to the next bus stop, which is called Nanhuayuan Siqu (南花园四区). The H21 bus from here to Shuǐ Chángchéng (水长城) stops at Zhuàngdàokǒu (¥8, one hour, every 30 minutes until 6.30pm). The last 916快 bus from Huáiróu back to Běijīng leaves Huáiróu at around 7pm.

➡ **Taxi** Around ¥700 to ¥800 return day trip from Běijīng.

Need to Know

➡ **Location** 80km from Běijīng

➡ **Price** no entrance fee

➡ **Opening hours** no official hours

EATING & SLEEPING

ZǍOXIĀNG YARD GUESTHOUSE $

(枣香庭院; Zǎoxiāng Tíngyuàn; ☎135 2208 3605; r ¥80-150) This modest guesthouse is housed in a 70-year-old courtyard building, which has traditional features such as wooden window frames and paper window panes, as well as more recent add-ons such as a shower room and dining area (you can also eat in the courtyard; English menu; mains ¥20 to ¥50). One room has a private bathroom. It's on your right on the main road, just before the bus drop-off. There are three other guesthouses on the pathway leading up to the Great Wall.

Jīnshānlǐng

The Jīnshānlǐng (金山岭) section of the Great Wall is completely restored, but it's so far from Běijīng that it sees far fewer tourists than other fully restored sections. It contains some unusual features such as Barrier Walls (walls within the Wall), and each watchtower comes with an inscription, in English, detailing the historic significance of that part of the Wall. The landscape here can be drier and starker than at, say, Jiànkǒu or Gǔběikǒu, but it's arguably more powerful, and it leaves you in no doubt that this is remote territory. This is the finish point of an adventurous 6½-hour hike from Gǔběikǒu.

Exploring the Wall

Hiking on the restored section of the Wall here is straightforward. There's an east gate and a west gate (about 2km apart), which means you can do a round trip (90 minutes) without backtracking; from the east gate, turn right at the Wall to find the west gate, then right again once back down on the road. If you need it, there's a **cable car** (缆车; lǎn chē; one-way/return trip ¥30/50) by the west gate ticket office. To find unrestored sections, turn right when you hit the Wall and just keep going. This stretch eventually leads to Gǔběikǒu (6½ hours), although you have to leave the Wall for an hour or two to skirt a small military camp.

Getting There & Away

➡ **Bus** A direct bus takes you from Wangjing West subway station (Line 13) to a point about 30 minutes walk from the Jīnshānlǐng ticket office. Come out of Exit C of the subway station and look over your right shoulder to see the red sign for the 'Tourist Bus to Jinshanling Great Wall' (金山岭长城旅游班车; Jīnshānlǐng Chángchéng lǚyóu bānchē), from where there are half-hourly buses to Jīnshānlǐng (¥32, 90 minutes, 7.30am to 4pm). From the bus drop-off point (a service station on a highway), walk back under the highway and keep going for about 2km to the east-gate ticket office. Note, when you return (turn right out of the east gate area), the bus will pick up passengers from the same side of the highway it dropped you off at; not from the side which has a police station beside it. Last bus back leaves the service station at 4.20pm.

➡**Taxi** Around ¥1000 to ¥1200 return day trip from Běijīng.

Need to Know

➡**Location** 142km from Běijīng

➡**Price** summer/winter ¥65/55

➡**Opening hours** no official hours

Beside the east gate entrance (东门; Dōngmén), is a hotel-lobby-like cafe (coffee ¥30, beer ¥12, mains ¥20 to ¥60) with an English menu and friendly staff who do their best with limited English.

Bādálǐng

The mere mention of its name sends a shudder down the spine of hardcore Wall walkers, but Bādálǐng (八达岭) is the easiest part of the Wall to get to (you can even get here by train!) and as such, if you are really pushed for time, this may be your only option. You'll have to put up with huge crowds of tourists, a lot of souvenir hawkers and a Wall that was completely renovated in the 1980s and so lacks a true sense of historical authenticity. The Bādálǐng Wall is highly photogenic, however, has good tourist facilities (restaurants, disabled access, cable cars etc) and can be visited on a half-day trip from Běijīng.

Exploring the Wall

Běijīng's most-visited chunk of brick-clad bastion ticks all the iffy Great Wall boxes in one flourish: souvenir stalls, T-shirt flogging hawkers, restaurants, heavily restored brickwork, little authenticity, guardrails and mobs of sightseers. On the plus side, the scenery is raw and striking and the Wall, which snakes off in classic fashion into the hills, is extremely photogenic. It dates back to Ming times (1368–1644), but underwent particularly heavy restoration work during the 1950s and 1980s, when it was essentially rebuilt.

There is a **cable car** (缆车; lǎn chē; one way/return ¥80/100, runs 8am to 4.30pm) from the bottom of the west car park, and a **toboggan ride** (¥30; called a 'sliding car' on the signs here), which descends to the east car park. There is also disabled access. ATMs can be found in the west car park.

Top Tip

Give the Bear Park a wide berth.

Getting There & Away

➡**Bus** The 877 (¥12, one hour, 6am to 5pm) leaves for Bādálǐng from the northern side of the Déshèngmén gateway (德胜门), about 500m east of Jishuitan subway station. It goes to east car park at Bādálǐng. From there, walk uphill a little, turn left through a covered souvenir-shop strip, then left again at the end and uphill to the ticket office, which is between two large fortified archways.

➡**Train** Getting here by train is the cheapest and most enjoyable option. Bādálǐng Train Station is a short walk downhill from the west car park; come out of the train station and turn left for the Wall (about 1km). Morning trains (¥6, 70 to 80 minutes) leave from **Běijīng North Train Station** (北京北站; Běijīng Běizhàn; Map p294; ☎5186 6223), which is connected to Xizhimen subway station, at the following times from Tuesday to Thursday: 6.12am, 8.34am, 10.57am and 12.42pm; and at the following times from Friday to Monday: 6.12am, 7.58am, 9.02am, 10.57am and 1.14pm and 1.35pm. Afternoon trains return at 1.40pm, 3.08pm, 5.30pm, 7.34pm and 9.33pm (Tuesday to Thursday); and at

CAMPING ON THE WALL

Although, strictly speaking, camping on the Great Wall is not allowed, many people do it; some of the watchtowers make excellent bases for pitching tents, or just laying down a sleeping bag. Remember, though; don't light fires and don't leave anything behind. You'll find fun places to camp at Zhuàngdàokǒu, Jiànkòu and Gǔběikǒu.

There are plenty of places to buy camping equipment in Běijīng, but one of the best in terms of quality and choice is **Sanfo** (三夫户外; Sānfū Hùwài; ☎6201 1333; www.sanfo.com; 3-4 Madian Nancun, 北三环中路马甸南村4之3－4号; ⏲9am-9pm). There are branches across the city, but this location on a side road of the middle section of the North 3rd Ring Rd stands out because it has three outlets side by side, as well as a few smaller cheaper camping shops next door. Turn right out of Exit D of Jiandemen subway station (Line 10) and walk south for about 800m, then cross under the 3rd Ring Rd and the camping shops will be on your right.

There's a smaller, easier-to-get-to **branch** (三夫户外; Sānfū Hùwài; Map p294; 9-4 Fuchengmen Dajie; 阜成门大街9－4; ⏲10am-8pm) about 200m south of Fuchengmen subway station.

1.40pm, 3.52pm, 4.14pm, 5.30pm, 8.06pm and 9.31pm (Friday to Monday).

➡**Taxi** Expect to pay around ¥600 to ¥700 for a round trip.

Need to Know

➡**Location** 70km from Běijīng

➡**Price** adult/student ¥45/25

➡**Opening hours** 6am to 7pm summer, 7am to 6pm winter

EATING

There are dozens of restaurants on the main drags leading up to the entrance to the Wall. Most are fast-food outlets or snack stalls.

YONG HE KING FAST FOOD $

(永和大王; Yǒnghé Dàwáng; mains ¥15-30; ⏲10am-9pm; 📋) Just up from the west car park, between a KFC and a Subway, try Yong He King for the Chinese version of fast food: rice meals, dumplings, noodles.

Hiking the Great Wall

Běijīng is within striking distance of a number of stretches of the Great Wall and that means there are plenty of excellent hiking opportunities for would-be adventurers. Following is a list of some of our favourite Great Wall hikes near the capital. Don't take any of these lightly, though. The Wall is incredibly steep in places, crumbling away in parts, often very exposed to the elements and at the unrestored sections usually has no sides. Wear shoes with good grip and take a rucksack so you have both hands free for clambering. And bring plenty of water.

Jiànkòu's Ox Horn to Mùtiányù

➡two hours (plus one-hour climb to the Wall)

Unrivalled for pure 'wild-wall' scenery, the Wall at Jiànkòu is very tough to negotiate. This short stretch, which passes through the 180-degree U-turn known as the Ox Horn, is equally hairy, but it soon links up with an easier, restored section at Mùtiányù. Access the Wall from hamlet No 1 in Xīzhàzi village (西栅子村一队; Xīzhàzi Cūn Yīduì). It takes an hour to reach the Wall from the village; from the sign that says 'this section of the Great Wall is not open to the public', follow a narrow dirt path uphill and through a lovely pine forest. When you reach a small clearing, go straight on (and down slightly), rather than up to the right. Later, when you hit the Wall, turn left. You'll climb/clamber up to, and round, the Ox Horn before descending (it's very slippery here) all the way to Mùtiányù where cable cars, toboggan rides and transport back to Běijīng await.

Zhuàngdàokǒu to Huánghuā Chéng

➡one hour (plus 20-minute climb to the Wall)

A short hop rather than a hike, and on a mostly restored part of the Wall, but this comes with stunning views of the Wall by a reservoir once you reach the summit of your climb. Access the Wall from Zhuàngdàokǒu village; turn right at the end of the village, by the small river, then follow the river (keeping it on your left) before turning right, up the hill between the houses, to climb a stony pathway. When you reach the Wall, turn right and keep going until you eventually descend to the main road by the reservoir. You can pick up buses, such as the H14, to Huáiróu from here (until 6pm).

Zhuàngdàokǒu to Shuǐ Chángchéng

➡two hours (plus 20-minute climb to the Wall)

Climb up to the Wall from Zhuàngdàokǒu village, and turn left at the Wall to be rewarded with this dangerous but fabulous stretch of crumbling bastion. The Wall eventually splits at a corner tower; turn left. Then, soon after you reach another tower from where you can see the reservoir far below you, the Wall crumbles down the mountain, and is impassable. Instead of risking your life, take the path that leads down to your left, just before the tower. This path eventually links up with the Wall again, but you may as well follow it all the way down to the road from here, where you'll be able to catch the H21 bus back to Huáiróu from the lower one of the two large car parks.

The Coiled Dragon Loop

➡2½ hours

This scenic but manageable hike starts and finishes in the town of Gǔběikǒu and follows a curling stretch of the Wall known as the Coiled Dragon. From the Folk Customs Village (the southern half of Gǔběikǒu), walk up to the newly reconstructed **Gǔběikǒu Gate** (古北口关; Gǔběikǒu Guǎn) but turn right up a dirt track just before the gateway. You should start seeing yellow-painted blobs, left over from an old marathon that was run here; follow them. The first section of Wall you reach is a very rare stony stretch of **Northern Qi Dynasty Wall** (1500 years old!). It soon joins up with the Ming-dynasty bricked version, which you then continue to walk along (although at one stage, you need to follow yellow arrows down off the Wall to the left, before rejoining it later). Around 90 minutes after you set off, you should reach a big sweeping right-hand bend in the Wall (the coil), with three towers on top. The first and third of these towers are quite well preserved, with walls, windows and part of a roof (great for camping in). At the third tower (called **Jiangjun Tower**), turn left, skirting right around it, then walk down the steps before turning right at a point marked with a yellow 'X' (the marathon went straight on here). Follow this pathway all the way back to Gǔběikǒu (30 minutes), turning right when you reach the road.

Gǔběikǒu to Jīnshānlǐng

➡6½ hours

This day-long adventure takes in some ancient stone Wall, some crumbling unrestored brick Wall and some picture-perfect, recently renovated Wall, as well as a 90-minute detour through the countryside. Bring plenty of water and enough food for lunch. Follow the first part of our Coiled Dragon Loop hike, but instead of leaving the Wall just after **Jiangjun Tower**, continue along the Wall for another hour until you reach the impressive **24-Window Tower** (there are only 15 windows left these days). Here, follow the yellow arrows off the Wall, to avoid a military zone up ahead, and walk down through the fields for about 25 minutes. Take the first right, at another yellow arrow, beside a vegetable plot, and climb the path back towards the Wall. After about half an hour you'll pass **Qing Yun Farmhouse**, where you may be able to buy food and drinks (but don't bank on it). It's a 25-minute climb up to the Wall from here (at the fork, the left path is easier). At the Wall, walk through the cute doorway to get up around the other side of the tower, then continue along the Wall to the restored section at Jīnshānlǐng. You'll have to buy a ticket from a lady at **Xiliang Zhuandao Tower**, from where it's about 30 minutes to **Little Jinshan Tower** (for the path, or cable car, down to the west gate), or about 90 minutes to **East Tower with Five Holes** (for the path down to the east gate, from where it's a 30-minute walk to the return bus to Běijīng).

Day Trips from Běijīng

Ming Tombs

Explore

The Unesco-protected Ming Tombs (十三陵; Shísān Líng) is the final resting place for 13 of the 16 Ming-dynasty emperors and makes for a fascinating half-day trip. The scattered tombs, each a huge temple-like complex guarding an enormous burial mound at its rear, back onto the southern slopes of Tiānshòu Mountain. Only three of the 13 tombs are open to the public, and only one has had its underground burial chambers excavated, but what you are able to see is impressive enough, and leaves you wondering just how many priceless treasures must still be buried here.

Top Tip

Keep an eye on the planned extension to the Changping subway line. The line will eventually reach the Ming Tombs and may be operational by the time you read this.

Getting There & Away

➡**Bus** Bus 872 (¥9, one hour, 7.10am to 7.10pm) leaves from the north side of Déshèngmén gateway (德胜门) and passes all the sights, apart from Zhāo Líng, before terminating at Cháng Líng. Last bus back is at 6pm.

Getting Around

➡**Bus** It's easy to bus-hop. Get off the 872 at Da Gong Men (大宫门) bus stop, and walk through the triple-arched Great Palace Gate (大宫门) that leads to Spirit Way. After walking the length of Spirit Way, catch bus 67 from Hu Zhuang (胡庄) bus stop (the first bus stop on your right) to its terminus at Zhāo Líng (¥1); walk straight on through the village to find the tomb. Then, coming back the way you came, catch another 67, or walk (2km; left at the end of the road, then left again) to Dìng Líng, from where you can catch bus 314 to Cháng Líng (¥1).

Need to Know

➡**Location** 50km from Běijīng

➡**Price** ¥35 to ¥65, combined ticket ¥135

➡**Opening Hours** 8am to 5.30pm

SIGHTS

CHÁNG LÍNG — TOMB

(长陵; admission ¥50, audio guide ¥50) The resting place of the first of the 13 emperors to be buried at the Ming Tombs, Cháng Líng contains the body of Emperor Yongle (1402–24), his wife and 16 concubines, and is the largest, most impressive and most important of the tombs here. Like all the tombs, it follows a standard imperial layout, a main gate (棱恩门; *lín'ēn mén*) leading to the first of a series of courtyards, and the main hall (棱恩殿; *líng'ēn diàn*).

Beyond this lie gates leading to the Soul Tower (明楼; Míng Lóu), behind which rises the burial mound surrounded by a fortified wall (宝成; *bǎo chéng*). Seated upon a three-tiered marble terrace, the standout structure in this complex is the Hall of Eminent Favours (灵恩殿; Líng'ēn Diàn), containing a recent statue of Yongle, various artefacts excavated from Dìng Líng, and a breathtaking interior with vast *nánmù* (cedar wood) columns. As with all three tombs here, you can climb the Soul Tower at the back of the complex for views of the surrounding hills.

DÌNG LÍNG — TOMB

(定陵; admission ¥65, audio guide ¥50) Dìng Líng, the resting place of Emperor Wanli (1572–1620) and his wife and concubines, is at first sight less impressive than Cháng Líng because many of the halls and gateways have been destroyed. It's the only tomb that has ever been opened, but many of the priceless artefacts were ruined after being left in a huge, unsealed storage room that leaked water. Other treasures – including the bodies of Emperor Wanli and his entourage – were looted and burned by Red Guards during the Cultural Revolution.

This, though, is the only tomb where you can climb down into the vast, but now empty, burial chambers.

The small **Museum of the Ming Tombs** (明十三陵博物馆; Míng Shísānlíng Bówùguǎn; admission with Dìng Líng ticket), just past the Dìng Líng ticket office, contains a few precious remaining artefacts, plus replicas of destroyed originals.

ZHĀO LÍNG — TOMB

(昭陵; admission ¥35) Zhāo Líng is the smallest of the three tombs, and many of its buildings are recent rebuilds. It's much less visited than the others, though, so is more peaceful, and the *bǎo chéng* (宝成; fortified

Ming Tombs

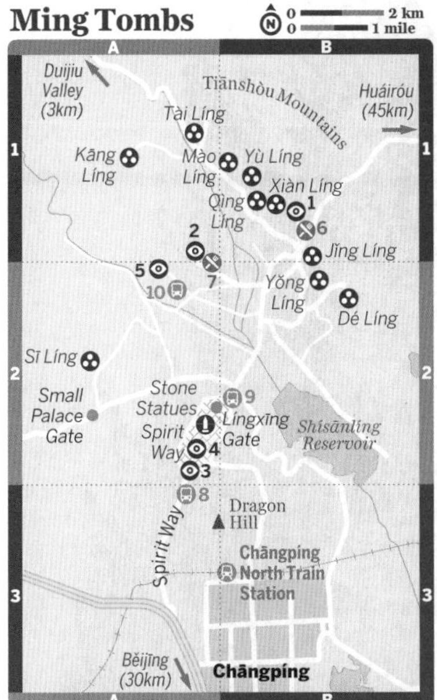

Ming Tombs

Sights	**(p184)**
1 Cháng Líng	B1
2 Dìng Líng	A1
3 Great Palace Gate	A2
4 Stele Pavilion	A2
5 Zhāo Líng	A2
Eating	**(p185)**
6 Ming Chang Ling Restaurant	B1
7 Nóngjiāfàn Kuàicān	A2
Transport	**(p184)**
8 Da Gong Men Bus Stop	A3
9 Hu Zhuang Bus Stop	B2
10 Terminus for Bus 67	A2

wall) surrounding the burial mound is unusual in both its size and form. The tomb, which is the resting place of Emperor Longqing (1537–72), is at the top end of the small village of Zhāolíng (昭陵村; Zhāolíng Cūn).

SPIRIT WAY ROAD

(神道; Shéndào; admission ¥35) The road leading up to the tombs is a 7km stretch called Spirit Way, about 1km of which is a ticketed tourist sight. Commencing from the south with a triumphal triple archway, known as the **Great Palace Gate** (大宫门; Dàgōng Mén), the path passes through **Stele Pavilion** (碑亭; Bēi Tíng), which contains a giant *bìxì* (mythical tortoiselike dragon) bearing the largest stele in China. From here, the site's famous guard of 12 sets of giant stone animals and officials ensues.

EATING

MING CHANG LING RESTAURANT CHINESE $

(明长陵餐厅; Míng Cháng Líng Cāntīng; Chang Ling Ming Tomb; ⏲8.30am-3pm) Simple but clean restaurant, with an English menu, just beside the Cháng Líng ticket office.

NÓNGJIĀFÀN KUÀICĀN CHINESE $

(农家饭快餐; mains ¥20-40; ⏲8.30am-5.30pm) Small restaurant in the car park at Dìng Líng (no English sign or menu). Dishes include *xīhóngshì jīdàn miàn* (西红柿鸡蛋面; egg and tomato noodles; ¥20), *zhájiàng miàn* (炸酱面; Běijīng-style pork noodles; ¥20), *huíguō ròu* (回锅肉; spicy cured pork; ¥28), *gōngbào jīdīng* (宫爆鸡丁; spicy chicken with peanuts; ¥26) and *yúxiāng ròusī* (鱼香肉丝; sweet and spicy shredded pork; ¥26).

Chuāndǐxià

Explore

Nestled in a valley 90km west of Běijīng and overlooked by towering peaks, the Ming-dynasty village of Chuāndǐxià is a gorgeous cluster of historic courtyard homes with old-world charm. The backdrop is lovely: terraced orchards and fields with ancient houses and alleyways rising up the hillside. Two hours is enough to wander around the village, but staying the night allows you to soak up its historic charms without the distraction of all the day-trippers.

Top Tip

Avoid weekends if possible; it can be uncomfortably overcrowded.

Getting There & Away

➡**Bus** Bus 892 leaves frequently from a bus stop 200m west of Pingguoyuan subway station (come out of Exit D and turn right) and goes to Zhāitáng (斋堂; ¥16, two hours, 6.30am to 5.50pm), from where you'll

1

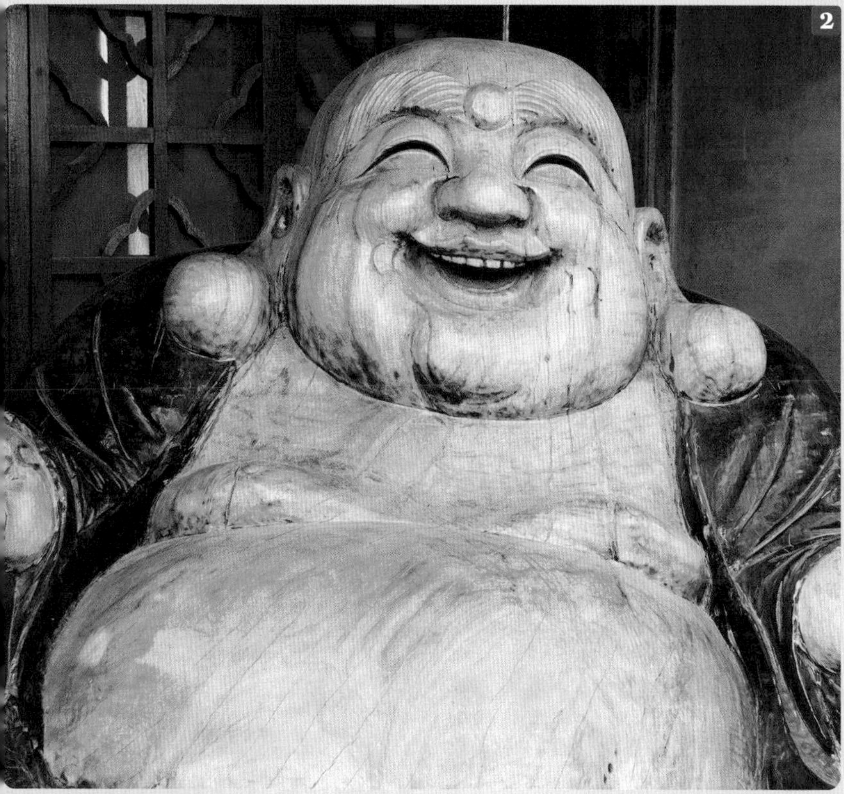

2

3

1. Ming Tombs (p184)
Stone statues on the Spirit Way, leading to the Ming Tombs.

2. Tánzhè Temple (p188)
Laughing Buddha at the largest, and one of the oldest, of all Běijīng's temples.

3. Chuāndǐxià (p185)
Nestled in a scenic valley, this Ming-dynasty village offers a gorgeous mix of charm and history.

have to take a taxi (¥20) for the last 6km to Chuāndǐxià. There's one direct bus to Chuāndǐxià, which leaves Pinguoyuan at 7am. The direct bus back to Pingguoyuan leaves Chuāndǐxià at 6.40am, but there are also two buses that go from Chuāndǐxià to Zhāitáng (¥3, 9.30am and 3.30pm). The last bus from Zhāitáng back to Pinguoyuan leaves at 5pm. If you miss that, you're looking at around ¥200 for a taxi.

Need to Know

➡**Location** 90km from Běijīng

➡**Price** ¥35

➡**Opening Hours** no official hours

SIGHTS

In the hills east of the village stands the small Qing-dynasty **Guāndì Temple** (关帝庙; Guāndì Miào). For panoramic photos of the village, climb the hill south of Chuāndǐxià (to your left as you approach the village) in the direction of the **Goddess Temple** (娘娘庙; Niángniáng Miào).

COURTYARD HOMES — HISTORIC HOUSES

The main attraction of Chuāndǐxià is the courtyard homes and the steps and alleyways that link them. It's great fun to just wander along the cobbled lanes and poke your head into ancient doorways. Many of the homes are from the Qing dynasty, while others remain from Ming times. Some have been turned into restaurants or guesthouses, meaning you can eat, drink tea or stay the night in a 500-year-old Chinese courtyard.

MAOIST SLOGANS — HISTORIC SITE

Chuāndǐxià is a museum of Maoist graffiti and slogans, especially up the incline among the better-preserved houses. Look for the very clear, red-painted slogan just past the Landlord's Courtyard (the village's principal courtyard), which reads: 用毛泽东思想武装我们的头脑 (*yòng Máozédōng sīxiǎng wǔzhuāng wǒmen de tóunǎo;* use Mao Zedong thought to arm our minds).

EATING & SLEEPING

Restaurant and guesthouse signs are clearly labelled in English, so places are easy to spot. Your best bet is to simply wander round and find what best suits you. Most restaurants have English menus. Specialities here include walnuts, apricots and roast leg of lamb.

CUAN YUN INN — CHINESE $$

(爨韵客栈; Chuànyùn Kèzhàn; 23 Chuāndǐxià Village, 爨低下村23号; mains ¥20-60; ⏲8am-8.30pm) The best place to sample roast leg of lamb (烤羊腿; *kǎo yáng tuǐ;* ¥200). On the right of main road as you enter the village. Photo menu.

GUCHENGBAO INN — INN $

(古城堡客栈; Gǔ Chéngbǎo Kèzhàn; ☎136 9135 9255; r ¥100, with attached bathroom ¥120; mains ¥20-40) This 400-year-old building is perched high above much of the village and enjoys fine views from its terrace restaurant. Rooms are in the back courtyard and are basic but charming. Each room has a traditional stone *kàng* bed, which sleeps up to four people, and can be fire-heated in winter.

The shared bathroom has no shower, but one new room comes with a small shower room, and lovely views. Guchengbao Inn is in the top left-hand corner of the village as you look up from just past the right-hand bend in the road.

Tánzhè Temple

Explore

The largest of all Běijīng's temples, and one of the oldest, 1700-year-old Tánzhè Temple (潭柘寺; Tánzhè Sì) dates from the Jin dynasty (AD 265–420), although it has been modified considerably since those days. It's attractively located amid trees in the mountains, and its ascending, terraced, temple grounds are overlooked by towering cypresses and pines, many of which are so old that their gangly limbs are supported by metal props. Visits around mid-April are recommended, as the magnolias are in bloom.

Getting There & Away

➡**Bus** Bus 931 leaves from Pingguoyuan subway station (turn right out of Exit D and wait at the first bus stop) and terminates at Tánzhè Temple (¥5, one hour). Last bus back: 6pm.

Need to Know

➡ **Location** 30km from Běijīng

➡ **Price** ¥55

➡ **Opening Hours** 8am to 5pm

SIGHTS

TÁNZHÈ TEMPLE BUDDHIST TEMPLE

(潭柘寺; Tánzhè Sì) The temple itself clings to the base of a forested hill in a series of terraced courtyards and hallways, running along three connected axes; central, east and west. The central axis has the temple's main hall, the **Mahavira Hall**, behind which is a large courtyard, shaded by a 1000-year-old gingko tree, dubbed the **Emperor Tree**. Overlooking the courtyard (to the right) is a cute **teahouse** with seating on a wooden balcony. The two-storey **Pilu Pavilion** at the back of the courtyard is the temple's highest point (with great views). The western axis includes two attractive octagonal **altars**, while the east contains the abbott's quarters, and was where visiting emperors would stay.

PAGODA FOREST CEMETERY

(下塔林; Xià Tǎlín) This astonishing collection of 75 ancient stupas, mostly from the Ming dynasty, but some dating back to the Liao (AD 907–1125) and even the Jin (AD 265–420), is in a slightly neglected garden beside where the bus drops you off. Made of bricks and built in a number of different sizes and designs, these stupas contain the remains of eminent monks from across the ages. There are actually four such graveyards in the area, but this is the largest and best preserved.

EATING & SLEEPING

There are cheap *nóngjiāyuàn* (农家院; village guesthouses) on the road leading up to the temple, offering rooms for ¥100 and meals for around ¥40.

JIĀFÚ FÀNDIÀN TEMPLE GUESTHOUSE $

(嘉福饭店; ☎6086 2781; Ānlè Hall, Tanzhe Temple; 潭柘寺安乐堂; r from ¥360; ❄) This is a treat. An ordinary, affordable guesthouse, which just happens to be located within the grounds of Ānlè Táng (安乐堂; Hall of Peace and Happiness), an old temple hall, now detached from the ticketed complex. Rooms are neat and simple, with attached bathrooms, and are located in the back courtyard.

The front courtyard contains a revered white-bark pine (白皮松; *báipí sōng*). Meals are available, but no English is spoken. It's down steps to the right just before the ticket office. To the left of the ticket office is **Jiāfú Bīnshè** (嘉福宾舍; ☎6085 1998; Tanzhe Temple; 潭柘寺; r from ¥799; ❄📶), a boutique courtyard hotel with more comfort but less charm.

Marco Polo Bridge & Wǎnpíng

Explore

The star attraction here is the famous 900-year-old Marco Polo Bridge (卢沟桥; Lúgōu Qiáo), but the unexpected bonus is the chance to see, at one end of the bridge, the enormous, war-torn, Ming-dynasty walls of the once heavily guarded Wǎnpíng Town (宛平城; Wǎnpíng Chéng).

Getting There & Away

➡ **Bus** Bus 662 comes here from Changchunjie subway station (Line 2). Come out of Exit A1 and the bus stop is in front of you on the right. Get off the bus at Lu Gou Xin Qiao (卢沟新桥) bus stop (¥1, 30 minutes) then turn right, beside a petrol station, and bear left to follow the road to bridge and the West Gate (400m).

➡ **Subway** Dawayao subway station (Line 14) is about a 1km walk from the East Gate of Wǎnpíng Town. Come out of Exit A, turn left at the junction and walk alongside the highway for about 600m before turning right down Chengnei Jie (城内街), which leads to the walls.

Need to Know

➡ **Location** 15km from central Běijīng

➡ **Price** ¥20

➡ **Opening Hours** 9am to 6pm

SHÍDÙ

Best visited during the summer rainy season, Shídù (十渡) is a scenic valley containing pinnacle-shaped rock formations, which tower over the Jùmǎ River. There is, potentially, some great hiking to be done here, but most people come for some good honest family fun: boating, kids rides, bungee jumping and riverside barbecues.

Shídù means '10 crossings': before the new road and bridges were built, you had to cross the Jùmǎ River 10 times while travelling along the gorge from Zhāngfāng (张坊) to Shídù.

Each crossing *(dù)* is like a small village. Most of the action takes place at the ninth crossing (九渡; *jiǔ dù*), where you'll find the Juma Amusement Park, a cable car, a bungee jump, a zip line, boat rides and loads of restaurants. Other crossings have more low-key attractions: bamboo rafts, dinghy rides etc. You can walk the valley along the river, or bus-hop from crossing to crossing. The eighth crossing (八渡; *bā dù*) has a quieter, villagelike feel to it, and is a nicer place to stay; try **Jiāyùn Nóngjiāyuàn** (佳运农家院; ☎134 3686 0728; r ¥80), with rooms off a small courtyard. It's about 100m past the *bā dù* bus stop.

To visit Shídù, take bus 836 from Liuliqiao East subway station (come out of Exit E then walk back on yourself to a bus stop 200m away). Shídù (¥20, two hours, 6am to 5pm) should be the last stop, but check with the bus conductor as some 836s don't go that far.

About 30 minutes before Shídù, at Zhāngfāng Village, you can visit the **Zhāngfāng Ancient Battle Tunnel** (张坊古战到; Zhāngfāng Gǔ Zhàndào; admission ¥20), a 1000-year-old underground military facility that was discovered by chance in 1991. Bus 836 stops here before it reaches Shídù; the entrance to the tunnels is inside the rebuilt ancient gateway, 200m ahead of the bus stop.

SIGHTS

MARCO POLO BRIDGE — BRIDGE

(卢沟桥; Lúgōu Qiáo; ¥20; ⊙9am-6pm) Described by the great traveller himself, this 266m-long granite bridge is the oldest bridge in Běijīng and is decorated beautifully with 485 individually carved stone lions. Dating from 1189, although widened in 1969, it spans the Yǒngdìng River, and was once the main route into the city from the southwest.

Despite the praises of Marco Polo, the bridge wouldn't have rated much in Chinese history were it not for the Marco Polo Bridge Incident, which ignited a full-scale war with Japan. On 7 July 1937 Japanese troops illegally occupied a railway junction outside Wǎnpíng. Japanese and Chinese soldiers starting shooting, giving Japan an excuse to attack and occupy Běijīng.

WĂNPÍNG TOWN — CITY WALLS

(宛平城; Wǎnpíng Chéng) FREE An astonishing sight, given that you are still within the confines of Běijīng's 5th Ring Rd, this double-gated, Ming-dynasty walled town is still lived in today. Although few of its original buildings still stand (residents live in newish brick bungalows), its 2km-long, 6m-high, battle-scarred walls date from 1640.

You can't walk on the walls, but you can walk around them or inside, around the town; enter via the West Gate, which is beside Marco Polo Bridge, or the East Gate, at the other end of the town's only proper road. On the outside of the southern wall, you can see scars from the Marco Polo Bridge Incident in the form of huge bullet holes.

MUSEUM OF THE WAR OF CHINESE PEOPLE'S RESISTANCE AGAINST JAPANESE AGGRESSION — MUSEUM

(中国人民抗日战争纪念馆; Zhōngguó Rénmín Kàng Rì Zhànzhēng Jìniànguǎn; entry with passport free, audio guide ¥120; ⊙9am-4.30pm) FREE This large, modern, propaganda-driven museum, on the north side of the main road in Wǎnpíng Town, is dedicated to the July 7th Incident (as it's called here) and the war with Japan which ensued. Includes English captions.

EATING

JĪNG CHUĀN — SICHUAN $

(京川; mains ¥20-40; ⊙11am-10pm) This simple Sìchuān restaurant, just inside the East Gate of Wǎnpíng Town, has a photo menu, rooftop seating and cold beer.

Sleeping

Běijīng's increasingly impressive hotel scene has something for everyone: a huge range of youth hostels, loads of business hotels, and all the international five-star hotel brands you'd expect of a city this size. The jewel in the crown, though, is its charming courtyard hotels, which offer a wonderful opportunity to experience life in Běijīng's unique hútòng (alleyways).

Hostels

Youth hostels offer much more than just dorm beds and budget prices. Many are hidden away in historic buildings down Běijīng's *hútòng,* with comfortable single and double rooms and staff tuned into foreign travellers' needs. Travel advice is often honest, impartial and knowledgeable, and staff members usually speak excellent English. They often rent bicycles, have free wi-fi, and tend to run worthwhile day trips and tours to places such as the Great Wall.

Courtyard Hotels

If you want history, try Běijīng's courtyard hotels, which allow you to uncover the city's *hútòng* ambience and inimitable courtyard residences. The downside is the smallish size of the rooms, but courtyard hotels come with an atmosphere that is uniquely Běijīng and a charm that other hotels can't imitate.

Luxury Hotels

The top-end bracket is crammed with options in most parts of town (apart from the Dōngchéng North neighbourhood). All the major international five-star hotels are represented.

Standard Hotels

Run-of-the-mill midrange Chinese hotels lack character, but can be good value as they often come with generous discounts. Expect clean rooms (although some rooms may be smoky) with TV, kettle, internet access through a cable, if not wi-fi, and small attached bathrooms. Staff at these types of places rarely speak much English.

Sadly, many of the city's cheapest guesthouses, often known as *zhāodàisuǒ* (招待所), still refuse to take foreigners because of the rigmarole involved with registering foreign guests with the local police.

Homestays & Long-Term Rentals

Homestays are a great way to experience Chinese culture (and improve your language skills). Běijīng also has a large couch-surfing community and short-term room rentals can be found at www.airbnb.com.

The rental market in Běijīng is good value. Prices start at around ¥4000 per month for a two-bed apartment. If you speak Chinese, just make enquiries at any local estate agent. If you don't, your easiest option is to check the accommodation pages of the websites of Běijīng's expat magazines.

Websites

These websites are useful for booking accommodation in Běijīng:

➡**ctrip.com** Hotel reservations.

➡**booking.com** Hotel reviews and reservations.

➡**hostelworld.com** Youth hostel reviews and reservations.

➡**chinahomestay.org** Homestays.

➡**chinastudyabroad.org** Homestays.

➡**thebeijinger.com** Long-term rentals.

➡**lonelyplanet.com/china/beijing/hotels** Hotel reviews and reservations.

NEED TO KNOW

Price Ranges

The following price ranges represent a standard double room per night:

$ under ¥400

$$ ¥400 to ¥1000

$$$ over ¥1000

Discounts

Discounts of 30% to 40% are the norm in ordinary, midrange, Chinese-run hotels. Hostels, courtyard hotels and boutique hotels tend to be more transparent, so will just charge the rack rates. Whatever the hotel, booking online – especially through large, well-established booking sites such as ctrip.com or booking.com – will often help you secure the best discounts.

Reservations

Hotel rooms are easy to find, although it's worth booking during public holidays. It's always advisable to book courtyard hotels, as they often have only four or five rooms in total.

Checking In

When checking into a hotel, you will need to complete a registration form, a copy of which will be sent to the local Public Security Bureau (PSB; Gōng'ānjú), and your passport will need to be scanned or photocopied.

Service Charge & Tips

A 15% service charge is levied at midrange and top-end hotels. Tipping is only expected in top-end hotels.

Lonely Planet's Top Choices

Temple Hotel (p195) Class and serenity in a Buddhist temple complex.

Great Wall Box House (p176) Renovated village hostel beside the Great Wall.

Qiánmén Hostel (p199) Fun, welcoming, heritage hostel.

Courtyard 7 (p198) Oozes Qing-dynasty charm.

Graceland Yard (p198) Boutique lodgings set around a long-abandoned temple.

Best by Budget

$

Qiánmén Hostel (p199) Historic hostel in Dashilar.

Běijīng Downtown Backpackers (p196) Great location. Great staff.

Three-Legged Frog Hostel (p199) Good, honest cheapie with a friendly welcome

Nostalgia Hotel (p196) Trendy alternative to the youth hostels

$$

Great Wall Box House (p176) Fabulous guesthouse beside the Great Wall.

Orchid (p197) The hipsters' *hútòng* hotel of choice.

Jǐngshān Garden Hotel (p194) Calm courtyard in central Běijīng.

$$$

Temple Hotel (p195) Utterly unique, Unesco-acclaimed temple conversion.

Opposite House Hotel (p201) Hotels don't come cooler than this.

Emperor (p198) Rooftop pool overlooking Tiān'ānmén Sq.

Aman at Summer Palace (p202) Pure indulgence on the city outskirts.

Côté Cour (p195) Exquisite rooms off a magnolia courtyard.

Courtyard 7 (p198) Bags of history. Plenty of class.

Best Courtyard Hotels

Courtyard 7 (p198) Former Qing-dynasty residence.

Temple Hotel (p195) Luxury lodgings off Buddhist-temple courtyards.

Graceland Yard (p198) Modest temple conversion with 500 years of history.

Jǐngshān Garden Hotel (p194) Pleasant courtyard in a quieter part of town.

Hulu Hotel (p194) Trendy new addition.

Best Hútòng Hostels

Qiánmén Hostel (p199) A hostel with history.

Běijīng Downtown Backpackers (p196) Nanluogu Xiang's best hostel.

Three-Legged Frog Hostel (p199) Fun, friendly and good value.

Red Lantern House West Yard (p198) Quality group of hostels in quieter Xīchéng.

Feel Inn (p194) A stone's throw from the Forbidden City.

Best City Escapes

Great Wall Box House (p176) Understated, friendly and on the Great Wall.

Brickyard Eco Retreat (p173) Quality lodgings close to the Great Wall.

Zǎoxiāng Yard (p179) Friendly family-run guesthouse, 20-minutes' walk from the Wall.

Where to Stay

Neighbourhood	For	Against
Forbidden City & Dōngchéng Central	Hugely historic. Highest concentration of sights. Good mix of ordinary hotels and *hútòng* accommodation.	Some parts are less residential than other neighbourhoods, and so can be eerily quiet in the evenings. Slim pickings on the nightlife front.
Drum Tower & Dōngchéng North	Běijīng's most desirable neighbourhood. Perfect for delving deep into the *hútòng*. Plenty of courtyard hotels. Cafes, bars and live music on your doorstep.	Budget backpackers may be priced out. No five-star hotels.
Temple of Heaven Park & Dōngchéng South	A real neighbourhood rather than a tourist area. Quiet.	A nightlife desert; not much in the way of standout eating options.
Běihǎi Park & Xīchéng North	Plenty of *hútòng* action, and the area by the lakes sees little motorised traffic, and so can be peaceful. Less touristy than Dōngchéng District.	Evening karaoke bars can ruin the lakeside ambience. Choice of accommodation, restaurants and bars is more limited.
Dashilar & Xīchéng South	Backpacker Central. Great choice of hostels, some historic. *Hútòng* vibe is still strong around Dashilar.	Extensive reconstruction has stolen some of the character from the area (particularly around Qiánmén), and seen restaurant prices rise, although hostel rooms are still cheap.
Sānlǐtún & Cháoyáng	Great for shopping, eating and nightlife.	Area lacks character and any historical narrative.
Summer Palace & Hǎidiàn	Less touristy.	Out of the way.

Forbidden City & Dōngchéng Central

FEEL INN HUTONG HOSTEL $

Map p284 (非凡客栈; Fēifán Kèzhàn; ☎6528 7418, 139 1040 9166; beijingfeelinn@gmail.com; 2 Ciqiku Hutong, off Nanheyan Dajie, 南河沿大街，磁器库胡同 2 号; dm ¥50-80, tw ¥240-300; ❄@📶) A small, understated hostel with a hidden, backstreet location, Feel Inn is tucked away amongst the alleys containing the little-known Pǔdù Temple, and yet is just a short walk from big-hitters such as the Forbidden City, Tiān'ānmén Sq and the shops on Wangfujing Dajie. Has simple, clean rooms, a small bar-restaurant, and wi-fi throughout.

BĚIJĪNG SAGA INTERNATIONAL YOUTH HOSTEL HUTONG HOSTEL $

Map p286 (北京实佳国际青年旅社; Běijīng Shíjiā Guójì Qīngnián Lǚshè; ☎6527 2773; www.sagayouthhostelbeijing.cn; 9 Shijia Hutong, 史家胡同 9 号; dm ¥70, d with/without bathroom from ¥259/200, tr ¥319; ❄@📶; ⓈDengshikou) Enjoying an interesting location on historic Shijia Hutong, this friendly hostel is a grey block, but the inside compensates with some character and staff members are helpful towards travellers. Rooms are basic but well kept, and it has a decent restaurant-cum-bar. Rents bikes (¥50) and does Great Wall trips.

BĚIJĪNG CITY CENTRAL INTERNATIONAL YOUTH HOSTEL HOSTEL $

Map p286 (北京城市国际青年旅社; Běijīng Chéngshì Guójì Qīngnián Lǚshè; ☎6525 8066, 8511 5050; www.centralhostel.com; 1 Beijingzhan Jie, 北京站街 1 号; 4–8-bed dm ¥60, s/d with shared bathroom ¥138/178, d ¥298-348; ⊖❄@📶; ⓈBeijing Railway Station) The first youth hostel you hit after exiting Běijīng Railway Station, this place is a decent choice if you can't be bothered lugging your heavy rucksack to nicer parts of the city. Rooms are pretty basic, but clean and spacious enough, and there's a large bar-cafe area with free wi-fi, internet terminals, pool tables and Western food.

The rooms with shared bathrooms are in the hostel proper, while those with private bathrooms are in the attached hotel (same reception).

YMCA HOTEL HOTEL $

Map p286 (创世商务酒店; Chuàngshì Shāngwù Jiǔdiàn; ☎6528 7782; 3 Dongdan Beidajie, 东单北大街 3 号; tw ¥338-688) This well-run place is neat and tidy, and comes with decent-sized rooms for the price. The windowless twins (¥338) are good value. All rooms come with wi-fi, TV, kettle and a clean shower room. Not much English spoken, though.

★JĬNGSHĀN GARDEN HOTEL COURTYARD HOTEL $$

Map p286 (景山花园酒店; Jǐngshān Huāyuán Jiǔdiàn; ☎8404 7979; www.jingshangardenhotel.com; 68 Sanyanjing Hutong, off Jingshan Dongjie; 景山东街，三眼井胡同 68 号; r ¥650-750; ❄@📶) This delightful, unfussy, two-storey guesthouse has bright spacious rooms surrounding a large, peaceful, flower-filled courtyard. First-floor rooms are pricier, but brighter than the ground-floor ones, and some have views of Jǐngshān Park from their bathrooms. Walking down Sanyuanjing Hutong from the direction of Jǐngshān Park, turn right down the first alleyway, and the hotel is at the end.

CITY WALLS COURTYARD HUTONG HOSTEL $$

Map p286 (城墙旅舍; Chéngqiáng Lǚshè; ☎6402 7805; www.beijingcitywalls.com; 57 Nianzi Hutong, 碾子胡同 57 号; dm/s/tw ¥100/240/480; ❄@📶; ⓈNanluoguxiang) This quiet hostel is on the pricey side for sure, but it's still an attractive choice because of its peaceful courtyard atmosphere and fabulous *hútòng* location – authentically hidden away from more touristy areas in one of the city's most historic neighbourhoods. All rooms have private bathrooms.

The maze of alleyways can be disorientating: from Jingshan Houjie, look for the *hútòng* opening just east of Jǐngshān Table Tennis Park. Walk up the *hútòng* and follow it around to the right and then left; the hostel is on the left-hand side.

HULU HOTEL COURTYARD HOTEL $$

Map p286 (壶庐宾馆; Húlú Bīnguǎn; ☎6543 9229; www.thehuluhotel.com; 91 Yanyue Hutong, off Dongsi Nandajie, 东四南大街，演乐胡同 91 号; r ¥798-1198) A stylish new addition to Běijīng's ever-growing brood of courtyard hotels, Hulu's converted *hútòng* space is minimalist throughout, with cool grey-painted wood beams, slate-tiled bathrooms and a cleverly renovated courtyard that combines its old-Běijīng roots with a modern, comfortable design. The atmosphere is laid-back, and the young staff speak excellent English. There are three grades of room (size increases with price), all of which have large double beds – no twins.

PARK PLAZA HOTEL $$

Map p286 (北京丽亭酒店; Běijīng Lìtíng Jiǔdiàn; ☎8522 1999; www.parkplaza.com/beijingcn; 97 Jinbao Jie, 金宝街 97 号; d from ¥900; ; Dengshikou) If you can't or don't want to stretch to a five-star hotel, this friendly place has a strong location and a comfortable, modern and well-presented four-star finish. It's hidden away behind its glitzier sister hotel, the Regent Běijīng.

★TEMPLE HOTEL HERITAGE HOTEL $$$

Map p286 (东景缘; Dōngjǐng Yuán; ☎8401 5680; www.thetemplehotel.com; 23 Shatan Beijie, off Wusi Dajie, 五四大街，沙滩北街 23 号; d ¥2000 ste ¥3000-4500) Unrivaled by anything else on the Běijīng hotel scene, this unique heritage hotel forms part of a renovation project that was recognised by Unesco for its conservation efforts. A team spent five years renovating what was left of Zhīzhù Sì (智珠寺; Temple of Wisdom), a part-abandoned, 250-year-old Buddhist temple, and slowly transformed it into one of the most alluring places to stay in the capital.

There are eight rooms, each presented immaculately, and each with its own story to tell. Some once formed part of the monks' dormitories during the Qing dynasty. Others are industrial in style, as befits their former incarnations as a television factory in the 1960s. The two-storey suites, meanwhile, have close-up views of the fabulous main temple hall, now used for art exhibitions or private events. The rooms are huge, and the atmosphere within the courtyard complex is serene.

★RED CAPITAL RESIDENCE COURTYARD HOTEL $$$

Map p286 (新红资客栈, Xīnhóngzī Kèzhàn; ☎8401 8886, 8403 5308; www.redcapitalclub.com.cn; 9 Dongsi Liutiao, 东四六条 9 号; r incl breakfast ¥1050; ; Zhangzizhonglu) Dressed up with Liberation-era artefacts and established in a gorgeous Qing-dynasty courtyard, this tiny but unique guesthouse – owned by American activist and author Laurence Brahm – offers a heady dose of nostalgia for a vanished age. Make your choice from three rooms decked out with paraphernalia that wouldn't look out of place in a museum.

Rooms and bathrooms are small, but beautifully decorated. What makes this place unique, though, is the cigar bar: it's housed below the courtyard in an underground bomb shelter! Booking is recommended, especially at weekends. Red Capital also operates a wonderfully rustic Great Wall retreat.

★CÔTÉ COUR COURTYARD HOTEL $$$

Map p286 (北京演乐酒店, Běijīng Yǎnyuè Jiǔdiàn; ☎6523 3958; www.hotelcotecourbj.com; 70 Yanyue Hutong, 演乐胡同 70 号; d/ste incl breakfast ¥1166/1995; ; Dengshikou) With a

ESCAPE TO THE GREAT WALL

As well as the accommodation options featured in our special Great Wall section, the following digs offer some luxury beside more remote parts of China's best-known icon.

Commune by the Great Wall (长城脚下的公社; Chángchéng Jiǎoxià de Gōngshè; ☎8118 1888; www.communebythegreatwall.com; r from ¥2500;) The Commune by the Great Wall is seriously expensive, but the cantilevered geometric architecture, location and superb panoramas are standouts. Positioned at the Shuǐguān Great Wall off the Badaling Hwy, the Kempinski-managed Commune may have a proletarian name, but the design and presentation are purely for the affluent. There is a kids' club to boot.

Shambhala at the Great Wall (新红资避暑山庄; Xīnhóngzī Bìshǔshānzhuāng; ☎8401 8886, 8403 5308; www.redcapitalclub.com.cn; 28 Xiaguandi Village, 怀柔县雁栖镇下关地村 28 号, Yanxi; r incl breakfast from ¥1050;) Doing its own thing miles from civilisation, Tibetan-themed Shambhala is owned by the same guys behind the wonderful city-centre courtyard hotel, Red Capital Residence. Once part of a Manchurian hunting lodge, the buildings here have been converted into Tibetan-style stone houses, while the restaurant specialises in Tibetan, Nepalese and Indian cuisine.

The houses are set around part of a 50-acre estate with a mountain backdrop and with Great Wall remains running through it.

calm, serene atmosphere and a lovely magnolia courtyard, this 14-room *hútòng* hotel makes a charming place to rest your head. The decor is exquisite – especially in the suite – and there's plenty of space to relax in the courtyard or on the extensive rooftop – perfect for a candle-lit evening drink.

Staff are sweet and friendly, and bicycles are available for rent (¥50). Nonguests can eat at the stylish rooftop restaurant (six-course set-dinner ¥298), which is open every evening from 6.30pm to 10pm. The courtyard is around 500 years old and was once the home of a troupe of musicians who performed for the imperial court.

RAFFLES BĚIJĪNG HISTORICAL HOTEL **$$$**

Map p286 (北京饭店莱佛士酒店; Běijīng Fàndiàn Láifóshì Jiǔdiàn; ☎6526 3388; www.raffles.com/beijing; 33 Dongchang'an Jie, 东长安街 33 号; r from ¥1800; ; Wangfujing) Sandwiched between two drab edifices (to the east the 1970s lines of the Běijīng Hotel, to the west a gawky Soviet-era facade), the seven-storey Raffles oozes cachet and grandeur. The heritage building dates to 1900, when it was the Grand Hotel de Pekin, and it stays true to its historic roots.

Illuminated in a chandelier glow, the elegant lobby yields to a graceful staircase leading to immaculate standard doubles that are spacious and well proportioned, decked out with period-style furniture and large bathrooms. The ground floor contains the hotel's most historic feature: the Writers Bar, once a common meeting place for Communist Party cadres, including Mao Zedong, and now a splendid spot for High Tea (2.30pm to 5.30pm, ¥158 to ¥168).

REGENT BĚIJĪNG LUXURY HOTEL **$$$**

Map p286 (北京丽晶大酒店; Běijīng Lìjīng Dàjiǔdiàn; ☎8522 1888; www.regenthotels.com; 99 Jinbao Jie, 金宝街 99 号; r from ¥1600; ; Dengshikou) Guest rooms at this lavish 500-room hotel are good value, being luxuriously styled and up to the minute. There's a full range of health and leisure facilities. Five restaurants round off the impressive picture.

RED WALL GARDEN COURTYARD HOTEL **$$$**

Map p286 (红墙花园酒店; Hóngqiáng Huāyuán Jiǔdiàn; ☎5169 2222; www.rwghotel.com; 41 Shijia Hutong, 史家胡同 41 号; d ¥1400-1600, ste ¥1780; ; Dengshikou) Despite its old *hútòng* location, there's nothing historic about this reconstructed courtyard hotel, but it offers top-end luxury rooms, complete with very comfortable beds and some beautiful pieces of traditional Chinese wood furniture, in a two-storey complex, which surrounds two sides of a huge, nicely landscaped, central courtyard. Wi-fi and nonsmoking throughout. Small bar. Decent restaurant.

HILTON BĚIJĪNG WÁNGFǓJǏNG LUXURY HOTEL **$$$**

Map p286 (北京王府井希尔顿酒店; Běijīng Wángfǔjǐng Xī'ěrdùn Jiǔdiàn; ☎5812 8888; www.wangfujing.hilton.com; Xiaowei Hutong, off Wangfujing Dongdajie, 王府井东大街校尉胡同; d ¥1550; ; Wangfujing) Modern and classy, this branch of the Hilton is one of Běijīng's best five-star offerings. Service is stellar and it has some of the largest guest rooms in the city.

Drum Tower & Dōngchéng North

BĚIJĪNG DOWNTOWN BACKPACKERS HUTONG HOSTEL **$**

Map p290 (东堂客栈, Dōngtáng Kèzhàn; ☎8400 2429; www.backpackingchina.com; 85 Nanluogu Xiang, 南锣鼓巷 85 号; dm ¥75-85, s ¥160, tw ¥160-210, ste ¥300; ; Beixinqiao) Downtown Backpackers is Nanluogu Xiang's original youth hostel and it hasn't forgotten its roots. Rooms are basic, therefore cheap, but are kept clean and tidy, and staff members are fully plugged in to the needs of Western travellers. Rents bikes (per day ¥20) and runs recommended hiking trips to the Great Wall (¥280), plus a range of other city trips. Rates include breakfast.

NOSTALGIA HOTEL HOTEL **$**

Map p290 (时光漫步怀旧主题酒店; Shíguāng Mànbù Huáijiù Zhǔtí Jiǔdiàn; ☎6403 2288; www.sgmbhotel.com; 46 Fangjia Hutong; 安定门内大街，方家胡同 46 号; r summer ¥388-408, winter ¥360-380) A good-value option if you don't fancy staying in a youth hostel, this funky hotel is housed in a small arts zone on trendy Fangjia Hutong. Rooms are dotted with retro knick-knacks, and have a different hand-painted mural in each. The bathrooms sparkle.

Staff on reception speak English, and there's lift access, but no restaurant. To find it, enter the small arts zone named after its address (46 Fangjia Hutong) and walk to the far left corner of the complex.

CONFUCIUS INTERNATIONAL YOUTH HOSTEL HÚTÒNG HOSTEL $

Map p290 (雍圣轩青年酒店; Yōngshèngxuān Qīngnián Jiǔdiàn; ☎6402 2082; 38 Wudaoying Hutong; 雍和宫大街，五道营胡同 38 号; dm/s/d/tw ¥80/120/138/158) One of the cheapest places that's open to foreigners in this area, Confucius has a handful of simple, no-frills rooms off a small, covered courtyard. No restaurant.

★ORCHID COURTYARD HOTEL $$

Map p290 (兰花宾馆; Lánhuā Bīnguǎn; ☎8404 4818; www.theorchidbeijing.com; 65 Baochao Hutong, 鼓楼东大街宝钞胡同 65 号; d ¥700-1200; ❄@📶; Ⓢ Gulou Dajie) Opened by a Canadian guy and a Tibetan girl, this place may lack the history of other courtyard hotels, but it's been renovated into a beautiful space, with a peaceful courtyard and some rooftop seating with distant views of the Drum and Bell Towers. Rooms are doubles only, and are small, but are tastefully decorated and come with Apple TV home entertainment systems.

They also do Great Wall tours, and can organise taxis for city tours (half-/full day ¥400/600) or Great Wall trips (¥700). Hard to spot, the Orchid is down an unnamed, shoulder-width alleyway opposite Mr Shi's Dumplings.

★DÙGÉ COURTYARD HOTEL $$

Map p290 (杜革四合院酒店; Dùgé Sìhéyuàn Jiǔdiàn; ☎6445 7463; www.dugecourtyard.com; 26 Qianyuan Ensi Hutong, 交道口南大街前园恩寺胡同 26 号; r small/large ¥897/1817; ❄@📶; Ⓢ Nanluoguxiang, Beixinqiao) This 19th-century former residence was originally home to a Qing-dynasty minister before being converted by a Belgian-Chinese couple into an exquisite designer courtyard hotel. Each of the six rooms is decorated uniquely with modern and artistic touches blended with overall themes of traditional China. Some of the wood furniture – four-poster beds, decorative Chinese screens – is beautiful.

Rooms are set around small, romantic, bamboo-lined courtyards, but space is at a premium – the small rooms really are small.

PEKING YOUTH HOSTEL HÚTÒNG HOSTEL $$

Map p290 (北平国际青年旅社; Běipíng Guójì Qīngnián Lǚshè; ☎8403 9098; pekinghostel@vip.163.com; 113 Nanluogu Xiang, 南锣鼓巷 113 号; dm/tw from ¥180/500; ❄@📶; Ⓢ Nanluoguxiang) Slick, colourful, but rather cramped rooms are located round the back of the flower-filled Peking Cafe, which opens out onto Nanluogu Xiang. Prices reflect the location rather than the size or quality of the rooms, or the quality of the service (staff can be a bit slack, especially in the busy cafe), but this is a sound choice nevertheless.

All the usual youth-hostel services are dished up, including bike hire and trips to the Great Wall.

ENGLISH-LANGUAGE SKILLS

Good English-language skills among hotel staff remain fitful. Youth hostels typically have excellent English-language speakers, as do five-star hotels – it's the ones in between that may not have staff fluent in English.

161 LAMA TEMPLE COURTYARD HOTEL COURTYARD HOTEL $$

Map p290 (北京 161 酒店－雍和宫四合院店; ☎8401 5027; beijing161lthotel@hotmail.com; 46 Beixinqiao Santiao; 北新桥三条 46 号; r ¥440 & ¥550) This hotel-cum-hostel, located on a *hútòng* that comes alive with restaurants in the evening, has 11 rooms, each themed on a different tourist sight in Běijīng. Rooms have a huge photo-mural to match their theme, and are small but spotless; the bathrooms likewise. The higher-category rooms come with a traditional wooden tea-drinking table, which can double as an extra single bed.

There's a small cafe in reception and some cute courtyard seating.

OLD BĚIJĪNG SQUARE HOTEL COURTYARD HOTEL $$

Map p290 (未名精品酒店; Wèimíng Jīngpǐn Jiǔdiàn; ☎8402 5337; weimingjiudian@163.com; 38 Baochao Hutong; 宝抄胡同 38 号; d with shared bathroom ¥480, d ¥680-980, ste ¥1380) This newly reconstructed courtyard hotel has been done with taste and charm, with plenty of natural light seeping through the glass roof into the central courtyard. Rooms are small (though bathrooms are tiny) but furnished well, and the staff are sweet. The hotel is hidden down an unmarked alley off Baochao Hutong, next door to a cheap hotel that doesn't accept foreigners.

★**COURTYARD 7** COURTYARD HOTEL $$$
Map p290 (四合院酒店; Sìhéyuàn Jiǔdiàn; ☎6406 0777; www.courtyard7.com; 7 Qianguloyuan Hutong, off Nanluogu Xiang, 鼓楼东大街南锣鼓巷前鼓楼苑胡同 7 号; r ¥900-1500; ❄@; Ⓢ Nanluoguxiang) Immaculate rooms, decorated in traditional Chinese furniture face onto a series of different-sized, 400-year-old courtyards, which over the years have been home to government ministers, rich merchants and even an army general. Despite the historical narrative, rooms still come with modern comforts such as underfloor heating, broadband internet, wi-fi, and cable TV.

The *hútòng* location – down a quiet alley, but very close to trendy Nanluogu Xiang – is also a winner. Breakfast is included.

Temple of Heaven Park & Dōngchéng South

EMPEROR HOTEL $$$
Map p293 (皇家驿站; Huángjiā Yìzhàn; ☎6701 7791; www.theemperor.com.cn; 87 Xianyukou St, Qianmen Commercial Centre, 前门商业区鲜鱼口街 87 号; r ¥1200; ❄📶🏊; Ⓢ Qianmen) Brand new, this modernist hotel comes with a spa and a pool on the roof that gives you a chance to laze in the sun while enjoying fine views over nearby Tiān'ānmén Sq. The cool, all-white rooms may not be huge, but the price is reasonable for a hotel of this quality and the location is perfect. Service is attentive and the atmosphere laid-back.

Běihǎi Park & Xīchéng North

SLEEPY INN HÚTÒNG HOSTEL $
Map p294 (丽舍; Lì Shè; ☎6406 9954; 103 Deshengmennei Dajie; 德胜门内大街 103 号; dm/tw ¥100/298; 📶) Facilities may not be as good here as in other larger hostels, but the location by Xīhǎi Lake is lovely, and staff members are friendly. Rooms are simple but clean, and there is bike rental and free wi-fi (although no computer terminals). This place has a small cafe, but no restaurant. Heading south along Deshengmennei Dajie, turn right at the stone bridge (but don't cross it) and Sleepy Inn is on the right after 50m.

RED LANTERN HOUSE WEST YARD COURTYARD HOTEL $
Map p294 (红灯笼; Hóng Dēnglóng; ☎6617 0870; 12 Xisi Beiertiao, 西四北二条 12 号; s ¥280, d & tw ¥360, ste ¥450; ❄@📶; Ⓢ Xisi) Previously the most engaging of the Red Lantern brood, West Yard was closed for wholesale renovations at the time of research, but will be open again by the time you read this. It was set around two lovely, quiet courtyards, and the rooms were thoughtfully and comfortably furnished in an old-Běijīng style. Book ahead. To find it, walk north on Xisi Beidajie from Xisi metro; it's two *hútòng* up on the left.

RED LANTERN HOUSE HUTONG HOSTEL $
Map p294 (仿古园, Fǎnggǔ Yuán; ☎8328 5771; www.redlanternhouse.com; 5 Zhengjue Hutong, 正觉胡同 5 号; 4–6-bed dm ¥85, d ¥220; ❄@📶; Ⓢ Jishuitan) Clean and simple rooms around a pleasant, covered courtyard, and a fantastic, nontouristy, *hútòng* location make this welcoming hostel a sound choice. All rooms come with shared bathrooms. If you want private bathrooms, or if this place is full, ask to see its laid-back, but less charming sibling, Red Lantern House East Yard. It's a couple of minutes' walk away in an alley off Zhengjue Hutong, with doubles and triples for ¥330 and ¥420.

DRUM TOWER YOUTH HOSTEL HOSTEL $
Map p294 (鼓韵青年旅舍; Gǔyùn Qīngnián Lǚshè; ☎8401 6565; www.24hostel.com; 51 Jiugulou Dajie, 旧鼓楼大街 51 号; 6-bed dm with/without bathroom ¥80/60, d & tw with/without bathroom ¥280/200; ❄@📶; Ⓢ Gulou Dajie) This large, dependable hostel, close to its namesake Drum Tower, was undergoing wholesale renovations at the time of research, but will be open again by the time you read this. Had clean, functional rooms, a roof terrace and an attached bar-restaurant.

★**GRACELAND YARD** COURTYARD HOTEL $$
Map p294 (觉品酒店; Juepin Jiudian; ☎159 1115 3219; www.graceland-yardhotel.com; 9 Zhengjue Hutong; 正觉胡同 9 号; s/d/tw/ste ¥599/699/799/1000, loft ¥899; @📶) Graceland is an exquisitely renovated courtyard hotel, housed within the grounds of the abandoned, 500-year-old Zhèngjué Temple. Each of the eight rooms is slightly different – there are singles, doubles, twins, a couple of fabulous loft rooms and a suite – but each is decorated with style, using traditional Buddhist-themed fur-

nishings. There's no restaurant – not even breakfast – but you're not short of eateries in the surrounding *hútòng*.

SHÍCHÀHǍI SHADOW ART HOTEL HOTEL $$
Map p294 (什刹海皮影酒店; Shíchàhǎi Píyǐng Jiǔdiàn; ☎136 8303 2251, 8328 7846; www.shichahaitour.com; 24 Songshu Jie, 松树街 24 号; tw & d ¥630-930) This slick, ultramodern, boutique hotel is somewhat at odds with the grainy textures of the old *hútòng* outside, but it offers a very comfortable stay in an interesting, mostly residential section of the Hòuhǎi Lakes area. Rooms are individually themed and mix modern design with touches of traditional China.

There's a small stage in the teahouse-lookalike lobby, where shadow-puppet shows are performed (for guests only) every Tuesday, Thursday and Saturday evening. There's no restaurant, but breakfast in the lobby is included.

There are larger, more expensive rooms in its equally natty sister hotel, **Shíchàhǎi Sandalwood Boutique Hotel** (什刹海紫檀酒店; Shíchàhǎi Zǐtán Jiǔdiàn; Map p294; ☎8322 6686; www.sch-hotel.com; 42 Xinghua Hutong; 兴华胡同 42 号; r ¥1020-1300), located a five-minute walk away, in Xinghua Hutong.

Dashilar & Xīchéng South

★**QIÁNMÉN HOSTEL** COURTYARD HOSTEL $
Map p296 (前门客栈; Qiánmén Kèzhàn; ☎6313 2370, 6313 2369; www.qianmenhostel.net; 33 Meishi Jie, 煤市街 33 号; 6-8 bed dm ¥70, 4-bed dm ¥80, with/without bathroom d & tw ¥280/240, tr ¥380/300; ❄@📶; ⓈQianmen) A five-minute trot southwest of Tiān'ānmén Sq, this heritage hostel with a cool courtyard offers a relaxing environment with able staff. The rooms are simple and not big but, like the dorms, they are clean, as are the shared bathrooms, and all were being upgraded at the time of writing. There's a decent cafe to hang out in too.

Despite the busy location, this is an easy place to switch off and appreciate the high ceilings, original woodwork and charming antique buildings. An affable old-hand, hostel owner Genghis Kane does his best to keep his standards high, while bikes can be rented for ¥20 a day and Great Wall tours arranged.

THREE-LEGGED FROG HOSTEL HUTONG HOSTEL $
Map p296 (京一食青年旅舍; Jīngyī Shí Qīngnián Lǚshè; ☎6304 0749; 3legs@threeleggedfrog-hostel.com; 27 Tieshu Xiejie, 铁树斜街 27 号; 6-bed dm with bathroom ¥65, 10-bed dm ¥55, d & tw ¥220, tr ¥270, f ¥339; ❄📶; ⓈQianmen) The name is a mystery but the decent-sized six-bed dorms with bathrooms are an excellent deal, while the rooms are compact but clean. All are set around a cute courtyard that's pleasant in the summer. It has a helpful owner – it's geared to foreign travellers – and a communal area out front that does Western breakfasts and evening beers.

LEO COURTYARD COURTYARD HOSTEL $
Map p296 (上林宾馆, Shànglín Bīnguǎn; ☎8316 6568; www.leohostel.com; 22 Shanxi Xiang, 陕西巷胡同 22 号; 4-bed dm without bathroom ¥60, 8/10-bed dm with bathroom ¥55/60, d/tw ¥140/160, tr ¥180; ❄📶; ⓈQianmen) It's a superb, historic, warren of a building with a racy past featuring courtesans and the imperial elite, but like most courtyard hotels the rooms are a little old-fashioned and the dorms on the small side. However, the once-sleepy staff have upped their game and are now helpful and the bathrooms are clean. It's down an alley off Dazhalan Xijie.

The attached bar-restaurant next door is a good place for a libation come sundown.

LEO HOSTEL HUTONG HOSTEL $
Map p296 (广聚园宾馆, Guǎngjùyuán Bīnguǎn; ☎6317 6288, 6303 3318; www.leohostel.com; 52 Dazhalan Xijie, 大栅栏西街 52 号; 4-bed dm with/without bathroom ¥80/70, 6-bed dm ¥65, 10-bed dm ¥55, 14-bed dm ¥45, d & tw ¥240, tr ¥270; ❄@📶; ⓈQianmen) Far less atmosphere than its venerable cousin Leo Courtyard, but the dorms and rooms are more modern and frankly better, despite some lumpy mattresses, even if the overall vibe is rather sterile. But there's a fair-sized communal area that does OK food, and it's close to Tiān'ānmén Sq and the surrounding sights. Always busy, it's worth booking ahead.

QIÁNMÉN JIÀNGUÓ HOTEL HOTEL $$$
Map p296 (前门建国饭店; Qiánmén Jiànguó Fàndiàn; ☎6301 6688; www.qianmenhotel.com; 175 Yong'an Lu, 永安路 175 号; d & tw ¥1500-1800, ste ¥2200-3500; 🚭❄@📶; ⓈCaishikou) Elegant in parts and popular with tour groups, this refurbished hotel with a vague Peking opera theme has pushed up

its prices to reflect its makeover. Business is brisk, so the staff are on their toes, and the rooms are spacious, bright and well maintained and a reasonable deal with the generous discounts (up to 50% off). Some English is spoken.

You can find the Líyuán Theatre to the right of the domed atrium at the rear of the hotel.

Sānlǐtún & Cháoyáng

SĀNLǏTÚN YOUTH HOSTEL HOSTEL $

Map p298 (三里屯青年旅馆; Sānlǐtún Qīngnián Lǚguǎn; ☎5190 9288; www.itisbeijing.com; Chunxiu Lu, 春秀路南口往北 250 米路东; 4/6 bed dm ¥80/70, d & tw with/without bathroom ¥280/220; Dongsishitiao, Dongzhimen) Sānlǐtún's only decent youth hostel, this place has efficient, amiable staff and is always busy. Rooms and dorms are functional and clean, although the shared bathrooms are a little pungent. Great Wall tours are available, as is bike hire (¥30 per day). There's an outdoor terrace for the summer and a good-value bar-restaurant area with a pool table.

HOTEL IBIS HOTEL $

Map p298 (宜必思酒店; Yíbìsī Jiǔdiàn; ☎6508 8100; www.ibis.cn-accorhotels.com; 30 Zhongfang Jie (Sanlitun Nanlu), 中纺街 30 号 (三里屯南路); r ¥349; Dongdaqiao) Compact and modern, albeit bland, rooms at this chain hotel outpost within walking distance of Sānlǐtún's main restaurant, bar and shopping zones and a subway stop. Its location alone makes it a decent deal. There's wi-fi and internet too, but don't expect to hear much, if any, English.

YOYO HOTEL HOTEL $

Map p298 (优优客酒店; Yōuyōu Kèjiǔdiàn; ☎6417 3388; www.yoyohotel.cn; Bldg 10 Dongsanjie Erjie, 三里屯北路东三街二街中 10 楼; r ¥339-379; Tuanjiehu) There's a boutique feel here, but the rooms, especially the bathrooms, are tiny. Nevertheless, they are excellent value for the location, and fine if you're not planning on spending too much time in the hotel. Staff members speak some English and are friendly, considering how rushed off their feet they usually are. There's wi-fi, as well as ADSL internet, in the rooms.

HOLIDAY INN EXPRESS HOTEL $$

Map p298 (智选假日酒店; Zhìxuǎn Jiàrì Jiǔdiàn; ☎6416 9999; www.holidayinnexpress.com.cn; 1 Chunxiu Lu, 春秀路 1 号; r ¥598; Dongsishitiao, Dongzhimen) There are 350 comfortable rooms at this well-located place with more personality than most chain hotels. Bright, pastel-coloured, clean rooms come with excellent beds (we love the big puffy pillows!). All are equipped with wide-screen TV's, free wi-fi and internet access via a cable. The lobby has Apple computers for the use of guests. Staff members are friendly and speak some English.

A HOTEL HOTEL $$

Map p298 (☎6586 5858; www.a-hotel.com.cn; East Gate of Worker's Stadium, 工人体育场东门; r ¥780-1080; Dongsishitiao, Tuanjiehu) Boutique-style on the cheap at this new hotel handily placed for restaurants and nightlife. Ignore the alarming wallpaper and striped-carpet patterns in the corridors, because the rooms themselves are sizeable, with beds raised up off the floor in the traditional Chinese *kàng*-style, circular, jacuzzi-like bath tubs and big-screen TVs as

FIVE-STAR LUXURY

If you fancy splashing the cash in west Běijīng – or your boss is paying – there's a cluster of international, five-star hotels in an area known as Financial Street (金融街; Jīnróng Jiē).

Ritz-Carlton (北京金融街丽嘉酒店; Běijīng Jīnróngjiē Lìjiā Jiǔdiàn; Map p294; ☎6601 6666; www.ritzcarlton.com; 1 Jinchengfang Dongjie; 金城坊东街 1 号; r from ¥2000) is probably the pick of the bunch, but there's also an excellent **Westin** (金茂北京威斯汀大饭店; Jīnmào Běijīng Wēisītīng Dàfàndiàn; Map p294; ☎6606 8866; www.starwoodhotels.com; 9 Jinrong Dajie; 金融大街乙 9 号; r from ¥1500) and an **Intercontinental** (北京金融街洲际酒店; Běijīng Jīnróngjiē Zhōujì Jiǔdiàn; Map p294; ☎5852 5888; www.ihg.com; 11 Financial St; 金融街 11 号; r from ¥1500), among others.

well. Wi-fi throughout. Opposite the east gate of the Worker's Stadium.

★OPPOSITE HOUSE HOTEL

BOUTIQUE HOTEL $$$

Map p298 (瑜舍; Yúshè; ☎6417 6688; www.theoppositehouse.com; 11 Sanlitun Lu, 三里屯路 11 号院 1 号楼, Bldg 1, Village; r ¥2300-3100; ; Ⓢ Tuanjiehu) With see-all open-plan bathrooms, American oak bathtubs, lovely mood lighting, underfloor heating, sliding doors, complimentary beers, TVs on extendable arms and a metal basin swimming pool, this trendy Swire-owned boutique hotel is top-drawer chic. The location is ideal for shopping, restaurants and drinking. No obvious sign. Just walk into the striking green glass cube of a building and ask.

Chinese motifs are muted: this is an international hotel with prices to match. It's not the sort of place to take the kids, but couples can splash out or sip drinks in trendy Mesh (p151).

ST REGIS

LUXURY HOTEL $$$

Map p298 (北京国际俱乐部饭店; Běijīng Guójì Jùlèbù Fàndiàn; ☎6460 6688; www.stregis.com/beijing; 21 Jianguomenwai Dajie, 建国门外大街 21 号; r from ¥4100; ; Ⓢ Jianguomen) An extravagant foyer, thorough professionalism and a tip-top location make the St Regis a marvellous, if costly, five-star choice, although 40% discounts are often available. Sumptuous and soothing rooms ooze comfort, 24-hour butlers are at hand to fine-tune your stay, while Chinese and Italian restaurants offer some of Běijīng's finest dining experiences. Shamefully, wi-fi access is ¥80 per day.

PARK HYATT

LUXURY HOTEL $$$

Map p298 (柏悦酒店; Bóyuè Jiǔdiàn; ☎8567 1234; www.beijing.park.hyatt.com; 2 Jianguomenwai Dajie, 建国门外大街 2 号; r ¥2500-6500; ; Ⓢ Guomao) Almost too cool for school, the beautiful Park Hyatt draws business types and cashed-up hipsters. Ride the ear-popping lift to reception on the 63rd floor to be greeted by a fantastic, panoramic view of the surrounding area. Big, light-filled rooms with stylish bathrooms, as well as top-notch service and all the facilities that come with a hotel of this standing.

For even more dramatic views, head to the 65th-floor China Bar (open 4pm to 1am) for evening drinks (cocktails from ¥70).

CONRAD

LUXURY HOTEL $$$

Map p298 (康莱德酒店; Kāngláidé Jiǔdiàn; ☎6584 6000; www.hilton.com/beijing; 29 Dongsanhuan Bei, 东三环北路 29 号; r ¥1800; ; Ⓢ Hujialou) Its all-white, Swiss-cheese-like facade of different-shaped windows ensures you can't miss the striking new Conrad. Rooms are equally slick and very big, the staff solicitous and the terrace of the Vivid Bar on the 5th floor is a hot-spot for Běijīng's beautiful people. The only drawback is the outrageous ¥120 per day charge for wi-fi in the rooms.

GALLERY

BOUTIQUE HOTEL $$$

Map p298 (瑞居; Ruìjū; ☎6551 5555; www.galleryhotelbj.com; 50 Gongrentiyuchang Beilu, 工人体育场北路 50 号; r ¥2500-3000; ; Ⓢ Dongsishitiao, Tuanjiehu) The red-glass block of a building doesn't look too promising from the outside, and the dim and pink interior lighting suggests a house of ill repute, but the rooms here are massive, very comfortable and nicely furnished. All come with not one but two giant TV's, while the baths are strategically positioned so you can dive in to the tub from your bed.

Summer Palace & Hǎidiàn

PEKING UNI INTERNATIONAL HOSTEL

HOSTEL $

Map p303 (未名国际青年旅舍; Wèimíng Guójì Qīngnián Lǚshè; ☎8287 1309, 6254 9667; www.pkuhostel.com; 150 Chengfu Lu, 成府路; 4-/6-/8-bed dm ¥80/70/60, d & tw ¥278-298, tw without bathroom ¥218; ; Ⓢ Wudaokou) Recently refurbished, this busy hostel is located in an office building and so lacks the character of many other hostels around town. But the dorms and rooms, while a little cramped, are clean and sound enough, as are the shared bathrooms, and there's a big communal area. Be sure to check the rooms before you decide, as some don't have windows.

It caters far more for domestic travellers (and students from the surrounding universities) than it does for foreigners. The staff are amenable, though, even if you won't hear much English spoken.

LTH HOTEL

HOTEL $

Map p303 (兰亭汇快捷酒店; Lántínghuì Kuàijié Jiǔdiàn; ☎6261 9226, 6261 8596; www.lthhotel.

com; 35-5 Chengfu Lu, 成府路 35-5 号; d & tw ¥298, tr ¥388; ❄📶; Ⓢ Wudaokou) Newish, modern hotel, unlike many in the area, with bright rooms (the ones with windows, anyway), compact bathrooms and a prime location close to the metro and the bar, cafe and club zone of Wǔdàokǒu. It's just to the side of the Dongyuan Plaza.

★AMAN AT SUMMER PALACE
HERITAGE HOTEL $$$

Map p302 (颐和安缦, Yíhé Ānmàn; ☎5987 9999; www.amanresorts.com; 1 Gongmen Qianjie, 宫门前街 1 号; r ¥4000, courtyard r ¥5200, ste ¥6400; 🚭❄@📶🏊; Ⓢ Xiyuan) Hard to fault this exquisite hotel, a candidate for best in Běijīng. It's located around the corner from the Summer Palace – parts of the hotel date back to the 19th century and were used to house distinguished guests waiting for audiences with Empress Cixi. Superbly appointed rooms are contained in a series of picture-perfect pavilions set around courtyards.

Stepping through the imposing red gates here is to enter a very different, very hushed and very privileged world. Choice restaurants, a spa, a library, a cinema, a pool, squash courts and, of course, silky-smooth service round off the refined picture. Try the daily afternoon tea (2pm to 5pm, ¥238) if you can't afford to stay here. Expect 15% discounts in the winter, but everything here comes with a 15% service charge.

Understand Běijīng

Běijīng Today

Běijīng has been transformed over the past 20 years. Unprecedented investment and massive population growth has helped fuel breakneck development. In terms of wealth and opportunities, Beijingers have never had it so good, but rapid transformation has come at a cost. Transport systems are full to bursting, pollution levels are at an all-time high, and the very fabric of traditional society is being threatened as age-old *hútòng* (narrow lanes) districts continue to make way for more modern alternatives.

Best on Film

Beijing Bicycle (2001) Follows a young and hapless Běijīng courier on the trail of his stolen mountain bike.
Lost in Beijing (2007) Close-to-the-bone, modern-day tale of a ménage-a-quatre. Banned in China.
The Last Emperor (1987) Bernardo Bertolucci's multi-Oscar-winning epic, charting the life of Puyi and the disintegration of dynastic China.
The Gate of Heavenly Peace (1995) Moving three-hour documentary that uses original footage from the six weeks preceding the 1989 Tiān'ānmén Square crackdown.

Best in Print

The People's Republic of Amnesia: Tiananmen Revisited (Louisa Lim; 2014) Engaging analyses of the social impact of the Tiān'ānmén crackdown.
Midnight in Peking (Paul French; 2012) Gripping account of the mystery surrounding the brutal murder in 1937 of Englishwoman Pamela Werner.
Rickshaw Boy (Lao She, translated by Shi Xiaoqing; 1981) A masterpiece by one of Běijīng's most beloved writers about a rickshaw-puller living in early-20th-century Běijīng.
Beijing Coma (Ma Jian; 2008) Novel revolving around the democracy protests of 1989 and the political coma that ensues.

Demolition & Gentrification

Liang Sicheng (1901–1972), the so-called 'father of modern Chinese architecture', once described Běijīng as an 'unparalleled masterpiece of city planning'. Běijīng – the last of China's imperial capitals – functioned as the moral and spiritual centre of the entire country; a cosmic focal point where the 'Son of Heaven' (the emperor) mediated between earthly and heavenly realms. Due to the city's divine nature, Chinese leaders throughout history paid special attention to the design of their capital. Even the slightest change to the configuration of the imperial city was regarded as an affront to tradition and thus to the established world order.

How times have changed. Today, shimmering superstructures, designed as free-standing landmarks, spring up around the city like individual monuments of modernity, jeopardising the forces of architectural yin and yang that once harmonised the whole structure of the city. Often making way for them are the older, more rundown neighbourhoods found in the city's ancient *hútòng*. The most recent high-profile example is the *hútòng* housing that was demolished to make way for the dazzling Galaxy Soho building.

Historic buildings, including *sìhéyuàn* (四合院; traditional courtyard houses), are often protected, and quite rightly so, but it's the *dàzáyuàn* (大杂院; densified courtyard compounds with many families living together) that continue to be threatened, either by being demolished to make way for modern superstructures, or by having their essence as residential communities squeezed out of them by large-scale gentrification projects.

Qiánmén, until recently the largest uninterrupted *hútòng* block in Běijīng, was demolished and rebuilt as a Qing-style shopping and residential district, just before the 2008 Olympics. Next up for 'renovation' is the charming residential *hútòng* district surrounding the historic Drum Tower and Bell Tower. Heritage preservation campaigners lobbied for development plans here to be scrapped, but after years of delays, they seem to have lost the battle. Demolition finally began in earnest in 2014, and although at the time of research it was still unclear exactly what would replace the dozens of *dàzáyuàn*, some residents had already begun moving out to the suburbs.

Pollution

Inevitably, rapid development brings increased pollution. The condition of the region's soil and water causes much concern to locals (Beijingers never drink their tap water), but perhaps most depressing is the sustained levels of the city's now infamous smog.

Air pollution counts hit record levels in January 2013, a month dubbed 'Airpocalypse' by the world's media. Expatriates began leaving in droves, but Beijingers are equally unimpressed with the often dire situation. In the first four months of 2014, residents lodged 12,599 formal complaints about the city's smog, a figure up 124% from the previous year. And any repeat visitor to the city will now notice a marked rise in the number of people wearing face masks.

The smog isn't continual – Běijīng still experiences days of wonderfully clear blue skies – but worryingly, it is on the increase.

Transport

In light of the pollution, the authorities can be commended for their continued investment in an increasingly impressive public transport system. Běijīng has an extensive fleet of natural-gas-powered and electric-powered buses, and its subway system is now the world's third largest (behind Seoul and Shànghǎi). The aim to have all city-centre residents live within 1km of a subway station is expected to be reached by 2015. And plans for a monorail system have been mooted.

Unfortunately, at the time of research, rumours were rife of a huge price hike in public transport fares, which have been heavily subsidised since 2007. It may alleviate overcrowding on the subway, but will surely only add to the congestion on Běijīng's already-clogged roads.

if Běijīng were 100 people

96 would be Han Chinese
2 would be Manchu
1 would be Hui
1 would be Mongul

Běijīng population over the years

(in millions)

population per sq km

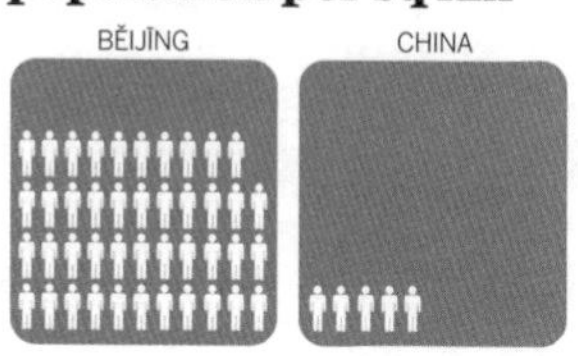

≈ 28 people

History

Běijīng's long and colourful history goes back some 3000 years, but the city didn't become the centre of Chinese rule until 1272 when Kublai Khan made it the capital of the Mongol-led Yuan dynasty. From that time on, with the exception of two brief interludes (1368–1421 and 1928–49), Běijīng has served as the seat of power for all of China.

The Mongols became the first 'barbarian' tribe to attempt to rule China. They ruled from Běijīng for just short of a century, from 1272 to 1368.

From the Beginning

The Great Capital of the Mongols

The place we now call Běijīng first rose to true prominence when it was turned into a capital city by Kublai Khan (1215–94), the founder of the Mongol-ruled Yuan dynasty. The Mongols called the city Khanbalik, and it was from here that the descendants of Genghis Khan (Kublai Khan was his grandson) ruled over the largest land empire in world history. This is where Marco Polo, one of many thousands of foreigners drafted to help the Mongols govern China, came to serve as an official. Běijīng was really only the winter capital for Kublai Khan, who chose to spend the summer months at Běijīng's sister city, Xanadu, which lay to the north, 1800m up on the steppes. This was called the 'Upper Capital', or 'Shàngdū' in Chinese, while Běijīng was 'Dàdū' or 'Great Capital'.

Běijīng seems a curious place to have been selected as capital of the Yuan empire, or indeed any empire. It lacks a river or access to the sea. It's on the very outer edge of the great northern plain, and very far indeed from the rich rice granaries in the south and the source of China's lucrative exports of tea, silk and porcelain. Throughout history the Han Chinese considered this barbarian territory, home to a series of hostile predatory dynasties such as the Liao (907–1125) and the Jin (1115–1234), who also both made Běijīng their capital. To this day Chinese historians describe these peoples as primitive 'tribes' rather than nations, perhaps a prejudice from the ancient antipathy between nomadic pastoralist peoples and the sedentary farmers who are the Chinese.

TIMELINE

500,000 BC

Peking man *(Sinanthropus pekinensis)* inhabits the Běijīng region; Peking man fossils are excavated at Zhōukǒudiàn in Běijīng municipality between 1923 and 1927.

pre-11th century BC

The first settlements in the Běijīng area are recorded (evidence suggests Paleolithic cultures living in the central areas of Běijīng).

c 600 BC

Laotzu (Laozi), founder of Taoism, is born. The folk religion of Taoism goes on to coexist with later introductions such as Buddhism.

Běijīng's First City Walls

Běijīng had first become a walled settlement back in AD 938 when the Khitans, one of the nomadic 'barbarian tribes', established it as an auxiliary southern capital of their Liao dynasty. When they were overthrown by Jurchens from Manchuria, the progenitors of the Manchus, it became Zhōngdū or 'Middle Capital'. Each of these three successive barbarian dynasties enlarged the walled city and built palaces and temples, especially Buddhist temples. They secured a supply of water by channelling streams from the otherwise dry limestone hills around Běijīng, and stored it in the lakes that still lie at the heart of the city.

The Lifeline of the Grand Canal

The Khitans relied on the Grand Canal to ship goods like silk, porcelain, tea and grain from the Yangzi River delta. Each successive dynasty shortened the Grand Canal. It was originally 2500km long when it was built in the 5th century by the Chinese Sui dynasty to facilitate the military conquest of northeast China and Korea. From the 10th century it was used for a different purpose: to enable these northern peoples to extract the wealth of central China. Běijīng's role was to be the terminus.

Remaining Traces

For 1000 years, half a million peasants spent six months a year hauling huge barges from Hángzhōu up the Grand Canal to Běijīng. You can still see the canal after it enters the city from Tōngzhōu, now a suburb of Běijīng, and then winds around the 2nd Ring Rd. The tax or tribute from central China was then stored in huge warehouses, a few of which remain. From Běijīng, the goods were carried out of the West Gate or Xīzhímén (where Xizhimen subway station is today), and taken up the Tánqín Gorge to Bādálǐng, which once marked the limits of the Chinese world. Beyond this pass, the caravans took the road to Zhāngjiākǒu, 6000ft above sea level where the grasslands of inner Asia begin.

End of 'Barbarian' Rule

The ultimate aim of the Khitans, Jurchens, Mongols and Manchus was to control the lucrative international trade in Chinese-made luxuries. Chinese dynasties such as the Song faced the choice of paying them off or staging a bloody resistance. The Southern Song did attack and destroy Běijīng, but when it failed to defeat the Liao dynasty of the Khitans it resorted to a strategy of 'using the barbarian to defeat the barbarian'. It made a pact with the Jurchens, and together they captured Běijīng in 1125. But instead of just helping to defeat the Khitans, the Jurchens carried on south and took the Song capital at Kāifēng. The Jurchens,

The Mongols referred to Zhāngjiākǒu as Kalgan, 'the Gate'. This trading route, leading to inner Asia's grasslands, was also the favourite route chosen by invaders, such as Genghis Khan.

551 BC

Confucius is born. His ideas of an ethical, ordered society that operated through hierarchy and self-development would dominate Chinese culture until the early 20th century.

5th–3rd century BC

The state of Yan, based about 50km southwest of Běijīng, conquers the state of Ji, and form a larger walled city called Yānjīng.

214 BC

Emperor Qin indentures thousands of labourers to link existing city walls into one Great Wall, made of tamped earth. The later stone-clad bastion dates from the Ming dynasty.

AD 938

Běijīng is established as auxiliary capital of the Liao dynasty. Běijīng's oldest street – Sanmiao Jie, or Three Temples St – dates to this time, when it was known as Tanzhou Jie.

History Books

The City of Heavenly Tranquility: Beijing in the History of China (Jasper Becker) Story of Běijīng's transformation from Ming capital to communist-capitalist hybrid.

The Penguin History of Modern China: The Fall and Rise of a Great Power 1850–2008 (Jonathan Fenby) Highly readable modern Chinese history.

The Siege at Peking (Peter Fleming) Account of the Boxer Rebellion.

The Dragon Empress (Marina Warner) Riveting biography of the Empress Dowager and fall of the Qing dynasty.

however, chose not to try to govern China by themselves and instead opted to milk the Southern Song dynasty.

Ming-Dynasty Běijīng

A True Chinese City

Běijīng can properly be said to have been a Chinese city only during the Ming dynasty (1368–1644), when Emperor Yongle used over 200,000 prisoners of war to rebuild the city, construct its massive battlements, rebuild the imperial palace and establish the magnificent Ming Tombs. He forced tens of thousands of leading Chinese families to relocate from Nánjīng, the capital founded by his father, and unwillingly settle in what they considered an alien land at the extremity of the Chinese world. Throughout the Ming dynasty, Běijīng was constantly under attack by the Mongols, and on many occasions their horsemen reached the very gates of the city. Mongol bandits roamed the countryside or hid out in the marshes south of the city, threatening communications with the empire.

Beefing Up the Great Wall

Everything needed for the gigantic enterprise of rebuilding the city – even tiles, bricks and timber – had to be shipped up the Grand Canal, but in time Běijīng grew into a city of nearly a million residents. Although farms and greenhouses sprang up around the city, it always depended on the Grand Canal as a lifeline. Most of the canal was required to ship the huge amounts of food needed to supply the garrison of more than a million men that Yongle press-ganged into building and manning the new Great Wall. The emperor was fearful of a resurgent Mongol threat. The Mongols had been pushed out of China as the Ming came to power in 1368, but they were still formidable, and by the dawn of the 15th century, they were itching to reconquer the rich lands to the south of the Great Wall. This Wall, unlike earlier walls, was clad in brick and stone, not pounded earth, and the Ming emperors kept enlarging it for the next 250 years, adding loops, spurs and watchtowers. For long stretches, the fortifications ran in two parallel bands.

The Forbidden City

Běijīng grew from a forward defence military headquarters into an administrative centre staffed by an elite corps of mandarins. They had to pass gruelling examinations that tested candidates' understanding of classical and Confucian literature. Then they were either assigned to the provinces or selected to work in the central government ministries, situated in what is now Tiān'ānmén Sq, south of the Meridian Gate and the entrance to the Forbidden City. Each day the mandarins and the generals entered the 'Great Within' and kowtowed before the emperor, who

1153

Běijīng becomes capital of the Jin dynasty when it is known as Zhōngdū ('Middle Capital'); the city walls are expanded and paper currency enters circulation.

1215

The Mongols, under Genghis Khan, break through the Great Wall at several points and sack Zhōngdū, razing it to the ground and slaughtering its inhabitants.

1264

The first Yuan emperor, Kublai Khan, sets about rebuilding the city his grandfather destroyed.

1272

Kublai Khan renames the city Dàdū (Great Capital), and officially unveils it as the capital of the Yuan dynasty. Běijīng is, for the first time, the capital of China.

lived inside, like a male version of a queen bee, served by thousands of women and eunuchs. Ming emperors were the only males permitted to live in the palace. Yongle established rigid rules and dreary rituals, and many of his successors rebelled against the constrictions.

Power of the Eunuchs

Under later Ming emperors, the eunuchs came to be more trusted and more powerful than the mandarins. There were 100,000 by the end of the Ming dynasty, more than in any other civilisation in history. A few became so powerful they virtually ruled the empire, but many died poor and destitute. Some used their wealth to build grandiose residences and tombs, or to patronise temples and monasteries located outside the walls.

A Centre for Arts & Science

Over time Běijīng became the most important religious centre in Asia, graced by more than 2000 temples and shrines. Daoists and Buddhists vied for the favour of the emperor who, as a divine being, was automatically the patron of every approved religious institution in the empire. As the residence of the emperor, Běijīng was regarded by the Chinese as the centre of the universe. The best poets and painters also flocked to Běijīng to seek court patronage. The Forbidden City required the finest porcelain, furniture and silverware, and its workshops grew in skill and design. Literature, drama, music, medicine, map-making, astrology and astronomy flourished, too, so the imperial city became a centre for arts and sciences.

Although early visitors complained about the dust and the beggars, most were awed and inspired by the city's size and magnificence. Ming culture was influential in Japan, Korea, Vietnam and other neighbouring countries. By the close of the 15th century the Ming capital, which had started out as a remote and isolated military outpost, had become a wealthy and sophisticated Chinese city.

The Fall of the Ming

Despite the Great Wall, the threat from the north intensified. The Manchus (formerly the Jurchens) established a new and powerful state based in Shěnyáng (currently the capital of Liáoníng province) and watched as the Ming empire decayed. The Ming had one of the most elaborate tax codes in history, but corrupt eunuchs abused their growing power. Excessive taxation sparked a series of peasant revolts. Silver, the main form of exchange, was devalued by imported silver from the new world, leading to inflation.

One peasant rebel army, led by Li Zicheng (1606–45), actually captured Běijīng. The last Ming emperor, Chongzhen (1611–44), called on the Manchus for help and after crossing the Great Wall at Shānhǎiguān,

1286

The Grand Canal is extended to Běijīng. Over time, the canal becomes a major artery for the transport of grain, salt and other important commodities between north and south China.

1368

Zhu Yuanzhang takes Dàdū and proceeds to level its palaces, renaming the city Běipíng (Northern Peace) and establishing the Ming dynasty.

1368–1644

The great city walls are reshaped and the Great Wall is rebuilt and clad with bricks, while the basic layout of modern Běijīng is established. Běijīng becomes the world's largest city.

1403–21

Emperor Yongle moves the capital south to Nánjīng, where the imperial palace is built. Běijīng is reinstated as capital in 1421 when the Forbidden City is completed (1406–20).

in current-day Héběi province, they helped rout Li Zicheng's army. The Manchus then marched on Běijīng, where Emperor Chongzhen hung himself on a tree on Coal Hill, the hill in Jǐngshān Park, which overlooks the Forbidden City.

Qing-Dynasty Běijīng

The Manchus Move In

The Manchus established the Qing dynasty in 1664, although it took several decades before they completed the conquest of the Ming empire. As a foreign dynasty, they took great pains to present themselves as legitimate successors to the Chinese Ming dynasty. For this reason they kept Běijīng as their capital and changed very little, effectively preserving Yongle's city. The Manchu imperial family, the Aisin Gioro Clan, moved in to the Forbidden City, and imperial princes took large courtyard palaces.

The Han Chinese were forced to wear their hair in a queue (pigtail) as a symbol of their subjugation to the ruling Manchus.

Summer Palaces

Soon the Aisin Gioro family began to feel that living inside the confines of the Forbidden City was claustrophobic. The great Emperor Kangxi (1654–1722) effectively moved the court to what is now called the Old Summer Palace, a vast parkland of lakes, canals and palaces linked to the city by the Jade Canal. The Manchus, like the Mongols, enjoyed hunting, riding, hawking, skating and archery. In summer, when Běijīng became hot and steamy, the court moved to Chéngdé, a week's ride to the north. At Chéngdé the court spent three months living in felt tents (or yurts) in a walled parkland.

Bannermen

The Manchu army was divided into regiments called banners, so the troops were called Bannermen (Qírén). Each banner had a separate colour by which it was known and its troops settled in a particular residential area in Běijīng. The Embroidered Yellow Bannermen, for example, lived near the Confucius Temple, and some of their descendants remain there today. Only a minority were actually ethnic Manchus – the rest were Mongols or Han Chinese.

Policing a Divided City

Běijīng at this stage was a Manchu city and foreigners called it the 'Tartar City' ('Tartars' being the label given to any nomadic race from inner Asia). The Han Chinese lived in the 'Chinese city' to the south of Tiān'ānmén Sq. This was the liveliest, most densely populated area, packed with markets, shops, theatres, brothels and hostels for provincial visitors. If Chinese people wanted to get to north Běijīng, they had to go

1420

The Temple of Heaven is constructed at the same time as the Forbidden City. The Gate of Heavenly Peace is completed, only to be burned down after a lightning strike in 1457.

1465

The Gate of Heavenly Peace is rebuilt, but is again torched by peasant rebels in 1644 prior to the arrival of Manchu soldiers. The reconstruction of the gate is completed in 1651.

1644

Manchu troops pour through the pass at Shānhǎiguān to impose the Qing dynasty on China; Emperor Chongzhen hangs himself from a tree in Jǐngshān Park.

1793

British diplomat Lord Macartney visits Běijīng with British industrial products, but is told by the Qianlong emperor that China has no need of his goods.

CHINA'S DYNASTIES

DYNASTY	CHINESE NAME	PERIOD OF RULE
Xià	夏	2070–1600 BC
Shāng	商	1600–1046 BC
Western Zhou	西周 (Xī Zhōu)	1046–771 BC
Eastern Zhou	东周 (Dōng Zhōu)	770–256 BC
Spring & Autumn	春秋 (Chūn Qiū)	771–476 BC
Warring States	战国 (Zhàn Guó)	476–221 BC
Qín	秦	221–206 BC
Western Han	西汉 (Xī Hàn)	206 BC– AD 9 & AD 23–25
Xīn	新	AD 9–23
Eastern Han	东汉 (Dōng Hàn)	AD 25–220
Three Kingdoms	三国 (Sān Guó)	220–265
Western Jin	西晋 (Xī Jìn)	265–317
Eastern Jin	东晋 (Dōng Jìn)	317–420
Southern & Northern	南北朝 (Nán Běi Cháo)	420–589
Suí	隋	581–618
Táng	唐	618–907
Five Dynasties & Ten Kingdoms	五代十国 (Wǔ Dài Shí Guó)	907–960
Kingdom of Dali	大理国 (Dà Lǐ Guó)	937–1253
Northern Song	北宋 (Běi Sòng)	960–1127
Southern Song	南宋 (Nán Sòng)	1127–1279
Liáo	辽	916–1125
Jīn	金	1115–1234
Western Xia	西夏 (Xī Xià)	1038–1227
Yuán	元	1271–1368
Míng	明	1368–1644
Qīng	清	1644–1911

all the way round the outside walls. The Bannermen posted at the gates prevented anyone from entering without permission. Up to 1900, the state provided all Bannermen families with clothing and free food that was shipped up the Grand Canal and stored in grain warehouses.

1850–68

The quasi-Christian Taiping Rebellion blazes north and east across China from Guǎngxī province, killing an estimated 20 million people in the process. Rebels fail to reach Běijīng.

1898

Emperor Guangxu permits major reforms, including new rights for women, but is thwarted by the Dowager Empress Cixi, who has many reformers arrested and executed.

1900

Boxer rebels commence the long siege of the Foreign Legation Quarter. The Hànlín Academy is accidentally burned down by rebels trying to flush out besieged foreigners.

1905

Major reforms in the late Qing, including the abolition of the 1000-year-long tradition of examinations in the Confucian classics to enter the Chinese bureaucracy.

Eunuchs tended to be Buddhists (while mandarins honoured Confucius), as it gave them hope they would return as whole men in a future reincarnation.

Fashioning Běijīng Culture

It was the Manchu Bannermen who really created a Běijīng culture. They loved Peking opera, and the city once had over 40 opera houses and many training schools. The sleeveless *qípáo* dress is really a Manchu dress. The Bannermen, who loved animals, raised songbirds and pigeons and bred exotic-looking goldfish and miniature dogs such as the Pekinese. And after the downfall of the Qing empire, they kept up traditional arts such as painting and calligraphy.

Language, Politics & Religion

Through the centuries of Qing rule, the Manchus tried to keep themselves culturally separate from the Chinese, speaking a different language, wearing different clothes and following different customs. For instance, Manchu women did not bind their feet, wore raised platform *patens* (shoes), and coiled their hair in distinctive and elaborate styles. All court documents were composed in the Manchu script; Manchu, Chinese and Mongolian script were used to write name signs in such places as the Forbidden City.

At the same time, the Qing copied the Ming's religious and bureaucratic institutions. The eight key ministries (Board of Works, Board of Revenue, Board of State Ceremonies, Board of War, Board of Rites, Board of Astronomy, Board of Medicines and Prefecture of Imperial Clan Affairs) continued to operate from the same buildings in what is now Tiān'ānmén Sq. The Qing dynasty worshipped their ancestors at rites held in a temple, which is now in the Workers Cultural Palace, a park immediately southeast of the Forbidden City. They also built a second ancestral temple devoted to the spirits of every Chinese emperor that ever ruled. For some time it was a girls' school, but it has since reopened as the Temple of Ancient Monarchs and can be visited.

Buddhist Ties

The study of Confucius was encouraged in order to strengthen the loyalty of the mandarins employed by the state bureaucracy. The Manchus carried out the customary rituals at the great state temples. By inclination, however, many of the Manchu emperors were either Shamanists or followers of Tibetan Buddhism. The Shamanist shrines have disappeared, but Běijīng is full of temples and stupas connected with Tibetan Buddhism. Emperor Qianlong considered himself the incarnation of the Bodhisattva Manjusri and cultivated strong links with various Dalai Lamas and Panchen Lamas. Many visited – a round trip usually lasted three years – and special palaces were built for them. The Manchus deliberately fostered the spread of Tibetan Buddhism among the warlike Mongols in the hope of pacifying them. Běijīng therefore developed into a holy city attracting pilgrims of all kinds.

1908

Two-year-old Puyi ascends the throne as China's last emperor. Local elites and new classes such as businessmen no longer support the dynasty, leading to its ultimate downfall.

1911

The Qing dynasty collapses and the modernisation of China begins in earnest; Sun Yatsen (fundraising in America at the time) is declared president of the Republic of China.

1912

Yuan Shikai, leader of China's most powerful regional army, goes to the Qing court to announce that the game is up: on 12 February the last emperor, six-year-old Puyi, abdicates.

1916

Yuan Shikai dies less than a year after attempting to establish himself as emperor. Yuan's monarchical claims prompted widespread resistance from Republicans.

The Jesuits

The arrival of the first Jesuits and other Christians made Běijīng an important centre of Christianity in China. Emperor Qianlong employed many Jesuits who built for him the baroque palaces that can still be seen in the ruins of the Old Summer Palace, which was burnt down by a combined force of British and French troops in 1860 during the Second Opium War.

Foreign Powers & the Fall of the Qing

Foreign Legation Quarter

After the military defeats of the Opium Wars, the Western nations forced the Qing emperors to allow them to open formal embassies or legations in the capital. Hitherto, the emperor had had no equal in the world – foreign powers could only send embassies to deliver tribute, and they were housed in tributary hostels.

The Dalai Lama's former Běijīng palace is now rented out by the government of the Tibet Autonomous Region.

Boxer Rebellion

The British legation was the first to open after 1860. It lay on the east side of Tiān'ānmén Sq and stayed there until the 1950s when its grounds were taken over by the Ministry of State Security. By 1900 there were a dozen legations in an odd foreign ghetto with an eclectic mixture of European architecture. The Foreign Legation Quarter never became a foreign concession like those in Shànghǎi or Tiānjīn, but it had banks, schools, shops, post offices, hospitals and military parade grounds. Much of it was reduced to rubble when the army of Boxers (a quasi-religious cult) besieged it in the summer of 1900. It was later rebuilt.

Republican China

After 1900 the last tribute barges arrived in Běijīng and a railway line ran along the traditional invasion route through the Jūyōng Pass to Bādálǐng. You can see the handsome clock tower and sheds of Běijīng's first railway station (Qiánmén Railway Station), recently restored as the Běijīng Railway Museum, on the southeast corner of Tiān'ānmén Sq. Běijīng never became an industrial or commercial centre – that role went to nearby Tiānjīn on the coast. Yet it remained the leading political and intellectual centre of China until the late 1920s.

For an insight into the sinful underworld of 1930s Běijīng, read Paul French's excellent 2012 crime thriller *Midnight in Peking*; a gripping account of the investigation into the brutal, 1937 murder of Englishwoman Pamela Werner.

Hotbed of Student Activity

In the settlement imposed after 1900, China had to pay the victors heavy indemnities. Some of this money was returned to China and used to build the first modern universities, including what are now the Oxford and Cambridge of China – Qīnghuá and Peking Universities. Běijīng's

4 May 1919

Students demonstrate in Běijīng against foreign occupation of territories in China and the terms that conclude WWI. The date of the protests leads to the name of the movement.

1927

The first shots of the Chinese Civil War are fired between the Kuomintang (KMT) and the communists. The war continues on and off until 1949.

1928

The nationalists move the capital to Nánjīng, and Běijīng is again renamed Běipíng. This is the first time the capital of the entire nation has been in Nánjīng for almost 500 years.

7 July 1937

The Marco Polo Bridge Incident signals the beginning of the Japanese occupation of Běijīng and the start of the Second Sino-Japanese War, which lasts until September 1945.

THE OPIUM WARS

A shameful chapter in British history, the First Opium War (1839–42), which led to the death of tens of thousands of Chinese people, was fought so that the British Empire could continue its illegal trade in opium.

Britain was struggling to pay for the huge, and ever-increasing, demand for Chinese tea back home. The Chinese thought little of the Wedgewood pottery, scientific instruments and woollen goods the British offered in return, and would only accept payment in silver. But Britain had another idea. Its conquest of Indian Bengal gave it access to massive amounts of opium, which it soon started smuggling into China and distributing among the population. The Chinese were soon hooked, and opium dens opened across the land.

But British law-breaking had not gone unnoticed and in 1839 Emperor Daoguang declared a war on drugs. A series of raids were ordered on the Western traders, and by the end of the year, Chinese officials had seized 20,000 chests (more than 1000 tons) of opium.

British traders were livid, and lobbied the government to give them backing to retaliate. Such was the size of the opium industry that the British government agreed and in 1840 a British fleet of 16 warships and 27 transports carrying 4000 men arrived in the Pearl River Delta. The technically advanced British military overwhelmed the Chinese and they trounced them in a series of battles all along the east coast, from Hong Kong up to Shànghǎi and beyond.

The bombardments lasted two years. Between 20,000 and 25,000 Chinese troops were killed. Britain lost just 69 men.

The war was eventually halted by the signing of the Treaty of Nanking, the first of what the Chinese now refer to as the 'Unequal Treaties'. The treaty granted Britain $21 million in compensation, the opening of five treaty ports, and the handing over of Hong Kong Island. But it still wasn't enough, and its failure to satisfy Britain's demands led to the Second Opium War (1856–60).

More bloody battles ensued, as this time the French joined forces with the British to devastate Chinese troops all the way up to Běijīng. With the Chinese armies defeated, the Qing court fled the capital, and the Allied troops, while stopping short of occupying the city, ransacked the Summer Palace and the Old Summer Palace before sitting down with Prince Gong on 18 October 1860 to ratify the Treaty of Tiānjīn, another devastatingly unequal treaty which had been drafted two years earlier.

The British, French and Russians were all granted a permanent diplomatic presence in Běijīng. The opium trade was legalised and Christians were granted full civil rights, including the right to own property, and the right to evangelise. It was a humiliating climax to a humiliating war that had been a shocking blow to the once powerful Qing dynasty, and in many ways it spelled the beginning of the end for the ancient civilisation that was China.

1946

Communists and the Kuomintang fail to form a coalition government, plunging China back into civil war.

1 October 1949

With the communist victory over the KMT, Mao Zedong announces the founding of the People's Republic of China from the Gate of Heavenly Peace.

1950s & 1960s

Most of Běijīng's city walls, gates and decorative arches are levelled to make way for roads. Work commences on its labyrinthine network of underground tunnels.

1956–57

The Hundred Flowers Movement promises an era of intellectual freedom, but instead leads to a purge of intellectuals, artists and thinkers who are labelled rightists and persecuted.

university quarter was established in the Hăidiàn district, near the Old Summer Palace (some campuses are actually in the imperial parkland). Intellectuals from all over China continued to gravitate to Běijīng, including the young Mao Zedong, who arrived to work as a librarian in 1921.

The last of the Foreign Legation Quarter's embassies left in 1967. Now most embassies are located east of the centre, in Cháoyáng District.

1919 May Fourth Movement

Běijīng students and professors were at the forefront of the 1919 May Fourth Movement. This was at once a student protest against the Versailles Treaty, which had awarded Germany's concessions in China to Japan, and an intellectual movement to jettison the Confucian feudal heritage and Westernise China. Mao himself declared that to modernise China it was first necessary to destroy it. China's intellectuals looked around the world for models to copy. Some went to Japan, others to the USA, Britain, Germany or, like Deng Xiaoping and Zhou Enlai, France. Many went to study Marxism in Moscow.

Modernising the City

As the warlords marched armies in and out of Běijīng, the almost medieval city began to change. Temples were closed down and turned into schools. The last emperor, Puyi, left the Forbidden City in 1924 with his eunuchs and concubines. As the Manchus adapted to the changes, they tried to assimilate and their presence faded. Western-style brick houses, shops and restaurants were built. City gates were widened and new ones added, including one at Jiànguóménwài to make way for the motorcar. Běijīng acquired nightclubs, cinemas, racecourses and a stock exchange; brothels and theatres flourished. Despite political and diplomatic crises, this was a period when people had fun and enjoyed a unique period of individual freedom.

Generalissimo Chiang Kaishek united most of the country under Chinese National Party (KMT, or Kuomintang in Chinese) rule and moved the capital to Nánjīng. Even after 1928, Běijīng's romantic air of decaying grandeur attracted Chinese and Western writers and painters trying to fuse Western and Chinese artistic traditions.

Some of 20th-century China's best literature was written in Běijīng in the 1920s and 1930s by the likes of Lao She, Lin Huiyin, Xu Zhimou, Shen Congwen and Qian Zhongshu.

Japanese Occupation

It all came to end when Japan's Kwantung Army moved down from Manchuria and occupied Běijīng in 1937. By then most people who could had fled, some to Chóngqìng in Sìchuān province, which served as Chiang Kaishek's wartime capital. Others joined Mao Zedong in his communist base at Yán'ān, in Shaanxi province. Many universities established campuses in exile in Yúnnán province.

1958

The Great Leap Forward commences ,but plans to rapidly industrialise China result in a disastrous famine that kills millions of Chinese.

1962

Liu Shaoqi and Deng Xiaoping introduce limited market reforms, leading to their condemnation in the Cultural Revolution.

16 May 1966

The Great Proletarian Cultural Revolution is launched by Mao Zedong in Běijīng; millions of Red Guards pack into Tiān'ānmén Sq. From August to September, 1772 Beijingers are killed.

1972

US President Richard Nixon meets with Mao Zedong in Běijīng, marking a major rapprochement during the Cold War, and the start of full diplomatic relations between the two countries.

During the Japanese invasion, the collection of imperial treasures was secretly removed, eventually ending up in Taiwan where they can still be seen in Taipei's National Palace Museum.

The Japanese stayed in Běijīng for eight years and, before their WWII defeat in 1945, had drawn up plans to build a new administrative capital in an area to the west of the city walls near Gōngzhǔfén. It was a miserable time for Běijīng, but the architecture was left largely untouched by the war. When the Japanese surrendered in August 1945, Běijīng was 'liberated' by US marines. The city once again became a merry place famous for its parties – the serious events took place elsewhere in China. When the civil war broke out in earnest between nationalists and communists in 1947, the worst fighting took place in the cities of Manchuria.

Communist Takeover

In 1948 the Communist Eighth Route Army moved south and encircled Běijīng. General Fu Zuoyi, commander-in-chief of the Nationalists' Northern China Bandit Suppression Headquarters, prepared the city for a prolonged siege. He razed private houses and built gun emplacements and dugouts along the Ming battlements. Nationalist planes dropped bags of rice and flour to relieve the shortages, some hitting skaters on frozen Běihǎi Lake. Both sides seemed reluctant to fight it out and destroy the ancient capital. The rich tried to flee on the few planes that took off from a runway constructed at Dongdan on Chang'an Dajie (Chang'an means 'Avenue of Eternal Peace'). Another airstrip was opened at Temple of Heaven Park by cutting down 20,000 trees, including 400 ancient cypresses.

EMPRESS DOWAGER CIXI

The Empress Dowager Cixi (1835–1908), a daughter of a Bordered Blue Bannermen, was a young concubine when the Old Summer Palace was burned down by foreign troops in 1860. Cixi allowed the palace to fall into decay, associating it with a humiliation, and instead built herself the new Summer Palace (Yíhé Yuán). She was left with a profound hatred and distrust of the Western barbarians and their ways.

Over the four decades in which Cixi ruled China 'from behind the curtain' through a series of proxy emperors, she resisted pressure to change and reform. After a naval defeat at the hands of the Japanese in 1895, young Chinese officials put forward a modernisation program. She had some of them executed outside Běijīng's walls, and imprisoned their patron and her nephew, Emperor Guangxu (1871–1908).

She encouraged the Boxers to attack Westerners, especially foreign missionaries in northern China, and when Boxers besieged the Foreign Legation Quarter in 1900, Cixi stood by. When the allied forces marched into Běijīng to end the siege, she fled in disguise, an ignominious retreat that marked the final humiliation that doomed the Qing dynasty. When Cixi returned in disgrace a year later, China's modernisation had begun in earnest, but it was too late to save the Qing dynasty – it fell in 1911.

1976

The death of Premier Zhou Enlai sparks spontaneous protests in Tiān'ānmén Sq; the mighty Tángshān earthquake is blamed on a cosmic correction after the death of Mao Zedong in September.

1976

Mao Zedong dies, aged 83. The Gang of Four are arrested by his successor and put on trial, where they are blamed for the disasters of the Cultural Revolution.

1977–79

With the death of Mao, the 'Běijīng Spring' sees the appearance of the short-lived 'Democracy Wall' in Xīdān. Deng Xiaoping's reformist agenda commences in 1979.

1980

The one-child policy is enforced. The state adopts it as a means of reducing the population, but at the same time imposes unprecedented control over the personal liberty of women.

On 22 January 1949 General Fu signed a surrender agreement, and on 31 January his KMT troops marched out and the People's Liberation Army (PLA) entered. A truck drove up Morrison St (now Wangfujing Dajie) blasting a continuous refrain to the residents of Běijīng (or Pěipíng as it was known then): 'Welcome to the Liberation Army on its arrival in Pěipíng! Congratulations to the people of Pěipíng on their liberation!' Behind it marched 300 soldiers in battle gear. A grand victory parade took place on 3 February with 250 assorted military vehicles, virtually all US-made and captured from the KMT over the previous two years.

'Communism is not love. Communism is a hammer which we use to crush the enemy.' Mao Zedong, quoted in *Time* (New York, 18 December 1950).

Mao's Běijīng

The People Stand Up

On 1 October 1949 Mao mounted the Gate of Heavenly Peace and declared the founding of the People's Republic of China, saying the Chinese people had stood up. He spoke only a few words in one of the very few public speeches he ever made.

Mao then moved into Zhōngnánhǎi, part of the chain of lakes and gardens immediately west of the Forbidden City and dating back to Kublai Khan. Marshal Yuan Shikai (1859–1916) had lived there too during his short-lived attempt to establish his own dynasty after 1911. Nobody is quite sure why he chose Běijīng as his capital, or why he failed to carry out his intention to raze the Forbidden City.

After 1949 many of new China's top leaders followed Mao's cue and moved their homes and offices into the old princely palaces *(wángfǔ)*, thus inadvertently preserving much of the old architecture.

China's first (and only) parliament was established in Běijīng in what was once the imperial elephant house, now out of sight in the sprawling headquarters of Xīnhuá, the state news agency.

Industrialisation

Mao wished to turn Běijīng into a city of production. Speaking to China's premier architectural historian, Liang Sicheng, as they stood on the Gate of Heavenly Peace looking south, Peng Zhen, the first Party Secretary of Běijīng, said that Chairman Mao wanted to make Běijīng into a large, modern city with lots of heavy industry.

Factories Galore

Thousands of factories sprang up in Běijīng and quite a few were built in old temples. In time Běijīng developed into a centre for steel, chemicals, machine tools, engines, electricity, vinegar, beer, concrete, textiles, weapons – in fact, everything that would make it an economically self-sufficient 'production base' in case of war. By the 1970s Běijīng had become one of the most heavily polluted cities in the world.

Mao worked as a library assistant at the former Peking University campus known as Hóng Lóu (the Red Building), now a small museum.

1987

The Last Emperor, filmed in the Forbidden City, collects an Oscar for Best Picture, and marks a new openness in China towards the outside world.

June 1989

Democracy protestors fill Tiān'ānmén Sq as parallel protests are held across the land. Běijīng imposes martial law; soldiers clear the streets, killing many in the process.

1997

Deng Xiaoping dies before having the chance to see Hong Kong returned to Chinese rule that same year. The reconstruction of Běijīng is launched.

25 April 1999

In the largest protest since the Tiān'ānmén Square crackdown, 10,000 practitioners of Fǎlún Gōng protest against harassment by state media outside Běijīng's central appeals office.

The Great Leap Forward

In the 1958 Great Leap Forward, the last qualms about preserving old Běijīng were abandoned. A new plan was approved to destroy 80% of the old capital. The walls were pulled down, but the series of ring roads planned at the time were never built.

The move to tear down the city's walls, widen the roads and demolish the distinctive *páilóu* (ceremonial arches) started immediately after 1949, but was fiercely contested by some intellectuals, including Liang Sicheng, who ran the architecture department of Qīnghuá University. So in the midst of the demolition of many famous landmarks, the municipal authorities earmarked numerous buildings and even old trees for conservation. However, it was all to no avail – Mao's brutal political purges silenced all opposition.

The Cultural Revolution

Those intellectuals who escaped persecution in the 1950s were savagely dealt with during the Cultural Revolution (1966–76). Qīnghuá University became the birthplace of the Red Guards (a mass movement of young radicals, mobilised by Mao). In the 'bloody August' of 1966, Běijīng's middle-school students turned on their teachers, brutally murdering some of them. Some reports estimate almost 2000 people were killed in Běijīng at this time. The number excludes those beaten to death as they tried to escape Běijīng on trains – their registration as residents of Běijīng having suddenly been cancelled.

End of the Mao Era

In Mao's time the geomantic symmetry of Běijīng was radically changed. The north–south axis of the Ming city was ruined by widening Chang'an Dajie into a 10-lane, east–west highway. This was used for huge annual military parades or when visiting dignitaries arrived and the population was turned out to cheer them. In the 1950s the centre was redesigned by Soviet architects and modelled on Moscow's Red Sq. Three major gates and many other Ming buildings, including the former government ministries, were demolished, leaving the concrete expanse of Tiān'ānmén Sq you see today.

In August and September of 1966, a total of 1772 people were killed during the Cultural Revolution in the capital, according to a report published by the *Beijing Daily* after 1979.

Mao used the square to receive the adulation of the millions of Red Guards who flocked to Běijīng from 1966 to 1969, but after 1969 Mao exiled the Red Guards, along with 20 million 'educated youth', to the countryside. From 1976 the square became the scene of massive anti-government protests – when Premier Zhou Enlai died in 1976 the large and apparently spontaneous protest in the square was quelled by the police. In 1976 Mao himself died.

22 July 1999

Two days after security forces abduct and detain thousands of Fǎlún Gōng practitioners, the government declares the movement an illegal organisation.

2001

Work commences on the immense National Grand Theatre, Běijīng's futuristic answer to the Shànghǎi Grand Theatre. The building is not completed for a further seven years.

2001

After winning the bid to host the 2008 Olympic Games, Běijīng embarks on a massive public-transport development project.

2002

Hu Jintao becomes China's new political leader when he is appointed general secretary of the Communist Party. He governs China for the next 10 years.

Reform & Protest

Calls for Democracy

Deng Xiaoping (1904–97), backed by a group of veteran generals, seized power in a coup d'état and threw Mao's widow, Jiang Qing (1914–91), and her ultra-leftist cronies into the notorious Qínchéng prison outside the city, where Mao had incarcerated so many senior party veterans. The prison still exists, not far from the Ming Tombs.

The Democracy Wall

At the third plenum of the 11th Party Congress, Deng consolidated his grip on power and launched economic reforms. At the same time thousands of people began putting up posters along a wall west of Zhōngnánhǎi, complaining of injustices under the 'Gang of Four' (Jiang Qing and her three associates) and demanding democracy. Deng initially appeared to back political reforms, but soon the activists were thrown into jail, some in the Běijīng No 1 Municipal Prison (demolished in the mid-1990s).

Rising Discontent

Many of the activists were former Red Guards or exiled educated youth. After 1976 they drifted back to the city, but could only find jobs in the new private sector running small market stalls, tailor shops or restaurants. After the universities opened, conditions remained poor and the intelligentsia continued to be treated with suspicion. Frustrations with the slow pace of reforms prompted fresh student protests in the winter of 1986. Peasants did well out of the first wave of reforms, but in the cities many people felt frustrated. Urban life revolved around 'work units' to which nearly everyone was assigned. The work unit distributed food, housing, bicycles, travel permits and almost everything else. Běijīng was still a rather drab, dispiriting place in the 1980s; there was much more to eat but everything else was in a lamentable state. For 30 years there had been little investment in housing or transport.

1989 Tiān'ānmén Square Crackdown

In January 1987 the party's conservative gerontocrats ousted the pro-reform party chief Hu Yaobang and, when he suddenly died in the spring of 1989, Běijīng students began assembling on Tiān'ānmén Sq. Officially they were mourning his passing but they began to raise slogans for political reform and against corruption. The protests snowballed as the Communist Party leadership split into rival factions, causing a rare paralysis. The police stood by as the protests spread across the country and workers, officials and ordinary citizens took to the streets. When the military tried to intervene, Beijingers surrounded the tanks. The students set up

Contrary to popular belief, the violence that shook the city – and the watching world – on 4 June didn't take place in Tiān'ānmén Sq itself, but in the surrounding streets.

1 August 2008

The Běijīng to Tiānjīn 'bullet train' begins operation; with a top speed of 330km/h, it sets a record for the fastest conventional train service in the world.

8 August 2008

Běijīng hosts the Olympic Games with a dramatic opening ceremony and a bravura performance that sees China topping the gold medals table.

2010

In a rare victory for heritage campaigners, Běijīng shelves its plans to redevelop the historic area surrounding the city's Drum and Bell Towers, but the reprieve is only temporary.

2011

Běijīng's best-known artist and political activist Ai Weiwei is seized at Běijīng Airport and placed under house arrest without explanation for almost three months.

tents on Tiān'ānmén Sq and went on a hunger strike. When the premier Li Peng held a dialogue with the students that was aired live on TV, student leaders sarcastically upbraided him.

Louisa Lim's 2014 book *The People's Republic of Amnesia: Tiananmen Revisited* is an excellent analysis of the impact the Tiān'ānmén Square crackdown has had on China.

The students created the first independent student union since 1919 and celebrated the anniversary of the May Fourth Movement with a demonstration in which over a million people took to the streets. For the first time since 1949, the press threw off the shackles of state censorship and became independent. When Soviet leader Mikhail Gorbachev entered on a state visit, and was enthusiastically welcomed as a symbol of political reform, it seemed as if the Chinese Communist Party (CCP), too, would embrace political change. Party General Secretary Zhao Ziyang led the reformist faction, but the older-generation leaders, led by Deng Xiaoping, decided to arrest Zhao and retake the city with a military assault. On the night of 3 June, tens of thousands of troops backed by tanks and armoured personnel carriers entered the city from four directions, bulldozing aside the hastily erected barricades.

Many people died – some say hundreds, some thousands – and by the early hours of 4 June the troops were in control of the square. In the crackdown that followed across the country, student leaders escaped abroad while the Communist Party arrested thousands of students and their supporters. In the purge of party members that followed, China's reforms seemed to be going into reverse.

Rapid Development

Economic Reform

Things began to change when Deng Xiaoping emerged from the shadows and set off in 1991 on a so-called 'southern tour', visiting his special economic zones in the south and calling for more and faster reform. Despite opposition in the party, he won the day. China began a wave of economic reforms, which transformed urban China and brought new wealth and opportunities to most urban residents, though the political system remained unchanged and some 40 million workers in state-owned factories lost their jobs. Deng's reforms pulled in a tide of foreign investment, creating two economic booms, after 1992 and 1998. Stock markets reopened, state companies were privatised and private enterprise began to flourish, especially in the service sector, which created millions of new jobs. Over 100 million peasants left the countryside to work on construction sites or in export-processing factories. The factories were moved out of Běijīng and the city once again became a 'centre of consumption'.

Běijīng boasted over 3679 historic *hútòng* (narrow alleyways) in the 1980s, but only 430 were left according to a field survey in 2006 by the Běijīng Institute of Civil Engineering & Architecture.

The Heritage Protection Battle

The economy was given a huge impetus by decisions to rebuild all major cities virtually from scratch, privatise housing and sell 50- or 70-year

June 2011

The high-speed rail link between Běijīng and Shànghǎi opens to the public, slashing train journey times between the two cities from 10 hours to just five.

2012

Blind civil-rights activist Chen Guangcheng, held in his village under virtual house arrest for almost two years, escapes and takes refuge in the US embassy in Běijīng.

July 2012

Seventy-seven people die and more than 65,000 are evacuated from their homes after Běijīng is hit by its worst floods in 60 years.

November 2012

Xi Jinping is appointed as China's new president as part of the nation's once-in-a-decade transfer of power.

land leases to developers. There was resistance by Party Secretary Chen Xitong to the destruction of Běijīng's centre. During the 1980s and early 1990s, Chen approved redevelopment plans that aimed to preserve and restore Běijīng's historic centre and characteristic architecture. Chen had earlier helped persuade many army and civilian work units to vacate historical sites they'd occupied during the 1970s. However, in 1995, he was ousted by Jiang Zemin, and imprisoned on corruption charges.

Designs to demolish the Forbidden City and erect new party headquarters on the site were drawn up in the late 1960s but never implemented. The palace was closed for nearly 10 years and became overgrown with weeds.

Rebuild & Relocate

Once the Party apparatus was under his direct control, President Jiang approved plans to completely rebuild Běijīng and relocate its inhabitants. This was part of the nationwide effort to rebuild the dilapidated and neglected infrastructure of all Chinese cities. The 'trillion-dollar' economic stimulus package was carried out with remarkable speed. In Běijīng more than a million peasants, housed in dormitories on construction sites, worked around the clock, and still do. New shopping malls, office blocks, hotels and luxury housing developments were thrown up at astonishing speed. Only a dictatorship with the vast human and industrial resources of China at its command could ever have achieved this.

Jiang wanted to turn Běijīng into another Hong Kong, with a forest of glass-and-steel skyscrapers. The new municipal leadership threw out the old zoning laws, which limited the height of buildings within the 2nd Ring Rd. It revoked existing land deeds by declaring old buildings to be dilapidated slums. Such regulations enabled the state to force residents to abandon their homes and move to new housing in satellite cities. Under the plan, only a fraction of the 67-sq-km Ming city was preserved.

Onwards & Upwards

Some see the rebuilding as a collective punishment on Běijīng for its 1989 rebellion, but others see it as the continuing legacy of Mao's Cultural Revolution and the late-Qing-dynasty reformers. Many of China's recent leaders have been engineers and ex–Red Guards, including former President Hu Jintao, who graduated from Qīnghuá University during the Cultural Revolution. Běijīng's state-of-the-art new architecture – the Bird's Nest, the CCTV Building, Galaxy Soho – seems designed to embody their aspiration to create a new, forward-looking, hi-tech society, and mark the realisation of the goal of a new modern China. Meanwhile the older parts of the city, such as its historic *hútòng* neighbourhoods, are hanging on by a thread.

Běijīng's so-called Underground City is connected by road and rail tunnels, which apparently still allow the top leadership to move around in secret.

January 2013

Běijīng's notoriously toxic air pollution reaches record levels. The month is dubbed 'Airpocalypse'.

October 2013

A car crashes beside Tiān'ānmén Sq, in what police describe as a terrorist suicide attack. Five people die: the three inside the vehicle, plus two tourists.

March 2014

Malaysia Airlines flight MH370 from Kuala Lumpur to Běijīng is declared missing, sparking the largest and most expensive multinational search and rescue effort in history.

March 2014

Four years after shelving the initial redevelopment plans, demolition work begins on the area surrounding the historic Drum and Bell Towers.

Historic Hútòng

The essence of Běijīng are its *hútòng*, the distinctive alleyways that cut across the centre of town. These enchanting passageways offer a very real glimpse of what Běijīng was like before the bulldozers and construction crews got to work, and are still home to almost 20% of the residents of inner Běijīng. Immersing yourself in the *hútòng* is an essential part of any visit to the capital and by far the best way to experience Běijīng street life in all its frenetic and fascinating glory.

The most significant *hútòng* have red street signs sporting the alley name. The *hútòng* name in Chinese also appears on a small metal plaque above doorways strung along each alley. A small blue plate over the doorway of a *sìhéyuàn* indicates a building protected by law.

Origins

Hútòng (胡同) first appeared in Běijīng in the Yuan dynasty (1271–1368), in the wake of Genghis Khan's army. With the city, then known as Zhōngdū, reduced to rubble in typical Mongol style, it was redesigned with *hútòng* running east–west. At first, their numbers were comparatively small – there were no more than 380 by the end of the Mongol reign over Běijīng – but they began to increase during the Ming dynasty. By the Qing dynasty more than 2000 *hútòng* riddled Běijīng, giving rise to the Chinese saying, 'There are 360 *hútòng* with names and as many nameless *hútòng* as there are hairs on a cow.'

The number of alleyways peaked in the 1950s, when there were reckoned to be over 6000. In recent decades the construction of office buildings and apartment blocks, as well as the widening of roads, has resulted in the demolition of many of them. However, it's likely that somewhere between 1000 and 2000 of these beguiling lanes have avoided the wrecking balls.

Venerable alleys include Zhuanta Hutong (砖塔胡同; Brick Pagoda Alley), dating from Mongol times and found west off Xisi Nandajie; and Nanluogu Xiang, which dates back 800 years and is now the best-known alley in town thanks to its emergence as a nightlife hub. Other *hútòng* survive in name only, like 900-year-old Sanmiao Jie (三庙街; Three Temple St) in Xuānwǔ District, which dates back to the Liao dynasty (907–1125). Long cited as the oldest *hútòng* of them all, little is left of the ancient alley as its courtyard houses were demolished in 2009.

Most *hútòng* lie within the loop of the 2nd Ring Rd. The most *hútòng*-rich neighbourhoods are in the centre and north of Dōngchéng District, closely followed by the northern part of Xīchéng District, especially the area around and to the west of Hòuhǎi Lakes. The *hútòng* here were the closest to the Forbidden City, and the nearer you lived to the imperial palace, the higher your status. For that reason, the *hútòng* immediately east and west of the Forbidden City were reserved for aristocrats and the city elite. It's in these *hútòng* that you'll find the oldest and most prestigious *sìhéyuàn* (courtyard houses), many of which are now government offices. Most date from the Qing dynasty, though many of the lanes are older.

The alleys around or close to the Forbidden City have been largely protected from the ravages of redevelopment. The houses further away were the homes of merchants and artisans, featuring more functional design with little or no ornamentation. It is these *hútòng*, especially the ones southeast and southwest of Tiān'ānmén Sq, that have suffered the most from the wrecking ball.

Walk through the once vibrant neighbourhood directly east of Qianmen Dajie (near Lìqún Roast Duck Restaurant), and you'll get a vivid impression of how many *hútòng* are clinging on in the face of property development. Nevertheless, the area around Dazahlan Xijie, itself a *hútòng*, still has many alleys, although they lack the aesthetic value of their posher counterparts to the north. But you can find *hútòng* of one sort of another in all Běijīng's neighbourhoods, even if some are relatively recent creations and are basically low-level housing rather than anything worthy of preservation. Wherever you choose to plunge into *hútòng* land, you'll be treading streets that have hundreds of years of history behind them.

The origins of the word *'hútòng'* are hazy. It was originally a Mongolian term, and could have referred to a passageway between *gers* (yurts), the traditional Mongol tents; or it might come from the word *'hottog'* (a well) – wherever there was water in the dry plain around Běijīng, there were inhabitants.

Imperial City Hútòng

The Imperial City failed to survive the convulsions of the 20th century, but the *hútòng* that threaded through the imperial enclave remain. Many bore names denoting their former function during imperial days. Zhonggu Hutong (钟鼓胡同; Bell and Drum Alley) was responsible for the provision of bells and drums to the imperial household. Jinmaoju Hutong (巾帽局胡同; Cloth and Cap Department Alley) handled the caps and boots used by the court, while Zhiranju Hutong (织染局胡同; Weaving and Dyeing Department Alley) supplied its satins and silks. Jiucuju Hutong (酒醋局胡同; Wine and Vinegar Department Alley) managed the stock of spirits, vinegar, sugar, flour and other culinary articles.

Candles were vital items during Ming and Qing times. Supply was handled by the Làkù, which operated from Laku Hutong (蜡库胡同; Candle Storehouse). The Jade Garden Hotel sits on the former site of the Cíqìkù (Porcelain Storehouse), which kept the Forbidden City stocked with porcelain bowls, plates, wine cups and other utensils.

West of Běihǎi Park, the large road of Xishiku Dajie (西什库大街; West Ten Storehouse St) gets its name from the various storehouses scattered along its length during Ming times. Among items supplied to the Imperial City from warehouses here were paper, lacquer, oil, copper, leather and weapons, including bows, arrows and swords.

There are also *hútòng* named after the craft workers who supplied the Forbidden City with its raw materials, such as Dashizuo Hutong (大石作胡同; Big Stonemason's Alley), where stonemasons fashioned the stone lions, terraces, imperial carriageways and bridges of the Imperial City.

Now-vanished temples are also recalled in *hútòng* names, such as the Guangming Hutong (光明胡同), south of Xi'anmen Dajie, named after the huge Guāngmíng Diàn (Guāngmíng Temple) that is no more.

The rectangular waffle-grid pattern of the *hútòng* stamps the points of the compass on the Běijīng psyche. You can still hear older locals exclaiming, *'wǒ gāoxìng de wǒ bù zhī běi le',* meaning 'I was so happy, I didn't know which way was north' (an extremely disorientating state of joy).

Hútòng Today

Hútòng land is now a hotchpotch of the old and the new, where Qing-dynasty courtyards come complete with recently added brick outhouses and stand beneath grim apartment blocks. Adding to the lack of uniformity is the fact that many *sìhéyuàn* were subdivided in the 1960s so that they could house more people.

The shortage of space, as well as the paucity of modern facilities such as heating, proper plumbing, private bathrooms and air-conditioning, is the main reason many *hútòng* dwellers have been happy to leave the alleyways for newly built high-rise flats. Older residents are more reluctant to abandon the *hútòng,* preferring the sense of living in a community, as opposed to a more isolated existence in the suburbs.

Foreigners long ago cottoned on to the charm of courtyard life and breached this conservative bastion, although many are repelled by poor heating, and neighbours who can be too close for comfort by Western standards. In addition, some *hútòng* homes still lack their own toilets, explaining the malodorous public loos strung along many alleyways. But other homes have been thoroughly modernised and sport such features as varnished wooden floors, fully fitted kitchens, split-level bedrooms and numerous bathrooms. Converted courtyards are prized and are much more expensive to buy or rent than even the swishest apartments.

While large numbers of old courtyard houses have been divided into smaller units, many of their historical features remain, especially their roofs. Courtyard communities are served by small shops and restaurants spread throughout the *hútòng*, making them very much their own self-contained worlds.

Many of the grandest *sìhéyuàn* are occupied by high-ranking CCP cadres or are government offices. Some of the *hútòng* off Nanluogu Xiang are known for the number of senior officials who live there, while former Premier Zhao Ziyang spent the last 15 years of his life under house arrest in a courtyard once occupied by Empress Cixi's hairdresser.

An Uncertain Future

A few years ago, it seemed that Běijīng's government had finally realised the aesthetic value of preserving the historic heart of the capital. Now, though, the future of the *hútòng* appears less certain. People are still being evicted from homes their families have occupied for generations, as local authorities continue to demolish whole alleys in the name of what they regard as progress.

The latest assault is taking place in the Drum and Bell Tower area, parts of which currently resemble a building site. Many of the surrounding *hútòng* are being levelled and are set to be replaced by a far less authentic re-creation of an 18th-century Qing-dynasty neighbourhood. To the distress of many Beijingers, local officials seem to have a vision of a gleaming, new Běijīng of shopping malls and apartment blocks that purposefully excludes the *hútòng*.

Despite laws that are supposed to protect them, it is telling that perhaps the best guarantee for the survival of a *hútòng* is whether it has commercial value. The successful remodelling of Nanluogu Xiang into a nightlife hotspot and tourist hub has been replicated elsewhere: some of the alleys off Gulou Dongdajie and Andingmen Dajie have also sprouted shops, bars, cafes and restaurants and have become almost as popular. As long as a *hútòng* is generating significant tax revenue for the local authority, officials appear willing to shield them from redevelopment.

Best Hútòng for Eating & Drinking

- *Nanluogu Xiang*
- *Beiluogu Xiang*
- *Fangjia Hutong*
- *Wudaoying Hutong*
- *Beixinqiao Santiao Hutong*
- *Banchang Hutong*

Old Walled Courtyards

Sìhéyuàn (四合院) are the building blocks of the *hútòng* world. Some old courtyards, such as the Lǎo Shě Museum, have been quaintly mothballed as museums, but many remain inhabited and hum with domestic activity inside and out. Doors to communal courtyards are typically left open, while from spring to autumn men collect outside their gates, drinking beer, smoking and chewing the fat. Inside, trees soar aloft, providing shade and a nesting place for birds.

Prestigious courtyards are entered by a number of gates, but the majority have just a single door. Venerable courtyards are fronted by large, thick, red doors, outside of which perch either a pair of Chinese lions or drum stones (*bǎogǔshí;* two circular stones resembling drums, each on a small plinth and occasionally topped by a miniature lion or a small dragon head). A set of square *méndāng* (wooden ornaments) above the gateway is a common sight. You may even see a set of stepping-on stones *(shàngmǎ shí)* that the owner would use for mounting his steed. The more historic courtyard gates are accessed by a set of steps, both topped with and flanked by ornate brick carvings – the generosity of detail indicates the social clout of the courtyard's original inhabitants.

Many of these impressive courtyards were the residences of Běijīng's officials, wealthy families and even princes; Prince Gong's Residence on Dingfu Jie is perhaps the most celebrated example. In more recent times, many were appropriated by work units to provide housing for their workforce. Others still belong to private owners, or are used by the government or universities, but the state ultimately owns all property in China, which leaves the fate of the *hútòng* in the hands of local authorities.

You can experience these delightful lanes to the full by spending a night in a *hútòng* courtyard hotel. There are also now restaurants, such as Dali Courtyard or Source, which allow you to dine inside a *sìhéyuàn*, as well as a growing number of cafes and bars located within former courtyard homes.

Wind-Water Lanes

By far the majority of *hútòng* run east–west, ensuring that the main gate faces south, so satisfying feng shui (geomancy, literally 'wind and water') requirements. This south-facing aspect guarantees maximum sunshine and protection from negative forces prevailing from the north. This positioning mirrors the layout of all Chinese temples, which nourishes the *yáng* (the male and light aspect) while checking the *yīn* (the female and dark aspect). Less significant north–south running alleyways link the main lanes.

Some courtyards used to be further protected by rectangular stones bearing the Chinese characters for Tài Shān (Mt Tài) to vanquish bad omens. Other courtyards preserve their screen walls or spirit walls *(yǐngbì)* – feng shui devices erected in front of the main gate to deflect roaming spirits. Běijīng's two most impressive spirit walls are the Nine Dragon Screens at the Forbidden City and in Běihǎi Park.

Trees provide *qì* (energy) and much-needed shade in summer, and most old courtyards have a locust tree at the front, which would have been planted when the *sìhéyuàn* was constructed.

Names

Some *hútòng* are christened after families, such as Zhaotangzi Hutong (赵堂子胡同; Alley of the Zhao Family). Other *hútòng* simply took their names from historical figures, temples or local features, while a few have more mysterious associations, such as Dragon Whiskers Ditch Alley (Lóngxūgōu; 龙须沟胡同). Many reflect the merchandise that was for sale at local markets, such as Ganmian Hutong (干面胡同; Dry Flour Alley), while some, such as Gongbei Hutong (弓背胡同; Bow Back Hutong), have names derived from their shape.

Other names reflect some of the rather unusual industries that coalesced around the Forbidden City. Young Girl Lane was home to future concubines and Wet Nurse Lane was full of young mothers who breastfed the imperial offspring; they were selected from around China on scouting trips four times a year. Clothes Washing Lane was the residence of the women who did the imperial laundry. The maids, having grown old in the service of the court, were subsequently packed off to faraway places until their intimate knowledge of royal undergarments was out of date and no longer newsworthy.

Some *hútòng* names conceal their original monickers, which were considered either too unsavoury or unlucky, in homophones or similarly sounding words, or are euphemisms for what actually went on there. Guancai Hutong (棺材胡同), 'Coffin Alley', was dropped for Guangcai Hutong (光彩胡同), which means 'Splendour Hutong'. Muzhu Hutong (母猪胡同), 'Mother Pig Hutong' or 'Sow Hutong', was elevated to the much more poetic Meizhu Hutong (梅竹胡同), or 'Plum Bamboo Hutong'. Rouge Hutong (胭脂胡同; Yanzhi Hutong) earned its name because it was the haunt of prostitutes, 'rouge' being old-Běijīng slang for a working girl.

For a bird's-eye panorama of Běijīng's *hútòng* universe, view the diorama of the modern city at the Běijīng Planning Exhibition Hall. The excellent NGO Běijīng Cultural Heritage Protection Centre (www.bjchp.org) is a great source on efforts to preserve the city's remaining *hútòng*.

Dimensions

Despite an attempt at standardisation, Běijīng's alleys have their own personalities and proportions. The longest is Dongjiaomin Xiang (东交民巷), which extends for 3km, while the shortest – unsurprisingly called Yichi Dajie (一尺大街; One Foot St) – is a brief 25m. Some people contest that Guantong Xiang (贯通巷; Guantong Alley), near Yangmeizhu Xijie, which is east of Liulichang Dongjie, is even shorter, at 20m.

THE CHANGING FACE OF HÚTÒNG LAND

One by-product of the commercialisation of some *hútòng* is that they cease to be the fascinating microcosms of local life they once were. Ten years ago, Nanluogu Xiang was still full of families who had lived there for generations and was lined with *xiǎomàibù* (small general stores) and greengrocers rather than bars.

Now, virtually none of those residents remain. Most have leased their courtyard homes as shops, restaurants, bars and cafes and used the sky-high rents to relocate to new apartment blocks in the suburbs. Whereas once kids played in the street on summer nights, while the adults sat fanning themselves or playing Chinese chess, now young Beijingers and domestic tourists stroll up and down, shopping, eating and drinking.

This transition from living communities into something far less organic is being mimicked elsewhere, eg at Wudaoying Hutong near the Lama Temple. Nearby Fangjia Alley is a bizarre mix of hip *hútòng* and old Běijīng, where you can sip an imported brew in a trendy bar while opposite locals sit on a doorstep and share a bottle of Yanjing beer.

The *hútòng* dwellers aren't complaining too much, though. On the contrary, it is now near impossible to buy a *sìhéyuàn* in such areas because their residents know they can guarantee their long-term future by renting them out instead. But if you're looking for a taste of truly authentic alley life, then you'll need to plunge into the *hútòng* that haven't been touched by the hand of Mammon.

Some *hútòng* are wide and leafy boulevards, whereas others are narrow, claustrophobic corridors. Běijīng's broadest alley is Lingjing Hutong (灵境胡同; Fairyland Alley), with a width of 32m, but the aptly named Xiaolaba Hutong (小喇叭胡同; Little Trumpet Alley), the city's smallest, is a squeeze at 50cm.

Chubby wayfarers would struggle even more in Qianshi Hutong (钱市胡同), situated not far from Qiánmén and Dàzhàlan – its narrowest reach is a mere 44cm, although it's a pathway rather than a genuine *hútòng*. Nor do all the lanes run straight: Jiuwan Hutong (九湾胡同; Nine Bend Alley) has no less than 13 turns in it.

During the Cultural Revolution, selected *hútòng* were rechristened to reflect the political fervour of the times. Nanxiawa Hutong was renamed Xuemaozhu Hutong, literally 'Study Mao's Writings Hutong', while Doujiao'er Hutong became Hongdaodi Hutong, or 'Red to the End Hutong'.

Tours

Exploring Běijīng's *hútòng* is an unmissable experience. Go on a walking or cycling tour and delve deep into this alternately ramshackle and genteel, but always magical, world. Best of all, just wander off the main roads in the centre of Běijīng into the alleyways that riddle the town within the 2nd Ring Rd. Getting lost is part of the fun of exploring the *hútòng*, and you don't have to worry about finding your way back because you'll never be far from a main road.

Good places to plunge into are the alleys to the west of Hòuhǎi Lakes, the area around Nanluogu Xiang, the roads branching west off Chaoyangmen Beixiaojie and Chaoyangmen Nanxiaojie, east of Wangfujing Dajie, and the lanes southwest of Tiān'ānmén Sq.

Hiring a bike is by far the best way to explore this historic world. But if you want to join a tour, the **China Culture Center** (Kent Center; ☎weekdays 6432 9341, weekends 6432 0141; www.chinaculturecenter.org; 29 Anjialou, Liangmaqiao Lu; Ⓢ Liangmaqiao) runs regular tours, or can arrange personalised tours. Call for further details, or check the website. **Bike Beijing** (www.bikebeijing.com) also does guided *hútòng* tours. Many hotels run tours of the *hútòng*, or will point you in the direction of someone who does. Alternatively, any number of pedicab touts infest the roads around Hòuhǎi Lakes, offering 45-minute or one-hour tours. Such tours typically cost ¥60 to ¥120 per person. If you want an English-speaking rickshaw rider, the Běijīng Tourist Information Centre opposite the north gate of Beihai Park can find you one.

Arts

Běijīng's arts scene has flourished over the past two decades, fuelled by China opening up to the outside world and the subsequent influx of new ideas from overseas. Lobotomised during the Cultural Revolution, the capital's creative faculties have sparked into life and found some space. Visual arts in particular have prospered. From its humble beginnings in the 798 Art District, Chinese contemporary art has achieved global recognition. But Běijīng is also the unofficial capital of China's film industry, the home of its finest bands and the best place to catch the enduring vitality of the traditional Chinese performing arts. Whatever your tastes run to, you'll find it in Běijīng.

Literature

In keeping with its well-read and creative reputation among ordinary and educated Chinese, Běijīng has been home to some of China's towering modern writers. The literary landscapes of Lao She, Lu Xun, Mao Dun and Guo Moruo are all forever associated with the capital. Venue of the inspirational May Fourth Movement, the first stirrings of the Red Guards and the democracy protests of 1989, Běijīng's revolutionary blood has naturally seeped into its literature. Over the past century, local writers have penned their stories of sorrow, fears and aspirations amid a context of ever-changing trends and political upheaval.

The eternal Běijīng versus Shànghǎi argument occurs in the arts too. The capital is grittier and edgier than its southern counterpart, and is slightly less obsessed with making money. For those reasons, and despite its authoritarian reputation as the centre of CCP power, Běijīng attracts far more creative talent than Shànghǎi.

The Birth of Modern Chinese Literature

The publication of Lu Xun's short story *Diary of a Madman* in 1918 had the same type of effect on Chinese literature as the leather-clad Elvis Presley had on the American music scene in the early 1950s. Until Lu Xun, novels had been composed in classical Chinese *(gǔwén)*, a kind of Shakespearian language far removed from colloquial speech *(báihuà)*. That maintained the huge gulf between educated and uneducated Chinese, putting literature beyond the reach of the common person and fashioning a cliquey lingua franca for officials and scholars.

The opening paragraph of Lu's seminal story uses that classical language. The stultifying introduction, peppered with archaic character use and the excruciatingly paired-down grammar of classical Chinese, continues as one solid block of text, without any new paragraphs or indentation. Then suddenly the passage concludes and the reader is confronted with the appearance of fluent colloquial - spoken - Chinese.

For Lu Xun to write his short story - itself a radical fable of palpable terror - in the vernacular was dynamite. Chinese people were at last able to read language as it was spoken and the short story's influence on creative expression was electric. Lu Xun's tale records the diary entries of a man descending into paranoia and despair. Fearful that those around him are engaging in cannibalism, the man's terrifying suspicions are seen as a critique of the self-consuming nature of feudal society. It is a haunting and powerful work, which instils doubts as to the madness of the narrator and concludes with lines that offer a glimmer of hope.

BĚIJĪNG BOOKSHELF

- *Beijing Coma* (Ma Jian, 2008) Novel revolving around protagonist Dai Wei's involvement with the pro-democracy protests of 1989 and the political coma that ensues.
- *Diary of a Madman and Other Stories* (Lu Xun, translated by William Lyell, 1990) Classic tale of mental disintegration and paranoia, and a critique of Confucianism in pre-revolutionary China from the father of modern Chinese literature. China's first story published in *báihuà* (colloquial speech), save the first paragraph.
- *Rickshaw Boy* (Lao She, translated by Shi Xiaoqing, 1981) A masterpiece by one of Běijīng's most beloved authors and playwrights about a rickshaw-puller living in early-20th-century China.
- *Blades of Grass: The Stories of Lao She* (translated by William Lyell, 2000) This collection contains 14 stories by Lao She – poignant descriptions of people living through times of political upheaval and uncertainty.
- *Kinder than Solitude* (Yiyun Li, 2014) Haunting novel in English by native Beijinger Yiyun Li that moves between 1990s Běijīng and the present-day US as it explores the complex relationship between three childhood friends.
- *The Maker of Heavenly Trousers* (Daniele Vare, 1935) Republished tale of old Běijīng with a splendid cast of dubious foreigners and plenty of insights into Chinese life in the capital in the chaotic pre-WWII days.
- *The Noodle Maker* (Ma Jian, translated by Flora Drew, 2004) A collection of interconnected stories as told by a state-employed writer during the aftermath of the Tiān'ānmén Square protests. Bleak, comical and unforgettable.
- *Midnight in Peking* (Paul French, 2012) True-life mystery of a brutal murder of an English girl in the Legation-era, with lots of juicy detail about the sinful underworld of pre-1949 Běijīng.
- *Black Snow* (Liu Heng, translated by Howard Goldblatt, 1993) Compelling novel about workers in Běijīng. Superbly written – a fine translation.
- *Peking Story: The Last Days of Old China* (David Kidd, 2003) A true story of a young man who marries the daughter of an aristocratic Chinese family in Běijīng two years before the 1949 Communist Revolution. The writing is simple, yet immersive.
- *Empress Orchid* (Anchee Min, 2004) Historical novel about Empress Cixi and her rise to Empress of China during the last days of the Qing dynasty. Good historical background of Běijīng and entertaining to read.
- *Beijing: A Novel* (Philip Gambone, 2003) A well-written account of an American working in a medical clinic in Běijīng who falls in love with a local artist. One of the few books out there to explore in-depth the intricacies of Běijīng gay subculture.

From this moment on, mainstream Chinese literature would be written as it was thought and spoken: Chinese writing had arrived in the modern age.

The text of *Diary of a Madman* (aka *A Madman's Diary*) can be downloaded for free at www.marxists.org, as can many of Lu Xun's other works. His novels can be picked up in translation at the Lu Xun Museum and are widely available in the West.

Pre-1989 Literature

Contemporary Chinese literature is commonly grouped into two stages: pre-1989 and post-1989. The 1949 ascendency saw literature gradually became a tool of state control and mere propaganda. Publishing was nationalised and most work in this period echoed the Communist Party line, with dull, formulaic language and cardboard characters in a socialist realist framework.

The Hundred Flowers Movement (1956–57) promised a period of open criticism and debate, but instead resulted in a widespread crackdown on intellectuals, including writers. During the Cultural Revolution (1966–76), writers either toed the line or were mercilessly purged. The much-loved Běijīng writer Lao She (1899–1966) was badly beaten and humiliated by Red Guards at the Confucius Temple in August 1966 and committed suicide the next day.

After Mao's death in 1976, Chinese artists and writers threw off political constraints and began to explore new modes of literary expression. Western books began to appear in translation for the first time, exposing Chinese authors to a wide array of literary techniques and styles.

One important writer to emerge during this period was Zhang Jie, who first drew the attention of literary critics with the publication of her daring novella *Love Must Not Be Forgotten* (1979). With its intimate portrayal of a middle-aged woman and her love of a married man, the book challenged the traditional mores of marriage. The authorities disparaged the book, calling it morally corrupt, but the book was extremely popular with readers and won a national book award.

Zhang went on to write the novels *Heavy Wings* (1980) and *The Ark* (1981). *The Ark,* about three women separated from their husbands, established Zhang as China's 'first feminist author'. Shen Rong was another talented female author. Her novella *At Middle Age* (1980) tells the plight of a Chinese intellectual who must balance her family life with her career as a doctor during the Cultural Revolution.

'Scar Literature' – novels exploring the traumatic impact of the Cultural Revolution on Chinese society – was the most significant of all the literary movements that flowered during the late 1970s and 1980s. It still flourishes today, with authors like Yu Hua, Jiang Rong and Ha Jin delving back into those dark days.

Post-1989 Literature

The tragic events of 1989 inspired a more 'realist' style of literature pioneered by writers such as Wang Shuo and Yu Hua. Wang, a sailor turned fiction writer, is famous for his satirical stories about China's underworld and political corruption. Wang's stories – dark, sometimes fantastic and taking jabs at just about every aspect of contemporary Chinese society – are notable for their inventive use of Běijīng slang; his style is similar to the way the Scottish author Irvine Welsh uses the Edinburgh vernacular in novels such as *Trainspotting.*

One of Wang's most contentious novels is *Please Don't Call Me Human.* Written after the Tiān'ānmén Square democracy protests, it provides a mocking look at the failures of China's state security system.

EXILES

Chinese authors living overseas, either through choice or because of their political views, have been responsible for some of the most effective writing about China in recent years. London-based Ma Jian left China after the Tiān'ānmén protests. His novel *Beijing Coma* (2008), which recounts the events of June 1989 from the perspective of a student left in a coma after being shot during the crackdown on the protestors, is the finest piece of fiction dealing with that momentous time.

Ma's masterpiece, though, is the remarkable *Red Dust* (2001), a memoir of the three years in the early 1980s Ma spent travelling around the remote edges of China, including Tibet, on the lam. Its opening chapters provide a fascinating snapshot of the then tiny community of bohemians in Běijīng and the suspicions they aroused among the authorities.

Native Beijinger Yiyun Li, who now lives in California, writes exquisite short stories. Both *A Thousand Years of Good Prayers* (2005) and *Gold Boy, Emerald Girl* (2010) reveal the lives of ordinary Chinese caught up in the sweeping cultural changes of the past 20 years and are told in memorable prose.

Another US-based author who writes in English is Ha Jin. His novel *Waiting* (1999) is a love story that spans two decades as its hero hangs on 18 years for official permission to get divorced so he can remarry. The harsher, more satirical *War Trash* (2004) examines the complicated web of loyalties – to family, country and political party – many Chinese struggled to reconcile in the wake of the communist takeover of China in 1949.

Wang's works appeal to a broad spectrum of Chinese society, despite being banned. He has written over 20 books as well as screenplays for TV and film. Books available in English include *Playing for Thrills* (2000) and *Please Don't Call Me Human* (1998).

In late February and March you have a choice of two literary festivals to attend. The Bookworm stages the International Literary Festival, while the Capital M Literary Festival is held at the Capital M restaurant. Both attract local and international authors – another sign of Běijīng's emergence as a true world city.

Like Wang, Yu Hua grew up during the Cultural Revolution and that experience is filtered through all his work. Yu, too, uses extreme situations and humour, and often violence, to illustrate his essentially absurd vision of modern-day China. But unlike Wang, Yu's novels are vast, sweeping affairs that cover decades. *To Live* (1992) follows the tribulations of one family from the founding of the new China through the Cultural Revolution. Its impact overseas helped turn Yu into a global name and his subsequent novels *Chronicle of a Blood Merchant* (1995), which moves from the 1950s to the 1980s, and *Brothers* (2005), a vicious, dark satire on the rush for riches that has characterised the last two decades in China, are all available in English translation.

Mo Yan (real name Guan Moye: 'Mo Yan' is a pen name that means 'don't speak' in Mandarin) has become a worldwide literary star since winning the Nobel Prize for Literature in 2012. His short stories and novels are less pitiless and abrasive than that of Yu Hua and Wang Shuo and, like the great Lu Xun, are essentially social commentary. Most of his work is available in English. The short story collection *Shifu: You'll Do Anything for a Laugh* (2002) provides a great introduction to his writing.

By far the biggest literary hit of recent years has been Jiang Rong's *Wolf Totem* (2004), which received widespread exposure in the West after being published in English in 2008. Set in the grasslands of Inner Mongolia, it's a lyrical, semi-autobiographical tale of a young Běijīng student 'sent down' to live among Mongolian nomads during the Cultural Revolution and the contrasts between their lives and the one he has left behind.

Of all the writers to emerge via the internet, Anni Baobei is the undisputed star. Nicknamed 'Flower in the Dark' by her legions of young female fans, her intense stories about lovelorn, lonely women searching for meaning in their lives have struck a huge chord with the one-child generation.

The advent of the internet has spawned a whole new generation of young writers who have sprung to fame by first publishing their work online. Now, legions of wannabe authors are posting their short stories, novels and poetry on websites. At the same time, the first writers from the one-child generation (born post-1980) to attract national attention have emerged. The work of Han Han and Guo Jingming will never win any literary prizes (indeed, both authors have been accused of plagiarism, or of merely being the front for teams of ghost writers), but their tales of urban youth have made them media icons and the best-selling authors in China.

Visual Arts

The founding of the new China in 1949 saw the individual artistic temperament suborned to the service of the state. Art was now for the masses and the socialist realist style emerged as the dominant style, with all human activity in paintings expressing the glory of the communist revolution.

Traditional precepts of Chinese classical painting were sidelined and foreign artistic techniques were imported wholesale. Washes on silk were replaced with oil on canvas while a realist attention to detail supplanted China's traditional obsession with the mysterious and ineffable. Landscapes were replaced with harder-edged panoramas in which humans occupied a central, commanding position. The entire course of Chinese painting – which had evolved in glacial increments over the centuries – was redirected virtually overnight.

Běijīng's Best Galleries & Art Districts

- *798 Art District*
- *Cǎochǎngdì*
- *Red Gate Gallery*
- *National Art Museum*

It was only with the death of Mao Zedong in September 1976 that the individual artistic temperament was once again allowed more freedom and painters such as Luo Zhongli employed the realist techniques they learned in China's art academies to portray the harsh suffering etched in the faces of contemporary peasants. Others escaped the suffocating confines of socialist realism to explore new horizons, experimenting with a variety of contemporary forms.

A voracious appetite for Western art put further distance between traditional Chinese aesthetics and artistic endeavour. One group of artists, the Stars, found retrospective inspiration in Picasso and German expressionism. The ephemeral group had a lasting impact on the development of Chinese art in the 1980s and 1990s, leading the way for the New Wave movement that emerged in 1985.

New Wave artists were greatly influenced by Western art, especially the iconoclastic Marcel Duchamp, and further challenged traditional Chinese artistic norms. The New Wave artist Huang Yongping destroyed his works at exhibitions, in an effort to escape from the notion of 'art'. Some New Wave artists adapted Chinese characters into abstract symbols, while others employed graphic images in a bid to shock viewers. Political realities became instant subject matter with performance artists wrapping themselves in plastic or tape to symbolise the repressive realities of modern-day China.

Yue Minjun's grotesque 'laughing' portraits of himself and friends, which are designed to convey a sense of boredom and mock joviality, have become perhaps the most recognisable images of Chinese contemporary art. Yue is now a globally known artist whose individual paintings sell for in excess of US$1 million.

Post-Tiān'ānmén

The disturbing events during and after June 1989 created artistic disillusionment with the political situation in China and hope soured into cynicism. This attitude was reflected through the 1990s in artworks permeated with feelings of loss, loneliness and social isolation. Two of the most important Běijīng artists during this period of 'Cynical Realism' were Yue Minjun and Fang Lijun.

Experiments with American-style pop art were another reaction to the events of 1989. Inspired by Warhol, some artists took symbols of socialist realism and transformed them into kitschy visual commentary. Images of Mao appeared against floral backgrounds and paintings of rosy-cheeked peasants and soldiers were interspersed with ads for Canon cameras and Coca-Cola. Artists were not only responding to the tragedies of the Tiān'ānmén protests but also to the rampant consumerism that was sweeping the country. Indeed, reaction to the rapid

SEX & THE CITY

Long a taboo subject in the arts, and Chinese society in general, sex has become one of the abiding themes of modern Chinese literature. The former poet Zhang Xianliang's *Half of Man is Woman* (1985), translated into English by Martha Avery, was a hugely controversial exploration of sexuality and marriage in contemporary China that went on to become an international bestseller. Zhang followed that with the clearly autobiographical *Getting Used to Dying* (1989), about a writer's new-found sexual freedom. The novel was banned in China until 1993.

In recent years, though, it has been female authors who have most successfully mined sexuality as a theme. The provocative *Beijing Doll* (2004), by Chun Shu, is a semi-autobiographical account of a high-school dropout who lives a life of casual sex, drink and drugs. The novel reveals the emergence of a shopping-mall- and punk-music-obsessed teenage tribe unimaginable in Běijīng even a few years before.

Annie Wang's *The People's Republic of Desire* (2006) also holds nothing back with its candid exploration of sexuality in modern Běijīng, while Anni Baobei (real name Li Jie) writes hugely popular short stories and novels that feature alienated young women caught up in dysfunctional or abusive relationships. *The Road of Others* (2012) collects some of her short stories in English translation.

modernisation of China has been a consistent theme of much Běijīng art from the 1990s to the present day.

Throughout the 1990s, artists who felt marginalised from the cultural mainstream found escape from political scrutiny by living together in ad hoc communes and setting up their own exhibitions in nonofficial spaces outside of state-run institutions. Most artists relied on the financial support of foreign buyers to continue working. Despite political pressure from authorities, some artists began to receive international attention for their art, sparking the beginning of a worldwide interest in and appetite for Chinese contemporary art. A defining moment for artists was in 1999, when 20 Chinese artists were invited to participate in the Venice Biennale for the first time.

Socialist realism has its roots in non-Chinese neoclassical art, the life-like canvases of Jacques Louis David and, of course, the output of Soviet Union painters. Infused with political symbolism and dripping with propaganda, it was produced on an industrial scale, with mechanical rules governing content and style.

Chinese art's obsessive focus on contemporary socio-economic realities makes much creativity from this period parochial and predictable, but more universal themes have become apparent over recent years and the art climate in Běijīng has changed dramatically. Many artists who left China in the 1990s have returned, setting up private studios and galleries. Government censorship remains, but artists are branching out into other areas and moving away from overtly political content and China-specific concerns.

With scores of private and state-run galleries, Běijīng is a fantastic city to witness the changing face of contemporary Chinese art. While traditional Chinese art is still practised in the capital, Běijīng has fully surrendered to the artistic currents that sweep the international sphere. And whereas once it was foreign buyers who drove the booming art market, increasingly it is now the new local rich who are acquiring art.

Today, Běijīng is home to a vibrant community of artists practising a diverse mix of art forms, from performance art, photography, installations and video art to film, although painting remains by far the most popular visual arts medium. Běijīng artists compete internationally in art events, and joint exhibitions with European and North American artists are frequent. At the same time, numerous Western artists have flocked to Běijīng in an aesthetic *entente cordiale.*

The capital hosts several art festivals, including the Dàshānzi International Arts Festival (every spring), SURGE Art Běijīng in May, and the Běijīng Biennale, held every two years in September/October, which attract artists, dealers and critics from around the world.

Music

China was a definite latecomer to pop and rock music. By the time Elvis and John Lennon were dead and punk had given way to floppy-fringed '80s new wave, Beijingers were still tapping their feet to 'The East is Red'. Like all of the arts, music was tranquilised during the Cultural Revolution as China's self-imposed isolation severed creative ties with the outside world.

Music festivals are catching on in a big way in China. In and around Běijīng, the Midi Music Festival and Strawberry are two of the best-organised and showcase both local and international acts.

It was a young, classically trained trumpet player named Cui Jian who changed all that. Cui swapped his horn for a guitar in the mid-'80s, founded a band and by 1989 was already a name to be reckoned with. But it was when his song 'Nothing To My Name' ('yī wú suǒ yǒu'), with its abrasive vocal style and lyrics describing feelings of loneliness and alienation, became the anthem of the 1989 Tiān'ānmén protests that he really kick-started the Chinese music scene.

Since those early days, Běijīng has always been China's rock-music mecca. The masses may still prefer the saccharine confections of mainstream Cantopop and Mandopop, but the capital is home to a medley of different bands who take their sonic inspiration from punk and indie, to blues, heavy metal, jazz and electronica.

Mostly, they labour in the twilight. Few local bands have record deals, or are able to make any money from putting out CDs or making music available for download. Indeed, the Chinese music industry in general suffers from widespread piracy – hardly any young Chinese would ever consider actually buying music. The upside for visitors is that bands have to rely on gigging to make a living, which means there's someone playing somewhere in Běijīng almost every night of the week.

There's an incestuous flavour to much of the scene, with frequent collaborations and musicians rotating between different groups. Some of the most popular and enduring bands are the postpunk/new wave–influenced Carsick Cars and Re-TROS, and the noise-pop trios Hedgehog and Snapline. But there are also bands riffing on reggae, rockabilly, ska, '70s-style hard rock and any number of indigenous folk styles. Jazz, too, has always been popular in China, a legacy of the foreign influence on pre-1949 Shànghǎi.

Hip-hop is in its infancy, but China has embraced electronic music in all its different glories. Clubgoers can get a groove on to house, drum and bass, techno and trance most weekends. The local DJ hero is Mickey Zhang; you'll see his name on flyers all over town. Check the local listings magazines for details of upcoming gigs and club nights.

For classical-music and opera lovers, as well as fans of classical Chinese dance, the National Centre for the Performing Arts is the hub of all activity, but there are other venues around the city too. The **Běijīng Music Festival** (www.bmf.org.cn), held for around 30 days during the months of October and November, features music performances by opera, jazz and classical artists from around the world, while an increasing number of orchestras and opera groups pass through town on a regular basis.

Traditional Chinese musical instruments include the two-stringed fiddle *(èrhú)* – famed for its desolate wail – the two-stringed viola *(húqín)*, the vertical flute *(dòngxiāo)*, the horizontal flute *(dízi)*, the four-stringed lute *(pípa)* and the Chinese zither *(zhēng)*. To appreciate traditional music in Běijīng, catch performances at the Lao She Teahouse, close to Tiān'ānmén Sq in the south of Xīchéng.

SCISSOR-HAPPY

A walk through the thought-provoking, sometimes controversial galleries of the 798 Art District, or its less commercial counterpart at Cǎochǎngdì, might make any visitor wonder about the fuss about freedom of expression and censorship in China. On the surface at least, artists appear to be enjoying more freedom than they have since 1949 and the beginning of communist rule.

But appearances, like art itself, can be deceptive. Painters may be enjoying a relative lack of scrutiny, with the CCP having sensibly decided that no picture ever inspired a revolution (and it's no coincidence that freedom has made the visual arts by far the most vibrant of China's creative industries), but that isn't the case for other mediums. Cinema, TV and literature, in particular, remain tightly controlled and there are serious limits to what can and can't be said. To overstep them no longer results in a prison sentence, as it does for political dissidents, but it still leads to a ban on making movies or publishing books that can last for a number of years.

Even worse than official censorship is the way 60-plus years of being constrained by the knowledge that art needs to satisfy the CCP's censors has created a culture of self-censorship. Many artists consciously, or unconsciously, hold back from doing anything that might antagonise the government.

This self-suppression is in part due to the fact that children are taught the CCP's vision of the world in school and that the Chinese education system remains dominated by rote-learning, which is not well-suited to nurturing creativity, out-of-the-box thinking and inventive criticism. Until this changes, the artistic ceiling in China will remain far lower than it should.

Peking Opera

The undisputed king of Peking opera was Mei Lanfang. Mei, who died in 1961, made his name playing female roles and introduced the outside world to China's most famous art form via overseas tours. Now, his name adorns one of Běijīng's top theatres and his former courtyard home is a museum.

Peking opera (aka Běijīng opera) is still regarded as the crème de la crème of all the opera styles in China and has traditionally been the opera of the masses. Intrigues, disasters or rebellions are common themes, and many opera narratives have their source in the fairy tales, stock characters and legends of classical literature.

The style of music, singing and costumes in Peking opera are products of their origins. In the past opera was performed on open-air stages in markets, streets, teahouses or temple courtyards. The orchestra had to play loudly and the performers had to develop a piercing style of singing, which could be heard over the throng. The costumes were a garish collection of sharply contrasting colours, because the stages were originally lit by oil lamps.

Dance styles as far back as the Tang dynasty (618–907) employed similar movements and techniques to those used in today's opera. Provincial opera companies were characterised by their dialect and style of singing, but when these companies converged on Běijīng they started a style of musical drama called *kunqu*. This developed during the Ming dynasty, along with a more popular variety of play-acting pieces based on legends, historical events and popular novels. These styles gradually merged by the late 18th and early 19th centuries into the opera we see today.

Musicians usually sit on the stage in plain clothes and play without written scores. The *èrhú,* a two-stringed fiddle that is tuned to a low register and has a soft tone, generally supports the *húqín,* a two-stringed viola tuned to a high register. The *yuèqín,* a sort of moon-shaped four-stringed guitar, has a soft tone and is used to support the *èrhú*. Other instruments are the *shēng* (a reed flute) and the *pípa* (lute), as well as drums, bells and cymbals. Last but not least is the *ban,* a time-clapper that virtually directs the band, beats time for the actors and gives them their cues.

Few props are used in Peking opera; instead the performers substitute for them with each move, gesture or facial expression having a symbolic meaning. A whip with silk tassels indicates an actor riding a horse, while lifting a foot means going through a doorway.

Apart from the singing and the music, the opera also incorporates acrobatics and mime. Language is often archaic Chinese, and the music is ear-splitting (bring some cotton wool), but the costumes and make-up are magnificent. Look out for a swift battle sequence – the female warriors, especially, are trained acrobats who leap, twirl, twist and somersault in attack.

If you get bored after the first hour or so, check out the audience antics – spitting, eating apples, plugging into a transistor radio (important sports match perhaps?) or loud tea slurping. It is lively audience entertainment fit for an emperor. Many theatres around town stage performances of Peking opera.

Cinema

Cinema in China dates to 1896, when a Spaniard with a film projector blew the socks off a crowd in a Shànghǎi teahouse garden. Although Shànghǎi's cosmopolitan gusto would help make the city the capital of China's film industry pre-1949, China's first movie – *Conquering Jun Mountain* (an excerpt from a Peking opera) – was actually filmed in Běijīng in 1905.

Like all the arts, China's film business went into a steep decline after 1949; the dark days of the Cultural Revolution (1966–76) were particularly devoid of creative output. While Taiwan's and Hong Kong's movie industries flourished, China's cinema business was satisfying political agendas with output focused on the glorification of the Communist Party. The film industry in China has yet to recover: taboo subjects still have directors walking on egg shells and criticism of the authori-

BEST FILMS ABOUT BĚIJĪNG

➡ *In the Heat of the Sun* (1994) Adapted from a Wang Shuo novel, a fantastic, dreamlike, highly evocative tale of Běijīng youth running wild during the latter days of the Cultural Revolution.

➡ *The Last Emperor* (1987) Bernardo Bertolucci's celebrated (seven Oscars including best director, best costume design and best cinematography) and extravagant epic charts the life of Puyi during his accession and the ensuing disintegration of dynastic China.

➡ *Summer Palace* (2006) Unusually explicit account of two students' intense love affair, set against the backdrop of the Tiān'ānmén Square protests, which got its director Lou Ye banned from making films for five years.

➡ *Farewell My Concubine* (1993) Charting a dramatic course through 20th-century Chinese history from the 1920s to the Cultural Revolution, Chen Kaige's film is a sumptuous and stunning narrative of two friends from Peking opera school whose lives are framed against social and political turmoil.

➡ *Cell Phone* (2003) Feng Xiaogang's funniest movie, a delicious satire of Běijīng's emerging middle classes centred on two men's extramarital affairs.

➡ *Lost in Beijing* (2007) Directed by Lu Yi, China's leading female director, this banned production examines the ménage a trois between a young female worker in a massage parlour, her boss and his wife against the backdrop of a rapidly changing Běijīng.

➡ *Beijing Bicycle* (2001) Eschewing the lavish colour of Fifth Generation directors and viewing Běijīng through a Realist lens, Wang Xiaoshuai's film follows young and hapless courier Guo on the trail of his stolen mountain bike.

➡ *The Gate of Heavenly Peace* (1995) Using original footage from the six weeks preceding the ending of the Tiān'ānmén protests, Richard Gordon and Carma Hinton's moving three-hour tribute to the spirit of the student movement and its demise is a must-see.

➡ *The World* (2005) Jia Zhangke's social commentary on the effects of globalisation is set in a Běijīng theme park called 'World Park', where workers and visitors play out their lives among replicas of the world's monuments.

➡ *Cala, My Dog!* (2003) Sly and subtle comedy about a Běijīng factory worker and avid gambler trying to raise the money to license the beloved family dog, while coping with his jealous wife and wayward teenage son.

➡ *Běijīng Love Story* (2014) The most popular of the recent wave of romantic comedies to hit China's cinemas follows five couples' turbulent relationships.

ties remains hazardous. Contemporary Chinese TV shows are mostly wooden and artificial, and are often costume dramas set in far-off, and politically safe, dynasties.

Western audiences awoke to a new golden age of Chinese cinema in the 1980s and 1990s when the lush palettes and lavish tragedies of Fifth Generation directors such as Chen Kaige and Zhang Yimou stimulated the right aesthetic nerves. Garlanded with praise and rewarded with several major film awards, rich works such as *Raise the Red Lantern* (Zhang Yimou; 1991) and *Farewell My Concubine* (Chen Kaige; 1993) redefined Chinese cinema, radiating a beauty that entranced Western cinema-goers and made their directors the darlings of Cannes and other film festivals. But with many of the early Fifth Generation films banned in their home country, few Chinese cinema-goers got to admire their artistry.

Sixth Generation film directors collectively shunned the exquisite beauty of the Fifth Generation, taking the opposite tack to render the

China's best-known director Zhang Yimou adapted Yu Hua's *To Live* for the screen in 1994. It is his masterpiece and confirmed Gong Li as China's greatest actress. But the movie remains banned in China and angered the authorities so much Zhang was prevented from making another film for two years.

angst and grimness of modern urban Chinese life. Their independent, low-budget works, often made without official permission, put an entirely different spin on mainland Chinese film-making. Zhang Yuan set the tone with *Mama* (1990), a beautiful but disturbing film about a mother and her autistic child. This low-key film, created without government sponsorship, had a huge influence on Zhang's peers.

Other notable Sixth Generation directors include Wang Xiaoshuai, whose *Beijing Bicycle* (2001) is a tale of a Běijīng youth seeking to recover the stolen bike that he needs for his job, and Lou Ye, whose dreamy, neo-noir style displayed in films like *Suzhou River* (2000) and *Summer Palace* (2006) mark him out from his more gritty contemporaries.

But it is Jia Zhangke who is the most talented of the film-makers who emerged in the 1990s. His debut *Pickpocket* (1997) is a remarkable portrait of a small-time criminal in a bleak provincial town, while its follow-up *Platform* (2000) was a highly ambitious tale of a changing China told through the story of a musical group who transform from being a state-run troupe performing patriotic songs, to a pop band. Subsequent movies such as *Still Life* (2006), *24 City* (2008) and *A Touch of Sin* (2013) have shown an increasing maturity that bodes well for the future, although like many Sixth Generation film-makers much of his work has never been seen in Chinese cinemas.

While the Sixth Generation were focusing on China's underbelly, an increasing number of directors have gone in the opposite direction by making unashamedly commercial movies. Native Beijinger Feng Xiaogang is the best of them and his clever comedies *Cellphone* (2003), *If You Were the One* (2008) and *Personal Tailor* (2013) have made him China's most bankable director. Following in his footsteps is Ning Hao, whose fun crime capers *Crazy Stone* (2006) and *Crazy Racer* (2009), as well as his Chinese-style western *No Man's Land* (2013), stormed the domestic box office.

An Uneasy Future

The optimism that accompanied the rise of the Fifth and Sixth Generations has begun to dissipate in the last couple of years. Cinema-going has always been a middle-class pastime in China, with ticket prices too high for most ordinary people and industrial-scale DVD piracy further reducing the potential audience. And with more and more Hollywood productions being shown in China now, the domestic film industry is discovering, as other film industries around the world have too, that it is very hard to compete with star-driven blockbuster movies.

Today, only a few directors who are able to attract domestic and overseas investment, such as Zhang Yimou and Chen Kaige, or who are seen as surefire bets, like Feng Xiaogang, can raise significant budgets to make movies in China. Increasingly, it is historical dramas or unchallenging romantic comedies that are dominating Chinese cinema screens. There is a real danger that the Chinese film industry will shrink into insignificance, in the face of Hollywood pressure and indifference from an audience no longer satisfied by the subject matter being approved by the CCP's censors.

A good place to see Chinese films by established and emerging directors is at the Běijīng Student Film Festival, a 20-day event held every April. Films are shown at various venues around the city – check local listing magazines for screening times.

Architecture

Whether it's the sublime Hall of Prayer for Good Harvests at Temple of Heaven Park or the extraordinary CCTV Building, Běijīng's shape-shifting architecture wows visitors across the generations. In the space of a few minutes, you can amble from an ancient *hútòng* (narrow alleyway) past the vermillion Forbidden City, trot alongside the mind-numbing Great Hall of the People and arrive at the vast and glittering sci-fi-style National Centre for the Performing Arts. In the process you will have spanned an architectural narrative of at least six centuries, and seen how Běijīng's buildings are as unique to the capital as the aroma of Peking duck.

Traditional Architecture

The oldest standing structure in the Běijīng municipality is the Great Wall. Although the wall dates from the 3rd century BC, most of what you will see is the work of Ming-dynasty (1368–1644) engineers, while the tourist sections have largely been rebuilt over the past 30 years or so.

In fact, while Běijīng as we know it today dates back to the Yuan dynasty (1271–1368), nearly all traditional architecture in the capital is a legacy of the Ming and Qing dynasties (1368–1911), although most Ming-era buildings were rebuilt during the Qing dynasty. A few fitful fragments have somehow struggled through from the Mongol era, but they are rare.

Standout structures from early dynasties include the magnificent Forbidden City (the largest architectural complex in China at 72 hectares), the Summer Palace, and the remaining *hútòng* and courtyard-style homes in the centre of the city. There are also fine examples of older temple architecture at places such as Temple of Heaven Park, Běihǎi Park and, further afield, at Tánzhè Temple.

Most historic buildings, however, date from the Qing dynasty (1664–1911) or later. Little survives from the Ming dynasty, although the conceptual plan of the city dates from Ming times. Old buildings were constructed with wood and paper, so fire was a perennial hazard (spot the huge bronze water vats dotted around the Forbidden City for extinguishing flames that could rapidly reduce halls to smoking mounds). Because buildings were not durable, even those that escaped fire were not expected to last long.

Home Sweet Home

Most residences in old Běijīng were once *sìhéyuàn*, houses situated on four sides of a courtyard. The houses were aligned exactly – the northern house was directly opposite the southern, the eastern directly across from the western. *Sìhéyuàn* can still be found within the 2nd Ring Rd, and although many have disappeared, an increasing number have been transformed into hotels.

Traditionally, the Chinese followed a basic ground plan when they built their homes. In upper-class homes as well as in palaces and temples, buildings were surrounded by an exterior wall and designed on a

BĚIJĪNG'S MOST NOTABLE BUILDINGS

➜ **CCTV Building** Designed by Rem Koolhaas and Ole Scheeren, this fantastic continuous loop of a building appears to defy gravity.

➜ **National Centre for the Performing Arts** Běijīng's most loved and most hated building – Paul Andreu's creation is either a masterpiece or a blot on the landscape. You decide.

➜ **Forbidden City** China's incomparably majestic imperial palace.

➜ **Hall of Prayer for Good Harvests** The *ne plus ultra* of Ming-dynasty design and a feast for the eyes.

➜ **Capital Museum** Cutting-edge example of modern Chinese museum design.

➜ **Legation Quarter** A too-rare example of thoughtful and tasteful restoration.

➜ **Great Hall of the People** This monster of Soviet-inspired socialist realist design, erected during the Great Leap Forward, would look right at home in Pyongyang.

➜ **National Stadium** The 2008 Olympics may be a distant memory, but this intricate mesh of steel, still known to Beijingers as the 'Bird's Nest', remains iconic.

➜ **Galaxy Soho** Curvacious and controversial, this sexy, space-station lookalike business and retail complex was plonked right next to a 15th-century Buddhist temple.

north–south axis, with an entrance gate and a gate to block spirits that might try to enter the building. Behind the entry gates in palaces and residential buildings was a public hall and behind this were private living quarters built around a central court with a garden. The garden area of upper-class gentry and imperial families spawned an entire subgenre of 'recreational architecture', which included gardens, pavilions, pagodas, ponds and bridges.

Religious Architecture

With today's religious renaissance drawing more and more Chinese people to prayer, Běijīng's temples and shrines are increasingly busy places of worship (although don't expect to be swept off your feet with religious fervour – atheism still rules over here). What isn't in doubt, though, is that temples are some of the finest structures in the city.

Buddhist, Taoist and Confucian temples may appear complex, but their layout and sequence of deities tend to follow quite strict schematic patterns. Temples are virtually all arranged on a north–south axis in a series of halls, with the main door of each hall facing south, as is done in courtyard houses and the halls of the Forbidden City.

To see how the Ming and Qing dynasties built Běijīng, visit the Běijīng Ancient Architecture Museum, which has a great scale model of the old imperial city and shows how the courtyard houses of the *hútòng* were constructed.

Chinese temples are strikingly different from Christian churches because of their open plan and succession of halls; buildings follow a hierarchy and are interspersed with breezy open-air courtyards. This allows the weather to permeate the empty spaces, changing the mood of the temple depending on the climate. The open-air layout also allows the *qì* (flow of vital or universal energy) to circulate, dispersing stale air and allowing incense to be liberally burned.

Large numbers of Běijīng's temples, such as the Big Buddha Temple, whose memory is commemorated in the street name Dafosi Dongjie, have vanished since the Qing dynasty. Others are in the process of disappearing, such as the small Guānyīn Temple just off Dazhalan Xijie, or remain shut, such as Guǎngfúguàn Taoist Temple.

Buddhist Temples

Although there are notable exceptions, most Buddhist temples tend to follow a predictable layout. The first hall is frequently the Hall of Heavenly Kings (Tiānwáng Diàn), where a sedentary statue of the smiling and podgy Bodhisattva Maitreya (Mílèfó), also known as the Monk with the Bag or the Laughing Buddha, is flanked by the ferocious Four Heavenly Kings.

Behind is the first courtyard, where the drum and bell towers often stand, if the temple is large enough, and smoking braziers for the burning of incense may be positioned. The largest hall is usually named the Great Treasure Hall (Dàxióng Bǎodiàn) where you will often discover a golden trinity of statues, representing the historic, contemporary and future Buddhas. You can often find two rows of nine *luóhàn* (Buddhists, especially monks, who have achieved enlightenment and passed to nirvana at death) on either wall to the side. In other temples the *luóhàn* appear in a crowd of 500, housed in a separate hall; the Azure Clouds Temple in Fragrant Hills Park has an example.

A statue of Guanyin (the Goddess of Mercy) often stands at the rear of the main hall, facing north, atop a fish's head or a rocky outcrop. The goddess may also be venerated in her own hall and often has a multitude of arms. The rear hall may house Sutras (Buddhist scriptures) in a building called the Scripture Storing Hall (Cángjīnglóu).

Sometimes a *tǎ* (pagoda) may rise above the main halls or may be the last vestige of a vanished temple. These were originally built to house the remains of Buddha, and later other Buddhist relics, and were also used for storing Sutras, religious artefacts and documents. Some pagodas can still be climbed for excellent views, but many are too fragile and are out of bounds. The most astonishing collection of pagodas in Běijīng can be found at Tánzhè Temple.

Many temples have been restored to their original purpose, but others are still occupied by residents or, in the case of Dàgāoxuán Temple, by the military. Some have been converted to offices (Bǎilín Temple), while the ancient Sōngzhùyuàn Temple has found a new lease of life as one of the city's trendiest restaurants.

Taoist Temples

As Taoism predates Buddhism and connects to a more primitive and distant era, Taoist shrines are more netherworldly and project more of an atmosphere of superstition and magic. Nonetheless, in the arrangement of their halls, Taoist temples appear very similar to Buddhist temples.

You will almost certainly see the shape of the circular *bāguà* (a circular figure made up of eight possible combinations of three parallel lines) reflected in eight-sided pavilions and diagrams. The *yīn-yáng* Taiji diagram is also a common motif. Effigies of Laotzu (the Jade Emperor), and other characters popularly associated with Taoist myths, such as the Eight Immortals and the God of Wealth, are customary.

Taoist temple entrances are often guarded by Taoist door gods, similar to those in Buddhist temples, and the main hall is usually called the Hall of the Three Clear Ones (Sānqīng Diàn) and devoted to a triumvirate of Taoist deities.

Confucian Temples

Běijīng's Confucius Temple is China's second largest after the temple in Qūfù in Shāndōng, the birthplace of the sage.

Confucian temples bristle with steles celebrating local scholars, some supported on the backs of *bìxì* (mythical tortoise-like dragons). A statue of Kongzi (Confucius) usually resides in the main hall, overseeing rows of musical instruments and flanked by disciples. A mythical animal, the *qílín* (a statue exists at the Summer Palace), is commonly seen. The *qílín* was a hybrid animal that appeared on earth only in times of harmony.

China's most legendary figure has endured a roller-coaster ride throughout Chinese history. These days, Confucius is enjoying an upswing with his vision of a 'harmonious society' now endorsed by the CCP. That's in marked contrast to the Cultural Revolution, when Red Guards savaged his teachings as one of the 'Four Olds'.

Rebuilding Běijīng

In 1949 Mao Zedong declared that 'Forests of factory chimneys should mushroom in Běijīng'. He didn't let ancient architecture stand in the way. When the mighty Xīzhí Mén was being levelled in 1969, the Yuan-dynasty gate of Héyì Mén was discovered within the later brickwork; it disappeared too.

For first-time visitors to Běijīng, the city can be an energising and inspiring synthesis of East and West, old and new. Yet after 1949 the characteristics of the old city of Běijīng – formidable and dwarfing city walls, vast and intimidating gates, unbroken architectural narrative and commanding sense of symmetry – were flung out the window.

Many argue (such as author Wang Jun in *Story of a City*) that the historic soul of Běijīng has been extirpated, never to return. It's a dismal irony that in its bid to resemble a Western city, Běijīng has lost a far larger proportion of historic architecture than have London, Paris or Rome.

Going, Going, Gone

Although Běijīng has been radically altered in every decade since 1949, the current building mania really picked up pace in the 1990s, with a housing renovation policy that resulted in thousands of old-style homes and Stalinist concrete structures from the 1950s being torn down and replaced by modern apartment buildings. In the following decade, office blocks began to mushroom across the city, prompting yet more demolition.

So much of Běijīng's architectural heritage perished in the 1990s that the capital was denied a World Heritage listing in 2000 and 2001. That led the government to establish 40 protection zones throughout the older parts of the city to protect the remaining heritage buildings. But according to Unesco, more than a third of the 62-sq-km area that made up the central part of the old city has been destroyed since 2003, displacing close to 580,000 people.

One of the hardest-hit areas was the central neighbourhood of Qiánmén, once the home of scholars and opera singers. Preservationists and residents have petitioned for government protection. However, a resolution passed in 2005 to protect Běijīng's historic districts did not include many places, including Qiánmén, which had been approved for demolition before the order was passed. Road widening has bulldozed its way through the area; Qianmen Dajie itself has been restored in a mock historic style, and the Dashilar area next door looks like being next in line for redevelopment.

While the pace of demolition has slowed, it still continues. In January 2012 the courtyard home of Liang Sicheng, known as the father of modern Chinese architecture, was pulled down despite being listed as a 'cultural relic'. Ironically, Liang had campaigned in the 1950s for the preservation of ancient Běijīng.

In with the New

Since 1949, replacing what has gone and integrating new architecture seem to have been done without much thought. The vast Legendale Hotel on Jinbao Lu is a kitsch interpretation of a Parisian apartment block curiously plonked in central Běijīng, while the glass grill exterior of the hip Hotel Kapok on Donghuamen Dajie is a jab in the eye of the staid Jade Garden Hotel next door. But it is the futuristic domelike National Centre for the Performing Arts that is perhaps Běijīng's most controversial building, thanks to its location so close to the Forbidden City. More recently, the curvacious, spaceship-lookalike Galaxy Soho complex drew complaints from heritage-preservation campaigners when it 'touched down' in an old *hútòng* neighbourhood, one block north of the 15th-century Zhìhuà Temple.

Those same campaigners now fear the worst for the future of the *hútòng*-rich neighbourhood surrounding the historic Drum and Bell Towers, which was undergoing wholesale redevelopment at the time of research.

Religion & Belief

Ideas have always possessed a certain volatility in China, and things have often come to a head in Běijīng: the Boxer Rebellion (1898–1900); the Tiān'ānmén Square protests (1989); the outlawing of the Fălún Gōng movement (1999). Nevertheless, today's Chinese are increasingly returning to religion after decades of state-orchestrated atheism.

Buddhism

Although not an indigenous faith, Buddhism (佛教; *Fójiào*) is the religion most associated with China. Many Chinese may not be regular temple-goers, but they possess an interest in Buddhism.

Chinese Buddhism arrived from India around 50 AD. The individualist nature of the dominant Theravada school of Buddhism didn't appeal to the group-oriented, ancestor-worshipping Chinese, so the relatively unimportant Mahayana School, characterised by worship of Bodhisattvas (菩萨, *púsà;* enlightened beings that postpone their entry into nirvana in order to help others), came to dominate in China.

David Aikman's *Jesus in Beijing: How Christianity is Transforming China and Changing the Global Balance of Power* (2003) predicts almost one third of Chinese will turn to Christianity within 30 years.

Ethnic Tibetans and Mongols in China practise a unique form of Mahayana Buddhism, known as Tibetan Buddhism or Lamaism (喇嘛教, *Lǎmajiào*), where priests, called lamas, are believed to be reincarnations of highly evolved beings; the Dalai Lama being the supreme patriarch.

Taoism

A home-grown philosophy-religion, Taoism (道教; *Dàojiào*) – perhaps the hardest of Chinese religions to grasp – is a natural counterpoint to Confucian order and correctness.

Taoism predates Buddhism in China and much of its religious culture connects to a distant animism and shamanism. In its earliest and simplest form, Taoism draws from the *Tao Te Ching* (道德经; *Dàodé Jīng, The Classic of the Way and its Power*), written in around 500 BC by the philosopher Lao-Tzu (老子; Lǎozi). It's a work of astonishing insight and sublime beauty. Devoid of a godlike being or deity, Lao-Tzu's writings instead endeavour to address the unknowable and ineffable principle of the universe, which he calls Tao (道; *Dào*), or 'the way'.

Falun Gong is a quasi-religious lifestyle philosophy that gained so much traction in the 1990s that it was labelled a cult by Chinese authorities, and subsequently outlawed. Its followers at the time numbered between 60 and 70 million.

Confucianism

Confucianism (儒教; *Rújiào*) is based upon the teachings of Confucius (孔子; *Kǒngzǐ*), a 6th-century BC philosopher. The central emphasis is on five basic hierarchical relationships: father-son, ruler-subject, husband-wife, elder-younger, friend-friend. Confucius believed that if each individual carried out his or her proper role in society, social order would be achieved.

Christianity

Christianity (基督教; *Jīdūjiào*) didn't really take a foothold in Běijīng until the arrival of the Jesuits in the 16th century. They made few converts, but they became popular figures in the imperial court, and helped

KNOW YOUR TEMPLES

All Chinese temples follow the same basic pattern. Built with careful respect for feng shui, they face southwards and are symmetrical along a north–south axis. The most important halls are at the rear. Entrance is from the south, through imposing gateways which open onto a courtyard protected by a spirit wall.

It is by the interior that you can tell the various types of Chinese temples apart.

Confucian Temples

Confucian temples are devoted to the memory of Confucius and the philosophers of Confucianism, and are the least noisy, colourful and lively of Chinese temples. Their courtyards are usually filled with stelae (stone tablets) dedicated to local scholars.

Běijīng's only Confucius Temple is the second largest in China.

Buddhist Temples

Buddhist temples often contain the same combination of deities. First is a hall containing huge, multicoloured statues of the angry looking Four Heavenly Kings. Next is often a chubby 'laughing Buddha' (Maitreya). There may be other halls with other deities, but the main hall usually contains three enormous Buddhas, side by side; the Buddhas of past, present and future. Around the back you will often find the multi-armed Guanyin, and at the sides of the main hall statues of *arhats* (Buddhist saints).

Central Běijīng's largest and most significant Buddhist temple is the Lama Temple (p84), although ancient **Tánzhè Temple**, nestled in the hills outside the city centre, is also hugely impressive.

Taoist Temples

Taoist temples tend to be the most colourful and gaudy. The main gates are painted with fierce-looking mythical heroes to scare off evil spirits. The halls can contain any number of different deities, the many-armed Guanyin among them. Other likely deities include the Eight Immortals and the Three Purities; believed to be the founders of civilisation.

Two of Běijīng's largest and most impressive Taoist temples are White Cloud Temple (p124) and Dōngyuè Temple (p141), both of which hold fascinating, traditional temple fairs (庙会; *miàohuì*) during Chinese New Year.

design the astronomical instruments you can still see at the Ancient Observatory (p69). Běijīng's first church, South Cathedral (p126; 1605), was built on the site of the house of the Jesuit priest Matteo Ricci.

The so-called 'Unequal Treaties' that followed the Opium Wars gave foreign missionaries the legal right to proselytise in China, but their new beliefs, and the general treatment of Chinese people by foreign powers at this time were not well received. Hostilities culminated in the Boxer Rebellion (1898–1900), a violent anti-Christian, anti-foreign movement, which was crushed by Allied troops.

Christianity has seen a revival in recent years. Most Chinese Christians belong to illicit house churches, rather than the state-recognised Protestant or Catholic churches, so the precise number of Christians is hard to fathom, but figures of over 100 million have been posited.

During the Cultural Revolution, many temples and churches in Běijīng served as warehouses or factories. Zhìzhù Temple, for example, was a television factory in the 1960s. It's now a heritage hotel.

Islam

Islam (伊斯兰教; *Yīsīlán Jiào*) in China dates to the 7th century, when it was brought by Arab and Persian traders along the Silk Road. The descendants of these groups gradually integrated into Han Chinese culture and today are distinguished primarily by their religion, rather than ethnic characteristics. In Chinese, they are called the Huí (回).

Niú Jiē Mosque, originally built in AD 996, is the oldest and largest mosque in Běijīng, and the spiritual centre for the 10,000 or so Huí Muslims living in the vicinity.

Survival Guide

Transport

ARRIVING IN BĚIJĪNG

Air

Most travellers will fly into Běijīng, although there are international train routes to and from Mongolia, North Korea, Russia and Vietnam, as well as trains to and from Hong Kong and Lhasa. Average flight times include: London 10 hours, New York 14 hours and Sydney 12 hours. Běijīng's international airport is Běijīng Capital International Airport (PEK). If coming from elsewhere in China, you may also fly into the small Nányuàn Airport (NAY).

Flights, cars and tours can be booked online at www.lonelyplanet.com. You can also purchase tickets in person at the **Civil Aviation Administration of China** (中国民航, Zhōngguó Mínháng, Aviation Bldg, 民航营业大厦, Mínháng Yíngyè Dàshà; Map p294; ☎6656 9118, domestic 6601 3336, international 6601 6667; 15 Xichang'an Jie; ⏰8.30am-6pm).

For good deals on flights to and from Běijīng, check the following websites:

C-trip (www.ctrip.com)

eLong (www.elong.net)

Travel Zen (www.travelzen.com)

eBookers (www.ebookers.com)

Expedia (www.expedia.com)

Běijīng Capital International Airport

Currently the world's second busiest airport, **Běijīng Capital International Airport** (北京首都国际机场, Běijīng Shǒudū Guójì Jīchǎng, PEK; ☎6454 1100) has three terminals. **Terminal 3** (三号航站楼; *sān hào hángzhànlóu*) deals with most long-haul flights, although international flights also use **Terminal 2** (二号航站楼; *èr hào hángzhànlóu*). Both are connected to the slick Airport Express, which links up with Běijīng's subway system. The smaller **Terminal 1** (一号航站楼; *yī hào hángzhànlóu*) is a 10-minute walk from Terminal 2. Free 24-hour shuttle buses connect all three terminals.

FACILITIES

All terminals have ATMs, money-changing facilities, information desks with English-speaking staff, booths selling local SIM cards, plenty of eating options and shops galore (although much less so at Terminal 1).

SLEEPING

If you need to stay by the airport, **Langham Place** (北京首都机场朗豪酒店, Lǎngháo Jiǔdiàn; ☎6457 5555; www.beijingairport.langhamplacehotels.com; 1 Erjing Lu, Terminal 3; 北京首都机场三号航站二径路1号; r from ¥1279; ❄@📶) lays on a free shuttle bus and is well regarded.

AIRPORT EXPRESS

The **Airport Express** (机场快轨; Jīchǎng Kuàiguǐ; Map p298; one way ¥25), also written as ABC (Airport Běijīng City), is quick and convenient and links Terminals 2 and 3 to Běijīng's subway system at Sanyuanqiao station (Line 10) and Dongzhimen station (Lines 2 and 13). Train times are as follows: Terminal 3 (6.21am to 10.51pm); Terminal 2 (6.35am to 11.10pm); Dongzhimen (6am to 10.30pm).

BUS

There are 11 different routes for the airport **shuttle bus** (机场巴士, jīchǎng bāshì; one way ¥15-24), including those listed here. They all leave from all three terminals and run from around 5am to midnight. Note that you may have to show a valid photo ID when buying your ticket.

Line 1 To Fāngzhuāng (方庄), via Dàběiyáo (大北窑) for the CBD (国贸; guó mào)

Line 2 To Xīdàn (西单)

Line 3 To Běijīng Train Station (北京站; Běijīng Zhàn), via Dongzhimen (东直门), Dongsi Shitiao (东四十条) and Chaoyangmen (朝阳门)

Line 7 To Běijīng West Train Station (西站; xī zhàn)

Line 10 To Běijīng South Train Station (南站; nán zhàn)

Coach service to Tiānjīn (天津, ¥82, 2½ hours, 7am to 11pm hourly)

CLIMATE CHANGE & TRAVEL

Every form of transport that relies on carbon-based fuel generates CO_2, the main cause of human-induced climate change. Modern travel is dependent on aeroplanes, which might use less fuel per kilometre per person than most cars but travel much greater distances. The altitude at which aircraft emit gases (including CO_2) and particles also contributes to their climate change impact. Many websites offer 'carbon calculators' that allow people to estimate the carbon emissions generated by their journey and, for those who wish to do so, to offset the impact of the greenhouse gases emitted with contributions to portfolios of climate-friendly initiatives throughout the world. Lonely Planet offsets the carbon footprint of all staff and author travel.

TAXI

A taxi should cost ¥80 to ¥100 from the airport to the city centre, including the ¥10 airport expressway toll; bank on it taking 40 minutes to one hour to get into town. Ignore unofficial drivers who may approach you as you exit customs and join the line for an official cab. When you get into the taxi, make sure the driver uses the meter (打表; *dă biăo*). Have the name of your hotel written down in Chinese to show the driver. Very few drivers speak any English.

CAR

The **Vehicle Administration Office** (车管所, chēguǎnsuǒ; ☎6453 0010; ⏲9am-6pm) on the 1st floor of Terminal 3 – look for the 'Traffic Police' sign – issues temporary driving licences for use in Běijīng municipality. Applicants must be between the ages of 18 and 70 and must hold a temporary Chinese visa (three months or less). The process involves checking out your home driving license and undergoing a simple medical test (including an eye-sight test). You'll also need two passport photos and copies and translations of your documents, although it can be arranged at the office. The whole procedure takes about 30 minutes and costs ¥10. Once you have the license, you can hire a car from **Hertz** (www.hertzchina.com), which has an office just along the corridor. Self-drive hire cars (自驾; *zìjià*) start from ¥230 per day (up to 150km per day), with a ¥10,000 deposit. A car-with-driver service (代驾; *dàijià*) is also available (from ¥660 per day).

Cars in China drive on the right-hand side of the road. Even skilled drivers will be unprepared for China's roads: cars lunge from all angles and chaos abounds.

Nányuàn Airport

The very small **Nányuàn Airport** (南苑机场, Nányuàn Jīchǎng, NAY; ☎6797 8899; Jingbeixi Lu, Nányuàn Zhèn, Fēngtái District, 丰台区南苑镇警备西路, 警备东路口) feels more like a provincial bus station than an airport, but it does service quite a few domestic routes. Airport facilities are limited to a few shops and snack stalls, and don't expect to hear much English.

BUS

The shuttle bus (机场巴士; *jīchǎng bāshì*) goes to Xīdàn (西单; ¥18, 1½ hours, 9am to last flight arrival) via Qiánmén (前门). You can pick up the subway at either destination.

TAXI

Around ¥60 to the Tiān'ānmén Sq area. Ignore drivers who approach you. Use the taxi queue. Make sure the driver uses the meter (打表; *dă biăo*).

Train

Běijīng has three major train stations for long-distance travel (Běijīng, Běijīng West and Běijīng South). Běijīng North is used much less.

Train Ticket Types

It is possible to upgrade (补票; *bŭpiào*) your ticket once aboard your train, but only on the rare occasions a better option is available.

SOFT SLEEPER

Soft sleepers (软卧; *ruăn wò*) are very comfortable, with four air-conditioned bunks in a closed compartment. Often, they cost as much as discounted airfares to the same destination.

All Z-class trains are soft-sleeper trains with up-to-date berths. A few T-class trains also offer two-berth compartments, with their own toilet. Tickets on upper berths are slightly cheaper than lower berths.

HARD SLEEPER

About half the price of soft sleepers, hard sleepers

TAKEN FOR A RIDE

A well-established illegal taxi operation at the airport attempts to lure weary travellers into a ¥300-plus ride to the city, so be on your guard. If anyone approaches you offering a taxi ride, ignore them and join the queue for a taxi outside.

BĚIJĪNG TRAIN INFORMATION

Běijīng Station

The most central of Běijīng's four main train stations, **Běijīng Train Station** (北京站; Běijīng Zhàn), which is linked to the subway system, is mainly for T-class trains *(tèkuài)*, slow trains and trains bound for the northeast; most fast trains heading south now depart from Běijīng South Train Station and Běijīng West Train Station. Slower trains to Shànghǎi also go from here.

DESTINATION	SCRIPT	CATEGORY	DURATION (HR)	DEPARTURES	FARE (¥)
Dàlián	大连	Z-series, soft sleeper	10½	8.27pm	372-388
Dàlián	大连	K-series, hard sleeper	12	8.06pm	239-255
Dàtóng	大同	K-series, hard sleeper	6	regular	99-107
Hā'ěrbīn	哈尔滨	D-series, soft seat	10	10.02am, 1.51pm, 3.15pm	306
Hā'ěrbīn	哈尔滨	T-series, hard sleeper	12	6.18am, noon, 6.57pm, 9.23pm	261-279
Jílín	吉林	T-series, hard sleeper	12	4.55pm	244-261
Shànghǎi	上海	T-series, soft sleeper	14	7.33pm	476-497

Běijīng South Train Station

The ultra-modern **Běijīng South Station** (南站; Nán Zhàn), which is linked to the subway system on Line 4, accommodates very high speed 'bullet' trains to destinations such as Tiānjīn, Shànghǎi, Hángzhōu and Qīngdǎo.

DESTINATION	SCRIPT	CATEGORY	DURATION (HR)	DEPARTURES	FARE (¥)
Fúzhōu	福州	D-series, 2nd-class seat	15	8.13am	765
Hángzhōu	杭州	G-series, 2nd-class seat	6	regular	538-629
Jǐ'nán	济南	G-series, 2nd-class seat	1½	regular	184-194
Nánjīng	南京	G-series, 2nd-class seat	4	regular	445
Qīngdǎo	青岛	G- and D-series, 2nd-class seat	5	regular	249-314
Shànghǎi (Hóngqiáo station)	上海虹桥	G-series, 2nd-class seat	5½	regular	553
Sūzhōu	苏州	G-series, 2nd-class seat	5	regular	523
Tiānjīn	天津	C-series, 1st/2nd class	30 min	regular	63/54

Běijīng north Train Station

The smaller **Běijīng North Station** (北站; Běi Zhàn) can be accessed from Xizhimen subway station.

DESTINATION	SCRIPT	CATEGORY	DURATION (HR)	DEPARTURES	FARE (¥)
Bādálíng Great Wall	八达岭	hard seat	75 min	regular	6
Hohhot	呼和浩特	K-series, hard sleeper	9	11.47pm	129-136

Běijīng West

The gargantuan **Běijīng West Train Station** (西站; Xī Zhàn) accommodates fast Z-series trains. It has its own subway stop on line 9. Public buses leave from the right of the station as you exit. Useful Bus 52 heads east past Xīdàn, Běijīng Train Station and Jiànguómén. For taxis, use the official taxi rank (underneath North Plaza) or walk a block away from the station and hail a cab on the street. Ignore drivers who approach you. Insist drivers use the meter (打表; *dǎ biǎo*).

DESTINATION	SCRIPT	CATEGORY	DURATION (HR)	DEPARTURES	FARE (¥)
Chángshā	长沙	Z-series, soft sleeper	13	6.01pm	504-527
Chángshā	长沙	T- and K-series, hard sleeper	14	regular	322-343
Chéngdū	成都	T- and K-series, hard sleeper	26-31	9am, 11.08am, 6.29pm, 9.52pm	389-486
Chóngqìng	重庆	T- and K-series, hard sleeper	25-30	5 daily	389-456
Fúzhōu	福州	Z-series, soft sleeper	20	2.47pm	426-456
Guǎngzhōu	广州	T- and K-series, hard sleeper	21	5 daily	426-456
Guìyáng	贵阳	T- and K-series, hard sleeper	29	3.58pm, 4.57pm	465-487
Hànkǒu (Wǔhàn)	汉口	Z-series, soft-sleeper	10	8.49pm	407-427
Kowloon (Hong Kong)	九龙	train Q97, soft-sleeper	24	1.08pm	584-611
Kūnmíng	昆明	T-series, hard sleeper	38	6.26am, 4.31pm	536-575
Lánzhōu	兰州	Z- and T-series, hard sleeper	17	5 daily	322-388
Nánchāng	南昌	Hard sleeper	11½	12.02pm, 2.06pm, 8.16pm	296-407
Shēnzhèn	深圳	T- and K-series, hard sleeper	24-29	8.12pm, 11.45pm	434-464
Shíjiāzhuāng	石家庄	D-series, 2nd-class seat	2	regular	81-86
Ürümqi	乌鲁木齐	T-series, hard sleeper	34	10.01am, 3.18pm	536-585
Wǔchāng (Wǔhàn)	武昌	Hard-sleeper	10	8.55pm, 9.55pm	261-279
Xī'ān	西安	Z- and T-series, hard sleeper	11-12	8 daily	254-288
Xīníng	西宁	T-series, hard sleeper	20-24	11.56am, 4.37pm, 8pm	353-428
Yíchāng	宜昌	K-series, hard sleeper	21½	11.11pm	310-331

For Lhasa (拉萨; Lāsà) in Tibet (西藏; Xīzàng), the T27 (hard seat/hard sleeper/soft sleeper ¥360/763/1186, 44 hours) leaves Běijīng West at 8pm, taking just under two days. In the return direction, the T28 departs Lhasa at 1.48pm and arrives at Běijīng West at 8.19am.

(硬卧; *yìng wò*) are the golden ticket everyone wants and are the hardest to obtain: book them well in advance. Normally comprised of six air-conditioned bunks in an open-ended doorless compartment, there is less room than in soft-sleepers, but they are still comfortable (clean bedding is provided). There is a small price difference between berths, with the lowest bunk (下铺; *xiàpù*) the most expensive, then the middle (中铺; *zhōngpù*), then the highest bunk (上铺; *shàngpù*).

As with all other classes, smoking is prohibited. Lights and speakers go out at around 10pm. Each compartment is equipped with its own hot-water flask.

SEATS

Soft-seat class (软座; *ruǎn zuò*) is more comfortable but not nearly as common as hard-seat class. First-class (一等; *yīděng*) and 2nd-class (二等; *èrděng*) soft seats are available in D-, C- and G-series high-speed trains. First class comes with TVs, mobile phone and laptop charging points, and seats arranged two abreast.

Second-class soft-seats are also very comfortable with courteous staff. On older trains, soft-seat carriages are often double-decker, and are not as plush as on the faster and more modern high-speed express trains.

Hard-seat class (硬座; *yìng zuò*) is not available on the faster and more comfortable C-, D- and G-series trains, and is only found on T-, K- and N-series trains and trains without a number prefix; a handful of Z-series trains have hard seat. Hard-seat class generally has padded seats, but it's a strain: unsanitary and noisy, packed to the gills and painful on long journeys. Hard-seat sections on newer trains are air-conditioned and less crowded

You should get a ticket with an assigned seat number, but if seats have sold out, ask for a standing ticket (无座、站票; *wúzuò* or *zhànpiào*), which gets you on the train, where you may find a seat, but will otherwise have to stand in the carriage or between carriages (with the smokers).

Buying Train Tickets

TICKET COUNTERS

There are no longer dedicated ticket offices for foreigners at the main stations in Běijīng, although there is sometimes a ticket window with a temporary 'for foreigners' sign attached to it. Otherwise, join any queue, but arm yourself with a few key Chinese phrases, or better still have a local write down what you want so you can show the ticket seller. Increasingly, ticket sellers at the three main stations speak a bit of English, but don't count on it.

PLANNING AHEAD

Never aim to get a hard-sleeper or soft-sleeper ticket on the day of travel – plan ahead. Most tickets can be booked in advance between two and 20 days prior to your intended date of departure. Buying hard-seat tickets at short notice is usually no hassle, but it may be a standing ticket rather than a numbered seat. It's normally no problem getting a same-day ticket on high-speed G-, D- and C-category trains to nearby destinations such as Tiānjīn. Tickets can only be purchased with cash, and you will need to show your passport to get them.

RETURN TICKETS

Tickets are one way only. If you want to buy tickets for a train between two destinations beyond the city you are buying your ticket in, it is often better to go to an independent ticket office that charges a commission.

BUSY PERIODS

As with air travel, buying train tickets around the Chinese New Year and during the 1 May and 1 October holiday periods ranges from very hard to impossible. At these times, touts swarm around the train stations selling black-market tickets; be wary of buying them as foreigners frequently get ripped off. You're better off trying one of the many independent train ticket offices dotted around the city – they charge a ¥10 mark-up per ticket. Or else ask at your hotel or hostel – they will usually take a mark-up of up to ¥50 per ticket.

ONLINE BOOKINGS

Tickets can be bought online at China DIY Travel (www.china-diy-travel.com/en), or at China Trip Advisor and Ctrip, although the last two

TRAIN CATEGORIES

CATEGORY	MEANING	TYPE
C	*chengji gāosù* (城际高速)	ultra-high-speed express
D	*dòngchē, héxiè hào* (动车和谐号)	high-speed express
G	*gāotiě* (高铁)	high-speed
K	*kuàisù* (快速)	fast train
T	*tèkuài* (特快)	express
Z	*zhídá tèkuài* (直达特快)	direct express (overnight)

INTERNATIONAL TRAINS

Mongolia

Two direct weekly trains leave from Běijīng Train Station to the Mongolian capital of Ulaanbaatar (乌兰巴托; Wūlánbātuō): the Trans-Mongolian Railway train (K3; hard sleeper/soft sleeper/delux ¥1222/1723/1883, 11.22am, 27 hours) goes via Ulaanbaatar en route to Moscow, and leaves every Wednesday. Meanwhile the K23 service has a train which leaves on Tuesdays (¥1222/1723/1883, 11.22am, 27 hours).

In the other direction, the K4 leaves Ulaanbaatar at 7.15am on Tuesday and arrives in Běijīng at 11.40am on Wednesday. The K24 departs from Ulaanbaatar at 7.15am on Thursday and reaches Běijīng the following day at 11.40am.

Russia

The Trans-Siberian Railway runs from Běijīng to Moscow (莫斯科; Mòsīkē) via two routes: the Trans-Mongolian Railway train (K3; hard sleeper/soft sleeper/delux ¥4050/5958/6523, 08.05am) and the Trans-Manchurian Railway train (K19; hard-sleeper/delux ¥3891/6044, 11pm). The K19 leaves Běijīng Train Station every Saturday at 11pm. It arrives in Moscow on Friday at 5.58pm.

The return K20 leaves Moscow at 11.45pm on Saturday and arrives in Běijīng on Friday at 5.46am.

Vietnam

There are two weekly trains from Běijīng to Hanoi (河内; Hénèi). The T5 (M2 in Vietnam) leaves Běijīng West Train Station at 3.57pm on Thursday and Sunday, arriving in Hanoi at 8.10am on Saturday and Wednesday.

In the other direction, the T6 (M1 in Vietnam) leaves Hanoi at 6.30pm on Tuesday and Friday and arrives at Běijīng West at 12.07pm on Friday and Monday. Only soft-sleeper tickets (¥2081) are available.

North Korea

There are four weekly services to Pyongyang (平壤; Píngrǎng; hard sleeper/soft sleeper ¥1017/1476). The K27 and K28 both leave twice a week from Běijīng Train Station, meaning there's a train on Monday, Wednesday, Thursday and Saturday. Each train leaves at 5.27pm and arrives the following day at 7.30pm.

Return trains leave from Pyongyang at 10.10am on Monday, Wednesday, Thursday and Saturday and arrive the following day in Běijīng at 8.31am.

Visas, Tickets & Tours

Visas aren't available at these border crossings. Ensure you arrange your visa beforehand.

You can only buy international tickets through travel agencies in Běijīng, not at train stations. For Mongolia, Russia and North Korea, buy tickets at the helpful office of the state-owned **CITS** (China International Travel Service; Zhōngguó Guójì Lǚxíngshè; Map p286; ☎6512 0507; 9 Jianguomennei Dajie, Běijīng International Hotel, Dōngchéng; ⏰9am-noon & 1.30-5pm Mon-Fri, 9am-noon Sat & Sun) housed round the back of the left-hand side of the lobby of the Běijīng International Hotel (北京国际饭店; Běijīng Guójì Fàndiàn), one block north of Běijīng Train Station. Trans-Siberian/Mongolian/Manchurian tickets can be bought from home, using Intourist Travel (www.intourist.com), which has branches in the UK, the USA, Canada, Finland and Poland.

For Vietnam, buy tickets at the office of **CRTS** (China Railway Travel Service; 中国铁道旅行社; Zhōngguó Tiědào Lǚxíngshè; Map p297; ☎5182 6541; 20 Beifengwo Lu, 北蜂窝路20号; ⏰9am-4pm). There's no English sign, but it's opposite the easy-to-spot Tiānyòu Hotel (天佑大夏; Tiānyòu Dàxià). Walk straight out of Exit C1 of Military Museum subway station, take the first right and CRTS will be on your left (10 minutes).

For help with booking a tour to North Korea, Běijīng's leading tour company to the area is **Koryo Tours** (www.koryogroup.com).

charge a hefty commission. If you read Chinese, or know someone who does, you can book online at the official Chinese ticket website www.12306.cn without paying any commission.

BULLET TRAIN TO TIĀNJĪN
You can book tickets in advance for the C-class 'bullet train' from Běijīng South to Tiānjīn, but trains are so frequent that you rarely have to wait more than half an hour for a train (except at public holidays) anyway.

Bus

There are numerous long-distance bus stations, but no international bus routes to Běijīng.

Bāwángfén Long-Distance Bus Station

Bāwángfén Long-Distance Bus Station (八王坟长途客运站; Bāwángfén Chángtú Kèyùnzhàn; 17 Xidawang Lu) is in the east of town, 500m south of Dawanglu subway station. Destinations include the following:

Bāotóu (包头) ¥130 to ¥150, 12 hours, 6pm

Chángchūn (长春) ¥221, 12 hours, 9am, noon, 6pm and 9pm

Dàlián (大连) ¥211 to ¥276, 8½ hours, 11am, noon, 2pm and 10pm

Hā'ěrbīn (哈尔滨) ¥301, 14 hours, 6pm

Shěnyáng (沈阳) ¥165, nine hours, regular 8am to 10pm

Tiānjīn (天津) ¥40, two hours, 10am and 5pm

Sìhuì Long-Distance Bus Station

Sìhuì Long-Distance Bus Station (四惠长途汽车站; Sìhuì Chángtú Qìchēzhàn; Jianguo Lu) is in the east of town, 200m east of Sihui subway station. Destinations include the following:

Bāotóu (包头) ¥130 to ¥150, 12 hours, 10.30am, 1.30pm and 2.30pm

Chéngdé (承德) ¥56 to ¥74, four hours, regular 5.10am to 5.30pm

Dāndōng (丹东) ¥180, 12 hours, 4pm

Jìxiàn (蓟县) ¥19 to ¥24, two hours, regular 5.10am to 7.30pm

Liùlǐqiáo Long-Distance Bus Station

Liùlǐqiáo Long-Distance Bus Station (六里桥长途站; Liùlǐqiáo Chángtúzhàn) is in the southwest of town, one subway stop from Běijīng West Train Station. Destinations include the following:

Dàtóng (大同) ¥100 to ¥132, 4½ hours, regular 7.10am to 6pm

Héféi (合肥) ¥299, 13 hours, 1.45pm

Luòyáng (洛阳) ¥129 to ¥149, 10 hours, six daily 8.30am to 10pm

Shíjiāzhuāng (石家庄) ¥75 to ¥90, 3½ hours, regular 6.30am to 8.55pm

Xiàmén (厦门) ¥479 to ¥519, 30 hours, 11am and 11.30am

Xī'ān (西安) ¥259, 12 hours, 5.45pm

Zhèngzhōu (郑州) ¥129 to ¥149, 8½ hours, nine daily 8.30am to 8.30pm

Liánhuāchí Long-Distance Bus Station

Liánhuāchí Long-Distance Bus Station (莲花池长途汽车站; Liánhuāchí Chángtú Qìchēzhàn) is a short walk north of Liùlǐqiáo Long-distance Bus Station. Destinations include the following:

Ānyáng (安阳) ¥84 to ¥100, 6½ hours, five daily 8am to 5.30pm

Luòyáng (洛阳) ¥130, 11 hours, 6.30pm

Yán'ān (延安) ¥256, 14 hours, 3pm

Zhàogōngkǒu Long-Distance Bus Station

Zhàogōngkǒu Long-Distance Bus Station (赵公口汽车站; Zhàogōngkǒu Qìchēzhàn) is in the south, 10 minutes walk west of Liujiayao subway station. Destinations include the following:

Jǐnán (济南) ¥114, 5½ hours, regular 6.30am to 7.30pm

Shànghǎi (上海) ¥340, 16 hours, two daily (4.30pm and 5pm)

Ferry

Tiānjīn International Cruise Home Port

The nearest major port is **Tiānjīn International Cruise Home Port** (天津国际游轮母港; *Tiānjīn Guójì Yóulún Mǔgǎng*). Express trains leave from **Běijīng South Train Station** (北京南站; Běijīng Nánzhàn) to Tiānjīn every half hour (¥55, 30 minutes). From there, take subway Line 9 to Citizen Plaza Station (市民广场; *Shìmín Guǎngchǎng*; ¥11, one hour), then take Bus 513 to the last stop (东疆游轮母港; *Dōngjiāng Yóulún Mǔgǎng*; ¥2, 40 minutes, 7am to 5pm). There's a ferry every other evening to Dàlián (大连; ¥260-880, 12 hours, 8pm) in Liáoníng province. It leaves on even numbers in the month (the return comes back on odd numbers). Boarding starts at 6pm and tickets can be bought on the day of travel. Currently, there are no services to Japan or South Korea from here, although that may change in the future.

GETTING AROUND BĚIJĪNG

Bicycle

Cycling is the most enjoyable way to get round Běijīng. The city is flat and almost every road has a bike lane, even if cars invade them. The quiet, tree-lined *hútòng* (alleys) are particularly conducive to cycling.

Bike Rental

The following are good options for renting bicycles (租自行车; *zū zìxíngchē*):

Bike Beijing (康多自行车租赁; Kāngduō Zìxíngchē Zūlìn; Map p286; ☎6526 5857; www.bikebeijing.com; 34 Donghuangchenggen Nanjie, 东皇城根南街34号; ⏱9am-6pm; Ⓢ China Museum of Art)

Natooke (耍(自行车店), Shuǎ (Zìxíngchē Diàn); Map p290; www.natooke.com; 19-1 Wudaoying Hutong, 五道营胡同19－1号; ⏱10am-7pm; Ⓢ Yonghegong-Lama Temple)

Giant (捷安特; Jié'āntè; Map p290; 77 Jiaodaokou Dongdajie, 交道口东大街77号; ⏱9am-7pm; Ⓢ Beixinqiao)

Bike stands around the Hòuhái Lakes also rent bikes (per hour ¥10). Hostels typically charge ¥20 to ¥30 per day for a standard town bike.

Buying a Bike

Giant (捷安特; Jié'āntè; Map p290; 77 Jiaodaokou Dongdajie, 交道口东大街77号; ⏱9am-7pm; Ⓢ Beixinqiao) For new bikes and equipment.

JH 2nd-hand Bike Shop (金典新桥信托商行; Jīndiǎn Xīnqiáo Xìntuō Shàngháng; Map p290; 43 Dongsi Beidajie, 东四北大街43号; ⏱9am-5pm; Ⓢ Beixinqiao) For classic old bone-rattlers.

Bike-Sharing Scheme

Běijīng has a bike-sharing scheme, although for now it remains restricted to Chinese nationals. There are plans to open it to foreigners at a later date, so check once you arrive. To use the bikes, you must have an ordinary Běijīng travel card (refundable deposit ¥20) that is activated for bike-rental use.

To do that, head to either Exit A2 of Tiantan Dongmen subway station or Exit A of Dongzhimen subway station. Both desks are only open Monday to Friday from 9.30am to 11.30am and from 2pm to 4pm.

You need to pay a ¥400 deposit to activate the card for bike use, and then ensure it has at least ¥30 on it.

Bike-sharing kiosks are dotted around the city. Swipe your card at one of them to get a bike; then swipe it again when you put it back. Bike use is free for the first hour, so if you use them cleverly, swapping bikes at another kiosk before your hour is up, it means free bikes! After the first hour, it's ¥1 per hour to begin with, before it starts rising in price to ¥2, ¥3 or ¥4 per hour, depending on how long you keep the bike for.

Subway

Massive, and getting bigger every year, the **Běijīng subway system** (地铁; Dìtiě; www.bjsubway.com; per trip ¥2; ⏱6am-11pm) is modern, safe and easy to use. At the time of writing, it appeared likely that fares would rise from the current ¥2 flat fare to distance-based pricing at the end of 2014. Get hold of a travel card (refundable deposit ¥20) if you don't fancy queuing for tickets each time you travel. If fares do go up, the card will get you a discount as it does already on all bus journeys within the municipality of Běijīng.

> **LEFT LUGGAGE**
>
> Left-luggage counters (行李寄存; *xíngli jìcún)* and lockers can be found at all the main Běijīng train stations. Prices are ¥5 to ¥10 per bag per day. They tend to be open from around 6am to 11pm.

Subway stations (地铁站; *dì tiě zhàn*) are signed with the subway symbol, a blue English capital 'D' in a circle.

You'll find a detailed pull-out subway map at the back of this book.

Taxi

Taxis (出租车; *chūzūchē*) are everywhere, although finding one can be a problem during rush hour, rainstorms and between 8pm and 10pm – prime time for people heading home after eating out.

Flag fall is ¥13, and lasts for 3km. After that it's ¥2 per kilometre. Drivers also add a ¥1 fuel surcharge. Rates increase slightly at night.

Drivers rarely speak any English so it's important to have the name and address of where you want to go written down in Chinese characters. Remember to keep your hotel's business card on you so you can get home at the end of the night.

Most Běijīng taxi drivers are honest and use the meter (打表; *dǎ biǎo*). If they refuse, get out and find another cab. The exception is for long, out-of-town trips to, say, the Great Wall, where prices are agreed (but not paid for!) beforehand.

Taxi Drivers & Companies

Miles Meng (☎137 1786 1403; www.beijingtourvan.blog.sohu.com) Reliable, English-speaking driver with a variety of decent-quality vehicles. Day-long trips to the Great Wall start at ¥650 per vehicle (for the Mùtiányù Great Wall area), and he is happy to drop you at one part of the Wall and pick you up at another to allow you to hike from A to B. See his blog for full list of prices.

Mr Sun (孙先生, Sūn Xiānsheng; ☎136 5109 3753) Only speaks Chinese but is very reliable and can find other drivers if he's busy. Does round trips to the Great Wall from ¥600.

Shǒuqì Jítuán (☎139 1137 3093) Local taxi company. Does round trips to the Great Wall for around ¥700. No English spoken.

Bus

Běijīng's buses (公共汽车; *gōnggòng qìchē*) have always been numerous and dirt cheap (from ¥1), but they're now easier to use for non-Chinese-speakers, with swipe cards, announcements in English, and bus-stop signs written in Pīnyīn as well as Chinese characters. Nevertheless, it's still a challenge to get from A to B successfully, and the buses are still as packed as ever, so you rarely see foreigners climbing aboard. At the time of writing, Běijīng's government had indicated that fares would rise in the near future.

If you use a travel card, you get 60% discount on all journeys. Useful routes:

1 Runs along Chang'an Jie, Jianguomenwai Dajie and Jianguomennei Dajie: Sihuizhan, Bawangfen, Yong'anli, Dongdan, Xidan, Muxidi, Junshi Bowuguan, Gongzhufen, Maguanying

4 Runs along Chang'an Jie, Jianguomenwai Dajie and Jianguomennei Dajie: Gongzhufen, Junshi Bowuguan, Muxidi, Xidan, Tian'anmen West, Dongdan, Yong'anli, Bawangfen, Sihuizhan

5 Deshengmen, Di'anmen, Beihai Park, Xihuamen, Zhongshan Park, Qianmen

15 Běijīng Zoo, Fuxingmen, Xidan, Hepingmen, Liulichang, Tianqiao

20 Běijīng South Train Station, Tianqiao, Dashilar, Tiān'ānmén Sq, Wangfujing, Dongdan, Běijīng Train Station

44 outer ring Xinjiekou, Xizhimen, Fuchengmen, Fuxingmen, Changchunjie, Xuanwumen, Qianmen, Taijichang, Chongwenmen, Dongbianmen, Chaoyangmen, Dongzhimen, Andingmen, Deshengmen, Xinjiekou

52 Běijīng West Train Station, Muxidi, Fuxingmen, Xidan, Gate of Heavenly Peace, Dongdan, Běijīng Train Station, Jianguomen

103 Běijīng Train Station, Dengshikou, China Art Gallery, Forbidden City (north entrance), Beihai Park, Fuchengmen, Běijīng Zoo

332 Běijīng Zoo, Weigongcun, Renmin Daxue, Zhongguancun, Haidian, Běijīng University, Summer Palace

These double-decker routes may also be useful:

2 Qianmen, north on Dongdan Beidajie, Dongsi Nandajie, Dongsi Beidajie, Lama Temple, Zhonghua Minzu Yuan (Ethnic Minorities Park), Asian Games Village

3 Jijia Miao (the southwest extremity of the 3rd Ring Rd), Grand View Garden, Leyou Hotel, Jingguang New World Hotel, Tuanjiehu Park, Agricultural Exhibition Center, Lufthansa Center

4 Běijīng Zoo, Exhibition Center, 2nd Ring Rd, Holiday Inn Downtown, Yuetan Park, Fuxingmen Dajie flyover, Qianmen Xidajie, Qianmen

Rickshaw

Rickshaws (三轮车; *sānlúnchē*) are less common these days, but you will still see them (both the cycle-powered ones and the motorised ones), especially around major tourist sights. Generally speaking they're more expensive than taxis, and foreign tourists are often heavily overcharged, so we don't advise using them.

Hútòng Tours

Rickshaw tours (one hour per person ¥100) can be taken around the Hòuhǎi Lakes and around the alleys by the Drum Tower, although they are aimed mostly at tour groups, and riders don't speak English.

Directory A–Z

Customs Regulations

Chinese customs generally pay tourists little attention. There are clearly marked 'green channels' (nothing to declare) and 'red channels' (something to declare) at the airport.

Duty Free Allowed to import 400 cigarettes or the equivalent in tobacco products and 1.5L of alcohol. Fresh fruit and meat prohibited. No restrictions on foreign currency, but declare any cash exceeding US$5000 (or equivalent).

DVDs Pirated DVDs and CDs are illegal exports from China and illegal imports into most other countries. If they are found, they will be confiscated.

Antiques Objects considered antiques require a certificate and red seal to clear customs. To get clearance, antiques must be inspected by the **Relics Bureau** (Wénwù Jiàndìng; ☎6401 4608; no English spoken). Anything made before 1949 is considered an antique; if made before 1795 it cannot legally be taken out of the country.

Discount Cards

Student Cards International Student Identity Card (ISIC; www.isiccard.com) may get half-price entry to some sights. Chinese signs at most sights clearly indicate that students pay half price – so push the point. If studying in China, your school will issue you with

PRACTICALITIES

➡ **DVDs** China is still a big market of pirated foreign movies and TV shows, as well as homegrown ones. You will see them for sale all over Běijīng. Bear in mind that some countries, especially the USA and Australia, take a dim view of people importing counterfeit DVDs. They will confiscate them and can impose large fines.

➡ **Newspapers & magazines** China's print media is state-run and subject to rigid controls. There are two main English-language newspapers, *China Daily* and *Global Times*. *China Daily* is a broadsheet, the *Global Times* a tabloid. Neither are exciting reads. Běijīng has a number of listings magazines in English – *Time Out Beijing*, *The Beijinger* and *City Weekend* – which are useful for finding out the latest bar, club and restaurant hotspots.

➡ **Smoking** While the dark days of people lighting up in hospitals are mostly a distant memory, China has an estimated 400 million smokers and many bars and restaurants still allow it.

➡ **TV & radio** China has a dedicated English-language channel – CCTV News – as well as the English-language China Radio International. Both follow the Chinese Communist Part (CCP) line and are an uncontroversial mix of news, current affairs shows and documentaries.

➡ **Weights & measures** China uses an approximation of the metric system for weights and measurements. The most common unit of weight travellers will encounter is the *jīn* (斤). One *jīn* is roughly half a kilo.

a student card, which is more useful for discounts.

Seniors People over 65 are frequently eligible for a discount; take passport as proof of age.

Free Sights Tickets must be purchased for most sights in Běijīng, although more and more museums are now free (need to show passport).

Museum Pass The annual **Běijīng Museum Pass** (¥120) gets you into over 100 museums.

Travel Card Free travel card (¥20 deposit) available at any subway or large bus station. It makes subway travel more convenient (and may make it cheaper if subway fares rise as expected) and gives 60% off all bus rides, including those out to the Great Wall.

Electricity

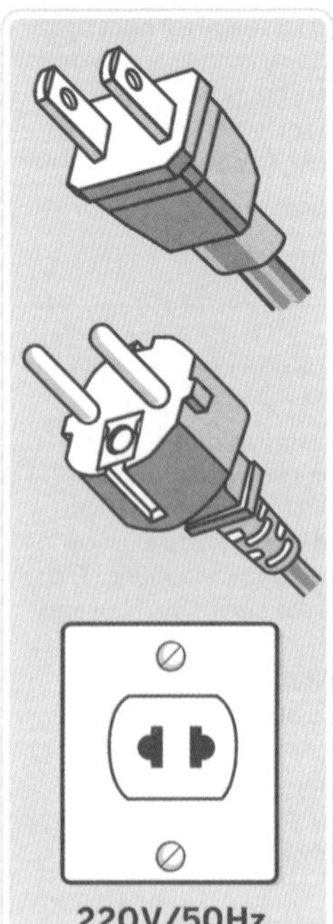

Embassies & Consulates

Embassies (大使馆; *dàshǐguǎn*) in Běijīng are open from 9am to noon and from 1.30pm to 4pm Monday to Friday, but visa departments, which are often in separate office blocks (check the embassy website), are sometimes only open in the morning. There are three main embassy areas: Jiànguóménwài, Sānlǐtún and Liàngmǎqiáo.

Embassies may turn down visa applications from foreigners who do not live in China. It's always best to arrange visas in your home country.

Jiànguóménwài Area

Irish Embassy (爱尔兰大使馆; Ài'ěrlán Dàshǐguǎn; Map p298; ☎8531 6200; www.embassyofireland.cn; 3 Ritan Donglu, 日坛东路3号)

Mongolian Embassy (蒙古大使馆; Ménggǔ Dàshǐguǎn; Map p298; ☎010-6532 1203; 2 Xiushui Beijie) There is a separate visa section (Map p298; ☎6532 6512; ⏲Mon-Fri 9am-11am). Other offices are in Hohhot (蒙古领事馆; Měnggǔ Lǐngshìguǎn; 5 Dongying Nanjie, 东影南街5号; ⏲9am-noon Mon, Tue & Thu) and Erenhot (☎151-6497-1992; Youyi Lu; ⏲9am-noon & 3-5pm Mon-Fri).

New Zealand Embassy (新西兰大使馆; Xīnxīlán Dàshǐguǎn; Map p298; ☎8531 2700; www.nzembassy.com/china; 3 Sanlitun Dongsanjie, 三里屯东三街3号)

Singapore Embassy (新加坡大使馆; Xīnjiāpō Dàshǐguǎn; Map p298; ☎6532 1115; www.mfa.gov.sg/beijing; 1 Xiushui Beijie, 建国门外大街秀水北街1号) Near Jianguomenwai Dajie.

Thai Embassy (泰国大使馆; Tàiguó Dàshǐguǎn; Map p298; ☎6532 1749; www.thaiembassy.org; 40 Guanghua Lu, 光华路40号)

UK Embassy (联合王国大使馆; Liánhé Wángguó Dàshǐguǎn; Map p298) Consular Section (英国大使馆; Map p298; ☎8529 6600; 21st fl, Kerry Center, 1 Guanghua Lu, 光华路1号家里中心21层)

Vietnamese Embassy (越南大使馆; Yuènán Dàshǐguǎn; Map p298; ☎010-6532 1155; http://vnemba.org.cn; 32 Guanghua Lu, 光华路32号) Other offices in Hong Kong (☎852-2591 4510; vnconsul@netvigator.com; 15th fl, Great Smart Tower, 230 Wan Chai Rd, Wan Chai) and Kūnmíng (☎0871-352 2669; 507, Hongta Mansion, 155 Beijing Lu).

Sānlǐtún Area

Australian Embassy (澳大利亚大使馆; Àodàlìyǎ Dàshǐguǎn; Map p298; ☎5140 4111; www.china.embassy.gov.au; 21 Dongzhimenwai Dajie, 东直门外大街21号)

Cambodian Embassy (柬埔寨大使馆; Jiǎnpǔzhài Dàshǐguǎn; Map p298; ☎6532

1889; 9 Dongzhimenwai Dajie, 东直门外大街9号)

Canadian Embassy (加拿大大使馆; Jiānádà Dàshǐguǎn; Map p298; 5139 4000; www.beijing.gc.ca; 19 Dongzhimenwai Dajie, 东直门外大街19号)

German Embassy (Map p298; 8532 9000; www.china.diplo.de) Hong Kong (852-2105 8777; 21st fl, United Centre, 95 Queensway, Admiralty) Other offices in Shànghǎi (德国领事馆; Déguó Lǐngshìguǎn; 021-3401 0106; www.shanghai.diplo.de; 181 Yongfu Rd; 永福路181号), Chéngdū (028-8528 0800; 25th fl, Western Tower, 19 Renmin Nanlu 4th Section) and Guǎngzhōu (020-8313 0000; 14th fl, Main Tower, Yuèhǎi Tiānhé Bldg, 208 Tianhe Lu).

Italian Embassy (意大利大使馆; Yìdàlì Dàshǐguǎn; Map p298; 8532 7600; www.ambpechino.esteri.it; 2 Sanlitun Dong'erjie, 三里屯东二街)

Laotian Embassy (老挝大使馆; Lǎowō Dàshǐguǎn; Map p298; 010-6532 1224; 11 Sanlitun Dongsijie, 三里屯东二街11号) Other offices in Hong Kong (852-2544 1186; 14th fl, Arion Commercial Centre, 2-12 Queen's Rd West, Sheung Wan), Kūnmíng (0871-316 8916; Ground fl, Kūnmíng Diplomat Compound, 6800 Caiyun Beilu) and Jǐnghóng (老挝领事馆; Lǎowō Lǐngshìguǎn ; 221 9355; 2/F, Bldg 2, Gaozhuang Xishuangjing, Xuanwei Dadao; 宣慰大道，告庄西双景综合楼2楼; 8.30-11.30am & 2.30-4.30pm Mon-Fri).

Nepalese Embassy (尼泊尔大使馆; Níbó'ěr Dàshǐguǎn; Map p298; 010-6532 1795; www.nepalembassy.org.cn; 1 Sanlitun Xiliujie, 三里屯西六街1号) Other offices in Hong Kong (852-2369 7813; www.nepalconsulatehk.org; 715 China Aerospace Tower, Concordia Plaza, 1 Science Museum Rd, Tsim Sha Tsui), Shànghǎi (021-6272 0259; 16a, 669 West Beijing Rd) and Lhasa (0891-681 3965; 13 Norbulingka Beilu; 10am-noon Mon-Fri).

Netherlands Embassy (荷兰大使馆; Hélán Dàshǐguǎn; Map p298; 8532 0200; www.hollandinchina.org; 4 Liangmahe Nanlu, 亮马河南路4号)

South African Embassy (南非洲大使馆; Nán Fēizhōu Dàshǐguǎn; Map p298; 6532 0171; www.saembassy.org.cn; 5 Dongzhimenwai Dajie, 东直门外大街5号)

Liàngmǎqiáo Area

Indian Embassy (印度大使馆; Yìndù Dàshǐguǎn; Map p298; 010-8531 2500; www.indianembassy.org.cn; 5 Liangmaqiao Beijie, 亮马桥北街5号) Other offices in Hong Kong (852-3970 9900; www.cgihk.gov.in; Unit A, 16th fl, United Centre, 95 Queensway, Admiralty) and Shànghǎi (021-6275 8881; 1008 Shànghǎi International Trade Centre, 2201 West Yan'an Rd).

Japan (日本大使馆, Rìběn Dàshǐguǎn; 8531 9800; www.cn.emb-japan.go.jp; 1 Liangmaqiaodong Jie, 亮马桥东街1号) Other offices in Hong Kong (852-2522 1184; www.hk.emb-japan.go.jp; 46-47th fl, One Exchange Sq, 8 Connaught Pl, Central), Shànghǎi (日本领事馆; Rìběn Lǐngshìguǎn; 021-5257 4766; www.shanghai.cn.emb-japan.go.jp; 8 Wanshan Rd; 万山路8号; 9am-12.30pm & 1.30-5.30pm Mon-Fri) and Qīngdǎo (0532-8090 0001; 59 Xianggang Donglu).

South Korean Embassy (南韩大使馆, Nánhán Dàshǐguǎn; Map p298; 010-8531 0700; 20 Dongfang Donglu, 东方东路20号) Other offices in Shěnyáng (024-2385 3388; 37 Nanshisan Weilu) and Qīngdǎo (0532-8897 6001; 101 Xianggang Donglu).

US Embassy (美国大使馆, Měiguó Dàshǐguǎn; Consular 8531 3300, Embassy 8531 3000; http://beijing.usembassy-china.org.cn; 55 Anjialou Lu, 亮马桥安家楼路55号, off Liangmaqiao Lu)

Other Areas

Russian Embassy (俄罗斯大使馆, Èluósī Dàshǐguǎn; Map p290; 6532 1381; www.russia.org.cn; 4 Dongzhimen Beizhongjie, 东直门内大街东直门北中街4号, off Dongzhimennei Dajie)

Emergency

Ambulance (120)

Fire (119)

Police (110)

Public Security Bureau (foreigners' section 8402 0101)

Gay & Lesbian Travellers

Although the Chinese authorities take a dim view of homosexuality, which was officially classified as a mental disorder until 2001, a low-profile gay and lesbian scene exists in Běijīng. Check out the following:

Spartacus International Gay Guide (Bruno Gmunder Verlag) Best-selling guide for gay travellers.

Utopia (www.utopia-asia.com/tipschin.htm)

Health

Apart from the thick layer of air pollution that sometimes blankets the city, Běijīng is a reasonably healthy place and you needn't fear tropical diseases such as malaria.

HEALTH ADVISORIES

It's a good idea to consult your government's travel-health website before departure.

- **Australia** (www.dfat.gov.au/travel)
- **Canada** (www.travelhealth.gc.ca)
- **New Zealand** (www.mfat.govt.nz/travel)
- **UK** (www.fco.gov.uk/en/travel-and-living-abroad)
- **US** (www.cdc.gov/travel)

Your greatest health and safety issue is likely to be crossing the road. Bear in mind that if you do require immediate treatment, taking a taxi to hospital will often be quicker than waiting for an ambulance.

It's worth taking your own medicine kit. It is also advisable to take your own prescription drugs with you, because they could be more expensive or hard to find in the capital. Antibiotics *(kàngjūnsù)* and sleeping pills *(ānmiányào)* are no longer prescription-free in Běijīng. If you require a specific type of drug, ensure you take an adequate supply. When looking for medications in Běijīng, take along the brand and the generic name so that pharmacy staff can locate it for you.

Vaccinations

Proof of vaccination for Yellow Fever is required if entering China within six days of visiting an infected country. If you are travelling to China from Africa or South America, check with a travel medicine clinic about whether you need the vaccine.

The following vaccinations are recommended for those travelling to China:

- **Adult diphtheria/tetanus (ADT)** A booster is recommended if it is more than 10 years since your last shot. Side effects include a sore arm and fever.
- **Hepatitis A** One shot provides almost 100% protection for up to a year; a booster after 12 months provides another 20 years' protection. Mild side effects include a sore arm, fever and headaches.
- **Hepatitis B** Now considered a routine vaccination for most travellers. Given as three shots over six months, this vaccine can be combined with Hepatitis A (Twinrix). In most people the course gives lifetime protection. Mild side effects include a sore arm and headaches.
- **Measles/mumps/rubella (MMR)** Two lifetime doses of MMR are recommended unless you have had the diseases. Many adults under the age of 35 require a booster. Occasionally a rash and flu-like illness occur about a week after vaccination.
- **Typhoid** Needed if spending more than two weeks in China. A single injection provides around 70% protection for two to three years.
- **Varicella (chickenpox)** If you haven't had chickenpox, discuss this vaccine with your doctor. Chickenpox can be a serious disease in adults and has such complications as pneumonia and encephalitis.

Under certain circumstances, or for those at special risk, the following vaccinations are recommended. Discuss these with a doctor who specialises in travel medicine.

- **Influenza** If you are over 50 years of age or have a chronic medical condition such as diabetes, lung disease or heart disease, you should have an influenza shot annually.
- **Japanese encephalitis** There is risk only in the rural areas of China. Recommended if travelling to rural areas for more than a month during summer.
- **Pneumonia (Pneumococcal)** This vaccine is recommended for travellers over 65 or those with chronic lung or heart disease. A single shot is given, with a booster in five years.
- **Rabies** Recommended if spending more than three months in China. Three injections given over a one-month period are required.

If you are pregnant or breastfeeding, consult a doctor who specialises in travel medicine before having any vaccines.

Diseases

BIRD FLU

'Bird flu' or Influenza A (H5N1) is a subtype of the type A influenza virus. This virus typically infects birds and not humans; however, in 1997 the first documented case of bird-to-human transmission was recorded in Hong Kong. The virus has been eliminated from most of the 63 countries infected at its peak in 2006, which saw 4000 outbreaks across the globe, but it remains endemic in China. Other variants of the virus, like H7N9, have emerged in China too.

Very close contact with dead or sick birds is the principal source of infection and bird-to-human transmission does not easily occur.

Symptoms include high fever and typical influenza-like symptoms with rapid deterioration, leading to respiratory failure and often death. It is not recommended for travellers to carry antiviral drugs such as Tamiflu; rather, immediate medical care should be sought if bird flu is suspected.

There is currently no vaccine available to prevent bird flu. For up-to-date information, check the World Health Organization website www.who.int/en.

HEPATITIS A
This virus is transmitted through contaminated food and water, and infects the liver, causing jaundice (yellow skin and eyes), nausea and extreme tiredness. There is no specific treatment available; you just need to allow time for the liver to heal, which might take many weeks.

HEPATITIS B
This disease is common in China and is transmitted via infected body fluids, including through sexual contact. The long-term consequences can include liver cancer and cirrhosis.

HIV & SEXUALLY TRANSMITTED INFECTIONS
The Chinese government takes HIV seriously, and overall HIV prevalence is low in the country. However, among certain high-risk groups – gay men, sex workers, intravenous drug users – prevalence of HIV and other sexually transmitted infections is comparatively high, reaching 20% among some groups in some areas. Consistently using condoms during any sexual encounter is an effective way to protect yourself from becoming infected and never, ever share needles.

If you have engaged in any risky behaviour while travelling, including unprotected sex or injecting drugs, you should get a check-up immediately. You can do this at most major Chinese hospitals or at any Centre for Disease Control (疾控中心; Jíkòng Zhōngxīn). There's one in every district of the city, including this one just off Nanluogu Xiang: **Dōngchéng Disease Prevention & Control Centre** (东城疾控中心; Dōngchéng Jíkòng Zhōngxīn; Map p290; ☎6404 0807; 5 Beibingmasi Huton, 东城区交道口南大街北兵马司胡同5号, off Nanluogu Xiang).

For up-to-date information on HIV in China, visit the website of UNAIDS China (www.unaids.org.cn).

INFLUENZA
Flu is common in Běijīng in winter. This virus gives you high fevers, body aches and general symptoms, such as a cough, runny nose and sore throat. Antibiotics won't help unless you develop a complication, such as pneumonia. Anyone travelling in winter could think about vaccination, but it is particularly recommended for the elderly or those with underlying medical conditions.

TRAVELLER'S DIARRHOEA
This is the most common problem faced by travellers in Asia. Most traveller's diarrhoea is caused by bacteria and thus responds rapidly to a short course of appropriate antibiotics. How soon you treat your diarrhoea will depend on individual circumstances, but it is a good idea to carry treatment in your medical kit.

TUBERCULOSIS (TB)
This is a rare disease in travellers that's contracted after prolonged close exposure to a person with an active TB infection. Symptoms include a cough, weight loss, night sweats and fevers. Children under the age of five spending more than six months in China should receive BCG (Bacillus Calmette-Guérin) vaccination. Adults are rarely immunised.

TYPHOID
This serious bacterial infection is contracted from contaminated food and water. Symptoms include high fever, headache, a cough and lethargy. The diagnosis is made via blood tests, and treatment is with specific antibiotics.

Environmental Hazards

AIR POLLUTION
Běijīng is one of the most polluted cities in the world. Although the government improved the situation prior to the 2008 Olympics and kept certain measures in place after the games (eg restricting car use), those with chronic respiratory conditions should ensure they have adequate personal medication with them in case symptoms worsen.

WATER
Don't drink the tap water or eat ice. Bottled water (but check the seal is not broken on the cap), soft drinks, alcohol and drinks made from boiled water (tea, coffee) are fine.

Internet Access

Hotels Almost all hotels provide wi-fi or broadband internet access (or both), although some charge a daily rate. Youth hostels have free wi-fi as well as computer terminals, but levy a small internet charge (around ¥10 per hour) to use them.

Internet cafes (网吧; *wǎngbā*) Generally easy to find, although may be tucked away down side streets. Generally open 24 hours. Standard rates are ¥3 to ¥5 per hour, but can be different priced zones within each internet cafe – the common area *(pǔtōng qū)* is the cheapest. Smoking is standard in internet cafes. Many internet cafes do not allow the use of a USB stick.

Internet cafes are required to see your passport before allowing you to go online, and a record of your visit may be made. You will be filmed or digitally photographed at reception by a rectangular metal box that sits on the counter of each licensed internet cafe in town. Usually you will then be given a card with a number (*zhèngjiànhào*) and password (*mìmǎ* or *kǒulìng*) to enter into the on-screen box before you can start.

Wi-fi cafes Most Western-style bars and cafes offer free wi-fi. Be prepared for occasionally slow connections and the sudden disappearance of sites for periods of time.

Censorship Some politically sensitive websites and some of the most popular social media websites, such as Twitter, Facebook and YouTube, are blocked in China. To access such websites here you will need to run your laptop or smartphone through a VPN (virtual private network).

Legal Matters

Drugs China's drug laws are harsh; foreign nationals have been executed for drug offences (trafficking in more than 50g of heroin can result in the death penalty).

Judicial system The Chinese criminal justice system does not ensure a fair trial, and defendants are not presumed innocent until proven guilty. China conducts more judicial executions than the rest of the world combined; up to 10,000 per year (270 per day) according to some sources, although estimates vary and the actual figure is hard to determine. If arrested, most foreign citizens have the right to contact their embassy.

Medical Services

Clinics

A consultation with a doctor in a private clinic will cost ¥500 and up, depending on where you go. It will cost ¥10 to ¥50 in a state hospital.

Bayley & Jackson Medical Center (庇利积臣医疗中心; Bìlì Jīchén Yīliáo Zhōngxīn; Map p298; ☎8562 9998; www.bjhealthcare.com; 7 Ritan Donglu, Cháoyáng; ⏰dental 9am-4pm Mon-Fri, medical 8.30am-6pm Mon-Sat) Full range of medical and dental services; attractively located in a courtyard next to Ritan Park. Dental check up ¥456; medical consultation ¥500.

Běijīng Union Hospital (协和医院; Xiéhé Yīyuàn; Map p286; ☎6915 6699, emergency 6915 9180; 53 Dongdan Beidajie, Dōngchéng; ⏰24hr) A recommended hospital, open 24 hours and with a full range of facilities for inpatient and outpatient care, plus a pharmacy. Head for International Medical Services (国际医疗部, Guójì Yīliáo Bù; ☎6915 6699), a wing reserved for foreigners which has English-speaking staff and telephone receptionists.

Běijīng United Family Hospital (和睦家医疗; Hémùjiā Yīliáo; ☎4008 919191, 24hr emergency hotline 5927 7120; www.unitedfamilyhospitals.com; 2 Jiangtai Lu, Cháoyáng; ⏰24hr) Can provide alternative medical treatments, along with a comprehensive range of inpatient and outpatient care. Has a critical care unit. Emergency room staffed by expat physicians.

Hong Kong International Medical Clinic (北京香港国际医务诊所, Běijīng Xiānggǎng Guójì Yīwù Zhěnsuǒ; Map p298; ☎6553 2288; www.hkclinic.com/en; 9th fl, Office Tower, Hong Kong Macau Center, Swissôtel, 2 Chaoyangmen Beidajie, Cháoyáng; ⏰9am-9pm, dental 9am-7pm) Well-trusted dental and medical clinic with English-speaking staff. Includes obstetric and gynaecological services and facilities for ultrasonic scanning. Immunisations can also be performed. Prices are more reasonable than at International SOS. Full medical check-ups start from ¥3000 for men, ¥3500 for women and ¥2200 for children. Dental check-up ¥350; medical consultation ¥690. Has night staff on duty too, so you can call for advice round the clock.

International SOS (国际SOS医务诊所, Guójì SOS Yīwù Zhěnsuǒ; Map p298; ☎24hr alarm centre 6462 9100, clinic appointments 6462 9199, dental appointments 6462 0333; www.internationalsos.com; Suite 105, Wing 1, Kunsha Bldg, 16 Xinyuanli, off Xin Donglu, Cháoyáng; ⏰9am-8pm Mon-Fri, 9am-6pm Sat & Sun) Offering 24-hour emergency medical care, with a high-quality clinic and English-speaking staff. Dental check up ¥930; medical consultation ¥1240.

Pharmacies

Pharmacies (药店; *yàodiàn*) are identified by a green cross. Several sizeable pharmacies on Wangfujing Dajie stock both Chinese medicine (*zhōngyào*) and Western medicine (*xīyào*). As with many large shops in Běijīng, once you have chosen your item you are issued with a receipt that you take to the till counter (*shōuyíntái*) where you pay, then you return to the counter where you chose your medicine to collect your purchase. Note that many pharmacies are effectively open 24 hours and have a small window or slit through which you can pay for and collect medicines through the night.

Běijīng Wángfǔjǐng Pharmaceutical Store (北京王府井医药商店, Běijīng Wángfǔjǐng Yīyào Shāngdiàn; ☎6524 0122; 267 Wangfujing Dajie, Dōngchéng; ⏰8.30am-

9pm) For a large range of Western and Chinese drugs.

Watson's (屈臣氏, Qūchénshì; Map p286; CC17 Oriental Plaza, 1 Dongchang'an Jie, Dōngchéng) Has many branches and is geared towards selling cosmetics, sunscreens, deodorants and the like.

Money

Rénmínbì (RMB), or 'people's money', is issued by the Bank of China. The basic unit of Chinese currency is the *yuán*, usually written in shops and on signs with its Chinese character (元). *Yuán* is also referred to colloquially as *kuài* or *kuàiqián*. There are also smaller denominations of *jiǎo* and *fēn*. Ten *jiǎo* – in spoken Chinese, it's known as *máo* – make up one *yuán*. Ten *fēn* make up one *jiǎo*, but these days *fēn* are rare because they are worth next to nothing.

ATMs

Most ATMs (取款机; *qǔkuǎnjī*) accept foreign credit cards and bank cards connected to Plus, Cirrus, Visa, MasterCard and Amex; a small withdrawal charge will be levied by your bank.

The following banks have extensive ATM networks:

Agricultural Bank of China (ABC) (中国农业银行; Zhōngguó Nóngyè Yínháng)

Bank of China (中国银行; Zhōngguó Yínháng)

China Construction Bank (中国建设银行; Zhōngguó Jiànshè Yínháng)

Industrial and Commercial Bank of China (ICBC) (工商银行; Gōngshāng Yínháng)

ATM screens almost always offer the choice of English or Chinese operation. There are ATMs in the arrivals hall at Běijīng Capital International Airport, and in many large department stores and hotels.

Banks

Bank of China (中国银行, Zhōngguó Yínháng; Map p286; ☎6513 2214; 19 Dong'anmen Dajie, 东城区东安门大街19号, Dōngchéng District) By the Dōnghuámén Night Market, this is one of dozens of branches around Běijīng with money-changing facilities.

HSBC (汇丰银行, Huìfēng Yínháng; Map p286; ☎6526 0668, nationwide 800 820 8878; www.hsbc.com.cn; 1st fl, Block A, COFCO Plaza, 8 Jianguomennei Dajie, Dōngchéng; ⏰9am-5pm Mon-Fri, 10am-6pm Sat) One of 12 branches in the capital.

Changing Money

Foreign currency can be changed at large branches of the main banks, and at the airport, hotel money-changing counters and at several department stores, as long as you have your passport. You can normally change foreign currency into rénmínbì at foreign-exchange outlets and banks at large international airports outside China, but rates may be poor. Hotels usually give the official rate, but some will add a small commission. Some upmarket hotels will change money for their own guests only.

Keep at least a few exchange receipts if you want to change any remaining rénmínbì back into another currency at the end of your trip.

Counterfeit Bills

Counterfeit notes are a problem across China, Běijīng included. Very few shopkeepers will accept a ¥50 or ¥100 note without first running it under an ultraviolet light. If you receive a note that doesn't seem right, hand it straight back.

Credit Cards

Credit is not big in China. In Běijīng, credit cards are relatively straightforward to use, but don't expect to be able to use them everywhere, and always carry enough cash. Where they are accepted, credit cards often deliver a slightly better exchange rate than in banks. Money can also be withdrawn at most ATMs on credit cards such as Visa, MasterCard and Amex. Credit cards can't be used to buy train tickets, but Civil Aviation Administration of China (CAAC; 中国民航; Zhōngguó Mínháng) offices readily accept international Visa cards for buying air tickets.

Money Transfers

Western Union (☎800 820 8668; www.westernunion.com) arranges money transfers that arrive in just 15 minutes. Counters can be found at branches of China Post and the Agricultural Bank of China.

Tipping

Almost no one in Běijīng asks for tips. Many midrange and top-end eateries include their own (often huge) service charge; cheap restaurants do not expect a tip. Taxi drivers do not ask for or expect tips.

Travellers Cheques

Travellers cheques cannot be used everywhere; always ensure you carry enough ready cash. You should have no problem cashing them at top-end tourist hotels, but they are of little use in budget hotels and restaurants. Most hotels will only cash the cheques of their guests. If cashing them at banks, aim for the larger banks such as the Bank of China or ICBC. Some banks won't change travellers cheques at the weekend.

Sticking to the major companies such as Thomas Cook, Amex and Visa is advisable, particularly if you plan to travel outside Běijīng. Keep your exchange receipts so you can change your money back to its original currency when you leave.

Opening Hours

China officially has a five-day working week. Saturday and Sunday are both holidays, but much remains open at weekends.

Banks, offices and government departments Normally open 9am until 5pm or 6pm Monday to Friday (some close for two hours in the middle of the day). Some banks have branches that are open at weekends. **Bank of China** branches are generally open weekdays from 9am to noon and 2pm to 4.30pm. Travel agencies, foreign-exchange counters in tourist hotels and some of the local branches of the Bank of China have similar opening hours, but are generally open on weekends as well, at least in the morning.

Museums & parks Most museums stay open on weekends and close on one weekday (usually Monday). Museums normally stop selling tickets half an hour before they close. Parks are generally open from 6am to around 9pm or later; they often open later and shut earlier in winter.

Shops & restaurants Generally open from 10am to 9pm, seven days a week, while restaurants tend to run from 11am to 11pm, although some shut in the afternoon between 2pm and 5.30pm. Some restaurants open specifically for breakfast (typically from 6am to 8.30am). Some restaurants may close for the week around Chinese New Year.

Internet cafes Usually 24/7.

Bars Běijīng's entertainment sector is working increasingly long hours, and it's possible to find something to eat and somewhere to drink at any hour of the day. Some bars close one day of the week.

Post

Large post offices are generally open daily between 9am and 6pm. Letters can be posted via your hotel reception desk, or at green post boxes around town.

Letters and parcels marked 'Poste Restante, Běijīng Main Post Office' will arrive at the **International Post Office** (国际邮电局, Guójì Yóudiàn Jú; Map p298; ☎6512 8114; Jianguomen Beidajie, Cháoyáng; ⏲8.30am-6pm), 200m north of Jianguomen Station. Outsized parcels going overseas should be sent from here (packaging can be bought at the post office); smaller parcels (up to around 20kg) can go from smaller post offices. Both outgoing and incoming packages will be opened and inspected. If you're sending a parcel, don't seal the package until you've had it inspected.

Letters take around a week to reach most overseas destinations. China charges extra for registered mail, but offers cheaper postal rates for printed matter, small packets, parcels, bulk mailings and so on.

Express Mail Service (EMS; 快递; Kuàidì) is available for registered deliveries to domestic and international destinations from most post offices around town.

Courier Companies

For international express posting of documents and parcels, with reliable pick-up services and drop-off centres:

DHL (敦豪快递, Dūnháo Kuàidì; ☎800 810 8000, 5790 5288; www.cn.dhl.com; Unit C18, 9 Jiuxianqiao Beilu, Cháoyáng, 朝阳区酒仙桥北路9号) This branch, beside Běijīng's 798 Art District is one of five, all on the outskirts of town.

FedEx (Federal Express, 联邦快递, Liánbāng Kuàidì; ☎6438 5560, toll-free landline 800 988 1888, toll-free mobile phones 400 886 1888; www.fedex.com/cn; Room 101, Tower C, Lonsdale Center, 5 Wanhong Lu, Cháoyáng, 朝阳区万红路5号蓝涛中心C座101; ⏲9am-9pm Mon-Sat) FedEx also has self-service counters in Kodak Express shops around town.

United Parcel Service (UPS快递, UPS Kuàidì; Map p298; ☎6505 5005, 800 820 8388; www.ups.com; Room 1822, China World Tower 1,1 Jianguomenwai Dajie, Cháoyáng, 朝阳区建国门外大街1号国际贸易中心1座1822室; ⏲9am-6pm Mon-Fri) One of four branches in Běijīng.

Public Holidays

China has 11 national holidays:

New Year's Day 1 January

Chinese New Year January or February

International Women's Day 8 March

Tomb Sweeping Festival 5 April

International Labour Day 1 May

Youth Day 4 May

International Children's Day 1 June

Birthday of the Chinese Communist Party 1 July

Anniversary of the Founding of the People's Liberation Army 1 August

Moon Festival end of September

National Day 1 October

The 1 May holiday is a three-day holiday, while National Day marks a week-long holiday from 1 October; the Chinese New Year is also a week-long holiday for many. It's not a great idea to arrive in China or go travelling during these holidays as the country tends to grind to a halt. Hotel prices rapidly shoot up during the May and October holiday periods.

Relocating

The following international companies can help you move house in Běijīng. Rates are typically around US$500 to US$1000 per cubic metre:

Asian Express (亚洲捷运(国际货运代理, Yàzhōu Jiéyùn; Map p298; ☎8580 1471; www.aemovers.com.hk; Room 1612, Tower D, SOHO New Town, 88 Jianguo Lu, Cháoyáng)

Crown Worldwide (Crown 国际货运代理, Crown Guójì Huòyùndàilǐ; ☎5801 8088; www.crownworldwide.com; 16 Xingmao Yijie, Tōngzhōu Logistics Park, Tōngzhōu District, 通州区马驹桥兴贸一街16号) Located in southeast Běijīng.

Safe Travel

Generally speaking, Běijīng is a very safe city compared to other similarly sized cities around the world. Serious crime against foreigners is rare, although on the rise.

Crime Guard against pickpockets, especially on public transport and in crowded places such as train stations. A money belt is the safest way to carry valuables, particularly when travelling on buses and trains. Hotels are usually secure places to leave your stuff and older establishments may have an attendant watching who goes in and out on each floor. Staying in dormitories carries its own set of risks, and while there have been a few reports of thefts by staff, the culprits are more likely to be other guests. Use lockers as much as possible.

Loss Reports If something is stolen, report it immediately to the nearest Foreign Affairs Branch of the Public Security Bureau (PSB). You will be asked to fill in a loss report before investigating the case. If you have travel insurance it is essential to obtain a loss report to claim compensation. Be prepared to spend many hours, perhaps even several days, organising it. Make a copy of your passport in case of loss or theft.

Road Safety The greatest hazard may well be crossing the road, a manoeuvre that requires alertness and dexterity. Traffic often comes from all directions (bikes, in particular, frequently ride the wrong way down streets), and a seeming reluctance to give way holds sway. If right of way is uncertain, drivers tend to dig in their heels. Ignore zebra crossings; cars are not obliged to stop at them, and never do. And take care at traffic light crossings: the green 'cross now' light doesn't necessarily mean that traffic won't run you down, as cars can still turn on red lights and bicycles, electric bikes and motor bikes rarely stop at red lights.

Scams

Teahouses Be wary of anyone luring you to cafes, teahouses or art galleries on Wangfujing Dajie, Tiān'ānmén Sq and other popular tourist areas. Foreigners have been scammed by English-speaking people who invite them to vastly overpriced tea ceremonies or art shows.

Taxis At Capital Airport never take a taxi from touts inside the arrivals halls, where a well-established illegal taxi operation attempts to lure tired travellers into a ¥300-plus ride to the city (one man acts as a taxi pimp for a squad of drivers).

Departure Tax Beware of fraudsters trying to sell you departure tax (now included in the price of your ticket) at Capital Airport.

Rickshaws Whenever taking a ride in a rickshaw, ask the driver to write the amount down on a piece of paper first (have a pen and paper ready), so there is no ambiguity about how much the trip will cost, otherwise you could be ripped off. And be clear as to which currency you are negotiating in.

Taxes

Four- and five-star hotels add a service charge of 15%, and smarter restaurants levy a service charge of 10%.

Telephone

Local calls from hotel-room phones are usually free, while international calls are expensive. If making a domestic phone call, public phones at newspaper stands (报刊亭; *bàokāntíng*) and hole-in-the-wall shops (小卖部; *xiǎomàibù*) are useful; make your call and pay the owner (a local call is around 5 *jiǎo*). Most public phones take IC (Integrated Circuit; *IC kǎ*) cards.

To make domestic long-distance or international calls, it's cheapest to use an IP (Internet Phone; *IP kǎ*) card. These calls can also be made from main telecommunications offices or 'phone bars' *(huàbā)*.

The country code to use to access China is ☎86; the code for Hong Kong is ☎852 and Macau is ☎853. To call a number in Běijīng from abroad, dial the international access code, dial the country code (☎86) and then the area code for Běijīng (☎010), dropping the first zero, and then dial the local number. For telephone calls within the same city, drop the area code *(qūhào)*.

Important city area codes within China include the following:

CITY	AREA CODE
Běijīng	010
Chéngdū	028
Chóngqìng	023
Guǎngzhōu	020
Hángzhōu	0571
Hāěrbì	0451
Hong Kong	852
Jǐnán	0531
Kūnmíng	0871
Nánjīng	025
Qīngdǎo	0532
Shànghǎi	021
Shíjiāzhuāng	0311
Tiānjīn	022
Xiàmén	0592

Mobile Phones

Mobile phone shops (手机店; *shǒujīdiàn*) such as China Mobile and China Unicom sell SIM cards, which cost from ¥30 to ¥100 and include ¥50 of credit. Note that numbers containing 4s are avoided by the Chinese, making them cheaper. You can top up credit with ¥20 to ¥100 credit-charging cards (充值卡; *chōngzhí kǎ*). Cards are available from newspaper kiosks and corner shops displaying the China Mobile sign.

The mobile phone you use in your home country should work (if it's unlocked) or you can buy a pay-as-you-go phone locally (from ¥300). China Mobile's local, nonroaming city call charge is 7 *jiǎo* per minute if calling a landline and 1.50 *jiǎo* per minute if calling another mobile phone. Receiving calls on your mobile is free from mobile phones and 7 *jiǎo* from landline phones. Roaming charges cost an additional 2 *jiǎo* per minute and the call receiving charge is the same. Overseas calls can be made for ¥4.80 per minute plus the local charge per minute by dialling ☎17951 – then follow the instructions and add 00 before the country code. Otherwise you will be charged the International Dialling Code call charge plus 7 *jiǎo* per minute.

Mobile phones are particularly useful for communicating messages to non-English speakers. You can phone restaurants and other venues from a taxi and hand the phone to the driver, so he knows where to go, or phone a Chinese-speaking friend and ask them to communicate your message.

Phonecards

For domestic calls, IC cards, available from kiosks, hole-in-the-wall shops, internet cafes and China Telecom offices, are prepaid cards in a variety of denominations that can be used in most public telephones. Note that some IC cards can only be used locally, while other cards can be used in phones throughout China, so check this when you purchase your card.

For international calls on a mobile phone or hotel phone and for long-distance domestic calls buy an IP card. International calls on IP cards are ¥1.80 per minute to the USA or Canada, ¥1.50 per minute to Hong Kong, Macau and Taiwan, and ¥3.20 to all other countries; domestic long-distance calls are ¥0.30 per minute. Follow the instructions on the reverse; English-language service is usually available. IP cards come in various denominations, typically with a big discount (a ¥100 card should cost around ¥40). IP cards can be found at the same places as IC cards. Again, some IP cards can only be used locally, while others can be used nationwide, so it is important to buy the right card (and check the expiry date).

Time

All of China runs on the same time as Běijīng, which is set eight hours ahead of GMT/UTC (no daylight saving during summer). When it's noon in Běijīng it's 4am the same day in London; 5am in Frankfurt, Paris and Rome; noon in Hong Kong; 2pm in Melbourne; 4pm in Wellington; and, on the previous day, 8pm in Los Angeles and 11pm in Montreal and New York.

Toilets

Over the last decade the capital has made its toilets less of an assault course of foul smells and primitive appliances, but many remain pungent. Make a beeline for fast-food outlets, top-end hotels and department stores for more hygienic alternatives. Toilet paper is rarely provided in streetside public toilets so keep a stash with you. Toilets are often squat versions, although most public toilets will have one sit-down toilet for disabled users (and inflexible Westerners). As a general rule, if you see a wastebasket next to the toilet, that's where you should throw the toilet paper.

The symbol for men is 男 (*nán*) and women is 女 (*nǚ*).

Tourist Information

Staff at the chain of **Běijīng Tourist Information Centers** (北京旅游咨询, Běijīng Lǚyóu Zīxún Fúwù Zhōngxīn; ⏲9am-5pm) generally have limited English-language skills and are not always helpful, but you can grab a free tourist map of town, nab handfuls of free literature and, at some branches, rustle up train tickets. Useful branches include the following:

Běijīng Train Station (Map p286; ☎6528 4848; 16 Laoqianju Hutong)

Capital Airport (☎6459 8148; Terminal 3, Capital Airport)

Hòuhǎi Lakes (Map p294; 49 Di'anmenxi Dajie, 地安门西大街49号, Hòuhǎi Lakes) Has an excellent, very detailed free map of all the *hùtòng* alleys surrounding the lakes of Hòuhǎi. Can also arrange rickshaw tours of the *hùtòng* with English-speaking riders.

Wángfǔjǐng (Map p286; 269 Wangfujing Dajie, 王府井大街269号, Wángfǔjǐng; ⏲9am-9pm) On the main shopping strip.

The **Běijīng Tourism Hotline** (☎6513 0828, press 1 for English; ⏲24hr) has English-speaking operators available to answer questions and hear complaints. **CITS** (China International Travel Service; Map p286; ☎8511 8522; www.cits.com.cn; Room 1212, CITS Bldg, 1 Dongdan Beidajie, Dōngchéng; ⏲9am-7pm) is more useful for booking tours, China-wide.

Hotels can offer you advice or connect you with a suitable tour, and some have useful tourist information desks that can point you in the right direction.

The best travel advice for independent travellers is usually dished out at youth hostels, although be aware that they will sometimes try to get you to sign up to one of their tours rather than give you impartial advice. Tours run by youth hostels are generally pretty good, though.

Travellers with Disabilities

If you are wheelchair bound or have a mobility disability, Běijīng can be a major obstacle course. Pavements are often crowded and in a dangerous condition, with high curbs often preventing wheelchair access. Many streets can be crossed only via underground or overhead walkways with steps. You will also have to stick to the main roads, as parked cars and bicycles often occupy the pavements of smaller alleys and lanes, forcing others on to the road. Escalators in subways normally only go up, but wheelchair lifts have been installed in numerous stations (although you may have to send someone down to find a member of staff to operate them). Getting around temples and big sights such as the Forbidden City and the Summer Palace can be trying for those in wheelchairs. It is recommended that you take a lightweight chair so you can collapse it easily when necessary, such as to load it into the back of a taxi. Most, but not all, hotels will have lifts, and while many top-end hotels do have rooms for those with disabilities as well as good wheelchair access, hotel restaurants may not.

Those with sight, hearing or mobility disabilities must be extremely cautious of the traffic, which almost never yields to pedestrians.

Visas

Applying for Visas

Citizens of 51 countries, including Australia, France, Germany, the UK and the USA, are allowed to stay for up to 72 hours in Běijīng without a visa. Citizens of every country except Japan, SIngapore and Brunei, require a visa for longer stays. Note that visas do not allow you to travel in areas of China, such as Tibet, that require special permits to visit.

Your passport must be valid for at least six months after the expiry date of your visa and you'll need at least one entire blank page in your passport for the visa. You may be required to show proof of hotel reservations and onward travel from China, as well as a bank statement showing you have $100 in your account for every day you plan to spend in China.

At the time of writing, prices for a single-entry 30-day visa were as follows:

- £30 for UK citizens
- US$140 for US citizens
- US$30 for citizens of other nations

Double-entry visas:

- £45 for UK citizens
- US$140 for US citizens
- US$45 for all other nationals

Six-month multiple-entry visas:

- £90 for UK citizens
- US$140 for US citizens
- US$60 for all other nationals

A standard 30-day single-entry visa can be issued from most Chinese embassies abroad in three to five working days. Express visas cost twice the usual fee. In some countries (eg the UK and the US) the visa service has been outsourced from the Chinese embassy to a Chinese Visa Application Service Centre, which levies an extra administration fee. In the case of the UK, a single-entry visa costs £30, but the standard administration charge levied by the centre is a further £36.

A standard 30-day visa is activated on the date you enter China, and must be used within three months of the date of issue. 60-day and 90-day tourist visas are reasonably easy to obtain in your home country but difficult elsewhere. To stay longer, you can extend your visa in China at least once, sometimes twice.

Visa applications require a completed application form (available at the embassy or downloaded from its website) and at least one photo (normally 51mm x 51mm). You normally pay for your visa when you collect it. A visa mailed to you will take up to three weeks. In the US and Canada, mailed visa applications have to go via a visa agent, at extra cost. In the US, many people use the **China Visa Service Center** (in the USA 800 799 6560; www.mychinavisa.com), which offers prompt service. The procedure takes around 10 to 14 days.

Hong Kong is a good place to pick up a China visa. However, at the time of writing only Hong Kong residents were able to obtain them direct from the **Visa Office of the People's Republic of China** (3413 2424; www.fmcoprc.gov.hk; 26 Harbour Rd, 7th fl, Lower Block, China Resources Centre, Wan Chai; 9am-noon & 2-5pm Mon-Fri). Single-entry visas processed here cost HK$200, double-entry visas HK$300, while six-month/one-year multiple-entry visas are HK$500. But China Travel Service (CTS) and many travel agencies in Hong Kong can get you a visa in two to three working days. Expect to pay HK$650 for a single-entry visa and HK$750 for a double-entry. Both American and UK passport holders must pay considerably more for their visas.

Be aware that political events can suddenly make visas more difficult to procure or renew.

When asked about your itinerary on the application form, list standard tourist destinations; if you are considering going to Tibet or western Xīnjiāng, just leave it off the form. The list you give is not binding. Those working in the media or journalism should profess a different occupation; otherwise, a visa may be refused or a shorter length of stay may be given. There are many different categories of visa. The eight most common are listed here (most travellers will enter China on an 'L' visa).

TYPE	ENGLISH NAME	CHINESE NAME
C	flight attendant	*chéngwù* 乘务
D	resident	*dìngjū* 定居
F	business, student or person on exchange program	*fǎngwèn* 访问
G	transit	*guòjìng* 过境
J	journalist	*jìzhě* 记者
L	travel	*lǚxíng* 旅行
X	long-term student	*liúxué* 留学
Z	working	*gōngzuò* 工作

Visa Extensions

The Foreign Affairs Branch of the local PSB – the police force – handles visa extensions. The visa office at the **PSB main office** (Map p290) is on the 2nd floor, accessed from the North 2nd Ring Rd. You can also apply for a residence permit here.

First-time extensions of 30 days are usually easy to obtain on single-entry tourist visas; further extensions are harder to get, and may only give you another week. Travellers report generous extensions in provincial towns, but don't bank on this. Popping south to Hong Kong to apply for a new tourist visa is another option.

Extensions to single-entry visas vary in price, depending on your nationality. At the time of writing, US travellers paid ¥185, Canadians ¥165, UK citizens ¥160 and Australians ¥100. Expect to wait up to five days for your visa extension to be processed.

The penalty for overstaying your visa in China is up to ¥500 per day. Some travellers have reported having trouble with officials who read the 'valid until' date on their visa incorrectly. For a one-month travel (L) visa, the 'valid until' date is the date by which you must enter the country (within three months of the date the visa was issued), not the date upon which your visa expires.

Residence Permits

Residence permits are available – normally issued for a period of one year at a time as a sticker in your passport – to people resident in China for work, who are married to Chinese citizens (although that doesn't guarantee you will be allowed to work while in China) and long-term students. Requirements are stringent; you will need to be sponsored by a Chinese company or university, or a foreign company with an office in China, and undergo a health check. Long-term residency permits, valid for five years and known as 'green cards', are available but are issued under even more stringent conditions.

Passports

Chinese law requires foreign visitors to carry their passport with them at all times; all hotels (and internet cafes) will insist on seeing it. You also need it to buy train tickets or to get into some tourist sights, particularly those which are free.

It's a good idea to bring an ID card with your photo in case you lose your passport. Even better, make copies or photos of your passport – your embassy may need these before issuing a new one. Report any loss to the local Public Security Bureau (PSB). Be careful who you pass your passport to, as you may never see it again.

Women Travellers

Women travellers generally feel safe in Běijīng. Chinese men are not macho and respect for women is deeply ingrained in Chinese culture.

As with anywhere else, you will be taking a risk if you travel alone. If you are concerned, a self-defence course can equip you with extra physical skills and boost your confidence before your trip. A whistle or small alarm can be a useful defence against an unpleasant encounter. For further tips, consult www.journeywoman.com.

Tampons *(wèishēng miántiáo)* can be found almost everywhere. It may be advisable to take supplies of the pill *(bìyùnyào)*, although you will find brands like Marvelon at local pharmacies.

Work

Over the past decade it has become easier for foreigners to find work in Běijīng, although having Chinese-language skills is now increasingly important.

Teaching jobs that pay by the hour are usually quite lucrative. If you have recognised ELT qualifications, such as TEFL, and/or experience, teaching can be a rewarding and profitable way to earn a living in Běijīng. International schools offer salaries in the region of ¥6000 to ¥10,000 per month to qualified teachers, with accommodation often provided. More basic (and plentiful) teaching positions will offer upwards of around ¥100 per hour. Schools regularly advertise in expat magazines, such as *The Beijinger;* you can visit its classified pages online at www.thebeijinger.com. Also hunt for teaching jobs on www.teachabroad.com. You could also try approaching organisations such as the British Council (www.britishcouncil.org), which runs teacher placement programs in Běijīng and beyond.

There are also opportunities in translation, freelance writing, editing, proofreading, the hotel industry, acting, modelling, photography, bar work, and sales and marketing. Most people find jobs in Běijīng through word of mouth; networking is key.

Doing Business

Difficulties for foreigners attempting to do business have eased up, but the China work environment can still be frustrating. Renting properties, getting licences, hiring employees and paying taxes can generate mind-boggling quantities of red tape. Most foreign business people who have worked in China say that success is usually the result of dogged persistence and finding cooperative officials.

If considering doing business in China, talk to other foreigners who are already working here. Alternatively, approach some business consultants for advice, or approach one of the following Běijīng business associations:

American Chamber of Commerce (中国美国商会, Zhōngguó Měiguó Shānghuì; Map p298; ☎8519 0800; www.amcham-china.org.cn; The Office Park, Tower AB, 6th fl, 10 Jintongxi Lu, Cháoyáng, 朝阳区金桐西路10号远洋光华国际AB座6层)

British Chamber of Commerce (中国英国商会, Zhōngguó Yīngguó Shānghuì; Map p298; ☎8525 1111; www.britishchamber.cn; Room 1001, China Life Tower, 16 Chaoyangmenwai Dajie, Cháoyáng, 朝阳门外大街16号中国人寿大夏1001室)

Canada-China Business Council (加中贸易理事会, Jiāzhōng Màoyì Lǐshìhuì; Map p298; ☎8526 1820; www.ccbc.com; Suite 11A16, Tower A, Hanwei Plaza, 7 Guanghua Lu, Cháoyáng, 朝阳区光华路7号汉威大夏A座)

China-Australia Chamber of Commerce (中国澳大利亚商会, Zhōngguó Àodàlìyà Shānghuì; Map p298; ☎6595 9252; www.austcham.org; 910, Tower A, U-Town Office Bldg, 1 Sanfengbeili, Cháoyáng, 朝阳区三丰北里1号 悠唐写字楼A座910室)

China-Britain Business Council (CBBC, 英中贸易协会, Yīngzhōng Màoyì Xiéhuì; Map p298; ☎8525 1111; www.cbbc.org; Room 1001, China Life Tower, 16 Chaoyangmenwai Dajie, Cháoyáng, 朝阳区朝阳门外大街16号, 中国人寿大夏1001室)

European Union Chamber of Commerce in China (中国欧盟商会, Zhōngguó Ōuméng Shànghuì; Map p298; ☎6462 2066; www.europeanchamber.com.cn; Room C-412, Lufthansa Center, 50 Liangmaqiao Lu, Cháoyáng, 朝阳区亮马桥路50号, 燕莎中心写字楼C-412室)

French Chamber of Commerce & Industry (中国法国工商会, Zhōngguó Fǎguó Gōngshānghu; Map p298; ☎6461 0260; www.ccifc.org; Room C-712, 7th fl, Office Bldg Lufthansa Center, 50 Liangmaqiao Lu, Cháoyáng, 朝阳区亮马桥路50号, 燕莎中心写字楼C-712室)

US-China Business Council (美中贸易全国委员会, Měizhōng Màoyì Quánguó Wěiyuánhuì; Map p298; ☎6592 0727; www.uschina.org; CITIC Bldg, Suite 10-01, 19 Jianguomenwai Dajie, Cháoyáng, 朝阳区建国门外大街19号, 国际大夏10-01室)

Business Cards

Business cards are essential in China. Cards are exchanged much in the same way as handshakes are in the West. To be caught without a card in a business setting is like attending an official function in jeans and trainers. Try to get your name translated into (simplified) Chinese and have it printed on the reverse of the card. You can get name cards made cheaply at local printers, but it's better to have some made before you arrive (try your local Chinatown). When proffering and receiving business cards, emulate the Chinese method of respectfully using the thumb and forefinger of both hands.

Volunteering

Many Westerners work in China with international development charities such as the following:

VSO (www.vso.org.uk) Provides you with useful experience and the chance to learn Chinese.

Go Overseas (www.gooverseas.com) Places volunteer teachers in Běijīng and elsewhere in China.

Joy in Action (JIA; www.joyinaction.org) Establishing work camps in places in need in south China.

World Teach (www.worldteach.org) Volunteer teachers.

Language

Discounting its many ethnic minority languages, China has eight major dialect groups: Pǔtōnghuà (Mandarin), Yue (Cantonese), Wu (Shanghainese), Minbei (Fuzhou), Minnan (Hokkien-Taiwanese), Xiang, Gan and Hakka. These dialects also divide into subdialects.

It's the language spoken in Běijīng which is considered the official language of China. It's usually referred to as Mandarin, but the Chinese themselves call it Pǔtōnghuà (meaning 'common speech'). Pǔtōnghuà is variously referred to as Hànyǔ (the Han language), Guóyǔ (the national language) or Zhōngwén or Zhōngguóhuà (Chinese). You'll find that knowing a few basics in Mandarin will not only come in handy in Běijīng, but also in many other parts of the country (although it may be spoken there with a regional accent).

Writing

Chinese is often referred to as a language of pictographs. Many of the basic Chinese characters are highly stylised pictures of what they represent, but around 90% are compounds of a 'meaning' element and a 'sound' element.

A well-educated, contemporary Chinese speaker might use between 6000 and 8000 characters. To read a Chinese newspaper you need to know 2000 to 3000 characters, but 1200 to 1500 would be enough to get the gist.

Theoretically, all Chinese dialects share the same written system. In practice, Cantonese adds about 3000 specialised characters of its own and many of the dialects don't have a written form at all.

Pinyin & Pronunciation

In 1958 the Chinese adopted Pinyin, a system of writing their language using the Roman alphabet. The original idea was to eventually do away with Chinese characters. However, tradition dies hard, and the idea was abandoned.

Pinyin is often used on shop fronts, street signs and advertising billboards. However, in the countryside and the smaller towns you may not see a single Pinyin sign anywhere, so unless you speak Chinese you'll need a phrasebook with Chinese characters.

In this chapter we've provided Pinyin alongside the Mandarin script. Below is a brief guide to the pronunciation of Pinyin letters.

Vowels

a	as in 'father'
ai	as in 'aisle'
ao	as the 'ow' in 'cow'
e	as in 'her' (without 'r' sound)
ei	as in 'weigh'
i	as the 'ee' in 'meet' (or like a light 'r' as in 'Grrr!' after c, ch, r, s, sh, z or zh)
ian	as the word 'yen'
ie	as the English word 'yeah'
o	as in 'or' (without 'r' sound)
ou	as the 'oa' in 'boat'
u	as in 'flute'
ui	as the word 'way'
uo	like a 'w' followed by 'o'
yu/ü	like 'ee' with lips pursed

Consonants

c	as the 'ts' in 'bits'
ch	as in 'chop', with the tongue curled up and back
h	as in 'hay', articulated from further back in the throat
q	as the 'ch' in 'cheese'
sh	as in 'ship', with the tongue curled up and back
x	as the 'sh' in 'ship'
z	as the 'ds' in 'suds'
zh	as the 'j' in 'judge', with the tongue curled up and back

The only consonants that occur at the end of a syllable are n, ng and r.

In Pinyin, apostrophes are occasionally used to separate syllables in order to prevent ambiguity, eg the word píng'ān can be written with an apostrophe after the 'g' to prevent it being pronounced as pín'gān.

Tones

Mandarin is a language with a large number of words with the same pronunciation but a different meaning. What distinguishes these homophones (as these words are called) is their 'tonal' quality – the raising and the lowering of pitch on certain syllables. Mandarin has four tones – high, rising, falling-rising and falling, plus a fifth 'neutral' tone that you can all but ignore. Tones are important for distinguishing meaning of words – eg the word ma has four different meanings according to tone: mā (mother), má (hemp, numb), mǎ (horse), mà (scold, swear). Tones are indicated in Pinyin by the following accent marks on vowels: ā (high), á (rising), ǎ (falling-rising) and à (falling).

Basics

When asking a question it is polite to start with qǐng wèn – literally, 'May I ask?'.

Hello.	你好。	Nǐhǎo.
Goodbye.	再见。	Zàijiàn.
How are you?	你好吗？	Nǐhǎo ma?
Fine. And you?	好。你呢？	Hǎo. Nǐ ne?
Excuse me.		
(to get attention)	劳驾。	Láojià.
(to get past)	借光。	Jièguāng.
Sorry.	对不起。	Duìbùqǐ.
Yes./No.	是。/不是。	Shì./Bùshì.
Please ...	请……	Qǐng ...
Thank you.	谢谢你。	Xièxie nǐ.
You're welcome.	不客气。	Bù kèqi.

What's your name?
你叫什么名字？ Nǐ jiào shénme míngzi?

My name is ...
我叫…… Wǒ jiào ...

Do you speak English?
你会说英文吗？ Nǐ huìshuō Yīngwén ma?

I don't understand.
我不明白。 Wǒ bù míngbái.

Accommodation

Do you have a single/double room?
有没有(单人/套)房？ Yǒuméiyǒu (dānrén/tào) fáng?

KEY PATTERNS

To get by in Mandarin, mix and match these simple patterns with words of your choice:

How much is (the deposit)?
(押金)多少？ (Yājīn) duōshǎo?

Do you have (a room)?
有没有(房)？ Yǒuméiyǒu (fáng)?

Is there (heating)?
有(暖气)吗？ Yóu (nuǎnqì) ma?

I'd like (that one).
我要(那个)。 Wǒ yào (nàge).

Please give me (the menu).
请给我(菜单)。 Qǐng gěiwǒ (càidān).

Can I (sit here)?
我能(坐这儿)吗？ Wǒ néng (zuòzhèr) ma?

I need (a can opener).
我想要(一个开罐器)。 Wǒ xiǎngyào (yīge kāiguàn qì).

Do we need (a guide)?
需要(向导)吗？ Xūyào (xiàngdǎo) ma?

I have (a reservation).
我有(预订)。 Wǒ yǒu (yùdìng).

I'm (a doctor).
我(是医生)。 Wǒ (shì yīshēng).

How much is it per night/person?
每天/人多少钱？ Měi tiān/rén duōshǎo qián?

air-con	空调	kōngtiáo
bathroom	浴室	yùshì
bed	床	chuáng
campsite	露营地	lùyíngdì
cot	张婴儿床	zhāng yīng'ér chuáng
guesthouse	宾馆	bīnguǎn
hostel	招待所	zhāodàisuǒ
hotel	酒店	jiǔdiàn
window	窗	chuāng

Directions

Where's a (bank)?
(银行)在哪儿？ (Yínháng) zài nǎr?

What's the address?
地址在哪儿？ Dìzhǐ zài nǎr?

Could you write the address, please?
能不能请你把地址写下来？ Néngbunéng qǐng nǐ bǎ dìzhǐ xiě xiàlái?

Can you show me where it is on the map?
请帮我找它在地图上的位置。 Qǐng bāngwǒ zhǎo tā zài dìtú shàng de wèizhi.

Go straight ahead.
一直走。 Yīzhí zǒu.

at the traffic lights
在红绿灯 zài hónglǜdēng

behind	背面	bèimiàn
far	远	yuǎn
in front of ...	……的前面	... de qiánmian
near	近	jìn
next to	旁边	pángbiān
on the corner	拐角	guǎijiǎo
opposite	对面	duìmiàn
Turn left.	左转。	Zuǒ zhuǎn.
Turn right.	右转。	Yòu zhuǎn.

Eating & Drinking

What would you recommend?
有什么菜可以推荐的? Yǒu shénme cài kěyǐ tuījiàn de?

What's in that dish?
这道菜用什么东西做的? Zhèdào cài yòng shénme dōngxi zuòde?

That was delicious.
真好吃。 Zhēn hǎochī.

The bill, please!
买单! Mǎidān!

Cheers!
干杯! Gānbēi!

I'd like to reserve a table for ...	我想预订一张……的桌子。	Wǒ xiǎng yùdìng yīzhāng ... de zhuōzi.
(eight) o'clock	（八）点钟	(bā) diǎn zhōng
(two) people	（两个）人	(liǎngge) rén

I don't eat ...	我不吃……	Wǒ bùchī ...
fish	鱼	yú
nuts	果仁	guǒrén
poultry	家禽	jiāqín
red meat	牛羊肉	niúyángròu

Key Words

bar	酒吧	jiǔbā
bottle	瓶子	píngzi
bowl	碗	wǎn
breakfast	早饭	zǎofàn
cafe	咖啡屋	kāfēiwū
chidren's menu	儿童菜单	értóng càidān
(too) cold	(太)凉	(tài) liáng
dinner	晚饭	wǎnfàn
food	食品	shípǐn
fork	叉子	chāzi
glass	杯子	bēizi
highchair	高凳	gāodèng
hot (warm)	热	rè
knife	刀	dāo
local specialties	地方小吃	dìfāng xiǎochī
lunch	午饭	wǔfàn
market	菜市	càishì
menu (in English)	(英文)菜单	(Yīngwén) càidān
plate	碟子	diézi
restaurant	餐馆	cānguǎn
(too) spicy	(太)辣	(tài) là
spoon	勺	sháo
vegetarian food	素食食品	sùshí shípín

Meat & Fish

beef	牛肉	niúròu
chicken	鸡肉	jīròu
duck	鸭	yā
fish	鱼	yú
lamb	羊肉	yángròu
pork	猪肉	zhūròu
seafood	海鲜	hǎixiān

Fruit & Vegetables

apple	苹果	píngguǒ
banana	香蕉	xiāngjiāo
carrot	胡萝卜	húluóbo
celery	芹菜	qíncài
cucumber	黄瓜	huángguā
fruit	水果	shuǐguǒ
grape	葡萄	pútáo
green beans	扁豆	biǎndòu
mango	芒果	mángguǒ
mushroom	蘑菇	mógū

Signs

入口	Rùkǒu	**Entrance**
出口	Chūkǒu	**Exit**
问讯处	Wènxùnchù	**Information**
开	Kāi	**Open**
关	Guān	**Closed**
禁止	Jìnzhǐ	**Prohibited**
厕所	Cèsuǒ	**Toilets**
男	Nán	**Men**
女	Nǚ	**Women**

onion	洋葱	yáng cōng
orange	橙子	chéngzi
pear	梨	lí
pineapple	凤梨	fènglí
plum	梅子	méizi
potato	土豆	tǔdòu
radish	萝卜	luóbo
spring onion	小葱	xiǎo cōng
sweet potato	地瓜	dìguā
vegetable	蔬菜	shūcài
watermelon	西瓜	xīguā

Other

bread	面包	miànbāo
butter	黄油	huángyóu
egg	蛋	dàn
herbs/spices	香料	xiāngliào
pepper	胡椒粉	hújiāo fěn
salt	盐	yán
soy sauce	酱油	jiàngyóu
sugar	砂糖	shātáng
tofu	豆腐	dòufu
vinegar	醋	cù
vegetable oil	菜油	càiyóu

Drinks

beer	啤酒	píjiǔ
coffee	咖啡	kāfēi
(orange) juice	(橙)汁	(chéng) zhī
milk	牛奶	niúnǎi
mineral water	矿泉水	kuàngquán shuǐ
red wine	红葡萄酒	hóng pútáo jiǔ
rice wine	米酒	mǐjiǔ
soft drink	汽水	qìshuǐ
tea	茶	chá
(boiled) water	(开)水	(kāi) shuǐ
white wine	白葡萄酒	bái pútáo jiǔ
yoghurt	酸奶	suānnǎi

Question Words

How?	怎么?	Zěnme?
What?	什么?	Shénme?
When?	什么时候	Shénme shíhòu?
Where?	哪儿	Nǎr?
Which?	哪个	Nǎge?
Who?	谁?	Shuí?
Why?	为什么?	Wèishénme?

Emergencies

Help!	救命!	Jiùmìng!
I'm lost.	我迷路了。	Wǒ mílù le.
Go away!	走开!	Zǒukāi!

Call a doctor!
请叫医生来! Qǐng jiào yīshēng lái!

Call the police!
请叫警察! Qǐng jiào jǐngchá!

I'm ill.
我生病了。 Wǒ shēngbìng le.

It hurts here.
这里痛。 Zhèlǐ tòng.

Where are the toilets?
厕所在哪儿? Cèsuǒ zài nǎr?

Shopping & Services

I'd like to buy ...
我想买…… Wǒ xiǎng mǎi ...

I'm just looking.
我先看看。 Wǒ xiān kànkan.

Can I look at it?
我能看看吗? Wǒ néng kànkan ma?

I don't like it.
我不喜欢。 Wǒ bù xǐhuan.

How much is it?
多少钱? Duōshǎo qián?

That's too expensive.
太贵了。 Tàiguì le.

Can you lower the price?
能便宜一点吗? Néng piányi yīdiǎn ma?

There's a mistake in the bill.
帐单上有问题。 Zhàngdān shàng yǒu wèntí.

ATM	自动取款机	zìdòng qǔkuǎn jī
credit card	信用卡	xìnyòng kǎ
internet cafe	网吧	wǎngbā
post office	邮局	yóujú
tourist office	旅行店	lǚxíng diàn

Time & Dates

What time is it?
现在几点钟? Xiànzài jǐdiǎn zhōng?

It's (10) o'clock.
(十)点钟。 (Shí) diǎn zhōng.

Half past (10).
(十)点三十分。 (Shí) diǎn sānshífēn.

Numbers

1	一	yī
2	二/两	èr/liǎng
3	三	sān
4	四	sì
5	五	wǔ
6	六	liù
7	七	qī
8	八	bā
9	九	jiǔ
10	十	shí
20	二十	èrshí
30	三十	sānshí
40	四十	sìshí
50	五十	wǔshí
60	六十	liùshí
70	七十	qīshí
80	八十	bāshí
90	九十	jiǔshí
100	一百	yībǎi
1000	一千	yīqiān

morning	早上	zǎoshang
afternoon	下午	xiàwǔ
evening	晚上	wǎnshàng
yesterday	昨天	zuótiān
today	今天	jīntiān
tomorrow	明天	míngtiān

Monday	星期一	xīngqī yī
Tuesday	星期二	xīngqī èr
Wednesday	星期三	xīngqī sān
Thursday	星期四	xīngqī sì
Friday	星期五	xīngqī wǔ
Saturday	星期六	xīngqī liù
Sunday	星期天	xīngqī tiān

Transport

boat	船	chuán
bus (city)	大巴	dàbā
bus (intercity)	长途车	chángtú chē
plane	飞机	fēijī
taxi	出租车	chūzū chē
train	火车	huǒchē
tram	电车	diànchē

I want to go to ...
我要去…… Wǒ yào qù ...

Does it stop at ...?
在……能下车吗? Zài ... néng xià chē ma?

At what time does it leave?
几点钟出发? Jǐdiǎnzhōng chūfā?

At what time does it get to ...?
几点钟到……? Jǐdiǎnzhōng dào ...?

I want to get off here.
我想这儿下车。 Wǒ xiǎng zhèr xiàchē.

When's the first/last (bus)?
首趟/末趟(车)几点走? Shǒutàng/Mòtàng (chē) jǐdiǎn zǒu?

A ... ticket to (Dàlián).	一张到(大连)的……票。	Yīzhāng dào (Dàlián) de ... piào.
1st-class	头等	tóuděng
2nd-class	二等	èrděng
one-way	单程	dānchéng
return	双程	shuāngchéng

aisle seat	走廊的座位	zǒuláng de zuòwèi
ticket office	售票处	shòupiàochù
timetable	时刻表	shíkè biǎo
window seat	窗户的座位	chuānghu de zuòwèi

bicycle pump	打气筒	dǎqìtóng
child seat	婴儿座	yīng'érzuò
helmet	头盔	tóukuī
mechanic	机修工	jīxiūgōng
petrol	汽油	qìyóu
service station	加油站	jiāyóu zhàn

I'd like to hire a ...	我要租一辆……	Wǒ yào zū yīliàng ...
4WD	四轮驱动	sìlún qūdòng
bicycle	自行车	zìxíngchē
car	汽车	qìchē
motorcycle	摩托车	mótuochē

Does this road lead to ...?
这条路到……吗? Zhè tiáo lù dào ... ma?

How long can I park here?
这儿可以停多久? Zhèr kěyi tíng duōjiǔ?

The car has broken down.
汽车是坏的。 Qìchē shì huài de.

I have a flat tyre.
轮胎瘪了。 Lúntāi biě le.

GLOSSARY

arhat – Buddhist, especially a monk, who has achieved enlightenment and passes to nirvana at death

běi – north; the other points of the compass are *nán* (south), *dōng* (east) and *xī* (west)

bīnguǎn – tourist hotel

bìxì – mythical tortoise-like dragons often depicted in Confucian temples

bodhisattva – one worthy of nirvana but who remains on earth to help others attain enlightenment

bówùguǎn – museum

bǔpiào – upgrade

cāntīng – restaurant

CCP – Chinese Communist Party, founded in Shànghǎi in 1921

Chángchéng – the Great Wall

chop – see *name chop*

CITS – China International Travel Service; the organisation deals with China's foreign tourists

dàfàndiàn – large hotel

dàjiē – avenue

dàshà – hotel, building

dàxué – university

dìtiě – subway

dōng – east; the other points of the compass are *běi* (north), *nán* (south) and *xī* (west)

dòngwùyuán – zoo

fàndiàn – hotel or restaurant

fēngshuǐ – geomancy, literally 'wind and water', the art of using ancient principles to maximise the flow of *qì*, or vital energy

gé – pavilion, temple (Taoist)

gōng – palace, temple

gōngyuán – park

gùjū – house, home, residence

hé – river

hú – lake

Huí – ethnic Chinese Muslims

hútòng – a narrow alleyway

jiāng – river

jiǎo – see *máo*

jiē – street

jié – festival

jīn – unit of measurement equal to 500g

jiǔdiàn – hotel

kǎoyādiàn – roast duck restaurant

kuài – colloquial term for the currency, *yuán*

Kuomintang – Chiang Kaishek's Nationalist Party, the dominant political force after the fall of the Qing dynasty

líng – tomb

lóu – tower

lù – road

luóhàn – see *arhat*

máo – colloquial term for *jiǎo*, 10 of which equal one *kuài*

mén – gate

miào – temple

name chop – a carved name seal that acts as a signature

nán – south; the other points of the compass are *běi* (north), *dōng* (east) and *xī* (west)

páilou – decorated archway

Pinyin – the official system for transliterating Chinese script into the Roman alphabet

PLA – People's Liberation Army

PRC – People's Republic of China

PSB – Public Security Bureau; the arm of the police force set up to deal with foreigners

qì – flow of vital or universal energy

qì gōng – exercise that channels *qì*

qiáo – bridge

qílín – a hybrid animal that only appeared on earth in times of harmony

rénmín – people, people's

renminbi – literally 'people's money', the formal name for the currency of China; shortened to RMB

shān – hill, mountain

shāngdiàn – shop, store

shìchǎng – market

sì – temple, monastery

sìhéyuàn – courtyard house

tíng – pavilion

wǔshù – martial arts

xī – west; the other points of the compass are *běi* (north), *nán* (south) and *dōng* (east)

yáng – positive, bright and masculine; the complementary principle to *yīn*

yīn – negative, dark and feminine; the complementary principle to *yáng*

yuán – the Chinese unit of currency; also referred to as RMB (see also *renminbi*)

zhōng – middle, centre

Behind the Scenes

SEND US YOUR FEEDBACK

We love to hear from travellers – your comments keep us on our toes and help make our books better. Our well-travelled team reads every word on what you loved or loathed about this book. Although we cannot reply individually to your submissions, we always guarantee that your feedback goes straight to the appropriate authors, in time for the next edition. Each person who sends us information is thanked in the next edition – the most useful submissions are rewarded with a selection of digital PDF chapters.

Visit **lonelyplanet.com/contact** to submit your updates and suggestions or to ask for help. Our award-winning website also features inspirational travel stories, news and discussions.

Note: We may edit, reproduce and incorporate your comments in Lonely Planet products such as guidebooks, websites and digital products, so let us know if you don't want your comments reproduced or your name acknowledged. For a copy of our privacy policy visit lonelyplanet.com/privacy.

OUR READERS

Many thanks to the travellers who used the last edition and wrote to us with helpful hints, useful advice and interesting anecdotes:

Adrienne Belai, Anna Barnett, Chris Egan, Stephane Desreumaux, Eric Rowell, Gary Kirchherr, Giuliana Taylor, Hayden Opie, John Rogers, Lorin Veltkamp, Maikel van Kasteren, Oliver Hawes, Phillip Li, Praveen Jolly, Ricardo Padilha, Richard Leow, Ryan Tandjung, Sonia Smith, Victorino Mijangos, Wilson Chia, Xiangdong Xu

AUTHOR THANKS

Daniel McCrohan

Firstly, a big *xièxie* to Kim, Sue and my auntie Pat for road-testing my research when they came to China. Thanks too to my friends in Běijīng for their hot tips, especially David Goodman-Smith, Darryl Snow, Sydney Bardwell and Zhao Jiewei. A doffed cap to my colleague David Eimer for keeping the other half of this book in such good shape. But of course, my biggest thanks, and all my love, to Taotao and our two amazing children; *wǒ ài nǐmen*.

David Eimer

Thanks to Daniel McCrohan for his diligent input, and to Damian Harper for his fine work on previous editions. Thanks also to Megan Eaves, Dianne Schallmeiner and Julie Sheridan at Lonely Planet for their guidance. Special gratitude goes to Wang Chenxi for her invaluable assistance.

ACKNOWLEDGMENTS

Cover photograph: portrait of Běijīng opera performer in traditional dress and make-up, Martin Puddy/Corbis
Illustration pp56-7 by Michael Weldon.

THIS BOOK

This 10th edition of Lonely Planet's *Beijing* guidebook was researched and written by Daniel McCrohan and David Eimer, who also wrote the 9th edition. The 8th edition was written by David Eimer and Damian Harper. This guidebook was produced by the following:

Destination Editor Megan Eaves
Commissioning Editor Joe Bindloss
Coordinating Editor Andrea Dobbin
Product Editor Bruce Evans
Senior Cartographer Julie Sheridan
Book Designer Virginia Moreno
Assisting Editors Victoria Harrison, Kate Evans
Cartographer Hunor Csutoros
Cover Researcher Naomi Parker
Thanks to Penny Cordner, Helvi Cranfield, Ryan Evans, Larissa Frost, Anna Harris, Diana Von Holdt, Jouve India, Andi Jones, Wayne Murphy, Claire Naylor, Karyn Noble, Averil Robertson, Dianne Schallmeiner, Ellie Simpson, Saralinda Turner, Samantha Tyson, Lauren Wellicome

Index

See also separate subindexes for:
- EATING P278
- DRINKING & NIGHTLIFE P279
- ENTERTAINMENT P279
- SHOPPING P279
- SPORTS & ACTIVITIES 279
- SLEEPING P279

Sights 000
Map Pages **000**
Photo Pages **000**

Sights 000
Map Pages **000**
Photo Pages **000**

EATING

Běijīng Maps

Sights
- Beach
- Bird Sanctuary
- Buddhist
- Castle/Palace
- Christian
- Confucian
- Hindu
- Islamic
- Jain
- Jewish
- Monument
- Museum/Gallery/Historic Building
- Ruin
- Shinto
- Sikh
- Taoist
- Winery/Vineyard
- Zoo/Wildlife Sanctuary
- Other Sight

Activities, Courses & Tours
- Bodysurfing
- Diving
- Canoeing/Kayaking
- Course/Tour
- Sento Hot Baths/Onsen
- Skiing
- Snorkelling
- Surfing
- Swimming/Pool
- Walking
- Windsurfing
- Other Activity

Sleeping
- Sleeping
- Camping

Eating
- Eating

Drinking & Nightlife
- Drinking & Nightlife
- Cafe

Entertainment
- Entertainment

Shopping
- Shopping

Information
- Bank
- Embassy/Consulate
- Hospital/Medical
- Internet
- Police
- Post Office
- Telephone
- Toilet
- Tourist Information
- Other Information

Geographic
- Beach
- Hut/Shelter
- Lighthouse
- Lookout
- Mountain/Volcano
- Oasis
- Park
- Pass
- Picnic Area
- Waterfall

Population
- Capital (National)
- Capital (State/Province)
- City/Large Town
- Town/Village

Transport
- Airport
- Border crossing
- Bus
- Cable car/Funicular
- Cycling
- Ferry
- Metro/MTR/MRT station
- Monorail
- Parking
- Petrol station
- Subway station
- Taxi
- Train station/Railway
- Tram
- Underground station
- Other Transport

Note: Not all symbols displayed above appear on the maps in this book

Routes
- Tollway
- Freeway
- Primary
- Secondary
- Tertiary
- Lane
- Unsealed road
- Road under construction
- Plaza/Mall
- Steps
- Tunnel
- Pedestrian overpass
- Walking Tour
- Walking Tour detour
- Path/Walking Trail

Boundaries
- International
- State/Province
- Disputed
- Regional/Suburb
- Marine Park
- Cliff
- Wall

Hydrography
- River, Creek
- Intermittent River
- Canal
- Water
- Dry/Salt/Intermittent Lake
- Reef

Areas
- Airport/Runway
- Beach/Desert
- Cemetery (Christian)
- Cemetery (Other)
- Glacier
- Mudflat
- Park/Forest
- Sight (Building)
- Sportsground
- Swamp/Mangrove

MAP INDEX

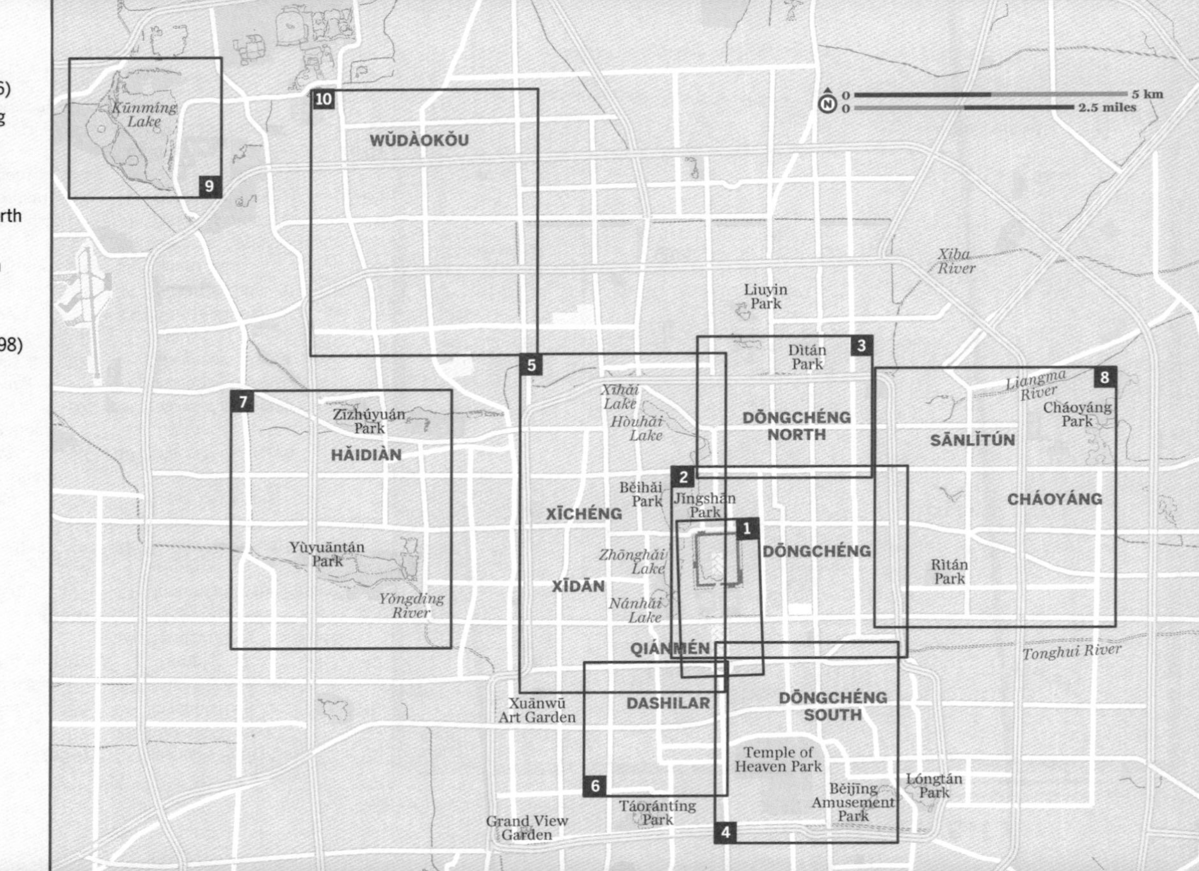

0 5 km
0 2.5 miles
Kūnmíng Lake
WǓDÀOKǑU
HǍIDIÀN
Zǐzhúyuán Park
Yùyuāntán Park
Yǒngdìng River
XĪCHÉNG
XĪDĀN
Xīhǎi Lake
Hòuhǎi Lake
Běihǎi Park
Zhōnghǎi Lake
Nánhǎi Lake
Jǐngshān Park
QIÁNMÉN
DASHILAR
Xuānwǔ Art Garden
Grand View Garden
Táorántíng Park
Liuyin Park
Dìtán Park
DŌNGCHÉNG NORTH
DŌNGCHÉNG
DŌNGCHÉNG SOUTH
Temple of Heaven Park
Běijīng Amusement Park
Lóngtán Park
Xiba River
Liangma River
Cháoyáng Park
SĀNLǏTÚN
CHÁOYÁNG
Rìtán Park
Tonghui River

FORBIDDEN CITY

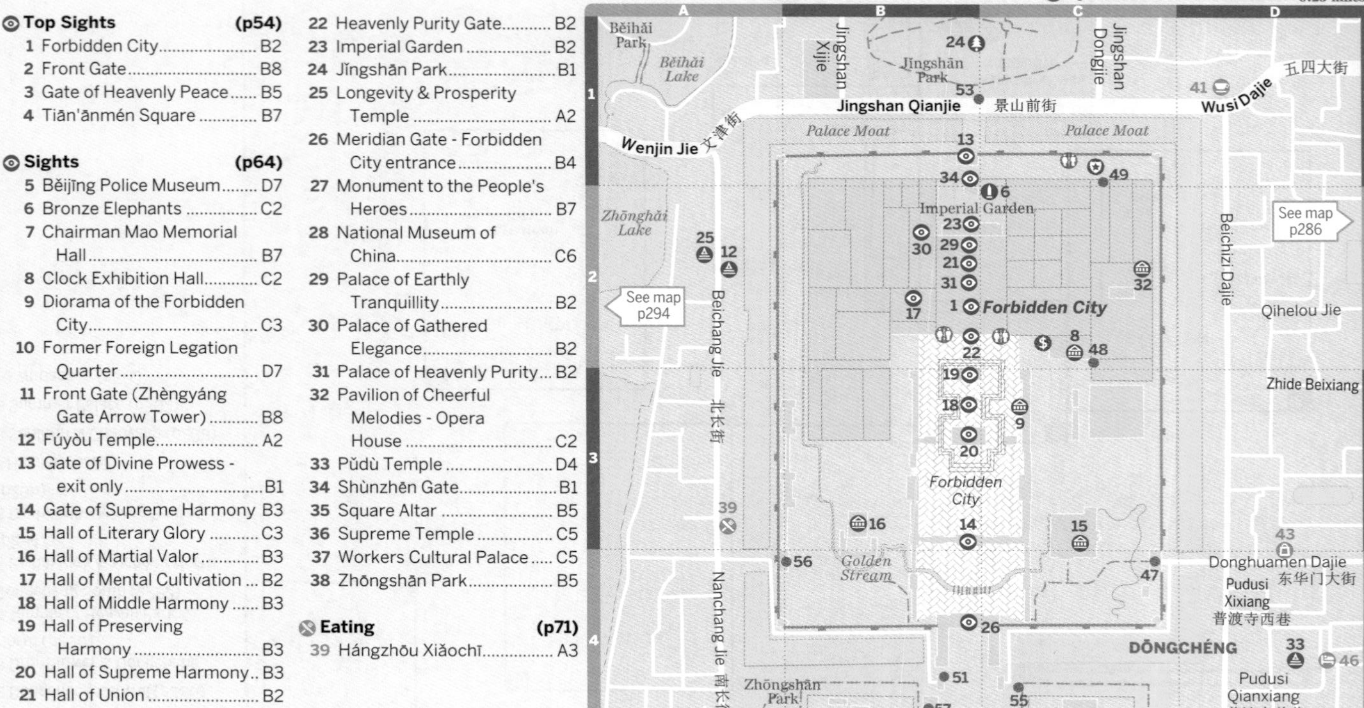

⊙ **Top Sights** **(p54)**

1 Forbidden City B2
2 Front Gate B8
3 Gate of Heavenly Peace B5
4 Tiān'ānmén Square B7

⊙ **Sights** **(p64)**

5 Běijīng Police Museum D7
6 Bronze Elephants C2
7 Chairman Mao Memorial Hall B7
8 Clock Exhibition Hall C2
9 Diorama of the Forbidden City C3
10 Former Foreign Legation Quarter D7
11 Front Gate (Zhèngyáng Gate Arrow Tower) B8
12 Fúyòu Temple A2
13 Gate of Divine Prowess - exit only B1
14 Gate of Supreme Harmony B3
15 Hall of Literary Glory C3
16 Hall of Martial Valor B3
17 Hall of Mental Cultivation B2
18 Hall of Middle Harmony B3
19 Hall of Preserving Harmony B3
20 Hall of Supreme Harmony B3
21 Hall of Union B2
22 Heavenly Purity Gate B2
23 Imperial Garden B2
24 Jǐngshān Park B1
25 Longevity & Prosperity Temple A2
26 Meridian Gate - Forbidden City entrance B4
27 Monument to the People's Heroes B7
28 National Museum of China C6
29 Palace of Earthly Tranquillity B2
30 Palace of Gathered Elegance B2
31 Palace of Heavenly Purity B2
32 Pavilion of Cheerful Melodies - Opera House C2
33 Pǔdù Temple D4
34 Shùnzhēn Gate B1
35 Square Altar B5
36 Supreme Temple C5
37 Workers Cultural Palace C5
38 Zhōngshān Park B5

Eating **(p71)**

39 Hángzhōu Xiǎochī A3

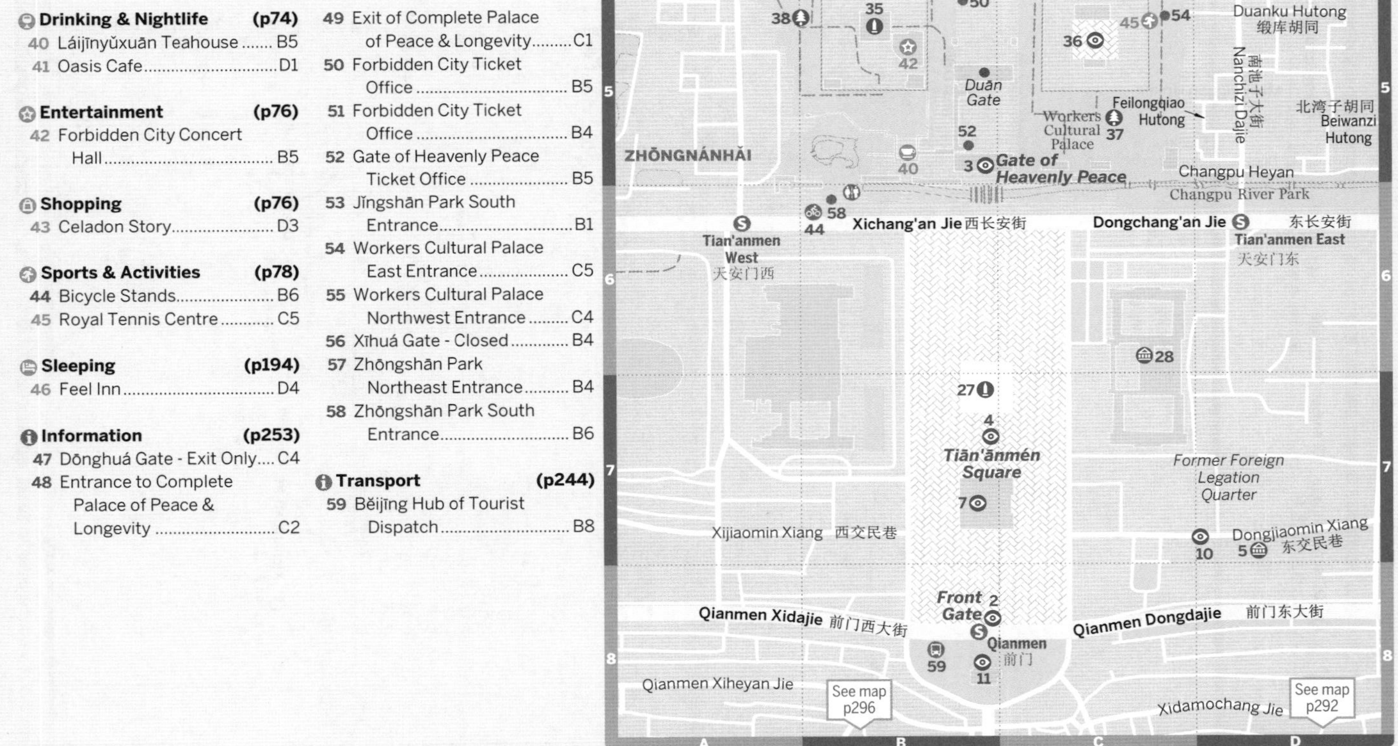

Drinking & Nightlife (p74)
40 Láijīnyǔxuān Teahouse B5
41 Oasis Cafe D1

Entertainment (p76)
42 Forbidden City Concert Hall B5

Shopping (p76)
43 Celadon Story D3

Sports & Activities (p78)
44 Bicycle Stands B6
45 Royal Tennis Centre C5

Sleeping (p194)
46 Feel Inn D4

Information (p253)
47 Dōnghuá Gate - Exit Only C4
48 Entrance to Complete Palace of Peace & Longevity C2
49 Exit of Complete Palace of Peace & Longevity C1
50 Forbidden City Ticket Office B5
51 Forbidden City Ticket Office B4
52 Gate of Heavenly Peace Ticket Office B5
53 Jǐngshān Park South Entrance B1
54 Workers Cultural Palace East Entrance C5
55 Workers Cultural Palace Northwest Entrance C4
56 Xīhuá Gate - Closed B4
57 Zhōngshān Park Northeast Entrance B4
58 Zhōngshān Park South Entrance B6

Transport (p244)
59 Běijīng Hub of Tourist Dispatch B8

Key on p288

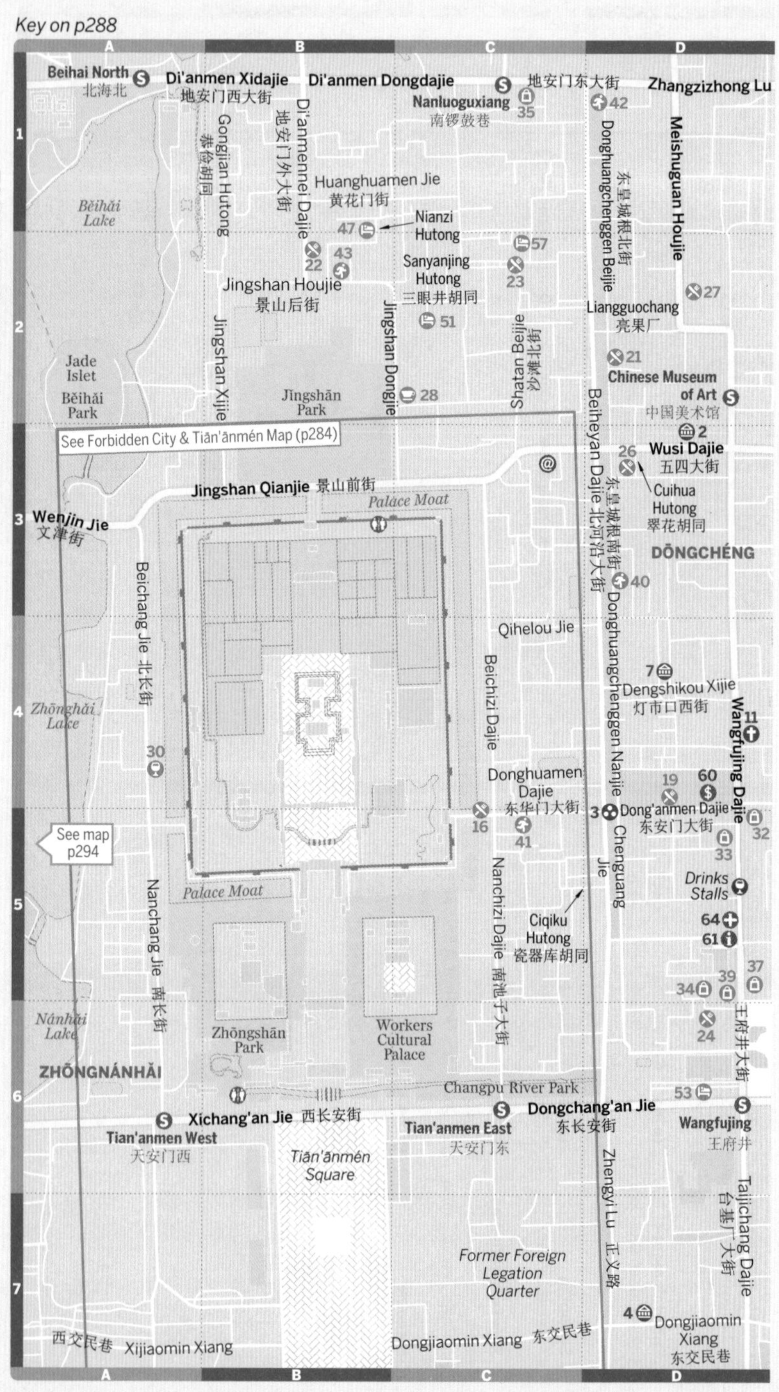

Beihai North 北海北
Di'anmen Xidajie 地安门西大街
Di'anmen Dongdajie
地安门东大街
Zhangzizhong Lu
Nanluoguxiang 南锣鼓巷
Gongjian Hutong 恭俭胡同
Di'anmennei Dajie 地安门外大街
Huanghuamen Jie 黄花门街
Nianzi Hutong
Sanyanjing Hutong 三眼井胡同
Jingshan Houjie 景山后街
Donghuangchenggen Beijie 东皇城根北街
Meishuguan Houjie
Liangguochang 亮果厂
Běihǎi Lake
Jade Islet
Běihǎi Park
Jingshan Xijie
Jingshan Dongjie
Jǐngshān Park
Shatan Beijie 沙滩北街
Chinese Museum of Art 中国美术馆
Wusi Dajie 五四大街
Cuihua Hutong 翠花胡同
See Forbidden City & Tiān'ānmén Map (p284)
Jingshan Qianjie 景山前街
Palace Moat
Wenjin Jie 文津街
Beiheyan Dajie 北河沿大街
东皇城根南街
DŌNGCHÉNG
Donghuangchenggen Nanjie
Qihelou Jie
Beichang Jie 北长街
Beichizi Dajie
Dengshikou Xijie 灯市口西街
Wangfujing Dajie
Zhōnghǎi Lake
Donghuamen Dajie 东华门大街
Dong'anmen Dajie 东安门大街
See map p294
Chenguang Jie
Drinks Stalls
Palace Moat
Nanchang Jie 南长街
Nanchizi Dajie 南池子大街
Ciqiku Hutong 瓷器库胡同
王府井大街
Nánhǎi Lake
Zhōngshān Park
Workers Cultural Palace
ZHŌNGNÁNHǍI
Changpu River Park
Xichang'an Jie 西长安街
Tian'anmen West 天安门西
Tian'anmen East 天安门东
Dongchang'an Jie 东长安街
Wangfujing 王府井
Tiān'ānmén Square
Zhengyi Lu 正义路
Taijichang Dajie 台基厂大街
Former Foreign Legation Quarter
Dongjiaomin Xiang 东交民巷
西交民巷 Xijiaomin Xiang
Dongjiaomin Xiang 东交民巷
A B C D
1 2 3 4 5 6 7
2 3 4 7 11 16 19 21 22 23 24 26 27 28 30 32 33 34 35 37 39 40 41 42 43 47 51 53 57 60 61 64

DŌNGCHÉNG CENTRAL
Zhangzizhonglu
张自忠路
See map p290
Dongsishitiao Lu
Dongsi Shitiao
东四十条
CHÁOYÁNG
Dongsi Batiao
东四八条
Dongsi Beidajie
东四北大街
Dongsi Liutiao 东四六条
See map p298
East 2nd Ring Rd 东二环
Chaoyangmen Beixiaojie
Qianliang Hutong
Dongsi
东四
Dongsi Xidajie
东四西大街
Chaoyangmennei Dajie
Chaoyangmen
朝阳门
Dongsi Nandajie
东四南大街
Baofang Hutong
演乐胡同
Yanyue Hutong
East 2nd Ring Rd 东二环路
Neiwubu Jie
Shijia Hutong
Dafangjia Hutong
Dengshikou Dajie
Lumicang Hutong
禄米仓胡同
Ganmian Hutong
Xitangzi Hutong
西堂子胡同
Jinyu Hutong
金鱼胡同
Dengshikou
灯市口
Jinbao Jie
Yabao Lu
Chaoyangmen Nanxiaojie
Shuaifuyuan Hutong
Dongdan Beidajie
东单北大街
Guanghua Lu
Jianguomen Beidajie
Dongzongbu Hutong
东总部胡同
Dongdan Santiao
东单三条
Oriental Plaza
建国门内大街
Dongdan
东单
Jianguomennei Dajie
建国门内大街
Jianguomen
建国门
建国门北大街
Beijingzhan Jie
Chongwenmennei Dajie
Dōngdān Park
Beijingzhan Dongjie
Beijing Railway Station (Beijing Zhan)
北京站
Běijīng Train Station
北京火车站
Tonghui River
See map p292
0 500 m
0 0.25 miles

DŌNGCHÉNG CENTRAL *Map on p286*

Sights (p64)
1 Ancient Observatory H6
2 China Art Museum D3
3 Dōng'ān Mén Remains D5
4 Former French Post Office D7
5 Galaxy Soho H3
6 Imperial Granaries H1
7 Lao She Museum D4
8 Poly Art Museum H1
9 Shèng Xī Fú Hat Museum E2
10 Shǐjiā Hútòng Museum F4
11 St Joseph's Church D4
12 St Michael's Church E7
13 Ten Fu's Tea Culture House E4
14 Zhìhuà Temple H4

Eating (p71)
15 Běijīng Dàdǒng Roast Duck Restaurant F5
16 Brian McKenna @ The Courtyard C5
17 Chuān Bàn H5
18 Crescent Moon Muslim Restaurant F1
19 Dōnghuámén Night Market D4
20 Dōngzi Lǘròu Huǒshāo G4
Grandma's (see 32)
21 Little Yúnnán D2
22 Mǎn Fú Lóu B2
23 Temple Restaurant C2
24 Wángfǔjǐng Snack Street D6
25 Wǔgē Jīchì F1
26 Yuèbīn Fànguǎn D3
27 Zuǒ Lín Yòu Shè D2

Drinking & Nightlife (p74)
28 Alley Coffee C2
29 Slow Boat Brewery Taproom F1
30 What? Bar A4

Entertainment (p76)
31 Cháng'ān Grand Theatre G6
Star City (see 36)

Shopping (p76)
32 Běijīng apm D5
33 Foreign Languages Bookstore D5
34 Háoyuán Market D5
35 Nanluogu Xiang C1
36 Oriental Plaza E6
37 Shèng Xī Fú Hat Store D5
38 Slow Lane F4
39 Wangfujing Dajie D5

Sports & Activities (p78)
40 Bike Beijing D3
41 Dragonfly Therapeutic Retreat C5
42 Imperial City Ruins Park D1
43 Jǐngshān Table Tennis Park B2
44 Mílún Kungfu School E4

Sleeping (p194)
45 Běijīng City Central International Youth Hostel G7
46 Běijīng Saga International Youth Hostel G4
47 City Walls Courtyard B1
48 Côté Cour F3
49 Hilton Běijīng Wángfǔjǐng E5
50 Hulu Hotel F3
51 Jǐngshān Garden Hotel C2
52 Park Plaza F4
53 Raffles Běijīng D6
54 Red Capital Residence F1
55 Red Wall Garden F4
56 Regent Běijīng E4
57 Temple Hotel C2
58 YMCA Hotel E5

Information (p253)
59 ATM E2
60 Bank of China D4
61 Běijīng Tourist Information Center D5
62 Běijīng Tourist Information Center G7
63 Běijīng Union Hospital E5
64 Běijīng Wángfǔjǐng Pharmaceutical Store D5
65 Citibank G6
66 CITS E5
67 HSBC G6
Watson's (see 36)

Transport (p244)
68 CITS - International Train Tickets G6

DRUM TOWER & DŌNGCHÉNG NORTH *Map on p290*

Top Sights (p84)
1 Bell Tower A4
2 Drum Tower A5
3 Lama Temple F3

Sights (p88)
4 Arrow Factory E3
5 Confucius Temple & Imperial College E4
6 Dadu Museum of Art E4
7 Dìtán Park E1
8 Fire God Temple D4
9 Mao Dun's Former Residence C6
10 Nanluogu Xiang C7
11 Qi Baishi's Former Residence B6

Eating (p93)
12 Bǎihé Vegetarian Restaurant G5
13 Bāozi Pù C5
14 Café De La Poste F4
15 Café Sambal A4
16 Chez Gérard E4
17 Chóngqìng Kǒngliàng Huǒguō F5
18 Dàlǐ Courtyard C5
19 Ghost Street F5
20 Jiānbing Savoury Pancake Vendour F4
21 Jīn Dǐng Xuān F2
22 Little Sheep G5
Noodle In .... (see 18)
23 Róng Tiān Sheep Spine B4
24 Source D7
25 Stuff'd E3
26 Tàn Huā Lamb BBQ F4
27 Taste C6
28 Vineyard Café E3
29 Wǔ Jīn Cafe E3
30 Xiǎo Yú Shān G5
31 Xù Xiāng Zhāi Vegetarian Restaurant E4
32 Yáng Fāng Lamb Hotpot B5
33 Yáojì Chǎogān B5
34 Yī Lóng Zhāi B6
35 Zhāng Māma D6
36 Zhāng Māma (Original Branch) D4

Drinking & Nightlife (p98)
37 Ball House B5
38 Black-tea Tea Room C4
39 Cafe Confucius E4
40 El Nido D4
41 Essence A5
42 Great Leap Brewing B6
43 Hippo G4
44 If C4
45 Irresistible Cafe B6
46 Mado B4
47 Mài C4
48 Mao Mao Chong Bar D7
49 Modernista B4
50 Niǎn Bar C4
51 Other Place C3
52 Salud C6
53 Three Trees Coffee C6
54 Zá Jiā A4

Entertainment (p101)
55 Jiāng Hú D6
56 Jiāng Jìn Jiǔ A5
57 Mao Livehouse C5
58 Pénghāo Theatre D6
59 Star Live F2
Tango KTV .... (see 59)
60 Temple Bar B5
61 Yúgōng Yíshān E7

Shopping (p102)
62 C Rock C5
63 Esy Dragon Gift Shop C5
64 Famous Tea of China C5
65 Giant E5
66 JH 2nd-hand Bike Shop F5
67 Jīngchéng Bǎixìng D4
68 Plastered 8 .... C6
69 Ruìfúxiáng A5
70 Tiān Yì Goods Market A7

Sports & Activities (p104)
71 Black Sesame Kitchen C6
72 Culture Yard F5
73 Drum & Bell Square A5
74 Jīnsè Fēilún Bike Shop D5
75 Mào'ér Lǎolǐ Health Club C6
76 Natooke E3
77 Qīngnián Hú Park B1
78 The Hutong F5

Sleeping (p196)
79 161 Lama Temple Courtyard Hotel G4
80 Běijīng Downtown Backpackers C6
81 Confucius International Youth Hostel E3
82 Courtyard 7 .... C5
83 DùGé C6
84 Nostalgia Hotel E4
85 Old Běijīng Square Hotel B4
86 Orchid B4
87 Peking Youth Hostel C6

Information (p253)
88 Dōngchéng Disease Prevention & Control Centre D6
89 Russian Embassy H4

Key on p289

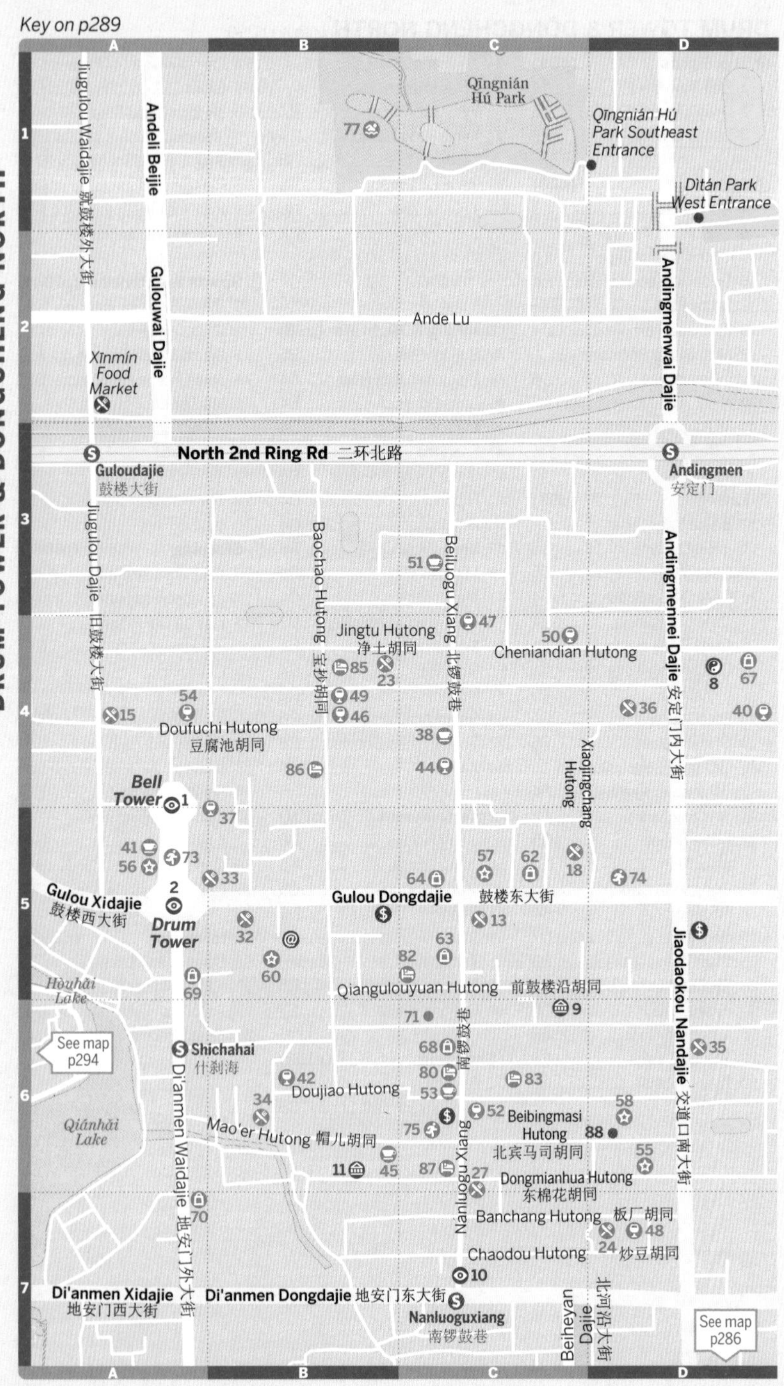

See map p294

See map p286

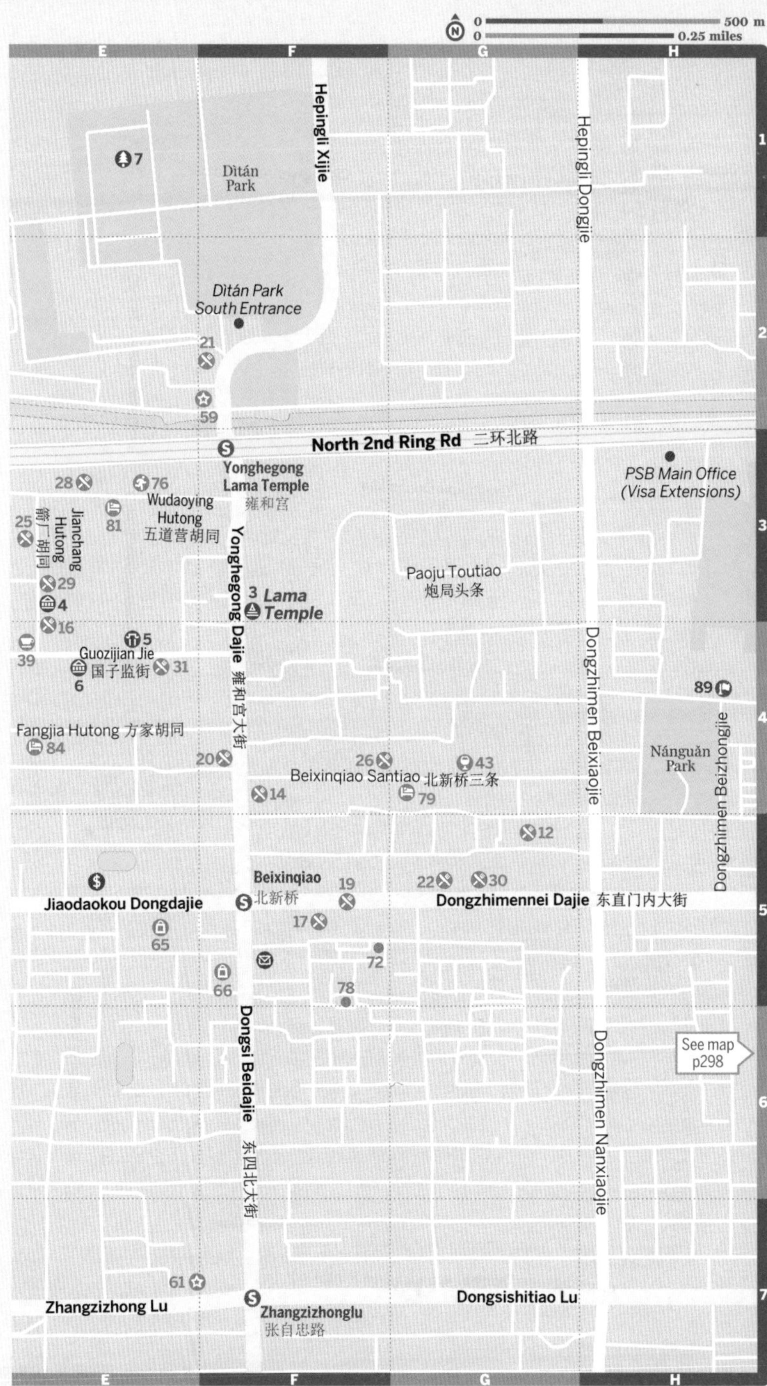
0 500 m
0 0.25 miles
E
F
G
H
1
2
3
4
5
6
7
7
Dìtán Park
Hepingli Xijie
Hepingli Dongjie
Dìtán Park South Entrance
21
59
North 2nd Ring Rd 二环北路
Yonghegong Lama Temple 雍和宫
PSB Main Office (Visa Extensions)
28
76
Wudaoying Hutong 五道营胡同
81
25
Jianchang Hutong 箭厂胡同
29
4
16
3 Lama Temple
Paoju Toutiao 炮局头条
Yonghegong Dajie 雍和宫大街
5
39
Guozijian Jie 国子监街
31
6
89
Dongzhimen Beixiaojie
Nánguǎn Park
Dongzhimen Beizhongjie
Fangjia Hutong 方家胡同
84
20
26
43
Beixinqiao Santiao 北新桥三条
14
79
12
Beixinqiao 北新桥
19
22
30
Jiaodaokou Dongdajie
Dongzhimennei Dajie 东直门内大街
17
65
72
66
78
Dongsi Beidajie 东四北大街
See map p298
Dongzhimen Nanxiaojie
61
Zhangzizhong Lu
Zhangzizhonglu 张自忠路
Dongsishitiao Lu

TEMPLE OF HEAVEN PARK & DŌNGCHÉNG SOUTH

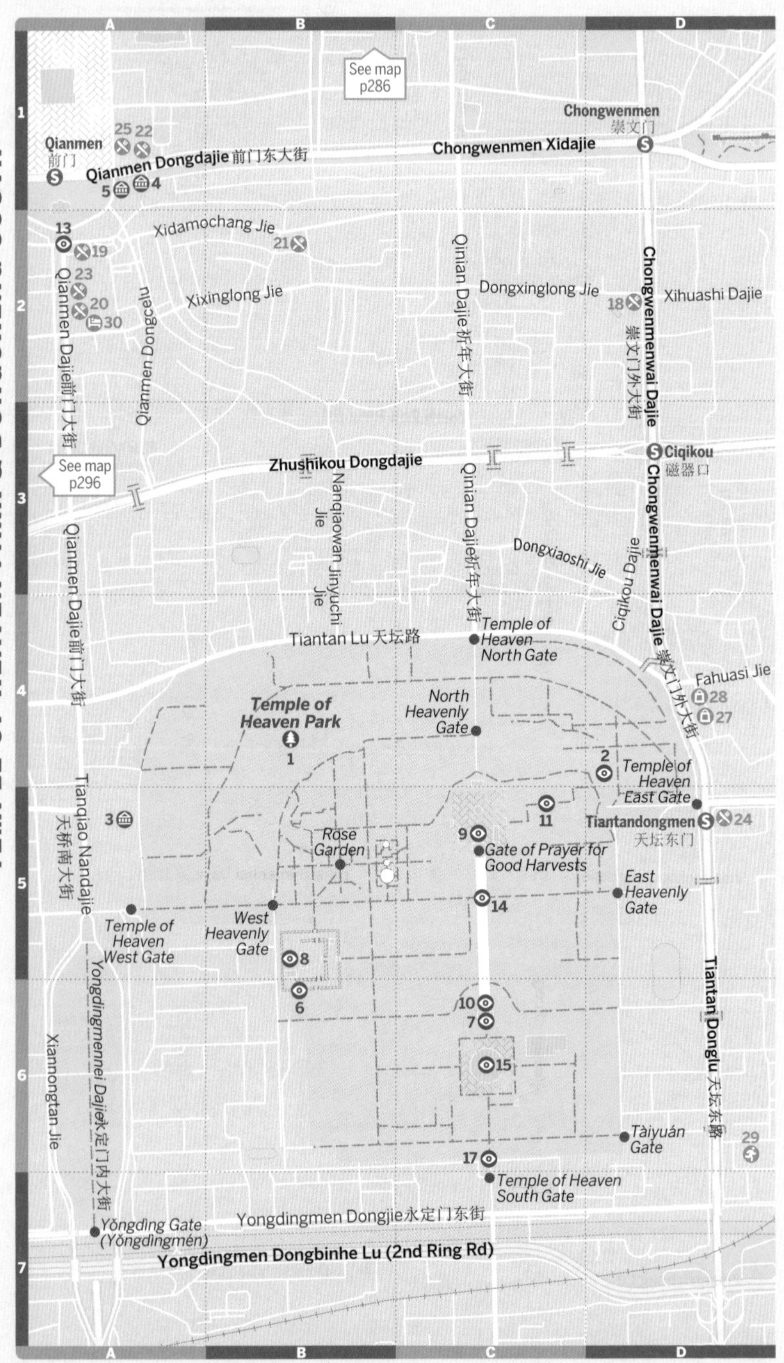

Top Sights (p108)

1 Temple of Heaven Park B4

Sights (p111)

2 Animal Killing Pavilion D4
3 Běijīng Natural History Museum A5
4 Běijīng Planning Exhibition Hall A1
5 Běijīng Railway Museum A1
6 Divine Music Administration B6
7 Echo Wall C6
8 Fasting Palace B5
9 Hall of Prayer for Good Harvests C5
10 Imperial Vault of Heaven C6
11 Long Corridor C5
12 Ming City Wall Ruins Park E1
13 Qianmen Dajie A2
14 Red Stairway Bridge C5
15 Round Altar C6
16 Southeast Corner Watchtower & Red Gate Gallery F1
17 Zhāohēng Gate C6

Eating (p113)

18 Biànyífāng D2
19 Capital M A2
20 Dūyīchù A2
21 Lìqún Roast Duck Restaurant B2
22 Lost Heaven A1
Old Běijīng Zhájiàng Noodle King .... (see 18)
23 Qiánmén Quánjùdé Roast Duck Restaurant A2
24 Wedomé D5
25 Xīn Tiān Yuàn A1

Entertainment (p115)

26 Red Theatre F4

Shopping (p115)

27 Hóngqiáo (Pearl) Market D4
28 Toys City D4

Sports & Activities (p115)

29 NTSC Tennis Club D6

Sleeping (p202)

30 Emperor A2

BĚIHǍI PARK & XĪCHÉNG NORTH

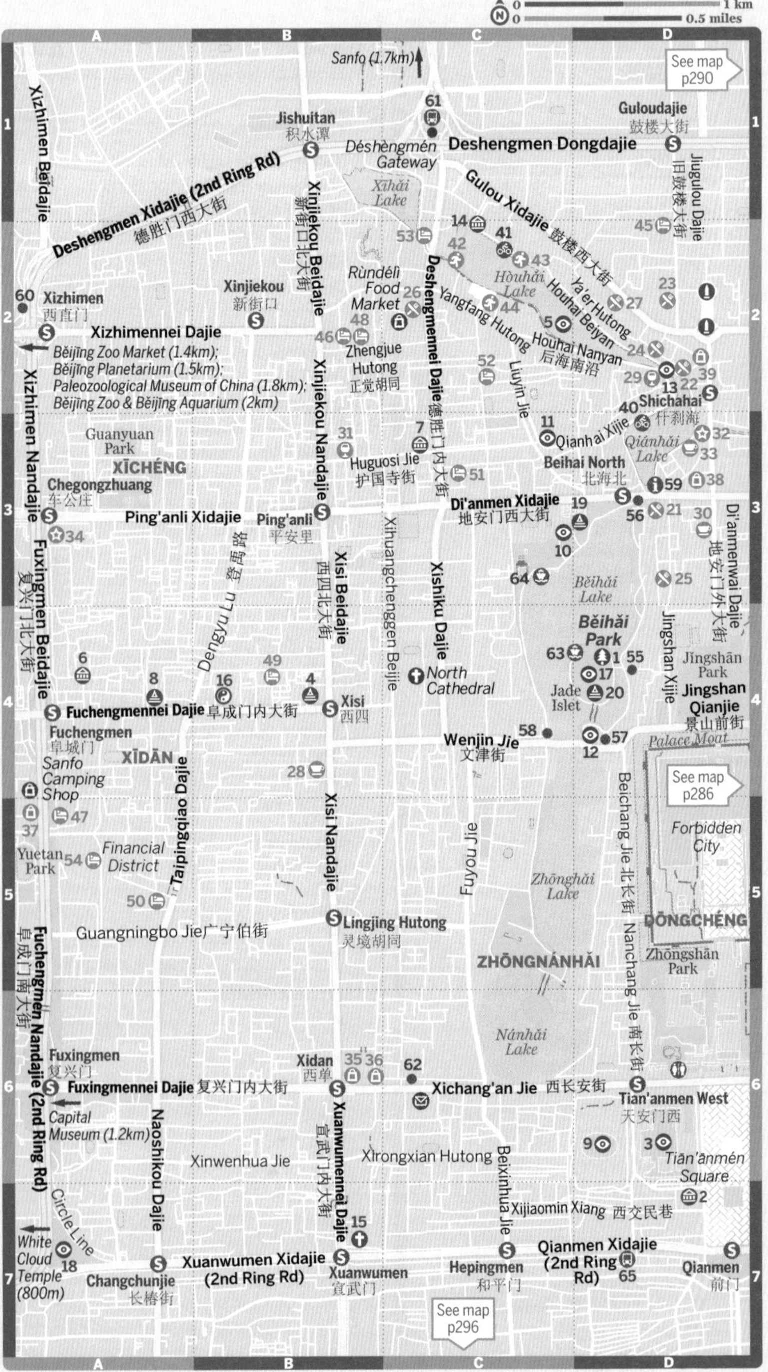

BĚIHǍI PARK & XĪCHÉNG NORTH

Top Sights (p118)
1 Běihǎi Park....D4

Sights (p120)
2 China Numismatic Museum....D7
3 Great Hall of the People....D6
4 Guǎngjì Temple....B4
5 Hòuhǎi Lakes....C2
6 Lu Xun Museum....A4
7 Mei Lanfang Former Residence....C3
8 Miàoyīng Temple White Dagoba....A4
9 National Centre for the Performing Arts (NCPA)....D6
10 Nine Dragon Screen....C3
11 Prince Gong's Residence....C3
12 Round City....D4
13 Silver Ingot Bridge....D2
14 Song Qingling Former Residence....C2
15 South Cathedral....B7
16 Temple of Ancient Monarchs....B4
17 White Dagoba....D4
18 Xībiànmén Watchtower....A7
19 Xītiān Fánjìng....D3
20 Yǒngān Temple....D4

Eating (p126)
21 Guǎnshì Chìbā....D3
22 Kǎo Ròu Jì....D2
23 Le Petit Saigon....D2
24 Lǐjì Fēngwèi Měishí Cāntīng....D2
25 Royal Icehouse....D3
26 Rùndélì Food Market....C2
27 Wang Pang Zi Donkey Burger....D2

Drinking & Nightlife (p128)
28 Await Cafe....B4
29 Hòuhǎi Bar Strip....D2
30 Le Grenadier....D3
31 NBeer Pub....B3
32 Tángrén Teahouse....D3

Entertainment (p128)
33 East Shore Jazz Café....D3
34 Mei Lanfang Grand Theatre....A3
National Centre for the Performing Arts....(see 9)

Shopping (p129)
35 77th Street....B6
36 Běijīng Books Building....B6
37 Sanfo (Fuchengmen)....A5
38 Three Stone Kite Shop....D3
39 Yandai Xiejie....D2

Sports & Activities (p120)
40 Bike Hire....D3
41 Bike Hire....C2
42 Golden Sail Water Sports Club....C2
43 Hòuhǎi Exercise Park....C2
44 Hòuhǎi Park....C2

Sleeping (p198)
45 Drum Tower Youth Hostel....D2
46 Graceland Yard....B2
47 Intercontinental....A5
48 Red Lantern House....B2
49 Red Lantern House West Yard....B4
50 Ritz-Carlton....A5
51 Shíchàhǎi Sandalwood Boutique Hotel...C3
52 Shíchàhǎi Shadow Art Hotel....C2
53 Sleepy Inn....C2
54 Westin....A5

Information (p253)
55 Běihǎi Park East Gate....D4
56 Běihǎi Park North Gate....D3
57 Běihǎi Park South Gate....D4
58 Běihǎi Park West Gate....C4
59 Běijīng Tourist Information Center....D3

Transport (p244)
60 Běijīng North Train Station....A2
61 Buses to Bādálǐng Great Wall and the Ming Tombs....C1
62 Civil Aviation Administration of China (CAAC)....C6
63 Ferry Dock (Jade Island)....D4
64 Ferry Dock (Northwest)....C3
65 Qianmen Xi Bus Stop (for Bus 901)....D7

DASHILAR & XĪCHÉNG SOUTH

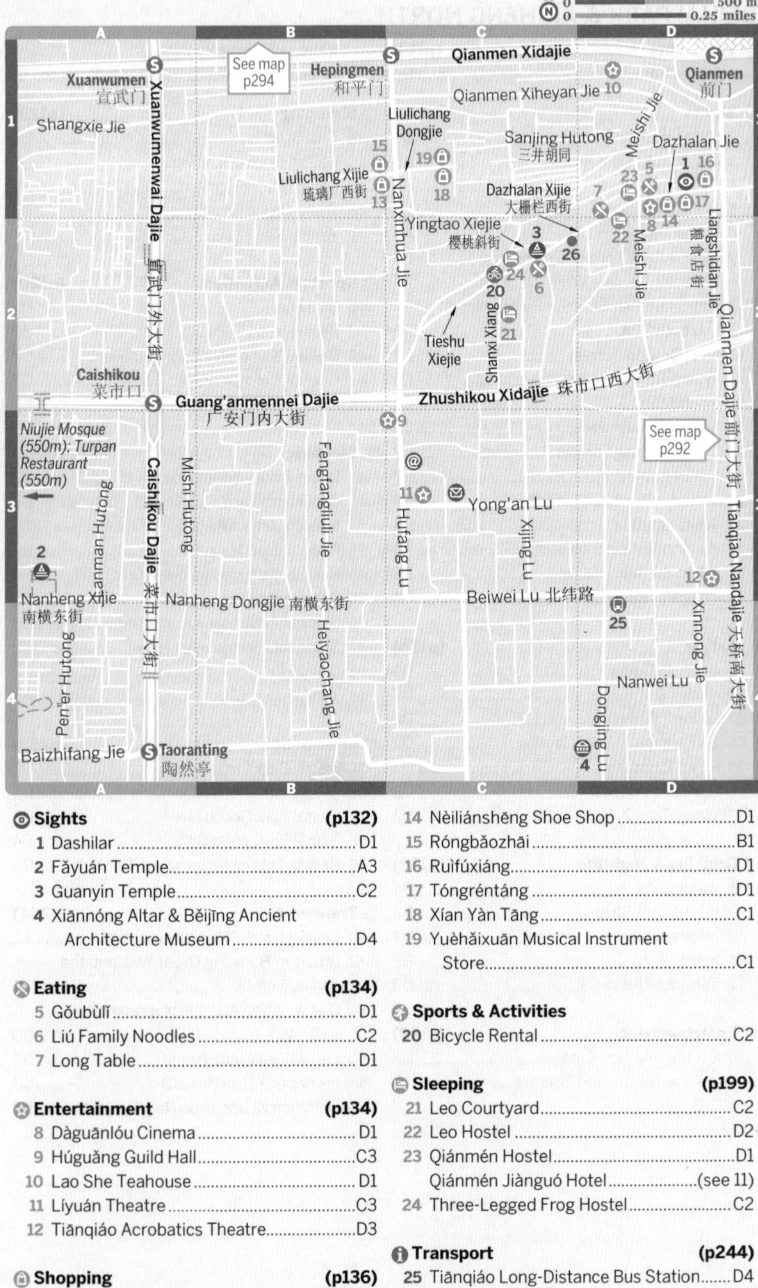

Sights (p132)

- 1 Dashilar D1
- 2 Fǎyuán Temple A3
- 3 Guanyin Temple C2
- 4 Xiānnóng Altar & Běijīng Ancient Architecture Museum D4

Eating (p134)

- 5 Gǒubùlǐ D1
- 6 Liú Family Noodles C2
- 7 Long Table D1

Entertainment (p134)

- 8 Dàguānlóu Cinema D1
- 9 Húguǎng Guild Hall C3
- 10 Lao She Teahouse D1
- 11 Líyuán Theatre C3
- 12 Tiānqiáo Acrobatics Theatre D3

Shopping (p136)

- 13 Cathay Bookshop B1
- 14 Nèiliánshēng Shoe Shop D1
- 15 Róngbǎozhāi B1
- 16 Ruìfúxiáng D1
- 17 Tóngréntáng D1
- 18 Xían Yàn Tāng C1
- 19 Yuèhǎixuān Musical Instrument Store C1

Sports & Activities

- 20 Bicycle Rental C2

Sleeping (p199)

- 21 Leo Courtyard C2
- 22 Leo Hostel D2
- 23 Qiánmén Hostel D1
- Qiánmén Jiànguó Hotel .... (see 11)
- 24 Three-Legged Frog Hostel C2

Transport (p244)

- 25 Tiānqiáo Long-Distance Bus Station D4
- 26 Train Ticket Office C2

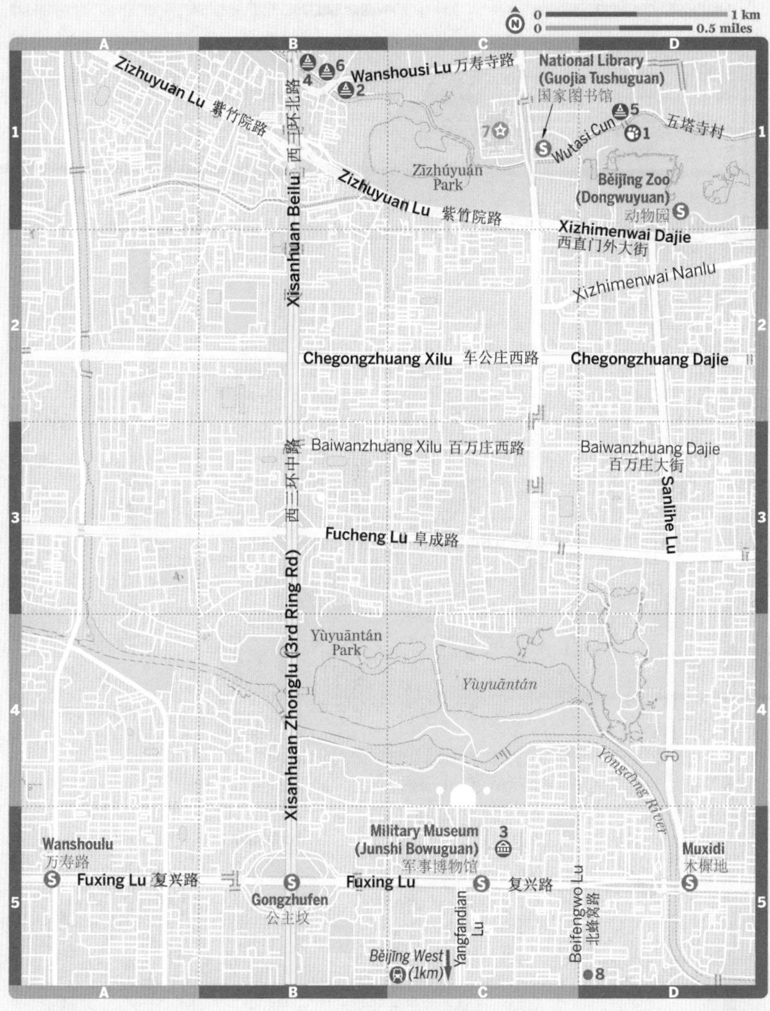

Sights (p161)

1 Běijīng Zoo (North Entrance)........ D1
2 Dragon King Temple Remains........ B1
3 Military Museum........ C5
4 Wànshòu Temple........ B1
5 Wǔtǎ Temple........ D1
6 Yánqìng Temple Remains........ B1

Entertainment (p168)

7 National Library Concert Hall........ C1

Transport (p244)

8 CRTS........ D5

SĀNLǏTÚN & CHÁOYÁNG

Key on p300

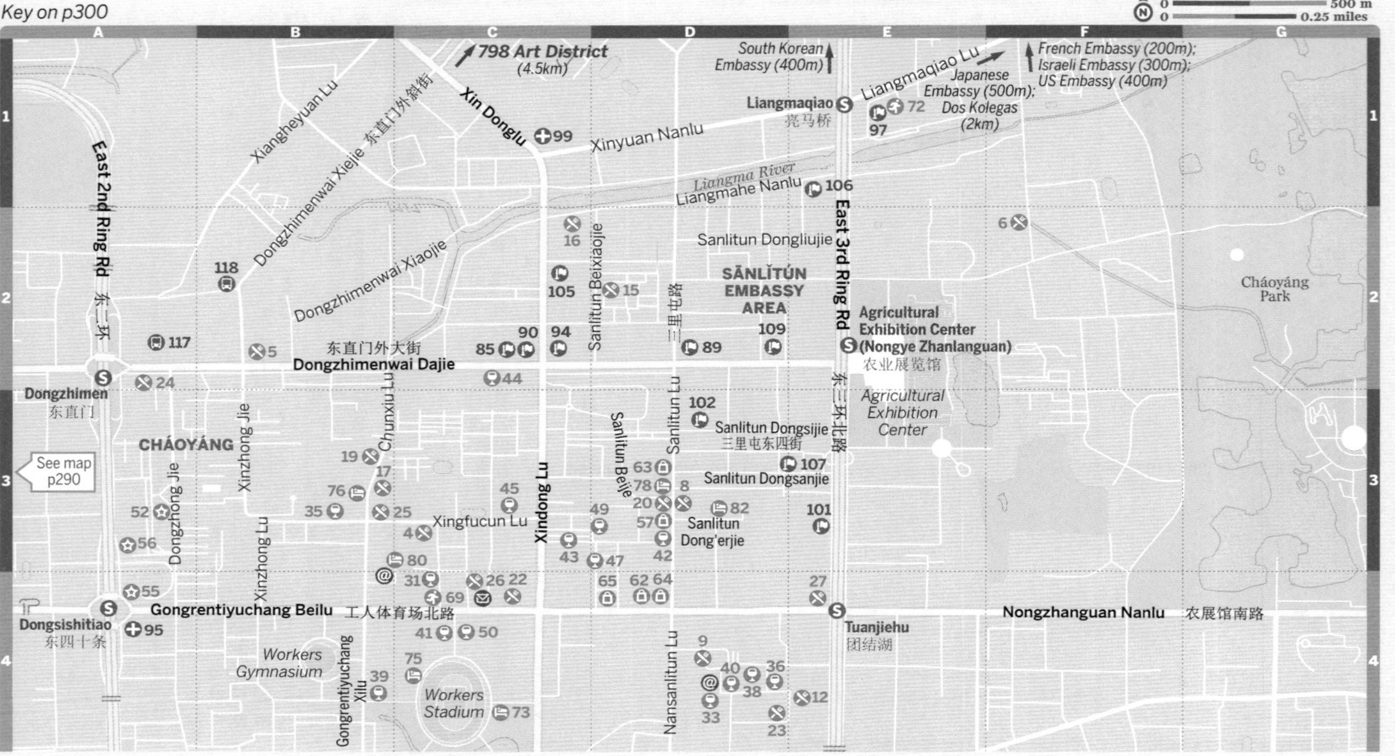

SĀNLǏTÚN & CHÁOYÁNG

SĀNLǏTÚN & CHÁOYÁNG *Map on p298*

Sights (p141)

1 CCTV Building E7
2 Dōngyuè Temple B5
3 Jiǔtiān Pǔhuā Gōng C5

Eating (p144)

4 April Gourmet C3
5 Bàodǔ Huáng B2
6 Bǎoyuán Dumpling Restaurant F2
7 Bellagio B5
Big Smoke (see 25)
Biteapitta (see 42)
8 Bocata D3
9 Bookworm D4
Carmen (see 42)
10 Desert Rose B6
11 Din Tai Fung G8
12 Duck de Chine E4
13 Elephant B6
14 Hóng Lú D5
15 In & Out D2
16 Indian Kitchen C2
17 Jīngzūn Peking Duck B3
18 Jíxiángniǎo Xiāngcài B5
19 Méizhōu Dōngpō Jiǔlóu B3
20 Mosto D3
21 Nàjiā Xiǎoguǎn C8
22 Nánjīng Impressions C4
23 Okra D4
24 Olé A2
25 O'Steak B3
26 Purple Haze C4
27 Rumi E4
28 Uighur Willow B6
29 Xiǎo Wáng's Home Restaurant D7
30 Yàn Lán Lóu C6

Drinking & Nightlife (p148)

31 Alfa C4
Apothecary (see 42)
Big Smoke (see 25)
32 Chocolate B6
33 d Lounge D4
34 Destination B5
First Floor (see 42)
35 Great Leap Brewing B3
36 Home Plate Bar B-Que D4
37 Ichikura E6
38 Janes and Hooch D4
39 Lantern B4
40 Local D4
Mesh (see 78)
Migas Bar (see 42)
41 Mix C4
42 Nali Patio D3
43 Nearby the Tree C3
44 Paddy O'Shea's C2
45 Parlor C3
46 Q Bar D5
47 Revolution D3
Second Floor (see 42)
Spark (see 61)
48 Stone Boat B7
49 Tree D3
50 Vics C4
Xiù (see 79)

Entertainment (p152)

51 Cháoyáng Theatre E6
52 East Gate Cinema A3
MegaBox (see 64)
53 Melody KTV C5
54 Partyworld KTV B6
55 Poly Plaza International Theatre A4
56 Universal Theatre (Heaven & Earth Theatre) A3